D1402745

PSYCHOPATHOLOGY
IN
CHILDHOOD

PSYCHOPATHOLOGY IN CHILDHOOD

Edited by
JULIANA RASIC LACHENMEYER, Ph.D.
MARGARET S. GIBBS, Ph.D.
Fairleigh Dickinson University

Gardner Press, Inc., New York

Library of Congress Cataloging in Publication Data
Main entry under title:

Psychopathology in childhood.

    Bibliography: p.
    Includes index.
    1. Child psychopathology. 2. Child psychotherapy.
I. Lachenmeyer, Juliana Rasic. II. Gibbs, Margaret S.
RJ499.P769   618.92'89   81-20282
ISBN 0-89876-014-3   AACR2

Gardner Press, Inc.

19 Union Square West

New York 10003

Library of Congress Cataloging in Publication Data

ISBN 0-89876-014-3

Designed by Raymond Solomon

Production by Publishers Creative Services Inc.

Printed in the United States of America

Contributors

THOMAS M. ACHENBACH, PhD.
Departments of Psychiatry and Psychology
University of Vermont
Burlington, Vermont

TEODORO AYLLON, PhD.
Psychology Department
Georgia State University
Atlanta, Georgia

ROBERT BRADLEY, PhD.
Center for Child Development and Education
University of Arkansas
Little Rock, Arkansas

STEPHEN COLE, M.D.
New York Veterans Administration Medical Center
New York, New York
and Family Institute of Westchester
White Plains, New York

DANIEL DOLEYS, PHD.
Center for Developmental and Learning Disorders
University of Alabama School of Medicine
Birmingham, Alabama

JAMES EGAN, M.D.
Children's Hospital, National Medical Center
Washington, D.C.
and George Washington University
School of Medicine
Washington, D.C.

MARGARET S. GIBBS, PHD.
Psychology Department
Fairleigh Dickinson University
Teaneck, N.J.

ARTHUR GREEN, M.D.
Department of Psychiatry
Columbia University College of Physicians and Surgeons
New York, New York
and Columbia Presbyterian Family Center and Crisis Nursery
New York, New York
and Babies Hospital
Columbia Presbyterian Medical Center
New York, New York

PHILIP C. KENDALL, PHD.
Psychology Department
University of Minnesota
Minneapolis, Minnesota

JULIANA RASIC LACHENMEYER, PHD.
Psychology Department
Fairleigh Dickinson University
Teaneck, N.J.
and Department of Psychiatry
North Shore University Hospital
Manhasset, N.Y.
and Department of Psychiatry
Cornell University Medical College
New York, New York

DENNIS R. MOORE, PHD.
Family Research Associates
Eugene, Oregon

CRIGHTON NEWSOM, PHD.
Suffolk Child Development Center
State University of New York
Stony Brook, N.Y.

VERNON PEGRAM, PHD.
Neurosciences Program
and Department of Psychiatry
University of Alabama School of Medicine
Birmingham, Alabama

DENNIS C. RUSSO, PHD.
Department of Psychiatry
Children's Hospital Medical Center
Boston, Mass.
and Department of Psychiatry
Harvard Medical School
Boston, Mass.

STEVEN J. SIMON, PHD.
Seven County Services, Inc.
Louisville, Kentucky

HAROLD SOLAN, MA., OD.
Psychology Department
Fairleigh Dickinson University
Teaneck, N.J.

LISA A. TEDESCO, PHD.
Psychology Department
State University of New York
Buffalo, N.Y.

EUGENE S. URBAIN, PHD.
Wilder Child Guidance Clinic
St. Paul, Minnesota

THORNTON A. VANDERSALL, M.D.
Department of Psychiatry
North Shore University Hospital
Manhasset, N.Y.
and Department of Psychiatry
Cornell University Medical College
New York, New York

DEBRA WEILER, PHD.
Neurosciences Program
University of Alabama School of Medicine
Birmingham, Alabama

CAROL WHALEN, PHD.
Program in Social Ecology
University of California
Irvine, California

Contents

Part II DISORDERS OF CHILDHOOD
Overview

PART III THERAPEUTIC APPROACHES WITH CHILDREN

Preface

The aim of this book is to present an integrated view of current knowledge of child psychopathology in a form that is useful to both the advanced student and the practicing clinician. Psychology has woefully neglected the study of mental and emotional disorders in children. The development of normal children has been carefully observed and recorded, and much has been written about psychopathology in adults. Children with psychological problems, however, have been ignored in both the laboratory and the consulting room. This is partly because our identification and understanding of pathology traditionally rests on internal dynamics (e.g., anxiety and defenses) that cannot be directly observed and that children are seldom capable of direct communication. Behavioral approaches to child psychopathology offer an alternative, since they do not require intrapsychic understanding of the child. Indeed, it appears that much of the recent advance in treatment of childhood disorders has come from the behavioral field; for instance, the treatment of autism and childhood schizophrenia, childhood phobias, and psychophysiological disorders. Physiological approaches have also proved promising to our understanding of such problems as learning disorders, psychophysiological disorders and autism and childhood schizophrenia.

In this volume we have tried to present and integrate all three of these important points of view. Each chapter on a major category of childhood psychopathology incorporates theories and studies from a psychodynamic, behavioral, and physiological viewpoint. The section on treatment of disorders contains chapters written by expert representatives of all three viewpoints, as well as several other perspectives. We hope that what emerges is a comprehensive survey of research, theory, and treatment for and about psychopathology.

Our point of view about childhood disorder is that it must be seen in the context of normal development. We assume a competency model of normal development. The child's problem can be viewed as a disruption of this pattern of growing coping skills, either through environmental or physiological causes. In this context, the research literature relating abnormal and normal development becomes important, and several chapters take this perspective. For instance, the chapters by Gibbs and by Achenbach look at identification and diagnosis of childhood disorders in terms of a continuum from the normal. Bradley and Tedesco, in their chapter on mental retardation, summarize the environmental factors that strengthen and impede normal development of intellectual capacities. Moore, on the child with behavior problems, relies heavily on the literature that explores the effects of discipline techniques in normal children. Kendall's chapter on problem-solving approaches in treatment also is an indication of our adherence to the competency model of normal development.

The section on treatment of childhood disorders is, by design, a sizable portion of the book. Our point of view is a pragmatic one: our knowledge remains limited, but we must treat troubled children and their families with the most effective modalities available. Certain disorders seem to respond prescriptively to certain treatment approaches, and these approaches deserve to be widely known. For other disorders, knowledge of a wide range of treatment possibilities allows the practitioner selectively to modify the therapy plan to fit the situation and the expectancies of the child and family.

In the treatment section, we have stressed both technique, in Cole's chapter on family therapy, and research on treatment approaches, in Whelan's chapter on the use of psychostimulants for hyperactive children. There are several reasons for the emphasis on research relation to treatment. First, from a prescriptive viewpoint, we need to be aware of the effectiveness of our techniques, e.g., what exactly can psychostimulants accomplish, and what are their limitations, for exactly what types of problem? Second, knowledge of the effectiveness of a technique may stimulate the clinicians to broaden their experience to learn new approaches; any one clinician's personal experience of "what works" is necessarily limited. And third, understanding the research literature on the various disorders and their treatment can provide the clinician with valuable clues to use in hypothesis-testing within an individual practice.

As is clear from the above examples, we consider this book to be useful both as a text for students who are learning child psychopathology and as a reference tool for experienced clinicians. That is, we have planned the book to be extensive enough to provide the student with the necessary breadth of coverage and intensive enough to provide new perspectives and ideas for long-term professionals.

Basically, we view our book as eclectic—and ourselves as eclectic as well. Juliana Lachenmeyer received her training in social, child, and behavioral psychology—in addition to her academic career as a behavioral consultant. Gretchen Gibbs was trained in a clinical psychology program that was strongly rooted in an interdisciplinary perspective and in addition to her academic career is a psychotherapist. We have found the differences between our points of view useful and rewarding to our own development, and hope that our ecumenical viewpoint will also prove useful to others.

This is the second book we have edited together. We have enjoyed it, and the joint effort has deepened an already strong friendship. We would like to thank our contributors, and those secretaries and students who have assisted us. This is also our second book published by Gardner Press, and we would like to thank Gardner Spungin for his ready availability and general helpfulness.

Introduction

This book is divided into three sections: classification systems, specific disorders of childhood and different approaches to therapy with children. In the first section Achenbach uses factorial analysis to come up with empirical approaches to classification. Gibbs in her chapter goes over current classification systems currently in use pointing out their weaknesses especially in relation to assessment and diagnosis of children. She focuses on the difficulties inherent in working with children and makes specific recommendations.

The second section of the book, on specific disorders has two chapters on special disorders of childhood. The first by Lachenmeyer reviews definitional problems, epidemiological research, and different etiological and treatment approaches to childhood depression, school phobia and anorexia nervosa, as well as outcome studies where available. The second chapter, by Doleys, Weiler, and Pegram, discusses etiology and treatment of enuresis, encopresis, and sleep disorders in children. Russo and Newsom in their chapter on psychotic disorders in children evaluate diagnostic, treatment, and prognostic factors in psychotic disorders and formulate a behavioral-inductive model, emphasizing empirical data and treatment. Bradley and Tedesco discuss research on the facilitating and inhibiting factors in the cognitive, social and physical home enviroment and how they affect mental development. Solan provides a broad overview of learning disabilities, discussing nutritional, and genetic factors—as well as psychological ones. The Moore chapter looks at control problems, agressive problems, and delinquent behavior from a social learning point of view. He focuses on the parent-child reciprocal interactions and views the family as the primary system responsible for early behavior patterns. He makes an interesting contrast to the systems' approach to the family found in Cole's chapter. The last chapter in this section is Green's on child abuse. The author covers current research on child abuse and discusses etiology and treatment from a psychodynamic point of view.

The last section of the book covers different therapeutic approaches. Ayllon and Simon present an overview of behavior therapy principles and then apply these to specific behavior problems with children. Kendall and Urbain present a more cognitive-behavioral approach, focusing on self-control procedures and problem-solving skills. The psychoanalytic view is presented by Egan with an illustrative case example. Cole offers a problem solving approach to family therapy. He reviews the system's assumptions and model. He then covers assessment and treatment with case illustrations. Whalen in the last chapter in the book discusses the interplay between research on the use of psychostimulants and their use in the treatment of hyperactivity. She then raises and answers a series of practical questions about the effects of psychostimulants on the behavior of children.

PART I
CLASSIFICATION

OVERVIEW

When a child is brought to the psycho-therapist's waiting room, a complicated process of diagnosis begins. As discussed in Chapter 1, the clinician must first determine if indeed the child needs treatment and, if so, what is the likelihood that the child will benefit from treatment. Assuming the determination is for treatment, the clinician must then decide what treatment plan would best be applied (given the type of problem), family attitudes and expectancies, severity and chronicity of the problem, and so forth. In addition, the child must be given a formal diagnosis, so that the family insurance company will pay for the treatment, the psychotherapist will be able to keep records of her or his work, and so that, if needed, the therapist can communicate impressions briefly to other professionals. In addition, a label is needed if the case will be used for any research purposes. As Prugh, Engel, and Morse (1975) have pointed out, two types of diagnosis are involved here: assessment and classification. That is, the formulation of a treatment plan involves an assessment of the patient's situation; research, communication, and record keeping require formal classification. These goals of diagnosis to some extent may even work at cross-purposes. Treatment cannot take place without consideration of the situational context, while research studies attempt to remove the situational context so that all extraneous variables can be controlled. Research and treatment also serve a kind of cross-fertilization, however, in that the clinician's treatment plan should reflect what is currently known about the diagnostic category, and each treated case has the potential for generating research questions.

Many of the problems in developing a diagnostic system revolve around the need to use it for both assessment and classification. The origins of the diagnostic system, as described in the next two chapters, were in medical attempts to establish treatment programs for specific disorders.

The official diagnostic system used today (Diagnostic and Statistical Manual-III, 1980) is still a product of the medical model. This is in spite of the fact that short descriptive labels have not proved conducive to a development of effective treatment approaches. It is also in spite of the fact that the medical model is not compatible with an understanding of psychopathology that does not have an organic basis.

As Chapter One and Chapter Two demonstrate, classification is moving away from the medical model in two new directions. In Chapter One, Gibbs describes identification of the disordered child and the pragmatic approach to assessment for treatment of childhood disorders, developed by Hobbs and his associates (1975a and b). She cites the research that indicates the importance of assessing the family context in planning treatment for children. Traditional classification systems are discussed in this chapter from a pragmatic viewpoint. Gibbs feels that the only major improvement in formal systems has been the development of a multiaxial approach.

Achenbach shows, in Chapter Two, the

progress made in empirical classification systems. One valuable contribution has been the discovery of the generality and usefulness of labeling disorders as Internalizing versus Externalizing. Factor analysis shows the existence of narrow-band syndromes within these two wider band categories. In addition, profiles for each child, of clusters of symptoms, can be drawn up in a system developed by Achenbach. Such profiles are useful to the treatment of the individual child, as well as to our understanding of what symptoms are associated with each other, thus forming clinical syndromes.

In short, both research findings and more sophisticated treatment strategies are leading to changing ideas about classification of childhood disorders, although the latest official system, DSM-III, has incorporated few of these new ideas.

REFERENCES

American Psychiatric Association. *Diagnostic and statistical manual of mental disorders* (3rd ed.) Washington, D.C., Author, 1980.

Hobbs, N. *The future of children: Categories, labels and their consequences.* San Francisco: Jossey-Bass, 1975. (a)

Hobbs, N. (Ed.), *Issues in the classification of children.* V.s I and II. San Francisco: Jossey-Bass, 1975. (b)

Prugh, D. G., Engel, M., & Morse, W. C. Emotional disturbance in children. In N. Hobbs (Ed.), *Issues in the classification of children.* V. II. San Francisco: Jossey-Bass, 1975.

CHAPTER 1

Identification and Classification of Child Psychopathology: A Pragmatic Analysis of Traditional Approaches

MARGARET S. GIBBS, Ph.D.

Anyone who is at all knowledgeable about psychopathology is aware that what is "abnormal" as applied to mental health cannot be well defined. The problems of identifying and classifying what is abnormal in children are greater.

Let us consider the case of Tommy, age six. Tommy is having bad dreams, is fearful of dogs, and has wet the bed once a week for the past five weeks. Tommy's mother is worried and brings him to a child guidance clinic. In his evaluation at the clinic he expresses some fearful fantasies and some œdipal themes. Tommy is accepted into treatment and has officially become "an abnormal child." His probable diagnosis under the most recent classification system will be adjustment disorder with anxious mood, a diagnosis primarily applied to adults. But, is Tommy an abnormal child? Are his problems different in kind or intensity from those of other children his age? Might he quickly outgrow his present symptoms? How do other mothers view similar behavior? If untreated, will he grow up to be neurotic? Will treatment help his present symptoms and reduce the likelihood of later problems? How will the experience of being labeled abnormal affect him?

While some of these questions may be relevant to adult problems as well, there is a special ethical question when we consider children's problems. Lacking perspective on themselves or on psychotherapy, children are very seldom self-referred. They cannot ask us for our help. This means we have a special obligation to identify those children who need treatment. On the other hand, to treat children who do not need our help may not only be a waste of time but an infringement of their rights. Treatment can do harm (Bergin, 1971), and while an adult can give informed consent to the process of psychotherapy in the same way as to a surgical operation with some associated risks, the child is not asked for or able to give an informed consent. Thus, any harmful effects due to treatment or to labeling the child with an emotional disorder are unethical, as well as pernicious.

Once children who can benefit from therapy are identified, there are further problems in classifying the nature of their disorders. Classification systems for emotional disorders reflect theories and philosophies of psychological disorder, and as such they have been the focus of much bitter dispute over the years (e.g., Szasz, 1969; Zigler and Phillips, 1961). The dissatisfaction with systems for children seems more pervasive, however. Few attempts have been made to develop a new adult nomenclature, but it seems as though almost every writer or organization in the field (Ackerman, 1953; Beller, 1962; Brown, 1937; Cameron, 1955; Fish, 1960; Fish and Shapiro, 1965; *GAP,* 1966; Pearson, 1949; Prugh, 1973; Rutter et al., 1969) has proposed a revised classification system for children! In 1966 the Group for the Advancement of Psychiatry reviewed previous systems of classification and found 24; since that time there have been several important additions.

Not only are there many systems for classifying children, they differ markedly, even within the same theoretical framework. For instance, the first *Diagnostic and Statistical Manual (DSM-I)* of the American Psychiatric Association (1952) contained only autism and childhood schizophrenia as specific disorders of children; DSM-III (1980) contains a list of 40 classifications, (plus those for mental retardation) that arise in childhood and adolescence. While this difference might be attributed to the greater knowledge that 26 years has produced, the fact of the matter is that we have hardly any greater empirical justification for the *DSM-III* classification system than for the *DSM-I.*

The confusion about and dissatisfaction with classification systems for children reflects the fact that research on disturbed children and their treatment has been neglected in favor of a focus on adults (Levitt, 1971). Recently progress has been made in classifying the actual behavioral symptoms children show. This chapter is followed by one by Achenbach reviewing empirical classification systems, and the reader should consider both chapters in conjunction with each other.

Identification and classification of childrens' problems are difficult for another reason. The point of view of this chapter is that the difficulty arises primarily from the dependency of children on their families and social environments. That is, the dependency of children means that they are not self-referred, and the identification of their problems rests on others. It means that their behavior is less stable, being more responsive to environmental changes and manipulations than is adult behavior. Their problems are more likely to be related to immaturity and specific developmental crises and are thus more likely to change with time. Their dependency means that they are more likely to be scapegoated as the cause of problems within a family system of pathology. Because of these factors, diagnostic syndromes lack consistency and do not differentiate normal from abnormal children. The foregoing points will be elaborated and supported later. I will also discuss the problems created by the labeling process for children. Diagnostic labels create the false impression that there is a stable disorder existing within the person, and the dependency of children means that this impression is especially false in their case. A more appropriate focus stresses the pragmatics of the interventions needed. A pragmatic approach requires emphasis on the interdependency of child and family, since family interventions have been shown to be more effective than treating the child alone. At the end of the chapter, I will consider traditional classification systems for children in the context of these considerations.

SPECIAL PROBLEMS IN IDENTIFYING CHILDREN WITH PSYCHOLOGICAL DISORDER

Parent Concern and Pathology

Since children seldom identify their own mental health problems, it is important to look at the characteristics of those persons (parents and school personnel) who identify the problem. As an example of how being referred by others may affect the validity of the referral process, it is well known that the number of boys referred for psychotherapy far exceeds the number of girls, although many more women than men enter therapy as adults. Many factors may operate to produce more referrals of boys, but some of these factors are reflections on the referral process itself. For instance, the greater aggression shown by boys makes them more troublesome than girls to their parents and teachers, and female teachers and parents are more likely to become upset by disruptive behavior in boys than in girls (Eme, 1979.)

Other research indicates that characteristics of parents may determine referral of children more than the characteristics of the children. For instance, Langner et al. (1974), in a broad epidemiological study, found that the best predictor of child referral was the mother's education. College-educated mothers were three times more likely to refer children than were mothers with a grade-school education. While the mother's education may make her more psychologically sophisticated, able to identify psychological problems, and aware of resources to provide help, it is also possible that such psychological sophistication and awareness lead to over-concern about the problems of one's children. Shepherd, Oppenheim, and Mitchell (1966) compared 50 children referred to a child-guidance clinic with 50 nonreferred children very carefully matched for similar type and severity of problems. They found the main factor discriminating referrals from nonreferrals was the mother's worry about the child. Nonreferred children were perceived as having temporary difficulties they would outgrow.

Other studies support the idea that parents of referred and nonreferred children see the same problems differently. Conners (1970) described differences in degree, not kind, between parents' descriptions of outpatient children and hypothesized that the factor operating in referral may be parents' threshold for tolerance rather than the actual behavior of children. Campbell and Steinert (1978) reported that ratings from mothers of clinic children fitted neatly into the pattern of Internalizing-Externalizing syndromes (see Chapter 2 by Achenbach), while ratings from mothers of control children were more heterogeneous. Teachers' ratings showed the Internalizing-Externalizing pattern even for the same control children. It would appear that mothers of nonreferred children generalize less about their children's problems, seeing them as discrete and unrelated, rather than as forming patterns. One would expect this attitude to reflect less worry and concern on their part. Finally, an interesting study by Piers (1972) found that there was little difference between the self-concepts of children referred to a clinic, as compared

to those of control children. Mothers of clinic children, however, underestimated their children's actual self-esteem, while parents of control children overestimated their self-esteem. According to Piers, "The answer to the question 'To what extent is a child mentally healthy because his parents think he is?' has not been resolved, but this study certainly indicates that differences between the two groups of parents are much wider than between the two groups of children." (p. 432)

Such findings about parental concern and/or over-concern as a central factor in the referral process can be explained in two general ways. Concern can be an artifact of education, cultural and subcultural expectations, psychological sophistication, and experience or lack of experience with children. Concern, especially over-concern, can also be seen as a reflection of the parents' own emotional problems. Every child care worker knows that parents often identify with their children and project their own problems onto them. In addition, it is often evident that the child is not the "real" problem but represents a focus that a troubled family is willing to accept.

There is some empirical support for the hypothesis that at least part of the parental concern leading to referrals reflects parental problems. The Shepherd et al. (1966) study (cited above), found clinic mothers more concerned about their children's problems and also found a trend for mothers of referred children to describe themselves as "suffering from nerves." Fourteen clinic mothers of 50 described themselves as anxious and easily upset, as mildly depressed, tired and unappreciated, and as finding it difficult to cope with their house, husband, and children, as compared to 6 of 50 nonclinic mothers. This difference does appear to be significant ($X^2 = 4$, d.f. $= 1$, $p < .05$), although not reported as such by Shepherd et al. In addition, there was a tendency for the severity of the child's problem to relate to whether a parent had been treated for or had been severely limited by an emotional disorder.

Several studies have compared the MMPIs of parents of children referred for therapy to those of parents of normal control children. Consistently, the parents of referred children show more pathology (Goodstein and Rowley, 1961; Liverant, 1959; Marks, 1961).

Ferguson and Allen (1978) reported a significant correlation between parents' ratings of their children's adjustment and their satisfaction with their own marriage. In addition, congruence between parent perceptions of the child and of themselves correlated with their ratings of the child's adjustment. This suggests that the amount of harmony in the marriage may be related to perception of the child as adjusted, as well as to the child's actual adjustment. Ferguson, Partyka, and Lester (1974) found that parent perceptions of children who had been referred to a clinic were less congruent than those of nonreferred children. Jacob's (1975) review of the literature found clarity and accuracy of communication between parents to be a factor relating to child disturbance. Parents' inability to agree on their child's emotional adjustment may reflect a family pathology that could bring about actual child disorder or a general family dissatisfaction that results in child referrals, irrespective of the child's needs. It should not be overlooked that having a disturbed child can disrupt the parents' communication patterns and parent adjustment. All three factors probably interact. The findings of Shepherd et al. (1966) and Piers (1972), showing larger parent differences than child differences for clinic versus control children, would indicate, however, that the differences between parents of referred and nonreferred children cannot be attributed solely to the children.

Reliability of Parent Judgments

The discussion of amount of congruence in parents' perceptions of their children raises the question of the reliability of the information given by parents at a child guidance clinic. This is a difficult question to research and much of the information bearing on it is indirect. Dreger et al. (1964) compared descriptions by the mothers of 17 children referred to clinics to the descriptions given by fathers or other close relatives who knew the child intimately. Percentages of agreement on the 229 items, all of which represented actual behavior rather than judgment or inference about behavior, ranged from 10 percent to 55 percent (The average agreement was 36 percent.) Correlations and significance levels are not reported, but this is an astonishing low level of agreement.

Lapouse and Monk (1959) reported the amount of agreement between 193 normal children and their mothers as to their problems. Percentages of agreement were higher than in the Dreger study, but the fact that this was a normal sample must also be kept in mind. For instance, 84 percent of mothers and children agreed on whether the child wet the bed, while only 54 percent of mothers and children agreed on whether the child had nightmares or whether the child had seven or more fears. Mothers' and children's perceptions are far from identical.

Children's self-ratings may be inaccurate or reflect different factors than parent ratings. Glennon and Weisz (1978) reported teacher, parent, and observational ratings of anxiety to correlate with each other, but none of these correlated with the child's self-rating of anxiety. The child's self-rating did correlate with a poor performance on IQ subtests traditionally related to anxiety; none of the adult ratings correlated with the subtest scores.

Miller (1964) reported that parents show greater agreement among themselves than clinicians show in ratings of child behavior. Parent ratings were also more likely to agree with teacher and clinician ratings than were teacher and clinician ratings to agree between themselves.

Identification of problems that depends on the child's past behavior is more difficult because it involves memory factors in the parents (Wenar, 1961). Since Mac-Farlane (1938), researchers have complained of the lack of accuracy of parents' memories about their children's development. Yarrow, Campbell, and Burton (1970) reported that parent recollections of child behaviors are not only inaccurate but also reflect the degree of parent sophistication about what is mentally healthy.

In summary, wide differences have been reported in reliability of parent perceptions about children. This is not surprising, given our previous discussion about family congruence and accuracy of parent communication as factors themselves in child pathology. More systematic study of parent reliability is needed to control for level of parent and child adjustment, family education, degree of structure of the interview or questionnaire, memory factors, and so forth.

Clinical Judgment

Perhaps clinicians, with their presumed perceptiveness about family dynamics, can ignore or weigh judiciously information given by over-concerned parents about their children and are thus able to assess children's problems accurately. The one study directly relating to this issue suggests not. McCoy (1976) asked doctoral candidates in clinical and counseling psychology to evaluate children's need for treatment. The judges were given film clips of normal children showing either positive or negative behavior and were shown parent reports that described either positive or negative behavior. Judgments as to need for treatment were based almost entirely on the content of the parent report. Thirty-eight of the 40 judges considered that at least one of these normal children needed treatment. "In general, judges seemed to treat the report data as though they were a valid and unbiased description of the child, representative of his overall functioning." (p. 714)

One further study sheds light on the relationship between parents' reports and clinical assessment. Forehand, Wells, and Sturgis (1978) commented that parent-report measures are traditionally accepted as accurate assessments. They made home observations of child noncompliance and investigated to what extent parent-report and clinic observations correlated with the child's behavior at home. Neither parent-report nor child behavior in the clinic predicted child behavior at home, although some of the mother's behavior in the clinic could be used to predict the child's behavior at home. This study indicates the complexity of making accurate clinical assessments of children, a complexity that is seldom recognized by clinicians if McCoy's (1976) findings can be generalized.

Validity of Referrals: Characteristics of Referred and Nonreferred Children

We have been considering some of the factors within families that determine which children are referred. We have discovered that in some cases referral of a child tells us more about family characteristics than it does about the child. In actuality, what are the differences between referred and nonreferred children?

Langner et al. (1974) made a large-scale epidemiological study that compared a random cross-section of 1034 urban families to 1000 families receiving welfare. Based on interviews with the mother (a source of which we, by this time, should be cautious), children were rated as to degree of impairment. Of the children in the random cross-sample 13.5 were rated as having marked or severe impairment. Almost 50 percent of these were referred for treatment, and the point-biserial correlation between amount of impairment and referral was .43. Of the children with "well" or "mild" impairment ratings, 7.4 percent were referred. The Langner et al. findings can be considered two ways. First, it should reassure us that there is at least some correlation between degree of impairment and referral, although the correlation is much smaller than one would expect or hope. (We must also remember that the mother is both the informant as to degree of impairment and the most common referral source, and that this may artificially inflate the amount of correlation.) Secondly, the study points to the existence of large numbers of apparently impaired children who are not receiving help.

Conners (1970), as previously mentioned, found significant differences in severity of symptoms between normal, neurotic, and hyperkinetic children. Few qualitative differences were found, however, and parent ratings were again the source of severity estimates.

Dreger et al. (1964) compared 372 children referred to clinics with 90 controls. Of eight factors derived from behavioral items and reflecting problems, referred children showed higher scores on four, nonreferred children on two, and no differences were obtained on two. Dreger et al. also report that control children scored higher on a ninth positive factor measuring confidence and sociality. Again, parents were the source of information.

Schectman (1970a) compared 62 children treated in a mental health clinic with 62 matched controls. Information for the referred children was obtained from clinic files and for the controls from interviews with the mother. Of 91 problem behaviors, only 21 discriminated between clinic and control children, and of these 21, control children appear to have scored higher on three. A later study by Schectman (1971) found only three of the 91 items to discriminate between referred and nonreferred black children.

In summary, referred children appear to receive more severe ratings on scales measuring pathology than nonreferred children, but the size of the difference is often smaller than one would predict. In addition, since parents in all cases are the prime referral source and informants about the severity of the child's problems, we cannot be sure how much of the reported difference in children lies in the perceptions of the parents. Studies on the existence of problems in normal children and studies of demographic variables in child pathology may shed more light on the validity of the referral process.

Problems in Normal Children

In general, surveys of normal children tend to identify relatively large proportions of children with difficulties ordinarily viewed as severe enough to be referred for help. For instance, Werry and Quay (1971) surveyed all children in kindergarten through second grade in Urbana, Illinois. The mean number of behavior symptoms per child, as rated by teachers, was 11.4 for boys and 7.6 for girls. Many symptoms were prevalent; 46 percent of boys were rated as disruptive; 23 percent of boys were rated as showing odd, bizarre behavior; 43 percent of boys were rated as having a short attention span, and so forth. Symptoms were more prevalent in boys than girls, and tended to decrease with age. Werry and Quay concluded that the diagnostic value of individual symptoms is

very limited.

Using mother's responses to a structured interview, Lapouse and Monk (1958, 1959 and Lapouse, 1966) also found normal children's behavior symptoms to be surprisingly high. Of 482 representative normal children aged six to twelve, 17 percent had wet the bed in the past year, 48 percent lost their tempers twice a week or more, and in particular, 43 percent had seven or more present fears and worries. For instance, 44 percent of all children were afraid of snakes, 38 percent feared little cuts and bruises, and 41 percent were afraid of anyone in the family getting sick, having an accident or dying. While mothers' reports as a source of information may be questioned, in this case the authors discovered that mothers *underreported* by 41 percent their children's own reports of fears!

Lapouse and Monk (1964) also found boys to show more behavioral symptoms, in general, than girls though girls were more fearful. Again, the total number of symptoms decreased in older children, though some types of symptoms were more frequent in older children. Schectman (1970) also found symptoms to decrease with age. Rosen, Bahn, and Kramer (1964) also showed that referral to out-patient clinics is age- and sex-related for children, with distinct increases and decreases of referrals with age, at somewhat different ages for boys and girls.

In conclusion, many characteristics of children often taken to be significant clinical symptoms, such as fearfulness, disruptiveness, and so forth, appear, in fact, to be the norm. In addition, "symptoms" appear to be linked to developmental stages, and the popular wisdom in which parents console each other that "this is a stage Mary will grow out of" appears to have a great deal of merit.

Longitudinal Studies

Since many "symptoms" seem to be normal markers of developmental states, one should question whether children might also outgrow the problems for which they are referred to psychotherapy. What is the continuity between childhood and adult psychopathology? Does the deviant child become the deviant adult?

In discussing this issue, we must distinguish between types of problems. The concept of the "environmentally responsive continuum" formed by Prugh, Engel, and Morse (1975) is relevant here. Some childhood disorders, such as brain syndromes and nonfamilial mental retardation, are attributed primarily to organic causes and would be expected to show little change in response to environmental change. With other disorders, the child is more clearly reacting to environmental factors and would be expected to show more response to changes in that environment. Therefore, followup studies of troubled children must specify the classification of the disorder. A further discussion of classification systems will be provided later. At this point we will simply use the broad, popularly accepted categories that have been employed in studies.

Robins has carried out the most careful and relevant followup study of troubled children (1966). She selected children referred 30 years earlier to a psychiatric clinic, contrasted them with a comparable sample of normal school children, and located them as adults. The clinic children were divided into those referred for antisocial behavior (theft, incorrigibility, and so forth,) and those referred for other reasons (learning problems, temper tantrums, nervousness, and so forth). Some of the children were treated at the clinic but the majority were simply evaluated—the clinic serving a consultant role to social workers in the area. Trained lay interviewers reached 491 adult subjects, 82 percent of the target group. Although interviewers knew which adults had been referred as children, they knew nothing of the reason for referral or any history material.

In general, both groups of patients showed more pathology as adults than did the control subjects. However, the patients referred for antisocial behavior were more disturbed than those referred for other problems. They were not only much more likely to be antisocial as adults (71 percent of the antisocial boys had adult arrest records), but were more socially isolated, had more psychiatric hospitalizations, and more

feelings of ill health. Specific antisocial symptoms in childhood predicted not only sociopathic diagnoses in adulthood but also alcoholism, chronic brain syndrome, and hysteria. While some other non-antisocial symptoms in childhood also predicted adult diagnoses, the majority (20 out of 31) did not.

"Included among those nonantisocial symptoms which appear related little or not at all to adult psychiatric status are some of the symptoms which most frequently bring children to psychiatric attention: fearfulness, hypersensitivity, shyness, tics, and speech defects. The evidence of the current study seems to be that these symptoms do not portend psychiatric illness, however much they may disturb parent-child relationships while they occur. Almost all of the common antisocial symptoms, on the other hand, did predict later difficulties." (Robins, 1966, pp. 151-152)

Robins, in her 1970 review of other follow-up studies, reiterated these conclusions. Antisocial childhood referrals seem most predictive of adult deviance; other types of referrals are less clearly related.

Other writers disagree about the relationship between neurotic-type disorders in childhood and adult disturbance. Morris, Soroker, and Burruss (1954) reported that children diagnosed (but not treated) as shy and withdrawn 16 to 27 years earlier mainly showed satisfactory adjustment as adults. Only 2 of the 34 were seen as "sick" and two-thirds were satisfactorily adjusted.

Miller et al., (1972) reported an interesting two-year follow-up study of school phobics who were therapeutic failures. Only 7 percent remained severely school phobic; the majority showed dramatic changes. Sixty percent of these children had additional treatment, however, which is a complicating factor.

Coolidge, Brodie, and Feeney (1964), on the other hand, found that 50 percent of supposedly cured school phobics showed fearful behaviors that could be traced back to their phobias. This is an example of what Levitt (1971) discussed as "developmental symptom substitution": while childhood problems may seem to disappear, they can also reappear in guises more related to later developmental stages.

Waldron (1976) followed up 24 school phobic subjects, 18 children diagnosed as having other neuroses and 20 controls. Average age at follow-up was twenty-two. Waldron found those children referred for help were far more disturbed as adults than the controls. Two problems exist with this study, however. First, the children appear to have been in treatment, although "No patient received adequate treatment by psychoanalytic standards." (p. 537) Second, Waldron conducted most of the follow-up interviews; although he did not know the child's previous record, it is likely that in the course of a three-and-a-half hour psychiatric interview, such information frequently appeared. The possibility of inadvertent experimenter bias is suggested by the difference in findings between clinical ratings of pathology and diagnoses made from rating scales. Clinical evaluation found 75 percent of the former patients to be at least mildly ill, compared to 15 percent of the controls. On the ratings scales, 69 percent of the former patients were mildly ill, compared to 35 percent of the controls—a much smaller difference. The discrepancy in results may also be due to other factors, as Waldron suggested.

In summary, children with neurotic-type problems appear in adulthood less well adjusted than controls. The amount of impairment varies and the best-designed of the studies found few specific symptoms to predict pathology in adulthood. Antisocial behavior in children, however, is a clearer sign of serious problems in adulthood.

Of the less "environmentally responsive" disorders, the most research has been carried out on mental retardation and psychoses in childhood. The results with regard to mental retardation are quite encouraging. Charles and Baller conducted successive follow-up evaluations of a group of mentally retarded children in Nebraska (Baller, Charles, and Miller, 1967; Charles, 1957). They looked at the children whose IQ ranged from 42 to 70, and who were referred to training programs, and in 1967 compared them with a group of children from the same school whose IQ ranged from 72 to 88, and with a group of average

IQ. Although the range of IQs in the groups had not changed, the functioning of the retarded and border-line groups was remarkably adjusted. While 96 percent of the control group was self-supporting, 90 percent of the border-line group was self-supporting, and about 80 percent of the retarded group was consistently employed. About two-thirds did not require welfare. Only 7 percent of the retarded group was institutionalized. About 30 percent of the original retarded group had died, however, probably indicating the organic basis of the retardation in many cases.

Other researchers, such as Kennedy (1948) and Bijou, Ainsworth, and Stockey (1943), have reported similar positive follow-ups of the retarded. The implication of the findings seems to be that intelligence as measured by IQ tests is not as highly correlated to adaptive functioning as it is often thought to be.

The follow-up studies of psychosis in childhood are more confusing. Bennett and Klein (1976) traced back the first cases of childhood schizophrenia to be diagnosed and of 12 found only one was able to live outside the hospital. Eggers (1978), however, in a careful and well-designed study found that of children with clear schizophrenic symptoms, 50 percent had at least a good social adaptation at follow-up, an average of 15 years later. Such large discrepancies in results are typical of other studies and are related to several factors, one of which is the age at which the psychotic diagnosis is made. Ignoring such factors, the most common figure for a later social adjustment for the psychotic child is about one-third. [Bender (1973) reported 37 percent social adjustment; Eisenberg and Kanner (1956) reported 27 percent good or fair outcomes; Lotter (1974) reported 37 percent good or fair outcomes; Rees (1975) reported 34 percent successful outcomes; Rutter, Greenfield, and Lockyer (1967) reported 39 percent good or fair outcomes.]

The chief factor in the differences between studies is probably the lack of agreement about the classifications of childhood psychosis. As Russo discusses in Chapter 6, both infantile autism and childhood schizophrenia lack consistency as diagnostic entities and both show similarities to and overlap with organic conditions. Knobloch and Pasamanick (1974), for instance, reported that of 39 autistic children, autistic behavior had disappeared at follow-up in three-fourths of them. However, most children showed poorer IQ or developmental quotient performance at follow-up, leading them to consider autism as "global aphasia," that is, a neurological rather than an schizophrenic condition. Eaton and Menolascino (1967) reported, in a five-year follow-up of psychotic children, that about a quarter showed clearer indication of neurological problems at that time. Many studies show poor prognosis to be strongly related to low intelligence in the children (Eggers, 1978; Knobloch and Pasamanick, 1974; Lotter, 1974; Rees and Taylor, 1975; Rutter et al., 1967), and this also suggests neurological impairment.

In summary, even in the case of disorders not considered to be environmentally responsive, a sizable proportion of children make acceptable adult adjustments. About one-third of children with diagnoses of psychosis in childhood make a later adjustment, and approximately 80 percent of children mildly and moderately retarded later make at least a marginal adjustment to society.

There appears to be some relationship between disturbance in childhood and later adjustment problems as an adult. We have mentioned that some of the long-term studies presented are complicated by the issue of what type of treatment, if any, was received by the child. Does treatment make the occurrence of future problems less likely? Let us examine studies that compare the outcomes of children who did and did not receive psychotherapy, with the recognition that most of these studies do not follow the child's progress into adulthood as far as those just presented.

Effects of Psychotherapy

Levitt several times (1957, 1963, 1971) reviewed the literature on psychotherapy with children. He used as a control group those children who are treatment defectors and found about two-thirds showing improvement. (This seems relatively congruent with the longitudinal studies we discussed of neurotic-type disorders in childhood.) Levitt found that in a variety of therapy studies there was approximately the same two-thirds rate of improvement, concluding that therapy is ineffective. Barrett, Hampe, and Miller (1978) reviewed more recent studies and concurred with Levitt. The Shepherd et al. (1966) study, mentioned earlier, discovered no difference between children who had received therapy for their emotional problems and those children matched for severity of problems who received no therapy. A slightly higher percentage of the treated children improved, but a higher percentage also deteriorated; neither difference was significant.

Such negative findings for the effectiveness of therapy are understandable when we consider how the cognitive immaturity of children affects their problems and how the dependency of children makes it difficult for them to make changes in their environment. Few therapies (outside of play therapy,) have been developed specifically for children; it may be that new, more effective therapeutic techniques could be generated if children's special needs were to be more directly considered.

If individual psychotherapy with children has not been shown to be generally effective, it is nevertheless the case that family approaches have been shown to be. Levitt (1971) cited several studies showing participation of the parents to improve therapy results for children. Love and Kaswan (1974) found treatment focused on the child alone to be less effective than treatment focused on the parents without the child's participation.

In addition, reviews of studies on the effectiveness of using parents as change agents for their children have found such procedures to be effective. Both Tavormina (1974) and Reisinger, Ora, and Frangia (1976) found parent counseling and instruction as to childrearing to be effective within a range of studies using both behavioral and psychodynamic approaches. Although some of the studies reviewed lacked precise methodology, recent studies (Tavormina, 1975; Martin, 1977) found interventions with parents improve in family problems.

Two basic conclusions seem warranted: (1) treatment of the child alone tends to be ineffective; and (2) treatment of the family system appears to be effective. If the appropriate unit for intervention with children's problems is the family, it then appears that to identify whom to treat and what problems are amenable, we must focus on dimensions within the family as a whole rather than within the child. We must consider larger social variables, such as social class.

Social Class Variation

Extremely clear-cut findings link adult mental disorder to social class (Dohrenwend, 1969, 1974). It is interesting that with children, the correlations are not so clear-cut. While IQs seem lower (see Chapter 7) and brain dysfunction seems more prevalent in lower-class children (Amante et al., 1977), there is some disagreement about emotional disorder.

Lapouse and Monk (1964) found negligible differences between number of symptoms in upper- and lower-class white children in their normal sample. The Langner et al. (1974) survey of welfare children and a normal cross-section of children in Manhattan showed welfare children to have more marked and severe disturbances than the cross-section children (23.1 to 13.5 percent). These differences are not large, however, and Conger and Coie (1975) pointed out that more welfare children are rated well or minimally disturbed than cross-section children (9.9 to 5.9 percent). Discussing several problems in measurement, they concluded that either there are no differences between the two groups of children or that measurement problems obscure real differences.

Harris (1974) found that lower-income parents of children attending an outpatient clinic reported that their children had more problems than higher income parents reported about their children attending the same clinic. This finding could, of course, be an artifact of the referral process; upper-class parents are quicker to refer their children for more minor problems (Shepherd

et al., 1966; Langner et al., 1974). When Conners (1970) compared clinic children to normal, he found social class to have a remarkably small effect on symptoms or factor patterns. Lapouse (1966) found mothers' ratings of maladjustment to be higher for lower-class children, although the lower-class children showed no more behavioral symptoms than middle-class children. Angelino (1956) reported that while the type of fear held by children was linked to their social class, there were no significant differences in number of fears held by upper and lower social-class children. He cited several other studies with similar findings.

Robins (1966) found the antisocial children in her study to come, as expected, largely from lower social-class backgrounds. However, the best predictors of later sociopathy were not social class but the extent of the child's antisocial behavior and the psychiatric status of the father. More disturbed fathers and more antisocial behavior in children were concentrated in the lower classes, but the predictive factors proved to be these individual characteristics rather than social class itself.

What can we conclude from these minor effects of social class on childhood psychopathology? Perhaps the negative impact of lower social class has immediate physical effects on brain functioning through inferior nutrition and medical care, but the negative psychological impact is slower to occur. It may be that the child is so dependent on the immediate environment that larger social factors have only an indirect influence. Whatever the explanatory factors, the findings are another indication that to discuss childhood disorder using principles derived from adult psychopathology seems not to work well.

Conclusions on Identifying Psychopathology in Children

About 50 percent of severely disturbed children are referred for treatment (Langner et al., 1974). This is important, since such children are the most likely to become severely disturbed adults. Improved procedures for identifying severely disturbed children would be valuable, and diagnostic categories, such as psychotic or delinquent, would seem *from these considerations* to be appropriate categories to have in use.

Less severely disturbed children, however, seem to be referred as a function of parental over-concern and family conflict. Their problems are often indistinguishable from those of normal, nonreferred children, and such problems seem specific to certain ages and developmental stresses, disappearing as the child matures. For these reasons, our present means of identifying children who need help are inefficient and ineffective, since they focus on the child as the source of the problem. Diagnostic systems that identify dimensions of the troubled family could, at least hypothetically, replace the diagnostic system for children who are not seriously disturbed.

Even for the severely disturbed child, it may be appropriate to question our labeling practices. It appears as though both severely troubled and mildly disturbed children are helped in treatment only when the parents are also treated; severe, as well as mild disturbance, occurs in a family context. Russo, in his chapter in this book, points out how few factors conclusively differentiate psychotic children from others. Two other issues are relevant here and need to be discussed. Even when a label accurately identifies a child to be in need of help, is it useful to provide that help? Secondly, what are the negative effects of applying the label to the child?

LABELING AND THE PRAGMATIC APPROACH

The labeling perspective has been attacked so frequently, so cogently, and from so many theoretical points of view, that there is little need be said about it. Sociologists and psychologists have shown that labels reflect social judgments and roles over which the labeled person has little control—with little to do with her or his behavior or personal characteristics (Carson, 1969; Goffman, 1961; Rappaport and Cleary, 1980; Sarbin, 1970; Scheff, 1966, 1975; Schur, 1971). When mental health professionals engage in the labeling process, they assume a judgmental and moralistic stance toward the labeled person that emphasizes the superiority of the judge, the dependency of the labeled person, and that is contrary to a helping role (Caplan and Nelson, 1973; Laing, 1967; Rogers, 1950; Szasz, 1969). All stress the most important point: labeling creates its own reality. A process of reification occurs in which saying something makes it so. The potential detrimental effects on the labeled person are obvious, and they have been amply demonstrated empirically (Larkin and Loman, 1977; Rist, 1970; Rosenhan, 1973; Rosenthal and Jacobson, 1968; Zimbardo, 1973).

When children, as compared to adults, are given labels, their dependency exacerbates the negative effects. First, children's greater dependency on the environment makes them more prone to be labeled on the basis of environmental factors outside their control. Rist (1970), for instance, found that by the eighth day of kindergarten, teachers labeled children's ability according to social-class variables, such as the child's dress and the father's occupation. Second, more dependency on the environment means that such labels have a more profound effect. As compared to an adult, the child is less aware of having been labeled, less capable of arguing with the person who does the labeling and less capable of changing behavior or changing external aspects of themselves that have been judged, such as clothes, haircut, cleanliness, braces, glasses, and so forth. (Perhaps every child has a memory of being forced to wear something that made him or her an object of ridicule.) In addition, adults can create a new environment for themselves, while children are completely incapable of leaving the environment in which they have received a negative label. In fact, the attempt itself to leave the environment is labeled as new deviance—school phobia, running away, truancy, withdrawal, and the whole gamut of "avoidance." One might speculate that much so-called deviance in children may represent a healthy attempt to escape the deleterious effects of labels. It may be that one of the reasons the model of adult psychopathology applies so poorly to children is that the defenses and behavior that serve defensive functions in adults are primarily maladaptive because more appropriate coping mechanisms are available; in the child the same avoidance mechanisms can be adaptive since other means of coping are more limited.

At any rate, the effect of the label can be far-reaching. Larkin and Loman (1977) showed that parents accept the labels given by professionals to innocuous behavior, and McCoy (1976), as previously mentioned, has shown that professionals accept parents' labels. The ability groups Rist (1970) reported, as formed at the eighth day of kindergarten, remained together for years. The Rosenthal and Jacobson (1968) findings on the effect of labels on children's IQ are well known.

Perhaps the most damaging effect of the label is on the child's self-image. The third way in which childhood dependency exacerbates labeling effects is through children's greater reliance on others for their self-evaluations. While inner sensations of competence and incompetence undoubtably effect self-esteem (White, 1960), there seems little question that the children's self-concepts are also formed by what they are taught to think about their competence. Thus, reflected appraisals, labels, conditions of worth, and so forth, affect the child's identity. Schur (1971) has given a particularly compelling account of how the label "juvenile delinquent" can transform the child into a delinquent.

It seems, then, that we must be especially careful to avoid the insidious effects of labels on children. Hobbs and his associates (1975a, 1975b), working on the federally funded Project on the Classification of Exceptional Children, have devoted a great deal of attention to this issue. Hobbs suggested that one method of diagnosis that may avoid negative labeling effects is simply to describe the child's assets and liabilities in the way that best facilitates interventions. This suggestion deserves careful consideration.

A Pragmatic Approach to Classification

To understand Hobbs' contribution, we must consider the basic practical purpose of medical diagnosis: the specification of appropriate therapeutic interventions. The approved American Psychiatric Association diagnostic systems for psychological disorders are based on the model for medical disorder. Spitzer, Sheehy, and Endicott (1977), in discussing the guiding principles of the American Psychiatric Association's *DSM-III*, described the purposes of medical diagnosis as four: communication between professionals; specification of treatment; information about outcome; and information about etiology. It can be argued that while communication between professionals constitutes a separate purpose for diagnosis, information about etiology and outcome is primarily of value in terms of their inevitable involvement with treatment specification. That is, notions about etiology and the course of a disorder indicate how the disorder should be handled. While occasionally they may be unrelated to treatment (as in electroshock as a treatment for depression), we generally find the lack of relationship an unsatisfactory state of affairs. Medicine is the healing profession; its basic purpose would seem to be healing.

Spitzer et al. stressed that *DSM-III* is based on the medical model. In fact, however, *DSM-III* is primarily descriptive. The explanation provided for this contradiction is that for most of the disorders covered, the etiology is unknown. Thus, there is also no attempt to discuss appropriate treatment for the disorders.

This is, then, the failure of the medical model. Whereas a single descriptive term—like diabetes or pneumonia—can suggest etiology and treatment for a medical disease, this is not currently possible for psychological disorders. It may be that our conceptualizations are still too primitive; this is the explanation favored by the *DSM-III* workers as to why their system is descriptive. It seems more likely, however, that the model itself is at fault. If, after a quarter century of arduous labor our descriptions of disorders still contain minimal implications for what we should do for the disorders, then perhaps we are going about it the wrong way. The multi-axial approach of *DSM-III* implies some recognition of the need for a changed approach, but the basic medical model has not been changed.

What needs revision within the medical model is the implication of a disorder residing like a tumor or a virus within the person. As we have tried to demonstrate, this model is particularly inappropriate with children. Hobbs makes this point clearly:

Finally, using the individual child as the basic unit for describing, classifying and programming (and neglecting to consider his family, his school, his community) has inherent limitations. . . . The child's exceptional status is defined in the first place by a complex matrix of relationships. Diagnosis and treatment must attend to these relationships, not to the child alone. (1975a, p. 104)

Broadening the context of child assessment has three important consequences: (1) we are more likely to label correctly which child-family units need help; (2) we avoid the negative effects of labeling the child as "owning" the disorder; and (3) we are better able to identify those parts of the system into which we can and should intervene. A family-enviornmental systems approach, then, is basically a pragmatic one. It is less likely to do harm through inaccurate or negative labels and more likely to guide appropriate intervention.

What Hobbs specifically suggests is that we make up a profile describing the child's assets and liabilities as they relate to the expectations held by significant others, keeping in mind the effect of the particular setting at the particlar time. Thus, to use Hobbs' example, aggressive behavior may be regarded as antisocial in one setting, whereas in another it is necessary for survival. Our treatment goals will obviously be different in these cases, and should develop naturally from the case profile. Information relating to other services needed by the child should also be indicated in the profile, for example, a need for tutoring, glasses, treatment for diabetes, neurological exam, drugs the family cannot afford, and other needs.

Hobbs' ideas seem sensible and sound. They represent what Prugh, Engel, and Morse (1975), working within Hobbs' commission, cited as *assessment*, rather than *classification* per se. That is, these writers distinguish between the considerations that apply to evaluation and clinical assessment and those that apply to a formal system of classification. The purposes of assessment—formulating treatment plans, etiology, and prognosis—are best served by multiple considerations and dimensions. A formal classification system serves other purposes: professional communication, research, epidemiological record keeping and surveying, and insurance claims. Hobbs is not addressing himself to classification, and we will discuss this later.

It seems that Hobbs' suggestions do not go far enough; the child and his symptoms (for example, "aggressive behavior") are still the focus of the formulations and the services needed. Classification systems bear some relationship to assessment formulations. They tend to summarize and abbreviate our formulations and emerge with a single label. No matter how innocuous this label sounds, once it become part of a system, it takes on negative connotations—e.g. the history of our labels for the retarded. Thus, "aggressive child" can come to have all the stigmatizing effects that Hobbs abhors, no matter how much detail of the social context he has supplied in the assessment.

When assessment focuses on the family and environment rather than the child still more than the focus in Hobbs' examples, it may be easier to avoid labeling the child. Take the following fictional formulation.

Mr. C. perceives his son, John, age nine, as inadequate, due to John's poor coordination for sports and his average grades and intellectual ability, inferior to Mr. C.'s own academic accomplishment as a lawyer. Failure to meet his father's expectations leaves John himself feeling inadequate and depressed; he has reacted with a rather severe withdrawal. Mrs. C. responds by overprotecting John and by anger at Mr. C., which leads to further sense of inadequacy and guilt in John. There is a need for: better information for Mr. C. on normal child behavior and maturation, exploration of Mr. C's expectations about himself, exploration of Mrs. C's perceptions of John and of herself, improved communication between parents with focus on problem-solving and conflict resolution, more experience of success for John (what does he do well? what new activities might he succeed in?), and more reinforcement for success for John (increased parental understanding, contact with the school to increase reinforcement from teachers).

If a single phrase "diagnosis" is to be gleaned from the description, it should be, not "depression" or "introverted disorder," but something like "incongruent family expectations." This may seem to be merely shifting the stigma from the child to the family, but at least the stigma is more easily dealt with by the family than by the child. It should be made clear, also, that the point is not to shift the burden and the "blame" to the father alone or to the mother and father. The child plays his part as well; with a different type of child there might be no problems whatsoever in the family. The shared responsibility should make blaming and scapegoating, both within the family and from without, less frequent, and make taking responsibility for change easier for all family members. And, obviously, it makes development of an appropriate treatment plan easier.

There are, of course, many disorders—organicity, retardation, psychosis, psychosomatic disorders—that apparently reside within the child. These are the less "environmentally responsive" disorders (Prugh, Morse, and Engel, 1975), that are less responsive to changes in the environment and correspondingly involve a higher degree of biological versus environmental causation of the disorder. This continuum appears to be an important dimension for assessment. The extent of physiological involvement in a child's problem should be assessed, with implications for treatment and prognosis.

While not all children's problems can be seen as family problems, they are nevertheless treated through the use and manipulation of the child's environment. This is not true or less true for adults who can usually take responsibility for their own treatment. Thus, for a child with epilepsy, drugs will be administered by the family; and an assessment is required of the family's level of responsibility, ability to afford medication, perceptions of the disorder, and of the side-effects of the drugs. Whether institutionalization will be needed depends not only on the severity and frequency of attacks but on the resources of the family: perceptions and expectations of the child; parents' ego strength; financial resources; existence of alternate parenting figures; presence of how many other children of what ages; parental sensitivity to cues of on-coming attacks; and so forth. While the amount of focus on the child's behavior necessary in a treatment plan will vary from problem to problem, there are always interventions needed on the family level as well, if only information, support, and advice.

I am not arguing that all childhood disorders should be given a family label but that, whenever possible, they should be. When they cannot be, one important dimension for a multi-axial system should be the amount of support or stress provided by the family or immediate environment. "Childhood epilepsy within a family of unusual resources" or "childhood epilepsy within a conflicted, anxious family" are possible types of labels that convey more information and less stigma for the child.

In the following section, I will discuss the formal classification systems currently available, using Hobbs' pragmatic approach and the research findings presented earlier as a framework in which to evaluate such systems. Phillips, Dragun, and Bartlett (1975), working as part of Hobbs' commission, have made some specific recommendations for a classification system for children, and it is appropriate to list these as part of the framework we will be using. They recommend: (1) a pragmatic system that is open to revision in response to experience with the system; (2) a system that incorporates research findings; (3) a system that avoids the application of adult models to children; (4) a system that regards children's problems in the context of maturational and developmental stages; (5) a multi-axial system providing information along several dimensions rather than a one-or two-word label; (6) a system that identifies the situational context of the child's behavior; (7) a system that fosters communication between professionals outside the mental health field (teachers, judges, police, and others.) and between these persons and mental health professions, rather than simply communication within the profession. We have already alluded to the need for all of the above, with the exceptions of (1) and (7), and these have obvious merit. We might also add recommendations for a system to (1) show more recognition of the variability and apparent deviations in "normal" child behavior; (2) label the problem as interactional whenever possible; (3) when not possible to label as interactional, in describing etiology and recommending treatment for the problem, identify family characteristics.

CURRENT CLASSIFICATION SYSTEMS

The above recommendations seemingly constitute an impossible classification system. Systems, by their very nature, do not deal well with situational contexts, maturational contexts, family contexts, interpersonal interactions, and so forth. Their purpose is nomothetic, not idiographic. They seek to reduce a complex, unique situation to a recognizable concept or two. The idea of portraying complexity and uniqueness is contrary to the idea of facilitating communication and research. That is, the functions of labels for treatment and for research may be contradictory. Treatment can only effectively operate within a specific context; research as a scientific discipline attempts to remove the specific context to reveal general laws.

How do we resolve this contradiction? We can, as Prugh, Engel, and Morse (1975) suggested, consider assessment and classification separately. We can provide, for the purposes of treatment, a formulation that includes all the contextual variables we consider relevant and then supply a classificatory phrase for research and recording purposes. The problem with this approach is that, given what we know about labels, the paragraph will tend to be ignored, and the one-word or short-phrase label will be reified.

A better solution seems to be to build complexity into the label, although more complex assessments will be needed for treatment purposes. This approach, essentially the multi-axial approach, specifies relevant dimensions on which the context of an individual's problem must be de-

scribed. A multi-axial approach has several potential advantages. It should tend to limit the deleterious effect of labels, because the context is embedded into the label. There should be no one word or phrase in the label that can be used pejoratively. A multi-axial approach should describe the context in a form relevant to treatment. It should tend to foster communication, since simple one-word or phrase diagnoses convey limited information. Finally, it should facilitate research, since it could identify relevant variables to investigate and control.

The development of multi-axial approaches is the most significant improvement in our classification systems. Let us look briefly at the background of classification systems for children.

Development of Major Classification Systems for Children

Although many authors developed classification systems of their own, the first system to have the backing of a nationwide organization, the American Psychiatric Association, was *DSM-I*. Published in 1951, it reflected the experience of psychiatrists during World War II and their need for a comprehensive diagnostic system. Perhaps because the nature of their wartime experience was quite unrelated to children, the system contained few references to children and no real attempt to classify their problems. The Group for the Advancement of Psychiatry (GAP) addressed itself to this unfilled need. In 1957 it published a report on the diagnostic process in child psychiatry, dealing with what we have called here assessment, and in 1966 it published what has been a standard for child classification. Although the concepts used were basically psychoanalytic, the GAP showed a laudatory concern for the contextual aspects of children's problems. The three basic aspects of its theoretical framework were in fact interactional: (1) the psychosomatic concept—the interaction between mind and body; (2) the developmental dimension—the need to look at the child in the context of stages of development; and (3) the psychosocial aspects of the child's interactions with family and society. Engel (1969) pointed out that the GAP system can thus be seen as the forerunner for multiple classification.

The system had many other positive features. It included the category of Healthy Responses to account for normal variations and situational and developmental crises. The category was not simply a label to apply when there was an absence of symptomatology; it made a statement that many childhood "symptoms" were in fact healthy reactions. The GAP system included an important category for Developmental Deviation (motor, sensory, psychosexual, and so forth) to account for such differences within a maturational context. While the classification system for adults was essentially retained in the rest of the major categories (Psychoneurotic Disorders, Personality Disorders, Psychotic Disorders, Psychophysiologic Disorders, Brain Syndromes, Mental Retardation, Other Disorders), many of these categories were adapted so as to make them more appropriate to the changeable situationalism of childhood disorder. Thus, children could be classified as Isolated Personality or Mistrustful Personality, rather than Schizoid or Paranoid. Overly Dependent, Overly Inhibited, and Oppositional were other Personality Disorders included as appropriate only to children, and there was an attempt to make Psychotic Disorders specific to the varieties shown in infancy, childhood, and adolescence.

In 1968, the American Psychiatric Association published its revised *DSM-II*, and in this revision more attention was given to childhood disorder than in the previous manual. Transient situational disorders of infancy, childhood, and adolescence were included. (Such problems were classified as Healthy Responses in the GAP system, a label with less potential negative implications.) There was no attempt to modify for children adult classifications of Personality Disorders or Psychoses (other than the inclusion of Schizophrenic Reaction, childhood type) and no inclusion of developmental deviations. *DSM-II*, however, did include a new major category, Behavior Disorders of Childhood and Adolescence, to account for disorders more stable than Situational Disorders but less stable than

Psychoses, Neuroses, and Personality Disorders. "This intermediate stability is attributed to the greater fluidity of all behavior at this age." (p. 50) Behavior Disorders included Hyperkinetic Reaction, Withdrawing Reaction, Overanxious Reaction, Runaway Reaction, Unsocialized Aggressive Reaction, Group Delinquent Reaction, and Other Reaction. These classifications included some of the "new" Personality Disorders proposed by the GAP, and also had the advantage that many disorders, including some antisocial behavior, could be given a classification with fewer permanent connotations than a Personality Disorder.

While *DSM-II* became the official classification system currently in use, some of the advantages of the GAP system (Bemporad, Pfeiffer, and Bloom, 1970) led to its continued use. Also in 1968, a new multiaxial classification system appeared (Rutter, Lebovici, Eisenberg, Sneznevskij, Sadoun, Brooke and Lin) that used many of the GAP concepts. The World Health Organization had organized a group to provide a basis for the revision of the International Classification of Diseases, and the result was a tri-axial classification of mental disorder in childhood. The first axis was the psychiatric syndrome; the second the child's intellectual level (regardless of etiology); and the third axis noted any associated or etiological factors, both physical and environmental. It was recognized that more work was needed in elaborating relevant environmental factors, and the WHO group merely suggested "two broad categories: factors of a social or material nature and factors of an emotional or attitudinal nature." (p. 52)

The actual categories for clinical classification proposed by the WHO group overlapped closely with the GAP recommendations (Prugh, Engel, and Morse, 1975). They included a category of Normal Variation, an Adaptation Reaction to refer to transient disorders, and Developmental Disorders. The category of psychoses was adapted to be relevant to infancy and childhood, and a Hyperkinetic Syndrome was included.

The American Psychiatric Association provided a more developed multi-axial system in *DSM-III*. It also adapted the system to the ninth revision of the International Classification of Diseases. *DSM-III* includes five axes. The first and second axes describe the current psychiatric syndrome, if relevant, (Axis 1), and the long-term personality structure, if relevant (Axis II). That is, there is an attempt to describe and differentiate between current and long-term functioning. Children's learning disorders, interestingly, are coded on Axis II. The rationale is that such developmental deviations are so common in conjunction with other childhood disorders that they should be routinely recorded.

The third axis consists of physical disorders relevant to the treatment or management of the emotional disorders. Such physical disorder need not be etiological but could, for instance, refer to the diabetes of a child with a conduct disorder. One is reminded of Hobbs' insistence that diagnosis contain a comprehensive assessment of the child's needs; in this perspective, the inclusion of physical factors seems to the good. Other factors, such as social and cognitive ones, might be more worthy of inclusion, however. The fact that all clinicians are required to apply this axis has had the unfortunate effect of emphasizing the medical model underlying this classification system. Adherence to the medical model is, of course, a point of contention between many psychiatrists and psychologists, (Schast and Nathan, 1977), and is one of the basic reasons the American Psychological Association has yet witheld its approval from *DSM-III*. (Foltz, 1980)

Axis IV indicates the specific psychosocial stressors and rates their severity. A long list of family factors relevant to the lives of children and adolescents is provided, such as "cold or distant relationship between parents," "parental intrusiveness," "inconsistent parental control," "insufficient social or cognitive stimulation," and so forth. Axis V is the highest level of adaptive functioning reached by the patient in the last year, considering occupation (or school performance), social relations and use of leisure time (more important when there is no occupation as with young children). These axes, if utilized, require the clinician to recognize and include the context and situation of an individual's problems. They represent an enormous step in our approach to classifying emotional disorder.

The actual classification of childhood disorders stresses that adult classifications are to be used whenever appropriate. Children's problems are considered to be of five varieties:

1) intellectual (mental retardation)
2) behavioral (attention deficit disorder; conduct disorder)
3) emotional (anxiety disorder; other disorders)
4) physical (eating disorders; stereotyped movement disorders; other disorders with physical manifestations)
5) developmental (pervasive developmental disorders; learning disabilities)

There are a total of 45 individual diagnoses within these five categories. There is no longer a category for childhood schizophrenia, although autism is retained as a separate diagnosis.

Evaluation of Current Classification Systems

Criticisms of each of the systems presented could be made from varying theoretical orientations, and all could certainly be criticized from a scientific viewpoint. Some of the specific categories used within some systems are more justifiable than others. Let us here restrict ourselves, however, to a critique from the pragmatic viewpoint—already described.

The multi-axial systems described, especially *DSM-III*, are contextual in the picture given of the child's disorder, and this is the greatest improvement shown. The use of concrete descriptive categories, as would be expected, has led to improved reliability in comparison to earlier diagnostic systems (Beitchman, Dielman, Landis, Benson and Kemp, 1978; *DSM-III*, 1980; Spitzer, Forman and Nee, 1979; Spitzer and Forman, 1979). One would also expect the use of more operational categories to provide for more ease in revision in response to research findings. In fact, *DSM-III* reports that reliability improved for adult classification in Phase Two of their study, using diagnostic criteria revised after a series of Phase One field trials. The reliability for childhood diagnosis, however, did not improve in Phase Two, and in fact tended to be lower.

An additional advantage of the atheoretical *DSM-III* approach is that it is probably more easily understood by nonprofessionals.

In some respects, however, the more theoretical GAP system is easier to apply and more open to construct validation. Our constructs about personality and classification may be primitive and widely different within different schools, but without the use of some constructs, it is hard to see how we will ever make much progress in understanding psychopathology.

As Achenbach argues in the following chapter, classification empirically arrived at may be used to form new constructs about psychopathology. One of the major criticisms of *DSM-III's* childhood classification system is that its long list of childhood syndromes does not appear to be connected with the extensive research cited by Achenbach. The American Psychological Association is considering, for this reason, formulating its own child classification system, (Foltz, 1980), concluding that there is enough evidence for an empirically-derived system.

The *DSM-III* system is also open to the criticism that its lists of disorders are over-inclusive. Garmezy (1978) protested that the system provides pathological labels and incorporates within a system of mental disorder many behaviors that are either normal or not appropriately treated by psychiatry or psychology. Garmezy pointed out that "Shyness Disorder" (in the final form of the manual "Avoidant Disorder") as defined could apply to millions of children, that "Reading Disorder" is caused by a multitude of interrelated factors and is poorly served by considering it a mental disorder, and that Developmental Disorders are not (as in the WHO system) treated as temporary deviations from the norm. Garmezy feels that the system is an attempt to enhance the status and scope of psychiatry, and as such is dangerous to the children it proposes to serve. The American Psychological Association (1981)

in its official statement on *DSM-III* has also questioned the broadening of the range and scope of categories of mental disorder.

All the recent classification systems presented, show recognition of developmental stages in their inclusion of developmental deviations as diagnoses. In the view of the author, however, none of the recent classification systems presented show enough recognition of the variability of normal behavior. With the exception of the GAP category of "Healthy Behavior," there is little room for placing the "normal" symptom in the context of adaptation. One of the most serious criticisms of all systems presented is their application of adult models of psychopathology to children. All systems presented that use the category of "neurosis" apply it to children exactly as to adults. Most also apply at least some of the adult categories of personality disorders and psychoses to children. The *DSM-III* recommendation that child categories are to be used only when adult diagnoses cannot be applied shows little recognition of the special nature of children's problems.

The *DSM-III* classification for children was criticized by the American Psychological Association (1981). Although adopting *DSM-III*, the Association specifically cited its poor applicability to disorders in childhood. The Association organized its own task force to develop a more dimensional behavioral classification (Foltz, 1980), with the understanding that the results of classification research would provide much of the basis for this new system. Achenbach in Chapter Two summarizes much of this research literature.

The remaining difficulty with all the systems presented is the absence of interactional labels. Children are still described as though they own the disorder, even though some family patterns are incorporated into Axis IV of *DSM-III*. From all the evidence we have reviewed, this seems an unfounded assumption for most of the continuum of innate to environmental etiology of children's problems.

One of the reasons for the lack of interactional labels is that it would appear to be difficult to reach agreement on what might be an appropriate system of interactional classification. Fisher (1976), however, in a review of 29 schemas and systems of family assessment, concluded that there is "surprising comparability" among the dimensions presented in different approaches. He provides an overview of family assessment dimensions with five categories: (1) Structural Descriptors (roles, alliances, patterns of communication, and so forth); (2) Controls and Sanctions (power, flexibility, exercise of control); (3) Emotions and Needs (methods for affective expression, need satisfaction, and so forth; (4) Cultural Aspects; and (5) Developmental Aspects. It appears that the first three categories alone could be used with some elaboration to provide useful descriptions of families.

To summarize, while *DSM-III* is the most developed multi-axial system, it lacks a theoretical basis and has not incorporated some of the strong points of earlier systems such as the GAP. All systems lack interactional labels.

PRACTICAL IMPLICATIONS

The dangers of harming children through unnecessary treatment and labels have been stressed so thoroughly that it is necessary to consider briefly the process that takes place for children who do need help. The following is an attempt to spell out for the psychologist, psychiatrist, or social worker working with children the fairly obvious implications of the point of view that has been expressed here.

First, the professional working with children should keep in mind the wide range of normal variation in behavior and development. Perhaps most professionals would benefit from more experience with "normal" children in a teaching or recreational setting. The professional would then be better able to identify the sophisticated parent or teacher who is overreacting to symptoms that are normal.

The professional should assess the severity of the problem within the framework of normal variation. Kessler (1966) suggested the following guidelines for parents to determine whether their child needs help; professionals might well keep them in mind as well in assessing the child's symptoms.

(1) Age appropriateness. The surveys of Lapouse and Monk (1964) and others about the occurrence of various symptoms at various ages should be kept in mind.

(2) Frequency.

(3) Number of troublesome behaviors. While the epidemiological studies demonstrate that many children have a significant "symptom," when a variety of problems show up in the child, there is more likely to be a need for help. Glidewell, Mensh, and Gildea (1957) found a positive relationship between number of symptoms and ratings of disturbance based on teacher or clinical observation. Robins (1966) found the number of problems in childhood to predict adult psychopathology.

(4) Social disadvantage. Symptoms that lead to the child being ostracized by others or that interfere with the child's ability to learn are more important.

(5) The child's inner suffering. This point will be elaborated later.

(6) Intractability. A symptom that persists over time in spite of attempts to deal with it is less likely to be a "stage." Glidewell, et al, (1957) also found that ratings of duration, frequency, and severity of child's symptoms made by the mother could be combined to form a measure that correlated with observational ratings of the child's disturbance.

Second, the professional should use an interactional assessment approach from the outset. This appears to make assessment more complex, since the parents and/or teacher must also be observed and understood. However, a number of new interactional techniques have been developed, and old techniques have been adapted to interactional assessment. Cromwell, Olson, and Fournier (1978) listed many of these. Brown (1975) pointed out many arguments in favor of family assessment besides those presented here: use of parents as mental health resources; greater likelihood of instructions being carried out if parents agree with the treatment plan; preventive benefits since parents become better problem-solvers; legal and ethical problems that arise when parents must give "informed" consent to assessment procedures from which they have been excluded; and improved validity of assessment when children are observed in their natural environment. She provided several sensible strategies for observation of the family and child. It appears that the hurdles to interactional assessment are surmountable.

Third, the professional should emphasize assessment rather than classification and use a multi-axial classification system. This point needs no further amplification.

Fourth, motivation for treatment should be carefully assessed. The course of action taken by the agency or school depends essentially on the family's motivation for help.

Family Motivated

If the family agrees, a treatment approach, stressing the family as a whole, will probably be preferable. Even for childhood disorders with a strong physiological component, evidence shows the value of enlisting the parents as change agents. The child may need individual assistance also, both of a psychological nature—behavioral techniques, catharsis, cognitive change, and so forth—and of a nonpsychological nature—medical treatment, tutoring, social activities, and so forth. It may be wise to involve the child's school. However, this individual assistance will almost always be more effective in the context of a family involvement and family change.

The family who is motivated only toward "helping Tommy," not toward change within the family unit itself, may still be considered the effective treatment unit. A good child-care professional knows how thin the line is between families who acknowledge their need for change and those who must identify the child as the target for change. The second type of family unit can often change as much as the first, if the professional is tactful and subtle in making plans and dealing with family reactions.

A word of caution is in order. In the attempt to avoid stigmatizing the child and to treat the family, sometimes the child's problems may be ignored. If the professional sees the child's problems as a consequence of conflict between the parents, marital therapy may be undertaken, the parents may get involved in their own problems, and the fact that the child is still showing the original symptoms may be overlooked. It should be kept in mind that the reason for treating the parents is that evidence shows this to be usually the most effective treatment for the child. The right of the child to receive help must not be overlooked, just as we must not overlook the possible negative effects of some treatments and labels.

Family Not Motivated

If the family motivation is limited, the professional can still work to mobilize and maximize whatever motivation exists. When there is none, however, the approach must change. It could be argued that it is these children, least likely to be helped by their families, who most need the help of outside agencies. In this case, the psychologist should first consider the possibility of individual treatment for the child, assuming that the parents will allow it.

In planning treatment in such cases, the child's motivation seems to be of paramount importance. Children's motivation must be assessed differently from adults', since they have vague and inaccurate ideas about treatment. The child's probable motivational response to treatment can be roughly estimated from the degree of inner suffering. As with adults, the child whose avoidance responses are working effectively to prevent pain and anxiety is less likely to become your therapeutic ally. While empirical support is lacking for the idea that motivation in children is crucial to their response to individual therapy, there is evidence that motivation in adults increases the likelihood of successful therapy. Clinical impressions would also support the idea for children that individual or group therapy is warranted for the child who is suffering.

When a child who suffers is identified by the school psychologist or another professional and the family refuses to allow treatment for the child, the professional must work with that limitation. Bringing the child's plight to the attention of helpful adults (the teacher, the teacher's aide, the camp counselor, the Big Brother or Sister, and others) who can listen and offer support and guidance may be the most appropriate step. The professional's role then becomes one of consultation. Groups such as Alateen may also be of help for older children.

Obviously, the most difficult situation exists when neither the family nor the child is motivated for help. The antisocial children discussed by Robins who grew up to be sociopathic and emotionally disturbed fall into this group. It could be that children who act out their problems instead of feeling them, and who thus alienate the important people in their environment, are the children least likely to receive informal help or to benefit from individual formal help. They thus become the population most at-risk as adults. Perhaps the most difficult task facing the child professional is to find new methods to reach such children.

For all children with unmotivated families, the environmental context in which the problem is seen must be widened beyond the family. What in the environment is supporting the child's behavior and what can be changed? Parents can in some cases be required to come to school for conferences; legal sanctions can be brought to bear in the case of child abuse. The child may be helped to form an interest in an activity that reinforces new behavior (Girl Scouts, YMCA, YWHA, and other activities). A change of program at school or a change of schools may help. Sanctions from the school or the police may have to be applied to the child. Institutionalization, when carefully planned, may be the only recourse for a child whose environment is extremely unhealthy and shows little possibility for change. While the foregoing is couched in somewhat behavioristic terms, what I have in mind is that the child-care professional function is like a skilled social worker who knows and uses all the resources of the community.

Obviously, awareness of environmental resources is important in working with all children. In the long run, advocacy procedures for children may be of use in increasing the kinds of interventions the child-care professional can use with disturbed children from unmotivated homes.

CONCLUSION

The dependency of children upon their families and wider environment makes classification systems for adult psychopathology inappropriate to them and renders our methods of identifying troubled children ineffective. Recent changes in classification systems for children stress the situational context through a multi-axial procedure. This is a decided improvement, but further change is needed: (1) identifying the children who need help; (2) assessing and classifying their problems; and (3) planning their treatments. All require an interactional approach. Specific recommendations have been made in these three areas.

REFERENCES

Achenbach, T., & Edelbrock, C. S. The classification of child psychopathology: A review and analysis of empirical efforts. *Psychological Bulletin*, 1978, *85*, 1275–1301.

Ackerman, N. W. Psychiatric disorders in children—Diagnosis and etiology in our time. In P. Hoch & J. Zubin, (Eds.) *Current problems in psychiatric diagnosis*. New York: Grune & Stratton, 1953.

Amante, D., Van Houten, V. W., Grieve, J. H., Bader, C. A., & Margules, P. H. Neuropsychological deficit, ethnicity, and socioeconomic status. *Journal of Consulting and Clinical Psychology*, 1977, *45*, 524–535.

American Psychiatric Association. *Diagnostic and statistical manual, mental disorders* (1st ed.). Washington, D.C., Author, 1952.

American Psychiatric Association. *Diagnostic and statistical manual of mental disorders* (2nd ed.) Washington, D. C., Author, 1968.

American Psychiatric Association. *Diagnostic and statistical manual of mental disorders* (3rd ed.) Washington, D.C., Author, 1980.

American Psychological Association, Proceedings for the year 1980. *American Psychologist*, 1981, *36*, 552–586.

Angelino, H., Dollins, J., & Mech, E. V. Trends in the "fears and worries" of school children as related to socioeconomic status and age. *Journal of Genetic Psychology*, 1956, *89*,

263–276.

Baller, W. R., Charles, D. C., & Miller, E. L. Mid-life attainment of the mentally retarded: A longitudinal study. *Genetic Psychology Monographs*, 1967, *75*, 235–329.

Barrett, C. L., Hampe, I. E., & Miller, L. C. Research on child psychotherapy. In S. L. Garfield & A. E. Bergin (Eds.) *Handbook of psychotherapy and behavior change: An empirical analysis*. New York: Wiley, 1978.

Beitchman, J. H.; Dielman T. E; Landis, J. R.; Benson, R. M. & Kemp, P. L. Reliability of the Group for the Advancement of Psychiatry diagnostic categories in child psychiatry. *Archives of General Psychiatry*, 1978, *35*, 1461-1468.

Beller, E. K. *Clinical process*. Glencoe, Ind.: Free Press, 1962.

Bemporad, J. R., Pfeifer, C. M., — Bloom, W. Twelve months' experience with the GAP classification of childhood disorders. *American Journal of Psychiatry*, 1970, *127*, 118–124.

Bender, L. The life course of children with schizophrenia. *American Journal of Psychiatry*, 1973, *130*, 783–786.

Bennett, S., & Klein, H. R. Childhood schizophrenia: 30 years later. *American Journal of Psychiatry*, 1966, *122*, 1121–1124.

Bergin, A. E. The evaluation of therapeutic outcomes. In A. E. Bergin & S. L. Garfield (Eds.), *Handbook of psychotherapy and behavior change: An empirical analysis*. New York: Wiley, 1971.

Bijou, S. W. Ainsworth, M. H., & Stockey, M. R. The social adjustment of mentally retarded girls paroled from the Wayne County Training School. *American Journal of Mental Deficiency*, 1943, *47*, 422–428.

Brown, L. K. Familial dialectics in a clinical context. *Human Development*, 1975, *18*, 223–238.

Campbell, S. B. & Steinert, Y. Comparisons of rating scales of child psychopathology in clinic and non-clinic samples. *Journal of Consulting and Clinical Psychology*, 1978, *46*, 358–359.

Cameron, K. Diagnostic categories in child psychiatry. *British Journal of Medical Psychology*, 1955, *28*, 67–71.

Carson, R. C. *Interaction concepts of personality*. Chicago: Aldine, 1969.

Charles, D. C. Adult adjustment of some deficient American children—II. *American Journal of Mental Deficiency*, 1957, *62*, 300–304.

Conger, A. J., & Coie, J. P. Who's crazy in Manhattan: A reexamination of "Treatment of psychological disorders among urban children." *Journal of Consulting and Clinical Psychology*, 1975, *43*, 179–182.

Conners, C. K. Symptom patterns in hyperki-

netic, neurotic and normal children. *Child Development*, 1970, *41*, 667–682.

Coolidge, J. C., Brodie, R. D., & Feeney, B. A ten-year follow-up study of sixty-six school-phobic children. *American Journal of Orthopsychiatry*, 1964, *34*, 675–684.

Cowen, E. L., Huser, J., Beach, D. R., & Rappaport, J. Parental perceptions of young children and their relation to indexes of adjustment. *Journal of Consulting and Clinical Psychology*, 1970, *34*, 97–103.

Cromwell, R. E., Olson, D. H. L., & Fournier, D. G. Tools and techniques for diagnosis and evaluation in marital and family therapy. *Family Process*, 1976, *15*, 1–47.

Dohrenwend, B. P. & Dohrenwend, B. S. Social and cultural influences on psychopathology. In M. R. Rosenzweig, and L.W. Porter, (Eds.) *Annual review of psychology*, V. 25, Palo Alto, Calif. Annual Reviews, 1974.

Dohrenwend, B. S. Dohrenwend, B. P. *Social status and psychological disorder: A causal inquiry*. New York: Wiley, 1969.

Dreger, R. M., Reed, M., Lewis, P., Overlade, D., Rich, T., Taffel, C., Miller, K., & Flemming, E. Behavioral classification project. *Journal of Consulting Psychology*, 1964, *28*, 1–13.

Eaton, L. & Menolascino, F. J. Psychotic reactions of childhood: A follow-up study. *American Journal of Orthopsychiatry*, 1967, *37*, 521–529.

Eggers, C. Course and prognosis of childhood schizophrenia. *Journal of Autism and Childhood Schizophrenia*, 1978, *8*, 21–36

Eisenberg, L. & Kanner, L. Early infantile autism 1943–1955. *American Journal of Orthopsychiatry*, 1956, *26*, 556–566.

Eme, R. F. Sex differences in childhood psychopathology: A review. *Psychological Bulletin*, 1979, *86*, 574–595.

Engel, M. Dilemmas of classification and diagnosis. *Journal of Special Education*, 1969, *3*, 231–239.

Ferguson, L. R. & Allen, D. R. Congruence of parental perception, marital satisfaction, and child adjustment. *Journal of Consulting and Clinical Psychology*, 1978, *46*, 345–346.

Ferguson, L. R., Partyka, L. B., & Lester, B. M. Patterns of parent perception differentiating clinic from non-clinic children. *Journal of Abnormal Child Psychology*, 1974, *2*, 169–181.

Fish, B. Drug therapy in child psychiatry: Psychological aspects. *Comprehensive Psychiatry*, 1, 55, 1960.

Fish, B. & Shapiro, T. A. A typology of children's psychiatric disorders. I. Its application to a controlled evaluation of treatment. *Journal of the American Academy of Child Psy-*

chiatry, 4, 32, 1965.

Fisher, L. Dimensions of family assessment: A critical review. *Journal of Marriage and Family Counseling*, 1976, 2, 367–382.

Foltz, D. Judgment withheld on *DSM-III*, New child classification pushed. *APA Monitor*, 1981, *11* (1), 1.

Forehand, R., Wells, K. C., & Sturgis, E. T. Predictors of child noncompliant behavior in the home. *Journal of Consulting and Clinical Psychology*, 1978, *46*, 179.

Garmezy, N. *DSM-III*: Never mind the psychologists; Is it good for the children? *The Clinical Psychologist*, 1978, *31*, 1–6.

Glennon, B. & Weisz, J. R. An observational approach to the assessment of anxiety in young children. *Journal of Consulting and Clinical Psychology*, 1978, *46*, 1246–1257.

Glidewell, J., Mensch, I., & Glidea, M. Behavior symptoms in children and degree of sickness. *American Journal of Psychiatry*, 1957, *114*, 47–53.

Goffman, E. *Asylums*. Garden City, N.Y.: Doubleday, 1961.

Goodstein, L. D. & Rowley, V. N. A further study of MMPI differences between parents of disturbed and non-disturbed children. *Journal of Consulting Psychology*, 1961, *25*, 460.

Group for the Advancement of Psychiatry. The diagnostic process in child psychiatry. *GAP Report No. 38*, 1957.

Group for the Advancement of Psychiatry. Psychopathological disorders in childhood: Theoretical considerations and a proposed classification. *GAP Report No. 62*, 1966.

Harris, S. L. The relationship between family income and number of parent-perceived problems. *International Journal of Social Psychiatry*, 1974, *20*, 109–112.

Hobbs, N. *The future of children: Categories, labels and their consequences*. San Francisco: Jossey-Bass, Inc., 1975. (a)

Hobbs, N. (Ed.) *Issues in the classification of children*. V.s I and II. San Francisco: Jossey-Bass, 1975. (b)

Jackson, B. The Revised Diagnostic and Statistical Manual of the American Psychiatric Association. *American Journal of Psychiatry*, 1970, *127*, 65–73.

Jacob, T. Family interaction in disturbed and normal families. A methodological and substantive review. *Psychological Bulletin*, 1975, *82*, 33–65.

Kennedy, R. J. R. *The social adjustment of morons in a Connecticut city*. Hartford: State Office Building, 1948.

Kessler, J. *Psychopathology of childhood*. Englewood Cliffs, N.J.: Prentice-Hall, 1966.

Knobloch, H. & Pasamanick, B. (Eds.) *Gesell and Amatruda's developmental diagnosis: The evaluation and management of normal and abnormal neuropsychologic development in infancy and early childhood (3rd ed.)*. Hagerstown, Md: Harper and Row, 1974.

Laing, R. D. The study of family and social contexts in relation to the origin of schizophrenia. In J. Romano, (Ed.) *Origins of Schizophrenia*. Amsterdam: Excerpta Medica, 1967.

Langner, T. S., Gersten, J. C., Greene, E. L., Eisenber, J. G., Herson, J. H., & McCarthy, E. D. Treatment of psychological disorders among urban children. *Journal of Consulting and Clinical Psychology*, 1974, *42*, 170–179.

Lapouse, R. The epidemiology of behavior disorders in children. *American Journal of Diseases of Children*, 1966, *3*, 594–599.

Lapouse, R. & Monk, M. A. An epidemiologic study of behavior characteristics in children. *American Journal of Public Health*, 1958, *48*, 1134–1144.

Lapouse, R. & Monk, M. A. Fears and worries in a representative sample of children. *American Journal of Orthopsychiatry*, 1959, *29*, 803–818.

Lapouse, R. & Monk, M. A. Behavior deviations in a representative sample of children: Variation by sex, age, race, social class and family size. *American Journal of Orthopsychiatry*, 1964, *34*, 436–446.

Larkin, W. E. & Loman, L. A. Labeling in the family context: An experimental study. *Sociology and Social Research*, 1977, *61*, 192–203.

Levitt, E. E. The results of psychotherapy with children: An evaluation. *Journal of Consulting Psychology*, 1957, *21*, 189–196.

Levitt, E. E. Psychotherapy with children: A further evaluation. *Behavior Research and Therapy*, 1963, *60*, 326–329.

Levitt, E. E. Research on psychotherapy with children. In A. E. Bergin & S. L. Garfield, (Eds.) *Handbook of psychotherapy and behavior change: An empirical analysis*. New York: Wiley & Sons, 1971.

Liverant, S. MMPI differences between parents of disturbed and nondisturbed children. *Journal of Consulting Psychology*, 1959, *23*, 256–260.

Lotter, V. Factors related to outcome in autistic children. *Journal of Autism and Childhood Schizophrenia*, 1974, *4*, 263–277.

Love, L. R., & Kaswan, J. K. *Troubled children: Their families, schools and treatments*. New York: Wiley, 1974.

MacFarlane, J. W. Studies in child guidance. I. Methodology of data collection and organization. *Monographs of Social Research in*

Child Development, 1938, *3*, No. 2.

Marks, P. A. An assessment of the diagnostic process in a child guidance setting. *Psychological Monographs*, 1961, *48*, 185–189.

Martin, B. Brief family intervention: Effectiveness and the importance of including the father. *Journal of Consulting and Clinical Psychology*, 1977, *45*, 1002–1010.

McCoy, S. A. Clinical judgments of normal childhood behavior. *Journal of Consulting and Clinical Psychology*, 1976, *44*, 710–714.

Miller, L. C. Q–sort agreement among observers of children. *American Journal of Orthopsychiatry*, 1964, *34*, 71–75.

Miller, L. C., Barrett, C. L., Hampe, E., & Noble, H. Comparison of reciprocal inhibition, psychotherapy, and waiting list control for phobic children. *Journal of Abnormal Psychology*, 1972, *79*, 269–277.

Morris, D. P., Soroker, E., & Burruss, C. Follow-up studies of shy, withdrawn children: Evaluation of later adjustment. *American Journal of Orthopsychiatry*, 1954, *24*, 743–754.

Pearson, G. H. J. *Emotional disorders of childhood*. New York: Norton, 1949.

Piers, E. Parent prediction of children's self-concepts. *Journal of Consulting and Clinical Psychology*, 1972, *38*, 428–433.

Prugh, D. G. Psychosocial disorders in childhood and adolescence: Theoretical considerations and an attempt at classification. In Joint Commission on Mental Health of Children, *The Mental Health of Children: Services, research and manpower*. Report of Task Forces IV and V. New York: Harper and Row, 1973.

Prugh, D. G., Engel, M., and Morse, W. C. Emotional disturbance in children. In N. Hobbs, (Ed.), *Issues in the classification of children*, Vol. II. San Francisco: Jossey-Bass, 1975.

Rappaport, J., & Cleary, C. P. Labeling theory and the social psychology of experts and helpers. In, M. S. Gibbs, J. R. Lachenmeyer, & J. Sigal (Eds.) *Community Psychology*, New York: Gardner, 1980.

Rees, S. C., & Taylor, A. Prognostic antecedents and outcome in a follow-up study of children with a diagnosis of childhood psychosis. *Journal of Autism and Childhood Schizophrenia*, 1975, *5*, 309–322.

Reisinger, J. J., Ora, J. P., & Frangia, G. W. Parents as change agents for their children: A review. *Journal of Community Psychology*, 1976, *4*, 103–123.

Rist, R. C. Student social class and teacher expectations: The self-fulfilling prophecy in ghetto education. *Harvard Educational Review*, 1970, *40*, 411–451.

Robins, L. N. Deviant children grown up. Baltimore: Williams and Wilkins, 1966.

Robins, L. N. Follow-up studies investigating childhood disorders. In E. H. Hare and J. K. Wing (Eds.), *Psychiatric epidemiology: Proceedings of the International Symposium held at Aberdeen University*. London: Oxford, 1970.

Rogers, C. R. *Client-centered therapy*. Boston: Houghton Mifflin, 1951.

Rosen, B., Bahn, A., & Kramer, M. Demographic and diagnostic characteristics of psychiatric outpatient clinics in the U.S. *American Journal of Orthopsychiatry*, 1964, *34*, 455–468.

Rosenhan, D. On being sane in insane places. *Science*, 1973, *179*, 250–259.

Rosenthal, R., & Jacobson, L. *Pygmalion in the classroom: Teachers' expectations and pupils' intellectual development*. New York: Holt, 1968.

Rutter, M., Greenfield, G., & Lockyer, L. A five to fifteen year follow-up study of infantile psychosis. II. Social and behavioral outcome. *British Journal of Psychiatry*, 1967, *113*, 1183–1199.

Rutter, M., Lebovici, L., Eisenberg, L., Sneznevskij, A. V., Sadoun, R., Brooke, E., & Tsung-Yi Lin. A tri-axial classification of mental disorders in childhood: An international study. *Journal of Child Psychology and Psychiatry*, 1969, *10*, 41–61.

Sarbin, T. R. A role theory perspective for community psychology: The structure of social identity. In D. Adelson & B. L. Kalis (Eds.), *Community psychology and mental health: Perspectives and challenges*. Scranton, Pa.: Chandler, 1970.

Schact, T., & Nathan, P. E. But is it good for the psychologists? Appraisal and status of *DSM-III*. *American Psychologist*, 1977, *32*, 1017–1025.

Scheff, T. J. *Being mentally ill: A sociological theory*. Chicago: Aldine, 1966.

Schur, E. *Labeling deviant behavior*. New York: Harper, 1971.

Shechtman, A. Psychiatric symptoms observed in normal and disturbed children. *Journal of Clinical Psychology*. 1970, *26*, 38–41.(a)

Shechtman, A. Age patterns in children's psychiatric symptoms. *Child Development*, 1970, *41*, 683–693. (b)

Shechtman, A. Psychiatric symptoms observed in normal and disturbed black children. *Journal of Clinical Psychology*. 1971, *27*, 445–447.

Shepherd, M., Oppenheim, A., & Mitchell, S. Childhood behavior disorders and the child guidance clinic: An epidemiological survey. *Journal of Child Psychology and Psychiatry*, 1966, *7*, 39–52.

Spitzer, R. L. 9 Forman, J. W. *DSM-III* field trials: II. Initial experience with the multiaxial system. American Journal of Psychiatry, 1979, 136, 818–820.

Spitzer, R. L., Forman, J. W.; & Nee, J. *DSM-III* field trials: I. Initial interrater diagnostic reliability. *American Journal of Psychiatry*, 1979, 136, 815–817.

Spitzer, R. L., Sheehy, M., & Endicott, J. *DSM-III:* Guiding principles. In, V. M. Rakoff, H. C. Stancer, & H. B. Kedward, (Eds.), *Psychiatric diagnosis.* New York: Brunner/Mazel, 1977.

Szasz, T. S. *Ideology and insanity.* Garden City, N.Y.: Doubleday, 1969.

Tavormina, J. B. Basic models of parent counseling: A critical review. *Psychological Bulletin*, 1974, *81* (11), 827–835.

Tavormina, J. B. Relative effectiveness of behavioral and reflective group counseling with parents of mentally retarded children. *Journal of Consulting and Clinical Psychology*, 1975, *43*, 22–31.

Wahler, R. G., House, A. E., & Stambaugh, E. E. *Ecological assessment of child problem behavior.* New York: Pergamon Press, 1976.

Waldron, S. The significance of childhood neurosis for adult mental health: A follow-up study. *American Journal of Psychiatry.* 1976, *133,* 532–538.

Wenar, C. The reliability of mothers' histories. *Child Development*, 1961, *32*, 491–500.

Werry, J. S. & Quay, H. C. The prevalence of behavior symptoms in younger elementary school children. *American Journal of Orthopsychiatry*, 1971, *41*, 136–143.

White, R. W. Competence and the psychosexual stages of development. In M. R. Jones, (Ed), *Nebraska Symposium on Motivation.* Lincoln: University of Nebraska Press, 1960.

Yarrow, M. R., Campbell, J. D., & Burton, R. V. Recollections of childhood: A study of the retrospective method. *Monographs of the Society for Research in Child Development*, 1970, *35*, No. 5.

Zigler, E., & Phillips, L. Psychiatric diagnosis: A critique. *Journal of Abnormal and Social Psychology*, 1961, *63*, 607–618.

Zimbardo, P. G. The mind is a formidable jailer: A Pirandellian prison. *New York Times Magazine.* April 8, 1973, *38.*

Zubin, J. But is it good for science? *The Clinical Psychologist*, 1977–1978, *31* (2), 1–7.

CHAPTER 2

Empirical Approaches to the Classification of Child Psychopathology

THOMAS M. ACHENBACH, Ph.D.

The first systematic psychiatric taxonomy emerged from nineteenth-century applications of organic disease models to behavior disorders. Progress in bacteriology provided a prototype disease model for all of medicine, and psychiatry's version of this prototype was the disorder known as *paresis*. Progressively better descriptions of symptom patterns during the early nineteenth century led to a definition of paresis as a combination of *mental* symptoms—including forgetfulness and irrationality—with *organic* symptoms of motor impairment, usually ending in death. Once the syndrome was identified, people who manifested it could be systematically compared with people who did not. By the middle of the nineteenth century, autopsy research revealed inflammation in the brains of many patients who died of paresis. Although it was not until the turn of the twentieth century that syphilitic infection was decisively proven to be the cause of paresis, the progress from observation of symptoms to the identification of a syndrome of symptoms that consistently occurred together, to documentation of the course of the syndrome, and then to research comparing people who did and did not manifest it, provided a model for the classification of other psychiatric disorders. The model held that—in the absence of known causes—classification based on careful description was the first step in a sequence that would culminate in the dis-covery of specific organic causes.

As the number of syndrome descriptions grew, there was an increasing need for an overarching framework within which to delineate their boundaries and group them into types and subtypes. The most influential effort of this sort was the classification system first published by Emil Kraepelin in 1883 and revised in nine more editions over the next 43 years. Initially guided by the tenets of descriptive diagnosis and the assumption that all mental disorders have organic causes, Kraepelin's system replaced a hodgepodge of idiosyncratic descriptions with a comprehensive taxonomy in which individual types and subtypes of disorders were to be distinguished from one another. In his later editions, Kraepelin added the course of a disorder as a criterion for diagnostic classification. For example, psychotics who improved could be classed as manic-depressive but not schizophrenic, because Kraepelin believed that manic-depressives recovered, whereas schizophrenics did not. Kraepelin also added categories for psychogenic disorders and for personality patterns that he regarded as bordering between illness and common eccentricity. Subsequent psychiatric taxonomies have continued to proclaim the ideal of descriptive diagnosis for disorders of unknown etiology, but what is considered "descriptive" depends on the theoretical orientation of the describer.

In the American versions of Kraepelin's

system, the progressive expansion of personality disorders and of disorders assumed to be psychogenic, the influence of psychoanalytic theory, and the formulation of categories in terms of Adolph Meyer's *reaction types* of the psychobiological unit (Winters, 1951), all served to obscure the original ideal of descriptive diagnosis. As a result, American taxonomies came to include mixtures of behavioral description, inferences about psychodynamics, theories of causation, and assumptions about the personalities, environments, and developmental histories of the people to be diagnosed. Although the adult categories of these systems could be applied to children, disorders peculiar to childhood went virtually unacknowledged until the late 1960s. Traditional taxonomic approaches are covered elsewhere in this book, but the following points should be noted here: (1) the original Kraepelinian ideal was to describe disorders as an initial step toward discovery of their (organic) causes; (2) descendants of this system were increasingly complicated by the inclusion of disorders assumed to have nonorganic causes and of personality patterns not readily conceptualized as diseases; (3) theories and treatments of psychopathology progressively diverged from the organic disease model in which Kraepelin's taxonomy was rooted; and (4) despite theoretical emphasis on the childhood origins of adult disorders, psychopathology in children received little notice.

EARLY EMPIRICAL EFFORTS

Against such a background, is it any wonder that alternative approaches to the classification of child psychopathology were sought? Although distinctions were often made between aggressive children and overinhibited children, and between psychotic (sometimes equated with "schizophrenic") and nonpsychotic children, these distinctions represented extremely crude ways of classifying behavioral patterns and severity. Beginning in the 1940s, Richard Jenkins and his colleagues sought to anchor global distinctions of this type in groupings of behaviors that tended to occur together, as reported in the case histories of children who were referred to mental health clinics. They did so by applying a combination of clinical judgment and statistical criteria to correlations between individual items scored from case histories (Hewitt and Jenkins, 1946). Support was found for groupings of characteristics that Jenkins designated as the Overinhibited Child, the Unsocialized Aggressive Child, and the Socialized Delinquent Child. In a more purely statistical analysis of correlations among items scored from another sample of case histories, Jenkins and Glickman (1946) found five syndromes for each sex: Overinhibited, Unsocialized Aggressive, Socialized Delinquent, Brain-Injured, and Schizoid.

The approach taken by Jenkins and Glickman reflected both a significant departure from the taxonomic tradition that had evolved from Kraepelin's work and a return to the original Kraepelinian ideal—but with a new twist. In the form that it had evolved, the taxonomic tradition was characterized by a variety of conflicting elements. It retained many of the categories introduced by Kraepelin, but redefined them in terms of diverse theoretical concepts without empirical support. In fact, disputes among competing factions eventually came to play a greater role than empirical data in determining the official psychiatric categories and definitions, as reflected in the first edition of the American Psychiatric Association's *Diagnostic and Statistical Manual of Mental Disorders* (DSM-I, American Psychiatric Association, 1952). Although an omnibus classification system of ill-defined phenomena, intended to serve many masters, can hardly be popular, the approach taken seems to have satisfied nobody, as the official taxonomy won the respect of neither clinicians nor researchers.

The Jenkins-Glickman work contrasted with the DSM-I approach by *empirically* identifying characteristics that actually occurred together and categorizing children according to the obtained syndromes in order to see whether the children differed in other ways as well. This was a return to Kraepelinian descriptive diagnosis, aided by statistical methods for assessing the co-variation among characteristics. To demonstrate how syndromes based on statistical correlation fulfilled the ideal of descriptive diagnosis, Jenkins and Glickman showed that the statistically intercorrelated physical, laboratory, and behavioral signs of paresis in children could collectively predict the clinical diagnosis of paresis. Furthermore, the behavioral signs alone predicted the diagnosis about as well as the combination of physical, laboratory, and behavioral signs. Statistical correlations among behaviors could thus provide an efficient empirical summary of a childhood version of the classical prototype syndrome of psychiatric taxonomy.

After identifying behavioral syndromes from case histories, Jenkins revised his syndromes through new analyses of the same data and of case histories from an institution for delinquents. He also assessed biographical data in the case histories of children whose problems resembled each of the syndromes. From differences in family backgrounds and other characteristics, Jenkins composed personality portraits thought to typify children manifesting the various syndromes (see Jenkins, 1973). It was on the basis of this work that several categories of behavior disorders of childhood and adolescence were added to the second edition of the American Psychiatric Association's *Diagnostic and Statistical Manual* (*DSM-II*, 1968). These were designated as the Hyperkinetic Reaction, Withdrawing Reaction, Overanxious Reaction, Runaway Reaction, Unsocialized Aggressive Reaction, and Group Delinquent Reaction. The first step toward reasonably differentiated categories of childhood disorders within the official taxonomy was thus based on empirical efforts to identify syndromes. However, the DSM-II provided no objective criteria for applying these categories and, as evident in the following sections, the task of constructing an empirically based taxonomy of childhood disorders was far from finished. The current edition of the *Diagnostic and Statistical Manual* (DSM-III; 1980) has more objective diagnostic content, but no greater empirical support for its childhood syndromes.

LATER EMPIRICAL EFFORTS

It should not be surprising that, as the first attempt at a new approach, Jenkins' findings left many questions unanswered. For example, his data were obtained from the case histories of a few selected agencies, using a particular list of items abstracted from these records. Would other sources of data—records of agencies with different clinical philosophies, direct reports by people who knew the children, or different criteria for recording items—produce different syndromes? Even among Jenkins' own studies, the findings were somewhat inconsistent, as the syndrome he originally called Brain-Injured emerged clearly from records of an agency that had served children affected by an epidemic of encephalitis. Likewise, the Runaway syndrome emerged only from the case histories of an institution for delinquents.

Another question was whether different methods of analysis would produce different syndromes. An affirmative answer is suggested by Jenkins' studies, which progressed from a largely subjective selection of intercorrelated items conforming to preconceived syndromes (Hewitt and Jenkins, 1946), to more objective criteria for retention of items on the basis of their intercorrelations but with subjective decisions as to size of correlations required for retention, and finally to reanalyses of the same data by computerized clustering of individual cases according to their similarities in behavior problems (Jenkins, 1966, 1969).

A third question was whether empirically obtained syndromes could improve on prose descriptions in fulfilling the various goals of classification. As the ultimate fate of Jenkins' syndromes was translation into the narrative format of the *DSM-II*, we will defer this question until we have considered the outcomes of other empirical efforts.

Factor Analyses of Behavior Checklists

Other than re-analyses of the data employed in Jenkins' early studies, it was not until the 1960s that further empirical efforts were launched. These new efforts took advantage of advances in multivariate statistical methods and computer technology that made it far easier to identify statistical relations in large quantities of data. Such aids cannot by themselves solve taxonomic problems, but they can help reduce complex relations among behaviors to conceptually manageable units. The primary method has been *factor analysis* of the correlations among items recorded on checklists of behavior problems. Although there are many varieties of factor analysis, those to be considered here have been directed at reducing large matrices of correlations among specific behavior problems to a smaller number of dimensions or vectors that summarize the co-variation among all the behavior problems. Each of the resulting vectors is known as a *factor*.

A factor consists of a set of weights assigned to all the items among which correlations were computed. These weights—termed *loadings*—can range from -1.00 to $+1.00$. The loading of each item on a factor can be thought of roughly as the correlation of that item with the dimension represented by the factor. In the computation of the first factor of a factor analysis, the combination of loadings obtained for all the items represents a quantitatively optimal way of summarizing the co-variation among the items. Items that correlate most highly with the largest number of other items will have the highest loadings on the first factor. Because the first factor rarely accounts for all the covariation among items, additional factors are computed to provide vectors of item loadings that summarize the remaining covariation among items. Each successive factor is defined primarily by a group of items that intercorrelate highly with one another. It is these items that have the highest loadings on the factor. Note that, because the typical factor analysis summarizes covariation among *items*, the factors represent syndromes of behavior problems that tend to occur together without necessarily representing types of *people*. The translation of covariation among items into categories of people requires other steps that will be discussed later.

The most useful factor analyses are usually those in which each factor has a few items with very high loadings and many items with low loadings. In such analyses, each item typically obtains high loadings on just a few of the factors and low loadings on the rest. When factor analyses yield several groupings of items like this, they are said to achieve *simple structure*—that is, they simplify the correlations among many items into a structure composed of a few well-defined dimensions.

Because the initial results of most factor analyses do not approximate simple structure, mathematical formulas have been developed to "rotate" the results into arrangements of loadings that more nearly approximate simple structure. Rotating a set of factors merely involves transforming all the loadings in some uniform way. For example, one of the most commonly used rotations, the *varimax rotation*, transforms the loadings to achieve simple structure by maximizing the variance among the squares of the loadings. (See Achenbach, 1978a, 1982, for further details of application to child psychopathology.)

Sources of Data

Psychiatric taxonomies have traditionally been based on clinicians' observations of their patients in clinical settings, and most of these patients have been adults. Such observations are of limited applicability to children. First, children do not readily adopt the role of patient in relation to mental health professionals; they neither seek mental health services nor do they spontaneously aid in the diagnostic process. Second, judgments as to whether children need help and what needs changing are typically made by others, especially parents and teachers. Third, the settings in which they are seen affect children's behavior more than that of adults; clinical settings in particular evoke unrepresentative behavior because children react to them with bewilderment, anxiety, withdrawal, or anger. Fourth, the pathological significance of children's behavior must be evaluated more in terms of its implications for further development than in terms of deviation from attained levels of biological, cognitive, occupational, and social functioning, as is true for adults. Fifth, children's dependent status makes them hostage to adults and to environmental conditions that they cannot change, whereas adults can alter their environments.

The susceptibility of children's behavior to diverse influences and the importance of the developmental and social context mean that there cannot be a single criterion situation or method for obtaining definitive observations. During the diagnostic process, clinicians see children briefly under circumstances unfamiliar to the children and in roles likely to evoke unrepresentative behavior. Teachers see children under a wider variety of conditions that are important for the child's overall adaptation, but generally in large groups in which the child's behavior and the teacher's judgment are both affected by the time of the school year, the type, and level of the class (for example, all-day first grade versus 45-minute junior or senior high school class), and the behavior of the child's classmates. Parents are typically the most crucial sources of information; despite their biases, they have been found to report a far higher proportion of bona fide behavior problems than do teachers, clinical interviewers, or observers placed in the school or home (Novick, Rosenfeld, Bloch, and Dawson, 1966). Furthermore, mothers' and fathers' reports of their children's behavior have been found to agree better than reports by clinicians or clinicians and teachers (Achenbach, Dickerson, and Edelbrock, 1982; Miller, 1964).

Although unbiased observers who have total access to children in their customary environments might be preferable to parents as an ideal source of data, the presence of observers significantly affects family interactions (White, 1977). The obstacles to accurate measurement of children's behavior problems thus resemble the obstacles to measuring the location and velocity of physical particles that led the physicist Heisenberg to formulate the Principle of Uncertainty: because any measurement procedure affects the target variable, there is no way of obtaining with certainty an exact measure of the target.

If absolute measures of behavior problems are impossible, how can we obtain valid measures of syndromes? Two answers are relevant. One answer is, despite the impossibility of obtaining precise knowledge of a specific instance of a phenomenon, statistical summaries of imperfectly measured individual instances can be used to describe the general course of a phenomenon. This strategy has solved the dilemma that the Principle of Uncertainty posed for particle physics, and it has formed the basis for behavioral research where absolute measurement is precluded both by the effects of measurement procedures and by the impossibility of obtaining measurements under conditions that are simultaneously standardized and ecologically valid. Thus, procedures, like factor analysis, are used to summarize relations among variables imperfectly measured across many individual cases, even though many of the cases may deviate from the summary pictures obtained.

A second answer to the question of uncertainty of measurement is that scientifically valid knowledge depends on obtaining convergent relations among observations of various types. No matter how accurate individual measurements are assumed to be, the infinite possibilities for misinterpretation, bias, and unrepresentativeness of findings mean that findings gain credibility primarily through convergent relations with other findings. Thus, findings are most useful when they can be corroborated through other types of observations of the same phenomena and/or through verification of predictions made on the basis of the findings. In considering empirical studies of child behavior problems we will seek convergent findings that emerge, despite the differing flaws and biases of each study. The sources of data have included ratings that, like those of the Jenkins studies, were made from pre-existing case histories compiled by mental health workers for clinical rather than research purposes, plus ratings made by mental health workers, parents, and teachers who had direct contact with the children and who filled out the behavior checklists to be analyzed. Studies of children not disturbed enough to be referred for mental health services will not be considered, as they would not be likely to reveal syndromes of clinical seriousness.

Findings

A detailed review of individual studies has been presented elsewhere (Achenbach & Edelbrock, 1978), and a summary of the findings will be presented here. In order to avoid undue attention to findings that are unlikely to be reliable or that failed to produce substantial groupings of behavior problems, the following criteria were employed: (1) because the effects of chance relationships on multivariate analyses increase as the number of variables increases, syndromes were excluded if they were based on analyses in which the number of subjects was less than twice the number of variables or totaled less than 100 altogether; (2) syndromes were excluded if they failed to include at least five items having factor loadings or average intercorrelations of at least .30; and (3) studies were excluded if they failed to produce at least two syndromes retained on the basis of the first two criteria.

In almost all studies where the methodology permitted it, syndromes roughly corresponding to the traditional distinction between aggressive and overinhibited children were found in data from case histories and direct ratings by mental health workers, parents, and teachers. Although these syndromes were given different names by different investigators, we designate them as representing *Undercontrolled* and *Overcontrolled* behavior. The various versions of the Undercontrolled syndrome—which was found in sixteen studies—generally included such items as *disobedience, lying, stealing, fighting, temper tantrums, destructiveness,* and *overactivity.* By contrast, the various versions of the Overcontrolled syndrome—found in twelve studies—included such items as *bodily complaints, fears, worrying, withdrawal,* and *excessive crying.*

The identification of the Undercontrolled and Overcontrolled syndromes in so many studies leaves little doubt that behavior problems group in this fashion in a wide range of children, as described by diverse observers. However, finer-grained analyses have shown that these may represent only the most general aspects of children's behavior patterns. By increasing the number of rated items, using more sensitive statistical analyses, and separately analyzing samples of children homogeneous with respect to age and sex, it has been possible to obtain greater differentiation among syndromes and to identify syndromes that are restricted to particular groups. Many of the additional syndromes have counterparts in two or more studies. A few of these studies have also included analyses aimed at clarifying the relations between the more general Undercontrolled and Overcontrolled dichotomy and the syndromes obtained through finer-grained analyses.

Second-order Factor Analysis. The primary approach to clarifying the relations between the more general and more specific syndromes has been through *second-order factor analysis.* In a second-order factor analysis, *first-order* factors are first computed as described earlier. *Factor scores* are then obtained for each subject in a sample on each of the first-order factors. To obtain a subject's factor score, his or her score on each item is multiplied by the loading that item received on the factor of interest. The products obtained by multiplying the loading times the score on each item are then summed to yield the subject's score on the dimension represented by the factor. If 10 factors were obtained from a factor analysis of 100 behavior problems, for example, 10 factor scores would be computed for each subject. A subject's factor score for the *first* factor would consist of the sum of his or her scores on all 100 original behavior problems after each had been multiplied by the loading it received on the first factor. The subject's factor score for the *second* factor would likewise consist of the sum of his or her scores on all 100 problems after each had been multiplied by the loading it received on the second factor, and so on for the computation of eight more factor scores.

An alternative procedure is simply to employ the items having the highest loadings (e.g., loadings of .30 or higher) on a factor as the definition of the syndrome represented by the factor. A subject's score for that syndrome is then obtained by summing his or her scores on just those items. This excludes items whose low loadings on a factor show that they bear little relation to the syndrome represented by the factor. Moreover, summing the scores actually obtained by the subject on the items rather than weighting them by the factor loadings reduces the influence of small differences among loadings, which may themselves be relatively unreliable (Wainer, 1976).

When a factor score has been obtained for each subject on each factor—using either of the procedures just outlined—these scores are intercorrelated, and the correlations are factor-analyzed to produce second-order factors composed of loadings for each of the first-order factors. In other words, each first-order factor is treated as if it were a single variable, and the second-order factors show which first-order factors group together.

Broad-band and Narrow-band Syndromes. Second-order analyses have revealed a hierarchical relationship between the Undercontrolled-Overcontrolled dichotomy and the factors obtained in fine-grained analyses, such that some of the finer-grained, first-order factors group together to form second-order Undercontrolled and Overcontrolled factors (Achenbach, 1966, 1978b; Achenbach & Edelbrock, 1979; Miller, 1967). For this reason, the Undercontrolled and Overcontrolled syndromes can be thought of as relatively "broad-band" groupings of

problems, whereas the finer-grained syndromes are more specific, "narrow-band" groupings.

Table 1 shows the number of studies of data from each type of source that have produced the two major broad-band syndromes, two other broad-band syndromes, and fourteen narrow-band syndromes. Of the two additional broad-band syndromes, the one labeled Pathological Detachment was not very uniform among the four studies that produced versions of it, but it included items indicative of thought disorder and disorganization. The remaining broad-band syndrome, labeled Learning Problems, like the narrow-band Academic Disability syndrome, comprised such items as *math problems, number problems,* and *concepts problems* in one version (Clarfield, 1974), and *spells poorly, reads poorly,* and *writes poorly* in another version (Miller, 1967). Because most of the items are so similar, this grouping might be viewed as a single problem of poor school performance rather than a syndrome of behavior problems.

As can be seen from Table 1, versions of the narrow-band Aggressive, Delinquent, Hyperactive, and Schizoid syndromes were found in from 10 to 14 studies, indicating

Table 1. Number of Studies in which Syndromes have been Identified through Multivariate Analyses

Source of ratings

Syndrome	Case histories	Mental Health workers	Teachers	Parents	Total
Broad band					12
Overcontrolled	2	1	5	4	16
Undercontrolled	3	3	5	5	4
Pathological detachment	3	—	1	—	2
Learning problems	—	—	1	1	
Narrow band					4
Academic disability	—	1	—	3	14
Aggressive	3	4	1	6	6
Anxious	1	2	1	2	10
Delinquent	3	1	—	6	6
Depressed	2	1	—	3	12
Hyperactive	3	2	1	6	3
Immature	—	1	—	2	3
Obsessive-compulsive	1	—	—	2	10
Schizoid	3	4	—	3	4
Sexual problems	1	2	—	1	3
Sleep problems	—	—	1	3	6
Social withdrawal	1	1	—	3	6
Somatic complaints	1	—	—	5	3
Uncommunicative	—	1		2	

[a]See Achenbach and Edelbrock, 1978, for details.

that they are quite pervasive across samples, methods of analysis, and sources of data. The Anxious, Depressed, Social Withdrawal, and Somatic Complaints syndromes—found in six studies each—also seem quite robust. However, the Sexual Problems syndrome—found in four studies—and the Immature, Obsessive-Compulsive, Sleep Problems, and Uncommunicative sydromes—found in three studies each—may be somewhat more restricted to particular groups of children, methods of analysis, or sources of data. It is obvious, for example, that syndromes, such as Sleep Problems, cannot be expected to appear in teachers' ratings. In fact, only one study of teachers' ratings produced narrow-band syndrome (Conners, 1969), and these were restricted to versions of the Aggressive, Anxious, Hyperactive, and Social Withdrawal syndromes. Because the number of syndromes produced is generally proportional to the number of items analyzed, and because studies of teacher ratings have employed relatively few items, it remains to be seen whether more differentiated syndromes can be obtained from teacher ratings. Work is presently under way to determine if teacher ratings on a 118-item checklist produce sydromes as differentiated as those obtained from parent ratings on a parallel version of the 118-item checklist (Achenbach & Edelbrock, in preparation).

RELIABILITY AND STABILITY OF SYNDROME RATINGS

One of the most common complaints about traditional taxonomies is that clinicians do not agree on the diagnostic classification of individual clients. Studies of agreement among clinicians, using traditional psychiatric diagnoses, in fact show only about 60 percent agreement in the assignment of clients to broad categories, such as psychotic versus neurotic—considerably less for diagnosis of specific disorders within the broad categories (Freeman, 1971; Sandifer, Pettus, and Quade, 1964; Tarter, Templer, and Hardy, 1975). Not only do clinicians show mediocre agreement with each other, but their own diagnostic judgments of the same data are inconsistent. Freeman (1971), e.g., found only 72 percent agreement between diagnoses made by child psychiatrists from case history materials and diagnoses made by the *same* psychiatrists from the *same* case history materials three months later.

Unlike traditional diagnostic categories, the syndromes summarized in Table 1 consist of ratings on specific behavior problems that can be quantified by computing factor scores and other summary indices of a child's standing in each syndrome. The scores obtained by the same children from ratings by different informants and from ratings by the same informants on different occasions can be statistically analyzed to determine the degree of agreement. Table 2 displays the averages of correlations obtained in different studies where the same people rated children twice at intervals ranging from one week to one month (test-retest reliability); where the same people rated children twice at intervals from one and a half to six months (short-term stability), and from fifteen months to five years (long-term stability); where different people rated the same children under similar circumstances (inter-rater reliability); and where different people rated the same children under different circumstances. As Table 2 shows, agreement was quite high for test-retest reliability and short-term stability; moderate for inter-rater reliability and long-term stability; and low for different raters, seeing children in different situations. Within each category, the degree of agreement was fairly similar for broad- and narrow-band syndromes.

FROM SYNDROMES TO PEOPLE

Although syndromes derived through factor analysis reflect co-variation among specific behaviors, additional steps are required to translate syndromes of this sort into categories. In addition to the need for reliable descriptions of phenomena, taxonomies must be evaluated in terms of their ability to facilitate communication about individual cases and to discriminate among individuals who differ in other important characteristics—such as the causes

Table 2. Reliability and Stability of Syndrome Ratings

Type of measure		Type of Syndrome	
	Type of rater	Broad band	Narrow band
Test-retest reliability (1 week to 1 month)	Parents	.90	.88
	Teachers	.87	.82
Short-term stability (1½ to 6 months)	Parents	.83	.77
	Teachers	.83	—
	Mental health workers	.59	.57
Long-term stability (15 months to 5 years)	Parents	.60	.52
Inter-rater reliability			
	Parents	.69	.69
	Teachers	.70	—
	Mental health workers	—	.72
Different raters seeing children in different contexts		.37	.19

Note: Figures are averages of correlations obtained in studies reported in detail by Achenbach, Dickerson, and Edelbrock (1980) and Achenbach and Edelbrock (1978); trest-retest reliabilities were not available for mental health workers ratings, nor were long-term stabilities available for mental health workers' orteachers' ratings of either broad-band or narrow-band syndromes.

and prognoses of their disorders, the kinds of management necessary, and the most appropriate treatments. In the absence of complete knowledge about etiology, prognosis, and differential treatment effectiveness, any taxonomy must be regarded as provisional, subject to change as more knowledge is accumulated. However, until complete knowledge is achieved, taxonomic approaches can be evaluated in terms of their ability to provide reliable descriptions, to facilitate communication, and to provide leads for determining differential etiologies, prognoses, and responses to treatment.

Classification by Individual Syndromes

Despite the numerous efforts to identify syndromes empirically, only a few of these have been carried to the next step whereby individual children are categorized according to the syndromes and are then compared on other characteristics. When this has been done, it has primarily involved the broad-band Overcontrolled and Undercontrolled syndromes, especially the versions of these syndromes identified by Achenbach (1966) and labeled Internalizing and Externalizing, respectively. Among disturbed children manifesting these two syndromes, it has been found that Externalizers performed worse than Internaliz-

ers in school and on standardized tests, were rated less favorably by teachers and peers, had more pre-existing social problems, and displayed less self-control on experimental measures of impulsivity, delay of gratification, and foresight (Achenbach, 1966; Achenbach and Lewis, 1971; Rolf, 1972; Rolf and Garmezy, 1974; Weintraub, 1973). Externalizers have also been found to display less disparity between their real-self and ideal-self images (Katz, Zigler, and Zalk, 1975) and to terminate sooner and improve less in psychotherapy than Internalizers (Achenbach and Lewis, 1971). Furthermore, parents of Externalizers have been found to differ from parents of Internalizers in being less strict with their child and less concerned about the child's problems, and in having more overt social problems, more marital separations, more overall pathology, and different Minnesota Multiphasic Personality Inventory (MMPI) profiles (Achenbach, 1966; Achenbach and Lewis, 1971; Anderson, 1969; Weintraub, 1973).

The Internalizing-Externalizing dichotomy has also been found related to long-term prognosis, as a follow-up study of disturbed adolescents when they had reached adulthood (mean age of 38 years) showed the following differences between demographically matched Internalizers and Externalizers (Hafner, Quast, and Shea,

1975): Internalizers had better academic records, completed more grades, were more likely to graduate from high school, had more friends, and received more favorable mental health ratings. Within-sex comparisons favored Internalizers over Externalizers of the same sex on indices of occupational, marital, and social adjustment. Other versions of the Overcontrolled-Undercontrolled dichotomy have also shown better outcomes for children manifesting the Overcontrolled syndrome (Lorion and Cowen, 1976; Lorion, Cowen, and Caldwell, 1974).

Profile Approaches

In the approach just discussed, children were classified into two broad-band categories on an either/or basis. In effect, this involves using the empirically-derived syndromes to place children into mutually exclusive categories in much the same fashion as is done with traditional taxonomies. The major differences are that the empirically-derived syndromes consist of specific sets of behaviors and that explicit, usually quantitative, criteria are employed to decide which syndrome a child's behavior most resembles. Another way to use empirically-derived syndromes is to score each individual on a profile of the narrow-band syndromes identified for his or her age and sex. Because few children show *all* the characteristics of one syndrome and *none* of any other syndrome, this approach preserves more information about children's overall behavioral patterns than does categorization on the basis of single syndromes, either those derived empirically and applied according to explicit decision rules or those of traditional taxonomies applied idiosyncratically.

Preserving maximal information about behavior patterns is especially important when assessing disturbed children, because few of their problems bear a one-to-one relation to a specific etiology such that removal of the cause automatically results in normal adaptation. Instead, even where specific organic etiologies are involved, many aspects of a child's adaptive pattern may be affected, including the development of social, academic, cognitive, and recreational skills. Once a child's development is significantly deflected from the normal course—even if the cause is temporary—the child is likely to adopt ways of coping that can become obstacles to healthy adaptation after the original cause is no longer present. For example, reading problems in the early grades have diverse causes, including slow maturation, specific perceptual-motor deficits, family stress, and teaching that is poorly matched to the needs of particular children. Many of these causal factors are either temporary or are correctable through appropriate intervention. However, by the time a reading problem is recognized, the child may have acquired a sense of inferiority, as well as behaviors for avoiding intellectual challenges and exposure of his or her deficiencies. Depending on other characteristics of the child, these behaviors can be primarily of the overcontrolled or undercontrolled kind, or some mixture thereof. Yet, even though they were evoked by difficulties with reading, the behaviors themselves can interfere with development in other areas as well as with attempts to overcome the reading problem. Likewise, hyperactivity may have a variety of relatively transient causes, and it may be reduced by stimulant drugs. Yet, follow-up studies of treated children show continuing maladaptation in school and social relationships despite a reduction in activity level (Weiss, Kruger, Danielson, and Elman, 1975).

The Child Behavior Profile. To take full advantage of the profile approach, it is necessary to take account of differences in the frequency and patterning of behavior problems among children differing in age and sex. In a program of research designed to do this, parents of clinically referred children aged four through sixteen filled out the Child Behavior Checklist, comprised of 118 behavior problem items, plus 20 social competence items for assessing children's involvement in sports, nonsports activities, organizations, jobs and chores, relationships with other people, and school (Achenbach, 1978b; Achenbach and Edelbrock, 1979). To derive profiles reflecting the patterns of problems characterizing children of each sex at different age levels, checklists are factor analyzed for each sex

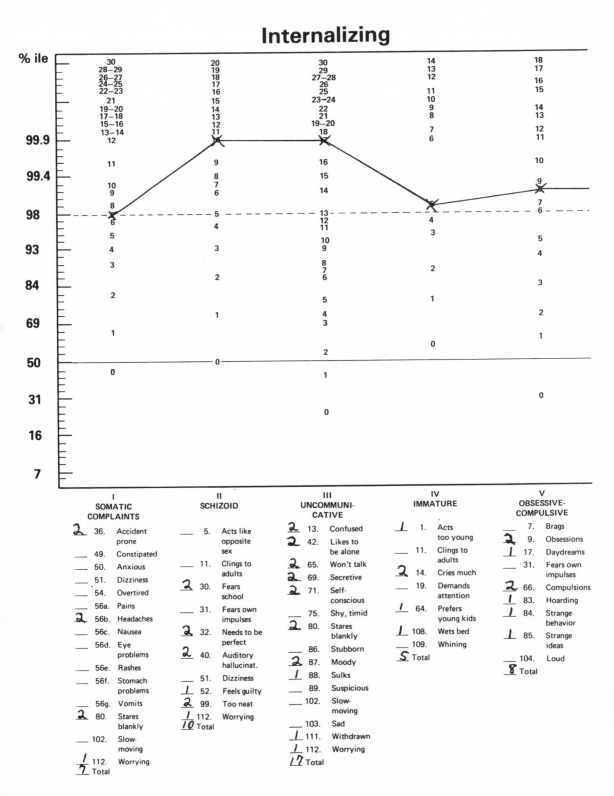

Figure 1. The Child Behavior Profile for Boys Aged 12-16.

Externalizing

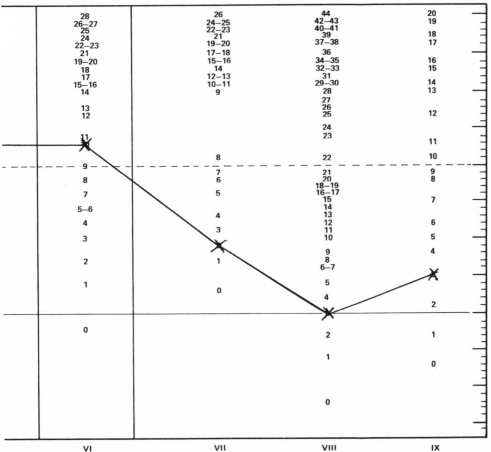

VI HOSTILE WITHDRAWAL	VII DELINQUENT	VIII AGGRESSIVE	IX HYPERACTIVE
_1_ 1. Acts too young	___ 20. Destroys own things	___ 3. Argues	_1_ 1. Acts too young
___ 12. Lonely	___ 21. Destroys others' things	___ 10. Hyperactive	___ 8. Can't concentrate
___ 20. Destroys own things	___ 23. Disobeys at school	___ 16. Cruel to others	___ 10. Hyperactive
___ 21. Destroys others' things	___ 39. Bad friends	___ 19. Demands attention	___ 23. Disobeys at school
_2_ 25. Poor peer relations	___ 43. Lies, cheats	___ 22. Disobeys at home	___ 41. Impulsive
___ 33. Feels unloved	_2_ 61. Poor school work	___ 27. Jealous	___ 44. Nailbiting
___ 34. Feels persecuted	___ 67. Runs away	___ 34. Feels persecuted	___ 45. Nervous
_2_ 35. Feels worthless	___ 72. Sets fires	___ 37. Fights	_2_ 61. Poor school-work
___ 37. Fights	___ 81. Steals at home	___ 41. Impulsive	___ 62. Clumsy
_2_ 38. Is teased	___ 82. Steals outside home	___ 45. Nervous	___ 74. Shows off
_1_ 48. Unliked	___ 101. Truant	___ 57. Attacks people	_3_ Total
___ 62. Clumsy	___ 105. Alcohol, drugs	___ 68. Screams	
_1_ 64. Prefers young kids	___ 106. Vandalism	___ 86. Stubborn	
_1_ 111. Withdrawn	_2_ Total	_2_ 87. Moody	
_10_ Total		_1_ 88. Sulks	
		___ 89. Suspicious	
		___ 90. Swearing	
		___ 93. Excess talk	
		___ 94. Teases	
		___ 95. Temper	
		___ 97. Threatens	
		___ 104. Loud	
		_3_ Total	

Figure 2.

at ages four to five, six to eleven, and twelve to sixteen. The items having the highest loadings on factors obtained for children of a particular age and sex are used to construct behavior problem scales that are then assembled into a scoring profile for children of that age and sex. By adding up the scores a child obtains for the behavior problems on each scale, a series of scores are computed that can be presented in the form of a profile. Figure 1 displays an example of the edition of the Child Behavior Profile that has been constructed for boys aged 12 to 16 (Achenbach and Edelbrock, 1979a). The behavior problem items are abbreviated versions of the items appearing on the Child Behavior Checklist from which the Profile is scored.

Note that there are nine behavior problem scales in the Child Behavior Profile for boys aged 12 to 16. These are composed of the items loading highest on nine factors found in factor analyses of Child Behavior Checklists filled out by parents of 450 disturbed boys. In order to determine how these first-order, narrow-band scales grouped together, they were subjected to second-order factor analysis. The second-order factor analysis showed that the five scales on the left (Somatic Complaints, Schizoid, Uncommunicative, Immature, Obsessive-Compulsive) formed one broad band grouping, whereas the three scales on the right (Delinquent, Aggressive, Hyperactive) formed a second broad band grouping. Because these groupings contained many of the items previously found in the internalizing and externalizing versions (Achenbach, 1966) of the Overcontrolled and Undercontrolled syndromes, they were labeled as Internalizing and Externalizing, respectively. An overall Internalizing score can be computed for a boy by adding up his scores on all the items of the Internalizing scales and likewise for Externalizing. A boy's behavior problem pattern can thus be viewed in terms of profile of scores on the narrow-band scales and/or in terms of the broad-band dichotomy. Because the narrow-band Hostile Withdrawal scale had moderate loadings on both the second-order Internalizing and Externalizing factors, it is excluded from the two broad-band groupings.

In order to assess a child's *deviance* from norms for children of the same age and sex, percentiles at the left of the Profile reflect the distribution of scores obtained in a survey of normal children (Achenbach & Edelbrock, 1981). Thus, compared to normal 12- to 16-year-old boys, the boy whose profile is shown in Figure 1 stands at the 98 percentile on the Somatic Complaints scale, the 99.9 percentile on the Schizoid and Uncommunicative scales, and the 50 percentile on the Aggressive scale. The boy's standing on the broad-band Internalizing and Externalizing syndromes can also be determined by reference to a table (not shown) that converts his scores into standard scores based on normal boys. A second page of the Profile displays the child's standing on three social competence scales, entitled Activities, Social, and School.

Age and Sex differences. With each of the age and sex groups for which editions of the Child Behavior Profile have been standardized to date, either eight or nine factors were obtained that were robust enough to warrant basing behavior problem scales on them. Second-order Internalizing and Externalizing groupings of the first-order scales were also found in each group. The names of the first-order, narrow-band scales and their relations to the second-order, broad-band groupings are portrayed in Table 3. Note that Aggressive and Somatic Complaints syndromes were found for all groups, although the exact composition of these scales differed somewhat from group to group. Versions of the Schizoid, Withdrawal, Hyperactive, Delinquent, and Depressed syndromes were also found for most groups, but their composition was more variable, and in some groups they included items that formed a separate syndrome in other groups. The Cruel syndrome was found for girls, whereas the Uncommunicative syndrome was found for boys. It should be pointed out, however, that the presence of such syndromes in data from only one sex does not necessarily mean that the *behaviors* are not reported for the other sex. It merely means that the behaviors do not consistently *occur together* in a discriminating fashion for that sex. Thus, *cruel to animals* is reported some-

Table 3. Behavior Problem Scales of the Child Behavior Profile

Edition	Internalizing scales[a]	Mixed scales	Externalizing scales[a]
Boys aged 4-5	1. Social withdrawal 2. Somatic complaints 3. Immature 4. Depressed	1. Sex problems	1.1 Delinquent 2. Aggressive 3. Shizoid
Boys aged 6-11	1. Schizoid 2. Depressed 3. Uncommunicative 4. Obsessive-compulsive 5. Somatic complaints	1. Social withdrawal	1. Delinquent 2. Aggressive 3. Hyperactive
Boys aged 12-16	1. Somatic complaints 2. Schizoid 3. Uncommunicative 4. Immature 5. Obsessive-compulsive	1. Hostile withdrawal	1. Hyperactive 2. Aggressive 3. Delinquent
Girls aged 6-11	1. Depressed 2. Social withdrawal 3. Somatic complaints 4. Schizoid-obsessive		1. Cruel 2. Aggressive 3. Delinquent 4. Sex problems 5. Hyperactive
Girls aged 12-16	1. Anxious-obsessive 2. Somatic complaints 3. Schizoid 4. Depressed withdrawal	1. Immature Hyperactive	1. Cruel 2. Aggressive 3. Delinquent

[a]Scales are listed in descending order of their loadings on the second-order Internalizing and Externalizing factors.

what more frequently for disturbed boys than disturbed girls, but among girls it occurs more consistently in conjunction with certain other behaviors to form a distinct syndrome. Combining data from both sexes would have obscured this tendency for behaviors to covary in a particular way for one sex but not for the other. Likewise, syndromes occurring in only one age group would have been obscured by combining data across age groups.

Classification by Profile Patterns

A profile approach like the one just described provides a much more complete picture of each child's behavior pattern than does classification into mutually exclusive categories in an either or fashion. When a child's behavior is reassessed at intervals or after treatment, the profile approach can also be used to measure changes across a broad spectrum of behavior rather than being restricted to a narrowly defined target syndrome, such as hyperactivity. However, a further step is needed to clas-sify children according to their profiles. This step is essential if the profile approach is to facilitate communication about classes of children and comparison of groups of children with respect to etiological factors, prognoses, and differential response to treatment.

In order to classify children according to profile patterns, it is necessary to select criteria for determining the degree of similarity between individual profiles. An approach used with adult MMPI profiles is to group profiles according to their two or three highest scores ("high points"). This has been relatively fruitful for high points that correlate well with existing diagnostic categories. For example, a strong relationship has been found between diagnoses of psychopathic personality (now called sociopathic or antisocial personality) and high points on the Psychopathic Deviate and Manic scales of the MMPI. This relationship is to some extent circular, however, as the Psychopathic Deviate scale was originally constructed from items found to discriminate between psychiatric patients diagnosed as psychopathic personalities and patients receiving other diagnoses.

Because child psychopathology lacks well-established diagnostic categories like those on which the MMPI scales were based, scales cannot be constructed and profile patterns cannot be validated by reference to diagnoses. The lack of accepted diagnostic categories for children's disorders may actually be a blessing in the long run, because using traditional diagnoses to validate new approaches risks perpetuation of categories that may in fact have little value. But in the short run, the lack of such categories means that not only the construction of profiles but also the search for correlates must be fundamentally empirical. Thus, the value of categories based on profile similarities must be established by determining whether the individuals so grouped have anything in common other than their profile patterns. Because grouping on the basis of high points neglects other characteristics of profiles, it is an inefficient way to begin constructing categories where individual scales are not already known to discriminate among diagnostic categories and where no categories command enough confidence to serve as validating criteria for profile patterns.

Cluster Analysis of Profiles. Just as factor analysis has been used to summarize co-variation among many *variables*, multivariate methods, known as *cluster analysis*, have been used to summarize similarities among the *profiles* of scores obtained by *individuals*. In contrast to classification by a few high points, cluster analysis of profiles is sensitive to the entire profile pattern. Although there are many methods of cluster analysis, one of the most effective for profiles of behavior problem scores is *centroid linkage* (Edelbrock, 1979). Suppose, for example, one wished to construct categories of Child Behavior Profile patterns that would efficiently reflect the different types of profiles present in a sample of 200 disturbed children. A computer program, using the centroid linkage strategy, first surveys the profiles obtained by the 200 children in order to find the two profiles whose patterns are most similar. (Various criteria for similarity are possible, but correlation coefficients have been found to be the most effective indices of similarity among Child Behavior Profile patterns.) When the two most similar individual patterns have been found (i.e., the two correlating most highly with one another), the average of their scores on each scale of the profile is computed. These averages form a new profile that is half way between the two original profiles on all scales. This average profile is called a *centroid*. As a quantitative summary of the two members of the first cluster, the centroid serves as the operational definition of the cluster.

In the next step, the computer program surveys the 198 individual profiles remaining in the sample and determines whether any one of them is more similar to the *centroid* of the first cluster than to any of the other 197 individual profiles. If a profile is found that is more similar to the centroid than to any individual's profile, then that profile is added to the initial cluster, and the centroid of the cluster is recomputed as the average of the original two members plus the new member. The computer program repeats this procedure, using the centroid computed from the three members of the initial cluster to seek new members. Whenever two individuals' profiles are found to be more similar than any unclustered individual's profile is to the centroid of an existing cluster, the two individuals are linked together to form a new cluster of their own. As larger clusters are formed, they are linked together whenever their centroids are more similar to one another than are the profiles of any remaining unclustered individuals. In this fashion, a hierarchical picture of the groups and subgroups of profile types is obtained for a sample of individual profiles.

The reliability of the profile types can be assessed by computing correlations between the centroids of clusters obtained in separate samples. If a particular cluster is replicated in different samples—as shown by high correlations between the centroids of versions of the cluster found in the different samples—this indicates that it reliably represents a category of individuals. After reliable profile types have been identified, new individuals can be classified according to the profile types by computing the correlation between their profile of scores and the centroid of each cluster to determine which profile type they most resemble.

When the above procedure has been followed with Child Behavior Profiles of disturbed children, highly reliable profile types have been found that efficiently classify most disturbed children (Edelbrock and Achenbach, 1980). For example, six profile types were found for boys aged twelve to sixteen. These can be descriptively summarized in terms of the Child Behavior Profile scales showing the highest points in the centroid of each pattern, but it should be remembered that—unlike MMPI high point classifications—each type is defined by its entire profile pattern. Designating them by their high points, the six types were: *Schizoid; Uncommunicative; Immature-Aggressive; Hyperative; Uncommunicative-Delinquent;* and *Delinquent.*

Although it is possible to interpret some of the profile types in terms of psychological theory, we will defer interpretation until empirical correlates have been established. To date, we have found some demographic correlates that suggest differential etiologic factors. We have also performed follow-up studies that show that—regardless of demographic background—children manifesting certain patterns seem to improve after mental health contacts, whereas children manifesting other patterns do not. In order to determine whether these interactions between profile pattern and outcome are affected by the type of treatment administered, we are presently conducting research in which matched groups of children who are similar in profile patterns and other characteristics receive different treatments. From this type of research, we hope to answer the following questions: (1) Are certain treatment approaches better than others across all profile types? (2) Do some profile types benefit only from particular treatments? (3) Do some profile types consistently have worse outcomes than other profile types, regardless of treatment? (4) If children can be identified who consistently show poor responses to current mental health services, can new approaches be found that help them? Whether or not one uses profiles of behavior problems to classify children, these are the types of questions that taxonomies should help to answer, and they are the questions that need answers if mental health services are to bring significant benefits to troubled children.

CONCLUSION

Modern psychiatric taxonomy originated with the application of organic disease models to behavior disorders in the nineteenth century. Taking paresis as a prototype, it was assumed that progressively better descriptions of symptoms would make it possible to distinguish among different disorders and that patients grouped by syndrome could then be compared to identify the organic causes of each syndrome. Kraepelin's (1883) classification system provided a comprehensive framework for descriptive diagnosis, although the later inclusion of the outcome of disorders as a criterion for diagnosis and the addition of psychogenic and personality disorders complicated the ideal of descriptive diagnosis. American descendants of Kraepelin's system were further complicated by the influence of psychoanalytic theory and Adolph Meyer's concept of reaction types, to the point that official taxonomies primarily reflected compromises among competing schools of thought.

Almost entirely neglected in the offical taxonomies until 1968, children's disorders first became the subject of empirical descriptive efforts in the 1940s. However, it was only in the 1960s and 1970s that research on child psychopathology reached the point where the need for a more differentiated taxonomy was widely recognized. In the absence of entrenched diagnostic categories, taxonomic efforts capitalized on the advent of high-speed computers and multivariate techniques to derive syndromes from correlations among behavior problems rated by mental health workers, parents, and teachers. Despite variations in the problems rated, the observers' vantage points, the subject samples, and the methods of analysis, two broad-band syndromes and several narrow-band syndromes have been found in many studies. The test-retest reliabilities and short- and long-term stabilities of these syndromes are quite satisfactory, although inter-rater reliabilities decline with increases in the differences between the types of raters and the situations in which they see children.

Children classified by the major broad-band syndromes in an either/or fashion have been found to differ in many ways, but scoring children on profiles comprised of the narrow-band syndromes found for their sex and age provides a more complete picture of their overall behavior patterns. Profiles can be used to assess change across a broad range of behavior, and profile types identified through cluster analysis can be used to group children for purposes of communication as well as for research on etiology, prognosis, and differential responsiveness to treatment.

REFERENCES

Achenbach, T. M. The classification of children's psychiatric symptoms: A factor-analytic study. *Psychological Monographs*, 1966, *80* (Whole No. 615).

Achenbach, T. M. *Development psychopathology.* 2nd Ed. New York: Wiley, 1982.

Achenbach, T. M. *Research in developmental psychology: Concepts, strategies, methods.* New York: Free Press, Div. of Macmillan, 1978. (a)

Achenbach, T. M. The Child Behavior Profile: I. Boys aged 6–11. *Journal of Consulting and Clinical Psychology*, 1978, *46*, 478–488. (b)

Achenbach, T. M., Dickerson, F. B., & Edelbrock, C. S. Relations between parent, teacher, and clinician reports of behavior problems in child and adolescent outpatients at intake and follow-up. Manuscript in preparation, 1982.

Achenbach, T. M., & Edelbrock, C. S. The classification of child psychopathology: A review and analysis of empirical efforts. *Psychological Bulletin*, 1978, *85*, 1275–1301.

Achenbach, T. M., & Edelbrock, C. S. The Child Behavior Profile: II. Boys aged 12–16 and girls aged 6–11 and 12–16. *Journal of Consulting and Clinical Psychology*, 1979, *47*, 223–233

Achenbach, T. M. & Edelbrock, C. S. Behavioral problems and competencies reported by parents of normal and disturbed children aged 4 through 16. *Monographs of the Society for Research in Child Development*, 1981, *46* (Serial No. 188.)

Achenbach, T. M., & Edelbrock, C. S. The Teacher's Report Form. In preparation.

Achenbach, T. M., & Lewis, M. A proposed model for clinical research and its application to encopresis and enuresis. *Journal of the American Academy of Child Psychiatry*, 1971, *10*, 535–554.

American Psychiatric Association. *Diagnostic and Statistical Manual of Mental Disorders.* Washington, D.C. Author, first edition, 1952; second edition, 1968; third edition, 1980.

Anderson, L. M. Personality characteristics of parents of neurotic, aggressive, and normal preadolescent boys. *Journal of Consulting and Clinical Psychology*, 1969, *33*, 575–581.

Clarfield, S. P. The development of a teacher referral form for identifying early school maladaptation. *American Journal of Community Psychology*, 1974, *2*, 199–210

Conners, C. K. A teacher rating scale for use in drug studies with children. *American Journal of Psychiatry*, 1969, *126*, 884–888.

Edelbrock, C. S. Mixture model tests of hierarchical clustering algorithms: The problem of classifying everybody. *Multivariate Behavioral Research*, 1979, *14*, 367–384.

Edelbrock, C. S., & Achenbach, T. M. A typology of Child Behavior Profile patterns: Distribution and correlates for disturbed children aged 6-16. *Journal of Abnormal Child Psychology*, 1980, *8*, 441–470.

Freeman, M. A reliability study of pscyhiatric diagnosis in childhood and adolescence. *Journal of Child Psychology and Psychiatry*, 1971, *12*, 43–54.

Hafner, A. J., Quast, W., & Shea, M. J. The adult adjustment of 1000 psychiatric and pediatric patients: Initial findings from a twenty-five-year follow-up. In R. D. Wirt, G. Winokur, and M. Roff (Eds), *Life history research in psychopathology, Vol. 4.* Minneapolis: University of Minnesota Press, 1975.

Hewitt, L., & Jenkins, R. L. *Fundamental patterns of maladjustment: The dynamics of their origin.* Springifeld, Ill.: State of Illinois, 1946.

Jenkins, R. L. Psychiatric syndromes in children and their relation to family background. *American Journal of Orthopsychiatry*, 1966, *36*, 450–457.

Jenkins, R. L. Classification of behavior problems of children. *American Journal of Psychiatry*, 1969, *125*, 1032–1039.

Jenkins, R. L. *Behavior disorders of childhood and adolescence.* Springfield, Ill.: Thomas, 1973.

Jenkins, R. L., & Glickman, S. Common syndromes in child psychiatry. *American Jour-*

nal of Orthopsychiatry, 1946, *16*, 244–261.

Katz, P. A., Zigler, E., & Zalk, S. R. Children's self-image disparity: The effects of age, maladjustment, and action-thought orientation. *Developmental Psychology*, 1975, *11*, 546–550.

Kraepelin, E. *Compendium der Psychiatrie*. Leipzig: Abel, 1883.

Lorion, R. P., & Cowen, E. L. Comparison of two outcome groups in a school-based mental health project. *American Journal of Community Psychology*, 1976, *4*, 65–73.

Lorion, R. P., Cowen, E. L., & Caldwell, R. A. Problem types of children referred to a school-based mental health program. *Journal of Consulting and Clinical Psychology*, 1974, *42*, 491–496.

Miller, L. C. Q-sort agreement among observers of children. *American Journal of Orthopsychiatry*, 1964, *34*, 71–75.

Miller, L. C. Louisville Behavior Checklist for males 6–12 years of age. *Psychological Reports*, 1967, *21*, 885–896.

Novick, J., Rosenfeld, E., Bloch, D. A., & Dawson, D. Ascertaining deviant behavior in children. *Journal of Consulting and Clinical Psychology*, 1966, *30*, 230–238.

Rolf, J. E. The social and academic competence of children vulnerable to schizophrenia and other behavior pathologies. *Journal of Abnormal Psychology*, 1972, *80*, 225–243.

Rolf, J. E., & Garmezy, N. The school performance of children vulnerable to behavior pathology. In D. Ricks, A. Thomas, & M. Roff (Eds), *Life history research in psychopathology*, *Vol. 3*. Minneapolis: University of Minnesota Press, 1974.

Sandifer, M. G., Pettus, C., & Quade, D. A study of psychiatric diagnosis. *Journal of Nervous and Mental Disease*, 1964, *139*, 350–356.

Tarter, R. E., Templer, D. I., & Hardy, C. Reliability of the psychiatric diagnosis. *Diseases of the Nervous System*, 1975, *36*, 30–31.

Wainer, H. Estimating coefficients in linear models: It don't make no nevermind. *Psychological Bulletin*, 1976, *83*, 213–217.

Weintraub, S. A. Self-control as a correlate of an Internalizing-Externalizing symptom dimension. *Journal of Abnormal Child Psychology*, 1973, *1*, 292–307.

Weiss, G., Kruger, E., Danielson, U., & Elman, M. Effect of long-term treatment of hyperactive children with methylphenidate. *Canadian Medical Association Journal*, 1975, *112*, 159–165.

White, G. D. Effects of observer presence on family interaction. *Journal of Applied Behavior Analysis*, 1977, *10*, 734.

Winters, E. (Ed). *The Collected papers of Adolf Meyer, Vol. 3*. Baltimore: Johns Hopkins Press, 1951.

PART II
DISORDERS OF
CHILDHOOD

Overview

This section of the book covers specific disorders found in children. In the first chapter in this section, Lachenmeyer looks at different etiological and treatment approaches to childhood depression, school phobia, and anorexia nervosa. The issue of childhood depression as a distinct clinical syndrome, as opposed to a transient and developmental disorder is discussed. Behavioral, cognitive, and psychoanalytic theories of depression are reviewed, and implications of these for etiology and treatment of children are presented. Definitional questions and typologies of school phobia are covered, and comparisons are made across treatment approaches on issues, such as a speedy return to school. An overview of the literature on anorexia nervosa indicates a high rate of weight recovery within the hospital using operant procedures but some questions still remain with treatment following hospitalization. Under all three disorders, epidemiological studies on patient and family characteristics are presented, as well as long term follow-up studies where available.

The second chapter by Doleys, Weiler, and Pegam describes some of the less common disorders of childhood: enuresis, encopresis, sleep disorders, and Gilles de la Tourette's syndrome. Assessment, etiology, and treatment of each of the disorders is presented. The authors make the argument that there are common characteristics in these disorders: all have a higher frequency in boys than girls, with overall rates probably underestimated; all have severe consequences for the family as well as the child; all are often said to be maturational and therefore often ignored; and treatment for all requires some knowledge of physiology.

Vandersall, on psychophysiological disorders in childhood, presents a brief historical review of psychosomatic concepts. Ulcerative colitis and asthma are discussed. The author concludes that the relationship between the physiological order and psychological factors is complicated and psychological factors are not always causative.

Russo and Newson, discussing psychosis in children, focus upon childhood schizophrenia and early infantile autism. They present a historical survey of both concepts. They review data on genetics, neurology, and psychological factors for each of the disorders with respect to childhood schizophrenia. They conclude that this is a heterogeneous group of children whose disorder began after infancy. They show general deficits in sensation, perception, cognition, and language. The authors discuss the functions of diagnosis and argue for a behavioral-inductive model that emphasizes empirical data and treatment outcomes rather than a deductive model. They conclude with a discussion of emerging trends in the treatment of psychotic children, such as classroom education and parent training.

Moore presents a social learning theory perspective to childhood behavior problems: control problems, aggressive behavior, and delinquent behavior. He is interested in how behavior develops and is maintained in a natural setting, acknowledging that the conditions that lead to a behavior may not be the same as those that can change it. He looks at the parent-child interaction and views the family as the locus for early-established behavior patterns. Interactive processes that seem to differentiate problem children from nonproblem children are presented from numerous data sources. Inconsistant and erratic parental attention and punishment are related to all three forms of child maladjustment. The type of behavior problem that develops varies according to the parental role model and the home atmosphere. Direct and indirect influences on the child in the community settings are also discussed. This view of the family presents an interesting contrast to the systems approach found in Cole's chapter.

Solan, discussing learning disabilities, reviews the learning procedures for diagnosing the disabled child, genetic factors related to the occurrence of learning disabilities, and descriptions of the kinds of impairments: perceptual, impulsivity, visual, reading readiness, and psychological difficulties. Current research on nutrition is also discussed.

Bradley and Tedesco focus upon the cognitive, social and physical aspects of the early home environment and their influence on mental development and intellectual functioning. Social class as a concept is examined and the relationship of social class to traditional intelligence tests and Piagetian tests is explored. Cognitive home environment is conceptualized as language stimulation, intellectuality, variety of stimulation, and acceleration of achievement. The social home environment is defined as responsiveness, warmth and nurturance, encouragement of independence and maturity, restrictiveness, and discipline techniques. Physical home environment involves games and toys, levels of sensory input, and organization of the environment.

The final chapter in this section, written by Green, is about child abuse. The term itself is defined. Parental and child characteristics, as found in research are discussed. The psychodynamics of the parent-child interaction are presented from an ego psychological point of view.

CHAPTER 3

Special Disorders of Childhood: Depression, School Phobia and Anorexia Nervosa[1]

JULIANA RASIC LACHENMEYER, Ph.D

CHILDHOOD DEPRESSION

Childhood Depression as a Unified Syndrome

Currently, there is much discussion about a unified syndrome of childhood depression. The concern centers around two basic positions. The first, based primarily on epidemiological research, suggests that at this time the existence of such a syndrome is doubtful. The second position is that such a syndrome constitutes a clinical entity.

With the use of epidemiological data, it has been argued that childhood depression, rather than being a distinct syndrome, may be a developmental condition that disappears in time. To determine whether this is a developmental condition or a separate syndrome, one must determine to what extent these symptoms appear in a normal population. Lapousse (1966) studied 482 children, aged 6 to 12. These children were randomly selected from a clinic population. The results, based on mother and teacher interviews, found

relatively high rates of overactivity (50 percent), children with seven or more fears (40 percent), past eneuresis (20 percent), and daily loss of temper (10 percent). These problems were reported significantly more often in the 6-to-8-year-old group than in the 9-to-12-year-old group. These deviant behaviors were only related to maladjustment in the lower socioeconomic status (SES) group.

Werry and Quay (1971) obtained data on the distribution of 55 behavior categories of 96 percent of a kindergarten through second grade school population in Urbana, Illinois sample of 1,753. Lefkowitz and Burton (1978) reanalyzed these data, looking at the prevalence of 16 behaviors associated with depression (Cytryn and McKnew, 1974; Malmquist, 1975). The results indicated that 20 percent of the general child population had symptoms of childhood depression that are associated with depression in a clinic population. Pearce (1977) reported that 23 percent of a child psychiatric clinic population displayed symptoms of depression. Shepherd, Oppenheim, and Mitchell (1971) collected data from parents and teachers, using 45 behaviors of 6,000 boys and girls aged 5 to 15—in England. Psychopathology was defined as statistical deviation from the norm; behavior that occurred in ten percent or less in either sex

[1]The author is grateful for the thoughtful and detailed comments on this chapter by John J. Stine and those by John Oldham on the psychoanalytic view of childhood depression.

or age grouping was defined as deviant. Again, the incidence of most behavior disorders seemed to decrease with age. However, two behavioral categories appeared to be unrelated to age: disobedience, which was at a relatively high rate (10 percent of the sample), and withdrawal behavior (3 percent of the sample).

The epidemiological studies repeatedly show that a high rate of symptoms associated with childhood depression are found in the general child population, and that these symptoms and other behavioral problems decrease with age. This suggests, to some extent, these problems are transient and developmental. Werry and Quay (1971) maintain that, given these findings, the diagnostic utility of unified syndrome childhood depression is limited. Lapousse's study (1966) further suggests that if one wanted to determine the rate of childhood disorders in the general population, the socioeconomic distribution of the clinic population should correspond to that of the population as a whole.

Those who hold the view that there exists a syndrome of childhood depression can be divided into those who see this syndrome as similar to that of adult depression, with perhaps some additional unique features (Gittleman-Klein, 1977; Beck and Kovacs, 1977), and those who see it as different from the adult syndrome and not manifested in overt depressive symptoms: "masked depression." Those who view childhood depression as similar to adult depression start out with a list of symptoms that constitute depression, and including dysphoric mood and self-deprecatory ideation, as well as other related symptoms. This list is used in one of two ways: either clinical observations are examined to see to what extent depressive symptoms are involved (McConville, Boag, and Purohit, 1973), or a population of clinic children are given a self-report questionnaire, based on the depressive-symptom list (Kovacs and Beck, 1977).

McConville et al. (1973) described three types of childhood depression in a group of 6-to-13-year-old inpatients. Based on entries from staff, 75 children were identified as ones in whom depression was a "prime target symptom." Clusters were developed from 15 depressive items that were determined to be high rate. These clusters led to the three types of depression. The first type was called "affective depression." This involved expressions of sadness, helplessness, and occasional hopelessness and was found to be most common among six-to-eight-year-olds. The second type was called "negative self-esteem" depression. These were children in whom "thought-feelings" about depression dominated, including feelings of negative self-esteem and being unloved. This appeared to be more common after the age of eight. The third group was called the "guilt depression" group. Children in this group reported feeling that they were wicked and should be dead. This group had the smallest number of children in it. They were eleven years of age or older.

A methodological problem with this and similar approaches is that the description of symptoms leads to a diagnosis that defines and then limits the class. These class criteria are applied to other cases and determine the absence or presence of the syndrome.

Kovacs and Beck (1977) maintain the position that since there is no a priori evidence that a depressive syndrome does not exist in children, one should assume that it may and develop measures to determine the rates of its occurrence. They maintain that either childhood depression does not occur before the ages of six or seven or because of the importance of verbal measures of assessment, it cannot be adequately assessed before then. For assessment of childhood depression, Kovacs & Beck (1977) devised the Child's Depression Inventory (CDI). The CDI is a short form of the Beck Depression Inventory (BDI) and consists of items from the BDI that are most highly correlated with the total BDI score. The language of the items has been modified for children. The purpose of both inventories is to assess the presence and severity of affective, cognitive, motivational, and vegetative factors in depression. Validation efforts on the BDI have used different patient and nonpatient populations (Albert, 1973, Albert and Beck, 1975). The form is a self-report in which each item has four levels, rated according to severity (0–3). A range of possible scores, based on the varying degrees of severity multiplied by the number of items, has been established. Four categories with numerical cutoffs, based on psychiatric populations have been determined: no depression, mild depression, moderate depression, and severe depression.

The CDI has been administered to school children along with self-report measures of adjustment. Teacher evaluations of student classroom performance were also obtained. The teacher evaluations were inversely related to self-reports of problems in adjustment. The adjustment picture resembled the CDI picture and clinical picture of depressed adults (Kovacs and Beck, 1977). In another study (Kovacs, Betof Celebre, Mansheim, Petty and Raynek, 1978), the interview schedule for Children (ISC) was administered. It consisted of 37 symptoms and symptom clusters as well as severity ratings. The interview was structured with specific interview questions listed. It focused upon the period two weeks prior to the interview, and it had three parts: the first was global ratings of symptoms of adult depression, the second part was masked depression items, and the third was mental status and observational behavioral ratings. Symptoms were rated on an eight-point scale of severity, with some yes or no answers (e.g., for suicide); mental status items were responded to by no, probable and definite. This was administered to 39 children who had consecutive admissions for partial or full hospitalization, referred from Philadelphia Child Guidance Clinic. The 20 control subjects were matched for age and had had no psychiatric contacts. A parents' questionnaire (PQ) consisting of twenty-five items that described potential behavior on the part of the child and social manifestations of depression as well as the CDI were also administered according to the Global. Depression ratings from the ISC, 14 percent of the clinic population had moderate to severe depressive symptoms, and 24 percent had mild depression. In the nonclinic population, no one had symptoms of severe depression; 5 to 10 percent had moderate depression; and 5 percent mild

depression. The CDI showed twice as much depression in the clinic population as in the nonclinic population. However, some items received high responses from both populations; the correlation between the CDI and ISC was fair (.55). The authors talk of "reasonable concurrent validity" (p.11). The correlation between the CDI and PQ was low (.20). The authors suggest that this may be due to lack of stability in behaviors across settings, parental tendency to minimize pathology in children, parents as poor observers of their child's behavior, and item or rating ambiguity of the PQ. The authors conclude that responses on the CDI show withdrawal from peers and reduced interest in play or school activities. They see it as similar to depression in adults, although children are less likely to be referred for the depression—more likely for lack of cooperation, difficulties in attention, or impaired performances accompanying depression.

This research is still preliminary. Kovacs and Beck (1977) are unsure as to whether some of the symptoms are developmental in nature and the extent to which childhood depressive symptoms may correspond to depressive symptoms in adults. Gittleman-Klein (1977) suggested that one should define four subgroups of childhood depression: a group in which there is pervasive endogenous depression, a second group of children with situational dysphoria, and two or more groups of children with mood disorders and other behavioral problems. She suggested that in quantifying hedonic response, one must consider different developmental levels. With younger children, one should rely on observing behavior in specific situations and less on interviews that can be used with older children. She maintained that one should have ratings on current clinical status of other mood states: attitudes (self-esteem and expressed goals); motor functioning (e.g., retardation); mutism; rigidity; biological functioning (e.g., sleep, eating, and elimination); social functioning with peers, siblings, and adults; school performances, including attention and achievement; and other neurotic syptoms.

Masked Depression

An alternative position that accepts childhood depression as a clinical entity is one that considers *masked depression*. Masked depression can occur in children with no overt depressive symptoms. The child has symptoms that are usually not associated with depression: behavior problems, hyperactivity, psychoneurotic reaction, and psychophysiological reactions. There are also psychopathological features that have depressive elements, such as negative self-evaluation and unwarranted feelings of rejection (Glaser, 1968; Toolan, 1962; Cytryn and McKnew, 1972; Bakin, 1972; and Renshaw, 1974). Malmquist (1972) includes obesity and anorexia as disorders that mask depression. One implication of this is that childhood depression is underdiagnosed. Ossofsky (1974) suggests that endogenous depression can be diagnosed in infancy and childhood—to be treated with imipramine. He argues that the soft neurological signs, associated with minimal brain dysfunction, may actually be depressive in nature. He equates hyperactivity with masked depression, especially when there has been precipitate labor. Cytryn (1977) cites research on fantasies as support for the motion of masked depression. The overtly depressed child will report fantasies about animals, cartoon figures, or inanimate objects experiencing negative things. The child with overt anxiety reactions will have similar fantasies—with the exception that there is a threat of harm that is not carried out. Children with behavior problems, such as aggression, delinquency, psychophysiological disorders, and school phobia report the same kind of fantasies as the overtly depressed child: harm happening to another. Cytryn (1977) suggests that if one looks at the histories of children with behavior problems, there are intermittent periods of overt depression, with verbal and nonverbal symptoms. Cytryn and McKnew (1974) maintain that masked depression is the most common form of depression in childhood, with little overt depressive behavior.

The concept of masked depression can be criticized on several grounds. Kovacs and Beck (1977) note that general somatic complaints included in masked depression for children are not put under such a label for adults. Gittleman-Klein (1977) points out that there is no evidence that hyperactivity and similar problems are defenses against depression. More general criticisms could also be made. First, to categorize so many diverse symptoms under one label does not have much utility. Second, since the concept of masked depression is inferred from depressive themes on projective tests and the similarity of these themes to the themes of overtly depressed children, the criticisms and reservations centering around the use of projective tests are relevant here. Third, the assumption is that since the themes expressed by two groups of children in fantasy are similar, that the underlying condition is the same can be questioned.

The epidemiological argument against viewing childhood depression as a unified syndrome has already been presented. The same argument is also made from other points of view. Gittleman-Klein (1977) states that there is no clear definitional picture of childhood depression. Currently, the clinical description includes a wide variety of states, and the syndrome is often inferred from disparate behavior, sometimes in the absence of clear mood change.

Lefkowitz and Burton (1978) conclude that diagnosis of childhood depression is premature, the symptoms appearing at a high rate in the normal population of children, the conceptualization presently is weak, and the methods of assessment are not valid or reliable. They suggest that because one has adequate models or theories of childhood depression based on adult depression, this does not mean the syndrome exists.

Lastly, from a behavior-therapy view, one might accept the notion of syndrome as a means of categorizing symptoms to enable better collection of information about etiology, disorders, and outcome. However, this view would point out that energies might be better directed toward changing specific dealing behaviors (overt or symbolic) rather than focusing upon what are or are not symptoms of a particular disorder and whether or not these symptoms form a unitary entity.

Theories of Depression

We will now review theories of depression—with specific application to children. When the theory has not been applied to children, implications for childhood depression will be discussed. What a therapist looks for affects what she or he sees. The information sought reflects a therapist's operating assumptions, if not formal theoretical orientation. With this in mind, treatment implications from each of the theoretical formulations will be discussed. The theories are psycho-analytic, cognitive, and behavioral approaches, which also include the learned helplessness theory of depression.

Psychoanalytic Theories Psychoanalytic theories of depression are for the most part, retrospective. They involve multiple concepts; some come from developmental processes (orality); some are concepts of pathological character formation (sadism); some are normal, unconscious defensive mechanisms (introjection, internalization); and others are pathological defensive operations (turning against oneself, narcissism, and ambivalence). One can look at the different theories historically. The original formulation was based on instinct theory; depression followed the loss of sufficient opportunity to gratify instincts. This was Freud's "actual neurosis": damming up of the libido. Depression is a result of regression to the oral-sadistic level of ego development.

A structural view emphasized the role of the superego. Rado (1928) wrote that characteristics predisposing one to depression are intense cravings for narcissistic identification, along with narcissistic intolerance. The individual predisposed toward depression is dependent on love objects for self-esteem. While identifying with parents, the child discovers that one can punish oneself in one's own mind and thereby reproduce anticipated punishment. In the depressed adult, the superego replaces the parents as the instrument of punishment. Punishment is endured by the ego because of the childhood experience that atonement through punishment wins love. Therefore, punishing oneself in this way reflects an unconscious desire to win love.

Rado pointed to the self-love of depression-prone individuals and the guilt and rage inherent in depression. Psychodynamic formulations of instinctual and structural theories focus upon the role of conflict. The conflict in depression usually involves an excessively powerful instinct or excessively strict superego.

Recent formulations revolve around object relations theory. Kernberg (1976) favors a restricted definition of object relations theory: the accumulation of dyadic or bipolar intrapsychic representation (self and object images) as reflections of the original infant-mother relationship and its later development into dyadic, triangular, and multiple internal and external interpersonal relationships; focus on simultaneous build up of self-composite structures derived from the integration of multiple self-images and object representations or internalized objects derived from the integration of multiple object images into more comprehensive representations of other; the nature of internalization is bipolar; each unit of the self and object image is established in a particular affective context. Malmquist (1977), in relating this approach to depression, speaks of "object relations" as relations to the significant others who gratify or deprive an infant. He speaks of "object constancy" as an introjection of images, qualities, and affects—associated with objects. These introjects can be positive or negative. He maintains that attachment and dependence is its own "discrete and endogenous system."

There are two specific psychoanalytic approaches to childhood depression to be considered: Spitz on hospitalism and Bowlby on mourning. Spitz is often cited as an illustration of the effect of loss of the mother on young children. If one goes back to the original study (1945, 1946), it becomes clear that stimulus deprivation is the salient factor. Two groups of children were studied. Both were under continuous institutional care for about one year for reasons other than physical illness. One of the institutions was a nursery in a penal institution for delinquents. Those delinquent females who were pregnant stayed in the nursery with their child for one year. The backgrounds of the parents included indications of maladjustment, feeblemindedness, or psychological abnormalities. The second institution studied was a foundling home in which the mother was well adjusted—but had no money. Both institutions were clean: food was nutritious; clothing was warm; and the medical attention was good. The differences between the two institutions were in the number of toys available, the amount of visual stimulation possible, the radius of locomotion possible, and the number of adults available to provide stimulation as well as access to other children. Greater stimulation in all these areas occurred in nursery group. It should be mentioned that in the nursery group each child had the full attention of either the mother, the mother of another child, or a pregnant woman. However, Spitz mentions that stimulation by the mother is always more intensive than that of the best trained nursery personnel. Although even Spitz referred to the intellectual, social, skeletal, and motoric retardation of the children, due to lack of stimulation and the absence of a mother, he and others in the psychoanalytic literature usually refer to this study as an example of anaclitic depression attributable to the absence of a mother figure during the crucial second half of the first year of life.

Spitz believes treatment involves the return of the mother. Although he states that this led to dramatic change, he questions the permanence of the change. For prevention, the implications of this approach are that no extensive separation between mother and child should occur during the critical period.

The studies themselves have been criticized on the ground that Spitz used the Hetzer-Wolf baby tests (1930) to measure the development of the children. These tests had been standardized on the poor of Vienna (Herring, 1937). They were not later restandardized for the United States populations (Lefkowitz and Burton, 1980). Pinneau (1955), reviewing the Spitz studies, says that they were carried out in such a way that they neither support nor refute his hypotheses. Two of the major weaknesses are the lack of information on the dates and places of the studies and on the

training of the research staff. There are also inconsistent reports on the number of children in the studies—and on their physical surroundings, physical health, and the amount of time to observe them. There was no comparability between the groups on socioeconomic status.

Bowlby (1961) said that the crucial period for separation is between the second half of the first year and the third birthday. He studied children aged 15 to 30 months who were put into residential nurseries or hospital wards for a limited period of time. They were children who had not previously been separated from their mothers. Bowlby mentioned three phases, each defined according to the attitude toward the mother that predominates. The first phase is the "protest phase" in which the child cries and angrily demands that the mother come back; at this time the child seems hopeful of getting the mother back. The second phase is the "despair phase" in which the child is still preoccupied with the absent mother, but the child seems to have given up hope for her return. These two phases may alternate. The third phase is "detachment": the child seems to have forgotten about the mother. When the mother returns, the child seems uninterested, not even appearing to recognize the mother. Tantrums and destructive episodes may appear in each of these phases. After the separation is over, detachment may still occur, depending on the length of the separation and the frequency of the visits from the mother during the separation. Bowlby talked of the detachment "breaking" into intense ambivalence that then leaves anxiety and rage. He stated that this is a variant of mourning in adults. In children, however, there are two differences: the time period is abbreviated, and the processes leading to detachment are apt to develop prematurely, because they coincide with and mask a yearning for or an anger at the lost love object, both of which exist at an unconscious level. The mourning processes for children take a course that in an adult is pathological. Bowlby suggested that the anger at the loved object and the attempt to recover the loved object are a normal part of a grief reaction. The pathology is apparent in the inability to express either the anger or the recovery attempt overtly. This is either repressed or split off. Therefore, the child has an active system within the personality but no overt or direct expression of it.

Thus, from a psychoanalytic point of view, depression occurs in childhood; it might be apparent but is usually masked. One explanatory model is the mourning process in adults (Bowlby, 1961). Malmquist (1977) suggested a working classification for the diverse manifestations of childhood depression (p. 50): (1) deprivation type syndromes (anaclitic depressions); (2) primary, physical illnesses such as in diabetes or reactive response to a disease; (3) separation-individuation problem; (4) object losses; (5) overdeveloped ego-ideal systems; (6) depressive equivalent; and (7) cyclothymic mood disturbances.

Cognitive Theories Beck (1967) sees childhood depression as similar to depression in adults. It involves affective change, cognitive change, motivational change, and vegetative and psychomotor disturbances. His approach rests on two assumptions: childhood depression is a syndrome or collection of symptoms, and diagnosis depends on change in the psychobiological system. If conceptualization of the self or of situations is negative, affect will also be negative. This can lead to indecision, avoidance wishes, and increased dependence on one's own negative view. The fundamental tenet of this approach is that affect is determined by the ways an individual structures experience. In the depressed individual, cognition is structured in negative terms; cognitions are faulty and distorted. Oneself, the world, and the future are viewed negatively. Evaluations are unrealistic, distorted, or illogical ways of thinking that do not correspond to reality. This is apparent in the depressed person's tendency to (1) make use of exaggerations or misinterpretation of events; (2) make extreme, absolute judgments in certain situations; (3) overgeneralize from a single incident; (4) focus upon particular details out of context and ignore more salient features of a situation; (5) draw inferences in the absence of evidence or even in the presence of contrary evidence; and (6) extract personally relevant meaning from unpleasant situations.

Negative thought patterns tend to center on themes of loss and deprivation. Actual losses are misinterpreted: overgeneralized or extravagant meanings are attached to them. A negative view of self is the primary determinant of selfblame. Certain unfavorable conditions (e.g., loss of parents, chronic rejection) make one more prone to rejection. Rizley (1973) using the BDI, found that depressed college students rated internal causal factors as more important determinants of failure but less important determinants of success than nondepressed students.

There have been criticisms of the cognitive approach. Izard (1972) said that this approach ignores the motivational properties of emotion; it has difficulties in accounting for the overt physiological and vegetative symptoms of depression, and the etiology of persistent negative views is obscure. The fact that negative cognitions occur consistently with depression is not an issue, but whether these are primary, with resulting affective changes, is in question. Beck states that the relationship between cognitions and affect is circular; cognitions lead to affect, and then affect leads to cognitions. He suggests that cognitive concepts are easily conceptualized and can lead to empirical verification.

Treatment from a cognitive view would focus upon the statements individuals make to themselves and how these influence affect and behavior. Attribution theory (Shaver 1975) is useful in looking at the relationship between causal attributions and behavior. Ellis' rational-emotive therapy would be one way of restructuring cognitions. Beck's CDI scale has already been discussed. Schachter's (1964) two-factor theory of emotions has implications for the relationship between thoughts and behavior, specifically in application to children. Schachter talks of a general physiological arousal; what differentiates each emotion is not the kind of arousal but rather the social context and the cognitive labeling of the arousal or to what one attributes the arousal. Children learn to label their emotions. Children can learn to mislabel their own or another's behavior. Children's mislabeling of the "cause" of whatever punishment or reinforcement they receive can lead to generalized tendencies to attribute reinforcement to themselves or to others as measured by Rotter's Internal-External Control of Reinforcement Scale (1966).

Behavioral Theories Ferster (1973) spoke of the depressed individual as experiencing an increase in avoidance and escape activity, an increase in latency of responding, and a distorted, incomplete, or misleading view of the environment. The depressed individual does not undertake the normal exploration of the environment—likely to lead to an extended behavioral repertoire. There are two broad classes of circumstances that can lead to a decrease in reinforcing behavior: a direct reduction of the frequency of reinforcable behaviors (such as erratic presentation of reinforcement, especially during infancy and early childhood when an individual's behavioral repertoire is increasing in complexity) and aversive stimuli that lead to escape and avoidance behavior. Inappropriate time-reinforcement, and intermittent schedules of reinforcement reduce the amount of behavior that is generated by reinforcement and the frequency with which the behavior occurs. Environmental changes can lead to a reduction of reinforcement when the individual lacks the appropriate responses to get reinforcement under new environmental conditions. Ferster recognized the role of evaluative self-statements in the initiations of behavior as well as an individual's perceptions of reality. Verbal statements are viewed as verbal behavior. If individuals do not accurately observe the environment, they are unlikely to emit behaviors that will produce reinforcement. Ferster also addressed the relationship of anger to depression. He saw anger as an operant that is unlikely to gain reinforcement from other people in the environment. This lack of reinforcement can lead to greater anger and also to suppression of anger.

Aversive control can lead to a reduction in the frequency of behavior. Moss and Boren (1972) stated two ways in which aversive control is related to depressive behavior. It is directly related, in that an aversive event can lead to the reduction of positive reinforcement. Most behavioral explanations for clinical depression focus upon this reduction of positive reinforcement. Aversive control also can lead to an anxiety response. Lazarus (1968) saw anxiety and depression as having different antecedents: anxiety is a response to aversive stimuli and depression a response to inadequate or insufficient reinforcement, although he states that depression can result from prolonged anxiety. This is similar to the position that Thomas and de Wald (1977) took in their discussion of experimental neurosis and depression: experimental neurosis usually includes a stage of agitation later followed by depression.

Lewinsohn (1974) had a somewhat different operant explanation for depression. A low rate of response-contingent reinforcement (*resconposre*) acts as an unconditioned stimulus for certain behaviors associated with depression, such as feelings of dysphoria and fatigue. A low rate of resconposre is an example of prolonged extinction; it will lead to a low rate of behavior.

The amount of resconposre is a function of the number of events that are potentially reinforcing for an individual, the number of potentially reinforcing events that can be provided by the environment, and the extent to which an individual has the requisite skills to emit behaviors that provide reinforcement. Thus, according to Lewinsohn (1974), the total amount of resconposre for a depressed individual should be less than that for a nondepressed individual; the onset of depression for any individual should be accompanied by a reduction in resconposre, the intensity of depression should covary with the rate of resconposre, and improvements should be accompanied by increases in resconposre.

Lewinsohn wrote about the distorted cognitions of the depressed individual. However, unlike Beck (1967), he did not see these as primary factors in depression but as a secondary elaboration of dysphoria, which in turn is a function of low resconposre. He also addresses the issue of the relationship of hostility to depression. Hostility and aggressive behavior in the depressed individual are secondary and are elicited by aversive stimulation.

The aggressive responses are due to low rate of resconposre. These responses tend to alienate others and isolate the depressed individual.

Lewinsohn gave two explanations of why depression may follow success: (1) external success does not necessarily mean that the number of potentially reinforcing events has increased; and (2) if an individual has worked hard to reach a goal and the reinforcer turns out to be weak, resconposre is low.

Costello (1978) suggested that the general loss of interest in the environment that occurs in depression is a function of general loss of reinforcer effectiveness. There are two possible antecendents: endogenous biochemical, neurophysiological changes or a disruption in a behavioral chain, with reinforcement at the end of the chain contingent the completion of the entire chain.

None of the behavioral formulations directly addresses the issue of childhood depression. The explanatory principles that are evoked could be applied to children. Implications for treatment from a behavioral point of view can involve skill training, consistent reinforcement of incompatible behaviors, problem-solving skills, and modification of evaluative self-statements.

Learned Helplessness—Seligman's (1974) "learned helplessness" model was derived from animal studies and can be considered behavioral in a broad sense. The early formulations suggested that the perception of outcomes as uncontrollable lead to three types of deficits: motivational deficits that lead to a failure to initiate instrumental responses, cognitive deficits that make it difficult for an individual to learn responses that can control outcomes, and deficits in affective responding. Although uncontrollability is sufficient to bring about motivational and cognitive deficits, it is not sufficient to bring about helplessness. For this, the individual must come to expect that future outcomes are uncontrollable. Perception of uncontrollability of positive events may lead to motivational and cognitive deficits (Goodkin, 1976; Welker, 1976; Griffiths, 1977) but is not likely to produce sad affect. It is also likely that attributions of lack of control will be made less often when outcomes are positive than when outcomes are negative. The number of trials over which one will have to experience uncontrollability in order to lead to helplessness will depend on the significance of the noncontingent events. If individuals have experienced control prior to experiencing noncontrol, they are less likely to develop helplessness.

Recently this model has been reformulated. First, distinction between personal helplessness and universal helplessness has been introduced. The attributions that an individual makes for noncontingency between behaviors and outcomes in the present become the determinants of expectations for future noncontingencies. When people believe that outcomes are more or less likely to happen to themselves than to relevant others, they will attribute these outcomes to internal factors or personal helplessness. When an individual believes that outcomes are as likely to happen to themselves as to relevant others, then external attributions are made (universal helplessness). This is similar to Rotter's (1966) Internal-External Locus of Control Scale. Rotter's scale focuses upon the individual's generalized perception of the source of reinforcement as being within his or her control or external to the individual, whereas Abramson, Seligman, and Teasdale (1978) looked at attributions based on the probability of certain outcomes for an individual compared to the probability of the same outcomes for some relevant other. Both universal and personal helplessness lead to cognitive and motivational deficits, but only attributions of helplessness lead to low self-esteem.

Second, the earlier formulation was vague whether helplessness was general across situations or specific and whether chronic or acute. Attributions are global or specific and transient or chronic (stable, unstable). Global attributions are those that affect a wide variety of outcomes (global-specific continuum). Attributions to global factors will recur even when the situation changes; attributions to stable factors will recur after a lapse of time.

Third, the intensity and severity of deficits is related to the chronicity and generality of the attributions. The intensity of the motivational and cognitive deficits increases with the strength or certainty of the expectation of noncontingency. The intensity of loss of self-esteem and affective changes will increase with the certainty and importance of events for which there is personal helplessness. If the attributions are global and/or stable, the individual will expect to be helpless in the distant future. This expectation leads to increased intensity in loss of self-esteem and affective deficits. If the attributions are internal, the deficits may also be more severe, because they are also more stable and global.

To summarize, the nature of the attributions that one makes concerning uncontrollability (i.e., personal helplessness/ universal helplessness, global/specific, and/or chronic/acute) are important. These attributions predict the recurrence of expectations, but the expectations *determine* the occurrence of deficits of helplessness.

Applying this model of depression, Abramson, Seligman, and Teasdale (1978) suggest four classes of deficits—self-esteem added to the earlier three. Motivational, cognitive, and self-esteem deficits come from uncontrollability. The affective deficit comes from the expectation that a negative outcome will occur. The intensity of affect and self-esteem deficits increases with the desirability of unobtainable outcomes or with aversiveness of unavoidable outcomes and with the strength or certainty of expectation of uncontrollability. Depression may occur with either universal or personal helplessness. Also, intensity of depression may depend on whether the helplessness is seen as universal or personal. Weiner (1974) found that failure that is attributed to internal factors leads to greater negative affect. Both personal and universal helplessness lead to negative cognitive sets, lowered affect, and motivational deficits. Hammen and Krantz (1976) found that depressives made more global, more stable, and more internal attributions for negative events. Klein et al. (1976) found that depressives make more external, specific, but less stable attributions for their success.

According to this reformulation, depression is most severe when (a) the estimated probability of a positive outcome is low or the estimated probability of an aversive outcome is high; (b) the outcome is highly positive or highly aversive; (c) the outcome is expected to be uncontrollable; and (d) the attribution for this uncontrollability is to a global, stable, internal factor. The treatment strategies are the following (Abramson, Seligman, and Teasdale, 1978):

(1.) Change the estimated probability of the outcome: reduce the probability of aversive events and increase the probability of desired events.
(2.) Make highly preferred outcomes less preferred: reduce the aversiveness of highly aversive outcomes or reduce the desirability of highly desired unattainable outcomes.
(3.) Change expectations from uncontrollability to controllability when outcomes are possible. If skills are not in an individual's repertoire, appropriate training should be done. If an individual has the skills but has distorted the expectations of response-outcome independence, modification of this expectation is useful.
(4.) Change unrealistic attributions for failure, unstable, specific factors and then change unrealistic attributions for success toward internal, stable, global factors.

Watson (1977), in a discussion of the earlier formulation of the learned helplessness hypothesis, stated that further research is needed on the variables that make controllable events appear uncontrollable. He suggested looking at environmental factors that may mask contingency and organismic variables, affecting an individual's acuity in perception of contingencies. Drawing from the general learning literature, some environmental factors that may mask contingencies are delayed reinforcement, inconsistent reinforcement, lack of clear discriminative stimuli, dysfunctional distribution of practice, and causal attributions that misattribute control to factors outside the individual. Some organismic variables might be lowered memory capacities that magnify the importance of delays between behavior and consequences, making recognition of reoccurrences difficult, and limited or inappropriate attentional function. Watson suggests further work is necessary on factors that influence perception of control and how these interference effects are generalized.

The question has been raised (Watson, 1977; Dweck, 1977) that if learned helplessness leads to depression, why are there not more depressed children than depressed adults? In absolute terms, children have less control over their environment than adults. One task of development is to teach realistic assessment of situations where one has control. Watson (1977) suggested that perception of lack of control depends on experience of control, which children do not have to any great degree. Dweck (1977) stated that for failure to control to be seen as affecting one's competence, it must occur in the face of necessity to control. These pressures occur in adolescence when one is expected to take on responsibility. Also, it is only in adolescence that the individual is capable of abstract thought so that helpless cognitions are generalized across time and situations.

Conclusion

The epidemological data do not seem to support the existence of a unitary syndrome of depression in children. They suggest that the depressive symptoms may be transitory. If one limits the definition of depression in children to low dysphoric mood and low rate of instrumental responses, the construct of childhood depression may be a useful tool for a clinician. Theories and research on adult depression are relatively advanced. Thus, the application of depression as a construct to an individual may lead to differential treatment in a therapeutic situation. Also, although reliable data are hard to obtain, childhood suicides occur and adults who are depressed often recall having thought about suicide when they were children (Gibbs, 1979). Further research is needed to differentiate the developmental phenomena from more durable and potentially harmful ones. However, the possible consequences of childhood depression are too severe to dismiss it as a construct because one cannot presently point to its existence as a unitary sydrome.

SCHOOL PHOBIA

This part of the chapter is intended to provide an overview of the available literature on school phobia. It will cover the various approaches to definition and diagnosis, epidemeological studies that describe characteristics of the school phobic child as well as some studies of their families, several treatment approaches (psychoanalytic, dynamic, and behavioral), drug treatment, and follow-up studies with some tentative implications for long term prognosis.

Definition

There is disagreement about the definition of school phobia. Typologies that have been developed center on one of three factors: differentiation by symptoms, differentiation by etiology, and further specification of anxiety-arousing factors in the school situation.

Kelly (1973) limited the definition to extreme reluctance to go to school as a result of extreme anxiety and a dread of some aspects of the school situation. Coolidge, Hahn, and Peck (1957) discussed two types of school disturbances: neurotic in the context of a sound personality, and characterological, where the disturbance is part of a more pervasive personality disturbance. Kennedy (1965) developed ten descriptive criteria to distinguish Coolidge's two types. These are: (1) the present illness is the first episode; (2) there is a Monday onset following absence due to physical illness on the previous Thursday or Friday; (3) acute onset occurs; (4) prevalence of children in lower grades is noted (5) the child expresses concern about death; (6) the mother's physical health is in question, either in reality or in the mind of the child; (7) there is good communication between the parents; (8) the mother and father are well adjusted in most areas; (9) the father is competitive with the mother in household management; and (10) the parents achieve understanding of dynamics easily

(p. 286). If seven of the ten criteria are present, the child is diagnosed as the neurotic school phobic (Type I). If fewer than seven criteria are evident, the child is diagnosed as the characterological school phobic (Type II). Prognosis is poorer with Type II.

Marine (1968) expanded these into four categories: simple separation anxiety; mild, acute school refusal (Kennedy's Type I); severe, chronic school refusal (Kennedy's Type II); and childhood psychosis with school refusal symptoms.

Waldron (1975), rather than differentiating by symptoms, developed a typology based on etiology. The categories are not mutually exclusive. The first category is school refusal as a consequence of separation anxiety in the context of a mutually hostile-dependent relationship between mother and child. This has been called the "family interaction type" (Johnson, Falstein, and Szurak, 1941; Waldfogel, Coolidge and Hahn, 1957). The second category is school refusal as a phobic response, involving defenses of displacement, projection, and externalization. It is different from other phobias only in that the presence of the mother is "more mandatory." The third category involves a conscious concern over what will happen to the parent while the child is away; there is an actual medical illness or threatened danger such as depression of the mother. In this case, school complaints are rationalizations that can be easily abandoned. This is not a phobia but rather an acute anxiety reaction (Davidson, 1961; Sperling, 1967). The fourth category is school avoidance due to fear of the real situation. This may be fear of failure and loss of self-esteem or fear of bodily harm. Waldron (1975) said that children with poor autonomy and poor self-esteem are more vulnerable to such crises. This is the situational characterological type (Milman, 1961, Leventhal and Sills, 1964; Lazarus, Davison and Polejka, 1965; Levanthal, Weinberger, Stander and Stearns (1967).

In practice, two factors play an important role in diagnosing a child as school phobic: school avoidance, accompanied by anxiety that occurs before adolescence. After adolescence, school avoidance is associated with many different problems (Miller, 1961; Coolidge, Willer, Tessman, and Waldfogel, 1960). The school phobic differs from the truant in that she or he is often a good student, whereas the truant is not. The school phobic child stays at home; the truant avoids the home. Therefore, the parents of the school phobic child are aware of his or her absences, whereas the truant's parents may not be aware of the absence. The school phobic child remains out of school continuously for periods at a time; the truant is intermittently absent (Gordon and Young, 1976).

Epidemiological Factors

Waldron, Shrier, Stone, and Tobin (1975) contrasted school phobics to other categories of neurotics on personal characteristics, individual family members, and family interaction. Patients were matched on sex, age, age at the time of referral, and year of referral. The study used the Group for Advancement of Psychiatry (GAP) classification system to diagnose patients seen in an out-patient clinic 1955–1961. They found that in the school phobic sample, 75 percent of the children experienced more than minimal separation anxiety, compared with 32 percent of the neurotic population; 75 percent experienced more than mild dependency, compared with 37 percent of the neurotic population. Approximately two-thirds of each group showed an excessive need to control others. Of the school phobic population. 56 percent appeared depressed, but only 26 percent of the neurotic population seemed depressed. Thirty-two percent of the school phobics showed unrealistic expectations compared with nine percent of the other neurotics. The school phobics showed preoccupation with mistreatment from individuals outside the family (18 percent), whereas none of the other children displayed this (defined as projection). The school phobics showed greater inhibition of fantasy (72 percent compared with 35 percent of the neurotics), and they had a greater number of problems in school before the currently diagnosed problems (62 percent contrasted to 38 percent).

In all, school phobia was associated with separation anxiety, excessive dependency, depression, overly high unrealistic expectations, projection of aggression onto others, inhibition of fantasy, and higher incidence of school problems before onset of the diagnosed problem.

The school-phobic child is described as both willful and passive. It is likely that this child is passive outside the home and willful at home. Resisting parental instructions or commands to go to school implies willfulness and even a large degree of control of interpersonal family relations on the part of the child. Most researchers mention somatic complaints on the part of the child, such as nausea, vomiting, and acute panic reactions (Leventhal and Sills, 1964; Talbot, 1957).

There are no consistent findings that indicate a higher proportion of either males or females among school phobics (Clyne, 1966; Kelly, 1973; Fuerst, 1969). There appears to be no relationship to socioeconomic status. There is disagreement as to whether one age group predominates. Gordon and Young (1976), in their review of several studies, suggested that the rates are evenly distributed between the ages of five to fifteen. There is no evidence pointing to a relationship between school phobia and birth order. (Chotiner and Forrest, 1974; Hersov, 1960; Johnson et al. 1941). Adams, McDonald and Huey (1966) reported that a relatively high rate of school phobics are second in birth order, although this does not appear to be significant when compared to the number of second born in the general population. Berg, Butler, and McGuire (1972) suggested that school phobics tend to be late in birth order when they come from families with three or more children.

Much has been written about the intelligence of the school phobic child relative to the general school population. Johnson (1964) reported that school phobic children tend to have average intelligence. Hampe, Miller, Barrett, and Noble (1973), using the WISC-R and a wide range of achievement tests, sampled from a population of school phobic children whose parents had sought help. They found the same distribution of intelligence that one would find in the general population. They explain the findings that children with school phobia appear to have higher than average intelligence by suggesting that when a child with lower intelligence refuses to go to school, the refusal is attributed to factors other than a phobic reaction and also that a child with lower intelligence is unlikely to conceptualize his or her reluctance to go to school as being due to fear.

Family Characteristics

Several studies suggest that the mother of the school phobic child had a deprived childhood (Eisenberg, 1958; Goldberg, 1953; Van Houten, 1948). Others suggest that she has an unresolved dependency conflict with her own mother (Buell, 1962; Coolidge, et al., 1957; Davidson, 1960; Eisenberg, 1958; Skynner, 1974). The mother is seen as someone who feels incompetent because she cannot live up to her own standards (Buell, 1962; Nurstein, 1963; Talbot, 1957; Waldfogel et al., 1957). Agras (1959) found that the mother often shows signs of depression and a lack of interest outside of the family.

There are conflicting descriptions of the fathers of school phobic children in the literature. Some studies report the father to be passive, dependent, ineffectual, and disinterested (Agras, 1959; Davidson, 1960; Goldberg, 1953; Jackson, 1964; Leton, 1962; Levenson, 1961; Skynner, 1974; Van Houten, 1948; Weiss and Cain, 1964). Waldfogel et al. (1957) described the father as actively involved. His competition with the mother undermines the mother's feeling of maternal adequacy. Hersov (1960) found both active and passive fathers in his sample. In some studies, the fathers were reported to be conscientious and hardworking (Buell, 1962; Chotiner and Forrest, 1974). Some authors reported that the father also has unresolved dependency conflicts (Choi, 1961; Goldberg, 1953; Talbot, 1957); some reported a pattern of heavy drinking (Agras, 1959; Choi, 1961) and a higher rate of psychological problems than with the "normal" child (Agras, 1959; Berg and McGuire, 1975; Jackson, 1964; Suttenfield, 1954). Marital relations are often poor, as is communication between parents (Choi, 1961; Chotiner and Forrest, 1974).

Psychoanalytic Approach

The psychoanalytic approaches look at anxiety about school attendance as having been displaced from the parent-child situation to the school. One view is that the mother is ambivalent toward the child, encouraging overdependence which itself satisfies her needs rather than those of the child. However, the mother feels trapped by the child and hostile. The mother's anger leads to feelings of guilt which leads the mother to overprotect the child. The mother is unable to set limits. The dependence of the child on the mother is inappropriate, and as the child gets older, this is perceptible to the child. This perception leads to guilt on the part of the child. The child fears that denial of his or her wishes will lead to death. The child recognizes the mother's ambivalence and strikes back. Often hostility toward the mother is displaced (Berg, Nichols and Pritchard 1969; Berg and McGuire, 1974). According to Johnson, Falstein, Szurek, and Svendsen (1941) separation anxiety is a predisposing factor that combined with two other factors, can lead to school phobia. These are acute anxiety precipitated by the occurrence of either a physical symptom or some kind of emotional conflict, for example, the birth of a sibling and an increase in anxiety in the mother due to some threat to her emotional satisfaction.

Shapiro and Jegeda (1973) concluded from their review of cases that four dimensions should be used to arrive at a diagnosis of school phobia as well as other syndromes: (1) a chronological age in relation to developmental stage and maturation of the nervous system; (2) the participation of external forces such as school and family with special attention to the mother; (3) the intrapsychic organization of the child in relation to his or her behavior and symptoms; and (4) the symptom in relation to the degree of manifest anxiety on a continuum of ego-alien or ego-syntonic. They point out that nursery schools are now common phenomena and that avoidance of school can start with a child's earliest experiences and can run through college. Data on adults who stay out of work suggest that some of them

have had previous histories of school refusal (Pittman, Langley, and de Young 1968). Not only is chronological age related to developmental stage, it in turn affects parental expectations. Parents and educators do not expect an anxious three-year-old to stay in school without ego supports. An anxious child at this age is not considered to be phobic. As the child gets older, expectations about ability to separate and cope are greater. The emphasis that a family places on independence varies. If the child senses early stress on independence and, if his or her dependency needs are great, a feeling of rejection can lead to anger at having too many responsibilities. If there is sufficient psychic structure, anger may turn to guilt. If the anxiety is overwhelming, it may interfere with other ego functions and pseudoneurotic schizophrenia may occur. Ego-syntonicity of the avoidence behavior has external causes and may have the support of either parents or a truant group. Readiness for treatment and cooperative motivation for a therapeutic alliance are important. The family values and unique psychic organization play a determining role in whether a phobia will develop. School philosophy may also affect the probability of school avoidance, given the other factors just discussed. If school practices are permissive and allow aggressive behavior on the part of the children, a child with strict upbringing at home may have trouble struggling to restrain aggressive impulses. If school practices are punitive and/or programs are structured, it may be difficult for impulsive children with insufficient ego structure. Whether truancy or phobia will develop depends on the kind of support the child gets from a peer or parent. Shapiro and Jegeda (1973) suggest that one should carefully match the type of school and social support for an individual child's ego structure. The concern about separation from the mother is not necessarily a symptom of separation anxiety. These authors point out that the intrapsychic organization can be Freud's hierarchy of helplessness, separation, castration, superego anxieties, or Mahler's symbiosis. These can all manifest themselves in a child clinging to his or her mother.

Shapiro and Jegeda (1973) suggested caution on the question of whether the therapist should insist on the child's speedy return to school. They said that if the child's ego is not sufficiently independent, or if the mother is too disruptive either silently or vocally, the efforts to get the child to return to school may fail. The child may temporarily need the support of the mother, or, when the child is older, true neurotic symptoms may emerge.

Eisenberg (1958) spoke of school anxiety as generalized separation anxiety that is due to resistance in the total individuation process. It is associated with sex role anxiety.

On the whole, psychoanalytic therapy with a school phobic child involves insight and improvement of strength and family equilibrium. There may be an early emphasis on symptom relief (i.e., the return to school) with a later focus on the underlying problems. However, there is not the uniform emphasis on a speedy return to school that one finds in dynamic and behavioral approaches.

Dynamic Approaches

Leventhal and Sills (1964) hypothesized that the school phobic child overvalues his or her self. The child has an unrealistic self-image. If this image is threatened in the school situation, the child becomes anxious. To avoid this threat to self-image, the child retreats home. This retreat may be reinforced at home. They stated that one should get information on how school personnel, school activities, classmates, and parents contribute to the school avoidance. Then, the therapist should address the child's fantasies, unrealistic self-image, and the power issue of school attendance. Confrontation on these issues is proposed, as is graduated pressure for an early return to school.

Radin (1968) wrote about a cycle underlying school phobia. Parental-faulty attitudes foster infantile feelings of omnipotence. These feelings do not allow for adequate ego identification. Through realistic evaluation in the school, the child's omnipotent self-image is threatened. The child tries to restore self-image at home and at the same time becomes angry with the parents for the self-deception and for further ego inflation. This is similar to the Leventhal-Sills (1964) formulation, with the addition of the child's ambivalence; the child's overdependence leads to an inadequate and weak ego, threatened by the outside world but unsatisfied with parental approval. It is similar to the psychoanalytic views in its emphasis on the deficiencies in the parent-child relationship. However, the focus is upon the child's anxiety and fears concerning self-esteem rather than fear of losing the parent. Treatment, according to Radin, involves the interruption of the cycle through insight that is achieved through fear reduction, correction of parental attitudes, and the replacement of fear with pleasure as a motive.

McDonald and Shepherd (1976) questioned the hypothesis that a child's unrealistic self-esteem leads to school avoidance. They pointed out that one sees the same type of parent-child relationships in families where there is no school phobia. Often only one child in such a family avoids school. Also, children who avoid school seem to have no difficulty in separating themselves from their mothers on other occasions.

A study by Nichols and Berg (1970) called into question the notion of the school phobic child as having unrealistic self-expectations. They found no significant differences between the self-evaluation of school phobic children and that of normal children, using the semantic differential. Along similar lines, it has been suggested that there is an inverse relationship between anxiety level and self-evaluation. If self-evaluation is high, it is not affected by criticism. Parents of children who have high self-evaluations are also likely to be firm and consistent giving clear statements of rules.

Behavioral Approaches

Behavioral approaches to school phobia focus upon it as an avoidance behavior accompanied by emotional responses. School itself may be directly or vicariously punishing; fears of parental loss may be verbally conditioned to school or school-related events; and school can be time away from reinforcement at home. With most behavioral approaches there is less emphasis on etiology and more on treatment. The primary emphasis is on the child's return to school and involvement of the parents. Studies have used both operant and respondent techniques.

Garvey and Hegrenes (1966) used *in vivo* desensitization. The child gradually approached school in a 12-step hierarchy over 20 consecutive days, including Saturday and Sunday. The child reported when there was anxiety. At this point the child was allowed to withdraw. There was reinforcement in the form of praise for accomplishments. Allyon, Smith, and Rogers. (1970) concentrated on reinforcement that was maintaining the school avoidance behavior. Smith and Sharpe (1970) used implosive therapy. They point out that aged 8-14, children are highly suggestible, so that an imagined technique is most effective. Tahmisian and Reynolds (1970) focused upon fear-arousing properties of the school situation as well as anxiety over parental separation. Imaginal desensitization was not effective because of the environmental contingencies, so they used parental reinforcement to shape approach behavior to school. Miller (1972) used both imaginal and *in vivo* desensitization to eliminate a child's fear of separation, fear of death, and the school situation. Hersen (1970) instructed the mother to be firm about school attendance, to reinforce approach responses, and to ignore somatic complaints.

Doleys and Williams (1977) attempted to make being in school more reinforcing than being out of school. Attendance behavior was shaped. The amount of time spent in school was increased if the child completed three consecutive days at a particular level without any disruptive incidents and if the amount of time spent in school was the same on Monday as it was on the previous Friday. School personnel were used as monitors and sources of positive reinforcement; teachers verbally reinforced quiet behavior and work behavior in the classroom. If the child cried or was disruptive, the child was warned that the parents would be called. Subsequently, the parents would be called without warning. In this way, the child was not removed from the classroom by school personnel or disciplined by them. Parents were given specific instructions if they were called. If the child was being disruptive when the parent arrived, the child would be removed from class, given two spankings, and confined to a small room. The child could return to class, if quiet and if he decided to return within ten minutes. If either was not the case, the child would be taken home, deprived of toys for the rest of the day or evening. The child would be released from the room only to return to school for a make-up period. This period occurred immediately after school or during the following morning. The make-up period was supervised by the therapists. Time was spent cleaning up the classroom so that this would not be a desireable activity. The child could go home after the make-up period only if she or he had been quiet; otherwise, it would be extended an additional ten minutes. The purpose of the make-up period itself was that disruptive behavior should not have the consequence of reducing the amount of time spent in school. At home, the parents were assisted in restructuring natural consequences. The child has a list of reinforcers available in the home (TV, etc.). They would chose one each day each time the parent was not called to school. There were additional reinforcers available at the end of the week after full attendance had been established. The fact that the home was made nonreinforcing during school hours on school days had no effect on the weekend.

Lazarus, Davison, and Polejka (1965) discussed both the operant and respondent aspects of anxiety in school phobia. First, they used desensitization to decrease anxiety. They found that the decrease in anxiety did not lead to an increase in school approach behavior, so operant techniques were introduced. They pointed out that although by the end of the treatment period it may be clear whether anxiety is a respondent or an operant response, at the beginning of treatment the role of anxiety is in doubt. The use of one or the other explanatory models has implications for different treatment strategies. If a child avoids school and at the same time appears anxious, an operant explanation of that anxiety would suggest that the reports of anxiety should be ignored. A respondent explanation for the anxiety would suggest that the child, when anxious, be allowed to withdraw from the situation and be given support. Lazarus et al., (1965) suggested that, given that there is always the possibility of error, one should initially make a decision based on the level of anxiety. If the child's anxiety is high, a respondent strategy should be used. The rationale for this is that when anxiety is high, an operant approach would increase sensitivity, leading to an avoidance or escape response from school. The latter would be strengthened as a response because of its anxiety-reduction consequences. Also, increased school avoidance would mean that the child would be unable to interact with peers and teachers and to make other responses that reduce anxiety. The inappropriate use of the respondent model, such as withdrawal from the anxiety-arousing situation or the use of relaxation, might reinforce the avoidance behavior. Lazarus et al. (1965) argued that an error along these lines is preferable.

Behavioral approaches focus upon treatment rather than etiology. The concern is: What factors are maintaining the school-avoidance behavior. Priority is given to getting the child back in school, usually through shaping, although sometimes desensitization is used. To maintain school attendance, reinforcement contingencies in the school (where possible) and in the home are changed. The latter, in effect, involves restructuring the parent-child interaction.

Drug Treatment

Gittelman-Klein and Klein (1973) saw separation anxiety as the central issue—anticipation anxiety as secondary. They did not see the school-phobic child as depressed, because she or he has not lost the capacity to anticipate pleasure. They studied the effects of imipramine, the rationale for the use of imipramine is that the drug has been used effectively with adult agoraphobics and their retrospective

histories show a high rate of school phobia. Baseline measures with follow-up measures at three and six week intervals were used. The dependent measures were school attendance that was rated by the mother on a seven-point scale ranging from complete refusal to regular attendance, psychiatric evaluations, mother's evaluation of the child, and the child's impression of the degree of change. These measures of change concentrated on the level of anxiety, the mood state, interpersonal functioning, and target symptom change. School attendance for the imipramine group improved by 81 percent compared with 47 percent for the placebo group. When the latter was effective, it was so within the first three weeks. At the end of this period, the imipramine group was at the same level as the placebo group. Further improvement in the imipramine group occurred within the second three-week period. All children—on imipramine—reported "feeling better." For the placebo group, some children went back to school without reporting "feeling better." In the children's self-ratings, the placebo and imipramine groups were indistinguishable after three weeks. The authors suggest that this may be due to dosage. The psychiatric ratings of symptoms suggest that somatic complaints and fear before school were reduced by the imipramine. The mother's ratings suggest that although the placebo was also effective, the imipramine was more effective in reducing anxiety. There were few side effects that were associated with the use of imipramine. It should be noted that other factors contributed to the results besides the imipramine/placebo conditions. The child had been told to expect a reduction in fear, and attempts were made to persuade the child to return to school. The caseworker was told to be firm about school attendance. Family members were advised to bring the child to school and to stay until the child's anxiety was reduced. The attendance at school was brought about gradually.

Follow-Up Studies

Follow-up studies occurring immediately after treatment point to conflicting results on the relationship of age to prognosis. Rodriquez, Rodriquez and Eisenberg (1959) claim that 89 percent of their clients under 11 years of age returned to school, whereas only 36 percent of those 11 or older returned. Skynner (1974) reports no relationship between treatment and age.

Gittelman-Klein and Klein (1973), as mentioned earlier, point out that adult agoraphobics have a high incidence of school phobia in their retrospective histories. They suggest some similarities in the clinical picture of school phobic children and adult agoraphobics. Both syndromes seem to be related to some loss. However, the unexplained panic attacks that occur with the agoraphobics do not occur with school phobic children. The somatic symptoms that the two describe are also different. The adults report dizziness, feelings of depersonalization, palpitations, and feelings of impending death; the children report nausea and vomiting. They found some depression in children but not the pessimism and inability to anticipate pleasure found in depressed adults. (Gittelman-Klein and Klein (1973) speculate on the possibility of school phobia as a precursor of adult depression or adult phobic anxiety states.)

Although there are several short-term follow-up studies, there are no longitudinal studies and very few long-term follow-up studies. Waldron (1976) followed up patients seen at a clinic from 1955 to 1962. Former school phobic patients were matched with other neurotic patients on the basis of age, sex, and year of referral. The mean age at the time of the follow-up was 22 years. The Menninger Clinic's Health-Sickness Ratings (HSR) (Luborsky, 1962, and Luborsky and Bachrach, 1974) and the Current and Past Psychopathology Scales (CAPPS) (Endicott and Spitzer 1972) were used, as well as an independent clinical assessment.

Contrasting the school phobics to the other neurotics, the school phobics were more likely to be dependent (29 percent compared with 6 percent); the school phobics had a greater tendency to somatize (42 percent versus 11 percent), the school phobics had greater difficulty in completing high school (25 percent versus 6 percent). In other ways the school phobics could not be distinguished from other neurotics.

Conclusion

Faulty self-evaluation processes from a dynamic view and conditioned anxiety with secondary gain from school avoidance from a behavioral point of view are two explanations for school phobia. Both the dynamic and behavioral positions give priority to the child's return to school. There is value in early school return, since continued school accordance leads to increased anxiety, with increased fear of teacher reaction and peer reaction as well as anxiety about accumulated school work. School refusal also affects the family negatively: a parent who cannot get a child to go to school has little control over the child and is not likely to experience being an effective parent. These feelings can further affect the parent-child relationship. The dynamic and behavioral formulations are also similar, in that they both focus upon the present and upon school and home conditions that appear to be related to the school avoidance. The psychoanalytic positions concentrate on the parent-child relationship and the level of development of the child's ego structure. Less emphasis is put on the immediate return to school. Long-term follow-up studies indicate that school phobic children mature with difficulties as adults.

ANOREXIA NERVOSA

Definition

There is some variation in the criteria used for the diagnosis of anorexia nervosa. Most studies state as one criterion a weight loss of at least 25 percent of the patient's original weight (Feighner, 1972; Halmi, Powers, and Cunningham, 1975). Brady and Rieger (1975) suggested that since the anorectic is frequently overweight at the time of initial dieting, a loss of weight of 30 percent below the standard weight for an individual's height is a more appropriate measure. To the age of onset (prior to the age of 30) and percentage of weight loss, Feighner (1972) added the following criteria: (1) a distorted attitude toward eating food or weight that overrides hunger, reassurances, and threats (this can involve a denial of illness, apparent enjoyment in weight loss with a desired body image of extreme thinness, or unusual hoarding or handling of food); (2) the absence of a medical illness to account for the weight loss; (3) no other known psychiatric disorder; and (4) at least two of the following: amenorrhea, lanugo (downy pelage), bradycardia (persistent resting pulse of 60 beats per minute or fewer), episodes of overactivity, and episodes of bulimia (compulsive overeating) or vomiting (self-induced or otherwise). These criteria are now more or less the standard ones used.

Epidemiological Research

Anorexia nervosa has been reported with increasing frequency both in clinical reports (Bruch, 1970; Thomä, 1967; Halmi, 1974; Duddle, 1973) and empirical studies. Theander (1970) puts the incidence at .25 annually per 100,000 in the population. Kendell, Hall, Halley, and Babigan (1973) figure it at 1.6 per 100,000. Nylander (1971) reports that one out of 150 adolescent girls have anorexia in its severe form. Crisp and Toms (1972), using information gained from anorectics about others with similar problems, put the rates at one out of 100 female adolescents between the ages of 16 and 18. These studies come from the United States, Scandanavian countries and England. Onset usually occurs before the age of 30, with some studies reporting treatment of children as young as nine (Brady and Rieger, 1975; Dally, 1967; Halmi, 1974; Kay and Leigh, 1954, Nemiah, 1950; Rowland, 1970; Theander, 1970). Death rates are usually reported at about 15 percent (Dally, 1969; Frazier, 1965; Nemiah, 1950). Van Buskirk (1977) in a review of the literature reported death rates that ranged from 10 to 23 percent.

Incidences of the disorder appear more frequently in middle and upper socioeconomic classes (Brady and Rieger, 1975; Crisp, Palmer and Kalucy, 1976). There seems to be no particular maternal or paternal personality type associated with an anorectic child (Bliss and Branch, 1960; Crisp, 1965). There seems to be no consistent relationship between family psychoses and anorexia and no apparent genetic factor, as reported in any twin studies. (Crisp, 1970). One should keep in mind that the number of subjects in these twin studies is quite small. Halmi, Goldberg, Eckert, Casper, and Davis (1977) in their study of 88 mothers and fathers of anorectics found that three of the mothers had been anorectic, as had four of the 130 siblings. This is somewhat higher than the incidence found in the general population as reported by Crisp (1970).

Descriptions of Anorectics

Halmi (1974) reviewed 94 cases of anorexia nervosa seen at the University of Iowa General and Psychopathic Hospitals between 1920 and 1972. She divided the cases into three groups, based on the age of onset: onset before 15, onset between the ages of 15 and 25, and onset after 25. The percentage of weight loss at the time of admission did not differ significantly between the three groups. Precipitating social events were more frequently identified in the onset over-25 group. Vomiting and laxative abuse also occurred more frequently in the later-onset group. There were few premorbid differences; obsessive-compulsive characteristics were found more often in the youngest onset group; anxiety was found more often in the oldest onset group, and a high rate of depression (72 to 85 percent) was found in all groups. There were greater numbers of somatic complaints and overactivity in the 15-to-25 onset group.

There are reports in the literature that anorectics are frequently overweight before they begin to diet. In this study, only one-third had been obese prior to onset. Obesity was more common in the group with the latest age of onset. Those who were initially obese reported slightly more feeding problems than those who were not (11 percent contrasted to 14 percent). Those who had not been obese showed more obsessive-compulsive traits than those who were both before and during the onset of the disorder. Both the normal weight and the obese groups were overactive and anxious. Both groups were to some extent depressed, although the normal weight group had a higher rate of depression (82 percent contrasted to 68 percent). The obese group reported more psychosomatic complaints (64 percent to 29 percent).

Garfinkel, Moldofsky, and Garner (1977) report that of their 42 patients, all had begun dieting at least one year prior to admission. Eleven patients had dieted less than two years, twelve between two and four years; 13 between four to six years; and six of their patients had dieted more than six years. Nineteen of the anorectics had no previous hospitalizations, eight had one prior hospitalization and 15 had between two to six hospital admissions. Sixty-two percent had marked food fads and only six had regular menstruation (of 42 total, two were males). Nineteen percent were frequently absent from work or school, while 21 percent did not attend work or school. Vomiting and purgative abuse was reported in one-third of the patients and bulimic episodes in one-half (Halmi et al. 1977; Halmi, Brodland, and Loney, 1973; Theander, 1970). According to Halmi et al. (1977) one-half of the anorectics they studied admitted having strong appetites. The majority of anorexics had above-average grade school and high school performances (Crisp, 1965; Halmi, 1974).

In terms of hospitalization, Halmi et al (1977) found that 52 percent of the patients were actively in favor of their own hospitalization; 23 percent were neutral about it; 20 percent were mildly opposed; and five percent were strongly opposed. However, in 71 percent of the cases, a person other than the patient was influential in bringing about the hospitalization.

Bruch (1977) stated that not only are the physical symptoms of the anorectics similar to those of victims of famine or chronic malnurishment but so are their behaviors and their psychodynamic formulations (narcissistic self-absorption, regression, splitting of the ego, and fragmented and psychotic-like thinking).

Family of the Anorectic

Crisp (1970) stated that one cannot always point to major difficulties in the parent-child relationship prior to onset of the disorder because the illness is a reponse to adolescent identity formation in someone with developmental objects and the absence of other defense mechanisms. Most of the anorectics come from intact families (Bruch, 1970; Halmi, Goldberg, Eckert, Casper, Davis, 1977; Theander, 1970). Halmi, Struss, Goldberg (1978) found no significant differences in the weight fluctuations of the parents of anorectics compared with controls. In terms of birth order, Halmi et al. (1977) reported 25 percent of the patients were first born, 36 percent second born, 30 percent third in birth order, and 7 percent fourth.

Halmi et al. (1977) asked parents questions about the anorectic child. In 80 percent of the cases the families identified excessive cooking by the anorectic. Both the families and patients rated the patient on the Hopkins Symptom Check List (SCL-Derogatis, Lipman, Rickels, Uhlenhuth, and Covi, 1974). These responses were compared with those of other neurotic patients and their families as well as normal controls. The scores for the anorectics were similar to those of anxious and depressed neurotics on obsessive-compulsive characteristics, depression, somatization, anxiety, and interpersonal sensitivity. Families were asked to rate patient symptoms that were most distressing to the patients. The families rated obsessive-compulsive characteristics first and depressive factors second, whereas the patients reported sleep disturbances and depression as the most disturbing characteristics. Parents described the patient's premorbid characteristics as well behaved (86 percent), perfectionistic (61 percent), and competitive and achieving (61 percent). Only 7 percent of the parents mentioned hyperactivity.

Pretreatment Predictors of Weight Gain

Goldberg, Halmi, Casper, Eckert, and

Davis (1977) correlated pretreatment variables with weight gain in the hospital. Greater degree of hyperactivity, lesser degree of the denial of the seriousness of the illness, greater report of hunger and appetite by the patient on a self-rating scale, greater appetite as rated from interview by the treating psychiatrist, lesser degree of psychosexual immaturity (self-rated), lesser tendency to overestimate the actual size of one's body parts, and fewer sleep disturbances (self-rated) were all associated with greater weight gain in the hospital. The measures were independent in that some were self-rating measures and others were done by the treating psychiatrist. The results, however, were intercorrelated. Halmi et al. (1977) in a separate report based on the same subjects found that a smaller amount of weight loss, the presence of precipitating factors in the onset of the illness, fewer complications in pregnancy and delivery, less hyperactivity reported in childhood, the presence of hypothermia, higher age of the mother at the patient's birth, and premorbid emphasis on eating were all related to greater weight gain in the hospital. Hypothermia, higher mother's age at the patient's birth and emphasis on eating in childhood also correlated highly with each other. The relationship between less weight loss and greater weight gain can be explained by the fact that those with greater weight loss may be more severely ill. The relationship of a precipitating environmental factor to weight gain might suggest that those who have not been exposed to explicit environmental stress might also be more severely ill or the presence of previous environmental stressors might suggest that these same patients might be more responsive to more positive environmental changes as well. Complications in pregnancy and delivery have been related to increased probability of minimal cerebral damage. Halmi et al. (1977) suggest that this predisposition may be related to less tolerance for and recovery from illness. A relationship between complications in pregnancy and delivery, hyperactivity and behavior problems has been reported elsewhere (Hertzig and Birch, 1966; Pasamanick and Knobloch, 1960; Pincus and Glaser 1966; Taft and Goldfarb, 1964). Halmi et al.

(1977) point out that hypothermia is an effective hypothalamic response to conserve energy during illness. Patients who cannot make this response probably have greater hypothalamic dysfunction. There are currently no hypotheses to explain why hypothermia, higher mother's age at birth of the patient, and emphasis on eating in childhood correlate with each other, and why higher mother's age at birth of the patient and emphasis on eating in childhood correlate with weight increase in the hospital.

Psychoanalytic Approach

Jessner and Abse (1960) described periods of oral deprivation followed by periods of gratification and closeness with the mother. This leads to ambivalence and displacement of anal defiance. It may be heightened by sibling rivalry, additional separations from the mother, and onset of Oedipal competition. The oral deprivation and overprotection interfere with individuation and differentiation of body and self-representations. For this reason pubescent genital strivings threaten the early tie to the mother. Pre-oedipal regressive wishes force the girl back to oral-anal drive discharge and ego functioning. Another formulation views anorexia as a rejection through starvation of the wish to be pregnant, with fantasies of oral impregnation. The unconscious fear of oral impregnation is denied through refusal of food and defeminization of the body through weight loss (Berlin, Boatman, Sheimo, and Szurek, 1951; Falstein, Feinstein, and Judas, 1956).

More recently the emphasis has shifted away from drive theory to early object relations theory. Selvini (1974) did not focus upon the eating function in the anorectic. The emphasis is on the helplessness of the ego rather than on oral-aggressive needs. The anorectic sees his or her body as an incorporating object that imposes a passive role on him or her. During latency, the child identifies with the mother through compliant surrender. The bad object is repressed. The massive repressive mechanism leads to splitting of the ego into the incorporating ego and the identifying ego. The anorectic experiences disturbed body image because the body is equated with the bad object and he or she is unable to recognize body needs and signals.

Sours (1969) said there is a wide spectrum of psychopathology and ego deviation in the developmental histories of anorectics. He suggested ineffective ego structures, instinctual fixation, and infantile object dependency. The feminine genital wishes push girls back to primary object relations and pregenital drive discharge. Fear of the merger of the self with an infantile inner object mobilizes a primitive identification with an omnipotent mother and gives magical devices to save herself from the merger. Through the mother's magic, the girl takes the mother's falsification of reality and use of masochistic maneuvers. The girl refuses food with the view of attaining autonomy. The ambivalence toward the mother is so powerful that all food is refused and hunger is denied. Aggression toward oneself is the basis of identification with the ambivalent love object. There appears to be indifference to inanition and denial of the possibility of death. This can only be done by denial of affect. The anorectic becomes delusional about her body.

Bruch (1970) differentiated between primary and secondary anorexia. In primary anorexia, pursuit of thinness is a motivating force. Food refusal is the means of accomplishing this. There are three areas of disturbed functioning. There is a disturbance in body image that is of delusional proportion. The illness is denied and appearance is defended as normal. There is also a disturbance of perception or cognitive interpretation of stimuli arising in the body. This involves two phases. The first is the failure of a motivating desire that leads to noneating and weight loss and uncontrollable impulses to gorge without awareness of hunger or satiety, followed by self-induced vomiting. The other aspect of this misperception is the overactivity and denial of fatigue, as well as failure of sexual functioning and absence of sexual feeling. The third area of disturbed functioning is the paralyzing sense of ineffectiveness that pervades all thinking and activities. The anorectic experiences herself as acting only in response to the demands

of others. Bruch (1970) stated that the first two areas of disturbed functioning are easily recognized. The overwhelming sense of ineffectiveness can be camouflaged by negativism and defiance.

Bruch stated that from birth there are two forms of behavior that require differentiation; those initiated from within the individual and those in response to external stimulation. Starting early in life the anorectic has deficits in self-initiated differentiation. The child does not learn to discriminate sources of sensation and does not learn control over them. There is misinterpretation of biological functioning and social roles, so that the fashion to be thin is internalized in an exaggerated and concrete way.

In terms of family dynamics, according to Bruch, the parents overvalue the child. They overprotect the child and are overly concerned and ambitious. They expect obedience and superior performance. As long as the child complies, all is well. As the child comes into adolescence, attempts at independence are unacceptable to the parents. The parents' need to control then comes out in the open. The illness is an escape from an overdemanding role and is an attempt to establish a sense of identity. The child's goal is perfection so that the concepts of being significant and worthwhile are unrealistic. The refusal to eat is a result of a fear of having no control over eating. Fear of not being in control is the basic issue. It is expressed in dependency on the home, open rejection of everything from the parents, and the inability to make decisions.

In terms of therapy, Bruch recommended that a nutritional program be first implemented, preferably away from the family. She argued that a behavioral program in its very efficiency at weight gain increases feelings on the part of the anorectic that she is not autonomous. She made a similar argument that emphasis on symbolic meaning of noneating and interpretations given to patients from a psychoanlaytic point of view, whether correct or not, confirm the patient's fear of being defective, incompetent, and dependent. She suggested that pointing out to the anorectic that she arouses anxiety and guilt in others indicates that she has an effect on others. Therapy should help the patient become aware that impulses, feelings, and needs originate from within herself. The patient should have an honest therapeutic relationship focusing on the patient's inner self-doubt with little or no attention to weight and dieting. It is difficult to get a systematic picture of the patients whom Bruch sees and what she actually does in treatment with what results. Her reports are informal descriptions or theoretical statement with case illustration.

Behavioral Approaches

A study by Bachrach, Erwin and Mohr (1965) was one of the first studies that used selective reinforcement. The patient was not allowed television, books or frequent visits by members of the nursing and medical staff. Social reinforcements such as staff attention, conversation, and praise were made contingent on eating behavior. Later, walks and visits from relatives were contingent on eating behavior. Leitenberg, Agras, and Thomson (1968) found that extinction of complaints and comments about eating difficulties did not lead to improvement in eating behavior. Conversation and attention contingent on eating were also unsuccessful. They decided to reinforce weight gain directly. A menu was planned allowing for 4,000 calories each day, distributed equally among four meals. There was no food allowed between meals. The meals lasted 30 minutes. They were eaten alone and without comment from the nursing staff. Patients were instructed to record each mouthful taken at each meal and to plot them along with daily weight gain. Praise and social attention were given for caloric intake and weight gain. Time out of the room and off the unit was made contingent on small increments of weight gain. When the reinforcers were no longer contingent, patients continued to gain weight. It was hypothesized that discharge from the hospital was seen by patients to be contingent on continued weight gain. Without privileges, the hospital was a dull place; privileges had to be earned. Therefore, patients ate to decrease the probability of staying in an unpleasant situation.

The perceived connection between eating and discharge was broken by contracting with the patients to stay for 12 weeks for "research purposes." This led to a decrease in weight under the no-contingent reinforcement conditions and an increase when reinforcement was reestablished.

Dally and Sargent (1966) used large doses of chloropromazine, as well as modified insulin therapy and bed rest. The patient was not allowed to get up from bed until a predetermined amount of weight was gained. It is not possible to differentiate the effect of the drug treatment from the effect of the enforced bed rest.

Azerrad and Stafford (1969) initially rewarded patients for weight increase. Weight loss led to a withholding of points until the weight was regained. After 12 days, points were also given contingent on the amount of food eaten. Points were translated into tokens that were then used to buy material objects and to get extra home visits. Scrignar (1971) worked with a 14-year-old girl on an outpatient basis. "Favorite" foods were used as reinforcement. Foods that were "liked very much" were made contingent on no vomiting the previous day and "liked" foods were allowed if vomiting occurred only after one or more meals. More preferred foods were given at the end of the meal. It should be noted, however, that Brady and Rieger (1975) questioned the diagnosis of this patient as anorectic and suggested that this was a case of hysterical vomiting. Hallsten (1965) combined systematic desensitization with visits from relatives made contingent on weight gain.

Blinder, Freeman, and Stunkard (1970) had six anorectic patients, all of whom were hyperactive as measured by recorded movement on a pedometer. The patients were allowed unrestricted movement outside the hospital contingent on weight gain of one-half pound above the previous morning's weight. This was effective for three of the six patients. Garfinkel, Kline, and Stancer (1973) wrote a verbal contract with each patient. The purpose of the contract was to increase the patient's responsibility for weight gain. The reinforcers for weight gain were physical activity, socializing off the ward, overnight and weekend passes, and progressively increasing privileges.

The Brady and Rieger (1975) study is a good example of how reinforcement programs should be individualized for each individual patient. These researchers made access to reinforcement contingent on a minimum daily weight gain. At first, the patient's weight was simply recorded. General activities were recorded to identify reinforcers. If patients gained one-half pound they would then receive six hours off the ward. If patients did not gain weight after three or four days, the therapist looked for more powerful reinforcers. For nine patients the opportunity to leave the ward was effective. Another three patients did not seem to be characterized by hyperactivity; thus socializing was used as a reinforcer. For another, studying was the reinforcer. A compulsive patient was contingently allowed access to her toothbrush, comb, and the like. For another, a token program was established with mail, phone, radio, and walks as backup reinforcers. A final patient in this report had only moderate success with the off-ward passes. This patient was resistant to taking chloropromazine, so the dosage was made contingent on weight gain. Most of the patients received phenothiazine during hospitalization, while some received tricyclic antidepressants. Some received both and some none. Brady and Rieger claim that there was no relationship between the drugs and weight gain. Since the two-year follow-up reported by Brady and Rieger (1975), the emphasis in the University of Pennsylvania program has shifted to hospitalization as only the beginning of treatment (Pertschuk, 1977). (This is discussed in greater detail in the section of follow-up studies).

Agras, Barlow, Chapin, Abel, and Leitenberg (1974) reported that social reinforcement given by the staff contingent on weight gain, but without any feedback on the weight gain, was not effective. Informational feedback as to weight gain without reinforcement from the staff led to small increases in caloric intake and weight gain. Reinforcement plus feedback led to substantial gains. Large meals also led to greater weight gain than did small meals.

To summarize, although the behavioral programs may vary in some specifics (number of meals, number of calories, weight gain specified for reinforcement, reinforcers), many basic elements are the same. First, priority is given to immediate weight gain. The rationale behind this is that the low weight presents a medical problem, and the anorectic is more amenable to therapy once a satisfactory weight has been attained. Second, the voluntary contractual nature of most of the programs is emphasized. A contract is developed, which represents the patient's desire to change. The contract should also help to minimize arguments over implementation of contingencies. Third, the focus during hospitalization has shifted from eating behavior to weight gain, which is seen as the patient's responsibility. In all the programs, the patient is left alone for a period of time during which the patient is supposed to eat. The eating behavior is not monitored, only the weight. The patient is also instructed in the use of feedback to aid in behavioral change. She or he counts and records the number of bites and graphs daily weight gain. Fourth, contingencies are made explicit to patients, staff, and other relevant individuals. Fifth, there is an emphasis on consistent application of contingencies. They are applied until the patient's weight is within the normal range. Sixth, there is no discussion or confrontation of issues centering around food, eating, or weight gain. Any discussion is limited to carrying out the contingencies. This should help to avoid power struggles centering around food, with issues of power and autonomy dealt with in other areas and to maximize the degree of patient choice. Issues of power and autonomy are dealt with around areas other than food. Seventh, reinforcers are individualized. If weight gain does not occur consistently for any given patient, other reinforcers are selected. Eighth, all behavioral programs now recommend behavioral family therapy for the patient upon discharge from the hospital. There are practical problems involved here inasmuch as when the patient leaves the hospital, although continued therapy can be strongly recommended, there is no structure to ensure that patients engage in behaviorally oriented family therapy. Also, this author has been unable to find any description of a behavioral-oriented family treatment program used following hospitalization

Family Approaches

Minuchin, Rosman, and Baker (1978) view anorexia as a psychosomatic illness. Treatment is based on a model of the psychosomatic family. The characteristics of the psychosomatic family are the same regardless of whether the symptoms are brittle diabetes, asthma, or anorexia. There are four characteristics of overall family functioning. No single characteristic is sufficient to initiate and maintain psychosomatic symptoms, but the four together seem to characterize the family process that underlies somatization. The family characteristics are enmeshment, overprotectiveness, rigidity, and lack of conflict resolution. Enmeshment refers to extreme proximity and intensity in family relations. In the enmeshed family changes within one family member or in the relationship between two members is felt throughout the system. Subsystem (e.g., parent subsystem or parent/child subsystem) boundaries are not clearly maintained. Also, individual family members are regulated by the system, so that there is little individual autonomy. The overprotectiveness is seen in the high degree of concern of family members for each other's welfare. The parents' overconcern tends to limit the autonomy and competence of the child. The child may use the psychosomatic symptoms to protect the family. The rigid family has difficulty handling change. They are easily affected by external events but are unable to cope. The enmeshment combined with the overprotectiveness and rigidity lead to a low threshold for conflict and no conflict resolution, which leads to an avoidance of conflict. Another key factor is the patient's symptom as the regulator of the family system. The support for the particular symptom is the child's involvement in the parental conflict. There are three conflict avoidance patterns of involvement of the child: triangulation, parent-child coalition, and detouring. Families may use each over time, but one pattern tends to predominate. In triangulation and parent child co-alition the spouse dyad is in conflict, and the child is an ally of one parent. In triangulation, the child is put in a position in which she or he cannot express herself or himself without siding with one parent against the other. In the parent-child coalition the child is in a stable coalition with one parent. In detouring, the spouse dyad appears to be united; the only family problem is the medically sick child who is either protected or blamed. The symptom bearer regulates the internal stability of the family. This leads to a continuation of the patient's symptoms and of the characteristics of the family organization. Liebman, Minuchin, and Baker (1974) point out that most therapies with anorectics follow a linear model rather than a systems model. A basic assumption of this system approach is that there is no beginning and no end to the interaction. The system can be activated at a number of points, and it has feedback mechanisms that operate at several points.

Actual therapy is usually conducted on an outpatient basis. If there is an inpatient period, operant conditioning procedures of reinforcement for weight gain are used. During this period confrontation over eating is avoided. It is emphasized that the parents have nothing to do with the program. Up to this point the inpatient program very much resembles the behavioral ones discussed earlier. At the end of the first week, the family (including siblings), pediatrician, and family psychiatrist (meeting with the family for the first time) have a luncheon meeting. This marks the beginning of the transition to an outpatient basis and is supposed to demonstrate that the pediatrician and psychiatrist can work together. At the end of the first lunch session a weight goal for discharge is established and a second lunch session is planned to explain the goals of outpatient treatment. The goals of the lunch sessions are to enable the patient to eat in the presence of the parents without the occurrence of a power struggle, thereby providing a new experience in relation to eating and to redefine the problem of the medically sick child into interpersonal, transactional problems within the family. The redefinition of the problem should decrease the centrality of the patient and the controlling powers of the symptom.

Rosman, Minuchin, and Liebman (1975) analyzed the goals and strategies of lunch sessions over a period of years. The first possible goal is to increase "parental executive effectiveness." The strategy is to have each parent try to get the child to eat. This redefines the problem as one of management. Observations indicate that usually one parent undermines or disqualifies the efforts of the other parent. For the most part, the effort by the individual parents fails. With some support from the therapist and their own anger, individual parents can combine their efforts and work together. Usually either they feed the patient or the patient spontaneously eats.

The second possible goal is to try to increase the distance between the parents and the child. The therapist again instructs each parent to try to get the child to eat. The therapist stops the unsuccessful attempts and points out the power of the "helpless child" who manipulates the "healthy parents." The family is told not to engage in any further contact over food. Eating is defined as a private issue between the therapist and the patient.

The third goal is to neutralize the family interactions with respect to eating. The patient may or may not eat in the presence of the parents. Any comments, positive or negative, on eating are discouraged. The therapist appears casual or indifferent toward eating and focuses upon family background and interpersonal problems. At some point, the patient begins to eat.

These strategies vary on the following dimensions: the degree to which parent-child confrontations are encouraged or discouraged, the level of emotional arousal during the session, and the intent of the therapist that the child eat or not eat. The choice of strategies, according to Rosman et al. (1975), should depend on an assessment of the family structure and style as well as the developmental state of the patient and the family. If there is a rigid family structure and the patient is overly resistant to the parents, the therapist should try either to increase parental executive effectiveness (model 1) or increase the distance between the parents and the child (model 2). With preadolescent children the parental executive model should be used so as to focus upon issues of control and to help parents become more competent. The second model, increasing distance between parents and child, should be used with older adolescents, where separation and autonomy issues are important. If there is a flexible family structure or if the child is already eating, the third model of neutralizing the family interactions around food should be used.

In the outpatient phase, the previous roles of the pediatrician and the psychiatrist are reversed. The psychiatrist takes on the primary responsibility for the patient, with the pediatrician in a supportive, consultant role. There are three goals for this phase of treatment. The first goal is the elimination of the symptom of food refusal and progressive weight gain. The second is to focus upon the dysfunctional family patterns that maintain the patient's symptoms. The third is to change the structure and function of the family system to prevent the reoccurence of the symptoms or the development of new symptoms. As mentioned earlier, weight gain is brought about through operant conditioning procedures. These procedures give the parents something concrete and thereby should decrease some of their anxiety and feelings of helplessness. The parents are told that it is their responsibility to enforce these procedures. If they work together, they can be successful. If the patient loses weight, then the parents are not working together. The functions of those instructions to the parents are to increase their managerial effectiveness and to get them to work together. Observations of these families indicate that they see the child as powerless rather than controlling and that often one parent will disqualify whatever the other says. The patient is told that it is her or his responsibility to herself or himself and to her or his parents to follow the procedures. As long as she or he follows them, she or he will be able to control her or his eating. A minimum weight gain is set for the week. If that is not reached by Friday, the patient must stay in the house for the weekend. She or he cannot have any visitors, and a member of the family must stay with her or him. Additional weight gain allows her or him to spend a greater part of the weekend out of the house or with friends. As weight gain continues, the focus shifts to interpersonal problems and then to school difficulties, community activities, and peer relations.

The family therapy approach to the problem of anorexia is based on a systems model. The basic aims are to redefine the status and concept of the patient within the family, to translate the "eating problem" into a problem of interpersonal relationships with the family, and to disengage the child from the problems of the parents. Operant conditioning procedures are used for both inpatient and outpatient treatments leading to weight gain. The family is the focus of treatment and is brought into treatment. Rosman et al. (1977) report an 88 percent effectiveness after a six month follow-up. They state that symptoms usually disappear between two and eight weeks after treatment has begun. The initial description of symptoms as well as the measures of success are often not systematic. This makes comparisons with other approaches difficult. It should also be noted that the family therapy cases reported by Rosman et al. (1977) had younger patients than those reported in other studies. Of 53 cases, 25 percent were between the ages of 9 and 12, 60 percent were between 13 and 16 and only 15 percent were between 17 and 21. One might assume that a family approach would be more effective with a younger child. Although the goals and strategies discussed seem to be excellent, they also appear to be systematized only after the fact. In retrospective studies, such as Rosman et al. (1977), this author has two reservations about the work as reported. First, Minuchin et al. (1978) report carrying out a specific manipulation. For example, the therapist whispers to the patient "Tell your mother that you are an ugly scarecrow because she doesn't love you." The purpose of this manipulation is to disengage the child from her mother. The way that it is supposed to work is that the specific intervention disrupts the system and starts a series of changes. Whether the specific manipulation actually has the intended effect and whether there are subsequent changes is not checked. To fol-

low through on the example, the child's statement can have a number of specific consequences other than disengagement. Having no history of making assertive statements to the mother, the child may feel very guilty, or the mother may emotionally withdraw after the session. Although disengagement is a possibility, it appears to be only one of several possible outcomes. A more structured approach could be tried. If the short-term goal is to have the child less dependent on the mother, she or he could be encouraged to make an appropriately assertive statement for which the therapist gives support. Rehearsal of this kind of statement and anticipating the mother's reactions are also possibilities. Another difficulty is that structures are applied by the therapist to what the therapist sees (e.g., disengagement, enmeshed boundaries). These structures then seem to take on a meaning of their own apart from the initial observations. For example, if the anorectic sits close to the mother and looks at her each time before speaking, the family is enmeshed. Rather than having these terms summarizing what is seen, they lead one to assume the presence many other behaviors. The initial observations are more or less forgotten. The goal has become to disengage the enmeshed family.

On a more positive note, no other therapeutic approaches attempt a systematic approach to the family. Also, within family context a major contribution is the redefinition of the sick role of the anorectic and the view of the power relations within the family: the relative ineffectualness of the parents and the effectualness of the sick child.

Follow-up Studies

Currently, there is a focus upon studies that look at patient outcomes some time after discharge. Dally and Sargent (1966) found no significant differences between patients who had been given chlorpromazine and bed rest and those who had been given nonspecific therapy. After three years approximately one-third of both groups were underweight. Browning and Miller (1968) had follow-up upon 36 anorectics who had been treated by a variety of methods. They found no relationship between the amount of weight that was gained while the patient was in the hospital and the weight that had been maintained at the time of the follow-up. Bhanji and Thompson (1974) looked at 11 patients who had been treated behaviorally. Of these, ten had gained weight while in the hospital. Seven patients were located after a median period of three years. Only three of them were at normal weight. Halmi (1975) found that seven months after the discharge of eight patients who were treated behaviorally, all but one were judged to be functioning adequately. Minuchin, Baker, Rosman, Liebman, Milman, and Todd (1975) reported that after a two-year period, 21 of the 25 patients treated with family therapy were recovered. The patients on the average were younger than those in other studies ($X = 13$ years) and the duration of the illness prior to treatment was shorter ($X =$ seven months). Brady and Reiger (1975) found that after a two-year period two out of 15 patients had died and three had failed to maintain their weight. Although ten had maintained an acceptable weight, only five functioned well in their daily lives. Pertschuk (1977) reported on 27 cases treated at the University of Pennsylvania in the period following the Brady and Rieger (1975) study. As mentioned earlier, the Brady and Rieger (1975) findings led to a change in emphasis in that program; hospitalization was seen as only the beginning of treatment. Recent studies go into more detail and are more systematic in their use of follow-up measures and reporting of results. According to Pertschuk (1977) of the 27 patients at the time of the follow-up study, 11 were within 20 percent of the normal weight. At discharge patients averaged 24 percent below normal weight. At the follow-up this figure had been reduced to 12 percent. Duration of illness and weight prior to hospital admission were unrelated to weight at the time of the follow-up. A rating system of general functioning based on vocational, social, and family adjustment was developed. The adjustment was assessed as good, fair or poor. All of those whose adjustment was poor at the time of the follow-up also had

eating problems. A good adjustment did not necessarily mean that there were no eating problems. Only two patients were determined to be fully recovered. Twelve patients required further hospitalization. Of these, ten were readmitted within six months of discharge; six were readmitted for serious weight loss, four following suicide attempts, and two for depression. The follow-up also indicated an increase in bulimia. None of the patients reported bulimia on admission to the hospital, but ten reported it at the time of the follow-up, and it was usually accompanied with compulsive vomiting. The correlation between the percentage of weight gained in the hospital and that gained at the time of the follow-up was not significant. All patients had been treated behaviorally while in the hospital. They had also all received psychotherapy on an outpatient basis. However, the type of psychotherapy varied. One effect of this is that there was no continuity in the type of treatment approach used in the hospital and on an outpatient basis: no statement can be made as to the long-term effectiveness of a behavioral treatment approach with anorecthics.

Garfinkel, Moldofsky, and Garner (1977) reported a one-year follow-up study on forty-two patients (40 females and two males). Twenty-six patients had been treated on an inpatient basis and 16 on an outpatient basis. A variety of treatment methods had been used; 31 patients received individual supportive psychotherapy, nine pharmacotherapy, five family therapy, two electroconvulsive therapy, and five consultation only. Operant conditioning was part of the hospital treatment for 17 patients. These were then compared to the 25 patients who experienced other forms of therapies. Those treated with operant techniques in the hospital were later treated by a variety of other therapies. At the time of the follow-up, clinical assessment was made on how the former patients related to males, peers, and family. Forty-one percent did well in two of the three areas, 46 percent did well in one of the three areas, and 5 percent did poorly in all three areas. In terms of educational and vocational adjustment, 49 percent attended school or work regularly and worked efficiently; 34

percent attended school or work regularly but worked below potential; 7 percent were frequently absent or performed poorly, and 10 percent did not work or attend school. A global adjustment score was also given based on weight, eating habits, menses, and measures of social, educational, and vocational adjustment already discussed. Four categories were developed: seven patients were considered to be "excellent," 14 "much improved," 13 "symptomatic," and eight were doing "poorly." If one collapsed these four categories into two, 50 percent were doing well at the time of the follow-up and 50 percent were doing poorly. Since discharge, ten had been rehospitalized; three had been rehospitalized more than once. Of these ten, eight had been rehospitalized for further episodes of weight loss and two for attempted suicide. An effort was made to look at what factors were related to the four different global adjustment scores reported at the time of the follow-up. A larger number of hospitalizations prior to admission to the Clinical Investigation Unit (CIU-Clark Institute of Psychiatry and University of Toronto) was related to poorer global scores. The "poor" outcome group initially had more incidents of bulimia and vomiting; however, there were no significant differences on food fads at the time of the follow-up. The degree of initial social adjustment was unrelated to adjustment at follow-up. The poor adjustment group had significantly worse scores at the initial assessment on educational and vocational adjustment than the other three groups, and the excellent group had better educational and vocational adjustment on initial assessment than the other three groups. Scores on the total initial global scale corresponded to those on the follow-up, with the poor-outcome group doing less well than the other groups and the excellent group doing better. Patients with poor outcomes had more subsequent hospitalizations and further incidences of weight loss. They tended to overestimate their body size. The excellent-outcome group tended to underestimate their body size. Those who underestimated their body weights also tended to weigh more. A comparison of those who underestimated their size and those who

overestimated their size at the time of the follow-up indicated that there was no difference between the two groups in age, age of onset, and percentage of weight loss. Those who overestimated their size had more prior hospitalizations and had poorer assessments on both the initial and follow-up global assessments. Also, whereas those who underestimated their size showed considerable improvement in their global scores from initial assessment to follow-up, those who overestimated their body size showed little change on their global scores.

Those treated in the hospital with operant conditioning techniques were compared to those treated with other therapies. On initial assessment the two groups did not differ in perception of body size or personality characteristics. The group treated through operant techniques was significantly younger than the other group at the time of onset and at the time of the assessment. They also weighed less at the assessment. On the follow-up measures the two groups were similar on their global assessment scores, on the percentage of change from their initial global assessment scores to their follow-up global assessment scores, and in their weight at follow-up. Of the 17 patients treated through operant techniques, six were rehospitalized, three more than once. It is not possible to make a statement about operant techniques with anorectics based on these findings, because patients treated behaviorally in the hospital were treated with a variety of other approaches on an outpatient basis. The patients in the hospitalization part of the study could have been grouped into three rather than two groups: inpatients treated by operant conditioning techniques, inpatients treated by other techniques, and those treated on an outpatient basis.

Russell (1977) conducted a follow-up study on forty-one patients, including three males. The program from which his patients come is based on a nonspecific "nursing regime" similar to that reported by Groen and Feldman-Toledaro (1966). It is referred to as educational; it is based on the assumption that the physician and nurse should act as substitute parents. The time of the follow-up ranged from four years to a maximum of ten years after discharge. Sixteen patients (13 females, three males) were reported as having maintained a good condition. This consisted of maintaining their body weight within 15 percent of the normal weight, normal menses for the females, and few psychological symptoms. The symptoms that occurred were mild anxiety or mild depression. An intermediate outcome group of 12 patients was described as maintaining a steady weight (two were obese), sporadic menstruation or absence of menses (one-half of the group), and "less than satisfactory" psychological, sexual and socioeconomic adjustment. The poor-outcome group of eleven patients had a mean weight that was 68 percent of the normal body weight, absent or sporadic menses, and severe depressive symptoms with "poor" sexual adjustment. Two deaths occurred. One resulted from a suicide following a leukotomy and another from status asthmaticus when the patient was emaciated.

The authors found no significant relationship between the outcomes at follow-up and various psychological disturbances, including the patient's fear of fatness, at the initial assessment. Although Theander (1970) found self-induced vomiting at the time of initial assessment to be related to outcome, this study found no relationship between vomiting and long-term outcome. Duration of the illness prior to initial assessment for the study as well as a later age of onset were related to outcome. Theander (1970) reported similar findings. Social class, educational achievement, and level of intelligence were unrelated to outcome, as were feeding difficulties in childhood, obesity preceeding illness, or presence of sibling rivalry. However, the presence of a disturbed relationship between the patient and other family members prior to the onset of the illness was related to a poor outcome. No predictions about outcome could be made from the patient's initial response to treatment, the degree of weight gain during hospitalization, any change in psychological symptoms, acceptance of a new feeding regime, duration of stay in the hospital, difficulty in maintaining the weight gained, or the use of antidepressants, electroconvulsive therapy, or chloropromazine.

Crisp, Kalucy, Lacey, and Harding (1977) looked at 350 patients seen in an English hospital over a 17-year period. They report that the following led to a poorer outcome: (1) later age of onset; (2) lower-class patients; (3) premorbid obesity; (4) excessive weight disorders, concern over weight control, and preoccupation with body shape within the family; (5) length of illness; (6) excessive compliance or behavior disorder during childhood and excessive somatic complaints within the disorder; (7) high levels of depression in parents at the time of assessment, along with obsessive traits in the mother and somatic complaints and extrovert traits in the father; (8) continued misperception of body size after weight restoration; (9) continued overeating and vomiting as means of weight control; and (10) poor motivation for treatment.

Problems with the Research Studies

There are several factors in the research studies that make comparison across the studies difficult. First, as late as 1966 different criteria for diagnosis were being used, e.g., Dally and Sargent (1966) used ten percent of premorbid weight as the criterion, while Bliss and Branch (1960) used 25 percent weight loss due to any psychological cause. Second, severity, length of illness, and age of onset are often difficult to determine, especially for patients who are first assessed in their twenties and thirties. Third, criteria for improvement are often not specified or may vary, for example, weight gain is usually not presented in terms of normal, average weight. Fourth, the criteria used to assess outcome before discharge or at the time of the follow-up are varied. Weight gain and weight maintenance, normal eating patterns, regular menses, adequate sexual functioning, improvement in interpersonal relationships, and resolution of intrapsychic and personal conflicts are all used as outcome measures. Actually, in practice, it appears that for discharge weight gain is the primary measure. Follow-up studies seem to focus more on different measures of functioning. The actual global measures vary from study to study. Fifth, the retrospective studies depend on the accuracy of the medical records.

Conclusion

A standard definition of anorexia nervosa has emerged that is based on a percentage of weight loss, a distorted attitude toward eating, and several physiological symptoms. There have been several studies describing the anorectic and her or his family, with few conclusive findings. One often-reported finding is that the anorectic comes from an intact family that sees itself as having no real problems other than its "sick child." The treatment approaches that have been reviewed are psychoanalytic, behavioral, and family therapy. All approaches now recognize that hospitalization and initial weight gain are only the beginning of treatment. All approaches see the problem as being more than a problem in eating behavior, and all refer to issues of autonomy and independence. Both family therapy and behavioral approaches use operant conditioning techniques to bring about weight gain on both an inpatient and an outpatient basis. Both also recognize the importance of work with the family. Although the behaviorists have not reported any systematic program for behaviorally oriented family therapy following hospitalization, they recognize such a need.

At the present time, few definitive statements can be made regarding outcomes at the time of follow-up. First, hospitalization is only the first part of treatment necessary for anorexics. No statement can be made about the effectiveness of different kinds of treatment following hospitalization: it is difficult to determine the kind and quality of treatment that patients receive after hospitalization; also there is no continuity between treatment during and after hospitalization. The kinds of outcome measures used at follow-up seem to be of three types: those related to weight gain and eating behavior, further hospitalization, and global adjustment measures. The rates of positive outcomes reported vary by the measures used and by individual studies. On the whole, one can say that the rate of successful adjustment is roughly half at the time of follow-up.

Two directions for future work are additional systematization of the work done by family therapists and application of a behaviorally oriented family approach that would be continued on an outpatient basis.

REFERENCES

Abramson, L. Y., Seligman, M. E. P., & Teasdale, J. D. Learned helplessness in humans: Critique and reformulation. *Journal of Abnormal Psychology*, 1978, *87*, 49–74.

Adams, P. O., McDonald, N. F., & Huey, W. P. School phobia and bisexual conflict: A report of 21 cases. *American Journal of Psychiatry*. 1966, *123*, 541–547.

Agras, S. The relationship of school phobia to childhood depression. *American Journal of Psychiatry*, 1959, *116*, 533–536.

Agras, W. S., Barlow, D. H., Chapin, H. N., Abel, G. G., & Leitenberg, H. Behavior modification of anorexia nervosa. *Archives of General Psychiatry*, 1974, *30*, 279–286.

Agras, W. S., & Werne, J. Behavior modification in anorexia nervosa. *In* R. A. Vigersky (Ed.), *Anorexia nervosa*. New York: Raven Press, 1977.

Albert, N., & Beck, A. T. Incidence of depression in early adolescence: A preliminary study. *Journal of Youth and Adolescence*, 1975, *4*, 301–307.

Albert N. Evidence of depression in an early adolescent school population. Unpublished manuscript, College of Villanova, Pennsylvania, 1973.

Ayllon, T., Smith, D., & Rogers, M. Behavioral management of school phobia. *Journal of Behavior Therapy and Experimental Psychiatry*, 1970, *1*, 125–138.

Azerrad, J., and Stafford, R. L. Restoration of eating behavior in anorexia nervosa through operant conditioning and environmental manipulation. *Behavior Research and Therapy*, 1969, *7*, 165–171.

Bachrach, A. J., Erwin, W. J., & Mohr, P. J. The control of eating behavior in an anorexic by operational conditioning techniques. In L. P. Ullman and L. Krasner (Eds.), *Case studies in behavior modification*. New York: Rinehart and Winston, 1965.

Bakwin, H. Depression—A mood disorder in children and adolescents. *Maryland State Medical Journal*, 1972, 55–61.

Beck, A. T. *Depression: Clinical, experimental and theoretical aspects*. New York: Harper Row, 1967.

Beck, A. T. *The diagnosis and management of*

depression. Philadelphia: University of Pennsylvania Press, 1973.

Beck, A. T. The development of depression: A cognitive model. In R. Friedman & M. Katz (Eds.), *Psychology of Depression: Contemporary theory & research.* Washington D. C.: Winston-Wiley, 1974.

Beck, A. T., Rial, W. Y., & Rickels, K. Short form of depression inventory: cross-validation. *Psychological Reports*, 1974, *34*, 1184–1186.

Beck, A. T., Ward, C. H., Mendelson, M., Mock, J., & Erbaugh, J. An inventory for measuring depression. Archives of General Psychiatry, 1961, *4*, 561–571.

Beck, A. T., Weissman, A., Lester, D., & Trexler, L. The measurement of pessisism: The hopeless scale. *Journal of Consulting and Clinical Psychology*, 1974, *42*, 861–865.

Bemis, K. M. Current approaches to the etiology and treatment of anorexia nervosa. *Psychological Bulletin*, 1978, *85*, 593–617.

Berg, I. Butler, A., & McGuire, R. Birth order and family size of school phobic adolescents. *British Journal of Psychiatry*, 1972, *121*, 509–514.

Berg, I., Collins, T., McGuire, R., & O'Melia, J. Educational attainment in adolescent school phobia. *British Journal of Psychiatry*, 1975, *126*, 435–438.

Berg, I., & McGuire, R. Are school phobic adolescents overdependent? *British Journal of Psychiatry*, 1971, *119*, 167–168.

Berg, I. & McGuire R. Are mothers of school phobic adolescents overprotective? *British Journal of Psychiatry*, 1*1974*, *124*, 10-13.

Berg, I., Nichols, K. & Pritchard, C. School phobia—its classification and relationship to dependency. *Journal of Child Psychology and Psychiatry*, 1969, *10*, 123-141.

Browning, C.H. & Miller, S.I. Anorexia nervosa: A study in prognosis and management. *American Journal of Psychiatry*, 1968, *124*, 1128-1132.

Berlin, I. N., Boatman, M. D., Sheimo, S. L., & Szyrek, S. A. Adolescent alternation of anorexia and obesity. *American Journal of Orthopsychiatry*, 1951, *21*, 387–419.

Bhanji, S., & Thompson, J. Operant conditioning in the treatment of anorexia nervosa: A review and retrospective study of 11 cases. *British Journal of Psychiatry*, 1974, *124*, 166–172.

Blinder, B. J., Freeman, D. M. A., & Stunkard, A. J. Behavior therapy of anorexia nervosa: Effectiveness of activity as a reinforcer of weight gain. *American Journal of Psychiatry*, 1970, *126*, 1093–1098.

Bliss, E. L., & Branch, C. H. H. *Anorexia nervosa:*

Its history, psychology and biology. New York: Paul Hoeber, 1960.

Bowlby, J. Childhood mourning and its implications for psychiatry. *American Journal of Psychiatry*, 1961, *118*, 481–498.

Brady, J. P., & Rieger, W. Behavioral treatment of anorexia nervosa. In T. Thompson & W. S. Duckens (Eds.), *Applications of behavior modification.* New York: Academic Press, 1975.

Browning, C.H. & Miller, S.I. Anorexia nervosa: A study in prognosis and management. *American Journal of Psychiatry*, 1968, *124*, 1128-1132.

Bruch, H. Psychological antecedents of anorexia nervosa. In R.A. Vigersky (Ed.), *Anorexia nervosa.* New York: Raven Press, 1977.

Bruch, H. Eating disorders: *Obesity, anorexia nervosa and the person within.* New York: Basic Books, 1973.

Bruch, H. Perils of behavior modification in treatment of anorexia nervosa. *Journal of American Medical Association*, 1974, *230*, 1419–1422.

Buell, F. A. School phobia. *Diseases of the Nervous System*, 1962, *23*, 79–84.

Choi, E. H. Father-daughter relationship in school phobia. *Smith College Studies in Social Work*, 1961, *31*, 142–178.

Chotiner, M. M., & Forrest, D. U. Adolescent school phobia: Six controlled cases studied retrospectively. *Adolescence*, 1974, *9*, 467†-480.

Clyne, M. B. *Absent: School refusal as an expression of disturbed family relationships.* London: Tavistock Publications, 1966.

Connell, H. M. Depression in childhood. *Child Psychiatry and Human Development*, 1972, *4*, 71–85.

Coolidge, J. C., Hahn, P. B., & Peck, A. L. School phobia: Neurotic crisis or way of life. *American Journal of Orthopsychiatry*, 1957, *1*, 125–138.

Coolidge, J. C., Willer, M. L., Tessman, E., & Waldfogel, S. School phobia in adolescence: A manifestation of severe character disturbance. *American Journal of Orthopsychiatry*, 1960, *30*, 599–607.

Coopersmith, S. *The antecedents of self-esteem.* London: Freeman, 1967.

Costello, C. G. A critical review of Seligman's laboratory experiments on learned helplessness and depression in humans. *Journal of Abnormal Psychology*, 1978, *87*, 21–31.

Crisp, A. H. A treatment regime for anorexia nervosa. *British Journal of Psychiatry*, 1965, *112*, 505–512.

Crisp, A. H. Reported birth weights and growth weights in a group of patients with primary anorexia nervosa (weight phobia). *Journal of Psychosomatic Research,* 1970, *50,* 14–23.

Crisp, A. H., Palmer, R. L., Kalucy, R. S. How common is anorexia nervosa? *British Journal of Psychiatry,* 1976, *128,* 549–554.

Crisp, A. H., Kalucy, R. S., Lacey, D. H., & Harding, B. The long-term prognosis in anorexia nervosa: Some factors predictive of outcome. In R. A. Vigersky (Ed.), *Anorexia Nervosa.* New York: Raven Press, 1977.

Crisp, A. H., & Toms, D. A. Primary anorexia nervosa or weight phobia in the male: Report on 13 cases. *British Medical Journal,* 1972, *1,* 334–338.

Cytryn, L. Discussion of Dr. Malinquest's chapter: Childhood depression: A clinical and behavioral perspective. In J. G. Schulterbrandt & A. Raskin (Eds.), *Depression in childhood: Diagnosis, treatment and conceptual models.* New York: Raven Press, 1977.

Cytryn, L., & McKnew, D. H. Proposed classification of childhood depression. *American Journal of Psychiatry,* 1972, *129,* 149–155.

Dally, P. *Anorexia nervosa.* London: Heinemann Medical Books, 1969.

Dally, P., & Sargant, W. Treatment and outcome of anorexia nervosa. *British Medical Journal,* 1966, 793–795.

Davidson, S. School phobia as a manifestation of family disturbance: Its structure and treatment. *Journal of Child Psychology and Psychiatry and Allied Disciplines,* 1960, *1,* 270–287.

Derogatis, L. R., Lipman, R. S., Rickels, K., Uhlenhuth, E. H. & Covi, L. The Hopkins Symptom Checklist (HSCL): A measurement of primary symptom dimensions. In P. Pichot (Ed.), *Psychological measurements in psychopharmacology: Modern problems in pharmacopsychiatry* (Vol. 7.) Basel: Karger, 1974.

Doleys, D. M., & Williams, S. C. The use of natural consequences and a make-up period to eliminate school phobic behavior: A case study. *Journal of School Psychology,* 1977, *15,* 44–50.

Duddle, M. An increase of anorexia nervosa in a university population. *British Journal of Psychiatry,* 1973, *123,* 711–712.

Dweck, C. S. Learned helplessness: A developmental approach. In J. G. Schulterbrandt & A. Raskin (Eds.),. *Depression in childhood: Diagnosis, treatment and conceptual models.* New York: Raven Press, 1977.

Eisenberg, L. School phobia: A study in the communication. *American Journal of Psychiatry,* 1958, *114,* 712–718.

Falstein, E. I., Feinstein, S. C., & Judas, I. An-

orexia nervosa in the male child. *American Journal of Orthopsychiatry,* 1956, *26,* 751–772.

Feighner, J. P. Diagnostic criteria for use in psychiatric research. *Archives of General Psychiatry,* 1972, *26,* 57–63.

Ferster, C. B. A functional analysis of depression. *American Psychologist* 1973, 857–870.

Frazier, S. H. Anorexia nervosa. *Diseases of the Nervous System,* 1965, *26,* 155–159.

Fuerst, E. School phobia. *Elementary School Guidance Counseling,* 1969, *3,* 184–189.

Garfinkel, P. E., Kline, S., & Stancer, H. Treatment of anorexia using operant conditioning techniques. *Journal of Nervous and Mental Disease,* 1973, *157,* 428–433.

Garfinkel, P. E., Moldofsky, H., & Garner, D. M. The outcome of anorexia nervosa: Significance of clinical features, body image and behavior modification. In R. A. Vigersky, (Ed.) *Anorexia nervosa.* New York: Raven Press, 1977.

Garvey, W. P., & Hegrenes, J. R. Desensization techniques in the treatment of school phobia. *American Journal of Orthopsychiatry,* 1966, *36,* 147–152.

Gibbs, M. S. Personal communication, 1979.

Gittelman-Klein, R. Definitional and methodological issues concerning depressive illness in children. In J. G. Schulterbrandt and A. Raskin (Eds.), *Depression in childhood: Diagnosis, treatment and conceptual models.* New York: Raven Press, 1977.

Gittelman-Klein, R., & Klein, D. F. Controlled Imipramine treatment of school phobia. *Archives of General Psychiatry,* 1973, *25,* 204–207.

Glaser, K. Masked depression in children and adolescents. *Annual Progress in Child Psychiatry and Child Development,* 1968, *1,* 345–355.

Goldberg, S. C., Halmi, K. A., Casper, R., Eckert, E. & Davis, J. Pre-treatment predictors of weight change in anorexia nervosa. In R. A. Vigersky (Ed.), *Anorexia nervosa.* New York: Raven Press, 1977.

Goldberg, T. B. Factors in the development of school phobia. *Smith College Studies in Social Work,* 1953, *23,* 227–248.

Goodkin, F. Rats learn the relationship between responding and environmental events: an expansion of the learned helplessness hypothesis, *Learning and Motivation, 1976, 7,* 382–393.

Gordon, D. A., & Young, R. D. School phobia: A discussion of aetiology. *Psychological Reports,* 1976, *39,* 783–804.

Griffiths, M. Effects of noncontingent success and failure on mood and performance, *Journal of Personality,* 1977, *45,* 442–457.

Groen, J. J., & Feldman-Toledano, Z. Educative treatment of patients and parents in anorexia nervosa. *British Journal of Psychiatry*, 1966, *112*, 671–681.

Hallsten, E. A. Adolescent anorexia nervosa treated by desensitization. *Behavior Research and Therapy*, 1965, *3*, 87–91.

Halmi, K. A. Comparison of demographic and clinical features in patient groups with different ages and weights at onset of anorexia nervosa. *Journal of Nervous and Mental Disease*, 1974, *158*, 222–225.

Halmi, K. A. Anorexia nervosa: Demographic and clinical features in 94 cases. *Psychosomatic Medicine*, 1974, *36*, 18–26.

Halmi, K. A., Brodland, G. & Loney, J. Prognosis in anorexia nervosa. *Annual of Internal Medicine*, 1973, *78*, 907–909.

Halmi, K. A., & Goldberg, S. C. Perceptual distortion of body image in adolescent girls. *Psychological Medicine*, 1977, *7*, 253–257.

Halmi, K. A., Goldberg, S., Eckert, E., Casper, R., & Davis, J. Pretreatment evaluation in anorexia nervosa. In R. A. Vigersky (Ed.), *Anorexia nervosa*. New York: Raven Press, 1977.

Halmi, K. A., Powers, P., & Cunningham, S. Treatment of anorexia nervosa with behavior modification. *Archives of General Psychiatry*, 1975, *32*, 93–96.

Halmi, K. A., Struss, A., & Goldberg, S. C. An investigation of weights in the parents of anorexia nervosa patients. *Journal of Nervous and Mental Disease*, 1978, *166*, 358–361.

Hammen, C. L., & Krantz, S. Effect of success and failure on depressive cognitions. *Journal of Abnormal Psychology*, 1976, *85*, 577–586.

Hampe, E., Miller, L., Barrett, C., & Noble, H. Intelligence and school phobia. *Journal of School Phobia*, 1973, *11*, 66–70.

Herring, A. An experimental study of the reliability of the Buhler Baby Tests. *Journal of Experimental Education*, 1937, *6*, 147–160.

Hersen, M. Behavior modification approach to a school phobia case. *Journal of Clinical Psychology*, 1970, *26*, 128–137.

Hersov, L. Refusal to go to school. *Journal of Child Psychology and Psychiatry*, 1960, *1*, 137–145.

Hetzer, H. & Wolf, K. Baby tests. In C. Buhler and H. Hetzer (Eds.), *The first year of life*. New York: John Day, 1930.

Hertzig, M. E., & Birch, H. G. Neurologic organization in psychiatrically disturbed adolescent girls. *Archives of General Psychiatry*, 1966, *15*, 590–598.

Izard, D. E. *Patterns of emotions*, New York: Academic Press 1972.

Jackson, L. Anxiety in adolescents in relation to school refusal. *Journal of Child Psychology and Psychiatry and Allied Disciplines*. 1964, *5*, 59–73.

Jessner, L., & Abse, D. W. Regressive forces in anorexia nervosa. *British Journal of Medical Psychology*, 1960, *33*, 301–312.

Johnson, A. M. School phobia: discussion. *American Journal of Orthopsychiatry*, 1964, *27*, 307–309.

Johnson, A. M., Falstein, E. J., Szurek, A. S., & Svendsen, M. School Phobia. *American Journal of Orthopsychiatry*, 1941, *11*, 702–711.

Kay, D. W. K., & Leigh, D. The natural history, treatment and prognosis of anorexia nervosa based on the study of 38 patients. *Journal of Mental Science*, 1954, *100*, 411–431.

Kelly, E. W. School phobia: A review of theory and treatment. *Psychology in the Schools*, 1973, *10*, 33–42.

Kendall, R. E., Hall D. J., Hailey A., & Babigan, H. M. The epidemiology of anorexia nervosa. *Psychological Medicine*, 1973, *3*, 200–203.

Kennedy, W. A. School phobia: rapid treatment of fifty cases. *Journal of Abnormal Psychology*, 1965, *70*, 285–289.

Kernberg, O. *Object relations theory and clinical psychoanalysis*. New York: Aronson, 1976.

Klein, D. C., Fencil-Morse, E., & Seligman, E. E. P. Learned helplessness, depression and attribution of failure. *Journal of Personality and Social Psychology*, 1976, *33*, 508–516.

Kovacs, M., & Beck, A. T. An empirical clinical approach toward a definition of childhood depression. In J. G. Schulterbrandt and A. Raskin (Eds.), *Depression in childhood: Diagnosis, treatment and conceptual models*. New York: Raven Press, 1977.

Kovacs, M., Betof, N. G., Celebre, J. E., Mansheim, P. A., Petty, L. K., & Raynek, J. T. *Childhood depression: Myth or clinical syndrome*. Unpublished manuscript, University of Pennsylvania School of Medicine, 1978.

Lang, P. J. Behavior therapy with a case of anorexia nervosa. In L. P. Ullman & L. Krasner (Eds.), *Case studies in behavior modification*. New York: Holt, Reinhart & Winston, 1965.

Lapousse, R. The Epidemeology of behavior disorders in children. *American Journal of Diseases of Children*, 1966, *111*, 594–599.

Lazarus, A. Learning theory and the treatment of depression. *Behavior Research and Therapy*, 1968, *6*, 83–89.

Lazarus, A. A., Davison, G. C., & Polejka, D. A. Classical and operant factors in the treatment of school phobia. *Journal of Abnormal Psychology* 1965, *70*, 225–229.

Lefkowitz, M. M., & Burton, N. Childhood depression: A critique of the concept. *Psy-*

chological Bulletin, 1978, 85, 716–726.

Leitenberg, H., Agras, W. S., & Thomson, L. E. A sequential analysis of the effect of selective positive reinforcement in modifying anorexia nervosa. *Behavior Research and Therapy,* 1968, *61,* 211–218.

Leitenberg, H., Agras, W. S., Thomson, L. E., & Wright, D. E. Feedback in behavior modification. *Journal of Applied Behavior Analysis,* 1968, *1,* 131–137.

Leton, D. A. Assessment of school phobia. *Mental Hygiene, 1962, 46,* 256–264.

Levenson, E.A. The treatment of school phobia in young adults. *American Journal of Psychotherapy,* 1961, *15,* 539-552.

Leventhal, T., & Sills, M. Self image in school phobia. *American Journal of Orthopsychiatry,* 964, *34,* 685–695.

Leventhal, T., Weinberger, G., Stander, R. J., Stearns, R. J. Therapeutic strategies with school phobia. *American Journal of Orthopsychiatry,* 1967, *37,* 64–70.

Lewinsohn, P. M. A behavioral approach to depression. In R. J. Freidman & M. M. Katz (Eds.), *The psychology of depression: Contemporary theory and research.* Washington, D.C.: Winston-Wiley, 1974.

Luborsky, L. Clinicans judgment of mental health: A proposed scale. *Archives of General Psychiatry,* 1962, *7,* 407–417.

Luborsky, L. E. & Bachrach, H. Factors influencing clinicians judgment of mental health. *Archives of General Psychiatry,* 1974, *31,* 292-299.

McConville, B. J. Boag, L. C., & Purohit, A. P. Three types of childhood depression. *Canadian Psychiatric Association,* 1973, *18,* 133–138.

McDonald, J. E., & Sheperd, G. School phobia: An overview. *Journal of School Psychology,* 1976, *14,* 291–306.

Malmquist, C. P. Depressive phenomena in children. In B. B. Wolman (Ed.), *Manual of child psychopathology.* New York: McGraw-Hill, 1972.

Malmquist, C. P. Depression in childhood. In F. Flach & S. Drajhi (Eds.), *Comprehensive textbook of depression.* New York: Wiley, 1975.

Malmquist, C. P. Childhood depression: A clinical and behavioral perspective. In J. G. Schulterbrandt & A. Rasken (Eds.) *Depression in childhood: Diagnosis, treatment and conceptual models.* New York: Raven Press, 1977.

Marine, E. School refusal—who should intervene? *Journal of School Psychology,* 1968, *7,* 63–70.

Millar, T. P. The child who refuses to attend school. *American Journal of Psychiatry,* 1961, *118,* 398–404.

Miller, P. M. The use of visual imagery and muscle relaxation in the counter-conditioning of a phobic child: A case study. *Journal of Nervous and Mental Disease,* 1972, *154,* 457–460.

Miller, W. R. Psychological deficit in depression. *Psychological Bulletin,* 1975, *82,* 238–260.

Miller, W. R., & Seligman, M. E. P. Depression and learned helplessness in man. *Journal of Abnormal Psychology,* 1975, *84,* 228–238.

Miller, W. R., & Seligman, M. E. P. Learned helplessness and the perception of reinforcement. *Behavior Research and Therapy,* 1976, *14,* 7–17.

Milman, D. School phobia in older children and adolescents: Diagnostic implications and prognosis *Pediatrics,* 1961, *28,* 462–471.

Minuchin, S. Baker, L. Rosman B., Liebman, R., Milman, L. & Todd, T. A conceptual model of psychosomatic illness in children. *Archives of General Psychiatry,* 1975, *32,* 1031–1038.

Minuchin, S., Rosman, B. L., & Baker, L. *Psychosomatic families.* Cambridge: Harvard University Press, 1978.

Moss, G. R., & Boren, J. H. Depression as a model for behavioral analysis. *Comprehensive Psychiatry,* 1972, *13,* 581–590.

Nemiah, J. C. Anorexia nervosa: A clinical psychiatric study. *Medicine,* 1950, *29,* 255–268.

Nichols, K. A. & Berg, I. School phobia and self-evaluation. *Journal of Child Psychology and Psychiatry,* 1970, *11,* 133–141.

Nowicki, S., & Strickland, B. R. A locus of control scale for children. *Journal of Consulting and Clinical Psychology,* 1973, *40,* 148–154.

Nurstein, J. P. Projection in later adjustment of school phobic children. *Smith College Studies in Social Work,* 1963, *33,* 210–229.

Nylander, I. The feeling of being fat and dieting in a school population. *Acta Sociomed. Scand.,* 1971, *3,* 17–26.

Ossofsky, H. Endogenous depression in infancy and childhood. *Comprehensive Psychiatry,* 1974, *15,* 19–25.

Pasamanick, B., & Knobloch, H. Brain and behaviors: Brain damage and reproductive causality. *American Journal of Orthopsychiatry,* 1960, *30,* 298–305.

Pearce, J. Depressive disorders in childhood. *Journal of Child Psychology and Psychiatry,* 1977, *18,* 79–83.

Pertschuk, M. J. Behavior therapy: Extended follow-up. In R. A. Vigersky (Ed.), *Anorexia nervosa.* New York: Raven Press, 1977.

Pincus, J. H., & Glaser, G. H. Syndrome of minimal brain damage in childhood. *New*

England Journal of Medicine, 1966, *275*, 27–35.

Pinneau, S. R. The infantile disorders of hospitalism and anaclitic depression. *Psychological Bulletin*, 1955, *52*, 429–452.

Pittman, F. S., Langsley, D. G., & DeYoung, C. D. Work and school phobias: A family approach to treatment. *American Journal of Psychiatry*, 1968, *124*, 1535–1541.

Radin, S. S. Psychotheraputic considerations in school phobia. *Adolescence*, 1968, *3*, 181–193.

Rado, S. Psychodynamics of depression from the etiological point of view. In W. Gaylin (Ed.), *The meaning of despair*. New York: Science House, 1968.

Renshaw, D. C. Suicide and depression in children. *Journal of School Health*, 1974, *44*, 487–489.

Rizley, R. Depression and distortion in the attribution of causality. *Journal of Abnormal Psychology*, 1978, *87*, 32–48.

Rodriquez, A., Rodriquez, M. & Eisenberg, L. The outcome of school phobia: A follow up study based on 41 cases. *American Journal of Psychiatry*, 1959, 116, 540–544.

Rosman, B. L., Minuchin, S., Baker, L., & Liebman, R. A family approach to anorexia nervosa: Study, treatment and outcome. In R. A. Vigersky (Ed.), *Anorexia Nervosa*. New York: Raven Press, 1977.

Rosman, B. L., Minuchin, S., & Liebman R. Family lunch session: An introduction to family therapy in anorexia nervosa. *American Journal of Orthopsychiatry*, 1975, *45*, 846–853.

Rotter, J. B. Generalized expectancies for internal versus external control of reinforcement. *Psychological Monographs*, 1966, *80*.

Rowland, C. Anorexia nervosa: A survey of the literature and a review of 30 cases. *International Psychiatry*, 1970, *1*, 37.

Russell, G. F. M. General management of anorexia nervosa and difficulties in assessing the efficacy of treatment. In R. A. Vigersky (Ed.), *Anorexia nervosa*. New York: Raven Press, 1977.

Schachter, S. The interaction of congnitive and physiological determinants of emotional states. In L. Berkowitz (Ed.), *Advances in experimental social psychology*. (Vol. 1). New York: Academic Press, 1964.

Schulterbrandt, J. G., & Raskin, A. (Eds.), *Depression in children: Diagnosis, treatment and coneptual models*. New York: Raven Press, 1977.

Scringnar, C. B. Food as the reinforcer in the outpatient treatment of anorexia nervosa. *Journal of Behavior Therapy and Experimental Psychiatry*, 1971, *2*, 31–36.

Seligman, M. E. P. Depression and learned helplessness. In R. J. Friedman & M. M. Katz (Eds.), The psychology of depression: Contemporary theory and research. Washington D.C.: Winston-Wiley, 1974.

Selvini, M. P. *Self starvation: From the intrapsychic to the transpersonal approach to anorexia nervosa*. London: Chancer Publishing Co., 1974.

Shapiro, T., & Jegeda, R. O. School phobia: A babel of tongues. *Journal of Autism and Childhood Schizophrenia*, 1973, *3*, 168–186.

Shaver, K. G. *An introduction to attribution processes*. Cambridge: Winthrop Publishers, 1975.

Shepherd, M. Oppenheim, B., & Mitchell, S. *Childhood behavior and mental health*. New York: Grune and Stratton, 1971.

Skynner, A. C. R. School phobia: A reappriasal. *British Journal of Medical Psychology*, 1974, *47*, 1–16.

Smith, R. E., & Sharpe, T. M. Treatment of a school phobia with implusive therapy. *Journal of Consulting and Clinical Psychology*, 1970, *35*, 2, 239–243.

Sours, J. A. The anorexia nervosa syndrome. *The International Journal of Psycho-Analysis*, 1974, *55*, 567–578.

Sperling, M. School phobias: Classification, dynamics and treatment. In R. Eissler, A. Freud, & H. Hartmann (Eds.). *The psychoanalytic study of the child* (Vol. 22). New York: International Universities Press, 1967.

Spitz, R. A. Hospitalism. An inquiry into the genesis of psychiatric conditions in early childhood. *Psychoanalytic study of the child* (Vol. 1). New York: International Universities Press, 1945.

Spitz, R. A. Hospitalism: A follow-up report. *Psychoanalytic Study of the child* (Vol. 2). New York: International Universities Press, 1946.

Suttenfield, V. School phobia—a study of five cases. *American Journal of Orthopsychiatry*, 1954, *24*, 368–380.

Taft, L. T., & Goldfarb, W. Prenatal and perinatal factors in childhood schizophrenia. *Developmental Medicine and Childhood Neurology*, 1964, *6*, 32–43.

Tahmisian, J. A., & Reynolds, W. Use of parents as behavioral engineers in the treatment of a school phobic girl. *Journal of Counseling Psychology*, 1970, *18*, 225–228.

Talbot, M. Panic in school phobia. *American Journal of Orthopsychiatry*, 1957, *27*, 286–295.

Theander, S. Anorexia nervosa: A psychiatric investigation of 94 female patients. *Acta Psychiatr Scand*, 1970, *214*, 1–194.

Thoma. H. *Anorexia nervosa*. New York: International University Press, 1967.

Thomas, E., & DeWald, L. Experimental neurosis: Neuropsychological analysis. In J. D. Maser & M. E. P. Seligman (Eds.), *Psychopathology: Experimental models.* San Francisco: W. H. Freeman, 1977.

Toolan, J. M. Depression in children and adolescents. *American Journal of Orthopsychiatry,* 1962, *32,* 404–414.

Van Buskirk, S. S. A two-phase perspective on the treatment of anorexia nervosa. *Psychological Bulletin,* 1977, *84,* 529–538.

Van Houten, J. Mother-child relationships in 12 cases of school phobia. *Smith College Studies in Social Work,* 1948, *18,* 161–180.

Waldron, S. The significance of childhood neurosis for adult mental health: A follow-up study. *American Journal of Psychiatry,* 1976 133, 532–538.

Waldron, S., Shier, D. K., Stone, B., & Tobin, F. School phobia and other childhood neuroses: A systematic study of children and their families. *American Journal of Psychiatry,* 1975, *132,* 802–805.

Waldfogel, S., Coolidge, J. C., & Hahn, P. B. The development, meaning and management of school phobia. *American Journal of Orthopsychiatry,* 1957, *27,* 754–776.

Watson, J. S. Depression and perception of control in early childhood. In J. G. Schulterbrandt & A. Raskin (Eds.), *Depression in childhood: Diagnosis, treatment and conceptual models.* New York: Raven Press, 1977.

Weiner, B. Achievement motivation and attribution theory. Morristown, New Jersey: General Learning Press, 1974.

Weiss, M., & Cain, B. The residential treatment of childhood and adolescents with school phobia. *American Journal of Orthopsychiatry,* 1964, *34,* 103–117.

Welker, R. L. Acquistion of a free operant appetitive response in pigeons as a function of prior experience with response-independent food. *Learning and motivation.* 1976, *7,* 394–405.

Werry, J. S., & Quay, H. C. The prevalence of behavior symptoms in younger elementary school children. *American Journal of Orthopsychiatry,* 1971, *41,* 136–143.

CHAPTER 4

Special Disorders of Childhood: Enuresis, Encopresis and Sleep Disorders*

DANIEL M. DOLEYS, Ph.D.
DEBRA WEILER, Ph.D.
AND
VERNON PEGRAM, Ph.D.

INTRODUCTION

The intention of this chapter is to describe briefly some of the less common disorders of childhood: enuresis, encorpresis, disorders of sleep, and Gilles la Tourette's syndrome. The most common of these disorders is enuresis, occurring in about 15 to 20 percent of younger children. The incidence of the other three disorders has been estimated to be approximately 3 percent or less of the general child population.

These diverse disorders do not appear to be linked to one another in any particular fashion. However, there are a set of characteristics common to each that justifies discussing them in a single chapter. First, in each case the disorder is found more frequently in boys than in girls. Usually, the ratio is 2 to 1 or 3 to 1. Second,

each disorder has severe and devastating consequences for the child and the family, if not remediated. Third, these problems, particularly in their formative stages, are typically ignored or relegated to the position of "maturational" disorders, and the parents are told that the child will "outgrow" the problem. Fourth, proper diagnosis and treatment require some knowledge or consultation in the area of anatomy and physiology. Finally, it is generally agreed that the incidence figures probably are underestimates.

ENURESIS

Functional nocturnal enuresis is a developmental disorder of childhood typically defined as persistent wetting of the bed in the absence of urological or neurological pathology (Campbell, 1970). A child can generally be considered enuretic if he/she is wetting the bed weekly beyond the age of three. There are numerous types of urinary incontinence (Lund, 1963). About 95 percent of all cases fall into the functional enuresis category.

*Preparation of this manuscript was supported in part by Project 910, U. S. Maternal and Child Health, H.S.M.S.A., Department of Health, Education and Welfare, as awarded to the Center for Developmental and learning Disorders, University of Alabama in Birmingham School of Medicine, Birmingham, Alabama.

Appreciation is expressed to Becky Dossett for her assistance in preparation of this chapter.

The two major types of nocturnal enuresis are persistent (continuous or primary) and acquired (discontinuous or secondary). The acquired enuretic has demonstrated a period of nighttime continence of at least six months. Nearly 85 percent of all nocturnal enuretics fall into the persistent category (deJonge, 1973). It is estimated that 15 to 20 percent of all five-year-olds are enuretic at night. This percentage decreases with age, so that only 2 percent of twelve- to fourteen-year-olds display nocturnal enuresis. Because of this substantial decrease in the incidence of enuresis with age, many physicians and other professionals choose not to treat the disorder in the younger (five- to ten-year-old) child, telling parents the child will "grow out of it" or "spontaneously stop.". There is, however, sufficient clinical and anecdotal evidence that many of the children who become dry do so only when the behavior is consequenced by trials of social restriction, embarrassment, punishment, and so forth. In addition, children who do not become dry until ten, eleven, or twelve years of age may be exposed to unnecessary ridicule and self-deprecation because of their wetting.

Although the enuretic child is often regarded as having emotional or psychiatric problems, the available data do not support this hypothesis. Several studies (Kolvin, Tounch, Currah, Garside, Norlan, and Shaw, 1972; Shaffer, 1973; Rutter, Yule — Graham, 1973) have failed to find a significant correlation between enuresis and any specific psychiatric or behavioral disorder.

Assessment

Adequate assessment of the enuretic child is a complex process. Merely gathering data on the number of wet nights per week is inadequate. Information relating to the bladder functioning (Yeates, 1973) should also be acquired. Medical examinations, urinalysis, and urine cultures are required to rule out contributing organic or urological pathology. Radiological examinations should be performed only when indicated. The clinical interview should be comprehensive and yield data relating to: (1) daytime and nighttime wetting; (2) history of the enuresis and previous treatment attempts; (3) brief medical history of family; (4) presence of other problem behaviors; and (5) home and family environment. Family problems and parents' inability to elicit compliance from their child are two of the many circumstances that would contraindicate immediate intervention for enuresis.

Precise behavioral records are needed as a baseline against which to evaluate the child's progress. Two- to four-week periods have been utilized. This also provides an opportunity to assess parental cooperation and motivation for treatment. Some children respond positively to self-monitoring and encouragement. Frequency of wet nights, wets per night, bladder capacity, and retention ability should be assessed. A more thorough discussion of the assessment procedures can be found elsewhere (Ciminero and Doleys, 1976; Doleys, 1978; Doleys, Schwartz and Ciminero, in press).

Etiology

Theories of etiology can be divided into three broad categories: medical-genetic, psychodynamic, and learning-behavioral. The medical-genetic approach views enuresis as a deficit in cortical control and draws upon data from sleep studies describing the presence of an arousal deficit in enuretic children. Bakwin (1961) supported a genetic interpretation noting the high rate of concordance among monozygotic as opposed to dyzygotic twins. Muellner (1960) proposed a maturation-developmental model, implicating the immature bladder as the main factor. Recently, Gerrard and his associates (Gerrard and Zaleski, 1976; Zaleski, Gerrard and Shokier, 1973) have hypothesized that enuresis may be a result of an allergic reaction which maintains the bladder in spasm, preventing the accumulation of urine and resulting in frequent voiding at very low bladder capacity.

The psychodynamic approach tends to interpret enuresis as a sign of some deeper underlying conflict or disturbance (Pierce, 1975; Sperling, 1965). The behavior is seen as evidence of regression, a bid for attention, a controlled expression of anger, equivalent of masturbation, or clinging to infancy. Sperling (1965) described it as an indicant of the child's "inability to tolerate instinctual or emotional tension" (p. 28). Therapy, therefore, focuses upon the presumed underlying problem rather than the enuresis itself.

A learning-behavioral model attends to the learning experiences of the child and the consequences of the enuresis (Atthowe, 1973; Lovibond and Coote, 1970; Yeates, 1973). Involvement of cortical control in conditioned inhibition of urination is acknowledged. Where the ability to exert such control is present but not in evidence, it is assumed to be a result of faulty or inadequate training. Nighttime wetting occurs because the cues emanating from bladder distention have not become discriminative leading to arousal of the child or inhibition of voiding. Treatment, therefore, focuses upon the development of bladder distention as an effective discriminative stimulus.

Treatment

The major treatment procedures are pharmacological, bladder expansion, and behavioral-conditioning. Although verbal psychotherapy has been reported in a small number of papers, its impact is limited, at best, and certainly does not appear to improve upon the rates of remission noted when no systematic therapy is applied (Doleys, 1978, 1979).

Drugs. A number of different dugs have been used in the treatment of enuresis. According to a review by Blackwell and Currah (1973), there is no conclusive support for the use of amphetamines. Imipramine hydrocloride (Tofranil), a trycyclic antidepressant, has been found to be significantly more effective than other drugs. The basis of its action is not well understood, though speculations include: (1) lightening of sleep; (2) inhibitory action on detrusor contraction; (3) heightened sphincter control; (4) relaxation of the detrusor allowing for increased bladder capacity; and (5) mood elevation (Blackwell and Currah, 1973; Kales, Kales, Jacobson, Humphrey, and Soldthos, 1977; Labay and

Boyarsky, 1972). The usual course of treatment is immediate reduction in enuretic episodes in over 85 percent of the cases. About 30 percent achieved total continence, and most relapse following drug withdrawal (Stewart, 1975). Dizziness, headaches, constipation, and disturbance in mood and sleep have been reported side effects. Deaths from imipramine toxicity, although rare, have occurred (Meadow, 1974), and raise serious questions about the use of imipramine and the supervision required.

Bladder Capacity. Several studies (Starfield and Mellits, 1968; Zaleski et al., 1973) have documented the presence of a small functional bladder capacity in enuretics as compared to nonenuretics. It is hypothesized that increased bladder capacity would benefit the enuretic child by allowing him to retain urine through the night or would result in stronger bladder cues which would be more likely to arouse him.

The general bladder expansion procedure requires a child to take in larger than usual quantities of liquid, refraining from voiding for increasing periods of time up to about thirty minutes (Doleys et al., 1977; Harris and Purohit, 1977). The frequency of trials, the length of treatment, and the delivery of reinforcements has varied across the studies.

Harris and Purohit (1977), in one of the more well-controlled studies, exposed eighteen children to thirty-five days of bladder expansion (retention) training. In spite of an average increase of nearly 35 percent in bladder capacity, the frequency of enuretic episodes decreased by an average of less than one per night per child. Similarly, Allen (1976) reported that none of the eight children who completed a ninety-day program of retention control training became dry at night.

Bladder expansion training does appear to be useful with the daytime enuretic and may facilitate treatment of the nighttime enuretic by encouraging the development of voluntary sphincter control where it is absent or not fully developed. By itself, it does not appear to be an effective treatment procedure for nocturnal enuresis. Moreover, this procedure results in complications for the child who has problems with urinary reflux.

Behavioral Conditioning. The urine alarm is perhaps the most researched treatment approach. In this procedure the child sleeps on a urine sensing device, which is triggered by the passage of small amounts of urine. When the alarm is activated, the child is to awaken, turn off the alarm, finish voiding in the bathroom, change night clothes and bedding, and return to bed. A recent review of studies published between 1960 and 1975 (Doleys, 1977), reporting on a total of 600 subjects ranging in age from four to fifteen years old, noted a 75 percent rate of remission with treatment duration ranging from five to twelve weeks. The relapse rate was 41 percent; 68 percent of these were successfully retreated. Variation in treatment procedures, sensitivity of urine alarm, criterion for dryness, and relapse were noted among the studies.

Two modifications of the standard urine alarm procedure hold promise for reducing the relapse rate. First is the overlearning procedure (Young and Morgan, 1972), which calls for increased intake of liquids prior to bedtime after seven to fourteen consecutive dry nights have been achieved under the standard procedure. Theoretically, it is assumed that the intake will result in higher degrees of bladder fullness, assuring that the child will have the opportunity to extend conditioning and strengthen the newly acquired behavior. Other studies have confirmed the potential utility of overlearning (Jehu, Morgan, Turner, and Jones, 1977; Taylor and Turner, 1975). The second innovation is the application of an intermittent alarm schedule (Finley, Beserman, Bennett, Clapp and Finley, 1973). Under this protocol, the alarm is operated only after a certain percentage of wetting episodes (usually 50 or 70 percent). Conceptually, this is seen as an intermittent schedule of reinforcement. Behaviors conditioned under such schedules are known to be more resistant to extinction (that is, relapse). The initial reports by Finley and his colleagues (Finley, et al., 1973; Finley and Wansley, 1976; Finley, Wansley, and Blenkran, 1977) have been very encouraging.

Most recently, Azrin, Sneed, and Foxx (1973, 1974) have introduced a multifaceted conditioning procedure for the treatment of nocturnal enuresis, called dry-bed training (DBT). This procedure incorporated positive practice, positive reinforcement, retention control training, night awakening, negative reinforcement, and full cleanliness training. Although a urine alarm was used, it was placed in the parents' room for the purpose of alerting them to the occurrence of a wet. The results of the initial study were very impressive, with 100 percent of twenty-four subjects obtaining dryness. Results of replication by Doleys et al. (1977) were not as remarkable and compared more to those obtained with standard urine alarms. Bollard and Woodroffe (1977), however, also replicated the dry-bed training, but had it administered totally by the parents, obtaining results similar to Azrin et al. (1974).

Summary

The treatment of nocturnal enuresis is a complex endeavor requiring trained professionals. Many of the critical issues in assessment and treatment were not covered in this brief space, but are discussed elsewhere (Doleys, 1978; Doleys, et al., in press). Selection of the proper equipment, parental cooperation, child compliance, and introduction of the procedure are but a few of the components of successful treatment. The urine alarm method appears to be the most researched and proven procedure to date. Dry-bed training certainly has produced remarkable results, but these have not been consistently replicated and the parental time is considerable. Bladder expansion exercises seem to have a limited, but perhaps useful role. Tofranil is relatively ineffective in the long run and may best be used as an adjunct to the urine alarm.

ENCOPRESIS

Functional encopresis is defined as "the passage of fecal material of any amount or consistency into clothing or other generally unacceptable areas in the absence of any organic pathology beyond the age of three years" (Doleys, 1978). The two major types of encopresis are the persistent and the acquired. In addition, encopresis can be of the retentive or nonretentive type (Anthony, 1957; Gavanski, 1971). In the first case the child retains for excessive periods before having a bowel movement, which is oftentimes artificially produced. The "pot refusal" syndrome has been used to describe children with normal bowel control, but who refused to sit on the commode. Prolonged retention can lead to overflow incontinence, a condition which, upon casual examination, mimicks diarrhea and has been referred to as "paradoxical diarrhea" (Davidson, 1958). Treatment, however, is very different. Walker (1978) suggested the use of three major categories: (1) manipulative soiler; (2) chronic diarrhea or irritable bowel syndrome; and (3) chronic diarrhea resulting from impactions or psychogenic megacolon. About 95 percent of cases would fall into the last category.

It is estimated that nearly 3 percent of children display functional encopresis (Levine, 1975; Yeates, 1973). Figures vary considerably and can go as high as 5.7 percent. There is common agreement that the actual incidence is probably much higher, but parents do not volunteer this information, and physicians do not routinely inquire about toileting habits. Encopresis is about three to four times more common in males than females, and is often accompanied by abdominal pain, lethargy, poor appetite, and loss of sensation to defecate (Levine, 1975). Nearly 30 percent may also be enuretic, and a majority will have impactions. Psychiatric, personality, or behavioral disorders are more common among encopretics than enuretics, but are still found in less than 30 percent of cases (Levine, 1975).

Assessment

Careful assessment of the encopretic child is important in selecting the most appropriate treatment approach. The child whose soiling is primarily a result of a lack of appropriate training will be best served by implementing a systematic and consistent toilet training regimen of the type described by Azrin and Foxx (1976). Different procedures are needed for the child who defecates frequently as opposed to the child who displays excessive retention.

A medical evaluation is needed to rule out organic pathology and to differentiate between functional encopresis and Hirschsprung's disease, a condition characterized by the absence of ganglion cells in part of the colon, which prohibits the development of bowel control (Ravitch, 1958). Unusual distention of the colon (megacolon) and impactions require a medical evaluation. Enemas, laxatives, stool softeners, and suppositories are often used as part of treatment. Medical consultation is required to ensure the best selection.

A second aspect of the evaluation involves a three-week baseline, during which specific behavioral records noting (1) frequency of soiling, (2) magnitude of each episode, (3) when and where each episode occurred, and (4) appropriate toileting behavior, are kept. Some children display situational specific patterns of soiling, remaining continent in certain settings. Others may be encopretic in response to stress, while still others may show an exaggerated fear of the toilet, preventing them from using it appropriately (Ashkenazi, 1975; Doleys and Arnold, 1975; Gelber and Meyer, 1965). Pain resulting from prolonged retention may be associated with toileting and may lead to the development of a conditioned avoidance response to the bathroom. "Pot refusal" behavior can result from the use of adversive procedures during toilet training. Furthermore, the assessment should evaluate the ability of the child to successfully undress, clean, and redress himself. All of these are necessary prerequisites to the development of appropriate toileting behavior and are oftentimes ignored.

Parental response to accidents and effects of previous treatment attempts are important to note. Parents should be encouraged to relax punitive measures in favor of a prescribed program. Many programs utilize removal of attention for soiling, positive reinforcement of appropriate defecation or clean pants, and the use of charts. If these procedures have already been systematically employed without success, there is little reason to suggest further replication. Some studies have noted a higher incidence of familial and marital problems in the family of encopretics (Wolters, 1974). When this exists, it may work against the development of a therapeutic environment and the consistent application of a program. Feelings of frustration or guilt by the parents should be assessed and laid to rest.

Etiology

Theories of etiology can be divided into medical, psychodynamic, and learning-behavioral. The medical view is adopted from a neuro-developmental model that emphasizes an examination of neural integrity and appropriate functioning of the physiological mechanisms involved in defecation. When it has been determined that the encopresis is not a result of organic pathology, the medical model usually leads to use of purgatives to avoid constipation.

As with enuresis, the psychoanalytically oriented therapist views encopresis as a sign or symptom of a deeper unconscious conflict. Hypothesized explanations include lack of parental love, pregnancy wishes, separation anxiety, aggression against the world, and traumatic separation during oral and anal stages of psychosexual development (Pierce, 1975; Silber, 1969). A power struggle over toileting is also seen as a controlling factor (Hilburn, 1968). Anthony (1957) has outlined other possibilities and interpretations focused upon what he called the "potting couple."

From a learning-behavioral perspective, primary encopresis may be viewed as an outcome of inadequate training, and acquired encopresis from the presence of reinforcing consequences. Appropriate toileting is seen as the final response in a chain of events which begins with sensing the need to defecate. Each behavior in the chain must be firmly established and contingencies arranged in such a fashion as to maintain appropriate toileting behavior.

Treatment

Psychotherapy. Although several studies have described the use of verbal psychoth-

erapy in the treatment of functional encopresis (Gavanski, 1971; McTaggert and Scott, 1959; Pinkerton, 1958), there appears to be little empirical evidence of its efficacy (Berg and Jones, 1964). Ashkenazi (1975) reported on three children who, although unsuccessfully treated by verbal psychotherapy and play therapy, later became continent when exposed to a behaviorally oriented treatment program.

Medical. Medical approaches to treatment of encopresis typically rely on the use of purgatives (laxatives, enemas) and dietary manipulation. These procedures are frequently useful. However, development of parent and child compliance, the acquisition of appropriate toileting behavior, and long-term maintenance of these behaviors, once they are established, are frequently not attended to. Several of the medical approaches have been described by Nisley (1976), Silber (1969), Ravitch (1958), and Davidson, Kugler, and Bauer (1963). The Davidson et al. study reported successful treatment of 90 of 119 encopretics. It is, however, obvious from Davidson's description that extensive counseling, feedback, monitoring, physician time, support, and encouragement were used. It is interesting that Silber (1969) advised parents not to engage in data-collecting procedures, to ignore episodes with incontinence, and not to discuss bowel habits with their children. Hospitalization of the encopretic child, although infrequently described in the literature, has been suggested as a means of producing temporary relief from the parents and convincing the child and the parents that continence is a reasonable goal (Ravitch, 1958).

Tofranil (imipramine) has been reported in the treatment of encopresis (Gavanski, 1971). It is speculated that imipramine has an inhibitory effect upon internal and external sphincter control, reducing the frequency of bowel movements. Controlled outcome studies on large numbers of subjects have not been accomplished with this procedure, and it would appear to be a consideration only for those children who engage in multiple soiling episodes each day and whose frequency cannot be controlled by other means.

Learning-Behavioral. The conditioning approach to the treatment of functional encopresis emphasizes the arrangement of environmental contingencies that will support the display of appropriate toilet behavior and lead to a decrease in the frequency of accidents. An array of different approaches have been utilized. They can be generally classified as those which involve: (1) positive reinforcement for appropriate behavior with no consequences for soiling; (2) punishment for soiling behavior; and (3) a multifaceted approaches utilizing a variety of behavioral procedures (Doleys, 1979).

Programs emphasizing the use of positive reinforcement in the treatment of encopresis fall into two groups. First are those that have made reinforcement contingent upon appropriate toileting behavior (Bach & Moylan, 1975; Keehn, 1965; Neale, 1963; Plachetta, 1976; Young & Goldsmith, 1972; Young, 1973). These regimens generally involve checking the child periodically and placing him on the commode. Positive reinforcement is made available contingent upon the child demonstrating appropriate bowel movements while sitting on the commode. Laxatives and stool softeners may be employed to ensure that the appropriate behavior is displayed. Most of these programs also involve fading of the checking procedure, so that the child gradually accepts greater and greater responsibility (Neale, 1963).

A second application of positive reinforcement is typified by programs described by Allyon, Simon and Wildman (1975), and Pedrini, and Pedrini (1971). Under these protocols, positive reinforcement was provided for clean pants rather than just appropriate toileting behavior. Logan and Gardner (1971) described a very interesting study using a seven-year-old partially deaf child in which a pant alarm was employed to detect episodes of soiling. Doleys et al. (1975) have cautioned against using reinforcement for clean pants alone. Some children might begin to retain as a means of producing clean pants. Clean pants are only a partial goal of treatment. More important goals are the display and strengthening of appropriate toileting behaviors.

Some studies (Edelman, 1971; Freinden

and VanHandel, 1970) have reported on the application of punishment procedures. Although positive results were noted, the exclusive use of punishment in the absence of positive reinforcement often results in emotional responses, tends to promote negative parent-child interactions, and can lead to excessive retention or attempts to escape the treatment environment. Many of the parents who seek treatment for their encopretic children have inadvertently tried various punishment procedures, making treatment more difficult than it might otherwise need to be.

Because of the multiplicity of factors related to the onset and maintenance of functional encorpresis, it is not surprising that multifaceted programs have become more frequently employed and are leading to the best results. Indicative of these programs are the ones described by Wright (1973, 1975; Wright and Walker, 1976, 1978), in which they combine positive reinforcement, negative reinforcement, periodic potting, the use of enemas and suppositories, and a fading procedure. Ashkenazi (1975) reported on a similar program, which also incorporated treatment for six of eighteen subjects who demonstrated a pot phobia reaction. Azrin and Foxx (1976) have introduced a comprehensive toilet-training program for the mentally retarded. Many of the components of this program have been utilized in the treatment of nonretarded children who display functional encopresis. Doleys et al. (1977), for example, described a program which utilized full cleanliness training, periodic potting, and token reinforcement for appropriate toileting.

Summary

Although the incidence of functional encopresis is unknown, there is agreement that it is probably much higher than is frequently reported. As was the case for enuresis, there appears to be no rationale for not introducing early treatment for the four- or five-year-old who is encopretic. Differential treatments may need to be applied, depending upon the circumstances surrounding the encopresis and whether or not it is of the persistent or acquired type. Although single-element conditioning programs have been reported, the studies have been conducted with small numbers of patients and will probably ultimately give way to the more multifaceted programs. Treatment frequently requires the use of suppositories or enemas and, therefore, should be done in conjunction with medical consultation. The use of purgatives by themselves is often inadequate and ignores the complex chain of behavior that makes up what we refer to as appropriate toileting. Precise assessment of the individual encopretic should be considered a necessity.

SLEEP DISORDERS

Normal Sleep Mechanisms

Sleep is divided into two major categories, rapid-eye-movement (REM) sleep and non-rapid-eye-movement (NREM) sleep. NREM sleep, sometimes referred to as slow-wave-sleep (SWS), is subdivided into stages 1, 2, 3, and 4. The stages are distinguished from one another by electroencephalographic (EEG) recordings in combination with electromyogram (EMG) and electrooculogram (EOG) recordings. Stage 1 occurs as a person falls asleep (stage 1 descending) and is characterized by the disappearance of theta waves (3–7 cps). The EEG pattern is low-amplitude and fast-frequency. In stage 1, the sleeper is awakened easily and may deny he has been sleeping (Battle, 1970).

Stage 2 is characterized on the EEG by the appearance of the K complex (slow frequency and high amplitude) and sleep spindles (bursts of high frequencey EEG waves, 12–16 cps). The stage is often referred to as "light sleep" and the sleeper may awaken easily.

Stages 3 and 4 are the deepest stages of slow-wave-sleep (SWS), because they are characterized by slow frequency ($\frac{1}{2}$–2 cps), high-voltage delta wave activity. Stage 3 may be differentiated from stage 4 by the presence of sleep spindles and K complexes with 20 percent to 50 percent delta activity. Stage 4 is characterized by more than 50 percent delta activity per page. The

vital signs begin to decrease, and the sleeper becomes more difficult to awaken in stage 3, while marked relaxation, rare movement, and slow response to awakening occur in stage 4 (Battle, 1970).

The quality and quantity of normal sleep varies as a function of age. Total sleep time is high in infancy and childhood and shows a significant decline in adolescence. Average sleep time decreases from sixteen hours per day in the neonate to about eight hours for age twelve, seven hours between ages twenty-five to forty-five, and approximately six and a half hours in old age (Hauri, 1977). The proportion of time spent in the sleep stages also varies with age. Stage 1 REM sleep is highest for infants (50 percent), and children (30 percent), with the largest decline occurring in age eighty and over (20 percent) (Feinberg, 1969). Stages 3 and 4 also decline with age from 15 percent to 20 percent at age twenty and gradually decrease until there is very little delta sleep by age sixty. Stage 1 increases as a function of age from 5 percent in childhood to about 15 percent of total sleep time in old age. Hauri (1977) noted that the decline of stages 3 and 4 and the increase of stage 1 with age imply that sleep becomes lighter and less efficient. In conjunction with this, the number of arousals from sleep (as indicated by EEG) increases linearly as a function of age, even when total sleep time remains constant (Feinberg, 1969).

Individual differences in total amount of sleep time are highly variable. The healthy adult requires on the average seven and a half hours sleep per twenty-four hours. However, some healthy adults may require only four hours sleep or less per twenty-four hours, while others may require ten to twelve hours. Also, individual variability in the amount of time spent in each stage is great, but the pattern in each individual tends to be repetitive night after night (Battle, 1970).

These same individual differences in sleep requirements may be found in children. Children who do not want to go to bed early may be viewed as behaviorally disruptive when in fact they are not tired or sleepy. Similarly, children who require less sleep than the "norm" for children their age may experience difficulty falling asleep at a predetermined time every night and may be viewed as having "sleep disorders". Powell (1972) notes, "It is usually not possible to impose on a child how long he should sleep and it is better to let him evolve his own habits of sleep naturally during the first year or two" (p. 198). This advice may well apply to older children with so-called "sleep problems".

Childhood Sleep Disorders

There are three major categories of sleep disorders common to children: insomnia (abnormally short sleep); hypersomnia (abnormally long or excessive daytime sleepiness); and parasomnia (disorders within sleep). There is some discrepancy in the literature concerning a precise definition of the parasomias. *DSM-III* (in accordance with the Nosology Committee of the Association of Sleep Disorders Centers) defines parasomnias as "dysfunctions associated with sleep, sleep stages, or partial arousals". The childhood parasomnias in particular appear to be best defined as dysfunctions associated with sleep stages and partial arousals within the night's sleep.

Insomnia. Insomnia may include all or one of the following: difficulty in falling asleep, difficulty in staying asleep, or too early final awakening (Kales and Kales, 1974). Insomnia due to a physiologic disorder is relatively uncommon in children. Often, parents may view a child's sleep behavior as insomnia when in fact it may be "normal" sleep behavior dependent upon the developmental period of the child. The incidence of insomnia in children is unreported but appears to be relatively uncommon.

Diagnosis of insomnia in children should be made with caution. Insomnia in the child frequently indicates family problems more often than insomnia secondary to an organic condition (Guilleminault and Anders, 1976). Jackson and Rawlins (1977) reported that insomnia may also be a symptom of "toddler negative behavior" resulting from social and emotional stress in the family. They also reported that this is normal behavior in which the child attempts to

exert his individuality by refusing to eat, sleep, and be toilet-trained. In such cases, the sleep disorder may best be treated by family psychotherapy. However, insomnia due to sleep apnea must be ruled out, and drug-dependent insomnia should be investigated after an organic condition has been ruled out. Drug-dependent insomnia was the most common cause of severe insomnia in one group of children studied (Guilleminault and Anders, 1976). Typically a child may experience difficulty in sleeping and is given a prescribed hypnotic. The child then develops a tolerance and dependency on the medication. Sudden withdrawal of the hypnotic can also result in insomnia in children due to dependency complications. The severity of a sleep disorder in a child "must be thoroughly appraised including its severity and etiology" before hypnotic medication is considered (Guilleminault and Anders, 1976.)

Hypersomnia and Excessive Daytime Sleepiness. Hypersomnia is defined by excessive somnolence. Chronic hypersomnia may be a symptom of a psychological disorder or a sign of CNS abnormality occurring from head trauma, brain tumor, or cerebrovascular disorder (Rechtschaflen and Dement, 1969). Hypersomnia may take the form of excessive nighttime sleep or excessive daytime sleep. The two primary sleep disorders affecting children are narcolepsy-cataplexy and the sleep-apnea syndrome, which produce excessive daytime somnolence (EDS).

Narcolepsy is characterized by an "irresistible" urge to sleep which commonly involves frequent naps of short duration. Cataplexy accompanies narcoleptic sleep attacks in approximately 80 to 88 percent of people with narcolepsy (Lewis, 1974; Guilleminault and Anders, 1976). Cataplexy is a loss of muscle tone and frequently occurs in response to sudden stimulation or emotion (Kales and Kales, 1974). It may involve complete loss of muscle tone, or it may be specific to certain groups of muscles. Sleep paralysis is frequently an auxillary symptom and may be experienced upon waking or prior to sleep onset, in which the child tries to move but cannot. Hypnagogic hallucinations frequently accompany sleep paralysis (Guilleminault and Anders, 1976; Kales and Kales, 1974). They are frequently auditory but may also be visual. The child may hear strange voices, see frightening shadows, and may then try to escape, but find he cannot move. The child may let out a scream and/or fall back asleep. He may remember the event as a nightmare, but there is usually amnesia for the event.

Sleep attacks may take forms other than what appear to be short naps. If the patient tries to fight off the sleep attack, a state of partial sleep may occur in which the patient may continue to walk, talk, and carry on activities in a semi-automatic way and later have no recollection of these activities (Lewis, 1974).

The general incidence of narcolepsy has been estimated from .03 percent to .05 percent (Guilleminault and Anders, 1976). The peak age of onset of narcoleptic EDS occurs between ages fifteen and twenty-five, with 20 percent of this population complaining of daytime sleepiness before age eleven (Guilleminault and Anders, 1976). EDS is often the first sign of narcolepsy and may be associated with hypnagogic hallucinations and sleep paralysis in childhood. Lewis (1974) reports that narcolepsy can begin at any age, but most typically occurs during adolescence. There is evidence that narcolepsy has a genetic basis (Kales and Kales, 1974) as the incidence in narcoleptic families is around 5 percent (Kessler, Guilleminault, and Dement, 1974).

Narcolepsy may be diagnosed by sleep lab EEG recordings. Recording of REM sleep onset in children with excessive daytime somnolence may suggest the diagnosis of narcolepsy, especially if cataplexy is present. However, REM onset may not be evident in those patients without cataplexy. In these cases multiple sleep latency tests in the laboratory may provide a more definitive diagnosis (Richardson, Carskadon, Flagg, Van Der Hood, Dement, & Miller, 1978). Differential diagnosis may include: Klein-Levine syndrome (affecting mostly adolescent boys), sleep apnea hypersomnia, hypothroidism, hypoglycemia, coma, and epilepsy (Zarcone, 1973; cited in Kales and Kales, 1974).

It is important to properly diagnose nar-

colepsy, because it may interfere greatly with learning, and as a result the child may be labeled slow, unmotivated, lazy, irresponsible, and even minimally brain damaged (MBD) (Guilleminault and Anders, 1976). The psychological impact on the narcoleptic and his parents may be great. It is important to aid parental understanding of cataplexy, sleep paralysis, and hypagogic hallucinations, which may be viewed as bizarre psychopathological behavior by the parents.

Investigators report limited success with Methyphenidate-hydrochloride (which suppresses REM sleep) for children with narcolepsy, but this drug does not control other narcoleptic symptoms. Imipramine and chlorimpramine are more effective for sleep paralysis, cataplexy, and hypnagogic hallucinations, but these drugs should not be prescribed before age ten (Guilleminault and Anders, 1976). Treatment of narcolepsy with Tofranil (imipramine) and Ritalin in small doses has been the most effective combination in adults. However, management of narcolepsy by daytime naps should always be considered before medication is prescribed. For example, some narcoleptics who only have two to three attacks per day can help their situation by taking scheduled brief naps at noon and/or right before supper, which appears to relieve some of the pressure to sleep.

Sleep apnea is defined as the periodic cessation of respiration during sleep. It is a universal occurrence in normal infants between one to three months of age (Gould, Lee, James, Sander, Teager, & Fineberg, 1977). The normal month-old infant has approximately eighty respiratory pauses every one hundred minutes, most with a duration of less than ten seconds (Gould et al., 1977). If sleep apnea continues into childhood it may be reported as insomnia, because the apnea episodes disturb deep sleep, which produces a lighter sleep with more general arousals (Guilleminault, Eldridge, & Dement, 1973). Most often the presenting symptoms will include "feeling tired", excessive daytime sleepiness, and snoring, which is described as loud "snorts" with intermittent periods of quiet sleep.

The three types of apnea most commonly described include: upper airway apnea, central apnea, and mixed apneas.. Upper-airway apnea is the most common and is created by a collapse of the upper airway. Respiratory effort does not cease, but there is no exchange of air. In central apnea, there is a cessation of respiratory effort, and the diaphragm ceases to move. Mixed apneas involve a lack of respiratory effort as well as upper airway collapse, followed by a resumption of respiratory effort with inability to maintain respiration successfully (Hauri, 1977).

Sleep apnea is estimated to affect more than 2 million adults and children in the United States (Karacan, Ware, Moore, Dervent, and Williams, 1977). An unusually high incidence (86 percent) of children with sleep apnea-hypersomnia are males (Guilleminault and Anders, 1976).

In older children the sleep apnea syndrome may be associated with insomnia, EDS, snoring, morning headache, poor school performance, and sometimes with nocturnal enuresis and cardiovascular abnormalities. Apnea may occur hundreds of times during the night. Each episode usually lasts between ten to thirty seconds, with some as long as 180 seconds. Guilleminault and Anders (1976) found the mean sleep apnea was 20.2 seconds, and the mean number of episodes in a seven-hour sleep period was 319 in the nine children they studied.

Sleep apnea may pose a serious threat to health, and it is important that it is diagnosed properly. Further, differentiation between sleep apnea and other sleep disorders is important because treatment with hypnotics is ineffective and can be fatal (Karacan et al., 1977). Sleep apnea is often misdiagnosed as narcolepsy, epilepsy, idiopathic or drug-induced insomnia, thyroid dysfunction, and general hypersomnia.

Snoring in association with EDS or fragmented sleep strongly suggests obstructive sleep apnea. If sleep apnea is suspected, a laryngoscopic examination of the upper airway is necessary in order to check for malformations of the neck and manible, and allergic reactions must also be excluded (Guilleminault and Anders, 1976). If malformations are found, the appropriate local treatment is necessary. The absence of obstructions suggests a neurologic

disorder (Guilleminault and Anders, 1976). Sleep apnea can be diagnosed when the patient is sleeping by measurement of blood gases, respiration, cardiac arohythmias, and loud snoring.

In cases of obstructive or mixed sleep apnea, tonsillectomy or adenoidectomy for children with hypertrophic tonsils or adenoids may produce relief. Obstruction of the upper airway, especially when accompanied by severe cardiac arrhythmias where immediate treatment is indicated, may be relieved by a tracheostomy.

At present, there is no adequate treatment for central apneas. Some relief with imipriamine has been obtained. Chronic phrenic nerve stimulation has also been utilized, but its efficacy is questionable (Hauri, 1977). Implantation of a diaphragm pacemaker in patients with central sleep apnea has been reported (Karacan, et al., 1977), but is yet a newly developed procedure under investigation. It is possible that the distinction between upper airway and central apnea is not a clear one. Sutter (1975) found that Pickwickian patients responded postively to sublingual medroxyprogesterone acetate therapy.

Parasomnias

Somnabulism and somniloquy are more commonly known as sleep-walking and sleep-talking, respectively. They may be considered parasominias because they are associated with partial arousal states in sleep.

Sleep-walking occurs in 1 to 6 percent of the population, with approximately 15 percent of all children between ages five and twelve walking in their sleep at least once (Anders, 1976; Guilleminault and Anders, 1976). Somnambulism occurs predominantly in males; affects more children than adults; and is often associated with nocturnal enuresis (Anders, 1976). There is often a family history for it and identical twins are concordant for the disorder six times as often an fraternal twins (Kales and Kales, 1974; Anders, 1976; Guilleminault and Anders, 1976).

Sleep-walking may be viewed as a rather harmless activity by parents but may often prove quite dangerous. Care should be taken to ensure the safety of the individual, as varying degrees of motor activity have been reported during somnambolistic episodes and sleepwalkers have been observed to open doors and windows.

Guilleminault and Anders (1976) described a typical somnambolistic episode in a sleep lab. First a body movement occurs which is followed by abrupt sitting up. The child's eyes are open but appear glassy and "unseeing". The child may leave the bed and his movements are clumsy. Mumbled and slurred speech with monosyllabic replies are often noted. The length of the episode while sitting in bed may vary from fifteen to thirty seconds and extend from five to thirty minutes or more when walking occurs (Guilleminault and Anders, 1976; Anders, 1976). Attempts to wake the sleepwalker are often difficult. There is frequently amnesia for the somnambolistic episode.

Sleep lab studies of children have revealed that sleepwalking occurs during NREM sleep and particularly in stages 3 and 4 (Kales and Kales, 1974; Jacobsen, Kales, and Kales, 1969). This information dispels myths of the sleepwalker acting out a dream, which if true should occur during REM sleep. Differential diagnosis includes psychologic disturbance, psychomotor epilepsy, and dissociative hysterical state similar to fugue states (Jacobsen et al. 1969).

Parents of the somnambolist often feel that the child's episodes indicate psychopathology. Psychological testing indicates that psychological disturbances do not appear to be primary factors in child and adolescent somnambolists. However, psychological disturbances are more frequent in adult somnambolists (Kales, Paulson, Jacobsen and Kales, 1966).

Psychomotor epilepsy may be ruled out, if there are no generalized seizures, by EEG studies and by response to external stimuli during the episode. Behavior associated with fugue states is often much more complex than that of the sleepwalker. It is often accompanied by a waking state of awareness, and psychopathology is more severe (Jacobsen et al., 1969).

Part of the treatment of somnambolism should include ensuring the safety of the child by locking doors and closing windows (Kales and Kales, 1974). In several cases, stage 4 suppressant drugs have decreased somnambolistic attacks (Jacobsen et al, 1969) and are currently under investigation. Limited success has been reported with the benzodiazepines (that is, diazepam or valium) which suppresses stages 3 and 4 effectively but without resultant clear-cut decreases in frequency of somnambolistic episodes (Kales et al., 1966; Kales and Kales, 1974). Perhaps the best hope for parent and child alike is the fact that sleepwalking is often outgrown with CNS maturation, usually with the onset of puberty.

Night terrors (pavor nocturnus) must be distinguished from nightmares. Nightmares are more frequent, occur in all ages, are not considered a disorder of arousal (Anders, 1976), and are characterized by less anxiety, easier arousal, and often with lengthy recall of content (Kales and Kales, 1974). Nightmares often cause the child to become fearful of going to bed, whereas there is amnesia for the night terror attack (or at most, fragments of content). Night terrors are characterized by extreme autonomic discharge, intense anxiety, perspiration, increased respiration, and quickened heart rate (Kales and Kales, 1974).

Night terrors occur more frequently in preschool children usually between the ages of two and four (Battle, 1970). They may occur in older children and adults. Information on incidence of night terrors is scant. Jacobsen et al. (1969) report 1 to 3 percent for one attack or more in children five to twelve years old. The frequency of night terrors drops spontaneously as the child matures.

In the course of a typical night terror, the child will sit up suddenly, often accompanied by a scream or cry and extreme mobility. The eyes are open and appear to be staring, breathing is increased in frequency, the face may appear pale, and the facial expression may appear to be one of terror. The child may continue this behavior for five to thirty minutes despite parental intervention. The child does not appear to respond to soothing or talking, usually does not awaken, and then falls back to sleep.

Night terrors may be the first sign of temporal lobe epilepsy or sleep apnea (Hauri, 1977). Differential diagnosis includes nightmares, sleep stage alteration associated with drug withdrawal (Kales and Kales, 1974) and psychopathology.

Night terrors in children rarely indicate psychological disturbance but more commonly indicate disturbance in adults (Kales and Kales, 1974). Jacobsen et al. (1969) stress the importance of parental understanding that night terror is only rarely a symptom of psychopathology in children. Night terrors seem instead to be related to a slight deviation from normal patterns of maturation (Jacobsen et al., 1969). However, persistent or increased incidence of night terrors in children or adults frequently indicates psychopathology and is associated with other symptoms (Kales and Kales, 1974). If psychopathology is suspected, appropriate psychological evaluation is indicated.

Diazepam is the drug of choice for severe cases of night terror and is still under investigation. It appears that Diazepam reduces the amount of stage 4 sleep. Comly (1975) has found success with methylphenidate. Medication is rarely required for most children with night terrors.

Jactatio capitis nocturna is a rhythmic head rocking or banging (Hauri, 1977) which sometimes extends to the upper body and is observed prior to or at sleep onset.

The rhythmic patterns usually subside as the child matures. They seem to serve as a tensional outlet (Battle, 1970) or a "comfort habit" like thumb-sucking prior to falling asleep. If rhythmic head and body rocking persist into adulthood, a neurological consultation may be in order (Hauri, 1977).

GILLES DE LA TOURETTE

Gilles de la Tourette is a rare syndrome characterized by multiple muscular tics. It was first described by Itard, but named after Tourette, a physician who gave an account of nine cases in 1885. Until the 1960s little scientific information was available relevant to the etiology, course, and treatment of the Tourette Syndrome. Since then, however, Shapiro and his colleagues (Shapiro, Shapiro, Bruun, and Sweet, 1978), Lucas (1964, 1967, 1973), and others have written extensively on this movement disorder. In contrast to earlier years, discussions and descriptions of the Tourette's syndrome have found their way into the popular media increasing the risk for over diagnosis.

Description and Incidence

The Tourette's syndrome is characterized by (1) age of onset between two and fifteen years; (2) multiple, rapid, stereotype, and involuntary muscular and verbal tics; (3) fluctuating clinical course (symptoms wax and wane, and change slowly over time); (4) temporary reduction or complete voluntary control of tics followed by tremor and an increase in the tics; (5) decrease in tics during nonanxious concentration or preoccupation, and a variety of psychosocial factors may be associated with an increase or decrease in symptoms; (6) symptoms always disappear during orgasm and sleep; and (7) the disorder is life long and chronic (Shapiro, et al. 1978).

There are several additional behaviors frequently associated with the syndrome which help to confirm the diagnosis, but which are not essential for its diagnosis: (1) copralalia (a burst of involuntary obscenities); (2) coprapraxia (obscene hand or motor movement); (3) echolalia (meaningless repetition of words or phrases); (4) echoproxia (spasmatic involuntary imitation of the movement of others); and (5) palilalia (phrases or words repeated with increasing rapidity). There are several clinical findings that have been associated with the Tourette's syndrome, but which are also nonessential for its diagnosis. These include a history of hyperactivity or perceptual problems in childhood or organic stigmata in adulthood, abnormal (nonspecific) EEGs, "soft signs" of neurological abnormalities, and subtle signs of organic dysfunction or psychological testing (Shapiro et al. 1978).

Tourette's syndrome usually begins with a single or multiple tic in the facial area. This tic may include eye blinks or mouth twitches, or the whole head may be involved in head-jerks to the side or back. These muscular tics are frequently accompanied by vocal tics or utterances which include a variety of meaningless, nondescript sounds. The patients will often attempt to disguise these sounds by making it appear that they are clearing their throat. Muscular tics involving the head, shoulders and/or arms follow in time. The progression of the tics tends to be cephalocaudae. Other vocal tics, such as stuttering and swearing (copralia) may be present. Perhaps one of the most confusing aspects of this syndrome is the waxing and waning of the behaviors. At one point, eye twitches and tongue extrusions may be the predominating characteristics, while weeks or months later these may be replaced by vocal or upper body tics.

Estimates of the incidence of muscular tics in the general population range from 12 to 23 percent. Although no incidence or prevalence data are confirmed, estimates of the occurrence of Tourette's are much lower. For example, Field, Corbin, Goldstein, and Klass (1966) reported only seven cases of Tourette's in 1.5 million patients seen at the Mayo Clinic prior to 1965. Woodrow (1974), however, noted a prevalence rate of 4 per 100,000. The mean age of onset of Tourette's is about seven years. Thirty percent of these cases develop before age eleven. The median age for diagnosis is sixteen years. There is, then, a mean lag of almost ten years from age of onset to diagnosis. Most Tourette's patients score in the normal range of intellectual functioning upon psychological testing. Three times as many males as females are diagnosed as Tourette's. This ratio is roughly the same as that found for the diagnosis of MBD, autism, and other specific developmental disabilities.

There is no evidence of any underlying psychopathological disorders. For a time, Tourette's syndrome was attributed to a manifestation of a variety of psychopathological factors. Shapiro's studies confirmed the views of other investigators and concluded that common psychopathological factors or dynamic conflicts are not characteristic of Tourette's patients, appear unrelated to the etiology, and are not clin-ically significant for diagnosis or treatment (Shapiro et al., 1978).

In Shapiro's first sample of thirty-four patients in the New York City area, 67 percent had an Eastern European Jewish background. Investigators interpreted these data to be a result of a higher concentration of Jewish people in that geographic area. Two subsequent samples which represented different geographical areas yielded only slightly smaller percentages. However, there were only .5 percent blacks represented in the total sample. More studies including a wider geographic and more representative sampling are needed to confirm the initial data.

In attempting to determine other correlates of the Tourette's syndrome, investigations have yielded no relationships between (1) mother's age at child's birth, (2) history of abortions, (3) birth history, (4) birth order, (5) mental illness, or (6) social class. Although Tourette's syndrome does occur more frequently in families who have family histories of tics, the difference is not statistically significant when compared to families with no such histories.

Etiology

Hypotheses about the etiology of Tourette's have been classified as psychological, psychophysiological, and neurological (Shapiro et al., 1978). Within the psychological category, there are many divergent views ranging from the psychoanalyst who alludes to an unconscious conflict, to the behavior therapist who relies upon a learning-conditioning model (Yates, 1970). Data supporting these views have been evaluated as inadequate, at best, and emanating from studies utilizing a small number of patients.

A psychophysiological model presumes the presence of a vulnerable physical symptom, which when combined with certain psychological factors such as stress reacts via tics. The data supporting this approach are not conclusive and are highly speculative (Shapiro et al., 1978).

The most tenable view seems to be the neurological one, which interprets the Tourette's syndrome as a central nervous system (CNS) dysfunction in the basal ganglion area characterized by excessive amounts of dopamine. Clinical and experimental findings which support this position include (1) the presence of neurological abnormalities, that is, "soft signs" found in over 53 percent of the patients; (2) history of developmental problems; and (3) EEG abnormalities. In addition, compounds known to block dopamine receptors have been effective in the treatment of Tourette's (Snyder, Taylor, Coyle, and Meyerhoff, 1970). This had led to the "dopamine hypothesis."

Treatment

Psychotherapy, behavior therapy, and drug therapy have all been applied in the treatment of the Tourette's syndrome. Shapiro et al. (1978) summarized a number of reports on the use of verbal psychotherapy, psychoanalysis, and family therapy. They concluded that such approaches have not been shown to be effective. There is, however, reason to believe that family therapy focused on reducing guilt and disruptions brought about the presence of a Tourette's child would be an important adjunct to other therapies with the patient. Similarly, a child who has displayed Tourette's for several years will often have been the target of cruel jokes and criticisms. Assistance in coping with this and in the development of a positive "self-conception" would be useful.

Behavior therapy has been applied in many instances, most of which are summarized by Shapiro et al. (1978). The theoretical foundation for the application of behavior therapy was initially presented by Yates (1958). Massed practice, overcorrection, punishment, and reinforcement of incompatible behaviors are but a few of the procedures that have been applied with varying degrees of success. In general, the use of inadequate measurement procedures, short follow-up, and the lack of adequate control groups or conditions have typified many of the behavioral studies in this area (Hersen and Eisler, 1973). Shapiro et al. (1978) have concluded that behavior therapy yields 20 to 25 percent success, a percentage similar to that obtained by nonspecific or specific psychotherapy or other "psychological treatments" (p. 356). They also point out the superiority of haloperidol (Haldol) in eight studies in which the two treatments were compared. A similar conclusion appears to have been made by Yates (1970), who noted the advantage of Haldol over the "tedious procedures of massed practice".

Haldol appears to be the treatment of choice for the Tourette's syndrome (Stevens & Blackly, 1966; Shapiro and Shapiro, 1968; and Abuzzhad and Anderson, 1974). Approximately 68 percent of cases treated improve over the initial six months of treatment with up to 89 percent showing beneficial results overall. The effective dosage varies. The side effects include akathisia (feeling of restlessness, urgency to move), akinesia (loss of muscle control), gastrointestional upset, extra pyramidal effects, "Spaced-out" look, and appearance of depression. Cogentin and barbiturates have been used effectively to control side effects.

Treatment with Haldol is only a partial answer, as evidenced by its differential effectiveness depending on family history. Ninety-three percent of patients with a positive family history of Tourette's are successfully treated; 70 percent with a family history of tics; and 43 percent where neither appeared. (Tourette Syndrome Association Newsletter, 1979). The therapeutic value of several other agents, including pimozidle (orap), Lecithin, and chlorine, is under investigation.

Although cognitive impairment has not been found in laboratory studies of the effects of Haldol upon test performance, reduced school performance has been identified in many children. Deficits in time discrimination, information acquisition, and processing have been noted by Goldstone and Lhamon (1976). Werry and Aman (1975) have suggested that the optimal dose for maintaining maximum cognitive functioning may differ from that for behavior-social functioning.

CONCLUSION

Enuresis, encopresis, disorders of sleep, and the Tourette's syndrome have received less attention from psychologists than many of the more common behavioral disorders described in this book. The sequelae of these special disorders, however, are equally or more traumatic. Disruption of the family and of the child's adjustment is inevitable. Assessment and treatment are complex and often long-term. While not often presented to the psychologist as the main problem for treatment, the association with other disorders should be looked for and attended to.

REFERENCES

Abuzzhad, F. S. & Anderson, F. O. Gilles de la Tourette's Syndrome: Cross cultural analysis and treatment outcome. *Clinical Neurology and Neurosurgery*, 1974, *1*, 66–74.

Allen, R. B. Bladder capacity and awakening behavior in the treatment of enuresis. Unpublished dissertation, University of Vermont, 1976.

Anders, T. F. What we know about sleep disorders in children. *Medical Times*, 1976, *4*, 75–80.

Anthony, E. J. An experimental approach to the psychopathology of childhood encopresis. *British Journal of Medical Psychology*, 1957, *30*, 146–175.

Ashkenazi, Z. The treatment of encopresis using a discriminative stimulus and positive reinforcement. *Journal of Behavior Therapy and Experimental Psychiatry*, 1975, *6*, 155–157.

Atthowe, J. M. Nocturnal enuresis and behavior therapy: A functional analysis. In *Advances In Behavior Therapy*, R. B. Rubin, J. Henderson, H. Fensterheim, & L. P. Ullman (Eds.), New York: Academic Press, 1973, vol. 4, pp. 263–270.

Allyon, T., Simon, S. J., & Wildman, R. W. Instructions and reinforcement in the elimination of encopresis: A case study. *Journal of Behavior Therapy and Experimental Psychiatry*, 1975, *6*, 235–238.

Azrin, N. H. & Foxx, R. M. *Toilet training in less than a day*. New York: Pocket Books, 1976.

Azrin, N. H., Sneed, T. J., & Foxx, R. M. Dry bed: A rapid method of eliminating bedwetting (enuresis) of the retarded. *Behaviour Research and Therapy*, 1973, *11*, 427–434.

Azrin, N. H., Sneed, T. J., & Foxx, R. M. Dry–bed training: Rapid elimination of childhood enuresis. *Behaviour Research and Therapy*, 1974, *12*, 1–10.

Bach, R. & Moylan, J. M. Parents administered behavior therapy for an appropriate urination and encopresis: A case study. *Journal of Behavior Therapy and Experimental Psychiatry*, 1975, *6*, 239–241.

Bakwin, H. Enuresis in children. *The Journal of Pediatrics*, 1961, *58*(6), 806–819.

Battle, C. V. Sleep and sleep disturbances in young children. *Clinical Pediatrics*, 1970, 675–682.

Berg, I., & Jones, K. V. Functional fecal incontinence in children. *Arch. of Disease in Childhood*, 1964, *39*, 465–472.

Blackwell, B. & Currah, J. The pharmacology of nocturnal enuresis. In I. Kolvin, R. C. MacKeith, & S. R. Meadow (Eds.), *Bladder control and enuresis*. Philadelphia: W. B. Saunders, 1973.

Bollard, R. J. & Woodroffe, P. The effect of parent–administered dry–bed training on nocturnal enuresis in children. *Behaviour Research and Therapy*, 1977, *15*, 159–165.

Braughton, R. J. Sleep disorders: Disorders of arousal? *Science*, 1968, *159*, 1070–1078.

Campbell, M. R. Neuromuscular uropathy. In *Urology* (vol. 2) M. F. Campbell & T. H. Harrison, (Eds.), Philadelphia: W. B. Saunders, 1970.

Ciminero, A. R. & Doleys, D. M. Childhood enuresis: Considerations in assessment. *Journal of Pediatric Psychology*, 1976, *4*, 17–20.

Comly, H. H. Successful treatment of night terrors. *American Journal of Psychiatry*, 1975, *132*, 761.

Davidson, M. Constipation and fecal incontinence. In cf2Pediatric Clinics of North America, H. Bakwin, (Ed.) Philadelphia: W. B. Saunders, 1958.

Davidson, M. D., Kugler, M. M., & Bauer, C. H. Diagnosis and management in children with severe and protracted constipation and obstipation. *Journal of Pediatrics*, 1963, *62*, 261–266.

de Jonge, G. A. Epidemiology of enuresis: A survey of the literature. In *Bladder Control and Enuresis*, I. Kolvin, R. C. MacKeith, & S. R. Meadow, (Eds.), Philadelphia: J. B. Lippincott, 1973.

Doleys, D. M. Behavioral treatments for nocturnal enuresis in children: A review of the recent literature. *Psychological Bulletin*, 1977, *84*, 30–54.

Doleys, D. M. Assessment and treatment of enuresis and encopresis in children. In M. Hersen, R. Eisler, & P. Miller, (Eds.), *Progress in behavior modification*. New York: Academic Press, 1978.

Doleys, D. M. Assessment and treatment of childhood encopresis. In A. J. Finch & P. C. Kendall (Eds.), *Treatment and research in child psychopathology,* New York: Spectrum, 1979.

Doleys, D. M. Assessment and treatment of childhood enuresis. In A. J. Finch & P. C. Kendall (Eds.), *Treatment and research in child psychopathology,* New York: Spectrum, 1979.

Doleys, D. M. Encopresis. In J. Ferguson & C. D. Taylor, (Eds.), *Advances in behavioral medicine.* New York: Spectrum, 1979 (in press).

Doleys, D. M. & Arnold, S. Treatment of childhood encopresis. Full cleanliness training. *Mental Retardation,* 1975, *13,* 14–6.

Doleys, D. M., Ciminero, A. R., Tollison, J. W., Williams, C. L., & Wells, K. Dry bed training: A comparison. *Behavior Therapy,* 1977, *8,* 541–548.

Doleys, D. M., Schwartz, M., & Ciminero, A. R. Elimination problems. In *Behavioral assessment of childhood Disorders,* E. J. Mash & L. G. Terdal (Eds.) New York: Guilford Press 1980.

Edelman, R. F. Operant conditioning treatment of encopresis. *Journal of Behavior Therapy and Experimental Psychiatry,* 1971, *2,* 17–73.

Field, J. R., Corbin, K. B., Goldstein, N. P., & Klass, D. W. Gilles de la Tourette's Syndrome. *Neurology,* 1966, *16,* 453–462.

Feinberg, I. Effects of age on human sleep patterns. In A. Kales (Ed.), *Sleep physiology and pathology.* Philadelphia: J. B. Lippincott, 1969, pp. 39–52.

Finley, W. W., Besserman, R. L., Bennett, L. F., Clapp, R. K., & Finley, P. M. The effect of continuous, intermittent, and "placebo" reinforcement on the effectiveness of the conditioning treatment for enuresis nocturna. *Behaviour Research and Therapy,* 1973, *11,* 289–297.

Finley, W. W., Wansley, R. A., & Blenkarn, M. M. Conditioning treatment of enuresis using a 70 percent intermittent reinforcement schedule. *Behaviour Research and Therapy,* 1977, *15,* 419–425.

Finley, W. W. & Wansley, R. A. Use of intermittent reinforcement in a clinical–research program for the treatment of enuresis nocturna. *Journal of Pediatric Psychology,* 1976, *4,* 24–27.

Fisher, C. F., Kahn, E., Edwards, A., & Davis, D. M. A psychophysiological study of nightmares and night terrors: The suppression of stage four night terrors with diazepam. *Archives of General Psychiatry,* 1973, *28,* 252–259.

Freinden, W. & VanHandel, D. Elimination of serling in an elementary school child through application of aversive technique. *Journal of School Psychology,* 1970, *8,* 267–269.

Gavanski, M. Treatment of non–retentive secondary encopresis with imipramine and psychotherapy. *Canadian Medical Association Journal,* 1971, *104,* 227–231.

Gelber, H. & Meyer, V. Behavior therapy and encopresis: The complexities involved in treatment. *Behaviour Research and Therapy,* 1965, *2,* 227–231.

Gerrard, J. W. & Zaleski, A. Functional bladder capacities in children with enuresis and recurrent urinary infections. In L. D. Dickey (Ed.), *Clinical ecology.* Springfield, Ill.: Charles C. Thomas, 1976.

Goldstone, S. & Lhamon, W. T. The effects of haloperidol upon temperal inferinatier processing by patients with Tourette's Syndrome. *Psychopharmeologia,* 1976, *50,* 7–10.

Gould, J., Lee, A. R., James, O. S., Sander, L., Teager, H., & Fineberg, N. The sleep state characteristics of apnea during infancy. *Pediatrics,* 1977, *59,* 182–194.

Guilleminault, C. & Anders, T. F. Sleep disorders in children, Part II. I. Schulman (Ed.), *Advances in pediatrics.* Chicago: Year Book Medical Publishers, 1976, pp. 151–172.

Guilleminault, C., Eldridge, F. L., & Dement, W. C. Insomnia with sleep apnea: A new syndrome. *Science,* 1973, *181,* 856–858.

Harris, L. S. & Purohit, A. P. Bladder training and enuresis: A controlled trial. *Behaviour Research and Therapy,* 1977, *15,* 485–490.

Hauri, P. *The sleep disorders.* Kalamazoo, Mich.: Upjohn Company, 1977.

Hersen, M. and Eisler, R. M. Behavioral approaches to the study and treatment of psychogenic ties. *Genetic Psychology Monographs,* 1973, *87,* 289–312.

Hilburn, W. B. Encopresis in Childhood. *Journal of the Kentucky Medical Association,* 1968, *66,* 978.

Jackson, H. & Rawlins, M. D. The sleepless child. *British Medical Journal,* 1977, *2,* 509.

Jacobsen, A., Kales, J. D., & Kales, A. Clinical and electrophysiological correlates of sleep disorders in children. In A. Kales (Ed.). *Sleep: physiology and pathology.* Philadelphia: J. B. Lippincott, 1969, pp. 109–118.

Jehu, D., Morgan, T., Turner, R., & Jones, A. A controlled trial of the treatment of nocturnal enuresis in residential homes for children. *Behaviour Research and Therapy,* 1977, *15,* pp. 1–16.

Kales, A. & Kales, J. D. Sleep disorders. *New England Journal of Medicine,* 1974, *290,* 487–499.

Kales, A., Paulson, M. J., Jacobsen, A., & Kales, J. D. Somnambulism: Psychophysiological Correlates II: Psychiatric interviews, psychological testing and discussion. *Archives of General Psychiatry*, 1966, *14*, 595–604.

Kales, A., Kales, J. D., Jacobsen, A., Humphrey, D. O., & Soldatos, C. R. Effects of imipramine on enuretic frequency and sleep stages. *Pediatrics*, 1977, 60, 431–436.

Karacan, I., Ware, C., Moore, C. A., Dervent, B., & Williams, R. L. Disturbed sleep as a function of sleep apnea: Too much sleep but not enough. *Texas medicine*, 1977, *73*, 49–56.

Keehn, J. D. Brief case report: Reinforcement therapy of incontinence. *Behaviour Research and Therapy*, 1965, *2*, 239.

Kessler, S., Guilleminault, C., & Dement, W. C. A family study of 50 REM narcoleptics. *Acta Neurologica Scandinavica*, 1974, *50*, 503–512.

Kolvin, T., Tounch, J., Currah, J., Garside, R. F., Norlan, J., & Shaw, W. B. Enuresis: A descriptive analysis and a controlled trial. *Developmental Medicine and Child Neurology*, 1972, *14*, 715–720.

Labay, P. & Boyarsky, S. The pharmacology of imipramine and its mechanism of action on enuresis. *Archives of Physical Rehabilitation*, 1972, *53*, 584.

Levine, M. D. Children with encopresis: A descriptive analysis. *Pediatrics*, 1975, *56*, 412–416.

Lewis, J. A. Sleep and its disorders. *American Journal of EEG Technology*, 1974, *14*, 218–224.

Logan, D. L. & Gardner, D. G. Effective behavior modification for reducing chronic soiling. *American Annals of the Deaf*, 1971, *116*, 382–385.

Lovibond, S. H. & Coote, M. A. Enuresis. In C. G. Costello (Ed.), *Symptoms of psychopathology*. New York: John Wiley & Sons, 1970.

Lucas, A. R. Gilles de la Tourette's disease in children: Treatment with phenothiazine drugs. *American Journal of Psychiatry*, 1964, *121*, 606–608.

Lucas, A. R. Gilles de la Tourette's disease in children: Treatment with haloperidol. *American Journal of Psychiatry*, 1967, *124*, 146–149.

Lucas, A. R. A report of Gilles de la Tourette's disease in two succeeding generations. *Child Psychiatry and Human Development*, 1973, *3*, 231–233.

Lund, C. J. Types of urinary incontinence. In C. J. Lund, (Ed.), *Clinical Obstetrics and Gynecology*, New York: Harper & Row, 1963.

McTaggert A. & Scott, M. A review of twelve cases of encopresis. *Journal of Pediatrics*, 1959, *54*, 762–768.

Muellner, S. R. Development of urinary control in children: A new concept in cause, prevention, and treatment of primary enuresis. *Journal of Urology*, 1960a, *84*, 714–716.

Neale, D. H. Behavior Therapy and encopresis in children. *Behaviour Research and Therapy*, 1963, *1*, 139–149.

Meadow, R. Drugs and bedwetting. *Archives of Disease in Childhood*, 1974, *49*, 257–267.

Nisley, D. D. Medical overview of the management of encopresis. *Journal of Pediatric Psychology*, 1976, *4*, 33–34.

Pedrini, B. C. & Pedrini, D. T. Reinforcement procedures in the control of encopresis: A case study. *Psyc. Reports*, 1971, *28*, 937–938.

Pierce, C. M. Enuresis and encopresis. In A. M. Friedman, H. I. Kaplan, & B. J. Sadock (Eds.), *Comprehensive textbook of psychiatry II*. Baltimore: Williams and Wilkins, 1975.

Pinkerton, P. Psychogenic megacolon in children: The implications of bowel negativism. *Archives of Disease in Children*, 1958, *33*, pp. 371–380.

Plachetta, K. E. Encopresis: A case study utilizing contracting, scheduling, and self–charting. *Journal of Behavior Therapy and Experimental Psychiatry*, 1976, *7*, 195–197.

Powell, B. W. Sleep disorders in childhood. *Practitioner*, 1972, *208*, 198–202.

Ravitch, M. M. Pseudo Hirschsprung's disease. *Annals of Surgery*, 1958, *148*, 781–795.

Rechtschaflen, A. & Dement, W. C. Narolepsy and hypersomnia. In A. Kales, (Ed.), *Sleep physiology and pathology*. Philadelphia: J. B. Lippincott, 1969, 119–130.

Richardson, G. S., Carskadon, M. A., Flagg, W., Van Der Hood, S., Dement, W. C., & Miller, M.M. Excessive daytime sleepiness in man: Multiple sleep latency measurement in narcoleptics and control subjects. *EEG and Clinic Neurophysiology*, 1978, *45*, 621–627.

Rutter, M., Vule, W., & Graham, P. Enuresis and behavioural deviance: some epidemiological considerations. In I. Kolvin, R. C. MacKeith and S. R. Meadow (Eds.) *Bladder control and enuresis* Philadelphia: W. C. Saunders, 1973.

Silber, D. L. Encopresis: Discussion of etiology and management. *Clinical Pediatrics*, 1969, *8*, 225–231.

Shaffer, D. The association between enuresis and emotional disorder: a review of the literature. In I. Kolvin, R. C. MacKeith, & S. R. Meadow (Eds.). *enuresis* Philadelphia: W. B. Saunder, 1973.

Shapiro, A. K., Shapiro, E. Treatment of Gilles de la Tourette's Syndrome with haloperidol. *British Journal of Psychiatry*, 1968, *114*, 345–350.

Shapiro, A. K., Shapiro, E. S., Bruun, R. D.,

and Sweet, R. D. *Gilles de la Tourette Syndrome*. New York: Raven Press, 1978.

Snyder, S. H., Taylor, K. H., Cogle, J. T., & Meyerhoff, J. L. The role of brain dopamine in behavioral regulation and the actions of psychotropic drugs. *American Journal of Psychiatry*, 1970, *127*, 199–207.

Sperling, M. Dynamic considerations and treatment of enuresis. *Journal of American Acd. Child Psychiatry*, 1965, *4*, 19–31.

Starfield, B. & Mellits, E. D. Increase in functional bladder capacity and improvements in enuresis. *Journal of Pediatrics*, 1968, *72*, 483–487.

Stevens, J. R. & Blacly, P. H. Successful treatment of the maladic des tics. *American Journal of Diseases of Childhood*, 1966, *112*, 541–545.

Stevens, J. R. & Turner, R. K. A clinical trial of continuous, intermittent, and overlearning "bell–and–pad" treatments for nocturnal enuresis. *Behaviour Research and Therapy*, 1975, *13*, 281–293.

Stewart, M. A. Treatment of bedwetting. *Journal of the American Medical Association*, 1975, *232*, 281–283.

Sutter, F. D., Zurllich, C. W., Geagh, C. E., Pierson, D. J., & Weil, J. V. Progesterone for outpatient treatment of Pickwichian Syndrome. *Annals of Internal Medicine*, 1975, *83*, 476–479.

Taylor, P.D. & Tarner, R.K. A clinical trial of continuous, intermittent, and overbearing "bell–and–pad" treatment for nocturnal enuresis. *Behaviour Research and Therapy*, 1975, *13*, 218–293.

Tourette Syndrome Association Newsletter, Bayside New York: Tourette Syndrome Association, 1979.

Walker, C. E. Toilet training, enuresis, encopresis. In P.R. Magrad (Ed.), *Psychological management of pediatric problems* (Vol. 1). Baltimore: University Park Press, 1978.

Werry, J. S. & Aman, M. F. Methylphenidote and haloperidol in children. *Archives of General Psychiatry*, 1975, *32*, 790–795.

Wolters, W. H. G. A comparative study of behavioral aspects in encopretic children. *Psychotherapy and Psychosomatics*, 1974, *24*, 86–97.

Woodrow, K.M. Gilles de la Tourette's disease-a review. *American Journal of Psychiotry*, 1974, 131, 1000–1004.

Wright, L. Handling the encopretic child. *Professional Psychology*, 1973, *4*, 137–144.

Wright, L. Outcome of a standardized program for treating psychogenic encopresis. *Professional Psychology*, 1975, *6*, 453–456.

Wright, L. & Walker, C. E. Behavioral treatment of encopresis. *Journal of Pediatric Psychology*. 1976, *4*, 35–37.

Wright, L. & Walker, E. C. A simple behavioral treatment program for psychogenic encopresis. *Behaviour Research and Therapy*, 1978, *16*, 209–212.

Yates, A. J. The application of learning theory to the treatment of tics, *Journal of Abnormal and Social Psychology*, 1958, *56*, 175–182.

Yates, A. J. *Behavior Therapy*. New York: John Wiley, 1970.

Yates, A. J. Tics. In C. Castello (Ed.), *Symptoms of psychopathology*, New York: John Wiley, 1970.

Yeates, W. K. Bladder function in normal micturition. In I. Kolvin, R. C. MacKeith, & S. R. Meadow (Eds.), *Bladder control and enuresis*. Philadelphia: W. B. Saunders, 1973.

Young, G. C. The treatment of childhood encopresis by conditioned gastroibol reflex training. *Behavior Resarch and Therapy*, 1973, *11*, 499–503.

Young, I. L. & Goldsmith, A. D. Treatment of encopresis in a day treatment program. *Psychotherapy: Theory, Res. & Practice*, 1972, *9*, 231–235.

Young, G. C. & Morgan, R. T. T. Overlearning in the conditioning treatment of enuresis. *Behaviour Research and Therapy*, 1972, *10*, 419–420.

Zaleski, A., Gerrard, J. W., & Shokier, M. H. K. Nocturnal enuresis: The importance of a small bladder capacity. In I. Kolvin, R. C. MacKeith, & S. R. Meadow (Eds.), *Bladder control and enuresis*. Philadelphia: W. B. Saunders, 1973.

Zarcone, V. Narcolepsy. *New England Journal of Medicine*, 1973, *228*, 1156–1166.

CHAPTER 5

Psychophysiological Disorders in Childhood

THORNTON VANDERSALL, M.D.

I will begin this discussion of psychophysiological disorders in childhood with a definition of the term and its implications for an understanding of childhood disorder. This will be followed by a brief review of the concepts of "disorder" and mind-body interactions in the causation and course of certain disorders of childhood with demonstrable physical alterations in structure or function. A history of our thinking about psychosomatic concepts will follow in the belief that a loosely defined area of evolving and changing conceptualization can be better understood with knowledge of its history. Finally, I will consider some of the "classical psychosomatic disorders" as they manifest themselves in childhood in the light of current thinking regarding these disorders.

DEFINITION

A parsimonious approach to an understanding of the term, psychophysiological disorders, would simply state that the term implies there are emotional influences operative in manifestations of any bodily disorder. A more rigorous and far-reaching definition of the term, and one much more commonly used in recent past decades, would state that psychological factors are necessary, or perhaps sufficient, for the causation, intensification, or prolongation of the physical disorders included under

this category. A decision as to how appropriate the use of the terms is in referring to any given condition must involve both a consideration of the meaning of the term "disorders," as well as a consideration of how psychological factors are related to or influence physical dysfunctions, commonly referred to as the mind-body problem.

Woodruff, Goodwin, and Guze (1974, p. 185) referred to a disease or disorder as any condition associated with discomfort, disability, or increased liability to those states that is viewed by healers and the public as requiring professional intervention. They point out that social, economic, and theological issues, as well as biological, may be involved at one time or another in deciding what is regarded as a disease. In a brief history of psychosomatic medicine, Kaplan (1975) has traced the evolution of the mind-body problem as it relates to disease. Primitive society viewed disease as caused by spiritual powers, and diseases were fought by spiritual means. Beginning with Greek and Roman civilization, the healers focused upon the body, evidenced by Galen's humors, while paying attention to the interrelationships of the body with the soul. During the Middle Ages, mysticism and religion dominated to create a regressive approach that harkened back to earlier ideas. The Renaissance and the following centuries through the nineteenth century focused increasingly, and with greater detail, upon the body alone in the causation and treatment of disease. Indeed, fascination with new-found understanding of body structure and function to an extent that excluded adequate considerations of social and emotional influences in disease process. Only in the twentieth century have we returned to a more holistic model that recognizes multiple causes of disorders and attempts to understand the relationships between mind and body in these disorders, as well as comprehending social and environmental influences on disease processes.

RECENT EVOLUTION

Beginning with its introduction by Heinroth in 1818, the term psychosomatic has served as an identifying label for this group of disorders and as a term implying interactions between mind and body. The term somatopsychic was also introduced in the early 1800s to indicate that bodily disorders could, in turn, influence emotional processes and responses. In the late 1950s, the American Psychiatric Association, in its classification of disorders, replaced the term psychosomatic with the term psychophysiologic. It was reasoned that psychosomatic implied a dualistic and separatist idea, such as was found in the older mind-body arguments, while the term psychophysiologic was believed to represent a simpler statement regarding the influence of psychological factors on bodily processes. However, as Sheehan and Hackett (1978) have pointed out, the term psychosomatic persists in current literature and may still deserve usage as a less cumbersome and a well-understood term.

At the beginning of theorizing, psychosomatic disorders were considered as involving those body systems that are under the control of the autonomic nervous system. This served as a differentiating factor from conversion reactions which usually involve the central nervous system innervation of skeletal muscle structures. We now recognize that neuro-endocrine and auto-immune systems play a crucial role in many psychosomatic disorders, so that the autonomic nervous system distinction is

overly simplistic and misleading. At the same time, however, it should be recognized that the early descriptions of conversion reactions by Freud (1905) were epochal in resolving the mind-body split and directing attention to the interrelationships that we consider in the psychophysiological disorders. In addition to Freud's unifying concepts, the work of Cannon and Selye in elaborating the body's response to any stress is also credited with a seminal and crucial influence on the development of our ideas about psychosomatic disorders.

Psychoanalytic theoriests such as Dunbar (1947) and Alexander (1948) exercised a massive influence over psychosomatic thinking in the 1930s and 1940s. Dunbar described specific personality profiles that were characteristic for the individual and determined how they organized and handled psychic energies. Dunbar believed that each psychosomatic disorder was associated with a specific personality organization.

Alexander elaborated an "organ specificity" theory that held that specific types of stresses evoked specific conflicts in individuals which, in turn, led to changes in specific organ systems. Thus the kind of stress experienced would determine the particular organ system that would be affected. The Alexander group saw the physical disorder as a manifestation of the biological component of the psychological conflict (Michels, 1978). Their group elaborated the seven "classical" psychosomatic disorders, and the attention of psychosomaticists was focused to a large extent upon these disorders for several decades. The seven disorders are hypertension, asthma, neurodermatitis, duodenal ulcer, rheumatoid arthritis, thyrotoxicosis, and ulcerative colitis.

While Alexander and his group were utilizing Freudian psychoanalytic theories as the springboard for their theorizing and research, others, such as Wolff (1950), were relying more on the background of Cannon and attempting to study the adaptive reactions of the body to stress. This group could be described as a nonspecific group in contrast to the specificity, championed by Dunbar and Alexander. Wolff believed that the psychosomatic disorder was a non-specific response to a nonspecific stress, having no particular psychic or symbolic meaning and serving only adaptive and reparative functions for the organism.

Certain later psychoanalytic theorists, such as Sperling (1946), postulated a potent deterministic role to psychological factors in the etiology of psychosomatic disorders. In her work with children with ulcerative colitis, Sperling focused upon primitive aggressive impulses and the discharge of those impulses through the symptoms. The bleeding in the child with ulcerative colitis was equated with the elimination of the hated and incorporated mother. The physical disorder served as the symbolic expression of the psychological conflict or emotion. The belief in such a literal translation of psychological conflict into physical symptoms led to such an intensification of psychoanalytic treatment, together with an almost concurrent avoidance of more conventional medical treatments, that the wisdom of such an extreme position was questioned not only by internists but also by some psychoanalysts (Karush, 1977).

No review of theoretical positions regarding psychosomatic disorders would be complete without some attention to the contribution of learning theory. Both respondent and operant conditioning may be viewed as changing visceral responses. Lachman (1972) attempted to create a theoretical framework that would characterize all psychosomatic disorders as learned responses. He began with the seemingly acceptable position that emotional behavior can be defined as "extensive and often pronounced patterns of reaction in structures innervated by the autonomic nervous system in response to stimulation of receptors." While there are situations wherein some nervous system responses to stimulation may be beneficial (i.e. increased pulse rate in shock, recoil reactions to flying objects, and so forth), when the stimulation is intense, certain psychosomatic "reactions," such as asthmatic attacks or transient rises in blood pressure, may be produced. If the stimulation continues in an intense way, Lachman postulated, a permanent structural change can be produced—the psychosomatic disease.

Lachman has labeled his theory of the causation of psychosomatic disorders the Autonomic Learning Theory. It states that "psychosomatic manifestations result from frequent or prolonged or intense implicit reactions elicited via stimulation of receptors."

Lachman elaborated and attempted to support his theory by calling attention to various ways that learning principles may operate within the framework of his theory. Stimulus-generalization learning can explain a new stimulus, associated in time or contiguity with the original stimulus, later eliciting the response independent of the original stimulus. Part of the original stimulus may have eliciting power at a later time. Symbolic equivalents (words) may replace actual events as elicitors of the response.

A lengthy critique of Lachman's theory is not appropriate here. However, it should be noted that his theory that prolonged intense stimulation may lead to structural disorder has not been substantiated in a physiological laboratory. Current neuroendocrine research, to mention only one frontier of understanding psychosomatic disorders, is revealing something of the great complexity of interactions in these disorders, the recognition of which argues against the acceptance of a simple explanation for the phenomena.

Learning models have been useful in understanding the causes of psychosomatic disorders, also providing some approaches to treatment of these disorders. Operant conditioning approaches have been used for centuries as an approach to debilitating, involuntary behavior patterns. More recently, many have recognized that techniques may be available to control or modulate unwelcome visceral responses. The use of operant conditioning to control visceral responses in adults has been facilitated by the use of devices that provide prompt measurement of internal biological functions—biofeedback. Miller (1978) pointed out that while the therapeutic effectiveness of feedback has not been definitely proved, there are many indications that devices may be helpfully used by intelligent and motivated individuals to gain a seemingly improved control over visceral responses.

Since motivation and understanding appear to be critical factors determing effectiveness of feedback, it is understandable that little work with children has been reported. Miller drew attention to a study that reported failure to learn heart rate change techniques in very young children and another study that found asthmatic children could increase respiratory flow rates by concentrating on frontalis muscle relaxation. Biofeedback techniques have been used in a number of conditions that occur in children, such as bruxism, enuresis, and encopresis. The alarm-ringing wet pad is familiar to everyone who deals with enuretic children. This might be considered as a biofeedback apparatus that may be successful with motivated children. (For a further discussion of this device and modifications of it, see Chapter 4). Miller notes some of the difficulties in evaluating the usefulness of biofeedback, citing the high natural recovery rate, the selection process already involved in those who present to use the techniques, and the placebo effect from instrumentation.

In a recent commentary, Knapp (1975) noted that classical conditioning has not been established as a necessary or sufficient cause of any major psychosomatic state. On the other hand, operant mechanisms may be well suited to adaptive ends and may yet be shown to play some role in the evolution of the complex states that are psychophysiologic disorders.

Lipowski (1977), discussing current theories of psychosomatic disorders, stressed the multidetermined nature of somatic functions. He noted that the present phase is marked by less emphasis on individual psychodynamics and more on responses to environmental stimuli. A social and ecological dimension has been added. Mirsky (1958) and Engel (1955) provided excellent examples of this current, holistic approach.

Mirsky, in his studies of duodenal ulcer, drew attention to a hereditary predisposition to the disorder existing by virtue of high pepsinogen secretory capacities in certain individuals.

A subset of these individuals, who have a personality style, involving a need for continuing dependency gratifications

without the ability to acknowledge the same, provide the second step in a pattern of causality that is completed when some particular dependent gratification becomes lost to them. Thus the individual (let us assume a new father) develops an active duodenal ulcer for the first time when his wife's attention is diverted from him to their newborn child.

Engel (1955) has further elaborated on object loss as a final precursor to the development of acute symptomatology in states such as ulcerative colitis. These theories take into account hereditary dispositions, evolved personality patterns of adaptiveness or maladaptiveness, cultural and ecological stresses, family dynamics, as well as the individual's inner psychic structure with its array of needs and wishes, as all being contributory in some way to the presence or absence of a particular disorder at any given time. Engel (1977) has recently summarized this general systems theory perspective in a synthetic article in *Science,* calling for the creation of a new biopsychosocial model as a blueprint for research, teaching, and action in health care.

ULCERATIVE COLITIS

Ulcerative colitis has been classified as one of the classic psychophysiological disorders. This disorder, which commonly begins in childhood and adolescence, is one of the major subgroups of inflammatory bowel disease. These disorders, of unknown cause, produce inflammatory and destructive changes of the intestinal tract. The three major subdivisions of inflammatory bowel disease are regional enteritis (Crohn's disease), granulomatous colitis, and ulcerative colitis. Regional enteritis is primarily a disease of the small intestine; ulcerative colitis of the large intestine, while granulomatous disease can be found in both the large and small intestine and, when involving only the small intestine, is usually referred to as Crohn's disease. In granulomatous disease, the inflammatory process involves the entire wall of the gut and is much more extensive and severe than the changes found in ulcerative colitis, where pathology is generally confined to the inner lining of the gut and consists of inflammatory changes followed by ulceration. The major symptoms of ulcerative colitis are pain, diarrhea, and bleeding from the intestinal tract.

There is a long history of observation and interest surrounding the emotional problems of patients with ulcerative colitis. Murray (1930) first reported a relationship between emotional factors and the onset of symptoms in patients with colitis, symptoms appearing when patients were faced with difficult emotional problems. It is interesting that the four cases Murray originally reported all first experienced symptoms as they contemplated marriage. In 1938, Wittkower attempted to classify the personality organization of 40 patients with colitis in England through intensive interviews. Thirty-seven of these patients were described as having "psychological abnormalities or definite psychological disorders well beyond the range of normal." Wittkower found that while the psychological background is not necessarily the cause of the obscure disorder—evidence has been given to demonstrate that ulcerative colitis is a disease of the mentally ill or maladjusted. Alexander and French (1940) spoke of the dependent needs of patients with colitis and characterized them as individuals who "do not receive from others what they believe they should." They describe the diarrhea as a wish for restitution and giving, as well as an aggressive expression. Diarrhea was equated with a statement such as, "I have the right to take and demand, for I always give sufficiently." Alexander and French thus viewed the intestinal tract as particularly well suited for the expression of psychological conflicts around giving and receiving, and their writings implied that the selection of the intestinal tract as a site of physiological disorder in these particular individuals was specifically psychologically determined.

Sperling (1946) went further in her ideas about specificity, believing that not only the selection of the system (gastrointestinal tract) was psychologically determined and mediated, but also the end organ changes (bleeding) within that system were psychologically determined. Karush (1975) has gone so far as to characterize Sperling as believing that the extent of bleeding in colitis patients was directly related to the degree of their own unconscious rage toward objects.

Engel (1955) has written extensively about many cases of ulcerative colitis. He viewed the bleeding episodes as tending to occur at times of disruption in human relationships when the patients experience a loss and cannot accomplish the work of grief, being left with a sense of hopelessness and helplessness. Engel admitted in his writings that he could not explain the choice of organ system for an expression of this type of grief and could not explain the intervening mechanisms between the psychological experience of loss and the physiological changes represented in a psychophysiological disorder. He thus retreated considerably from the specificity of such earlier workers as Alexander and Sperling.

Ulcerative colitis, together with asthma, probably has the richest literature about children with a psychophysiological disorder. Prugh (1951) attempted to demonstrate specific correlations between exacerbations of gastrointestinal symptoms and various types of emotional stress experienced by children. He was not able to establish the correlation in all cases, but where it was observed, he found it to be associated with emotions of fear or grief. In this study he characterized the parents as rigid and inconsistent, and he noted that the children were passive and overly dependent on the parental figures, particularly the mother.

Finch and Hess (1962) wrote about 17 children with ulcerative colitis. They found dominating mothers and passive, ineffectual fathers. Again, the children were described as dependent and constricted in their personality pattern. They, too, were unable to demonstrate a reason for the choice of the gastrointestinal tract as a vehicle for the expression of emotional conflict. Both the Prugh (1951) study and Finch and Hess (1962) tend to be somewhat impressionistic. Other reports of ulcerative colitis in children (Hijmans and Enzer, 1962) were not able to demonstrate significant emotional factors that influence or precede the onset of symptoms in any significant number of childhood cases.

In summary, the literature on ulcerative colitis in childhood reveals that almost invariably one finds other family members affected with serious bowel disease, suggesting a strong genetic-constitutional predisposition to the disorder. Psychopathological family dynamics may or may not be present. When difficulty is found, it tends to manifest itself in an emotional unavailability of the father to the patient and an overly close tie between the mother and the patient. The personalities of the children with ulcerative colitis showed an unusually large percentage of passive, minimally communicative, and dependent children who had difficulty dealing appropriately with emotions of anger and rage. However, the literature does not support any distinct association between a specific personality profile and the presence of colitis. While some exacerbations or attacks of the disorder appear to be related to object loss, this finding is not consistent, and the overall literature cannot support a theory of organ specificity wherein the intestinal tract would serve as the system selected to express emotions that center about object loss and its attendant emotions. The only safe assumptions regarding colitis is that we do not know its cause, and we are unable to determine whether the dependent posture of the child with ulcerative colitis, together with the family interactions that tend to be observed, is part of the emotional pathology that causes the disease or is a manifestation of the emotional posture that results from this chronic disorder.

My personal experience with children who have ulcerative colitis has led me to be careful and parsimonious in thinking about these disorders. Experience with a large number of patients with colitis cannot substantiate that psychological problems are either necessary or sufficient to produce the disorder of ulcerative colitis in childhood. Adaptation to this disorder seems to vary with the severity of the physical problems and the adaptive skills of the patient as well as with the appropriateness of supports from the family and other help-

ers. There are instances where physical impairment clearly produces a stress that impairs adaptation. At other times, individuals with colitis may undertake stressful life events successfully without exacerbating the disease. Attacks of bleeding, diarrhea, and pain may appear when the environment and the psychological adaptation of the child appear to be quite optimal and relatively conflict free. There were very few instances where stress could be found to correlate with exacerbations of the process. Psychological factors are as important in this disorder as they are in any other serious physical disorder. Children with ulcerative colitis should be approached with the same openminded, fact-finding approach we would use with any other patient or client in the belief that the findings regarding these individuals' intrapsychic operations will be as varied as those of any other person who consults us.

ASTHMA

Asthma, along with ulcerative colitis, is one of the two common psychophysiological disorders beginning in and observed during childhood. Asthma is defined as a diffuse obstructive disease of the airways in which chemical, allergic, infectious, auto-immune, and psychological factors may play varying and significant roles in causation. The same paradigm that was used for an understanding of ulcerative colitis in childhood can be used to organize our thinking about asthma. While the interrelationship of mind and body in the production of disease has been a concern to man for centuries, during most of the nineteenth century conceptual models were used that viewed disease as a physical dysfunction of the body due in almost all instances to some foreign, invading agent. In the twentieth century, recognizing the power of the mind on bodily processes, the early psychosomaticists began to elaborate specific ways in which the mind exerted this influence. As it was in ulcerative colitis, in asthma the initial hypothesis was that some specific personality profile would be associated with the development of asthma. Other hypotheses predicted that specific intrapsychic conflicts would lead to asthma because the respiratory organs were uniquely suited through their functioning to dramatize and symbolize these particular conflicts. Most observers and workers, finding themselves unable to support concepts of such specificity, moved toward attempts to characterize the types of conflicts that might be found generally in groups of asthmatics. Else, they distinguished between those groups of asthmatics where psychological factors seem to play a significant role and those groups of asthmatics were psychological factors might play minor or only secondary roles in causation of intensification of the symptoms.

Gerard (1948), writing in the early Alexander and French work, spoke of the overanxiety and lack of self-confidence manifested by children with asthma and the parents' overprotective attitude. The attack was seen as a reaction to the danger of separation or rupture of this overt close tie. As Egan (1978) has stressed, the threat of an impending separation is fundamentally different from anxiety about being separated. Thus, it was not viewed as incongruous that fears of separation might precipitate attacks, while actual separation was observed to alleviate attacks. During this early formulating period, Sperling intensely observed a number of asthmatic children in and out of hospital settings—just as she had done with children with ulcerative colitis. The hypothesis she formulated about these children at that time has been maintained, defended by her up to the present. In a more recent article (1968), she clearly ennunciated her ideas that a specific quality in the relationship between the mother and the child, the "psychosomatic type" of relationship, was necessary for the development of the symptom in the constitutionally predisposed child. Sperling characterized the "psychosomatic type" of relationship as one in which the child is rejected by his mother only when the child is healthy and evidenced strivings of independence. Conversely, the child is rewarded for being sick and helpless by virtue of the care and attention given at that time. Sperling observed that the child's illness was compliance with the mother's unconscious wishes and her need for con-

trol of the child, who in illness became dependent upon her. The aggression and rebelliousness that the child experienced by this maternal control were not expressed overtly but were discharged through the somatic symptoms. Such formulations led to the characterization of the asthmatic wheezing of the child as a "cry for help."

Others, such as Jessner (1955) and her group in Boston, echoed these ideas by speaking about asthma in the child as resulting from a number of influences, such as allergic constitution, early respiratory infections, ordinal position (first borns predominating), and special emotional conflicts of the mother relating to her own struggles about dependence-independence with her own mother. This same group (Long, Lamont, Whipple, Bandler, Blom, Burgin, and Jessner, 1958) experimented in an attempt to determine whether the child's improvement, separated from the parent, was due to removal from the allergen producing the disorder, or separation from the parent and the attendant emotional conflicts. Nineteen children with asthma with a history of strongly positive skin tests to house dust were hospitalized to separate them from the parents. When free of asthmatic symptoms, they were sprayed with house dust. None of the children responded with wheezing, leading the group to conclude that emotional factors must be predominant in the particular group they sampled.

A large body of work with asthmatic children over the last decade has been directed at understanding the effects of separation of asthmatic children from their parents. The Jewish National Home for Asthmatic Children in Denver and several other institutions have treated children with a combination of pharmacologic and psychologic approaches after removal of the children from their homes and parents. Purcell et al. (1961) in Denver have made many contributions to our understanding of the effects of the "parentectomy." They divided asthmatic children into a rapidly remitting group (RR) and a steroid-dependent (SD) group. As the titles suggest, the RR group referred to children who rapidly improved and remained symptom-free after separation from their parents. The SD group, on the other hand, required continuous maintenance with steroids for symptom control. Psychological determinants played a greater role in the RR group than in the SD group. Chemical and allergic factors were believed to predominate in symptom production in the SD group. In a later study to further distinguish between the effects of allergens and parent-child psychological conflicts in the production of symptoms (Purcell, Brady, Chai, Maser, Molk, Gordon, and Means, 1969), the Purcell group kept children in their own homes with alternate caretakers and removed the parents. Thus, the allergic factors were presumed to be the same. With the removal of the parents, the RR group of children demonstrated an improvement in symptoms even though they remained in their own homes.

A number of studies on adults with asthma characterize the disorder as multidetermined. A generalized abnormality in the function of adrenergic receptors has been demonstrated in both child and adult asthmatics (Elliot, 1975). While the possibility exists that such abnormalities may be the result of the common treatment of asthma with adrenergic agents, there are increasing suggestions that some difference in biochemical reactivity may characterize the entire asthmatic population.

In a review of the work done by their group and others, Stein (1976) has called attention to many indicators of the ways in which psychosocial factors influence resistance to infection and neoplasia—as well as immune responses. He acknowledged that the physiologic mechanisms that mediate these responses need further clarification. He directed particular attention to the influence of the hypothalmus on immune responses in an attempt to provide some detail regarding the specific physiology of the hypothalmus in its presumed mediating role between psychosocial influences and immune responses such as the hypersensitivity reaction that characterizes much asthma.

Animals with hypothalamic lesions are protected against the anaphylactic reactions and bronchospasm that are, to a lesser degree, part of all asthmatic attacks. It is apparent that we are only at the threshold of understanding the ways in which psychosocial factors, constitutional variations, and biochemical factors interact to produce the states we call psychosomatic disorders.

The role of learning and conditioning in the production of symptoms was illuminated in a study by Luparello, Lyons, Bleecker, and McFadden (1968). They measured airway resistance in 40 asthmatic subjects who were led to believe that they were participating in a study that would measure the constricting effect on the airway of various pollutants. Rather than nebulizing an allergen or agent that might produce attacks, as the subjects expected, they were subjected to the nebulization of plain salt water. Nineteen of the 40 individuals responded with a marked increase in airway resistance, and 12 developed full-blown asthmatic attacks. Each of these asthmatic attacks were rapidly reversed by the introduction of another nebulizer that they were told contained a drug known to relieve attacks when in fact the nebulizer also contained only salt water. Forty control subjects with no airway disease showed no reaction whatsoever or change in airway resistance to the nebulized salt water solution.

Thus, with asthma as with ulcerative colitis, we are faced with a condition that is multidetermined, and the role of each determinant varies in importance from case to case. Effective treatment in many or most cases will benefit from teamwork approach. Some individuals will require extensive medical management but will benefit from psychological intervention and support. Some will appear to respond simply to environmental manipulation, whether that involves changes in allergens only or an actual separation from parents. In other situations, improvement can be produced simply through psychological attention to the child and the family.

OTHER PSYCHOPHYSIOLOGICAL DISORDERS

There are five additional psychophysiological disorders in the "classical" group. In addition to ulcerative colitis and bronchial asthma, this group includes hypertension, peptic ulcer, rheumatoid arthritis, thyrotoxicosis, and neurodermatitis. It was at one time postulated that in each of these disorders psychological factors would be necessary and sufficient for the production of the disease. With the single exception of rheumatoid arthritis, which does manifest itself in a juvenile form, all of the remaining classic psychosomatic disorders are rare in children. Attempts to link specific personality profiles with specific disorders, as well as attempts to characterize the physiologic disorder as the end point of a specific intrapsychic conflict, have been as unsuccessful in these disorders as in asthma and colitis. There are also many parallels in the history of our understanding of all these disorders. For these reasons I will not discuss in detail the five remaining disorders.

Discussions of psychophysiological disorders in childhood usually include references to disorders of eating and elimination. A major eating disorder of great current interest, anorexia nervosa, is covered in another chapter of this book. Obesity represents the other extreme in manipulation of the appearance of the body. It has been considered together with anorexia by some authors (Bruch, 1973) in the belief that a similar psycho-endocrine axis may be involved in both disorders, and that both disorders may eventuate from similar personality conflicts worked out on opposing poles of a common adaptive axis. For this reason, obesity will not be considered in this discussion. (Enuresis and encopresis are discussed in the chapter on special disorders.)

There are additional disorders that occur in childhood, often included in reviews such as this. In the interest of brevity, however, headache, psychogenic pain, accident proneness, and diabetes will not be discussed here. Some writers (e.g., Kolb, 1977) have been so inclusive as to describe psychophysiological disorders to include all disturbances of the organs of internal economy, all disturbances of instinctual functions, and all disturbances involving the body image as a whole. While there is conceptual justification for such a potentially broad-based stance, in that physio-

logical and psychological processes are involved in every human disorder, I believe a case might also be made for limiting consideration of psychophysiological disorders to a small number of situations in which a definite disease process exists that involves both functional and structual changes and in which psychological factors would play a necessary, if not sufficient, role in causation.

It is perhaps in the belief that we cannot comfortably define any disease under that definition, given our present state of knowledge, that the new third edition of the Diagnostic and Statistical Manual of Mental Disorders, prepared by the American Psychiatric Association, does not include in the major descriptive group, a section on psychophysiological disorders. DSM-III approaches this group of disorders by creating two categories in a section entitled, *Other Disorders*. Thus, following specification of the physical disorder, the diagnostician may state whether psychological factors *probably* affect the physical disorder mentioned or psychological factors *definitely* affect the physical disorder described. Many are complaining about the "loss" of the psychosomatic disorders from the psychological lexicon. However, the honesty and rigor involved in determining *whether* psychological factors influence physical disorders may provide, at this stage of our understanding, a simple reentry point for the psychologist in the search for that complex answer as to the *ways* in which psychosocial factors influence physical disease processes.

CONCLUSION

This discussion of psychophysiological disorders has focused upon the two most common, classic psychophysiological disorders of childhood. The changes in our understanding of these disorders over the last half-century have been reviewed in an attempt to demonstrate how this represents our current approach to age-old problems involving mind-body dualism, the concept of disease, and the difficulties with reductionistic models. It is proposed that the disorders described here can best be understood by utilizing an open-minded and hard-headed approach that recognizes multiple, interacting contributants in the initiation, perpetuation, and amelioration of these disorders (Lipowski, 1968; Engel, 1977).

REFERENCES

Alexander, F. & French, T. M. *Studies in psychosomatic medicine*, New York: Ronald Press, 1948.

American Psychiatric Association Task Force on Nomenclature and Statistics. *Diagnostic and statistical manual of mental disorders* (3rd ed.) Washington, D.C., 1980.

Bruch, H. *Eating Disorders*. New York: Basic Books, Inc., 1973.

Dunbar, F. *Emotions and bodily changes*. New York: Columbia University Press, 1954.

Egan, J. Asthma: Psychological treatment. In B. B. Wolman, J. Egan, & A. O. Ross (Eds.) *Handbook of treatment of mental disorders in childhood and adolescence*, Englewood Cliffs, N.J.: Prentice-Hall, Inc., 1978.

Ellis, E. F. Asthma. In Vaughan, V. C., III, McKay, R. J., & Nelson, W. E. (Eds.) *Nelson testbook of pediatrics* (10th ed.), Philadelphia: W. B. Saunders Co., 1975.

Engel, G. L. Studies of ulcerative colitis; III, The nature of the psychologic processes. *American Journal of Medicine*, 1955, *19*, 231–256.

Engel, G. L. The need for a new medical model: A challenge for biomedicine. *Science*, 1977, *196*, 129–136.

Finch, S. M. & Hess, J. H. Ulcerative colitis in children. *American Journal of Psychiatry*, 1962, *118*, 819–826.

Freud, S. (Fragment of an analysis of a case of hysteria) *Standard edition of the complete psychological works of Signumd Freud* (Vol. 7), J. Strachey, Ed. and trans. London: Hogarth Press, 1953. (originally published, 1905.)

Gerard, M. W. Bronchial asthma in children. In F. Alexander & French, T. M., (Eds.) *Studies in psychosomatic medicine*. New York: Ronald Press, 1948.

Hijmans, J. C. & Enzer, N. B., Ulcerative colitis in childhood. *Pediatrics*, 1962, *29*, 389–403.

Jessner, L., Lamont, J., Long, R., Rollins, N., Whipple, B., & Prentice, N. Emotional impact of nearness and separation for the asthmatic child and his mother. In *The Psychoanalytic Study of the Child*, Vol. 10, New York: International Universities Press, 1955.

Kaplan, H. I. History of psychophysiological medicine. In A. M. Freedman, H. I. Ka-

plan, & B. J. Sadock (Eds.) *Comprehensive textbook of psychiatry*, (2nd ed.). Baltimore: Williams & Wilkins Co., 1975.

Karush, A. & Daniels, G. E., Flood, C., O'Connor, J. F. *Psychotherapy in chronic ulcerative colitis*. Philadelphia: W. B. Saunders Co., 1977.

Knapp, P. H. Current theoretical concepts in psychosomatic medicine. In A. M. Freedman, H. I. Kaplan, & B. J. Sadock (Eds.) *Comprehensive textbook of psychiatry* (2nd ed.). Baltimore: Williams & Wilkins Co., 1975.

Kolb, L. C. *Modern clinical psychiatry*, (9th ed.). Philadelphia: W. B. Saunders Co., 1977.

Lachman, S. J. *Psychosomatic disorders: A behavioristic interpretation*. New York: John Wiley & Sons, Inc., 1972.

Lipowski, Z. J. Review of consultation psychiatry and psychosomatic medicine. *Psychosomatic Medicine*, 1968, *30*, 395–422.

Lipowski, Z. J. Psychosomatic medicine in the seventies, *American Journal of Psychiatry*, 1977, *134*, 233–244.

Long, R. T., Lamont, J. H., Whipple, B., Bandler, L., Blom, G. E., Burgin, L., & Jessner, L. A psychosomatic study of allergic and emotional factors in children with asthma. *American Journal of Psychiatry*, 1958, *114*, 890–899.

Luparelllo, T., Lyons, H. A., Bleecker, E. R., & McFadden, E. R., Jr. Influences of suggestion on airway reactivity in asthmatic subjects. *Psychosomatic Medicine*, 1968, *30*, 819–825.

Michels, R. Personal communication, Sept. 5, 1978.

Miller, N.E. Biofeedback and visceral learning. *Annual Review of Psychology*. 1978, *29*, 373–404.

Mirsky, I. A. Physiologic, psychologic, and social determinants in the etiology of duodenal ulcer. *American Journal of Digestive Diseases*, 1958, 3 (New Series) 285–314.

Murray, C. D. Psychogenic factors in the etiology of ulcerative colitis and bloody diarrhea. *American Journal of the Medical Science*, 1930, *180*, 239–248.

Prugh, D. G. The influence of emotional factors on the clinical course of ulcerative colitis in children. *Gastroenterology*, 1951, *18*, 339–354.

Purcell, K., Bernstein, L., & Bukantz, S. C. A preliminary comparison of rapidly remitting and persistently steroid-dependent asthmatic children. *Psychosomatic Medicine*, 1961, *23*, 305–310.

Purcell, K., Brady, K., Chai, H., Maser, J., Molk, L., Gordon, N., & Means, J. The effect on asthma in children of experimental separation from the family. *Psychosomatic Medicine*, 1969, *31*, 144–164.

Sheehan, D. V. & Hackett, T. P. Psychosomatic disorders. In A. M. Nicholi, Jr. (Ed.) *The Harvard guide to modern psychiatry*. Cambridge, Mass.: Belknap/Harvard Press, 1978.

Sperling, M. Psychoanalytic study of ulcerative colitis in children. *Psychoanalytic Quarterly*, 1946, *15*, 302–329.

Sperling, M. Asthma in children; an evaluation of concepts and therapies. *Journal of the American Academy of Child Psychiatry*, 1968, *7*, 44-58.

Stein, M., Schiavi, R. C., & Camerino, M. Influence of brain and behavior on the immune system. *Science*, 1976, *191*, 435–440.

Wittkower, E. Ulcerative colitis; personality studies. *British Medical Journal*, 1938, *2*, 135–136.

Wolff, H. G. & Itase, C. C. *Life stress and bodily disease.* Baltimore: Williams & Wilkins Co., 1950.

Woodruff, R. A., Jr., Goodwin, D. W., & Guze, S. B. *Psychiatric diagnosis.* New York: Oxford Press, 1974.

CHAPTER *6*

Psychotic Disorders of Childhood*

DENNIS C. RUSSO, Ph.D.
AND
CREIGHTON D. NEWSOM, Ph.D.

Frequently, professionals engaged in work with the abnormal child will encounter clients whose behavioral disturbance is profound, with pervasive deficits in language, social behavior, affect, play and cognitive development. As a diagnostic class, these children are often labeled psychotic, schizophrenic, or autistic and present to the clinician a difficult series of decisions regarding treatment and prognosis.

The psychotic disorders of children represent an area rich in controversy regarding etiological speculation as well as the proper conceptualization for and the procedures of treatment. In this chapter we will review psychotic disorders, as they are manifested in children. As an initial step a study of the historical roots, theoretical and diagnostic classifications, and demographics of these disorders will be undertaken. From this study, two general epistemologies emerge: inductive and deductive. These methods for the study of psychotic disorders will be compared with respect to their ability to differentiate the behavioral characteristics of these disorders reliably, to provide a probable course

*Manuscript preparation supported by Project #917, Maternal and Child Health Service, U. S. Department of Health Education and Welfare, and the resources of the Behavioral Medicine Center, Department of Psychiatry and Behavioral Sciences, Johns Hopkins University School of Medicine.

of treatment on the basis of this diagnosis, and to serve as a foundation for continued research into treatment. Lastly, a survey of current behavioral treatment strategies and research will provide for the evaluation of the prognosis of the psychotic child from this perspective.

HISTORICAL ROOTS

As an area of study, the concept of psychosis in childhood is a newcomer relative to attempts to classify and describe adult psychopathology. There are several reasons for this delay and they were characteristic not only of historical psychiatric endeavor, but also highly dependent upon the development of scientific advances in medicine and child development.

The development of theoretical perspectives in the classification and diagnosis of psychosis in childhood has historically followed behind that of major theoretical formulation for adults (Goldfarb, 1970). As a particular new formulation has occurred in the adult literature, it has almost universally been followed by attempts to generalize the conceptulization to children. For example, Kraepelin's (1919) formulation of "dementia praecox" in adults was extended to children by DeSanctes (1925) as "dementia praecocissima" and further extended by Hulse (1954) to "dementia infantilis." Only recently has the conceptualization of psychopathology in childhood generated sufficient interest for its study independent of adult disorders.

Advances in medicine and child development have also supported this independence in thought and inquiry. Early formulations of psychosis in children strongly focused upon neurological degeneration as a primary cause of these conditions (DeSanctes, 1925; Goldfarb, 1970). As advances in both neurodiagnostics and psychiatric thought occurred, it became apparent that the explanation of psychosis as neurological degeneration was, in most cases, inappropriate, and emphasis was placed on conflict and adaptation as primary determinants, following Bleuler's (1952) model for adult schizophrenia.

Early workers were further handicapped by the general lack of knowledge available about normal child development. Since the diagnosis of deviancy is largely dependent upon established norms of behavior and thought, classification of children at young ages, when extreme behavioral heterogeneity in development is the rule, was difficult. More recent theorizing (Bender, 1960; Kanner, 1943; Eisenberg, 1966) has therefore had the advantage of a wide variety of inputs to theoretical formulation. Consequently, current speculation has attempted to provide bases for differentiating subgroups of children exhibiting extreme behavioral deviance.

Although current literature suggests a number of distinct theoretical psychoses, we will limit this review to the two major diagnostic divisions, childhood schizophrenia and early infantile autism, since these conditions are the most commonly encountered and account for the vast majority of the published studies in this field. The basis for this review will be the experimental studies defining the functional deficits that occur in these children, rather than adopting the more popular strategy of reviewing and contrasting the major individual theorists who have attempted to provide explanation and categorization of this group of children. Review at the level of data may provide for a more comprehensive understanding of psychosis in childhood than is obtainable within the confines of theoretical structure. Addition-

ally, by focusing on what we know about these children empirically, new directions for future inquiry may become apparent.

CHILDHOOD SCHIZOPHRENIA

History of the concept

Until the latter half of the nineteenth century, childhood psychoses were either lumped in with "amentia" (mental retardation) or denied altogether by the medical profession. In 1867 the famous British psychiatrist, Maudsley, shocked his colleagues in that overly moralistic era by publishing a textbook that not only argued that "insanity" could exist in childhood, but also presented a classification scheme which distinguished seven different syndromes (Kanner, 1973). Unfortunately, he also proposed an early version of the "blame the parents" attitude in suggesting that "neurotic" parents pass on a genetic predisposition to develop the condition. But Maudsley nevertheless legitimized the concept of psychosis in childhood, and articles and books addressed to the topic began to appear in the closing decades of the century.

The next major step in isolating childhood schizophrenia was taken by DeSanctes, an Italian physician in 1925. He proposed that children who were apparently intact neurologically and intellectually, yet displayed bizarre behavior, be classified as cases of "dementia praecocissima," or "very early mental deterioration." The term was a downward extension of Kraepelin's "dementia praecox" (1919), and it came to be translated as "childhood schizophrenia" after Bleuler (1952) used "schizophrenia" to describe the conditions discussed by Kraepelin.

There was widespread acceptance of childhood schizophrenia as a diagnostic category by the 1930s. A set of criteria for the application of the diagnosis was published in Potter's (1933) classic article, which described six symptoms highly reminiscent of Bleuler's criteria for the diagnosis of adult schizophrenia. Potter's criteria were the following:

(1) a generalized retraction of interests from the environment;
(2) dereistic thinking, feeling, and acting;
(3) disturbances of thought, including blocking, condensation, perseveration, incoherence, and diminution of speech, sometimes to the point of mutism;
(4) defective emotional rapport;
(5) diminution, rigidity, and distortion of affect;
(6) alterations of behavior resulting in either hyperactivity or immobility, or bizarre stereotyped behaviors.

Potter's criteria were so broad that "childhood schizophrenia" was applied to all children whose psychoses were of unknown origin. It continues to be the only "official" diagnosis of any "functional" childhood psychosis, because it is the only category for severe childhood disturbance in the 1968 edition of the *Diagnostic and Statistical Manual* of the American Psychiatric Association.

After the publication of Potter's criteria, several attempts were made to discriminate additional psychotic syndromes and to divide childhood schizophrenia into subtypes. Examples of the former were Mahler's (1952) description of "symbiotic psychosis," Rank's (1949) discussion of "atypical" children, and Kanner's (1943) elucidation of "early infantile autism." Only Kanner's syndrome has been successful in capturing substantial professional attention, as we will see below. Efforts to subdivide childhood schizophrenia have also been made by Bender and Goldfarb. Bender (1960) distinguished six different types of schizophrenia by using terms applied to nonpsychotic conditions to emphasize the more obvious symptoms: pseudodefective, pseudoneurotic, pseudopsychopathic, psychosomatic, psychotic-episodes type, and latent type. Goldfarb (1961) took a more empirical approach, using psychological, neurological, and developmental data to argue that at least two classes of childhood schizophrenia existed, "organic" and "nonorganic," distinguished on the basis of the presence or absence of evidence of brain damage. Neither Bender's nor Goldfarb's classifications have enjoyed general acceptance. Bender's system is insufficiently objective to be reliable, and Goldfarb's bifurcation

is unacceptable to the majority of workers who assume that childhood schizophrenia always includes some degree of organic dysfunction, whether or not that dysfunction is identifiable with current neurological and biochemical assessment procedures.

By the 1950s it was abundantly clear that a general acceptable description of childhood schizophrenia was urgently needed. A British group of 13 clinicians defined nine diagnostic criteria which have come to be widely used since their publication in 1961 (Creak, 1961). The list attempted to cover all the deviant behaviors that are commonly seen in schizophrenic children.

Not all the behaviors need be present; often, the presence of four or five results in the diagnosis. Creak's nine points are the following:

(1) gross and sustained impairment of emotional relationships with people;
(2) apparent unawareness of personal identity;
(3) pathological preoccupation with particular objects or certain characteristics of them, without regard for their accepted functions;
(4) sustained resistance to change in the environment;
(5) abnormal perceptual experience;
(6) acute, excessive, and seemingly illogical anxiety;
(7) mutism or immature or bizarre speech;
(8) distortion in motility patterns;
(9) serious retardation in which islets of normal, near normal, or superior intellectual function may appear.

An important omission in Creak's criteria is a specification of age of onset. During the 1960s and 1970s, studies in England (Kolvin, 1971), Japan (Makita, 1966), and Russia (Vrono, 1974) indicated bimodal distributions of ages of onset for childhood psychosis. In each study there is one peak for children whose conditions begin before three years of age and a second peak for those whose conditions begin in late childhood or early adolescence. As a result of this observation, as well as some information that early-onset psychoses differ from late-onset psychoses in important ways, it is becoming increasingly common for workers to restrict the diagnosis of childhood schizophrenia to children showing late onset. This tendency is reflected in the classification scheme of the Committee on Child Psychiatry of the Group for the Advancement of Psychiatry (1966). The GAP criteria for "schizophreniform psychotic disorder" is essentially an expanded version of Creak's criteria, but with the significant addition of an age of onset between six and thirteen years. The rationale behind this particular age range is not given, but at least an attempt was made to distinguish childhood schizophrenia as a condition distinct from the early-onset psychoses and the degenerative conditions of early childhood.

As this brief survey has indicated, relatively little progress has been made over the past 100 years in elucidating the concept of childhood schizophrenia. Although most workers can agree that certain behavioral excesses and deficits must be present for the diagnosis to be made, there is little consensus on which signs are primary and which are secondary, with the result that, in practice, idiosyncratic weighting of the diagnostic criteria is commonplace. The category continues to be a very broad one, including characteristics as diverse as severe retardation as well as superior intelligence, mutism as well as age-appropriate but perseverative and illogical verbalizations, and catatonic immobility as well as hyperactivity. The condition obviously remains in great need of parsing into subtypes on the basis of experimental medical and psychological research (rather than clinical intuition). It is to be expected that in the future, workers will consider the condition as "the group of childhood schizophrenias," in a manner parallel to Bleuler's conception of adult schizophrenia as a group of related but distinct conditions. Finally, as the observant reader will have noticed, this historical survey has been concerned with advances in description, rather than progress in the elucidation of the causes of childhood schizophrenia. The simple explanation for this approach may be bluntly stated by noting that no progress has been made in discovering the causes of this disorder, with the exception of the elimination of a few hypothesized explanations, as will be seen when we consider etiology. And the reasons for this lack of progress are equally clear. The disorder is

extremely rare and extremely complicated, unlikely to succumb to any single "breakthrough" solution; and it attracts only a handful of persistent investigators in each generation. Closely related to the preceding two points is that research into its medical and psychological aspects is very poorly supported by any national agency, in comparison with many other areas of medical and psychological research.

Epidemiology

The exact frequency of childhood schizophrenia will not be known until further refinement and standardization of diagnostic criteria have been achieved. Treffert (1970) surveyed the records of all the children aged 12 and under who were seen in the mental health facilities of the state of Wisconsin from 1962 to 1967. He found the prevalence of children diagnosed with childhood schizophrenia to be 3.1 per 10,000. This figure includes children with the syndrome of infantile autism, but it excludes children not yet brought to the attention of an agency; it is probably an underestimate of the true prevalence rate. The ratio of males to females was 3.4 to 1. There was no evidence of an effect of birthorder. Werry (1972) reviewed a number of epidemiological studies of childhood psychosis, sometimes defined very broadly, and found varying prevalance rates, but none greater than 6 per 10,000. Thus, the incidence of childhood schizophrenia is quite low, even when allowances are made for variability in diagnostic criteria and sampling procedures. There is no reliable evidence indicating that socioeconomic level, ethnic grouping, cultural milieu, or parental education or intelligence are factors in childhood schizophrenia (Goldfarb, 1970).

Etiology

In considering the etiology of childhood schizophrenia, it is very important to distinguish between theory and data. Although this *caveat* might seem obvious, it deserves emphasis because theoretical speculation is so predominant over experimental knowledge in this area of psychopathology that it tends to blur the distinction between the two. In this section, we will concentrate on empirical research. This emphasis reflects our assumption that inductive theorizing, which builds upward from data to theory, will ultimately succeed in producing durable knowledge, where deductive theorizing, which makes predictions from speculation, has failed. We present such evidence as there is from the genetic, neurological and psychological sciences.

Genetics. There are no obvious chromosome abnormalities that can account for childhood schizophrenia (Book, Nichtern, and Gruenberg, 1963). The evidence suggesting genetic influence in the disorder is indirect, consisting of a twin study and family histories. Kallman and Roth (1956) studied 52 sets of twins whose schizophrenia began at 8.8 years (males) and 11.1 years (females). The concordance rate between 17 monozygotic pairs was 70.6 percent, while for thirty-five dizygotic pairs it was 17.1 percent, suggesting a significant degree of hereditability in childhood schizophrenia.

Several studies have reported prevalance rates of parental schizophrenia. Meyers and Goldfarb (1962) studied the families of 45 early school-age schizophrenics and found that 28 percent of the mothers, 13 percent of the fathers, and 8 percent of the siblings were schizophrenic. Bender and Grugett (1956) reported that 43 percent of the mothers and 40 percent of the fathers were "mentally ill" (possibly schizophrenic) in a large sample of schizophrenic children. These figures seem to be very high, perhaps due to Bender's tendency to be generous in using the term "schizophrenia" with both children and adults. Kallman and Roth (1956), in the study cited earlier, applied very strict diagnostic criteria and reported the combined parental schizophrenia rate to be 9 percent. The highly varying rates of parental schizophrenia evident in the studies just cited apparently result from differences in diagnostic criteria, cultural backgrounds of the samples, and intactness of the families studied, as discussed by Goldfarb (1970). Even if the hypothesis of genetic determination, at least in some cases, could be

substantiated, we are far from knowing how such genetic deviations are expressed, since biochemical assays have yet to expose reliable differences between schizophrenic children and controls.

Neurology. There are no obvious structural abnormalities in childhood schizophrenia. However, a number of studies have suggested that neurological immaturity or impairment is present in many cases. Creak (1963) found that 54 of the 100 schizophrenic children in her sample were either uniformly or selectively retarded in developmental milestones. Kennard (1949, 1959) found abnormal EEG records more frequently in schizophrenic children than in normal members of their families or in other severely disturbed children. Goldfarb (1961) reported that 17 of 26 schizophrenic (including some autistic children) exhibited "soft" neurological signs. Prenatal and perinatal complications are much more prevalent in infants who later become schizophrenic than in their siblings or normal controls (Taft and Goldfarb, 1964). Gittelman and Birch (1967) studied 97 schizophrenic children in a special education setting and determined that 75 percent of them had signs of neurological dysfunction, and 35 percent had histories of prenatal or perinatal complications.

Evidence for neurological abnormalities, based on the direct examination of brain tissue, is very scarce. Darby (1976) surveyed the literature on autopsy findings in childhood psychosis and identified six cases of childhood schizophrenia. Various degenerative conditions, such as cerebral lipidosis, were present in five of the six cases. No conclusions can be drawn from so small a sample, and it is important to remember that negative findings (i.e., autopsies showing no abnormalities) are much less likely to be reported than are cases showing marked damage.

These and other studies (e.g., Taterka and Katz, 1955; White, DeMyer, and DeMyer, 1964) indicate that neurological abnormalities are prevalent in schizophrenic children. Presumably, such abnormalities contribute to the etiology of the condition in important, if still unknown, ways. As for those schizophrenic children who show neither "hard" nor "soft" neurological signs, it remains for future research to determine which of these children have subtle, so far undetected, neurological problems.

Psychological Factors. In considering psychological factors, we are concerned with sensation, perception, cognition, language, and family interaction. At the present time, studies in these areas have failed to provide any definitive leads to the etiology of childhood schizophrenia. They have, however, served to eliminate some hypotheses and to clarify the nature of the disorder.

Sensation and perception: There are no simple sensory defects that might enter into an account of the etiology of childhood schizophrenia. Tests for visual, auditory, and tactile acuity fail to differentiate schizophrenic from normal children (Goldfarb, 1961).

When stimuli become more complex and demand organized processing and selective responding, schizophrenic children show clear deficits. For example, schizophrenics are inferior to normals in speech reception thresholds (Hoberman and Goldfarb, 1963), tactile location, visual figure-ground discrimination, Gestalt closure (Goldfaarb, 1961), figure orientation (Fuller, 1965), visual and tactile exploration of objects (Schopler, 1966), WISC block design, and memory for designs (Safrin, 1964). Birch and Hertzig (1967) have shown that schizophrenic children are deficient in matching stimuli across modalities, such as vision and touch.

Cognition. Given the foregoing perceptual limitations, it is not surprising to find that schizophrenic children also experience serious cognitive disabilities. Studies of the performance of schizophrenic children on a number of tasks requiring various reasoning skills indicate that schizophrenic children tend to be very concrete, i.e., they are responsive to certain obvious physical features of objects and situations, to the neglect of their abstract functional or social significance (Norman, 1954). In sorting objects according to color and form, for example, schizophrenic children have shown vague, overgeneralized responses, based on only one aspect of the stimuli, and have great difficulty in learning a more abstract

approach (Goldfarb, 1961; Friedman, 1961). Most of the evidence documenting the existence of cognitive disabilities comes from studies of the scores of schizophrenic children on standardized intelligence tests. Pollack (1967) summarized thirteen reports and found that in each study the mean IQ of the schizophrenic group was lower than the mean IQ of the control group. One third of all the schizophrenic children had IQs below 70. In Goldfarb's (1961) investigation, the mean WISC IQ for the normal group was 102; for the "nonorganic" schizophrenic group it was 92; and for the "organic" group it was 62. Although some schizophrenic children have IQs in the average or superior range, such children are uncommon. Gittelman and Birch (1967) found only 18 percent of their sample of ninety-seven schizophrenic children had IQs of 90 above, while 56 percent had IQs below 69.

Language. One of the most compelling features of schizophrenic children is their deviant speech. Schizophrenic children deviate significantly from normals in phonation, rhythm, and articulation (Goldfarb, Braunstein, and Lorge, 1956). Stereotypy and repetition are present to a high degree (Wolff and Chess, 1965). Rutter (1965a) reported that 7 percent of the speaking children in his sample of psychotic children exhibited immediate or delayed echolalia, and 25 percent showed pronominal reversal. Other studies have indicated that the language of schizophrenic children is at a low developmental level and is generally characterized by limitations in the amount of speech, lack of questions and informative statements, idiosyncratic word meanings, limitations in comprehension, and little use of gesture (Cunningham, 1968; deHirsch, 1967; Fish, Shapiro, Campbell, and Wile, 1968; Goldfarb, Goldfarb, and Scholl, 1966; Rutter, 1965; Shapiro and Fish, 1969; Weber, 1965; Weiland and Legg, 1964).

Some of the difficulties encountered in attempts to communicate with schizophrenic children can be appreciated in reading the following transcript of a conversation between one of the authors (C.D.N.) and a 12-year-old mildly retarded schizophrenic boy we will call Billy (B). The adult (A) lets Billy take the lead and tries to follow as topics shift rapidly and sudden changes occur in affect and in attentiveness to the adult.

B: Hey. Good morning.

A: Good morning. How are you today?

B: I'm going to a party.

A: You're going to a party? Where's the party going to be?

B: (Hiding face with shirt) (Unintelligible)

A: I can't hear you. Pull your shirt down.

B: The show is start at one o'clock!

A: The show is starting at one o'clock. Very nice. What kind of show is it going to be?

B: Cartoon time.

A: Cartoon time?

B: Cartoon comin' over.

A: Cartoon's coming over?

B: Halloween costume (Covers face with hands)

A: Halloween costume? Put your hand down.

B: What's a matter? (Crying)

A: Put your hand down, Billy.

B: (Crying)

A: Why are you crying?

B: What?

A: Why are you crying?

B: (Crying; stands up and starts to leave.)

A: I'm here. Come sit down over here.

B: (Sits, continues to cry). (Unintelligible)

A: What? I can't understand you. What'd you do in school today?

B: (Crying stops abruptly.) No more. I'm going to Margie's house.

A: When?

B: Tonight.

A: What are you going to do there?

B: Huh?

A: What are you going to do there?

B: Go swimming!

A: Does she have a pool?

B: Yes. Go in.

A: You're gonna go in the water? Very nice.

B: Michael goin' Margie's. Have apple-sauce? I saw Star Wars at the movies.

A: You saw Star Wars?

B: Hey. Would you turn on the fan, please?

A: No, let's leave the fan off.

B: Hey. What is that called? What's that called? What's that called?

A: They're called Smarties candy (Gives B and few pieces.)

B: Huh? Watch me? (eats candy).

A? I'm watching.

B: You like it?

A: Yes.

B: Making noise?

B: Huh?

A: It's not making any noise. It's quiet.

B: Huh? Huh?

A: Do you like them, Billy? Do those taste good?

B: (Crying.)

A: What's wrong?

B: (Crying.) Have some?

A: Yes, you can have some more.

B: No thank you.

A: Okay. You don't have to eat them.

B: Yes, yes. (Crying.)

A: Go ahead and take them.

B: Huh? Smarties?

A: Yes.

B: May I have them?

A: You may have all of them.

B: Huh?

A: You may have all of them.

B: Where?

A: Right here in this room.

B: Oh . . . Stick her tongue at me. Mary Jane stick her tongue at me. At me.

A: I don't think Mary Jane would stick her tongue at you.

B: No! Mrs. (unintelligible)

A: Mrs. Who?

B: Space Dust make a noise down the hatch.

A: Yes, it does.

B: Hi.

A: Hi Billy. How are you?

B: Want to sing a song.

A: You want to sing a song?. Sing me a song, please, Billy.

B: What?

A: Do you know a good song? All right, sing me a song.

B: (Singing.) Billy's going swimming to-day . . .

A: Very nice. Can you finish that song?

B: Hold it.

A: Okay.

B: I'm goin' to a horse race. Goin' to a horse race.

A: Where?

B: Mommy's takin' me!

A: Mommy's taking you? Where?

B: I've gotta leave the show at one o'clock.

A: Why?

B: Because it's a puppet show?

A: Because it's a puppet show?

B: Yeah.

A: Oh. Today there's a puppet show.

B: What?

A: Today there's a puppet show. Do you like puppets?

B: Huh.

A: Do you like puppets?

B: Oh. I forgot the balloons.

A: You forgot the baloons?

B: There's a circus. Animals.

A: Oh, I don't think the circus animals are coming.

B: Yes it is!

A: Think so?

B: Yes. Wanna go now?

A: Do you want to go now? We can go now.

B: Are you ready?

A: I'm ready. Okay, let's go.

B: No! Wanna talk first.

A: You want to talk first? Okay.

B: (Sings) Oh, goin' to Margie's house, goin' to Margie's house.

This sample is typical of the speech of schizophrenic children. Retarded language development is evident in the constricted sentence lengths, frequent lack of inflections, failures to use the appropriate verb tense, and numerous elliptical constructions. The "schizophrenic" flavor of Billy's speech is due to the abrupt changes in topic, suggesting looseness in associations, equally abrupt shifts in affect, unnecessary repetitions, and frequent failures to attend to the adult's speech.

Parental Factors There is no scientifically valid evidence that the child-rearing practices or the personalities of the parents of schizophrenic children have any etiological significance. There are a number of subjective clinical observations and methodologically inadequate studies purporting to identify psychopathology in parents (see Behrens and Goldfarb, 1958; Boatman and Szurek, 1960; Despert, 1938; Kaufman, Frank, Heims, Herrick, and Willer, 1959; Rank, 1949; Singer & Wynne, 1963). Ob-jective, replicable studies, however, fail to lend any support to this line of speculation. Klebanoff (1959) investigated the child-rearing attitudes of mothers of schizophrenic, brain-damaged, and normal children. The most pathological attitudes were found in the mothers of the brain-damaged children, the next most in the others of the schizophrenic children, and the least in the mothers of normal children. Klebanoff concluded that the moderately pathological attitudes of the mothers of schizophrenics were the result rather than the cause of the children's condition, since the more seriously pathological attitudes of the mothers of brain-damaged children were certainly the result rather than the cause of the children's condition. Pitfield and Oppenheim (1964) measured attitudes important in child-rearing in the parents of schizophrenic, Down's syndrome, and normal children, and attributed the slight differences in their group's responses to the problems presented by each group of children rather than to differences in degree of psychopathology in the parents. About the worst that can be said of parents of schizophrenic children as a group is that they tend to be "indulgent," "uncertain" (Pitfield and Oppenheim, 1964), and unclear in communicating with their children (Goldfarb, Goldfarb, and Scholl, 1966). While these characteristics might be expected to exacerbate existing difficulties in rearing a deviant child, it is implausible that they could produce and maintain the extremely deviant behavior patterns characteristic of childhood schuzophrenia.

In summary, the data on childhood schizophrenia suggest a group of heterogeneous children who show general deficits in sensation, perception, cognition, and language. Equally apparent is the fact that etiological study has failed to produce evidence of factors common to the children and therefore definitive of psychosis. However, childhood schizophrenia, as a broad class, has been found to begin after infancy and early childhood, a finding that has been used to differentiate it from early-onset psychoses, such as infantile autism, which we will review next.

EARLY INFANTILE AUTISM

History of the concept

In 1943 Leo Kanner reported his conclusions from observations of 11 children who shared certain characteristics that seemed to distinguish them from children with other severe disorders. These children exhibited the following features:

(1) a profound inability to form social relationships;
(2) an anxiously obsessive desire for the preservation of sameness;
(3) a fascination with objects, which are handled skillfully;
(4) mutism or noncommunicative speech which includes immediate and delayed echolalia and pronominal reversal;
(5) normal physical appearance, suggesting intelligence;
(6) a good rote memory.

Kanner emphasized that the syndrome was in evidence in infancy. Initially, he believed that the underlying abnormality was also present from birth (Kanner, 1943), but he subsequently described the same syndrome in children with histories of apparently normal development up to the age of two years (Kanner and Eisenberg, 1955). Additionally, Kanner and Eisenberg (1955) asserted that the features absolutely essential for the diagnosis were the first two listed above, social aloofness and insistence on the maintenance of sameness.

Kanner's descriptions struck a responsive chord in other clinicians who then reported similar observations (e.g., Bakwin, 1954; Despert, 1951; van Krevelen, 1952). Several earlier accounts of children who would now be considered autistic were noticed, such as Itard's (1962) account of the "wild boy" of Aveyron (e.g., Darr and Worden, 1951; Vaillant, 1962). Almost immediately, however, problems in making the diagnosis arose due to a tendency on the part of clinicians to overgeneralize it and to see it in many more children than Kanner originally intended. Rutter (1978) attributed much of this confusion, which continues to the present, to Kanner's failure to communicate his impressions in a clear and easily understood manner. For example, the use of the term "autism"—in naming the syndrome—resulted in the assumption that a *withdrawal* from existing social relationships into an active fantasy life was intended, as in Bleuler's use of "autism" in describing schizophrenia in adults. Instead, Kanner was referring to a failure in the *development* of relationships and symbolic thinking.

Efforts to refine Kanner's criteria and to make the diagnostic process more objective have been conducted by several investigators. Rimland, in his landmark treatise on autism (1964), published a checklist that is filled out by a child's parents and contains a large number of specific items regarding early history and characteristics derived from Kanner's descriptions (1943, 1944). The checklist is scored by subtracting the number of responses not considered to be characteristic of autistic children from the number of responses considered to be characteristic of them. The criterion for diagnosing autism is a score of +20 or more, i.e., 20 or more "autistic" than "nonautistic" responses. Rimland (1971) analyzed 2,218 checklists completed on children who had been clinically diagnosed as autistic and found that only about 10 percent of them met the criterion for autism. This substantiated Kanner's impression that only about 10 percent of the children sent to him as autistic actually fitted the early infantile autism syndrome he had described.

Other students of autism recognized "Kanner's syndrome" as valid but overly narrow and restrictive, and they have defined "autism" in accordance with their interpretations of published research and personal clinical observations. Ornitz and Ritvo (1968, 1976) have emphasized perceptual dysfunction as a key component in autism. They define autism in terms of five subclusters of symptoms:

1. *disturbances of perception,* believed to be due to faulty modulation of sensory input and motor output by the brain, which results in over- and under-responsiveness to stimuli in the same child at different times
2. *disturbances of developmental rate,* as shown by spurts and plateaus in development and by the special abilities sometimes seen in chil-

dren who are otherwise severely retarded

3. *disturbances of relating,* including poor eye contact, delayed or absent social smile, apparent aversion to physical contact, inappropriate manipulation of objects, and inability to form strong relationships with peers and adults
4. *disturbances of speech and language,* either mutism or fixation at a given level of language development, with echolalia, reversal of pronouns, and atonal, uninflected speech
5. *disturbances of motility,* or repetitive, stereotyped behaviors such as body rocking, hand-flapping, head-banging, and lunging and darting movements

DeMyer and her colleagues (DeMyer, Churchill, Pontius, and Gilkey, 1971), have used the following criteria for autism in a continuing series of studies at Indiana University:

1. emotional withdrawal from people before age three
2. lack of speech for communication
3. nonfunctional, repetitive use of objects
4. failure to engage in role play, alone or with other children

Sixty-six autistic children identified by these crtieria have been subdivided into three groups by level of socialization (DeMyer, 1976). The *high* autistic group is characterized by a mixture of communicative and noncommunicative speech and some islets of social relatedness in a background of withdrawal. The *middle* autistic group shows severe withdrawal, noncommunicative speech, but some adaptive behavior commensurate with its chronological age level. The *low* autistic children resemble the middle children with the exception that all their verbal and adaptive behaviors are below the level expected for their chronological ages. Some objective validity for this clinical differentiation is indicated by the fact that the groups were shown to differ substantially in mean IQ.

In a recent, comprehensive review of the literature, Rutter (1978) argued that four diagnostic criteria distinguished autism from other severe disorders of childhood. According to Rutter, all of these criteria must be present for the diagnosis to be made in the child of four years or younger.

1. onset before the age of 30 months
2. impaired social development that is below the child's intellectual level. Specifically, there is a lack of attachment behavior and a relative failure of social bonding, as well as nondiscriminating use of eye contact
3. delayed and deviant language development that includes failure to initate, failure to engage in imaginative play, abnormal patterns of babbling, lack of comprehension, lack of gesture, immediate and delayed echolalia, I-You pronominal reversal, lack of conversational speech, and difficulty in talking about things outside the immediate situation
4. insistence of sameness, indicated by stereotyped play patterns, abnormal preoccupations with certain objects or activities, rigid routines, and resistance to changes in the environment

Rutter's criteria constitute what is essentially a definition of autism as the term is commonly used today. As such, it retains the points emphasized in Kanner's (1943) criteria, but broadens the concept of autism to include more children than Kanner probably intended. Thus, it is becoming increasingly common to find that most professionals use "autistic" rather loosely to refer to children having many of the behaviors mentioned by Rutter (1978) and that they use "Kanner's syndrome" or "classically autistic" to refer to children who closely match Kanner's original description. That is, "autism" has become a large category that distinguishes children with this label from children who are labeled with "childhood schizophrenia," "mental retardation," "neurosis," and "organic brain syndrome," for example, while "Kanner's syndrome" is used to denote a subcategory of autistic children. If this trend in usage continues, it is likely that other subcategories of autistic children will evolve. One indication that such a trend may be developing is apparent in Coleman's *The Autistic Syndromes* (1976), where the argument is made (and supported with objective data) that "familial autism," "purine autism," and "celiac autism" are reliably distinguishable subcategories.

Epidemiology

Two very sound epidemiological surveys indicate that in every 10,000 children, four to five will be autistic. Lotter (1966) screened all the children in Middlesex County, England, and investigated those whose records suggested autism through structured interviews with parents and teachers, examination of medical records, and observation and testing of the children. Three groups were identified. Group A, the "nuclear" autistic group, consisted of children who showed Kanner's two cardinal symptoms of social aloofness and resistance to change to a marked degree and yielded a prevalence rate of 2.0 per 10,000. Group B, the "nonnuclear" group, had many autistic characteristics, but did not strongly evidence Kanner's two features and yielded a prevalence rate of 2.5 per 10,000. Group C consisted of nonautistic children who nevertheless had some autistic features. Combining the two autistic groups results in a prevalence figure of 4.5 per 10,000 children aged eight to ten. The ratio of males to females was 2.75:1 in the nuclear group and 2.4:1 in the nonnuclear group. Wing, Yeates, Brierley, and Gould (1976) replicated Lotter's study in a large borough of London, studying all children five to fourteen years of age. They identified 2.0 per 10,000 "nuclear" autistic children and 2.8 per 10,000 "nonnuclear" autistic children, for a total prevalence of 4.8 per 10,000.

Kanner observed that most of the parents of the autistic children he saw were highly intelligent and generally employed in professional occupations. Subsequent research has supported this observation, although it is not applicable to the extent that Kanner originally supposed. The more classically autistic children of higher intelligence often have parents who fit Kanner's description (Lowe, 1966; Lotter, 1967; Rutter, Bartak, and Newman, 1971), while lower functioning, non-Kanner syndrome children often do not (Lotter, 1967; Ritvo, Cantwell, Johnson, Clements, Benbrook, Slagle, Kelly, and Ritz, 1971).

Etiology

Although the etiology of autism remains to be explained, research in this area has expanded greatly since Kanner first reported the syndrome. As research efforts have multiplied, particularly during the 1960s and 1970s, a strong shift has occurred away from speculative, psychodynamic theorizing about parental psychopathology toward medical and psychological observations regarding dysfunctional organic and behavioral processes.

Genetics. As in the case of childhood schizophrenia, no chromosome abnormalities have been detected in autistic children (Judd and Mandell, 1968; Spence, 1976). Only one to three percent of autistic children have siblings who are also autistic (Coleman and Rimland, 1976; Kanner and Lesser, 1958; Rimland, 1971; Rutter, 1965b). This rate is too low to indicate any simple mode of inheritance; some polygenic mechanism would have to be assumed if autism is to be accounted for genetically. Evidence from twin studies has yet to be obtained because there are too few cases to permit any conclusions (Rimland, 1971). The incidence of severe mental illness among the relatives of autistic children is about the same as for normal children, but incidence of relatives with Down's syndrome may be higher (Herzberg, 1976).

Biochemistry. Investigations of biochemical factors in autism are becoming increasingly common as the field generally expands and improved assay techniques become available. Another source of motivation for such studies is the hope that autism might be susceptible to a straightforward biochemical explanation in the way that the retardation syndrome associated with phenylketonuria was.

Serotonin is a neurotransmitter that controls one of the sleep phases. Schain and Freedman (1961) reported that some autistic children have elevated levels of serotonin, a finding that has stimulated several additional studies. Outside the brain, serotonin is transported in blood platelets and can therefore be studied in ordinary blood samples. Boullin, Coleman, and O'Brien (1970) found a marked elevation in the efflux of serotonin from the platelets of five of six Kanner's syndrome children in comparison to those of normal children. This finding was replicated in another group of

Kanner's syndrome children, but not in non-Kanner's syndrome autistic children (Boullin, Coleman, O'Brien, and Rimland, 1971). However, more recent research suggests that elevated serotonin is not uniquely associated with Kanner's syndrome, since it also occurs in various other psychiatric groups and in some normals (Coleman, 1973; Takahaski, Kanai, and Miyamoto, 1976). Other biochemical substances that might serve as "markers" for autism, possibly leading to a pharmacological or dietary treatment, are being investigated (Coleman, 1976), but there is currently no optimism about the immediate future.

Neurology. The evidence for neurological abnormalities in autism comes from clinical assessments and experimental studies concerned with hypotheses about the possible sites of damage. Lotter (1967) found that the clinical records of 27 percent of his nuclear autistic group and 41 percent of his nonnuclear autistic group contained evidence of some degree of neurological dysfunction. Schain and Yannet (1960) found that 42 percent of the mixed autistic children they studied had seizures of varying types early in life (birth to six years). Rutter, Bartak, and Newman (1971) reported that 29 percent of the autistic children they observed over a twelve- to twenty-year-follow-up developed epileptic seizures in adolescence or adulthood. DeMyer (1976) found that 75 percent of the large group of autistic children she evaluated showed signs of neurological dysfunction. A virus known to be associated with brain damage, rubella, is capable of producing autism. Chess (1971, 1977) has reported the occurrence of Kanner's syndrome in 11 of 243 cogential rubella children. Another 11 were judged to be autistic—to a less severe degree.

In EEG studies, significant numbers of autistic children show abnormalities, but there is no consistency across studies that points to a specific organic dysfunction. Hutt, Hutt, Lee, and Ounsted (1964, 1965) found low-voltage irregular records in three- to six-year-old autistic children, suggesting chronically high states of cortical arousal. Studying older autistic children (mean CA 9.0 years), Hermelin and O'Connor (1968) found no difference in arousal between autistic and normal children in a darkened room. Autistic children adapted more readily to intermittent light stimulation than normals or Down's syndrome children, and they showed more arousal to continuous sound stimulation than the two control groups. Ornitz and his colleagues have hypothesized that the vestibular nuclei in the brainstem are the site of the primary dysfunction in autistic children. In several experimental studies they have shown that certain functions mediated by the vestibular system are diminished in these children, including ocular nystagmus after rotation in a Baronay Chair (Ornitz, Brown, Mason, and Putnam, 1974; Ritvo, Ornitz, Eviatar, Markhan, Brown, and Mason, 1969), and rapid-eye movements usually associated with dreaming sleep (Ornitz, Forsythe, and de la Pena, 1973; Ornitz, Ritvo, Brown, LaFranchi, Parmelee, and Walter, 1969). These findings have been used as a basis for postulating that autism is a disorder of "perceptual inconsistency" (Ornitz, and Ritvo, 1968), in which the homeostatic regulation of sensory input and motor output is defective.

Other investigators have noticed that the deficits and skills usually attributed to autistic children are reminicent of recent findings regarding hemispheric localization of functions. Autistic children are known to be deficient in linguistic and logical abilities (predominantly left-hemisphere functions) and more skillful in musical and visuospatial abilities (predominantly right-hemisphere functions). Blackstock (1979) obtained experimental evidence suggesting that right-hemisphere information-processing is common among autistic children. For example, given a choice between verbal and musical auditory stimulation, nine-year-old autistic children preferred music while normal children showed no preference. This deviant lateralization is slow to develop. In his electrophysiological study, Tanguay (1976) reported that two- to five-year-old autistics, unlike normal children, show no significant differences in right *versus* left hemispheric responsiveness to auditory stimulation. Barry and James (1978) found that autistic children show a developmental lag in establishing dominant hand usage, compared to normal and retarded children, indicating delayed cerebral lateralization.

Psychological Factors. Studies of psychological factors in autism have provided a much clearer picture of the handicaps associated with this disorder than we had as little as ten years ago. Findings in the areas of sensation and perception, cognition, language, and parental characteristics seem likely to contribute to accounts of etiology, although crucial pieces of the puzzle are still missing.

Sensation and Perception. Studies of sensory functioning in large numbers of autistic children have not been reported, so it is not known to what extent sensory deficits exist in this population. It is generally assumed that such deficits occur no more often than among normal children, because Goldfarb's (1961) study of sensory functioning in childhood schizophrenia included some autistic children and, as noted earlier, no differences between the psychotic and normal groups were found. However, one of the earliest clinical signs of autism is unresponsiveness to certain sounds and a tendency to look "through" adults rather than making eye contact with them. Generally, these anomalies are found to result from attentional, rather than sensory, irregularities, as the work on stimulus overselectivity to be discussed indicates. But, it should be noted that the question of undiagnosed sensory problems in individual cases is often never answered satisfactorily, especially among more retarded autistic children who are not able to be tested conclusively by standard clinical examination procedures. Reliable techniques are still being developed and have yet to be applied to large numbers of autistic children (Fulton and Lloyd, 1969; Newsom and Simon, 1977).

Perceptual abnormalities of various kinds have been disclosed by a number of experimental studies (Newsom, 1978). Autistic children have difficulty learning simple visual discriminations (e.g., Koegel and Rincover, 1976; Koegel and Wilhelm, 1973); auditory discriminations (Hingtgen and Coulter, 1967; Reynolds, Newsom, and Lovaas, 1974), and imitative responses (Varni, Lovaas, Loegel, and Everett, 1978). The source of the difficulty for many au-

tistic children is their tendency to attend to only one feature of the stimulus situation while ignoring other relevant features—a phenomenon described as "stimulus overselectivity" (Lovaas, Schreibman, Koegel, and Rehm, 1971). These authors taught autistic children to make a simple response (pressing a lever) when presented with a compound stimulus, consisting of light, white noise, and tactile pressure. In tests with each of the components presented in isolation, the children responded to only one of the components (which differed across children) and remained unresponsive to the other two. Lovaas et al. (1971) concluded that autistic children cannot handle information presented to several modalities simultaneously; that, in a sense, they cannot see and hear at the same time. Further research has indicated that stimulus overselectivity can occur *within* either the visual or the auditory modality (e.g., Koegel and Wilhelm, 1973; Schreibman and Lovaas, 1973; Reynolds, Newsom, and Lovaas, 1974). Some investigators have found that overselectivity is associated with developmental level, often occurring in retarded and very young normal children, and have suggested that it may be due to a maturational lag in autistic children (Lovattana and Kraemer, 1974; Schover and Newsom, 1976; Wilhelm and Lovaas, 1976). The deficit is not irremediable; several experiments have shown that overselectivity can be exploited or overcome in teaching discriminations if special training procedures are used (Koegel and Schreibman, 1977; Rincover, 1978b; Schreibman, 1975; Schreibman, Koegel and Craig, 1977).

Cognition. Among the specific cognitive deficiencies of autistic children are delays and arrests in the development of short-term memory, temporal concepts, sequencing, sensory integration, and causal reasoning (Bryson, 1972; Dalgleish, 1975; Frith, 1970a,b, 1972; Frith and Hermelin, 1969; Hermelin, 1976). Global indicators of cognitive ability are provided by intelligence tests, showing that most autistic children are retarded, with about half in the severely and profoundly retarded ranges. From 50 to 60 percent of autistic children have IQs below 50 (Chess, 1971; Lotter, 1967; Rutter and Lockyer, 1967). DeMyer,

Barton, Alpern, Kimberlin, Allen, Yang, and Steele (1974) studied 115 autistic children over a period of five years, testing them with various standardized intelligence tests. Ninety-four percent of their patients had overall IQs in the retarded range (i.e., less than 68) at the time of initial evaluation. At follow-up, patients whose IQs had been over 50 showed a greater increase in IQ than did patients whose IQs had been less than 50. Greater gains occurred in performance scores than in verbal scores.

Language. The language abnormalities of autistic children are noticeable very early. As toddlers, they often do not babble normally and fail to imitate (Bartak, Rutter, and Cox, 1975; Ricks, 1975; Rutter, 1965a). Later, they show comprehension deficits, being unable to follow even simple commands unless they are accompanied by gestures and occur in a familiar situation. About 50 percent of autistic children never gain useful speech. In those who do learn to speak, there are several characteristic abnormalities. Immediate and delayed echolalia are common. The child repeats something just heard or something heard hours or days before. Immediate echolalia is often related to the child's ability to understand speech. Carr, Schreibman, and Lovaas (1975) have shown that autistic children are much more likely to echo a verbalization that they have no appropriate response for than one for which they do. Immediate echolalia results in another characteristic abnormality, pronominal reversal, in which the child substitutes "you" for "I" in making requests. For example, an autistic child might say "You want a cookie?" when "I want a cookie" is meant because he is echoing an adult's question which was previously associated with the object (Bartak and Rutter, 1974). Autistic children are usually poor in talking about things outside of the immediate environment and often exhibit immature grammatical forms (Rutter, 1978). The more verbal children tend to attach idiosyncratic meanings to words and create unusual metaphors (Kanner, 1946; Rutter, 1965a).

Parental Factors. On the basis of his clinical observations, Kanner (1943) described the parents of autistic children as cold, ob-

sessive, and mechanical in their child-rearing practices. He suggested that the parents might have a mild form of the disorder, which they passed on to some of their offspring genetically (Kanner, 1943, 1973). Other observers, most notably Bettelheim (1967), have gone further and argued that the parents hate and reject their child, who then becomes autistic as a defense against their hostility. This assumption is completely gratuitous and, as Rimland (1964) puts it, "pernicious," resulting in much unnecessary guilt among the parents on whom it has been inflicted.

Rutter, Bartak, and Newman (1971) investigated the parents of autistic children and aphasic children, using questionnaires and structured interviews. There were no differences between the two groups of parents on measures of psychiatric illness, obsessionability, emotional warmth toward the child, enthusiasm, and empathy. Neurotic or depressive problems had occurred in about half the mothers in each group, presumably as reactions to caring for a handicapped child. DeMyer, Pontius, Norton, Barton, Allen, and Steele (1972) used semistructured interviews to obtain information on child-rearing practices from the parents of autistic, brain-damaged, and normal children. They found no evidence that the parents of the autistic children engaged in practices or attitudes that might have caused the child's disorder.

Infantile autism, at this point in time, represents a general label applied to a particular subgroup of psychotic children. Factors such as early onset, preservation of sameness, and social aloofness have been utilized as a rationale for the independent study of autism. Whether this differentiation between autism and childhood schizophrenia is justified is as yet unanswerable. For, like childhood schizophrenia, no conclusive data have been generated to suggest a common etiology. Intense disagreement exists even as to which subgroup of psychotic children is autistic. The creation of this "convenient fiction" of autism has, however, provided secondary benefits in terms of public awareness, increased funding, and program availability. Despite these benefits, the data suggest no empirical reason for the current classification of these children with pervasive behavioral, perceptual, and cognitive deficits.

MODELS OF DIAGNOSIS

In attempting to abstract the criterion attributes of the particular diagnostic categories reviewed, the reader may feel that years of observation and speculation have produced little in the way of a firm course of action with regard to the diagnosis of the psychotic child. Some of this confusion may disperse, however, if attention shifts from particular theoretical positions to the consideration of the basic epistemologies, or ways of obtaining knowledge, that have been applied to the study of severely handicapped children. The choice of a basic epistemology represents a primary determinant of the probability of success in the diagnosis and treatment of psychosis in childhood.

Functional Diagnosis. The particular course of treatment, the manifestations of the psychoses, the presenting behavioral components, and, indeed, the very definition of psychosis itself are likely to be different depending upon the choice of approach. In clinical practice, this choice should be made based upon more than mere intuitive feelings that a particular approach is "right." It can be argued that it is the responsibility of the clinician to select from among the various approaches the one that is most efficacious in producing client improvement. Although therapist perception and training always influence this process, there are certain objective criteria by which any diagnosis can be evaluated.

Ideally, the attachment of a diagnostic label to the presenting symptom complex should be indicative of a number of factors. The first factor involves differential labeling of the disease or constellation of behaviors. That is, diagnosis should discriminate condition A from condition B, allowing for a clear sorting of individuals to receive a particular label.

A second function of diagnosis may relate to etiology. By the identification of a common set of indicators, the clinician hopes to understand the genesis of the entity and events or pathological states pro-ducing the condition. With certain conditions, independent tests can be made to confirm the validity of diagnosis.

Third, diagnosis may provide some indication of the course of a disorder. Knowledge of this course may provide further diagnostic confirmation; previous states of a known disorder, by history, may be used as evidence of the correctness of diagnosis.

A fourth function of diagnosis is to assist in the selection of treatments. Information as to the label, etiology, and course to date of the disorder may provide, in a prescriptive fashion, the next treatment of probable success or at least suggest several alternatives that might be of benefit.

Fifth, diagnosis should suggest some aspects of prognosis. The first four factors, the histories of similar clients, and the current state of treatment knowledge should provide a prediction of outcome and a rough yardstick by which to assess progress.

All of these factors lead to the notion that diagnosis should be functional. The process of diagnosis should provide information that is essential to outcome. When the understanding of the etiology, course, treatment, and prognosis of a particular symptom complex is limited, the value of a diagnostic label may be increasingly questioned. Ideally, diagnosis should provide utilizable information on all of these dimensions. In practice, this is seldom the case. With respect to the psychotic disorders of childhood, such as autism, its value is open to question (Lovaas and Newsom, 1976).

Wender (1971) has discussed the issues of the functionality and importance of diagnosis in psychiatric disorders, particularly minimal brain dysfunction. As with this disorder, the psychotic disorders of childhood are often diagnosed upon the basis of a number of behavioral symptoms which have been said to be representative of an underlying disease—or abnormality. The population of children with a particular diagnosis is often, under this "polythetic" scheme, quite heterogenous. The usefulness of such diagnostic procedures relates to the five purposes of diagnosis listed above. Mere labeling for classification of demographic purposes does not serve the client. Clearly, the empirical value of diagnosis is the primary variable to consider, and such value has yet to be demonstrated in the field of childhood psychosis. In the remainder of this chapter, we will take the stance that diagnosis of psychotic conditions, and the theoretical speculation upon which it is based, should properly be secondary to the design and evaluation of treatment programs designed to reduce the maladaptive behaviors of psychotic children, simultaneously developing and maintaining more adaptive behaviors.

TWO EPISTEMOLOGIES FOR THE STUDY OF PSYCHOSIS

The individual theories of psychosis, relating the disorders to dynamic, genetic, biochemical, or developmental factors, are based upon a logical structure in which a series of postulates and corollaries is derived from a set of basic assumptions. The logical structure of a theory is often well-conceived and consistent, leading to one particular conclusion. In this regard, theory construction is based upon a set of operations in logic rather than upon outcome. In the study of childhood psychosis, the major efforts in theory-building have, as we have seen, focused upon description and classification, with little empirical benefit to the children classified and described. With a comparison of two general epistemologies, deductive and inductive, a number of issues may be resolved, if treatment and prognosis, rather than diagnosis and classification, represent the primary dimensions of inquiry in these profoundly disturbed children.

Deductive Approaches.

A common factor in all diagnostic and classification schemes reviewed above is their reliance on a deductive model. That is, the theories assume that specific circumstances, such as biochemical or genetic deficits, or other primary states that render the child vulnerable to environmental circumstances, exist that define and discriminate the psychoses. As we will see, these basic assumptions, constituting a deductive approach, largely predetermine the directions and methods of study of these populations.

Whether or not a deductive model is, in itself, a valuable tool for inquiry is not the primary question. It might be strongly argued that deductive approaches have been a great benefit to the study of phenomena in the natural and biological sciences (Kuhn, 1970; Skinner, 1950). Rather, the issue to be dealt with is whether or not deductive approaches are the methods that are likely to produce the greater benefits in the study of psychosis in children, deserving therefore the largest share of scientific endeavor.

The primary characteristic of the deductive approach is its emphasis on the generation of theory. In the case of psychoses, the attempt is to explain the characteristics of a particular subgroup of children in terms of some criterion set of discriminative events or processes that relate to the etiology and definability of the subgroup. Often the generation of theory requires the statement of certain assumptions about the things we must accept as given because we are unable to assess their validity empirically. For example, most theoreticians assume that psychosis derives from some underlying genetic or metabolic defect as yet unknown to science. Other assumptions may relate to the process of development, such as the "primary circular autistic reaction" postulated by Bettelheim (1967). Irrespective of the particular assumption, the builder of theories must then, through logical reasoning, create a series of postulates of the variety, "If X is true, then Y follows." A complete theory, when appropriately constructed, is difficult to challenge with this dimension, since its logic is internally consistent. This forces speculation to focus upon the correctness of basic assumptions or upon segments of the logical structure amenable to empirical test. Since basic assumptions of a theory are rarely accessible experimentally, the main research focus has involved studies to assess the empirical validity of theoretical postulates. The "hypothesis-testing model" (Sidman, 1960) focuses upon generation of "critical" predictions of the theory. For example, Bettelheim's notions of a hostile and rejecting environment (1967) may be tested experimentally through the study of children in different environments, representing a continuum of warmth and trust. Positive experimental findings are taken to support theory, while negative findings are typically seen as the basis for theory modification to explain conflicting facts. The job of the theory-builder is to design "critical" experiments to support the theory, while its opponents seek to provide contradictory experimental evidence (Skinner, 1950).

A close look at this model suggests a number of inherent difficulties in its assessment. First, it may be argued that the deductive approach contains a number of built-in biases. Since theory has at its core certain assumptions, this is likely to represent a primary area of bias. Psychological experimentation has clearly demonstrated that experience is likely to influence perception and thought (Bruner and Goodman, 1947; Postman and Brown, 1952). The theory-builders are no less susceptible to the influence of their prior experience than other individuals. Professional training is not likely to reduce this potential for bias (Grosz and Grossman, 1968; Heine, 1953; Kass and O'Leary, 1970).

Bias is not likely to end at assumptions. Once constructed, the theory must be empirically tested. Proponents of a theory bear implicitly the responsibility for its experimental support. The desire for positive outcome, based upon belief of the individual in the theory and the issues of professional credibility and social pressure to produce verification, are likely to produce bias in even "objective" experimentation and testing (Chapman and Chapman, 1971; Mischel, 1968).

Finally, since theory is likely to organize and define the boundaries of the experimental work, the generation of experimental questions is limited. Therefore, a theory that is a "good" logical representation of what actually exists is likely to be productive, whereas a "bad" theory may produce years of dead-end research. In psychosis research, since we are as yet unable to differentiate these factors, the value of deductively based research itself may be questioned.

Since to date no hard neurological or biochemical data have clarified the development of children, classified as psychotic, continued reliance on deductively-based theory may remain unproductive. Under these conditions of uncertainty, it is appropriate to consider another approach to the study of children with pervasive behavioral disturbance.

Inductive Approaches.

An alternative strategy would be based upon an inductive model. Inductive science is based on a constructive process by which existing data are compiled to build a theory. As data are produced on specific events, their aggregation may produce a better understanding of some general phenomenon. Induction requires the empirical specification of the conditions under which a behavior occurs, rather than relying on a conceptual attribution. For example, self-injurious behavior (SIB), one of the classes of behaviors associated with psychosis in children, has been extensively studied (e.g., Lovaas and Simmons, 1969; Carr, Newsom, and Binkoff, 1976; Favell, McGimsey, and Jones, 1978). The sum of the individual investigations of factors that influence this behavior has, in recent years, provided better understanding of the function of this behavior and its treatment (Newsom, Carr, and Lovaas, 1979; Russo, Carr, and Lovaas, 1980).

A primary difficulty with inductive science is that it is a slow process. Elucidating the variables that control the occurrence of many of the numerous symptoms associated with psychosis has not yet led us to an understanding of the "whole child" or, indeed, indicated whether any common pathology or process exists across all children—or even all self-injurious children, for example. Despite the lack of rapid understanding of "psychosis" as an "underlying condition," it is clear that much progress has been made in the treatment of these children (Lovaas and Newsom, 1976).

Although slow, inductive science has allowed for the progressive evaluation of more complex variables. Early studies in childhood psychosis were designed to ask the simple question: Do the behaviors psychotic children exhibit follow the same laws of learning that hold for other organisms? These studies (c.f. Ferster and DeMyer, 1961; Lovaas and Simmons, 1969; Lovaas, Schaeffer and Simmons, 1965) manipulated powerful consequences, such as food, attention, and cutaneous shock to elucidate the orderly relationship between a behavior—such as self-injurious behavior—and operations—such as reinforcement and punishment. The outcome of these studies showed that psychotic behavior was indeed lawful, setting the stage for the generation of more complex questions about the nature of psychotic behaviors (Lovaas, Baer, and Bijou, 1965).

A second generation of studies designed on the basis of earlier outcomes was then able to frame questions such as, "Can the operations found effective in controlling individual behaviors be pooled to produce a program of productive instruction?" The generation of receptive and expressive language repertoires in autistic children (Lovaas, Berberich, Perloff, and Schaeffer, 1966) is an excellent example of this constructive process.

Refinement of these procedures has also accompanied this process. As it became clear that manipulation of powerful variables, such as food and pain, produced changes, it also become apparent that these early methods could be made more efficient through the study of newly observed phenomena arising out of these attempts. For example, Lovaas, Schreibman, Koegel, and Rehm (1971) posed the question, "Why, during language training, were sudden decreases observed in correct responding when certain visual stimuli were temporarily eliminated?" The research on stimulus overselectivity (Lovaas et al., 1971; Lovass and Schreibman, 1971) suggested an explanation and led to more productive and efficient treatment programs (Schreibman, 1965; Rincover, 1978; Rincover and Koegel, 1977b). The application of an inductive model in which the operations that produce changes in a behavior are evaluated, as opposed to speculative theoretical explanations of behavior, has demonstrated the ability to account for more of the repertoire of the psychotic child. As we will see, the empirical results of the application of the inductive model have also contributed to the directions taken in current treatment efforts.

By adopting this approach, certain biases inherent in deductive reasoning are lessened. Since inductive approaches study by empirical procedures, the relationships among variables, there can be no "negative" results (Sidman, 1960). Under this scheme, well-controlled research in which particular variables fail to influence the behavior studied also provide facts useful in the aggragation of knowledge. This "variable discovery" research is not immune to the introduction of systematic bias (Kass and O'Leary, 1970). However, since the purpose of this research is to discover the relationships between variables, direct and systematic replication studies are likely to increase confidence in empirical findings. This is particularly true when results are discussed in terms of change in the dependent measure rather than as an attempt to support theory.

Ethical Considerations. Apart from issues of scientific applicability, several other factors must be considered in the selection of an epistemological approach to the study of childhood psychosis. These issues relate to the responsibility inherent in work with children, their rights as patients, and their right to effective treatment. Considerations of this nature are often the result of a general consensus among professionals and the lay community (Risley, 1975). As such, they provide no absolute answers. All scientists and practitioners in helping professions must address their responsibility to those individuals whom they study or seek to serve. As we will review later in this chapter, little data has been generated to indicate that most approaches to childhood psychosis produce beneficial changes. Under these circumstances, unproven, theoretically-based treatments may provide the child no benefit. It would seem to be the responsibility of therapists to select treatments of proven clinical efficacy and to evaluate the impact of these procedures in an empirical fashion to ensure continued progress.

A Behavioral-Inductive Model

Based upon the foregoing review, it would seem that diagnosis, as a precursor to treatment, should have particular characteristics. Primarily, diagnosis should lead to the prescription of treatment and the empirical evaluation of outcome. Traditional diagnosis, based upon deductive models, has failed generally to produce more than a label for the child. Whether children with the pervasive deficits described previously can or should be categorized by 1, 10, or 20 labels makes little difference in the absence of an equal number of specific treatment regimens. Clearly, faced with a child whose symptomatology is often unique in the number, severity, and duration of abnormal behaviors he evidences, diagnostic labels that are nonfunctional in treatment prescription should be considered secondary. While diagnosis and classificatory systems serve to illustrate particular classes of children epidemiologically and, through common effort by national advocacy groups, may certainly increase public awareness and funding, they have not as yet influenced the long-term prognosis of children they identify.

Another, behavioral alternative is present. While less satisfying to those with a theoretical bent, it recognizes the individual differences among children and the lack of a common treatment. By identifying each of the behavioral deficits (e.g., self-injurious behavior, self-stimulation, echolalia), a prescriptive treatment may be developed, based upon existing procedures, program availability, and other factors —such as age of the child. Based on the severity and type of problem behaviors, it may also be predictive of treatment course and prognosis.

Therefore, in an effort to consider the current knowledge base for the treatment of psychotic children, we will review the literature pertinent to the development of empirically-based remediational strategies. While the literature on treatment from all perspectives has increased exponentially in recent years, we limit the review to those studies that serve as the foundations of current inductive efforts in treatment development and conceptualization.

TREATMENT

A wide variety of medical and psychological treatment interventions have been used with psychotic children. No cures are available, and treatments intended to produce global, nonspecific improvement —psychotherapy, pharmacotherapy, play therapy, and electroconvulsive shock—have met with minimal or no success (Bender, 1955; Campbell, 1978; Eisenberg and Kanner, 1956; Ney, Palvesky, and Markely, 1971). However, when specific behavioral deficits are targeted and treated with behavior modification procedures, significant positive changes in those behaviors often occur. Examples of adaptive behaviors that have proven trainable through operant conditioning techniques are visual attention (Brooks, Morrow, and Gray, 1968; Foxx, 1977; Marr, Miller, and Straub, 1966; McConnell, 1967); imitation (Brawley, Harris, Allen, Fleming, and Peterson, 1969; Hingtgen, Coulter, and Churchill, 1967; Lovaas, Freitas, Nelson, and Whalen, 1967; Metz, 1965); verbal language (Lovaas, 1966, 1977; Lovaas, Berberich, Perloff, and Schaeffer, 1966; Risley and Wolf, 1967; Sailor and Taman, 1972; Stevens-Long and Rasmussen, 1974); sign language (Carr, Binkoff, Kologinsky, and Eddy, 1978); play and social contact (DeMyer and Ferster, 1969; Hingtgen, Sanders, and DeMyer, 1965; Hingtgen and Trost, 1966; Koegel, Firestone, Kramme, and Dunlap, 1974; Lovaas, Schaeffer, and Simmons, 1965; Romanczyk, Diament, Goren, Trunell, and Harris, 1975; Wolf and Risley, 1967); and pre-academic and academic skills (Hewett, 1964; LaVigna, 1977; Lovaas, Freitas, Nelson, and Whalen, 1967; Martin, England, Kaprowy, Kilgour, and Pilek, 1968; Rincover, 1978b; Rincover and Koegel, 1977a,b; Rosenbaum and Breiling, 1976; Russo and Koegel, 1977; Schreibman, 1975). Among the maladaptive behaviors that have been successfully treated are echolalia (Carr, Schreibman, and Lovaas, 1975; Lovaas, 1977; Risley and Wolf, 1967); stereotyped, repetitive behavior (Foxx and Azrin, 1973; Lovaas, Schaeffer and Simmons, 1965; Rincover, 1978a); and self-injurious behavior (Baroff and Tate, 1968; Carr, Newsom and Binkoff, 1976; Favell, McGimsey and Jones,

1978; Lovaas and Simmons, 1969; Risley, 1968; Romanczyk and Goren, 1975; Solnick, Rincover and Peterson, 1977; Tate and Baroff, 1966).

The self-injurious behavior of psychotic children provides an excellent example of the development of behavioral technology in analysis and treatment deserving especial mention as a particularly successful area of inductive inquiry. As a class of behaviors, self-injury is viewed across a wide variety of abnormal children with disorders, such as autism (Lovaas and Koegel, 1973); childhood schizophrenia and mental retardation (Frankel and Simmons, 1969); genetic disorders, such as the Lesch-Nyhan (Lesch and Nyhan, 1964) and Cornelia de Lange syndromes (Bryson, Sakoti, Nyhan & Fish, 1971); and sensory neuropathies and dysautonomia (Landwirth, 1964). Mild self-injury is also an accompaniment of normal development in 9 to 17 percent of young children under two years of age (Ilg and Ames, 1955; Schintoub and Soulairac, 1961). Due to the heterogeneity of populations in which this behavior is seen, the varying typographies across children and the life-threatening nature of self-injury, it has received study as a separate behavior, as well as a symptom of the conditions with which it is associated (Russo, Carr, and Lovaas, 1980).

Children in whom self-injury is present often exhibit high rates of banging their heads against their fists or environmental objects, biting themselves, and gouging at flesh or eyes. Additionally, self-injury may take the form of persistent vomiting or rumination or the induction of organic states such as seizures. A first question, behaviorally, was whether these severe, bizarre behaviors responded to the principles of learning. That is, could the rate or intensity of SIB be changed, using operant procedures? Russo, Carr, and Lovaas (1980) have divided these initial studies into two groups, defined by the operations that were used to modify behavior.

The first operation, positive social reinforcement, was found to be correlated with increases in SIB (Lovaas, Freitag, Gold, and Kassorla, 1965; Lovaas and Simmons, 1969; Wolf, Risley, Johnston, Harris, and Allen, 1967). Specifically, studies showed that at-tention provided, contingent upon the occurrence of self-injury, caused increases in the rate and intensity of these behaviors (Lovaas et al., 1965), while removal of attention or extinction produced decreases and eventual elimination of the behaviors (Bucher and Lovaas, 1968; Lovaas and Simmons, 1969). Second, other studies showed that punishment procedures can control SIB. The application of a small number of localized cutaneous shocks has been demonstrated effective in reducing self-injurious behavior in a number of studies (Corte, Wolf, and Locke, 1971; Lovaas, Schaeffer, and Simmons, 1965; Risley, 1968; Risley, Johnston, Harris, and Allen, 1967).

These initial studies demonstrated not only that self-injurious behaviors were lawful, but that behavioral treatments could be highly effective in managing them. Current research has therefore continued to study the direct application of consequences to self-injurious behavior, as well as to evaluate other procedures in which treatment efforts are focused upon manipulation of antecedents to self-injury or upon training of incompatible responses. These recent efforts have attempted to provide alternatives to punishment procedures and to integrate current behavioral knowledge into treatment.

Direct attempts to reduce self-injury have focused upon the manipulation of consequences contingent upon the occurrence of self-injury. Removing or withholding social attention contingent upon self-injury through the use of extinction (Jones, Simmons, and Frankel, 1974; Myers, 1975) or time-out procedures (Gardner, 1969; Hamilton, Stevens, and Allen, 1967; Wolf, Risley, and Mees, 1964) continue to be viable treatment for SIB.

Punishment procedures have represented the most widely studied class of treatments for children with self-injurious behavior. Localized cutaneous shock, applied via an inductorium, a special belt (Galbraith, Byrick, and Rutledge, 1970) or a helmet (Yeakel, Salisbury, Greer, and Marcus, 1970), has demonstrated rapid suppression of self-injurious behavior (Corte, Wolf, and Locke, 1971; Lichstein and Schreibman, 1976; Lovaas and Simmons, 1969; Tate and Baroff, 1966). In some cases, overcorrection represents another punishment procedure that has been effectively utilized as an alternative to electric shock (Azrin, Gottlieb, Hughart, and Weslowski, 1975; Harris and Romanczyk, 1976).

However, procedures, based upon direct treatment, bring about several concerns. The use of extinction or time-out procedures, for example, often result in thousands of self-injurious responses before the rate approaches zero. Punishment procedures have been criticized for their specific, often transitory, effects. Further ethical questions have been raised about selecting punishment as a first attempt at treatment because it may involve pain (in the case of electric shock, it always does). While for many children these procedures are effective and necessary, as a last resort, recent research suggests several potential alternatives that take into account the function of self-injury for the child. Earlier studies, suggesting attention-seeking (Lovaas et al., 1965) and escape functions of self-injurious behavior (Wolf et al., 1967), are stimulating the development of these alternative strategies of treatment. Carr (1977), in a major review of self-injury, proposed that the motivation for self-injury be considered in the design of treatment. He suggested that SIB may function to provide: positive reinforcement to the child through the attention of others; negative reinforcement when environmental demands cease contingent upon its occurrence; or sensory feedback to the child, as a kind of self-stimulating behavior. Consideration of the motivation of self-injurious behavior in the individual child might therefore lead to the design of effective treatments. For example, Carr, Newsom, and Binkoff (1976) demonstrated the control of self-injury in a child in which this behavior provided an escape function by terminating environmental demands. Through the careful manipulation of the social context in which demands were presented, these authors achieved a reduction in self-injury, despite the fact that no direct consequences were applied.

Differential reinforcement of other behavior (DRO) has also been reported as successful in reducing self-injury (Frankel, Moss, Schofield, and Simmons, 1976; Myers, 1975; Peterson and Peterson, 1968). In this procedure, reinforcement is provided for any behavior other than self-injury that occurs during a specified time interval. By gradually increasing the length of the interval, the absence of SIB for longer periods may be shaped.

Favell, McGimsey and Jones (1978) provided an excellent example of what can be accomplished by careful evaluation of SIB and other responses in the child's repertoire. Favell et al. studied children who actively restrain themselves to prevent self-injury (Frankel and Simmons, 1976; Lovaas and Simmons, 1969). They found that the provision of restraint as a reinforcer for unrestrained periods of no self-injury, a DRO procedure, combined with the introduction of toys and activites, was effective in reducing SIB, as well as increasing opportunities for more positive interactions between the staff and the child. Another procedure in which positive behavior is strengthened through compliance training procedures also showed promise in reducing self-injury and other problem behaviors (Cataldo and Russo, 1979; Russo, Cataldo, and Cushing, 1977).

All of these procedures have in common their emphasis on the development of new adaptive repertoires that can be "taught" and maintained by naturally occurring positive reinforcers. By providing indirect treatments for self-injury, they suggest ethical alternatives to punishment and other direct treatments. The careful study of antecedents to self-injury may also serve to facilitate generalization and maintenance of treatment effects (Russo, Carr, and Lovaas, 1980).

This review of self-injury has indicated that an inductive approach has provided for a more efficacious analysis of this problem behavior than was previously available with hypothetical, deductive approaches that assumed feelings of anger or guilt in the child were major determinants of SIB and prescribed reassurance and warmth as treatments (Bettelheim, 1967; Hartman, Kris, and Lowenstein, 1949). A number of other reviews of self-injury (Bachman, 1972; Carr, 1977; Frankel and Simmons, 1976; Russo, Carr, and Lovaas, 1980; Smolev, 1971) may be consulted for additional information on this interesting problem.

Emerging Trends

The procedures developed in the studies cited above form the technological basis for the emergence of new trends in the treatment of psychotic children. Two of the most important of these trends are classroom educational programs and parent training efforts.

Classroom education. Until recently, most psychotic children were placed in large, custodial mental hospitals where they often did not have a school program. Parents who could not bring themselves to institutionalize their children and kept them at home were essentially on their own, since there were no public school classrooms and very few private schools for psychotic children. Some parents met the challenge of rearing and teaching their children admirably (e.g., Park, 1968; Copeland, 1973), while others were much less successful (e.g., Greenfeld, 1978). As the result of public education and lobbying efforts by parents' organizations, such as the National Society for Autistic Children, Public Law 94-142 was enacted in 1975, requiring school districts to provide classrooms for handicapped children. Currently, educational programs for psychotic children are increasingly numerous and classroom education now constitutes the most common form of treatment for these children.

Several guidelines for the development of classroom programs for psychotic children have been presented (Carr, 1976; Elgar, 1966; Everard, 1976; Gallagher and Wiegerink, 1976; Halpern, 1970; Hamblin, Buckholdt, Ferritor, Kozloff, and Blackwell, 1971; Lansing and Schopler, 1978; Oppenheim, 1974; Rincover, Koegel, and Russo, 1978; Wing, 1976). Additionally, certain investigators have attempted to solve some of the specific problems involved in educating psychotic children: the lack of trained teachers; the difficulty of instructing psychotic children in a group rather than individually; and the need for procedures that will effectively teach essential skills in spite of the child's handicaps.

Koegel, Russo, and Rincover (1977) designed and tested procedures to train teachers in the use of fundamental behavior modification skills. During pretesting, they found that children who were being taught individually were not making any progress in learning simple pre-academic tasks, because their teachers were using essential skills less than 50 percent of the time. After the teachers were trained through demonstrations, reading, and supervised practice in the correct use of five skills, such as giving instructions clearly and consistently, prompting, and appropriate consequences, their rate of using the skills averaged 90 percent; all the children made significant progress.

A major problem in educating psychotic children in a classroom is that behaviors acquired in one-to-one training often do not generalize to a group setting (Bijour, 1972; Koegel and Rincover, 1974; Peterson, Cox, and Bijour, 1972). Koegel and Rincover (1974) solved this problem by devising a procedure for gradually increasing the child-teacher ratio from one-to-one to eight-to-one situation. An essential component of this procedure was the reduction in reinforcement density from a fixed-ratio 1 schedule to a variable-ratio 8 schedule. As each child learned to make a gradually increasing number of correct responses before being rewarded, successively larger groups of children were brought together for instruction. In the eight-to-one situation, the children maintained behaviors previously learned in one-to-one training and, in addition, they learned new behaviors as group instruction continued. In a second phase of this research, Rincover and Koegel (1977a) developed a procedure for individualizing instruction within the group-setting by teaching the children to engage gradually in lengthening sequences of behavior without continuous supervision by the teacher.

The importance of the development of procedures, like those just described, is highlighted by the finding that some autistic children exposed to them are able to "graduate" into normal public school classrooms, deriving the benefits of interaction with their normal peers. Russo and Koegel (1977) have presented a method of integrating an autistic child into a normal class of 20 to 30 children that combines features of the teacher- and child-training procedures they had previously developed in collaboration with Rincover.

Another line of research on the education of psychotic children is concerned with the development of ways of presenting classroom tasks that enchance their probability of being learned despite the child's perceptual and cognitive handicaps (e.g., Koegel and Rincover, 1976; Rincover, 1978b; Russo, Koegel, and Lovaas, 1978; Schreibman, 1975). For example, Schreibman (1975) and Rincover (1978b) presented techniques for teaching discriminations to autistic children even when stimulus overselectivity occurs. In their approach, the teacher guides the child to respond correctly by exaggerating a distinct feature of the correct stimulus early in training and then fading it out. For example, in teaching a difficult discrimination between two numbers like 5 and 3, the straight horizontal line atop the 5 might be used as a distinctive-feature prompt, since it is not contained in the 3. That line would be exaggerated in width and length initially, and then the exaggeration would be gradually reduced during training trials. Ultimately the child is responding correctly without the exaggeration prompt.

The results of some follow-up studies suggest that educational treatment of psychotic children is associated with academic and social benefits (Lockyer and Rutter, 1969; Rutter and Bartak, 1973; Rutter, Greenfeld, and Lockyer, 1967). It is important to note that the type of educational program provided makes a considerable difference in whether or not the children show progress. Rutter and Bartak (1973) found that autistic children in a highly structured, goal-oriented classroom made much more progress in language, reading, and arithmetic during a four-year period than did children in either a class that mixed a fair amount of structure with free play or a class that focused entirely upon free play in a permissive atmosphere. There were no differences between the groups in social responsiveness or deviant behavior. Apparently, psychoanalytic theory that a warm, trusting relationship with an adult in the absence of specific skill

training will help psychotic children is actually detrimental to their progress.

Parent Training. Several events set the stage for the emergence of parent training as a major treatment modality for psychotic children. First, by the mid-1960s it was no longer possible to make gratuitous assumptions about parental psychopathology the cause of childhood psychosis, as the evidence against this hypothesis mounted. Freed of the burden of being labeled patients in need of psychotherapy, parents could begin to participate as cotherapists in the treatment of their children alongside professional therapists. Second, the development of behavior modification procedures, many of which are relatively easy to learn and to apply, provided a body of skills that could be taught to parents in a brief period of time. Third, it became evident to professionals that the behavioral gains they produced in psychotic children in their clinics were lost when the children were discharged to settings where the adults were ignorant of behavior modification procedures (Lovaas, Koegel, Simmons, and Long, 1973). Therefore, it became imperative to train parents in the use of these procedures if the children's gains were to be maintained and expanded.

Wolf, Risley, and Mees (1964) conducted the first attempt to train the parents of an autistic child in behavior modification skills. They initially had the parents observe, gradually taking over treatment as the child was moved from the hospital to the home. Since that study was published, several models that involved parents in treatment have developed. At the UCLA Autism Project, directed by Lovaas, parents are required to be at clinic sessions and to participate in treatment as apprentices to experienced graduate-student therapists. They are required to read instructional manuals and to record their child's progress. Therapists visit the home 10 to 20 hours weekly, helping the parents generalize their newly acquired skills to that setting. As the parents gradually become more skillful and take over the main responsibilities of treatment, the project therapists begin to assume the role of consultants (Lovaas, 1978).

Another model of parent training involves the coordination of school and home programs (Lansing, and Schopler, 1978; Schopler and Reichler, 1971). In Schopler's project, curricula for home teaching and the necessary techniques are developed jointly by teachers and parents and recorded in a "Home Program," which is then used both at home and in the child's classroom. Parents and teachers observe each other working with the child, making adjustments in the program during weekly sessions.

A third model of parent training consists exclusively of training in the home (Hemsley, Howlin, Berger, Hersov, Holbrook, Rutter, and Yule, 1978). In the Hemsley et al. (1978) program, the child's major difficulties are identified and evaluated in meetings between parents and a psychologist. A functional analysis of the problems is made with the parents to determine the conditions under which each problem occurs. Treatment plans are drawn up and implemented step by step by the parents in daily training sessions. The psychologist teaches the parents general principles of behavior modification through instruction, readings, and modeling. Visits to the home occur once or twice a week in the early stages of treatment and once a month or less after treatment is established.

Research on parent training has begun to reveal some of the essential components and the results of these efforts. Koegel, Glahn, and Nieminen (1978) evaluated various parent-training procedures and found generalizable skills were acquired only when parents were taught the general principles underlying specific techniques. Hemsley et al. (1978) found that the children involved in their home-based treatment program made significant behavioral gains, especially in language skills, while control children whose parents were not trained remained the same over six-month and eighteen-month follow-up periods.

Other recent treatment developments that will undoubtedly become more important are systematic prevocational training programs (e.g., Byron, 1975) and "teaching homes." or foster homes with trained, professional parent substitutes where family living skills can be taught effectively in a naturalistic setting (Russo,

Glahn, Miners, and Lovaas, 1974). Developments, such as these, provide the basis for much more optimism about the future for psychotic children and their families than was possible as little as 15 years ago.

Summary

Having reviewed the literature on psychosis in childhood, it is increasingly apparent that there exists great diversity in current thought and practice. Attempts to diagnose differentially children with severely deviant behavior are often based upon theoretical orientation rather than upon a set of attributes that are suggestive of treatment and outcome.

As a society, we are faced with large numbers of children, who are clearly outside developmental and behavioral norms, and for whom therapeutic services are required. The basis for these services should not be merely theoretical, but should consider outcome as well. The necessity for coordinated service programs involving home and school, or institutional environments whose programs are educational rather than custodial, cannot be understated or ignored.

At the same time that increased programs for treatment are required, one should not ignore continued research on the etiology and development of psychosis. Most workers hold that the psychoses of childhood, as well as adulthood, may have an undefined neurological or biochemical base. The scientific understanding of these causal variables is a necessary step, but clearly not sufficient toward the development of effective treatments. That is, even if a biological cause for childhood psychosis and any or all of its behavioral manifestations were found, we still would be faced with the task of bringing to this group of behaviorally deficient children a program of educational, language, and social skills training. In lieu of a major medical breakthrough, research to develop treatment procedures based upon an understanding of the behavioral, intellectual, and perceptual deficits of these children is required.

THE PROGNOSIS FOR PSYCHOTIC CHILDREN

Despite steady increases in treatment technology for behavior change in psychotic children, what is likely to be their prognosis? How well will they be able to fit within the increasingly less-restrictive environments being developed for them? Specifically, is the psychotic child any more likely to benefit from treatment today than 15-20 years ago?

It can be stated unequivocally that research has generated a far more sophisticated understanding of the function and control of deviant behaviors. However, while initial behavior change and the factors that produce it have been extensively studied, it is not at all clear that behaviors changed as a result of these treatments are likely to be maintained over time unless specific conditions are arranged to facilitate their continued performance (Lovaas et al., 1973; Stokes and Baer, 1977). Therefore, while research continues as to the conditions under which psychotic behavior may be changed, we have been led to an increased emphasis on the creation of environments and procedures to produce continued behavioral gains. The prognosis for the success of the psychotic child is tied wholly to these endeavors and cannot be considered independently. The research reviewed in the treatment section of this chapter serves as a final point for this review in its suggestion of emphasis for the conduct of future research. Two general issues following from that review are particularly pertinent in considering the prognosis of the psychotic child: the design of consistent and continuous therapeutic environments and the early identification and treatment of children with psychotic behaviors.

Therapeutic Environments. Behaviorally induced changes in psychotic children are extremely fragile. They do not maintain themselves well in the post-treatment environment unless specific conditions are programmed (Lovaas et al. 1973). Recent research has therefore been undertaken to provide consistent environments in which the knowledge gained through research may be combined in comprehensive programs for behavior change. As the psychotic child goes from home to school, or to any other activity, his therapeutic program must accompany him. As previously stated, the classroom has provided a primary area for this study (Rincover, Koegel, and Russo, 1978). Current research has been designed to evaluate the characteristics of the classroom that produce maximal learning (Koegel and Rincover, 1974; Rincover and Koegel, 1977a), investigate efficient instructional strategies (Russo, Koegel, and Lovaas, 1978), develop advanced skills, such as observational learning (Varni, Lovaas, Koegel, and Everett, in press), and create programs to ensure the opportunity for educational advancement within the mainstream of education (Russo and Koegel, 1977). Besides the design of curriculum and classroom environments, procedures to train teachers to become effective behavior therapists have also been devised (Koegel, Russo, and Rincover, 1977). The sum of this research has made possible the design of comprehensive educational programs with documented benefits to the psychotic child (Rincover & Koegel, 1977b; Rincover, Koegel, and Russo, 1978).

The family home, a second major treatment environment, has also received increased attention. Programs to train parents in the same skills as teachers such that congruent cross-environment programs may be developed have been devised and evaluated (Koegel, Glahn, and Nieminen, 1978; Kozloff, 1973). These training programs, if disseminated on a large scale, offer promise to maintain children within the mainstream of community life, providing at least an alternative to the institutionalization that has been the traditional fate of the psychotic child.

A large number of children are, however, currently in institutions. For these children, therapeutic environments are needed that approximate conditions to be encountered in community settings. Rather than treating children in the context of an institutional ward, where the changing shifts, physical environment, and learning programs are unlike any to be found in home or community environments, new models, more closely approximating mainstream environments, are required. Group home facilities ("teaching homes") are currently in operation, and research is under way to determine their effectiveness in returning institutionalized psychotic children to the community (Russo, Glahn, Miners, and Lovaas, 1974; Glahn, Lovaas, and Russo, 1977). Through a focus on home living environments, operated by professional "teaching parents," children may progress through a series of programs that are designed to provide a slow transition from institution to community. The concurrent training of their natural parents is used to facilitate their transfer to the community.

While all of these programs are still in development and evaluation, and research is continually required for program refinement, the application of the basic principles learned in earlier research has provided the empirical base for their development. Although it is uncertain what the final prognosis for these children will be, the systematic alternatives being developed offer consistent behavioral treatment environments—previously unavailable.

Early Identification and Treatment. The design of environments for the psychotic child is, in a number of senses, a reactive attempt to provide service for those children who have been previously underserved. A second conceptual strategy represents a preventive approach and provides a promising alternative. By identifying and treating children at an early age, Lovaas (1977) suggested that we may have greater impact of treatment and significantly improve the prognosis for these children. Children between the ages of one and four years who are identified as psychotic are much less behaviorally deficient relative to their normal peers than are older psychotic children. Therapeutically, much less training is required at this age to close the behavioral gap between the psychotic and the normal preschool child. Further, the younger child has had less opportunity to engage in psychotic behaviors; therefore, the deviant repertoire is less likely to have become generalized and is more likely to respond to contingency procedures in the home and clinic environments (Lovaas and Newsom, 1976).

CONCLUSION

This review of the psychotic disorders of childhood has attempted to evaluate the current data base regarding the known diagnostic, treatment, and prognostic factors. It has been specific in its intent to bypass current and historical theorizing and, instead, to focus on a more basic epistemological level. What emerges from such a study is that deductive, theoretical speculation has so far failed to produce the comprehensive understanding for which it has been known in other fields of endeavor. A behavioral-inductive model to guide research and treatment has been suggested as a potential alternative. In its insistence on empirical data, the focus upon treatment as opposed to diagnosis, and the demonstrated ability to deal with successively more comprehensive aspects of the behavior of psychotic children, this model appears to provide strong justification for its use as a conceptual approach to the study of childhood psychosis. While the most likely breakthrough in understanding these children will be in biochemical/structural studies, recent advances, characterized by the development of comprehensive environmentally-based treatments, provide the clearest immediate potential for the improvement of the behavioral deviations observed in psychotic children.

REFERENCES

Azrin, N. H., Gottlieb, L., Hughart, L., Wesolowski, M. D., & Rahn, T. Eliminating self injurious behavior by educative procedures. *Behavior Research and Therapy*, 1975, *13*, 101–111.

Bachman, J. A. Self-injurious behavior: A behavioral analysis. *Journal of Abnormal Psychology*, 1972, *80*, 211–244.

Bakwin, H. Early infantile autism. *Journal of Pediatrics*, 1954, *45*, 492–497.

Baroff, G. S., & Tate, B. G. The use of aversive stimulation in the treatment of self-injurious behavior. *Journal of the American Academy of Child Psychiatry*, 1968, *7*, 454–460.

Barry, R. J., & James, A. L. Handedness in autistics, retardates, and normals of a wide age range. *Journal of Autism and Childhood Schizophrenia*, 1978, *8*, 315–323.

Bartak, L., & Rutter, M. The use of personal pronouns by autistic children. *Journal of Autism and Childhood Schizophrenia*, 1974, *4*, 217–222.

Bartak, L., Rutter, M., & Cox, A. A comparative study of infantile autism and specific developmental receptive language disorder. I. The children. *British Journal of Psychiatry*, 1975, *126*, 127–245.

Behrens, M., & Goldfarb, W. A study of patterns of interaction of families of schizophrenic children in residential treatment. *American Journal of Orthopsychiatry*, 1958, *28*, 300–312.

Bender, L. The development of a schizophrenic child treated with electric convulsions at three years of age. In G. Caplan (Ed.), *Emotional problems of early childhood.* New York: Basic Books, 1955.

Bender, L. Treatment in early schizophrenia. *Progress in Psychotherapy*, 1960, *5*, 177–184.

Bender, L. & Grugett, A. A study of certain epidemiological factors in a group of children with childhood schizophrenia. *American Journal of Orthopsychiatry*, 1956, *26*, 131–145.

Bettelheim, B. *The empty fortress.* New York: Free Press, 1967.

Bijou, S. W. The technology of teaching handicapped children. In S. W. Bijour & E. Ribes-Inesta (Eds.), *Behavior modification: Issues and extensions.* New York: Academic Press, 1972.

Birch, H., and Hertzig, M. Etiology of schizophrenia: An overview of the relation of development to atypical behavior. Paper presented at the Internal Conference on Schizophrenia, Rochester, March, 1967.

Blackstock, E. G. Cerebral asymmetry and the development of early infantile autism. *Journal of Autism and Childhood Schizophrenia*, 1978, *8*, 339–353.

Blueler, E. *Dementia praecox or the group of schizophrenias.* (Joseph Zinkin, Trans.) New York: International Universities Press, 1952.

Boatman M. J., & Szurek, S. A. A clinical study of childhood schizophrenia. In D. D. Jackson (Ed.), *The etiology of schizophrenia.* New York: Basic Books, 1960.

Book, J., Nichtern, S., & Gruenberg, E. Cyto–genetical investigation in childhood schizophrenia. *Acta Psychiatrica Scandinavia.* 1963, *39*, 309–323.

Boullin, E. J., Coleman, M., & O'Brien, R. A. Abnormalities in platelet 5–hydroxytryptamine efflux in patients with infantile autism. *Nature.* 1970, *226*, 371–372.

Boullin, D., Coleman, M., O'Brien, R., & Rimland, B. Laboratory prediction of infantile autism based on 5–hydroxytryptamine efflux from blood platelets and their correlation with the Rimland E2 score. *Journal of Autism and Childhood Schizophrenia*, 1971, *1*, 63–71.

Brawley, E. R., Harris, F. R., Allen, K. E., Fleming, R. S., & Peterson, R. F. Behavior modification of an autistic child. *Behavioral Science*, 1969, *14*, 87–97.

Brooks, B., Morrow, J. & Gray, W. F. Reduction of autistic gaze aversion by reinforcement of visual–attention responses. *Journal of Special Education.* 1968, *2*, 307–309.

Bruner, J. S., & Goodman, C. C. Value and need as organizing factors in perception. *Journal of Abnormal and Social Psychology*, 1947, *42*, 33–44.

Bryson, C. Short–term memory and cross–modal information processing in autistic children. *Journal of Learning Disabilities*, 1972, *5*, 25–35.

Bryson, V., Sakati, N., Nyhan, W. L., & Fish, C. H. Self–mutilative behavior in the Cornelia de Lange syndrome. *American Journal of Mental Deficiency*, 1971, *76*, 319–324.

Bucher, B. & Lovaas, O. I. Use of aversive stimulation in behavior modification. In M. Jones (Ed.), *Miami Symposium on the Prediction of Behavior, 1967: Aversive Stimulation.* Coral Gables, Fla.: University of Miami Press, 1968.

Byron, R. A prevocational training program utilizing behavior modification techniques with behaviorally disoriented adolescents. In *Proceedings of the Annual Meeting and Conference of the National Society of Autistic Children, 1975.* Albany, N.Y.: National Society for Autistic Children, 1975.

Campbell, M. Pharmacotherapy. In M. Rutter & E. Schopler (Eds.), *Autism: A reappraisal of concepts and treatment.* New York: Plenum, 1978.

Carr, E. G. The motivation of self–injurious behavior: A review of some hypotheses. *Psychological Bulletin*, 1977, *84*, 800–816.

Carr, J. The severely retarded autistic child. In L. Wing (Ed.), *Early childhood autism: Clinical, educational and social aspects* (2nd ed.) London: Pergamon, 1976.

Carr, E. G., Binkoff, J. A., Kologinsky, E., & Eddy, M. Acquisition of sign language by autistic children. I. Expressive labeling. *Journal of Applied Behavior Analysis*, 1978, in press.

Carr, E. G., Newsom, C. D., & Binkoff, J. A. Stimulus control of self–destructive behavior in a psychotic child. *Journal of Abnormal Child Psychology*, 1976, *4*, 139–153.

Carr, E. G., Schreibman, L., & Lovaas, O. I. Control of echolalic speech in psychotic children. *Journal of Abnormal Child Psychology*, 1975, *3*, 331–351.

Cataldo, M. F. & Russo, D. C. Developmentally disabled in the community: Behavioral/Medical considerations. In L. A. Hamerlynck (Ed.), *Behavioral systems, for the developmentally disabled: II. Institutional, clinic, and community environments.* New York: Bruner/Mazel, 1979, 105–143.

Chapman, L. J., & Chapman, J. P. Associatively based illusory correlation as a source of psychodiagnostic folklore. In L. D. Goodstein & R. T. Lanyon (Eds.), *Readings in personality assessment.* New York: John Wiley and Sons, 1971.

Chess, S. Autism in children with congenital rubella. *Journal of Autism and Childhood Schizophrenia*, 1971, *1*, 33–34.

Chess, S. Follow–up report on autism in congenital rubella. *Journal of Autism and Childhood Schizophrenia*, 1977, *7*, 69–81.

Coleman, M. Serotonin and central nervous system syndromes of childhood: A review. *Journal of Autism and Childhood Schizophrenia*, 1975, *3*, 27–35.

Coleman, M., (Ed.), *The autistic syndromes.* Amsterdam: North Holland, 1976.

Coleman, M., & Rimland, B. Familial Autism. In M. Coleman (Ed.), *The autistic syndromes.* Amsterdam: North Holland, 1976.

Copeland, J., & Hodges, J. *For the love of Ann.* London: Arrow Brooks, 1973.

Corte, H. E., Wolf, M. M., & Locke, B. J. A comparison of procedures for eliminating self–injurious behavior of retarded adolescents. *Journal of Applied Behavior Analysis*, 1971, *4*, 201–213.

Creak, M. Schizophrenic syndrome in childhood: Progress report of a working party. *Cerebral Palsy Bulletin*, 1961, *3*, 501–504.

Creak, M. Childhood psychosis: A review of 100 cases. *British Journal of Psychiatry*, 1963, *109*, 84–89.

Cunningham, M. A. A comparison of the language of psychotic and nonpsychotic children who are mentally retarded. *Journal of Child Psychology and Psychiatry*, 1968, *9*, 229–244.

Dalgleish, B. Cognitive processing and linguistic reference in autistic children. *Journal of Autism and Childhood Schizophrenia*, 1975, *5*, 353–363.

Darby, J. Neuropathologic aspects of psychosis in children. *Journal of Autism and Childhood Schizophrenia*, 1976, *6*, 339–352.

Darr, G. C., & Worden, F. G. Case report twenty–eight years after an infantile autistic disorder. *American Journal of Orthopsychiatry*, 1951, *21*, 559–570.

Davison, G. C. A social learning therapy programme with an autistic child. *Behaviour Research and Therapy*, 1964, *2*, 149–159.

de Hirsch, K. Differential diagnosis between asphasic and schizophrenic language in children. *Journal of Speech and Hearing Disorders*, 1967, *32*, 3–10.

DeMyer, M. K. Motor, perceptual–motor and intellectual disabilities of autistic children. In L. Wing (Ed.), *Early childhood autism: Clinical, educational and social aspects* (2nd ed.). London: Pergamon, 1976.

DeMyer, M., Barton, S., Alpern, G., Kimberlin, C., Allen, J., Yang, E., & Steele, R. The measured intelligence of autistic children. *Journal of Autism and Childhood Schizophrenia*, 1974, *4*, 42–60.

DeMyer, M. K., Churchill, D., Pontius, W., & Gilkey, K. A comparison of five diagnostic systems for childhood schizophrenia and infantile autism. *Journal of Autism and Childhood Schizophrenia*, 1971, *1*, 175–189.

DeMyer, M. K., & Ferster, C. B. Teaching new social behavior to schizophrenic children. *Journal of the American Academy of Child Psychiatry*, 1962, *1*, 443–461.

DeMyer, M., Pontius, W., Norton, J., Barton, S., Allen, J., & Steele, R. Parental practices and innate activity in autistic and brain–damaged infants. *Journal of Autism and Childhood Schizophrenia*, 1972, *2*, 49–66.

De Sanctes, S. La neuropsychiatria infantile. *Infanzia Anormale*, 1925, *18*, 663–661.

Despert, J. L. Schizophrenia in childhood. *Psychiatric Quarterly*, 1938, *12*, 366–371.

Despert, J. L. Some considerations relating to the genesis of autistic behavior in children. *American Journal of Orthopsychiatry*, 1951, *21*, 335–350.

Eisenberg, L. Psychotic disorders in childhood. In R. E. Cook, (Ed.), *Biological basis of pediatric practice.* New York: McGraw–Hill, 1966.

Elgar, S. Teaching autistic children. In J. K. Wing (Ed.), *Early childhood autism: Clinical, educational and social aspects.* London: Pergamon, 1966.

Everard, M. P. (Ed.). *An approach to teaching autistic children.* London: Pergamon, 1976.

Favell, J. E., McGimsey, J. F., & Jones, M. L. The use of physical restraint in the treatment of self–injury and as positive reinforcement. *Journal of Applied Behavior Analysis*, 1978, *11*, 225–241.

Ferster, C. B. & DeMyer, M. K. The development of performances in autistic children in an automatically controlled environment. *Journal of Chronic Diseases*, 1961, *13*, 312–345.

Fish, B., Shapiro, T., Campbell, M., & Wile, R. A classification of schizophrenic children under five years. *American Journal of Psychiatry*, 1968, *124*, 1415–1423.

Foxx, R. M. Attention training: The use of overcorrection avoidance to increase the eye contact of autistic and retarded children. *Journal of Applied Behavior Analysis, 1977, 10,* 489–499.

Foxx, R. M., & Azrin, N. H. The elimination of autistic self–stimulatory behavior by overcorrection. *Journal of Applied Behavior Analysis*, 1973, *6*, 1–14.

Frankel, F., Moss, D., Schofield, S., & Simmons, J. Q. Case Study: Use of differential reinforcement to supress self–injurious and aggressive behavior. *Pyschological Report*, 1976, *39*, 843–849.

Frankel, F. & Simmons, J. Q. Self–injurious behavior in schizophrenic and retarded children. *American Journal of Mental Deficiency*, 1976, *80*, 512–522.

Friedman, G. Conceptual thinking in schizophrenic children. *Genetic Psychology Monographs*, 1961, *63*, 149–196.

Frith, U. Studies in pattern detection in normal and autistic children: Reproduction and production of color sequences. *Journal of Experimental Child Psychology*, 1970, *10*, 120–130 (a).

Frith, U. Studies in pattern perception in normal and autistic children: Immediate recall of auditory sequences. *Journal of Abnormal Psychology*, 1970, *76*, 413–421 (b).

Frith, U. Cognitive mechanisms in autism: Experiments with color and time sequence production. *Journal of Autism and Childhood Schizophrenia*, 1972, *2*, 160–173.

Frith, U., & Hermelin, B. The role of visual and motor cues for normal, subnormal, and autistic children. *Journal of Child Psychology and Psychiatry*, 1969, *10*, 153–163.

Fuller, G. The objective measurement of perception in determining personality disorganization among children. *Journal of Clinical Psychology*, 1965, *2*, 305–307.

Fulton, R. T., & Lloyd, L. L. *Audiometry for the retarded.* Baltimore: Williams & Wilkins, 1969.

Galbraith, D. A., Byrick, R. J., & Rutledge, J. T. An aversive conditioning approach to the inhibition of chronic vomiting. *Canadian Psychiatric Association Journal*, 1970, *15*, 311–313.

Gallagher, J. J., & Wiegerink, R. Educational strategies for the autistic child. *Journal of Autism and Childhood Schizophrenia*, 1976, *6*, 15–26.

Gardner, W. I. Use of punishment procedures

with the severely retarded: A review. *American Journal of Mental Deficiency*, 1969, *74*, 86–103.

Gittelman, M., & Birch, H. Childhood schizophrenia: Intellect, neurologic status, perinatal risk, prognosis, and family pathology. *Archives of General Psychiatry*, 1967, *17*, 16–25.

Glahn, T. J., Lovaas, O. I., & Russo, D. C. Teaching homes: An alternative to institutionalization for psychotic children. Unpublished manuscript, 1977.

Goldfarb, W. *Childhood schizophrenia.* Cambridge, Mass.: Harvard University Press, 1961.

Goldfarb, W. Childhood psychosis. In P. H. Mussen (Ed.), *Carmichael's manual of child psychology,* (Vol. 2). New York: Wiley, 1970.

Goldfarb, W., Braunstein, P., & Lorge, I. A study of speech patterns in a group of schizophrenic children. *American Journal of Psychiatry*, 1966, *122*, 1220–1227.

Goldfarb, W., Goldfarb, N., & Scholl, H. The speech of mothers of schizophrenic children. *American Journal of Psychiatry*, 1966, *122*, 1220–1227.

Greenfeld, J. *A place for Noah.* New York: Holt, Rinehart & Winston, 1978.

Grosz, H. J., & Grossman, K. G. Clinician's response style: A source of variation and bias in clinical judgements. *Journal of Abnormal Psychology*, 1968, *73*, 207–214.

Group for the Advancement of Psychiatry. Psychopathological disorders in childhood: Theoretical considerations and a proposed classification. *Report No. 62, 1966, 6,* 173–343.

Halpern, W. I. Schooling of autistic children. *American Journal of Orthopsychiatry*, 1970, *40*, 665–671.

Hamblin, R. L., Buckholdt, D., Ferritor, D., Kozloff, M., & Blackwell, L. *The humanization process.* New York: Wiley, 1971.

Hamilton, J., Stephens, L., & Allen, P. Controlling aggressive and destructive behavior in severely retarded institutionalized residents. *American Journal of Mental Deficiency*, 1967, *71*, 852–856.

Harris, S. L. & Romanczyk, R. G. A brief report on treating self–injurious behavior with overcorrection. *Behavior Therapy*, 1976, *7*, 237.

Hartman, J., Kris, E., & Lowenstein, R. M. Notes on the theory of aggression. *The psychoanalytic study of the child*, 1949, *3*, 1–36.

Heine, R. W. A comparison of patients' reports on psychotherapeutic experience with psychoanalytic, nondirective, and Alderian therapists. *American Journal of Psychotherapy*, 1953, *7*, 16–23.

Hemsley, R., Howlin, P., Berger, M., Hersov, L., Holbrook, D., Rutter, M., & Yule, W. Treating autistic children in a family context. In M. Rutter and E. Schopler (Eds.), *Autism: A reappraisal of concepts and treatment.* New York: Plenum, 1978.

Hermelin, B. Coding and the sense modalities. In L. Wing (Ed.), *Early childhood autism: Clinical, educational and social aspects* (2nd ed.). London: Pergamon, 1976.

Hermelin, B., & O'Connor, N. Measures of the occipital alpha rhythm in normal, subnormal, and autistic children. *British Journal of Psychiatry,* 1968, *114,* 603–610.

Herzberg, B. The families of autistic children. In M. Coleman (Ed.), *The autistic syndromes.* Amsterdam: North Holland, 1976.

Hewett, F. M. Teaching speech to an autistic child through operant conditioning. *American Journal of Orthopsychiatry,* 1965, *35,* 927–936.

Hewett, F. M. Teaching reading to an autistic boy through operant conditioning. *The Reading Teacher,* 1974, *17,* 613–618.

Hingtgen, J. N., & Coulter, S. K. Auditory control of operant behavior in mute autistic children. *Perceptual and Motor Skills,* 1967, *25,* 561–565.

Hingtgen, J. N., Coulter, S. K., & Churchill, D. W. Intensive reinforcement of imitative behavior in mute autistic children. *Archives of General Psychiatry,* 1967, *17,* 36–43.

Hingtgen, J. N., Sanders, B. J., & DeMyer, M. K. Shaping cooperative responses in early childhood schizophrenia. In L. P. Ullmann & L. Krasner (Eds.), *Case studies in behavior modification.* New York: Holt, Rinehart and Winston, 1965.

Hingtgen, J. N., & Trost, F. C. Shaping cooperative responses in early childhood schizophrenics: II. Reinforcement of mutual physical contact and vocal responses. In R. Ulrich, T. Stachnik, & J. Mabry (Eds.), *Control of human behavior.* Glenview, Ill.: Scott, Foresman, and Company, 1966.

Hoberman, S., & Goldfarb, W. Speech reception thresholds in schizophrenic children. *Journal of Speech and Hearing Research,* 1963, *6,* 101–106.

Hulse, W. C. Dementia infantilis. *Journal of Nervous and Mental Diseases,* 1954, *319,* 417–477.

Hutt, C., Hutt, S. J., Lee, D., & Ounsted, C. Arousal and childhood autism. *Nature,* 1964, *204,* 908–909.

Hutt, S. J., Hutt, C., Lee, D., & Ounsted, C. A behavioral and electroencephalographic study of autistic children. *Journal of Psychiatric Research,* 1965, *3,* 181–197.

Ilg, F. L. & Ames, L. B. *Child behavior.* New York: Harper, 1955.

Itard, J. M. G. *The wild boy of Aveyron.* (G. & M. Humphrey, trans.) New York: Appleton–Century–Crofts, 1962. (Originally published, 1894).

Jones, F. H., Simmons, J. Q., & Frankel, F. An extinction procedure for eliminating self–destructive behavior in a 9–year–old autistic girl. *Journal of Autism and Childhood Schizophrenia,* 1974, *4,* 241–250.

Judd, L., & Mandell, A. Chromosome studies in early infantile autism. *Archives of General Psychiatry,* 1968, *18,* 450–457.

Kallman, F., & Roth, B. Genetic aspects of preadolescent schizophrenia. *American Journal of Psychiatry,* 1956, *112,* 599–606.

Kanner, L. Autistic disturbances of affective contact. *Nervous Child,* 1943, *2,* 181–197.

Kanner, L. Early infantile autism. *Journal of Pediatrics,* 1944, *25,* 211–217.

Kanner, L. Irrelevant and mataphorical language in early infantile autism. *American Journal of Psychiatry,* 1946, *103,* 242–246.

Kanner, L. Childhood psychosis: A historical overview. In L. Kanner, *Childhood psychosis: Initial studies and new insights.* Washington, D.C.: V. H. Winston & Sons, 1973.

Kanner, L., & Eisenberg, L. Notes on the follow–up studies of autistic children. In P. H. Houch & J. Zubin (Eds.), *Psychopathology of childhood.* New York: Grune & Stratton, 1955.

Kanner, L. & Lesser, L. Early infantile autism. *Pediatric Clinics of North America,* 1958, *5,* 711–730.

Kass, R. E., & O'Leary, K. D. The effects of observer bias in field–experimental settings. Paper presented at *Symposium on Behavior Analysis in Education.* University of Kansas, April 9, 1970.

Kaufman, I., Frank, T., Heims, L., Herrick, J., & Willer, L. Parents of schizophrenic children: Four types of defense in mothers and fathers of schizophrenic children. *American Journal of Orthopsychiatry,* 1959, *29,* 460–472.

Kennard, M. Inheritance of electroencephalogram patterns in children with behavior disorders. *Psychomosomatic Medicine,* 1949, *11,* 151–157.

Kennard, M. The characteristics of thought disturbance as related to electroencephalographic findings in children and adolescents. *American Journal of Psychiatry,* 1959, *115,* 911–921.

Klebanoff, L. Parental attitudes of mothers of schizophrenic, brain–injured and retarded, and normal children. *American Journal of Orthopsychiatry,* 1959, *29,* 445–454.

Koegel, R. L., Firestone, P. B., Kramme, K. W., & Dunlap, G. Increasing spontaneous play by suppressing self–stimulation in autistic children. *Journal of Applied Behavior Analysis,* 1974, *7*, 521–528.

Koegel, R. L., Glahn, T. J., & Nieminen, G. S. Generalization of parent–training results. *Journal of Applied Behavior Analysis,* 1978, *11*, 95–109.

Koegel, R. L., & Rincover, A. Treatment of psychotic children in a classroom environment: I. Learning in a large group. *Journal of Applied Behavior Analysis,* 1974, *7*, 45–59.

Koegel, R. L., & Rincover, A. Some detrimental effects of using extra stimuli to guide learning in normal and autistic children. *Journal of Abnormal Child Psychology,* 1976, *4*, 59–71.

Koegel, R. L., Russo, D. C., & Rincover, A. Assessing and training teachers in the generalized use of behavior modification with autistic children. *Journal of Applied Behavior Analysis,* 1977, *10*, 197–205.

Koegel, R. L., & Schreibman, L. Teaching autistic children to respond to stimultaneous multiple cues. *Journal of Experimental Child Psychology,* 1977, *24*, 299–311.

Koegel, R. L., & Wilhelm, H. Selective to the components of multiple visual cues by autistic children. *Journal of Experimental Child Psychology,* 1973, *15*, 442–453.

Kolvin, I. Psychoses in childhood—a comparative study. In M. Rutter (Ed.), *Infantile autism: Concepts, characteristics, and treatment.* London: Churchill–Livingstone, 1971.

Kovattana, P. M. & Kraemer, H. C. Response to multiple visual cues of color, size, and form by autistic children. *Journal of Autism and Childhood Schizophrenia,* 1974, *4*, 251–261.

Kozloff, M. A. *Reaching the autistic child: A parent training program.* Champaign, Ill.: Research Press, 1973.

Kraeplin, E. *Dementia praecox.* M. R. Barcley, trans. Edinburgh: Livingstone, 1919.

Kuhn, S. *The structure of scientific revolutions.* (2nd Ed., Enlarged.) Chicago: University of Chicago Press, 1970.

Landwirth, J. Sensory radicular neuropathy and retinitis pigmentosa. *Pediatrics,* 1964, *34*, 519.

Lansing, M. D., & Schopler, E. Individualized education: A public school model. In M. Rutter & E. Schopler (Eds.), *Autism: A reappraisal of concepts and treatment.* New York: Plenum, 1978.

LaVigna, G. W. Communication training in mute autistic adolescents using the written word. *Journal of Autism and Childhood Schizophrenia,* 1977, *7*, 135–149.

Lesch, M., & Nyhan, W. L. A familial disorder of uric acid metabolism and central nervous system function. *American Journal of Medicine,* 1964, *36*, 561–570.

Lichstein, K. L. & Schreibman, L. Employing electric shock with autistic children. *Journal of Autism and Childhood Schizophrenia,* 1976, *6*, 163–174.

Lockyer, L., & Rutter, M. A five to fifteen year follow-up study of infantile psychosis—III. Psychological aspects. *British Journal of Psychiatry,* 1969, *115*, 865–882.

Lotter, V. Epidemiology of autistic conditions in young children. I. Prevalance. *Social Psychiatry,* 1966, *1*, 124–137.

Lotter, V. Epidemiology of autistic conditions in young children. II. Some characteristics of the parents and children. *Social Psychiatry,* 1967, *1*, 163–173.

Lovaas, O. I. A program for the establishment of speech in psychotic children. In J. K. Wing (Ed.), *Early childhood autism: Clinical, educational and social aspects.* London: Pergamon, 1966.

Lovaas, O. I. *The autistic child: Language development through behavior modification.* New York: Irvington, 1977.

Lovaas, O. I. Alternatives to hospitalization for autistic children. Paper presented at Annual Convention of National Society for Autistic Children, Orlando, Fla., 1977.

Lovaas, O. I. Parents as therapists. In M. Rutter & E. Schopler (Eds.), *Autism: A reappraisal of concepts and treatment.* New York: Plenum, 1978.

Lovaas, O. I., Baer, D. M., and Bijou, S. W. Experimental procedures for analyzing the interaction of symbolic social stimuli and children's behavior. *Child Development,* 1965, *36*, 237–247.

Lovaas, O. I., Berberich, J. P., Perloff, B. F., & Schaeffer, B. Acquisition of imitative speech by schizophrenic children. *Science,* 1966, *151*, 705–707.

Lovaas, O. I., Freitag, G., Gold, V. J., & Kassorla, I. C. Experimental studies in childhood schizophrenia. I. Analysis of self-destructive behavior. *Journal of Experimental Child Psychology,* 1965, *2*, 67–84.

Lovaas, O. I., Freitas, L., Nelson, K., & Whalen, C. The establishment of imitation and its use for the development of complex behavior in schizophrenic children. *Behaviour research and therapy,* 1967, *5*, 171–181.

Lovaas, O. I., and Koegel, R. L. Behavior therapy with autistic children. In C. E. Thoreson (Ed.), *Behavior Modification in Education.* Seventy-second yearbook of the National Society for the Study of Education. Chicago: University of Chicago Press, 1973.

Lovaas, O. I., Koegel, R. L., Simmons, J. Q., & Long, J. S. Some generalization and follow-up measures on autistic children in behavior therapy. *Journal of Applied Behavior Analysis*, 1973, *6*, 131–165.

Lovaas, O. I. & Newsom, C. D. Behavior modification with psychotic children. In H. Leitenberg (Ed.), *Handbook of behavior modification and behavior therapy*. New York: Appleton-Century-Crofts, 1976.

Lovaas, O. I., Schaeffer, B., & Simmons, J. Q. Experimental studies in childhood schizophrenia: Building social behavior in autistic children by use of electric shock. *Journal of Experimental Research in Personality*, 1965, *1*, 99–109.

Lovaas, O. I., Schreibman, L., Koegel, R. L., & Rehm, R. Selective responding by autistic children to multiple sensory input. *Journal of Abnormal Psychology*, 1971, *77*, 211–222.

Lovaas, O. I., & Simmons, J. Q. Manipulation of self-destruction in three retarded children. *Journal of Applied Behavior Analysis*, 1969, *2*, 143–157.

Lowe, L. H. Families of children with early childhood schizophrenia: Selected demographic information. *Archives of General Psychiatry*, 1966, *16*, 26–30.

Mahler, M. S. On child psychosis and schizophrenia: Autistic and symbiotic infantile psychoses. *Psychoanalytic Study of the Child*, 1952, *7*, 286–305.

Makita, K. The age of onset of childhood schizophrenia. *Folia Psychiatrica et Neurologica*, 1966, *20*, 111–121.

Marr, J., Miller, E., & Straub, R. Operant conditioning of attention with a psychotic girl. *Behaviour Research and Therapy*, 1966, *4*, 85–87.

Martin, G. L., England, G., Kaprowy, E., Kilgour, K., & Pilek, V. Operant conditioning of kindergarten-class behavior in autistic children. *Behavior Research and Therapy*, 1968, *6*, 281–294.

McConnell, O. L. Control of eye contact in an autistic child. *Journal of Child Psychology and Psychiatry*, 1967, *8*, 249–255.

Metz, J. R. Conditioning generalized imitation in autistic children. *Journal of Experimental Child Psychology*, 1965, *2*, 389–399.

Meyers, D., & Goldfarb, W. Psychiatric appraisal of parents and siblings of schizophrenic children. *American Journal of Psychiatry*, 1962, *118*, 902–915.

Meyers, D. Extinction, DRO, and response cost procedures for eliminating self-injurious behavior: A case study. *Behavior Research and Therapy*, 1975, *13*, 190.

Mischel, W. *Personality and Assessment*. New York: John Wiley and Sons, 1968.

Newsom, C. D. The role of sensory reinforcement in self-stimulatory behavior. Unpublished doctoral dissertation, University of California, Los Angeles, 1974.

Newsom, C. D. Perception and memory in autistic children. Paper presented at the annual convention of the American Psychological Association, Toronto, August, 1978.

Newsom, C. D., Carr, E. G., & Lovaas, O. I. The experimental analysis and modification of autistic behavior. In R. S. Davidson (Ed.), *Modification of behavior pathology*. New York: Gardner Press, 1979.

Newsom, C. D., & Simon, K. M. A simultaneous discrimination procedure for the measurement of vision in nonverbal children. *Journal of Applied Behavior Analysis*, 1977, *10*, 633–644.

Ney, P., Palvesky, E., & Markely, J. Relative effectiveness of operant conditioning and play therapy in childhood schizophrenia. *Journal of Autism and Childhood Schizophrenia*, 1971, *1*, 337-349.

Norman, E. Reality relationships of schizophrenic children. *British Journal of Medical Psychology*, 1954, *27*, 127–141.

Oppenheim, R. C. *Effective teaching methods of autistic children*. Springfield, Ill.: Charles C. Thomas, 1974.

Ornitz, E. M., Brown, M. B. Mason, A., & Putnmam, H. H. Effect of visual input on vestibular nystagmus in autistic children. *Archives of General Psychiatry*, 1974, *31*, 369–375.

Ornitz, E. M., Forsythe, A. B., & de la Pena, A. The effect of vestibular and auditory stimulation on the rapid-eye-movements of REM sleep in autistic children. *Archives of General Psychiatry*, 1973, *29*, 786–791.

Ornitz, E. M., & Ritvo, E. R. Perceptual inconstancy in early infantile autism. *Archives of General Psychiatry*, 1968, *18*, 76–98.

Ornitz, E. M., & Ritvo, E. R. The syndrome of autism: A critical review. *American Journal of Psychiatry*, 1976, *133*, 609–621.

Ornitz, E. M., Ritvo, E. E., Brown, M. B., LaFranchi, S., Parmelee, T., & Walter, R. D. The EEG and rapid eye movements during REM sleep in normal and autistic children. *Electroencephalography and Clinical Neurophysiology*, 1969, *26*, 167–175.

Park, C. C. *The seige*. London: Colin Smythe, 1968.

Peterson, R. F., Cox, M. A., & Bijou, S. W. Training children to work productively in classroom groups. *Exceptional Children*, 1971, *37*, 491–500.

Peterson, R. F., & Peterson, L. R. The use of positive reinforcement in the control of self-destructive behavior in a retarded boy. *Journal of Experimental Child Psychology*, 1968, *6*, 351–360.

Pitfield, M., & Oppenheim, A. N. Childrearing attitudes of mothers of psychotic children. *Journal of Child Psychology and Psychiatry*, 1964, *5*, 51–57.

Pollack, M. Mental subnormality and childhood schizophrenia. In P. H. Hoch & J. Zubin (Eds.), *Psychopathology of mental development*. New York: Grune and Stratton, 1967.

Postman, L., & Brown, D. R. The perceptual consequences of success and failure. *Journal of Abnormal and Social Psychology*, 1952, *47*, 213–221.

Potter, H. W. Schizophrenia in children. *American Journal of Psychiatry*, 1933, 1253–1270.

Rank, B. Adaption of the psychoanalytic technique for the treatment of young children. *Journal of Abnormal Child Psychology*, 1974, *2*, 253–263.

Reynolds, B. S., Newsom, C. D., & Lovaas, O. I. Auditory overselectivity in autistic children. *Journal of Abnormal Child Psychology*, 1974, *2*, 253–263.

Ricks, D. M. Vocal communication in pre-verbal normal and autistic children. In N. O'Connor (Ed.), *Language, cognitive deficits and retardation*. London: Butterworth's, 1975.

Rimland, B. *Infantile autism: The syndrome and its implications for a neural theory of behavior*. New York: Appleton-Century-Crofts, 1964.

Rimland, B. The differentiation of childhood psychosis: An analysis of checklists for 2218 psychotic children. *Journal of Autism and Childhood Schizophrenia*, 1971, *1*, 161–174.

Rincover, A. Sensory extinction: A procedure for eliminating self-stimulatory behavior in developmentally disabled children. *Journal of Abnormal Child Psychology*, 1978, *6*, 299–310 (a).

Rincover, A. Variables affecting stimulus fading and discriminative responding in psychotic children. *Journal of Abnormal Psychology*, 1978, in press (b).

Rincover, A., & Koegel, R. L. Treatment of psychotic children in a classroom environment: II. Individualized instruction in a group. *Journal of Abnormal Child Psychology*, 1977, *5*, 123–136 (a).

Rincover, A., & Koegel, R. L. Research on the education of autistic children: Recent advances and future directions. In B. B. Lahey and A. E. Kazdin (Eds.), *Advances in clinical child psychology*. Vol. 1. New York: Plenum Press, 1977 (b).

Rincover, A., Koegel, R. L., & Russo, D. C.

Some recent research on the education of autistic children. *Education and Treatment of Children*, 1978, *1*, 31–45.

Risley, T. The effects and side effects of the use of punishment with an autistic child. *Journal of Applied Behavior Analysis*, 1968, *1*, 21–34.

Risley, T. R. Certify procedures not people. In W. S. Wood (Ed.), *Issues in evaluating behavior modification*. Champaign, Ill.: Research Press, 1975.

Risley, T., & Wolf, M. Establishing functional speech in echolalic children. *Behaviour Research and Therapy*, 1967, *5*, 73–88.

Ritvo, E. R., Cantwell, D., Johnson, E., Clements, M., Benbrook, F., Slagle, P., Kelly, P., & Ritz, M. Social class factors in autism. *Journal of Autism and Childhood Schizophrenia*, 1971, *1*, 297–310.

Ritvo, E. R., Ornitz, E. M., Eviatar, A., Markham, C. H., Brown, M. B., & Mason, A. Decreased post-rotatory nystagmus in early infantile autism. *Neurology*, 1969, *19*, 653–658.

Romanczyk, R. G., Diament, C., Goren, E. R., Trunell, G., & Harris, S. L. Increasing isolate and social play in severely disturbed children: Intervention and postintervention effectiveness. *Journal of Autism and Childhood Schizophrenia*, 1975, *5*, 57–70.

Romanczyk, R. G., & Goren, E. R. Severe self-injurious behavior: The problem of clinical control. *Journal of Consulting and Clinical Psychology*, 1975, *43*, 730–739.

Rosenbaum, M. S., & Breiling, J. The development and functional control of reading comprehension behavior. *Journal of Applied Behavior Analysis*, 1976, *9*, 323–333.

Russo, D. C., Carr, E. G., and Lovaas, O. I. Self-injury in pediatric populations. In J. Ferguson and C. B. Taylor (Eds.), *Comprehensive handbook of behavioral medicine. Vol 3: Extended Applications and Issues*. Holliswood, N.Y.: Spectrum Publications, 1980, 23–41.

Russo, D. C., Cataldo, M. F., & Cushing, P. C. Compliance training and response-response relationships in the treatment of multiple behavior problems. Unpublished manuscript, 1977.

Russo, D. C., Glahn, T. J., Miners, W., & Lovaas, O. I. Use of teaching homes for the treatment of psychotic children. Paper presented at the meeting of the American Psychological Association, New Orleans, September, 1974.

Russo, D. C., & Koegel, R. L. A method of integrating an autistic child into a normal public-school classroom *Journal of Applied*

Behavior Analysis, 1977, *10*, 579–590.

Russo, D. C., Koegel, R. L., & Lovaas, O. I. A comparison of human and automated instruction of autistic children. *Journal of Abnormal Child Psychology*, 1978, *6*, 189–201.

Rutter, M. Speech disorders in a series of autistic children. In A. W. Franklin, (Ed.), *Children with communication problems*. London: Pitman, 1965 (a).

Rutter, M. The influence of organic and emotional factors on the origins, nature and outcome of childhood psychosis. *Developmental Medicine and Child Neurology*, 1965, *7*, 518–528 (b).

Rutter, M. Diagnosis and definition of childhood autism. *Journal of Autism and Childhood Schizophrenia*, 1968, *8*, 139–161.

Rutter, M., & Bartak, L. Special educational treatment of autistic children: A comparative study. II. Follow-up findings and implications for services. *Journal of Child Psychology and Psychiatry*, 1973, *14*, 241–270.

Rutter, M., Bartak, L., & Newman, S. Autism—a central disorder of cognition and language? In M. Rutter (Ed.), *Infantile autism: Concepts, characteristics and treatment.* London: Churchill-Livingstone, 1971.

Rutter, M., Greenfeld, D., & Lockyer, L. A five to fifteen year follow-up study of infantile psychosis. II. Social and behavioral outcome. *British Journal of Psychiatry*, 1967, *113*, 1183–1199.

Rutter, M., & Lockyer, L. A five to fifteen year follow-up study of infantile psychosis. I. Description of the sample. *British Journal of Psychiatry*, 1967, *113*, 1169–1182.

Safrin, R. Differences in visual perception and in visual motor functioning between psychotic and non-psychotic children. *Journal of Counsulting Psychology*, 1964, *28*, 41–45.

Sailor, W., & Taman, T. Stimulus factors in the training of prepositional usage in three autistic children. *Journal of Applied Behavior Analysis*, 1972, *5*, 183–190.

Schain, R., & Freedman, D. Studies on 5-hydroxindole metabolism in autistic and other mentally retarded children. *Journal of Pediatrics*, 1961, *58*, 315–320.

Schain, R., & Yannet, H. Infantile autism: An analysis of 50 cases and a consideration of certain relevant neurophysiologic concepts. *Journal of Pediatrics*, 1960, *57*, 560–567.

Schopler, E. Visual versus tactile receptor preferences in normal and schizophrenic children. *Journal of Abnormal Psychology*, 1966, *71*, 108–114.

Schopler, E. & Reichler, R. V. Parents as cotherapists in the treatment of psychotic children. *Journal of Autism and Childhood Schizophrenia*, 1971, *1*, 87–102.

Schover, L. R., & Newsom, C. D. Overselectivity, developmental level, and overtraining in autistic and normal children. *Journal of Abnormal Child Psychology*, 1976, *4*, 289–298.

Schreibman, L. Effects of within-stimulus and extra-stimulus prompting on discrimination learning in autistic children. *Journal of Applied Behavior Analysis*, 1975, *8*, 91–112.

Schreibman, L., Koegel, R. L., & Craig, M. S. Reducing stimulus overselectivity in autistic children. *Journal of Abnormal Child Psychology*, 1977, *5*, 425–436.

Schreibman, L., & Lovaas, O. I. Overslective response to social stimuli by autistic children. *Journal of Abnormal Child Psychology*, 1973, *1*, 152–168.

Shapiro, T., & Fish, B. A method to study language deviation as an aspect of ego organization in young schizophrenic children. *Journal of the American Academy of Child Psychiatry*, 1969, *8*, 36–56.

Shintoub, S. A., & Soulairac, A. L'enfant automultilateur. *Psychiatrie de l'Enfant.* 1961, *3*, 111–145.

Sidman, M. *Tactics of scientific research: Evaluating experimental data in psychology.* New York: Basic Books, 1960.

Singer, M., & Wynne, L. C. Differentiating characteristics of the parents of childhood schizophrenics, childhood neurotics, and young adult schizophrenics. *American Journal of Psychiatry*, 1963, *120*, 234–243.

Skinner, B. F. Are theories of learning necessary? *Psychological Review*, 1950, *57*, 193–216.

Smolev, S. R. Use of operant techniques for the modification of self-injurious behavior. *American Journal of Mental Deficiency*, 1971, *76*, 295–305.

Solnick, J., Rincover, A., & Peterson, C. Some determinants of the reinforcing and punishing effects of timeout. *Journal of Applied Behavior Analysis*, 1977, *10*, 415–424.

Spence, M. A. Genetic studies. In E. R. Ritvo (Ed.), *Autism: Diagnosis, current research and management.* New York: Spectrum, 1976.

Stevens-Long, J., & Rasmussen, M. The acquisition of simple and compound sentence structure in an autistic child. *Journal of Applied Behavior Analysis*, 1974, *7*, 473–749.

Stokes, T. F., & Baer, D. M. An implicit technology of generalization. *Journal of Applied Behavior Analysis*, 1977, *10*, 349–367.

Taft, L., & Goldfarb, W. Prenatal and perinatal factors in childhood schizophrenia. *Developmental Medicine and Child Neurology*, 1964, *6*, 32–43.

Takahashi, S., Kanai, H., and Miyamoto, Y. Reassessment of elevated serotonin levels in blood platelets in early infantile autism. *Journal of Autism and Childhood Schizophrenia,* 1976, *6,* 317–326.

Tanguay, P. Clinical and electrophysiological research. In E. R. Ritvo (Ed.), *Autism: Diagnosis, current research and management.* New York: Spectrum, 1976.

Tate, B. G., & Baroff, G. S. Aversive control of self-injurious behavior in a psychotic boy. *Behaviour Research and Therapy,* 1966, *4,* 281–287.

Taterka, J., & Katz, J. Study of correlations between electroencephalographic and psychological patterns in emotionally disturbed children. *Psychosomatic Medicine,* 1955, *17,* 62–72.

Treffert, D. A. The epidemiology of infantile autism. *Archives of General Psychiatry,* 1970, *22,* 431–438.

Vaillant, G. E. John Haslam on early infantile autism. *American Journal of Psychiatry,* 1962, *119,* 365.

Van Krevelen, D. A. Early infantile autism. *Acta Paedopsychiatrica,* 1952, *91,* 81–97.

Varni, J. W., Lovaas, O. I., Koegel, R. L., & Everett, N. L. An analysis of observational learning in autistic and normal children. *Journal of Abnormal Child Psychology,* 1978, in press.

Vrono, M. Schizophrenia in childhood and adolescence. *International Journal of Mental Health,* 1974, *2,* 7–116.

Weber, J. L. The speech and language abilities of emotionally disturbed children. *Canadian Psychiatric Association Journal,* 1965, *10,* 417–420.

Weiland, I. H., & Legg, D. R. Formal speech characteristics as a diagnostic aid in childhood psychosis. *American Journal of Orthopsychiatry,* 1964, *34,* 91–94.

Wender, P. H. *Minimal brain dysfunction in children.* New York: Wiley 1971.

Werry, J. S. Childhood psychosis. In H. C. Quay and J. S. Werry (Eds.), *Psychopathological disorders of childhood.* New York: Wiley, 1972.

White, P., DeMyer, W., & DeMyer, M. EEG abnormalities in early childhood schizophrenia: A double blind study of psychiatrically disturbed and normal children during promozene sedation. *American Journal of Mental Deficiency,* 1976, *81,* 26–31.

Wilhelm, H. & Lovaas, O. I. Stimulus overselectivity: A common feature in autism and mental retardation. *American Journal of Mental Deficiency,* 1976, *81,* 26–31.

Wing, L. The principles of remedial education for autistic children. In L. Wing (Ed.), *Early childhood autism: Clinical, educational and social aspects* (2nd ed.). London: Pergamon, 1976.

Wing, L., Yeates, S., Brierly, L., & Gould, J. The prevalence of early childhood autism: A comparison of administrative and epidemiological studies. *Psychological Medicine,* 1976, *6,* 89–100.

Wolf, M. M., Risley, T., Johnston, M., Harris, F., & Allen, E. Application of operant conditioning procedures to the behavior problems of an autistic child: A follow-up and extension. *Behavior Research and Therapy,* 1967, *5,* 103–111.

Wolf, M. M., Risley, T., & Mees, H. Application of operant conditioning procedures to the behavior problems of an autistic child. *Behaviour Research and Therapy,* 1964, *1,* 305-312.

Wolff, S., & Chess, S. Analysis of the language of fourteen schizophrenic children. *Journal of Child Psychology and Psychiatry,* 1965, *6,* 29–41.

Yeakel, J. A., Salisbury, L. L., Greer, S. L., & Marcus, L. F. An appliance for autoinduced aversive control of self-injurious behavior. *Journal of Experimental Child Psychology,* 1970, *10,* 159–169.

CHAPTER 7

Environmental Correlates of Mental Retardation

ROBERT H. BRADLEY, Ph.D.
LISA A. TEDESCO, Ph.D.

Mental development has been a paramount concern of research psychologists almost since the inception of psychology. Galton's classic studies on the hereditary bases of human abilities; Binet's development of intelligence tests; Terman's longitudinal investigation of genius; studies at Berkeley and at the Fels Institute concerning home factors related to mental growth; Burt's twin studies; Skeel's examination of institutionally reared infants; Jensen's and Shockley's controversial data on heritability of intelligence; and Mercer's work on adaptive behavior: these efforts and others like them have been empirical watersheds in the accumulation of knowledge pertaining to cognitive development in humans. This accumulated evidence disembogues on each bank of the nurture-nature confluence. Emphasis on research of the relative contributions of "nature and nurture" has only diverted efforts to define those environmental conditions that retard the development of intellectual potential. At this juncture in the history of research on home environment, we know environment has an influence, and it is becoming more evident what these powerful factors are. Thus, the major focus of this chapter concerns the cognitive, social, and physical aspects of early home environment and experience—and their influence on mental development and intellectual functioning.

This chapter emphasizes the richness of the past generation of research. With careful conceptualization and more precise measurement, social scientists have advanced theory, explanation, and analysis of human growth and development. Beginning with Bloom's landmark publication, *Stability and Change in Human Characteristics* (1964), and Hunt's *Intelligence and Experience* in the early 1960s through a series of studies on the effects on education begun in infancy (Caldwell, 1970; Klaus and Gray, 1967; Levenstein, 1970; and Heber and Garber, 1975) and investigations on the effects of schooling (Coleman, Campbell, Hobson, McPartland, Mood, Weinfold and York, 1966; Jencks, 1972; Shipman and associates, 1976; and Harnischfeger and Wiley, 1977), continuing with an amalgam of studies concerning home environment and community factors related to intellectual development (Elardo, Bradley, and Caldwell, 1975; Yarrow, Rubenstein, and Pederson, 1975; White, Watts, and Associates, 1973; Deutsch and associates, 1967) and contributions to theory of the reciprocity between adult and infant (Bell, 1968; and Wholwill, 1973), the advances in knowledge have been considerable.

The purpose of this chapter, then, is to review existing research findings pertaining to the relation between cognitive, social, and physical home environment and mental development—both the factors that seem to inhibit development and factors that facilitate it. The major emphasis is on those general factors in the home environment that appear to show the strongest relation to intellectual development. Little will be said, for example, about more specialized information, such as the particular roles that siblings or fathers play in children's development—albeit the research on such relationships is advancing rapidly and reveals important attributes. Some attention will be given to literature dealing with socioeconomic factors and possible interactions between contextual and home factors.

SOCIAL CLASS, THE ASSESSMENT OF INTELLIGENCE AND MENTAL RETARDATION

A great deal of controversy surrounds the human faculty referred to as "intelligence." One must understand that many criticisms have been aimed at the use of traditional measures of intelligence as indices of mental capability, especially among minority and lower socioeconomic groups (Golden and Birns, 1976). It is not our intention to discuss these criticisms. Our intent is to cite evidence which, taken as a whole, leads to the conclusion that higher social class is related in some coarsely defined, complicated fashion to more advanced levels of mental development. We chose the broad term, "mental development," over the more narrow one, "intelligence," in an effort to present a more complete picture of the evidence relating social class to mental development. In addition, the relation of social class and nontraditional measures of mental development, specifically Piagetian and culture-fair measures are discussed.

The Definition of Social Class.

Until recently, the most common means of assessing the quality of a child's environment were social class designations. Davis (1944) explained that the pivotal meaning of social class to students of human development is that it defines and systematizes different environments for

children of different classes. At present there is no complete agreement on what constitutes social class (Adler, 1972). However, Brown (1965) described four conditions that must be present before the existence of social classes can be affirmed: (1) the population must be aware of classes and agree on their number; (2) life styles must be uniform within these classes and unique between them; (3) social interaction must be sharply patterned on class; and (4) data on each of these factors must indicate the same boundaries between classes. Many social scientists have chosen to employ the term "socioeconomic status" or "SES" instead of "social class," because SES implies a continuous ranking from high to low and does not require assumptions about class consciousness, life styles, and so forth. A major stimulus to modern research in the area of social class differences was the development of an objective scale, called the Index of Social Characteristics (ISC), to measure a family's socioeconomic status (Warner, Meeker, and Eells, 1949). The scale is based on weighted ratings of four characteristics: occupation, source of income, house type, and dwelling area. the ISC was later modified by Hollingshead and Redlich (1958) and called "Index of Social Position." This index, subsequently used in many studies, comprised a number of weighted criteria: occupation of family head (weighted 9), residence (weighted 6), and education of family head (weighted 5).

Traditional IQ Tests and Social Class.

There is ample documentation of a positive relationship between SES and performance on traditional IQ tests. Estimates of the correlation average about .30 to .40, depending on the scales employed (Anastasi, 1958; Coleman, et al., 1966; Dreger and Miller, 1960, 1968; Eells, Davis, Havighurst, Herrick, Tyler, 1951; Plowden, 1967). This relationship usually does not appear until age two or three (Baley, 1965; Golden and Birns, 1968; Hindley, 1960; Knobloch and Pasamanick, 1960; Willerman, Broman, and Fiedler, 1970). However, it seems likely that SES-related variables that influence intellectual development and learning ability are operating during the preverbal period, but are simply not displayed in infant development test scores, which reflect mainly sensorimotor development. When more refined infant tests are employed that can reveal variations in central processes and abilities, such as the Uzgiris-Hung Scales (1966), SES differences can be identified in the performance of infants as young as seven months of age (Wachs, Uzgiris, & Hunt, 1971). One highly significant study of older children was done by Kennedy, Van de Riet, and White (1973). This work involved the administration of the Stanford-Binet Intelligence Test to a stratified random sample of 1,800 first- to sixth-grade black children, selected to represent the black population of the southeastern states. These investigators found that the higher SES children had higher IQ scores; with about 25 IQ points separating the lowest from the highest SES groups (79.39 ± 11.72 versus 105 ± 12.79). This study is significant in that it isolated SES from racial factors (since only black children were studied), and yet a significant SES effect upon IQ scores remained. Another, by Lesser, Fifer, and Clark (1965), examined the mental abilities of six- and seven-year-old children of differing SES backgrounds from four different racial-ethnic groups. Their measure of mental ability included scales tapping numerical ability, reasoning, verbal ability, and spatial ability. The finding of particular interest to the present discussion is that over the entire sample (40 middle-class and 40 lower-class children from each of 4 racial-ethnic groups = 320 children), the middle-class children performed better than the lower-class children.

Piagetian Tests and Social Class.

Piaget (1950, 1963) provided a detailed theory of the course of cognitive development. As a part of his theory, Piaget (1952) has given central emphasis to the child's acquisition of conservation. The ability to conserve refers to whether the child can recognize that certain properties of objects remain invariant after undergoing a transformation. For example, a child who is a conserver would say that the same amount of water is present even after it is poured from a short flat bowl into a tall thin glass. To Piaget, the acquisition of conservation signals the child's transition from a prelogical to a logical mode of thought. According to Kohlberg and DeVries (1969), the behavior pattern, known as "conservation," is not specific to any particular culture; rather it is thought of as an "equilibrated structure resulting from the interaction between the structures of the child's earlier schemeta and the structure of the physical world." In an attempt to assess the impact of the environment upon the development of conservation, Almy, Chittenden, and Miller (1966) studied middle- and lower-class children from the kindergarten year through early elementary grades. Each child was given five trials and three chances to offer explanation on tasks, including conservation of number, conservation of liquid, and reproducing a stair design with blocks. Almy found that when the middle-class children reached second grade, 48 percent were able to conserve on all tasks, but of the lower-class group, only 23 percent did so. The attainment of conservation was accomplished by the lower-class group approximately one year after the middclass group. In a similar study, Peisach (1967) reported that the correlation between SES and conservation score is significant and increases with age: .26 ($p<.05$) with kindergarten children and .48 ($p<.001$) with second graders. Other studies (Gouin-Decarie, 1967; Uzgiris, 1967; Wachs, Uzgiris, and Hunt, 1971) have provided evidence that children from deprived environments evolve object permanence and object handling concepts at a slower rate than infants from middle-class environments, although there are some contrary findings (Lewis, 1971; Golden and Birns, 1968). In one interesting study, relating sensorimotor measures to social class, Tulkin (1973) found that middle-class 10-month-old girls tended to be more "reflective" in making choices than lower-class girls.

Culture-fair Tests and Social Class.

About mid-century, Davis (1948), in a text called *Social-Class Influence Upon Learn-*

ing, protested against the common practices of using standardized intelligence tests with low SES and/or black children. He contended that the emphasis such tests gave to verbal skills reflected the values of tests that would not be culturally biased. Davis and Eells (1953) subsequently deisgned a nonlanguage test, known as the Davis-Eells Games, which focused upon human abilities that were free from subcultural influences. Cultural bias was said to be absent, since the test developers tried to include only items common to life experiences in many environmental contexts. As the test is entirely pictorial and directions are given by the examiner, there is no reading requirement that could presumably be prejudicial. In spite of the earnest attempt to develop culture-fair tests, educational psychologists (DeCecco, 1968; Divesta and Thompson, 1970), today largely agree that these tests have not proven useful. The same high-SES children who score well on standard intelligence tests score well on the cutlure-fair tests.

Golden and Birns (1976) concluded their review of social class and intellectual development by stating that "the most consistent finding is that cognitive measures that involve language are related to social class as early as the first year of life, and that starting at two years of age such verbal measures are highly correlated with children's performance on standard intelligence tests." (p. 320)

Shortcomings of the Concept of "Social Class".

The above studies, which described the home environment in terms of general sociological characteristics, were successful in identifying social class as an important variable related to parental and child behavior. However, descriptions of background factors, such as parental education and occupation, are principally indicative of what parents *are,* rather than what parents *do* to foster or retard mental development in their children. In retrospect, these research efforts appear to have laid the groundwork for more analytic, process-oriented studies of the home environment.

In recent times a growing number of educators and social scientists have become dissatisfied with the use of status variables as environment indices. One reason for this dissatisfaction is that social-status characteristics have failed to explain much of the variability in children's performance in school or on intelligence tests. As Bloom (1964) noted, social class rarely explains more than 25 percent of this variance. Illustrative of the problem is a study by Kahl (1953), who found that, within the same socioeconomic level, families with an aspiration of "getting ahead" were more interested in education than those with a "getting by" tendency. He found that the level of aspiration on the part of the parents was a more crucial factor than their social class; it explained more of the variability in the educational achievement of their children than did their social class designation (when the IQs of the children were matched). In a similar vein, Littman, Moore, and Pierce-Jones (1957) conducted an investigation of social-class differences in performance among an Oregon sample. They found a very wide range for all types of behavior in their middle- and lower-class samples. They concluded that this within-group variation overrode any slight mean difference existing in the two groups. Dramatic differences in parental and child behavior among representatives of the "lower" class were likewise reported by Malone (1963) and Pavenstedt (1965), who described vast differences in child-rearing practices among families labeled as "lower-class."

The point to be made is that the literature on social class and SES differences has traditionally paid insufficient attention to the extensive *intraclass variation* found in most studies. Moreover, statistically significant between-class differences are generally of small magnitude. As Bloom (1964) reasoned, the use of general indices of social status or class obscures many of the important differences among *environments,* almost in the same way that the use of IQ scores masks many of the important differences among individuals. According to Davé (1963), sociological labels are of little functional value to the educator. He explained that such classifications "fail to provide practical hints to the teacher, counselor, and educational administrator as to what remedial action should be taken when the home environment is found to be deficient." (p. 6) This point was further elaborated upon by Walberg and Marjoribanks (1976) in their review of research on family environment and cognitive development. They contended that there is little, if any, direct effect of status variables on cognitive performance unmediated by environment process variables; that is, "more comprehensive measures of the family environment are likely to mediate these effects completely." (p. 543)

Cynthia Deutsch (1973) believes that the discovery of any SES-behavior relationship is only a beginning.

All too many studies . . . have stopped at the first step, implying a view on the researcher's part that SES is a stable, specific, and rather homogenous entity—a demographic attribute whose dimensions are the same for all who share it . . . (p. 244).

She also stressed the notion that SES should not be viewed as a unitary variable, but as a conglomerate, so that the search for SES-development relationships amounts to the dissection out of the SES matrix of certain component variables that can be related to certain developmental skills. For example, a statement to the effect that low SES is highly correlated with low reading skills tells little about the aspects of life in the low-SES homes that mediate this relationship, leaving us totally bewildered when trying to explain the outstanding reading performance sometimes found in children from low SES homes.

Thus, that the use of SES and other family status variables is a system of shorthand to express a myriad of life-styles, values, and family dynamics is a point well made by individuals critiquing this area of research (Clasen, 1966; Deutsch, 1973; White, 1977). On many levels, use of those broad, family descriptors masks the real relations of processes in the home environment contributing to intellectual development.

In addition to the theoretical arguments advanced for the superiority of process over status measures of environmental

quality, there have been several empirical investigations whose results may be interpreted as leading to the same conclusion. Marjoribanks (1972) found a significant residual relationship between parental behavior toward children and the child's scores on the Primary Mental Abilities Test with SES partialed out. Similarly, Elardo, Bradley, and Caldwell (1975) recorded correlations ranging from .4 to .7 between specific measures of the early home environment assessed during various SES measures and three-year Binet IQs. Moreover, Bradley, Caldwell, and Elardo (1977) found that HOME scores alone predicted children's IQ about as well as did the combination of HOME and SES, whereas when SES was used alone, there was significant loss in predictive power—particularly among blacks. This finding corroborated Havighurst's conclusion that SES and race are substantially confounded in the United States.

A related reason that measures of specific environmental processes may be superior to SES indices in assessing environmental quality is that SES tends to be relatively static. The underlying notions of most social class indices remain as economic level and prestige attribution, producing an index of the family position in a status hierarchy (Lavin, 1965; Deutsch, 1973). Thus, status variables are broad categorizations of home background that do not easily lend to any manipulation or observations of flux and change. By comparison, the environmental processes are reflective of particular conditions at a given time. Previous research has demonstrated that children's developmental scores wax and wane in response to changes in environmental conditions (McCall, Appelbaum and Hogarty, 1973). Thus, environmental process measures can be of more use than SES measures in guiding an appropriate intervention strategy.

ENVIRONMENTAL PROCESSES AND COGNITIVE DEVELOPMENT

It behooves social scientists, responding to educational and developmental questions, to take a close look at the historical research of the last decade. Freeburg and Payne (1967) have argued that research on parental influence, child-rearing practices, and parent-child relations—specifically related to cognitive/mental functioning, prior to the mid-1960s—was not explicit or articulate. The War on Poverty, Headstart, and the Coleman Report served to underscore the lack of explanation and analysis produced from sociological status conceptualizations of home environment that emphasizes setting particulars—variables that cut across the more gross distinctions of parental education and occupation. For this reason, this view of environment has been labeled the *process* approach, focusing upon what parents *do,* interacting with their children, to influence mental development.

Results, obtained from studies dealing with twelve major types of environmental processes, will be described here to clarify the current state of knowledge in this area. These twelve processes categorize the home environment as *cognitive, social,* and *physical.* These processes were selected because they have been the subject of the greatest number of investigations, and they have been most frequently identified as bearing a relation to cognitive development in children. The twelve processes are not considered to operate independently, but they represent separate perspectives on the environment and involve different measurement tools. The relation of the twelve processes to cognitive development is examined from a developmental perspective—that is, the relation between each process and mental performance will be examined during each of four developmental periods: birth to age one; one to three years; three to six years; and six to twelve years. Finally, this review will concentrate on investigations of environmental processes that utilized interviews and observations about natural environments. Studies that used experimental designs or data collected in laboratory settings will not be the main subject for consideration.

Cognitive Home Environment and Experience

Language Stimulation. One environmental factor that has shown a consistently strong relation to measures of cognitive development is the quality and quantity of language used in the home. Quantity and quality of language is generally indicated by degree of environmental labeling, further identification of objects, feelings, or situations in relational terms, e.g., similarities and differences, degree of language abstraction, and complexity of syntactic structures or grammatical forms used by the adults in the young child's environment. The literature is replete with such evidence.

Elardo, Bradley, and Caldwell in a series of studies on home environment (Elardo, Bradley, & Caldwell, 1975, 1977; Bradley & Caldwell, 1976a, 1976b, 1979; and Bradley, Elardo, & Caldwell, 1979) found that mother's verbal and emotional responsiveness was significantly correlated with measures of cognitive development throughout the first nine years of life. Mother's use of language in the first year of life, while not correlated with concurrent infant measures, was moderately related to IQ and ITPA scores during the preschool years. These studies, involving predominantly lower- to lower-middle-class families (about two-thirds black), also revealed that the mother's verbal performance during the second and third years of a child's life was even more strongly related to the child's eventual cognitive performance. Language stimulation during the three- to six-year period was moderately related to both children's IQ and eventual school achievement test scores. Further investigation by these researchers indicated that the verbal and emotional responsivity of mother was correlated about .5 during the preschool years. The observed relations were somewhat stronger for males than females and for whites than blacks. One interesting finding involved a cross-lagged panel analysis, involving maternal language and child Bayley MDI scores at ages one and two. During this period no primary direction of effect was noted. Instead, results suggested that there may have been a kind of reciprocal effect. The onset, form, and developmental causes of very young children's ability to manipulate or alter their early environment, suggesting this reciprocity, is the research frontier educationists and developmentalists currently face. Similar results were reported by Clarke-Stewart (1973); Wachs, Uzgiris, and Hunt (1971); and Gordon (1974). In an investigation of 36 first-born infants from low SES backgrounds, Clarke-Stewart (1973) found no relation between mother's verbal stimulation of the infant prior to age one and the infant's Bayley MDI score during the same developmental period. However, moderate to rather high correlations were obtained for infant measures in the second year of life. One interesting finding from the Clarke-Stewart study was that child's language correlated .55 with nonresponsive maternal speech, prompting Clarke-Stewart to conclude that modeling of language—more than reinforcement—is important in early acquisition. In another study, dealing with language stimulation prior to age one, Tulkin and Covitz (1975) reported that for middle-class girls, maternal vocalization correlated about .4 with IQ at age six. (The correlation with ITPA was not significant.) Moreover, the amount of reciprocal vocalization between mother and daughter correlated .5 with ITPA. However, the same results did not obtain with lower-class girls.

A number of researchers have investigated the relation of maternal language during the second and third years of life and children's cognitive functioning —among them Wachs, Uzgiris, and Hunt (1971). Their study of 102 children from lower SES homes in Indiana showed that home scores were related (as high as .7) to a variety of subtests from the Infant Psychological Development Scale beginning at around fifteen months of age. A subsequent study conducted on 39 children (Wachs, 1976) indicated similar results. White, Watts, and their associates (1973) also found that the quantity and quality of mother's language distinguished those homes with potentially competent children and those with potentially incompetent children, regardless of the social status of the family.

Wulbert, Inglis, Kriegsman, and Mills (1975) compared the home environments of three groups of preschool-aged children: normal, language-delayed, and language-disabled. It was their contention that the

language environment of language-delayed children was deficient as compared with the other two groups. Findings from their study provided substantiation for such an hypothesis. Hanson (1975), who studied 60 male and 50 female middle-class white children from the Fels Longitudinal Study, found that the direct teaching of language to children measured when the children were 5½ years old was correlated .33 with IQ for males and .37 for females. Modeling language correlated .29 for males and .36 for females. Bradley and Caldwell (1979) obtained similar findings with mostly lower-class black and white children. In contrast, Ware and Garber (1972) reported no significant relation between language stimulation in the home and children's performance on the Preschool Inventory among Mexican-American and black four-year-olds. However, their study was limited due to the very small number of items in their environmental measures.

Marjoribanks (1972) described a somewhat detailed cross-sectional study of 92 middle-class and 95 lower-class 11-year-old Canadian boys whose mothers were interviewed using a 188-item environmental process measure. The instrument was partially based on Murray's need-press theory, one of the subscales being Press for English language. This environmental factor correlated .50 with verbal scores; .27 with number scores; .18 with spatial scores; and .28 with reasoning scores on the Primary Mental Abilities Test. She and Hanes (1977) found that press for language development was significantly related to reading achievement in white follow-through children, but not black children. In a study with children approximately the same age as those in the Marjoribanks (1972) study, Jones (1972) observed that opportunity for the use and development of language was the best predictor of verbal ability among boys in St. Johns, Newfoundland. Hanson (1975) found that the direct teaching of language correlated .30 with IQ for males at age nine and a half; .60 for females. Parental modeling of language correlated .25 and .64 for males and females, respectively. Among children just entering school, Henderson and Merritt (1968) found that language models in the home significantly differentiated the high-potential and low-potential Mexican-American students in Tucson, Arizona. In a related study, Henderson, Bergan, and Hurt (1972) obtained a .59 correlation between valuing language and school-related behavior and children's performance on the Boehm Test of Basic Concepts.

Language stimulation appears to bear an important relation to mental development throughout the first twelve years of life, with the exception that no significant correlations were obtained for mental test measures during the first year of life. This finding may reflect the highly motor content of infant tests during the intial year and the fact that infants possess limited language skills during that period. This is true particularly in view of the fact that environmental scores in the first year are significantly related to later mental scores. Language stimulation showed a generally moderate relation with mental scores (.3 to .6), with significant relations observed for a wide variety of populations. There was evidence of a sex difference when children reached school—with higher correlations for females. In addition, there was evidence that the relation was stronger for whites than blacks. Whether or not the association between language stimulation and cognitive development is actually weaker among blacks is not clear. The findings we reviewed may be an artifact of the limitation of both environmental and developmental measures used. The research we reviewed does not make it clear as to the relative importance of modeling language or encouragement of language in cognitive development, although evidence such as that presented by Clarke-Stewart (1973) suggests that modeling is important. It is also not clear what degree of reciprocity may exist between the young child's degree of control over early experience and parental language use. The Bradley Elardo, and Caldwell (1979) study suggested this early developmental phenomenon. This is a parallel finding with studies conducted by Rheingold and Eckerman (1975) and Carew (1975a; 1975b) that attest to this existence of early pro-active behavior, rooted in early adult-child experience.

Intellectuality in the Home. The level of intellectuality in the home and the amount of emphasis placed on intellectuality have been considered important to achievement and intelligence among school age children. Researchers, using this as a predictor variable, have defined it as the extent to which stimulus-induced maturation and development of mental skills occurred, including conceptual thinking, problem solving, and transformation of material. In general, however, this environmental factor has not been given great attention in studies of preschool-age children, particularly studies of children under three years of age. The Clarke-Stewart (1973) study of first-born children of low socioeconomic status backgrounds is one of few investigations of this type of environmental process among children in infancy. Even in this study, intellectuality was primarily measured not in terms of anything done directly in interaction with the infant. Instead, intellectuality involved maternal behaviors, such as knowledge of child development, use of imagination, desire to experiment, and Peabody Picture Vocabulary score. Intellectuality composed of these processes was correlated .37 with Bayley MDI scores during the first year of life and about .3 with Bayley scores, scores on object permanence and language during the second year of life. The data, as shown in this study, showed that intellectuality was substantially correlated with a maternal factor described as optimal care by Clarke-Stewart. Hanson's (1975) re-analysis of the Fels data showed that models of intellectual interests in the home when the child was three were not significantly related to IQ in either males or females. This same environmental variable, when measured aged five, was correlated .34 with IQ among males and .50 for females. In their study of Mexican-American and black four-year-olds, Ware and Garber (1972) found no significant relationship between rewards for intellectual attainment and children's performance on the Preschool Inventory.

In contrast to the general paucity of studies, relating intellectuality in the home during the preschool years to children's cognitive attainment, there have been numerous studies in the elementary school years, among them the classic studies by

Bloom (1964), Dave (1963), and Wolf (1964), at the University of Chicago. Dave (1963) selected 60 fourth-grade children by random stratified sample from each social class in Illinois. Mothers were interviewed and rated on their intellectual interests and activities in the home. This rating correlated .72 with achievement and .55 with IQ. Follow-up investigations reported by Wolf (1964; 1977) showed that intellectuality in the home, albeit broadly defined, was correlated about .7 with fifth grade IQ and .6 with ninth-grade aptitude test scores. Using a similar measure, Henderson and Merritt (1968) found that intellectuality in the home differentiated between high- and low-potential Mexican-American first graders in Arizona. In another study, Henderson, Bergan, and Hurt (1972) showed that intellectual guidance was not significantly related to achievement among Mexican-American and Anglo first-graders. Day (1973), who also used an environmental measure patterned after the Chicago group, found no relation between the intellectual environment of the home — broadly defined—among fourth-grade Anglos, designated as high and low achievers. He did, however, find such a difference among Mexican-Americans. It should be noted in this context the Anglo families scored higher in intellectuality than did Mexican-American families. Variability among the Anglo group was somewhat limited and, thus, may have contributed to the failure to find significant differences among high- and low-achieving groups. In one of the more comprehensive cross-sectional studies of the relation between intellectuality and development, Marjoribanks (1972) reported that press for intellectuality was correlated .61 with verbal ability among middle- and lower-class 11-year-old boys representing five ethnic groups in Ontario, Canada. Correlations were less with number ($r = .5$), spatial ($r = .3$), and reasoning ($r = .3$) abilities. These relationships remained significant even when social class and ethnic groups were considered. Hanson (1975) found that models of intellectual interests were correlated .34 with IQ for males and .61 for females when the children were nine. By comparison, rewards for intellectual attainment were correlated

with achievement among whites more so than blacks (Shea and Hanes, 1977).

Relatively little is known about the importance of modeling intellectual interests or encouragement of intellectual pursuits for children under three—albeit the process would not be meaningful at this developmental period. Findings for the preschool era are also largely lacking, and the findings that exist are equivocal. More attention should be paid to the potential importance both of modeling and of reinforcement of intellectual behaviors during this period. It may prove useful to examine both these facets of intellectuality in the home for their relevance to mental growth. Intellectuality in the home appears to bear a rather consistent relationship to cognitive development among school-age children. There was some evidence that intellectuality—rather broadly defined in terms of modeling and provisions of opportunities for intellectual activities—may be more strongly associated with mental development than direct reward for intellectual attainment. This relationship needs further examination particularly among lower socioeconomic groups.

Variety of Stimulation. Skeels and Dye (1939) believed that children should have a variety of sensory and social experiences to develop properly. Using their studies, they found that institutionalized infants were generally limited in the number and type of such experiences, concluding that the lack of experiences contributed to a variety of health and developmental problems observed in institutionalized children. Piaget's theory of cognitive development posits that sensory and social experiences are the grist of qualitative improvements in a child's ability to think. It is through encounters with varied events and objects that children learn to reason in increasingly more sophisticated and effective ways.

The research findings of Skeels, Dennis, and others (1973), regarding the deleterious consequences of limited sensory and social experiences, plus theories of cognitive development, such as Piaget's, have served to germinate several research investigations into the relation between the variety of stimulation available to a child and cognitive development among non-institutionalized children. In a study of 41 black five-month-old children from the Washington, D.C. area, Yarrow et al. (1973, 1975) found that level and variety of social stimulation measured when the child was five months old was correlated about .3 with scores of the Bayley Mental Development Index. Scores on this environmental variable were also correlated to several types of more specific competencies assessed through the Bayley scales, particularly goal orientation. In contrast to the findings of Yarrow et al., Elardo, Bradley, and Caldwell (1975) observed no significant relationship between variety in daily stimulation at age six months and performance on the Bayley MDI at six months. Correlation between these two variables at one year was also negligible. However, six-month scores on variety in daily stimulation were correlated .27 with Bayley MDI at 12 months and .31 with IQ at age three. Twelve-month scores on variety of daily stimulation were correlated about .3 with IQ at 54-months and about .3 with three-year scores on the Illinois Test of Psycholinguistic Abilities (Bradley and Caldwell, 1976; Elardo, Bradley, and Caldwell, 1977). Wachs, Uzgiris, and Hunt (1971) reported that at age seven months, the variety of colors in the room correlated about .4 - .5 with Infant Psychological Development Scales scores. Taking the child to visit a neighbor was also correlated about .5 - .7. Thus, there is evidence that variety in stimulation during the first year of life is related to cognitive development. However, the relationship among basically normal children is a modest one, which seems more pronounced when relatively specific environmental measures and focused developmental measures are used. Differences in findings may principally reflect differences in the manner in which the environment was analyzed.

Wachs and his colleagues also report findings, based on measures of the environment taken during the second year of life. More specifically, they found that at 15 months, color variety in the home was correlated .4 to .7 with Infant Psychological Development Scale scores, whereas visiting within and outside the neighborhood

were negatively related to IPDS scores. At 18 months the pattern was essentially the same: family travel was correlated .4 to .9, while visiting outside the neighborhood was correlated -.5. At 22 months, child excursions to areas downtown became correlated with IQ. A related study, published by Wachs (1978), indicated that the presence of decorations in the child's room at 15-17 months was correlated about .4 to .5 with 31-month IQ. By comparison, visiting neighbors was not correlated with IQ, while the number of strangers in the home was negatively related (about -.5). Elardo, Bradley, and Caldwell (1975, 1976, 1977) found that 24-month scores on variety in daily stimulation were correlated .5 with IQ at age three, .4 with 54-month IQ scores, and .6 with three-year ITPA scores. The Elardo, Bradley, and Caldwell (1977) study also indicated that the relationship between variety of stimulation and language development was more pronounced for males, and that no race differences were apparent. A final investigation worth noting, in which the relation between variety of experience and cognitive development was considered, was conducted by Moore (1968) in England. The study showed that a variety of toys, books and experiences, assessed at age two and a half was correlated .4 and .3 with IQ for boys and for girls, respectively. This correlation remained high (about .5 to .7) even with social class partialed out.

Relatively few studies examining the effects of variety of stimulation during the later preschool years have been reported. In one of the studies, Bradley and Caldwell (1979) investigated the association between variety of stimulation assessed at age three and again at age four and a half among mostly lower to lower middle-class children (65 percent black). Variety of stimulation was correlated about .5 with IQ at the same points in time. Using results from a smaller group of students, Bradley and Caldwell (1978) reported that variety of stimulation measured in the preschool years was correlated around .3 to .4 with achievement during the primary grades. Ware and Garber (1972) also examined the relation between learning opportunities outside the home and children's scores on the Preschool Inventory among Mexican-American and black four-year-olds. They observed no evidence of a significant relationship; however, the range of environmental scores for their sample was rather small.

Several researchers have reported investigations of the relation between the variety of outside experiences children have during elementary school and the children's achievement. Davé (1963) examined the relation between activeness of the family and children's academic achievement among a representative group of children from Chicago. He found them to be correlated about .6. He also found a correlation of about .5 with IQ in the same children. Henderson, Bergan, and Hurt (1972), who used a measure of the environment similar to the one used by Davé (1963), found that extended interests and community involvement among family members were related to the performance of Mexican-American and Anglo-American first graders in Arizona. Similar findings were reported by Shea and Hanes (1977). Specifically, they found that learning opportunities outside the home were moderately related to reading achievement of five- and six-year-old children, especially white children. Outside learning opportunities were also related to vocabulary and comprehension scores for seven-year-old children. The Head Start Longitudinal Study (Shipman, 1976) utilized somewhat different types of environmental measures than the other three studies, one of which looked at a variety of stimulation in terms of the number of places the child accompanied the mother. This variable was correlated only about .2 with achievement at ages nine and ten.

Among the studies reviewed, there appears a somewhat consistent picture of the relation between variety of stimulation and cognitive development. Variety of stimulation throughout the first twelve years of life is moderately correlated with measures of cognitive development, with correlations commonly in the .4 to .6 range. The relationship appears to hold for both sexes and across a broad spectrum of ethnic and socioeconomic groups. Generally lacking are longitudinal studies; thus, the possible long-term effects of variety in stimulation for any given period are presently difficult to gauge. The few studies that have appeared indicate a significant relation between the two variables.

Acceleration of Achievement. For years McClelland and his colleagues (1953) have contended that societal differences in the emphasis placed by the family on achievement tends to be instrumental in determining the level of achievement motivation. Their research in comparative psychology generally confirms the assertion. For example, countries where achievement is highly valued, such as Japan, the United States, and The Federal Republic of Germany, produce citizens with higher achievement motivation than countries where achievement is not as highly prized, such as Italy and Mexico. McClelland postulates that societal differences in how much achievement is valued are manifested in child-rearing practices related to achievement, particularly the direct encouragement and acceleration of achievement efforts and outcomes.

The general emphasis placed on achievement in the United States and northern Europe is partially responsible for the rather large number of investigations regarding the role of parental encouragement of, involvement in, and demand for achievement in increasing intelligence and achievement in children. Bayley and Schaeffer (1963) found that parental achievement demands during the first year of life were not related to mental test scores for boys prior to age one, but that they were slightly related to mental test performance in girls. Achievement demands during the initial year of life showed about the same pattern of relations vis-à-vis mental test scores up to age five. These early demands appeared to be related about .2 to .3 with mental test performance in boys after age five, but not girls. Similar findings were reported in a series of studies published by Elardo, Bradley, and Caldwell (1975, 1976, 1977). In essence, six-month scores on maternal involvement with the child were not correlated to six-month Bayley MDI scores, but were related about .3 with three-year and four and a half-year IQ scores and with three-year scores on the

Illinois Test of Psycholinguistic Abilities. The observed relations were higher for females than males. Twelve-month maternal involvement scores showed somewhat higher correlations with all dependent cognitive measures. In another study, a factor called optimal care, which had heavy weightings on maternal stimulation and responsiveness during the first year of life, was correlated .67 with children's competence in the second year of life (Clarke-Stewart, 1973). Gordon (1974) reported that mother-baby teaching transactions in the first year were correlated about .3 to .4 with the infant's performance on cognitive tasks but not performance on the Bayley scales.

Hanson (1975), using data from the Fels Longitudinal Study, reported that for both males and females, parental involvement with the child was mildly related to the child's IQ at age three. However, emphasis on school achievement and models of task orientation was not significantly related to achievement. McCall, Appelbaum, and Hogarty, also using the Fels data, showed evidence that attempts to accelerate achievement in the first three years of life differentiated between the children with increasing and decreasing IQ profiles. Returning to the Bayley and Schaeffer (1963) study for age two and three findings, parental achievement demands at this age were correlated about .3 with IQ for girls, but not for boys. The relationship appears to have reversed itself in later years. Parental demands around age three were correlated about .3 with IQ for boys after age five, but not for girls.

A detailed observational study regarding parents' attempts to encourage intellectual and achievement pursuits was undertaken by White and Watts (1973). They found that parents of potentially competent children spent more time with the child in intellectually valuable activities and gave more overt encouragement to such activities than did parents of children identified as potentially lacking competence. Furthermore, intellectually valuable experiences *provided for* the child prior to two years of age and IQ at age three were found to be more strongly related (r = .4 to .6), than child-constructed experience (r = .35).

Substantial correlations appeared for IQ at age three and child-constructed activity after two and a half years of age (r = .57). Thus, not until two and a half years of age did child-initiated competent behavior significantly correlate with age three IQ test performance. This relationship held across social classes.

Further indications of the importance of the impact of acceleration behaviors in the second and third years of life came from a series of studies by Bradley, Caldwell, and Elardo (1975, 1976, 1977; 1979). Maternal involvement with children assessed at age two was correlated .5 with children's IQ at ages three and four and a half. It also correlated .5 with performance on the Illinois Test of Psycholinguistic Abilities at age three. Particularly interesting were findings from a cross-lagged panel analysis that involved measurement of the child on the Bayley MDI at six, twelve, and twenty-four months and measurement of the mother's involvement with the child at the same time points. The panel analysis results indicated that from six to twelve months of age, the mother's involvement with the child may be shaped by the child's developmental capacity to respond with a type of reciprocal alertness. That is, the child's early, yet-to-be-refined mechanisms for accommodation and assimilation of environment and experience seem to direct the influence of maternal involvement. However, with the 12 and 24 month age period, a greater degree of influence from maternal behavior to child competence is able to be observed. In contrast to findings from most studies, Kagan and Freeman (1963) did not observe a significant relationship between acceleration of achievement between one and three years old and child's IQ. However, acceleration of achievement in the later preschool period was correlated .6 with IQ for girls during that period but not boys. A somewhat lower correlation (about .35) was observed between acceleration of achievement in the preschool years and later IQ for girls. Again, no significant relationship was obtained for boys. Similarly, Ware and Garber (1972) failed to observe a significant relationship between rewards for intellectual attainment and children's scores on the Preschool Inventory at age four. However, the environmental measure used appeared severely limited. One study that did find evidence of a relation between the two variables was that by Bradley and Caldwell (1978). They found that stimulations of academic behavior measured at age three were correlated .3 with IQ at age three and .4 with IQ at age four and a half. Stimulation of academic behavior at age 54 months was correlated .5 with IQ. Stimulation of academic behavior during the preschool years was also correlated about .3 with IQ and composite achievement test scores for children in the primary grades. Based on their studies of maternal teaching styles used with preschool children from middle-class and lower-class backgrounds, Hess and Shipman (1971) concluded that optimal maternal communication "implies high levels of specificity in both labeling and focusing behavior. This included not only orientation and feedback but also pre-response instructions, where specificity occurred least frequently. It also implies a preference for eliciting the child's interest in the task through engagement and for maintaining it through encouragement and praise." (p. 193)

Studies examining the relation between acceleration of achievement and children's cognitive development during the elementary school years generally showed a significant relationship. For example, Shea and Hanes (1977) found that reading press was a good predictor of achievement in both black and white samples, although rewards for intellectual attainment were not. Similarly, Henderson and his colleagues (1972) recorded a correlation of .6 between valuing language and school-related behavior and scores on the Boehm Test of Basic Concepts among Mexican-American and Anglo-American first graders. In a study of 11-year old Canadian fifth-grade boys, Marjoribanks (1972) observed a substantial correlation (.66) between press for achievement and boys' scores on number and verbal abilities. Lesser correlations were obtained for spatial and reasoning abilities. Crandall, Dewey, Katkovsky, and Preston (1964) obtained different results from their analysis of data from the Fels Longitudinal Study.

Specifically they found no significant relation between boys' achievement test scores and the following parental behaviors: standards for achievement, participation in intellectual activities, positive reaction to achievement behaviors, and negative reaction to achievement behaviors. By contrast, girls' achievement test scores were correlated .5 with mother's standards for achievement; .4 with mother's positive reaction to achievement behaviors; and -.3 with mother's negative reaction to achievement behaviors. The only paternal behavior significantly related to girls' achievement was negative reaction toward achievement behaviors. Participation of neither parent in the girls' intellectual activities appeared to be related to achievement. A number of other studies have been done that have investigated the relation between parental acceleration of achievement and child cognitive development during the elementary school years. Among the studies reviewed, all showed substantial relations between the two with correlation generally ranging from .4 to .7 (Greenberg and Davidson, 1972; Trotman, 1977; Dave, 1963; Wolf, 1964; Henson, 1975). These studies indicated a strong relationship across groups varying in race, social class, and sex.

In sum, parental behaviors designed to accelerate achievement—such as encouragement and reward of achievement efforts, involvement in achievement activities, modeling of achievement behaviors, and teaching the child—appear to be related to cognitive development in children throughout the first twelve years of life. There is some evidence to indicate that the relationship becomes stronger across those years—albeit this assertion is difficult to prove conclusively given multiple problems obtaining to the measurement of cognitive abilities across that period of the life span. The relation appears to hold for both males and females, although perhaps more so for females early in life. It also appears to hold across social class and ethnic groups. It would be of theoretical benefit to examine the primary direction of effect between parent behavior and child competency for various periods in childhood. It would also be of value to examine the relation between parent behavior and child competency with parents' intelligence controlled.

Social Home Environment and Experience

Responsiveness. Freudian and neo-Freudian theorists have long postulated that a mother's responsiveness to her child is central to the child's psychosocial development. In essence, the cornerstone of optimal social and intellectual development and trust in the environment is the appropriateness of the mother's behavior in response to the child's needs (Erikson, 1950). Maternal responsiveness is also a central tenet in theories of attachment (Ainsworth, 1973) and bonding (Klaus and Kennel, 1970). In order for an infant to become securely "attached" or "bonded" to the mother, the mother must correctly anticipate the infant's needs by inducing and reacting appropriately to the infant's signals. To the degree that the mother's behavior adequately anticipates and meets the child's needs, it is possible to set up a mother-child relationship that is mutually satisfying. Each comes to know what to expect from the other. This milieu of reciprocity and trust then operates as a base from which the infant can form positive alliances and engage in reinforcing encounters with the broader social and physical environment. These encounters, in turn, serve to promote optimal development.

Major social learning theories that have included expectancy variables in their formula for establishing the probability for human behavior tend to posit the importance of early maternal responsiveness as conducive to a child's achievement behaviors. An example of this occurs in the social learning model of Rotter (1966). A person's belief regarding how much control he or she can exercise over the outcome of a specific situation is one of two major factors determining the likelihood that the person will make an effort to obtain the outcome; the second factor is how much the individual desires or values the outcome. If a person thinks that a desired outcome is obtainable, he or she is likely to exhibit proactive behavior. These generalized beliefs in the efficacy of one's actions have their roots in the pattern of reinforcements experienced early in life. If care givers have been responsive—that is, if they have provided reinforcements on a rather frequent and predictable basis—the child develops a sense of personal effectiveness. Research tends to show that early encounters with the environment, particularly those with primary caregivers, are integral to the development of competence (White, 1959) and achievement motivation (McClelland et al., 1953; Crandall & Battle, 1970). In essence, intrinsic motives like competence and exploration serve as incentives for children to learn from the environment. The appropriateness of a caregiver's responsiveness serves to frustrate or to facilitate these processes.

Partly because so many different theories place importance on the appropriateness of a mother's responses to a child, there have been a substantial number of research investigations dealing with the relation between maternal responsiveness and cognitive development. Yarrow and his colleagues (Yarrow, et al., 1973; Yarrow, et al. 1975) reported on a rather involved study of the relation between responsiveness and cognitive development among five-month-old urban black infants. They found that mother's contingent responsiveness to the infant's positive vocalizations was related to the infant's vocalization during exploration and manipulation of novel stimuli. Contingent responsiveness to the infant's distress was moderately correlated (.3 to .4) to performance on the Bayley scales, specifically with performance on the motor subscales and with cognitive motivational items. Yarrow also examined the relation between the responsiveness of the inanimate environment and cognitive development. Results indicated that the child's motor performance and cognitive motivational behaviors were related to the availability of responsive toys, objects, and other stimuli. Elardo, Bradley, and Caldwell (1975) observed similar findings in a sample of lower to lower-middle-class children (about 60 percent black) in Little Rock, Arkansas. Specifically, the verbal and emotional responsivity of the primary caregiver as measured when the infant was six months old was not significantly related to Bayley MDI scores. (The same pattern was observed between twelve month environment and development scores.) However, scores on emotional and verbal responsivity during the first year of life, they were significantly correlated to IQ and language scores assessed at age three (Elardo, Bradley, and Caldwell, 1977). Clarke-Stewart (1973) and Beckwith (1971) also reported no significant correlation between maternal responsiveness and infant's scores on general measures of mental development during the first year of life. Like the studies of Elardo, Bradley, and Caldwell (1975, 1977), however, Clarke-Stewart observed significant correlations between maternal responsiveness during the first year of life and measures of infant cognitive performance after the first year. Tulkin and Covitz (1975) found that maternal responses to the infant's frets at 10 months were correlated .5 with scores on the Illinois Test of Psycholinguistic Abilities at age six for middle-class but not working-class children. Responsiveness to infant's vocalizations at 10 months was not significantly related to ITPA scores for either group. Bradley and Caldwell (1976) also reported no significant relation between maternal responsivity at six months and child IQ at 54 months.

Another interesting finding pertaining to the relation between maternal responsiveness and infant competence in the first year of life can be found in the cross-lagged panel study of these variables reported by Bradley, Elardo, and Caldwell (1979). Specifically, these researchers examined the interrelationships among maternal responsiveness and child Bayley MDI scores assessed at three points in time: 6 months, 12 months, and 24 months. No primary direction of effect was observed between maternal and child variables either between six and 12 months or between 12 and 24 months. Two plausible related interpretations emerge from these findings. First, mother and child frequently reach a kind of synchrony between maternal responsiveness and child behavioral competence in the first year of life. Second, the child plays an important role in establishing the pattern of the relationship. Early sensitivity, alertness, or certain tem-

peramental qualities (Thomas, Chess, and Birch, 1977) may assist in the establishment and maintenance of mother-child interactional responsivity patterns (see also Bell, 1968; Sameroff, 1975; Lewis and Rosenblum, 1976). In essence, the behavior of mother and child are to a significant degree stimulated and modulated by the other. It might be especially interesting to examine the role played by sibling order in establishing this relationship, since there is some evidence to indicate that maternal responsiveness wanes for later children.

The Bayley and Schaefer analysis of the Berkeley Growth Study (1964) found that mother's ignoring of a child in the first three years of life was not correlated to mental test scores in the first year of life. It was, on the other hand, correlated about -.3 with IQ for girls during the 13 to 36 month period and about -.4 with IQ for boys after age three. In a series of studies by Bradley, Elardo, and Caldwell (1975, 1976, 1977), it was shown that maternal responsivity assessed at twenty-four months was correlated .5 with IQ at ages 36 and 54 months, plus .52 with scores on the Illinois Test of Psycholinguistic Abilities at age three. Correlations were slightly higher for males than females and slightly higher for whites than blacks. The intensive observational study conducted by White, Watts, and their associates (1973) provided additional information regarding the relationship between maternal responsiveness (in the form of encouragement) and intellectual development during the second and third years of life. The behavior of mothers whose children were predicted to be competent (Type A) was compared to the behavior of mothers whose children were predicted to lack competence (Type C). Results showed that Type A mothers were more responsive in the sense that they overtly encouraged their children's participation in intellectually valuable activities. The difference between Type A and Type C mothers was most pronounced after the children reached two. In the period from two to three years, the ratio of encouragement to discouragement for Type A mothers was 3:1, for Type C it was only 4:3. Another clear difference in the two groups of mothers was that Type A mothers spent substantially greater amounts of time on a daily basis facilitating their children's involvement in activities.

Despite the seeming importance of responsiveness to development, there have been relatively few investigations to directly examine the relation of this variable to cognitive development in children over three. The reasons for the dearth of studies are not entirely clear, although it should be mentioned that there have been several studies of related variables such as nurturance and attention. In one study where parental responsiveness was considered, Shipman (1976) found that this environmental variable was modestly correlated (.2 to .3) with achievement at ages 9-10 among children in the Head Start Longitudinal Study. Henderson, Bergan, and Hurt (1972) also found that attention from parents was significantly related to performance on the Boehm Test of Basic Concepts among 60 lower SES Mexican-American first graders and 66 middle SES Anglo-American first graders. The paucity of data for older children precludes useful generalization about the strength of the relation between parental responsivity and cognitive development. Further studies are needed to clarify the relationship. It may well be that specifically focused responsiveness, such as willingness to assist children in academic areas where they are having difficulty and continued encouragement of their academic and intellectual pursuits, will show a strong association with intellectual and academic attainment. Investigation of possible sex differences would appear essential in view of previous findings regarding sex differences in achievement (Stein, 1973).

In sum, the research reviewed appears to indicate that a pattern of responsive social interaction between mother and child, conducive to cognitive development, may be established in the first year of life. Failure to find significant correlations between maternal responsiveness and general measures of mental performance in the first year may reflect limitations in the content and psychometric properties of the cognitive measures for children of this age, more so than the absence of a relationship. The general lack of significant correlations between maternal responsiveness in the first year of life and measures of child competence in the fifth and sixth year may be a partial function of the changing nature of maternal responsiveness, as the child matures, physically and socially, and as the child's interactions with other persons and objects take on greater importance. However, Yarrow's finding that maternal responsiveness was correlated with infant cognitive/motivational behaviors as early as five months suggests the budding of an important relationship between maternal responsiveness and the infant's confidence and eagerness to interact with the environment. It would be valuable to determine whether the relation between maternal responsiveness and infant cognitive/ motivational behavior early in life mediates the observed relation between maternal responsiveness and child competence in subsequent years.

Warmth and Nurturance. The child who experiences a responsive familial environment also tends to experience an environment that is warm and nurturant. While these two dimensions are to some degree separable, there is both conceptual and empirical overlap. For example, when Shaefer (1971) produced a circumplex model of maternal behavior, he found that warmth, nurturance, and responsiveness tended to cluster along the same axis— although they were not identical.

The research findings pertaining to warmth and nurturance will be treated in a separate section from the research on responsivity for several reasons. First, and most importantly, the dimensions as they have been operationalized in the literature are separable to some degree. There are parents who are affectionate and loving, but who through ignorance, inattentiveness, or other factors are not particularly responsive in the ways assessed in some research projects. Contrariwise, some parents respond appropriately to an infant's vocalizations or requests for physical care, but the responses may be rather mechanical and not filled with warmth. Second, the measurement instruments for the two dimensions have differed somewhat. Items assessing responsivity have often focused on transactions between mother and child (i.e., mother responds positively to infant vocalizations). Items assessing warmth have frequently only catalogued an adult behavior (i.e., mother kisses child).

The studies examined tend to present a rather vague, poorly delineated portrait of the relation between warmth and cognitive development. Clarke-Stewart (1973) found that warm physical contact was not correlated with cognitive measures during the first two years of life. Bayley and Schaefer (1964) obtained similar results during the first year, but a correlation of about .5 between expressions of affection and girls' mental test performance between 13 and 36 months. By contrast, Yarrow, et al. (1973) obtained a correlation of .3 between mother's positive affect at five months and children's social responsiveness, goal-directed behaviors, and manipulation of novel stimuli. Similarly, Gordon (1974) found a .3 correlation between baby-mother affectional transaction and the infant's responsive behavior, but not other cognitive behaviors. Thus, there appears to be a very weak relationship between parental warmth during the first year of life and the infant's cognitive performance with, perhaps, the exception of a modest association with infant's social responsiveness and involvement in novel situations.

The pattern of relations between nurturance and cognitive development between one and three years of age appears to be a little more consistent. For example, Engel and Keane (1975) found the mother's affectionate contact was correlated .6 with Bayley PDI scores at 18 months and .4 at 22 months. There was not a significant relation between affectionate contact and Bayley MDI score, however. Using data on 124 children from the Berkeley Guidance Study, Honzik (1967) found that a close mother-daughter relationship about age two was associated with cognitive development during the preschool years, while a close father-daughter relation early in life appeared more strongly related to development after age seven. For sons, the relationship with mother appeared most crucial after age eight. Rather similar findings emerged from the Berkeley Growth studies (Bayley and Schaefer, 1964). Specifically, mother's expression of affection between one and three was correlated about .5 with girls mental test performance during the period from 13 to 54 months, but not thereafter. No significant correlation was obtained for boys. Unlike findings from the Guidance Study, the Berkeley Growth Study showed no significant correlation between mother's expression of affection and boys mental test performance after age five. However, mother's positive evaluation correlated about .3 with IQ among boys after age five. Kagan and Freeman (1963), in their analysis of data from the Fels longtiudinal study, did not observe a significant relation between acceptance and affection around one to three years old and IQ for males during the same period or thereafter. Like the Guidance and Growth studies cited above, Kagan and Freeman (1963) observed a correlation of .5 between maternal acceptance and affection and girls' IQ during the ages one to three. A weaker relation obtained between acceptance during the one to three year period and subsequent IQ. In one of the more interesting analyses, Moore (1968) observed a correlation of about .4 between the emotional atmosphere of the home and IQ in both sexes at age three. Emotional atmosphere of the home assessed at age three was also correlated about .6 with IQ and achievement at age eight plus reading scores at age seven. Moore (1968) also examined the relationship between emotional atmosphere of the home and cognitive competence in children with social class partialed out. Using this partial correlation procedure, he obtained a coefficient of .35 between emotional atmosphere and IQ in boys at age three. The partial correlation between emotional atmosphere assessed at around age three and cognitive measures at age seven and eight ranged from .4 to .5 for both sexes.

In contrast to most of the studies reviewed, there were two studies in which there was no evidence of a relation between maternal warmth and children's development (Baumrind and Black, 1967; McCall et al., 1973). In the McCall study, however, there was some evidence that parents who were coercive tended to have children whose relative mental performance between age two and age seventeen decreased. In sum, there is general evidence that warmth and nurturance in the period from about one year old to three years old are moderately related to mental performance for girls during this period and abates thereafter. The evidence for males is equivocal but generally indicative of a weaker relationship during the one- to three-year period. There is greater evidence that warmth and nurturance in the second and third years of life are associated with later cognitive performance.

Relatively few studies have been reported on the relation of warmth and nurturance in the later preschool years and cognitive development. Radin (1972) looked closely at this relationship among a group of 31 white and 21 black lower-class children enrolled in the Early Education Project at Ypsilanti, Michigan. She found that maternal warmth correlated about .4 with IQ and Peabody Picture Vocabulary score measured during the later preschool years. It was also correlated about .3 with residual IQ gain and .4 with academic motivation. In a subsequent investigation of paternal nurturance and its relation to cognitive development in boys, Radin (1973) observed a correlation of .5 with IQ at ages five and six among middle-class boys. For lower-class boys, a correlation of .6 with IQ at age five, and .4 at age six was reported. Similar results were obtained by Bradley and Caldwell (1979) in their study of mostly lower- to lower-middle-class children in Little Rock, Arkansas. Sixty-five percent of this sample was comprised of black children. Parental pride, affection, and warmth assessed at age three were correlated .4 with IQ at three and four and a half. The same environmental process variable measured at around five years old was correlated about .3 with IQ at age five and .4, with composite achievement scores during the primary grades. Contrary to results from these studies, Kagan and Freeman (1963) found no significant relationship between acceptance and affection on the part of mothers and IQ scores for either boys or girls.

Included in the studies of the relation of warmth and cognitive development among school-age children is one described by Henderson, Bergan, and Hurt (1972). They found that attention of parents was significantly related to performance of first grade Mexican-American and Anglo-American children on the Boehm Test of Basic Concepts. Greenberg and Davidson (1973), in their investigation of disadvantaged urban black fifth graders, discovered that parental awareness of the child as an individual differentiated between high-achieving and low-achieving students. Crandall, Dewey, Katkovsky, and Preston (1964) obtained different results in a study of mostly white middle-class families from Detroit. Indeed, for girls they observed negative correlations between mother's affection and nurturance and achievement. For boys, no significant relation was observed.

In general, the relation between warmth and nurturance and cognitive development appears to depend on the time that the environmental variable is measured, the time that the cognitive measure is given, and the sex of the child. Maternal warmth during the first three years appears moderately related to competence for girls during the same period but very little for boys. It appears more strongly related to subsequent performance in boys. Warmth during the preschool years appears moderately related to mental test scores during that period, while the relation with later competence is less clear. The limited data on older children suggest perhaps a weak relationship during the school years. Finally, negative findings pertaining to the relation for girls need replication on a broader sample. These findings suggest, however, that too close a relationship could lead to complacency or involve restrictions in cognitive behavior (see Bayley and Schaefer, 1964).

Encouragement of Independence and Maturity. One of the principal societal values espoused in the United States is the development of independence and responsibility in its citizens. This facet of our social mores has led us to incorporate in our child-rearing practices an encouragement of independence. The link between encouragement of independence in young children and cognitive development is not a strong one. However, it is generally believed that highly dependent children tend not to be active in attempting to solve problems they encounter, thus missing many opportunities to learn from the experience.

Research investigations into the link between fostering independence in the first year of life and the child's cognitive competence indicate a mild negative relation—if any. For example, Gordon's (1974) study of low-income families in Florida obtained a -.3 correlation between maternal push for independence and children's performance on several cognitive tasks. No correlation was observed between maternal push and children's performance on the Bayley Scales. Similarly, Bayley and Schaefer (1964) found a correlation of approximately .2 between the fostering of dependency and mental test scores among mostly middle-class girls in the first year of life. No significant correlation was obtained for boys.

In general, it appears that a press for independence has little effect on the very young child's true needs. Lacking in the studies reviewed are data dealing with the longer term consequences of an early push for independence.

Several studies have been published that deal with the press for independence during the second and third years of life. The fostering of dependency correlated about .3 with IQ among girls only in the Berkeley Growth sample. Additionally, excessive contact between mother and child was correlated about .2 with mental test performance among girls (Bayley and Schaefer, 1964). Three reports involving data from the Fels Longtitudinal Study have reported findings in this area (Kagan and Freeman, 1963; McCall, et al., 1973; Hanson, 1975). All indicate negligible relations between such factors as general babying and general protectiveness and the child's mental test performance. A problem with the studies examining press for independence during the second and third years of life is that most focused on assessing parental behaviors thought to encourage dependence rather than on behaviors thought to encourage independence. It may be that investigations into behaviors that encourage independence would reveal a somewhat different picture, particularly parental behaviors that would facilitate the child's choosing or developing his own strategy to solve a problem.

Kagan and Freeman (1973) found that parental babying during the later preschool years was correlated about -.4 with IQ for girls at age five, while protectiveness was correlated about -.2. These parental behaviors held the same relation to children's intellectual performance at age nine. Bradley and Caldwell (1979), in their study of predominantly lower to lower-middle-class families in Little Rock, Arkansas, found that parental modeling and encouraging of social maturity at age three was correlated about .4 with IQ. However, modeling and encouraging of social maturity at four to five years of age produced no correlation with children's IQ. Finally, two studies involving a predominantly middle-class sample showed no significant relationship between independence-training and cognitive performance (Hanson, 1975; Baumrind and Black, 1967).

As with the earlier developmental periods, there is little evidence that encouragement of independence has a positive impact on cognitive attainment during the preschool period. There is some evidence that babying of children after three years may be related to poorer performance (Bayley and Schaefer, 1964; Bradley and Caldwell, 1979). Further investigations in this area are needed to determine the relationship between these behaviors and restrictiveness on the part of parents. In addition, there is a need to determine how such behaviors are related to fostering opportunities for the child to learn from social encounters outside the home.

Emphasis on performing independently during the early school years appears to have a positive relation to cognitive development. Hanson's (1975) reanalysis of the Fels data revealed a .3 correlation with IQ for boys at age nine and a .4 correlation for girls. Similarly, Marjoribanks (1972) found a correlation of .4 between press for independence and achievement among 11-year-old Canadian boys.

In sum, there is little evidence that encouraging independence prior to age six facilitates cognitive development in children. On the other hand, for school-aged children there is some evidence of a modest relationship. Generally lacking are the kinds of detailed studies needed to delineate fully the nature of the relationship. Also lacking are research studies delineating early experiences that influence the development of proactive, cooperative skills necessary to both cognitive and social problem solving situations. It may be useful to identify several different categories of independence and dependence behaviors and then develop information pertaining to each category and children's cognitive performance.

Restrictiveness. Since the time psychoanalytic theory was articulated, restrictiveness has been considered detrimental to children's health and development. However, several studies (Bayley & Schaefer, 1964; Clarke-Stewart, 1973; Elardo, et al., 1975) show little relationship between restrictiveness during the first year of life and mental test performance during the same period. The results pertaining to mental test scores later in life are mixed. Some studies show no significant relationship between restrictiveness in the first year and mental tests during later years; some studies show a weak negative relation (Bayley and Schaeffer, 1964; Clarke-Stewart, 1973). In one of the more interesting investigations, Clarke-Stewart (1973) reported that maternal restrictiveness during the last quarter of the first year of life was not related to Bayley MDI scores during the same period among a group of 36 children from lower-class families balanced for race and sex. However, responsiveness was correlated -.43 with a composite competence factor, -.37 with object permance, -.41 with Bayley MDI, and -.34 with length of involvement with objects—all measured during the first half of the second year of life.

Elardo, et al. (1975) observed a correlation of -.41 between avoidance of restriction and punishment assessed at 24-months and 3-year IQ scores among a group of predominantly lower to lower-middle-class children, of which about 60 percent were black. Other related studies found that 24-month scores on this environmental factor correlated -.28 with IQ at age 54 months (Bradley & Caldwell, 1976) and -.38 with scores on the Illinois Test of Psycholinguistic Abilities for males at age three (Elardo, et al., 1977). In the latter study, there was no significant result for females

and no race differences obtained. Kagan and Freeman (1963), using data from the Fels Longitudinal Study on a sample mostly from middle-class children of above average intelligence, found that restrictiveness during the two- to three-year-old period was correlated -.32 with IQ in males at age three and a half and -.51 for females. In addition, restrictiveness during this age period showed a correlation of about -.4 with IQ for both sexes up through age nine. In a similar study conducted by Engel and Keane (1975) of urban black infants, a correlation of -.40 between maternal prohibitions and Bayley PDI scores at 22 months was observed. Their interpretation of these results suggests that mothers tend to be more restrictive with children who were more physically active. White and Watts, (1973) concluded from their intensive examination of maternal behavior that mothers of competent children were more restrictive when the child was younger than two, but less restrictive thereafter.

Relatively few investigations have been reported on the association between parental restrictiveness after age three and children's cognitive development. Baumrind and Black (1967) examined this association among 83 middle-class preschool children with respect to restrictive behavior of both parents. Their results indicated that boys' IQ at about age five was weakly related to maternal restrictiveness (.3), but not related to paternal restrictiveness. For girls, no significant relations were observed. Seventeen middle-class and 13 lower-class fathers were observed for restrictiveness when their sons were five in a study directed by Radin (1973). IQ was measured at age five and again at age six. Results showed that for middle-class boys, paternal restrictiveness was correlated .47 with IQ at age 5 and -.32 at age six, while for lower-class boys, it was -.41 and -.23, respectively. Hanson's (1975) reanalysis of the Fels data involved an examination of two variables related to restrictiveness: freedom to explore the environment and freedom to engage in verbal expression. Concurrent relations between these variables and children's IQ at age five and a half revealed an interesting pattern. Freedom to engage in verbal expression was correlated .3 with IQ in boys and .6 in girls. Freedom to explore the environment showed no significant relation for either sex. Essentially the same results obtained when the children were nine years old.

In general, the modest level of association observed between restrictiveness and cognitive development may partially reflect the dearth of cases for which there was evidence of extreme restrictiveness. From the data that are available for the first three years of life the results seem to indicate a mild negative relationship for girls. However, restrictiveness during this period appears to have little sustained effect. There is also some evidence that mild restrictiveness early in life is conducive to development (Bayley and Schaefer, 1964; White and Watts, 1973). Perhaps restrictiveness over certain behaviors increases a child's ability to control and organize the environment and concomitantly increases the likelihood of benefiting from certain types of social learning activities (i.e., increased verbal experience may result when physical activity is reduced). Further examination of this phenomenon is needed among older, as well as younger, children. Another area in need of further exploration is the effect of restriction over different types of child activities. In the Hanson (1975) study, freedom to explore the physical environment was not significantly related to IQ, whereas freedom to engage in verbal expression was. It may well be that restrictiveness pertaining to certain activities is not as detrimental as restrictiveness pertaining to verbal experience, involvement with appropriate play materials, and the like. In conclusion, while this review did not reveal substantial evidence that mild restrictiveness has long-term deleterious consequences for mental development, it is likely that more pronounced restrictiveness does. Furthermore, the studies reviewed did not deal with such cognitively related issues as creativity and moral development.

Discipline Techniques. The issue of what kind of discipline strategy is most effective in facilitating social and moral development is a longstanding one in psychology. There have also been sustained interests in the relation between discipline and achievement motivation, achievement, and creativity. Theorists have argued that children need to develop sufficient internal controls in order to persist when faced with demanding cognitive tasks; that parents should avoid punishing intrinsic exploratory and competence drives; and that parents should be consistent with discipline and expectations for childrens' behavior. This is thought to engender confidence in children regarding the condition under which they must operate and confidence about what they can do to be successful in attaining a desired goal. Because of the widespread interest in the relation between discipline and development in children, there have been several studies that have examined the issue, some of which have investigated discipline practices considered detrimental to development and some of which have investigated discipline practices considered conducive to development.

In a series of studies conducted at the Center for Child Development and Education in Little Rock, Arkansas, Elardo, Bradley, and Caldwell (1975, 1976, 1977) found no significant relation between avoidance of restriction and punishment measured when children were six and twelve months old and measures of mental development during the first four and a half years of life. There was, however, a somewhat narrow range of scores on the measure of restriction and punishment. Bayley and Schaefer (1964), in their analysis of the Berkeley Growth data, found that punishment, use of fear to control, and strictness were correlated .4 with mental test scores for boys in the first year of life. By contrast, strictness was correlated -.3 with mental test scores for girls. Punishment, use of fear to control, strictness during the first three years of life, and mental test performance were correlated -.6, -.5, and -.3, respectively, for girls, but not to any degree for boys. Interestingly, in a later developmental period, from five to eighteen years of age, punishment, use of fear to control, and strictness were correlated -.2, -.4, and -.4 respectively, for boys, but not for girls.

McCall, et al. (1973) have described changes in developmental performance of children from the Fels Longitudinal study across the two and a half to seventeen-age period. Throughout this period the children were periodically assessed with mental tests. From these assessments a profile was developed for each child based on performance at each assessment point. The profiles were then subjected to a cluster analysis in order to identify several major patterns of performance across two and a half to seventeen-year period. Of five isolated patterns there were two increasing ones, two decreasing ones, and a single stable one. McCall and his colleagues found, via a discriminant function analysis, that severity of penalties in the first three years of life was associated with decreasing mental test profiles. Kagan and Freeman (1963), in an earlier analysis of the Fels Study, found that for girls severity of penalties, justification of penalties, coerciveness, and criticism were correlated with mental test scores in the first three years of life -.5, -.4, -.4 and .5, respectively. For boys, only coerciveness was significantly correlated. These early maternal variables showed substantially the same correlations with mental test performance up through age nine for girls. For boys, however, severity of punishment and coerciveness were correlated about -.4 with IQ at age five and a half but not age nine. Similar findings were reported by Caldwell and her colleagues in Little Rock, Arkansas. Specifically, avoidance of restriction and punishment on the part of the primary caregiver measured at twenty-four months was correlated .4 with three years IQ, .3 with four and a half year IQ, and .4 with ITPA scores at age three for females. No race differences were observed in the relations obtained. The one study in which no significant evidence of deleterious influences occurring from punishment of the child during the one to three-year period was conducted by Engel and Keane (1975). Indeed, the only significant correlation observed was a positive one between punishment and Bayley PDI score at 18 months. However, the researchers interpreted this finding as indicating parents' attempts to deal with a physically active child.

Physical punishment during the later preschool years does not seem as strongly associated with decrements in IQ as does physical punishment earlier in life. For instance, Baumrind and Black's (1967) study of middle-class children in California showed that neither punishment nor consistent discipline were significantly related to IQ among boys or girls. For boys, father's strictness concerning orderliness was moderately related to intelligence (.27), but mother's strictness was not. In the Kagan and Freeman (1963) study, severity of criticism and severity of punishment were not related to IQ, whereas justification of punishment and coerciveness were correlated .6 and -.4, respectively. For boys, justification of punishment assessed at five and a half years of age was correlated .5 with IQ at age nine, while coerciveness correlated -.3. Severity of punishment and severity of criticism produced no significant relationships with later IQ. For girls, severity of punishment and coerciveness assessed at age five and a half were correlated about -.4 with age nine IQ, while justification of punishment and criticism correlated about .6. Bradley and Caldwell (1978) found that physical punishment measured at age three was correlated -.2 with IQ at age three and -.3 with IQ at age four and a half. Physical punishment measured in the four- to six-year period was not correlated to IQ or achievement. Thus, there is general evidence that physical punishment (at the levels of intensity recorded in the studies reviewed) wanes in importance during the preschool years in terms of its relationship to cognitive development. By comparison, discipline techniques more directly involving concepts of fairness continue to show significant relations with mental development.

Relatively few studies have been done on the relationship between parental discipline strategies and mental performance during elementary school years. Those that have been done indicate a very modest level of relationship, if any.

In sum, punishment during the early years of a child's life seems to be negatively related to cognitive performance, with some evidence indicating that punishment during this period has a lasting effect. The use of physical punishment during later years appears to bear little relation to cognitive performance—albeit extreme cases of punishment appear to have been rarely recorded in the studies reviewed. Justification of punishment and coerciveness after age three indicated a modest relation to cognitive attainment. Generally lacking in the studies examined were investigations of discipline variables, such as consistency. There was some evidence of sex differences in the relation between discipline techniques and mental development: girls generally suffer more from harsh forms of discipline. There was also some evidence that fathers and mothers may play somewhat different roles in the relationship. Both of these sex-related differences are in need of further study, both in intact and single-parent families. Finally, an issue to be addressed is the mediational property of social-cultural influences on discipline and punishment patterns in child-rearing, and the relative effect this has on intellectual expression across the life span.

Physical Home Environment and Experience

Toys, Games, and Materials. Piaget postulated that children below about two years old use a sensorimotor type of thinking. Thinking is in terms of actions. For this reason, much of a child's early learning is based on experiences with real objects, in observing their actions. Partly because of Piaget's research on infant thinking, child development researchers have become more concerned with the importance of the toys, games, and materials that very young children have available for learning. A number of investigations conducted during the last decade have shown a rather consistent and pronounced relation between the amount, variety, and appropriateness of the toys and materials children have and their cognitive performance.

Studies conducted at the Center for Child Development and Education in Little Rock, Arkansas, involved the examination of this relationship throughout the first five years of life. The family's score on the scale Provision of Appropriate Play Materials assessed when the infant was six months old was not significantly correlated with the infant's performance on the Bayley at six months (Elardo et al., 1975). However,

it was correlated .41 with the child's three-year Binet IQ score and .44 with 54-month IQ. The appropriateness of play materials measured at 12 months was correlated .35 with 12-month Bayley scores and .56 with three-year IQ scores. Provision of Appropriate Play Materials, assessed at 24 months, showed a correlation of .64 with IQ at age three and .56 with IQ at age four and a half (Bradley and Caldwell, 1976). In a related study, Elardo et al. (1977) found that six-month scores on this environmental process measure were correlated .33 with age three ITPA scores, a somewhat higher correlation obtained for whites than blacks. The 24-month assessment of Provision of Appropriate Play Materials was correlated .55 with age three ITPA, with somewhat higher correlations for blacks and females.

Clarke-Stewart (1973) found that the number and variety of toys available to a child during the nine- to twelve-month period was not significantly correlated to Bayley MDI during the same period. It was, however, correlated about .3 to .4 with competence and about .45 with Bayley MDI in the second year of life, but not with performance on the Uzgiris-Hunt scales of mental development.

Wachs and his colleagues reported on several detailed studies of home environment and cognitive development that involved an assessment of toys and books present in the home. Results from a study of 102 predominantly lower SES children indicated that the availability of books and toys during the second year of life was significantly correlated with several scales from the Infant Psychological Development Scale at 22 months, but not at 15 and 18 months (Wachs, Uzgiris, and Hunt, 1971). Using another example, Wachs (1976) observed a substantial relationship between the number of audiovisually responsive toys and children's performance on object permanence and the development of schemas throughout the second year of life. Children's scores on the use of objects as means scale were related to the same environmental variable after the child was 18 months old. In a follow-up study, Wachs (1978) reported that the presence of audiovisually responsive toys in the second year of life was correlated .6

with IQ at age two and a half years. Tulkin and Covitz (1975) found that the number of environmental objects available in the home at age two was correlated .40 with middle-class girls' performance on the Illinois Test of Psycholinguistic Abilities at age six, but not their Peabody Picture Vocabulary scores. For working-class girls the correlations were .55 with ITPA and .40 with PPVT. Moore (1968) reported results from longitudinal study of 61 children from London who were generally representative of the regional population. He found that the toys, books, and experiences present in children's homes at age two and a half was correlated .4 and .3 with age three IQ for boys and girls, respectively. Even with social class partialed out, the correlations remained .36 and .14 for boys and girls, respectively. When Moore (1968) correlated the two and a half-year home environment scores with IQ at age eight, he observed a .6 correlation for both sexes (about .45 with social class partialed out). Correlations with reading scores at age seven were .5 for boys and .7 for girls. Partialing out social class dropped the correlation to .34 for boys with no effect on the correlation for girls.

Several research studies have been done on the relation of the availability of toys and materials in the later preschool years and the children's development. The research of Ware and Garber (1972) among Mexican-American and black four-year-olds provided information on such a relationship. They found that the availability of materials for learning in the home correlated .3 with children's scores on the Preschool Inventory. Similarly, Bradley and Caldwell (1978) found in a study of mostly lower to lower-middle-class families (about 65 percent black) that the availability of toys, games, and reading materials at age three was correlated .47 with three-year IQ and .48 with four and a half-year IQ. Scores on this environmental process variable, measured at 54 months old, correlated .55 with IQ at 54 months. Scores on the variable taken when the children were about five to six years old correlated .4 to .5 with achievement test scores in the primary grades. The Wulberg, Inglis, Kriegsman, and Mills (1975) study revealed that the

amount and *appropriateness* of toys during the preschool years significantly differentiated homes of language-delayed and normal children.

Investigations seeking to determine the association between the presence of learning materials and cognitive development during the school years have typically not focused on enumerating toys, but have most often catalogued the number and types of reading materials present. As a case in point, Keeves (1972) randomly selected 231 twelve-year-old boys from Australia and recorded the use of books in the home. This was significantly related to math achievement, even with previous math achievement controlled. The same pattern emerged with respect to science achievement. Shipman (1976) described findings from the Head Start Longitudinal Study that involved an examination of the relation of home factors and achievement. The 1212 nine- and ten-year-old participants were selected from the Southern, mid-Atlantic and Northwest regions of the United States. About 65 percent were black. Shipman found that the number of possessions and books a child had correlated .3 to .4 with achievement. Shea and Hanes (1977) reported on a study of black and white follow-through participants from Florida. In the group materials for learning in the home demonstrated a significant relation to achievement.

Based on the studies reviewed, it appears that there is a rather consistently strong relation between the availability of toys and other learning materials in the home and children's cognitive development. The exact meaning of this observed strong association is not completely clear. Indeed, multiple factors may be operating to make the correlations substantial. For example, having appropriate toys and materials available may partially reflect the affluence of the family, and it may partially reflect the general education level of parents, both of which may contribute in other ways to children's cognitive development. However, there is at least some evidence to suggest that the relation between learning materials and cognitive development is not solely a function of these socioeconomic variables (Moore, 1968). A second explanation for the high correlation may be that toys, as well as being a source of learning per se, serve as a vehicle to facilitate learning from parents when parents play and instruct their children while using toys. This would include the opportunity to hear parents talk and to learn some problem-solving skills from them regarding the toys. Similarly, toys and games may serve to facilitate learning via modeling and instruction from older siblings. These areas appear fruitful for future studies.

Level of Sensory Input. Parke (1978) noted that stimulation in the home settings "can be conceptualized not merely as specific objects or events that impinge on the child, but (also) . . . the amount of non-specific background noise (p. 35)." Studies of the effects of background noise on cognitive attainment have been relatively rare in psychological literature; however, existing findings point to a deleterious effect once the intensity and duration of the noise goes beyond a moderate level. In a study of 10-month old baby girls, Tulkin and Kagan (1972) observed that working-class homes were noiser and more crowded than middle-class homes. Children from these homes had more interaction with adults and more time to watch TV. Working-class children also tended to show poorer cognitive performance. With respect to the types of observation and interview studies reviewed for this paper, the largest amount of data developed was in studies by Wachs and his colleagues (Wachs, 1976, 1978; Wachs, Uzgiris, and Hunt, 1971). Wachs et al. (1971) found that high noise level in the homes of children about nine to eleven months old was correlated -.4 to -.9 with subscales from the Infant Psychological Development Scale (1971), as measured between nine and eleven months. Noise level, assessed during the second year of life, was correlated -.4 to -.6, with subscales of the Infant Psychological Development Scale. In addition, Wachs (1978) reported noise level measured at two years of age correlated from -.4 to -.7 with age two and a half IQ. High noise level in the homes of five-year-olds has been reported to interfere with ability to maintain attention in cognitive tasks (Heft, 1976). Additional investigations into the effects of internal

noise in a home, conducted by Wohlwill and Heft (1977), led them to conclude that "for the children from the noisier homes, it appears that their ability to selectively attend to the relevant stimulus features in each situation was adversely affected by the high noise levels in their homes in spite of their apparent adaptation to these conditions" (p. 132). Finally, in a study done by Michelson (1968), third graders from homes having high noise levels scored lower on spelling and language tests and were rated lower on creativity by their teachers.

Parke (1978), in his review of literature pertaining to the effects of sensory stimulation on cognitive development, noted that excessive stimulation is not restricted to noises emanating from within the home, but may involve noises originating from sources in the external environment (i.e., highways, airports, factories). He described a study by Cohen, Glass, and Singer (1973) that involved an investigation of the cognitive consequences of living close to a heavily traveled expressway. Children living in lower-floor apartments adjacent to an expressway showed decrements in auditory discrimination, as compared with children living on upper floors. Children living on lower floors also revealed impaired performance on reading tests. Impairments were particularly noticeable among children who had resided in the apartments for four or more years. Parke (1978) concluded his review of excessive auditory stimulation by stating that "these studies provide impressive support for the view that too much noise either inside or outside the home environment—that the child cannot control or escape—is negatively related to early cognitive development and later school achievement." (p. 140)

On the other hand, there is evidence that too little sensory stimulation can lead to retardation just as can too much. Classic studies, such as those performed by Spitz and Wolf (1946) and Dennis and Majarian (1957), on institutionalized infants indicated that cognitive and social development are dependent on a modicum of auditory, visual, tactile, and kinesthetic stimulation. Studies conducted by Barnard and her colleagues on low-birthweight infants in the intensive-care nursery setting showed the importance of providing sensory stimulation, particularly contingent stimulation, for children's development. Yarrow, Rubenstein, Pederson, and Jankowski (1973) observed that among five-month-old urban children the amount of tactile stimulation available correlated about .3 with two cognitive-motivational variables. Kinesthetic stimulation correlated about .3 to .6 with a variety of general and specific abilities; visual and auditory stimulation correlated about .3 with social responsiveness. Thus, it appears that a curvilinear relationship may exist between sensory input and mental development; a modest level of sensory input is necessary to support normal cognitive development. However, there is need for additional studies to be conducted on older children, like those performed by Yarrow and his colleagues (1975) on infants, to determine the relationship of sensory input to development throughout childhood.

Organization of the Environment. Parents and other caregivers provide both direct support for children's development by giving appropriate kinds of stimulation and indirect support for development through organizing the environment so the child can receive maximum benefit. As Parke (1978) has noted, "This secondary role may be even more important than the role as stimulator, since the amount of time that infants spend interacting with the inanimate environment far exceeds their social interaction time." (p. 11) Organization of the child's environment so that it is maximally conducive to development does not appear to be a unitary behavioral dimension. It includes such features as making certain that the child's environment contains no health or safety hazards; that it is free from clutter and obstructions; and that events occur with a relative degree of regularity. The concern for regularity and/or predictability in the environment is especially noteworthy. There is a growing body of evidence in the psychological and sociological literature that frequent, drastic change is a threat to mental health (Holmes & Rahe, 1967; Dean & Lin, 1977). Relatedly, studies utilizing a social learning model

have shown that individuals tend not to engage in productive behaviors unless they believe that events and outcomes are to some extent controllable. This internalized sense of control appears to depend on the individual's having experienced a history of reinforcements that is generally consistent.

Despite the seeming importance of organizing a child's environment, the number of studies relating this environmental process to cognitive development are limited. Elardo et al. (1975) examined the relationship beginning at six months old. Among a group of lower-class and middle-class subjects (about 60 percent black), they found that organization of the environment assessed at six months was correlated about .2 with six-month and twelve-month Bayley MDI scores, and .4 with three-year Binet IQ scores. In a follow-up study, Bradley and Caldwell (1976) reported that six-month scores on organization of the environment were correlated about .3 with IQ at age four and a half. Twelve-month scores on organization of the environment demonstrated about the same pattern of relationship to cognitive measures.

Wachs (1976), studying the environments of lower-class children in the Midwest, found that items indicating regularity of daily routine in the second year of life were correlated .3 to .7 with subtests on the Infant Psychological Development Scale. Wachs (1978) also reported that these types of items were correlated about .3 to .6, with IQ measured at 31 months. In their study of IQ profiles from the Fels participants, McCall et al. (1973) found that clarity of policy regulations and enforcement in the third year of life significantly discriminated between children with increasing and decreasing IQ profiles. Elardo et al. (1975) reported essentially the same results in their study. Organization of the environment assessed at two years of age correlated .4 with three-year IQ scores and .3 with IQ to 54 months (Bradley and Caldwell, 1976). In a separate study, these same researchers observed a correlation of about .3 between organization of the environment and scores on the Illinois Test of Psycholinguistic Abilities at age three, with females showing a slightly higher relation than males and whites a slightly higher relation than blacks.

Among the investigations reviewed, only one examined the relation between organization of the environment and cognitive development during the later preschool period. In that study, Bradley and Caldwell (1979) reported that children whose homes were rated as safe, clean, and organized when they were three had higher IQs at age three. The four and a half year score on this environmental process variable correlated about .3 with IQ at the same age period. A safe, clean, organized environment during the preschool period was correlated from .3 to .4 with achievement test scores in the primary grades.

The Greenberg and Davidson (1972) study of urban fifth graders showed that structure and orderliness in the home differentiated between high and low achievers. Related studies, such as the one managed by Dave (1963), indicated that academic guidance (a kind of environmental organization) was correlated .5 with IQ and .6 with achievement among fifth graders in Illinois. Williams (1976) involved reanalysis of Mosychuk's (1972) data from Canada showed that the expectations dimensions of the environment was correlated .5 with IQ among 10-year-olds.

In sum, from the studies reviewed, it appears that organization of the environment bears an important relation to children's cognitive development. However, the investigations to date reveal a sketchy portrait, one lacking in essential details. Important, unspecified variables include physical and temporal organization of environment and experience, and the effect on development of stability and change in the environment.

ENVIRONMENT AND TEMPERAMENT: THE DEVELOPMENT OF INDIVIDUAL DIFFERENCES

Regardless of whether data on environment/development relationships have been obtained from experimental or natural environments, environmental processes demonstrate differential associations with development among members of the group studied. That is, all children whose homes contain ten books and five toys requiring fine motor manipulation do not show the same IQ gains during the period from one to three years of age. The association between any particular environmental process and cognitive development is not an exact one, but depends on other characteristics of the child *as well as other environmental events and transactions.* Undoubtedly the number of individual difference variables that interact with environmental processes to affect cognitive development is legion. It is not the intent of this chapter to attempt a comprehensive review. Instead, the remainder of this chapter will focus on one variable, infant temperament, and the potentially important role it plays in relationships of the environment and development.

Temperament, or behavioral style as it is sometimes called, refers to relatively stable dispositions that appear to be at least partially based in genetics, partially based in constitutional differences, acquired in utero or at birth, and that affect a child's behavior across a broad array of situations (Buss and Plomin, 1975; Chess and Thomas, 1977). These temperamental characteristics, which can be reliably measured at about six months, show a substantial relation to the development of behavioral disorders (Thomas, Chess, and Birch, 1968), to academic achievement and school adjustment (Carey, Fox, and McDermott, 1977; Chess, Thomas, and Cameron, 1977) and are generally considered the basis from which personality traits emerge (Buss and Plomin, 1975).

Research on infant temperament conducted by a number of investigators has revealed that temperamental characteristics tend to be stable across time (Chess, 1977; Buss and Plomin, 1975; McDevitt, 1976). However, while the dispositions are considered to have a genetic or constitutional base, they are not considered immutable. As Chess and Thomas (1977) have emphasized, "A given pattern of temperament does not, as such, result ipso facto in any fixed psychological outcome. Normal and deviant development is at all times the result of a continuously evolving interaction between a child that has individual characteristics and significant features of an intrafamilial and extrafamilial environment." (p. 219) Their position is consonant with that of Sameroff (1975), who propounded a notion that linear relations between antecedents and consequences are nonexistent. Development proceeds through a sequence of regular restructuring of relations within and between the organism and environment. Thus, while children's basic temperaments predispose them to different levels of adjustment and success, the exact level results from a particular history of transactions with the environment. Thus, any developmental treatment of individual differences must emphasize environmental and constitutional differences beyond baseline genetic endowment explanation.

Of particular interest to this chapter are reactions of children with different temperaments to various components of the environment. The findings from the New York Longitudinal Study and others showed that temperament interacts with parent behaviors and environmental stress factors (Thomas et al., 1968; Graham, Rutter, and George, 1973; Buss and Plomin, 1975; Cameron, 1977). These studies indicated that the adequacy of an organism's functioning is dependent on the degree to which the properties of its environment are in accord with the organism's characteristics and style of behaving. Optimal development requires that opportunities and demands be consistent with the organism's capacities and dispositions (Thomas et al., 1968). Buss and Plomin (1975) contended that stress arises from a "mismatch" between the organism and its environment. Thomas and his colleagues have reported on several clinical case histories (1978; 1977). However, studies of Cameron (1977) and Buss and Plomin (1975) appear to have the greatest generalizability; the latter found little correlation between child temperament and parent practices. By contrast, Cameron (1977) found significant relations between negative temperament changes and such parental factors as intolerance, inconsistency, and conflict. The apparent contradiction between the two studies may have resulted from the wide disparity in research methodology used. Buss and

Plomin's study was not developmental, involved a narrow range of parental variables, and utilized a different set of temperaments. Their temperament factors were fewer in number, more global in scope, and more strongly tied to genetics.

Graham and his colleagues (1973) concluded that when predicting behavior of children a "simple uni-directional explanatory model seems inadequate." (p. 29) The child's temperament influences environment as well as vice versa. Moreover, a broader array of intrafamilial and extrafamilial environmental factors must be considered to accurately predict the course of development. Bell (1974) made a similar argument. There is a certain range of child behavior that is tolerable to a caregiver. Beyond that range the caregiving system breaks down. For example, a fussy infant may be ignored by the caregiver, ignoring the infant may lead to more fussing, the fussing to more ignoring, ad infinitum. If certain infant behaviors do not exceed tolerable limits, they may at least circumscribe caregiver behaviors. Carey (1972) found that colicky babies have different temperaments than normal babies: they were less manipulable and responsive. For such infants, the majority of mother's time was spent in caregiving rather than social interaction. In an interesting related piece of research, Levenstein (1969) reported a comparison between those children who appeared to benefit from participation in her intervention program (i.e., showed significant IQ gains) and those who did not. Those showing the least IQ gains were judged by home visitors as being higher in negative affect, in addition to being much lower in cognitive and social maturity. The first of these characteristics is quite similar to the temperament variable, negative mood, described by Chess, Thomas, and their colleagues.

The concerns of the present chapter with respect to temperament are twofold. First, how and to what extent do various temperament variables interact with environmental variables to affect development? Second, to what extent are these changes beneficial to development? Clarification of the interaction between environmental factors and basic dispositions in children will remain one of the most challenging tasks in developmental psychology during the next decade. Further delineation of the relation should prove of enormous benefit to theory development and to the practical business of advising caregivers on how to construct and appropriate learning environment for the children in their care.

THE ROLE OF ENVIRONMENTAL PROCESSES IN MENTAL RETARDATION

Environment and experience become critical variables in human development when one considers that 75 to 85 percent of the diagnosed retarded population have no apparent brain abnormality (United States Public Health Service, 1962). This is to say that the majority of the retarded population today are mildly retarded and that their condition is heightened when confronted with unfavorable environment, lacking in appropriate social, emotional, and cognitive experiences.

What is missing for the retarded child? Experience along the environmental process dimensions discussed throughout this' chapter begins to explain the role of caregivers as teachers of "how" to interact with the environment. Such knowledge is key to the developing individual's capacity to maximize use of the environment for learning. The foundation of intellectual growth and development is the construction and selection of environment and experience. The child changes, develops, and learns through the organization of behaviors in her/his repertoire with aspects of environmental demands or pressures (Kessen, 1968). If limitations in early environment exist, the child may experience a low degree of subsequent success in responding to novel problems presented in differing environments. Parents select and construct environments and experiences in which their children transact. Hence, if they guard against experiential variability, the later the selection the child makes in terms of environmental experiences to develop his/her competence may be equally low in variability. This suggests a notion of environmental development concurrent with human development, which when taken

together, manifest themselves as future displays of achievement or intellect in challenging environments (especially, the school setting).

Problems with future expressions of intelligence through use of the environment are further explained by cumulative deficit (Deutsch, 1967) and the "problem of the match" (Hunt, 1961). Early restrictions have been shown to accumulate in their deleterious effects. That is, activity on the environment is dependent on prior degree or quality of experience. The research specification of such experiences, throughout this chapter, clearly directs the educational practitioner or clinician to practices for remediation of experientally deficient children.

The notion of match is particular to the intellectual or achievement level of individuals and the environmental circumstances they encounter. If level of development, fostered by home experience, is incongruous with expected performance demanded by a new environment, as the classroom learning environment, then these latter experiences remain unassimilated. Again, specification of early experience and environment aids in the development of remediation.

REFERENCES

Adler, S. Social class bases of language: A reexamination of socioeconomic, sociopsychological, and sociolinguistic factors. *Asha*, 1973, *15*, 3–9.

Ainsworth, M. The development of infant–mother attachment. In B. Caldwell & H. Riccuiti (Eds.), *Review of child development research*, Vol. 3. Chicago: University of Chicago Press, 1973.

Almy, M., Chittenden, E., & Miller, P. *Young children's thinking: Studies of some aspects of Piaget's theory.* New York: Teachers College Press, 1966.

Anastasi, A. *Differential psychology* (3rd ed.). New York: Humanities Press, 1958.

Baumrind, D. & Black, A. Socialization practices associated with dimensions of competence in preschool boys and girls. *Child Development*, 1967, *38*, 291–327.

Bayley, N. Comparisons of mental and motor test scores for ages 1–15 months by sex, birth order, race, geographic location, and education of parents. *Child Development*, 1965, *36*, 379–412.

Bayley, N. & Schaefer, E. Correlations of maternal and child behaviors with the development of mental abilities: Data from the Berkeley Growth Study. *Monographs of the Society for Research in Child Development*, 1964, *29* (Whole No. 6).

Beckwith, L. Relationships between attributes of mothers and their infants' IQ scores. *Child Development*, 1971, *42*, 1083–1097.

Bell, R. A reinterpretation of the direction of effects in studies of socialization. *Psychological Review*, 1968, *75*, 81–95.

Bell, R. Contributions of human infants to caregiving and social interaction. In M. Lewis and L. Rosenblum (Eds.), *The effect of the infant on its caregiver*. New York: Wiley & Sons, 1974.

Bernstein, B. *Class, codes, and control*. London: Rutledge & Kegan Paul, 1971.

Bloom, B. *Stability and change in human characteristics*. New York: Wiley & Sons, 1964.

Bradley, R. & Caldwell, B. Early home environment and changes in mental test performance from 6 to 36 months. *Developmental Psychology*, 1976, *12*, 93–97.

Bradley, R. & Caldwell, B. The relation of infants' home environments to mental test performance at fifty–four months: a follow–up study. *Child Development*, 1976, *47*, 1172–1174.

Bradley, R. & Caldwell, B. Home Observation for Measurement of the Environment: A validation study of screening efficiency. *American Journal of Mental Deficiency*, 1977, *81*, 417–420.

Bradley, R. & Caldwell, B. Home Observation for Measurement of the Environment: A revision of the preschool scale. *American Journal of Mental Deficiency*, 1979, *84*, 235–244.

Bradley, R., Caldwell, B., and Elardo, R. Home environment, social status, and mental test performance. *Journal of Educational Psychology*, 1977, *69*, 697–701.

Bradley, R., Caldwell, B., and Elardo, R. Home environment and cognitive development in the first two years: a cross–lagged panel analysis. *Developmental Psychology*, 1979, *15*, 246–250.

Brown, P. & Elliott, R. Control of aggression in a nursery school class. *Journal of Experimental Child Psychology*, 1965, *2*, 103–107.

Buss, A., & Plomin, R. *A temperament theory of personality development*. New York: John Wiley and Sons, 1975.

Caldwell, B. M., On designing supplementary environments for early child development. *BAEYC Reports*, 1968, *10*, 1–11.

Caldwell, B., & Richmond, J. The children's center in Syracuse, New York. In Dittman, L. (Ed.) *Early child care: The new perspectives*. New York: Atherton Press, 1968.

Cameron, J. Parental Treatment, children's temperament, and the risk of childhood behavioral problems, Part I. *American Journal of Orthopsychiatry*, 1977, *47*, 568–576.

Carew, J. V. *Social class, everyday experience and the growth of intelligence in young children*. Paper presented at the meeting of the Third Biennial Conference of the International Society for the Study of Behavioral Development, Guildford, England, 1974.

Carew, J. V. *Observed intellectual competence and tested intelligence: Their roots in the young child's transactions with his environment*. Paper presented at the meeting of Society for Research in Child Development, Denver, 1975.

Carey, W. Measuring infant temperament. *Journal of Pediatrics*, 1972, *81*, 414.

Chess, S. and Thomas, A. Temperamental individuality from childhood to adolescence. *Journal of Child Psychiatry*, 1977, *16*, 218–226.

Chess, S., Thomas, A., & Cameron, M. Temperament: Its significance for early schooling. *New York University Education Quarterly*, 1976, *24*.

Clarke–Stewart, K. A. Interactions between mothers and their young children: characteristics and consequences. *Monographs of the Society for Research in Child Development*, 1973, *38* (Whole No. 6–7).

Clausen, J. A. Family structure, socializations and personality. In L. Hoffman & H. Hoffman (Eds.), *Review of child development research* (Vol. 2). New York: Russell Sage Foundation, 1966.

Coddington, R. The significance of life events as etiologic factors in the diseases of children—II—A study of a normal population. *Journal of Psychosomatic Research*, 1972, *16*, 205–213.

Cohen, S., Glass, D., & Singer, J. Apartment noise, auditory discrimination and reading ability in children. *Journal of Experimental Social Psychology*, 1973, *9*, 407–422.

Coleman, J., Campbell, D., Hobson, C., McPartland, J., Mood, A., Weinfold, J., & York, R. *Equality of educational opportunity*. Washington, D.C.: U. S. Government Printing Office, 1966.

Crandall, V. and Battle, E. The antecedents and adult correlates of academic and intellectual achievement effort. *Minnesota Symposia on Child Psychology*, vol. 4. Minneapolis: University of Minnesota Press, 1970, pp. 36–93.

Crandall, V., Dewey, R., Katkovsky, W., and

Preston, A. Parents' attitudes and behaviors and grade school children's academic achievements. *Journal of Genetic Psychology*, 1964, *104*, 54–66.

Davé, R. The identification and measurement of environmental process variables that are related to educational achievement. Unpublished dissertation, University of Chicago, 1963.

Davis, A. Socialization and the adolescent personality, Chapter XI in the *Forty–Third Yearbook of the National Society for the Study of Education*. Part 1, 198–215, 1944.

Davis, A. Social class influences upon learning. Cambridge, Mass., Harvard University Press, 1948.

Davis, A. and Eells, K. *Manual: Davis–Eells test of general intelligence or problem solving ability*. New York: World, 1953.

Day, S. Home factors influencing achievement of disadvantaged students. *Dissertation Abstracts International*, 1973, *34*, 555A.

Dean, A. & Lin, N. The stress–buffering role of social support. *Journal of Nervous and Mental Disease*, 1977, *165*, 403–417.

DeCecco, J. The psychology of learning and instruction: *Educational Psychology*, Englewood Cliffs, N.J.: Prentice–Hall, 1968.

Dennis, W. *Children of the Creche*. New York: Appleton–Century–Crofts, 1973.

Dennis, W. & Najarian, P. Infant development under environmental handicap. *Psychological Monographs*, 1957, *71* (Serial No. 436).

Deutsch, C. P. Social class and child development. In B. M. Caldwell & H. N. Riccuiti (Eds.), *Review of child development research* (Vol. 3). Chicago: University of Chicago Press, 1973.

Deutsch, M. Social intervention and the malleability of the child. In M. Deutsch & Associates (Eds.)., *The disadvantaged child*. New York: Basic Books, Inc., 1967.

Deutsch, M. and associates. *Social class, race and psychological development*. New York: Holt, Rinehart, and Winston, 1968.

Divesta, F., & Thompson, G. *Educational psychology: Instruction and behavioral change*. New York, Appleton–Century–Crofts, 1970.

Dreger, R., & Miller, K. Comparative psychological studies of Negroes and whites in the United States. *Psychological Bulletin*, 1960, *57*, 361–402.

Dreger, R., & Miller, K. Comparative psychological studies of Negroes and whites in the United States: 1959–1965. *Psychological Bulletin*. 1968, *70*, 1–58.

Eells, K., Davis, A., Havighurst, R., Herrick, V., & Tyler, R. *Intelligence and cultural differences*. Chicago: Universiity of Chicago Press, 1951.

Elardo, R., Bradley, R., & Caldwell, B. The relation of infant's home environments to mental test performance from six to thirty–six months: A longitudinal analysis. *Child Development*, 1975, *46*, 71–76.

Elardo, R., Bradley, R., & Caldwell, B. A longitudinal study of the relation of infants' home environments to language development at age three. *Child Development*, 1977, *48*, 595–603.

Ells, K., Davis, A., Havighurst, R., Herrick, V., & Tyler, R. *Intelligence and cultural differences*. Chicago: University of Chicago Press, 1951.

Engel, M. & Keane, W. Black mothers and their infant sons: Antecedents, correlates, and predictors of cognitive development in the second and sixth year of life. Paper presented at the annual meeting of the Society for Research in Child Development. Denver, 1975.

Erikson, E. *Childhood and society*. New York: Norton, 1950.

Escalona, S., & Corman, H. The impact of mother's presence upon behavior the first year. *Human Development*, 1971, *14*, 2–15.

Freeburg, N., & Payne, D. Parental influence on cognitive development in early childhood: A review. *Child Development*, 1967, *38*, 65–87.

Golden, M., & Birns, B. Social class and cognitive development in infancy. *Merrill–Palmer Quarterly*, 1968, *14*, 139.

Gordon, I. An investigation into the social roots of competence. Final report to the National Institute of Mental Health, 1974.

Gouindecarie, T. *Intelligence and affectivity in early childhood*. New York: International Universities Press, 1965.

Graham, P., Rutter, M., & George, S. Temperament characteristics as predictors of behavior disorders in children. *American Journal of Orthopsychiatry*, 1973, *43*, 328.

Greenberg, J., & Davidson, H. Home background and school achievement of black urban ghetto children. *American Journal of Orthopsychiatry*, 1972, *42*, 803–810.

Hanson, R. Consistency and stability of home environmental measures related to IQ. *Child Development*, 1975, *46*, 470–480.

Havighurst, R. The relative importance of social class and ethnicity in human development. *Human Development*, 1976, *19*, 56–64.

Heft, H. An examination of the relationship between environmental stimulation in the home and selective attention in your children. Unpublished Ph.D. Dissertation, Pennsylvania State University, 1976.

Henderson, R., & Merritt, C. Environmental backgrounds of Mexican–American children with different potentials for school success. *Journal of Social Psychology,* 1968, *76,* 101–106.

Henderson, R., Bergan, J., & Hurt, M. Development and validation of the Henderson Environmental Learning Process Scale. *Journal of Social Psychology,* 1972, *88,* 185–196.

Hess, R. & Shipman, V. Early experience and the socialization of cognitive modes in children. *Child Development,* 1965, *36,* 869–886.

Hindley, C. The Griffiths Scale of Infant Development: Scores and predictions from 3 to 18 months. *Journal of Child Psychology and Psychiatry,* 1960, *1,* 99.

Hollingshed, A. & Redlich, F., *Social class and mental illness: A community study.* New York: Wiley and Sons, 1958.

Holmes, T. and Masuda, M. Life change and illness susceptibility. In B. Dohrenwend and B. Dohrenwend (Eds.), *Stressful life events: Their nature and effects,* New York: Wiley and Sons, 1974.

Holmes, T., & Rahe, R. The social readjustment rating scale. *Journal of Psychomatic Research,* 1967, *11,* 213–218.

Honzik, M. Environmental correlates of mental growth: Prediction from the family setting at 21 months. *Child Development,* 1967, *38,* 337–364.

Hunt, J. *Intelligence and experience.* New York: Ronald Press Company, 1961.

Jencks, C. *Inequality: A reassessment of the effect of family and schooling in America.* New York: Basic Books, 1972.

Jones, P. Home environment and the development of verbal ability. *Child Development,* 1972, *43,* 1081–1086.

Kagan, J., & Freeman, M. Relation of childhood intelligence, maternal behaviors, and social class to behavior during adolescence. *Child Development,* 1963, *34,* 889–911.

Kahl, J. Educational and occupational aspirations of "common–men" boys. *Harvard Educational Review,* 1953, *23,* 186–203.

Keeves, J. *Educational environment and student achievement.* Stockholm: Almquist & Wiksell, 1972.

Kennedy, W., Van De Riet, V., & White, J. A normative sample of intelligence and achievement of Negro elementary school children in southeastern United States. *Monographs of the Society for Research in Child Development,* 1963, *28,* (Whole No. 6).

Kessen, W. The construction and selection of environments. In D. C. Glass (Ed.), *Environmental influences: Proceedings of a conference under the auspices of the Russell Sage Foundation and the Rockefeller University.* New York: The Rockefeller University Press and the Russell Sage Foundation, 1968.

Klaus, R., & Gray, S. The early training project for disadvantaged children: A report after five years. *Monographs of the Society for Research in Child Development,* 1968, *33,* (Whole No. 4).

Klaus, M., & Kennell, J. Mothers separated from their newborn infants. *Pediatric Clinics of North America,* 1970, *17,* 1015–1037.

Knobloch, H., & Pasamanick, B. Environmental factors affecting human development before and after birth. *Pediatrics,* 1960, *26,* 210–218.

Kohlberg, L., & De Vries, R. Relations between Piaget and psychometric measures of intelligence. Paper presented at the conference on National Curriculum of the Child. Urbana, Illinois, 1969.

Lavin, D. E. *The prediction of academic performance: A theoretical analysis and review of research.* New York: Russell Sage Foundation, 1965.

Lesser, G., Fifer, G., & Clark, D. Mental abilities of children in different social class and cultural groups. *Monographs of the Society for Research in Child Development,* 1965, *30,* (Whole No. 102).

Levenstein, P. Individual variation among preschoolers in a cognitive intervention program in low–income families. Proceedings of Conference on Council for Exceptional Children or Early Childhood Education, New Orleans, 1969.

Levenstein, P. Cognitive growth in preschoolers through verbal interaction with mothers. *American Journal of Orthopsychiatry,* 1970, *40,* 426–432.

Lewis, M. Infant development in lower–class American Families. Paper presented at the biennial meeting of the Society for Research in Child Development, Minneapolis, Minnesota, 1971.

Lewis, M. & Rosenblum, L. Friendship and peer relations. *The origins of behavior,* Vol. IV, New York: Wiley and Sons, 1975.

Littman, R., Moore, R., & Pierce–Jones, J. Social class differences in child rearing: A third community for comparison with Chicago and Newton, Massachusetts. *American Sociological Review,* 1957, *22,* 694–704.

Maher, B. *Principles of psychopathology.* New York: McGraw–Hill, 1966.

Malone, C. Some observations on children of disorganized families and problems of acting out. *Journal of the American Academy of Child Psychiatry,* 1963, *2,* 22.

Marjoribanks, K. Environment, social class, and

mental abilities. *Journal of Educational Psychology*, 1972, *43*, 103–109.

McCall, R., Appelbaum, M., & Hogarty, P. Developmental changes in mental performance. *Monographs of the Society for Research in Child Development*, 38: 3, 1973, *38* (Whole No. 3).

McClelland, D., Atkinson, R., Clark, R., & Lowell, E. *The achievement motive.* New York: Appelton, 1953.

Michelson, W. The physical environment as a mediating factor in school achievement. Paper presented at the annual meeting of The Canadian Sociology and Anthropology Association, Calgary, Alberta, 1968.

Moore, T. Language and intelligence: A longitudinal study of the first eight years, Part II. Environmental correlates of mental growth. *Human Development*, 1968, *11*, 1–24.

Mosychuk, H. Differential home environments and mental ability patterns. Unpublished doctoral dissertation, University of Alberta, 1972.

Nuckolls, C., Cassel, J., & Kaplan, B. Psychosocial assets, life crisis and the prognosis of pregnancy. *American Journal of Epidemiology*, 1972, *95*, 431–441.

Parke, R. Children's home environments: Social and cognitive effects. In I. Altman & J. Wohlwill (Eds.), *Children and the environment.* New York: Plenum, 1978.

Pavenstedt, E. A comparison of the child–rearing environment of upper–lower, and very low–lower class families. *American Journal of Orthopsychiatry*, 1968, *35*, 39–98.

Piaget, J. *The psychology of intelligence.* New York: Harcourt, Brace, 1950.

Piaget, J. *The origins of intelligence in children.* New York: International University Press, 1952.

Piaget, J. *The psychology of intelligence.* Paterson, N.J.: Littlefield–Adams, 1963.

Plowden, B. (Ed.). *Children and their primary schools.* A report of the Central Advisory Council for Education, England. London: Her Majesty's Stationary Office, 1967.

Radin, N. Maternal warmth, achievement motivation, and cognitive functioning in lower class preschool children. *Child Development*, 1971, *42*, 1560–1565.

Radin, N. Observed paternal behaviors as antecedents of intellectual functioning in young boys. *Developmental Psychology*, 1973, *8*, 369–376.

Ramey, C., Mills, R., Campbell, F., & O'Brien, C. Infants' home environments: A comparison of high–risk families and families from the general population. *American Journal of Mental Deficiency*, 1975, *80*, 40–42.

Rheingold, H., & Eckerman, C. Some proposals for unifying the study of social development. In M. Lewis & M. Rosenblum (Eds.), *Friendship and peer relations.* New York: Wiley, and Sons, 1975.

Rotter, J. Generalized expectancies for internal versus external control of reinforcement. *Psychological Monographs*, 1966, *80* (Whole No. 609).

Ruch, L. A multidimensional analysis of the concept of life change. *Journal of Health and Social Behavior*, 1977, *18*, 71–83.

Sameroff, A. Early influences on development, fact or fancy? *Merrill–Palmer Quarterly*, 1975, *21*, 267–294.

Schaefer, E. Development of hierarchical, configurational models for parent behavior and child behavior. *Minnesota Symposia on Child Psychology*, (Vol. 5). Minneapolis: University of Minnesota Press, 1971.

Sears, R., Maccoby, E., & Levin, H. *Patterns of child rearing.* Evanston, Ill.: Row and Peterson, 1957.

Shea, J. & Hanes, M. *The relationship between measures of home environment and school achievement of follow–through children.* Paper presented at the meeting of the American Educational Research Association, New York, 1977.

Shipman, V., McKee, J., & Bridgeman, B. *Disadvantaged children and their first school experience.* Head Start Longitudinal Study, New Jersey, Educational Testing Service, 1976.

Skeels, H. & Dye, H. A study of the effects of differential stimulation on mentally retarded children. *Proceedings of the American Association on Mental Deficiency*, 1939, *44*, 114–136.

Solomon, D., Houlihan, K., Busse, T., & Parelius, R. Parent behavior and child academic achievement, achievement striving and related personality variables. *Genetic Psychology Monographs*, 1971, *83*, 173–273.

Spitz, R., & Wolf, K. Anaclitic depression. *Psychoanalytic Study of the Child*, 1946, *2*, 313–342.

Thomas, A. & Chess, S. *Temperament and development.* New York: Brunner/Mazel, 1977.

Thomas, A., Chess, S., & Birch, H. *Temperament and behavior disorders in children.* New York: New York University Press, 1968.

Trotman, F. Race, IQ and the middle class. *Journal of Educational Psychology*, 1977, *69*, 266–273.

Tulkin, S. Social class differences in infants' reactions to mother's and stranger's voices. *Developmental Psychology*, 1973, *8*, 137.

Tulkin, S., & Covitz, F. Mother–infant interaction and intellectual functioning at age six. Presented at the biennial meeting of the Society for Research in Child Development, Denver, 1975.

Tulkin, S., & Kagan, J. Mother–child interaction in the first year of life. *Child Development*, 1972, *43*, 31–41.

United States Public Health Service. *A proposed program for national action to combat mental retardation.* Report of the President's Panel on Mental Retardation, 1962.

Uzgiris, I. Ordinality in the development of schemas in relating to objects. In J. Hellmeth (Ed.), *Exceptional infant, Vol. 1: The normal infant.* Seattle: Special Child Publications, 1967.

Uzgiris, I., & Hunt, J. An instrument for assessing infant psychological development. Mimeographed paper, University of Illinois, 1966.

Wachs, T. Utilization of a Piagetian approach in the investigation of early experience effects: A research strategy and some illustrative data. *Merrill–Palmer Quarterly*, 1976, *22*, 11–29.

Wachs, T., Uzgiris, I., & Hunt, J. Cognitive development in infants from different age levels and different environmental backgrounds: An explanatory investigation. *Merrill–Palmer Quarterly*, 1971, *17*, 283–317.

Wachs, T. The relationship of infants' physical environment to their Binet performance at 2½ years. *International Journal of Behavioral Development*, 1978, *1*, 51–65.

Walberg, H. & Marjoribanks, K. Family environment and cognitive development: Twelve analytic models. *Review of Educational Research*, 1976, *45*, 517–552.

Ware, W., & Garber, M. The home environment as a predictor of school achievement. *Theory into Practice*, 1972, *11*, 190–195.

Warner, W., Meeker, M., & Eells, K. *Social class in America: A manual of procedure for the measurement of social status.* Chicago: Science Research Associates, 1949.

White, B., & Watts, J. *Experience and environment.* Prentice–Hall, Englewood Cliffs, N.J., 1973.

White, R. Motivation reconsidered: The concept of competence. *Psychological Review*, 1959, *66*, 297–333.

White, K. R. *The relationship between socioeconomic status and academic achievement.* Unpublished doctoral dissertation, University of Colorado, 1976.

Wiley, D., & Harnischfeger, A. Explosion of a myth: Quantity of schooling and exposure to instruction, major educational vehicles. *Educational Researcher*, 1974, *3*, 7–12.

Willerman, L., Broman, S., & Fiedler, M. Infant development, preschool I.Q. and social class. *Child Development*, 1970, *41*, 69–77.

Wohlwill, J. *The study of behavioral development.* New York: Academic Press, 1973.

Wohlwill, J. and Heft, H. Environments fit for the developing child. In H. McGurk (Ed.), *Ecological factors in human development.* Amsterdam: North Holland Publishing Co., 1977.

Wolf, R. The measurement of environments. In Anastasi (Ed.), *Testing problems in perspective*, Princeton, N.J.: Educational Testing Service, 1965.

Wulbert, M., Inglis, S., Kriegsman, E., & Mills, B. Language delay and associated mother–child interactions. *Development Psychology*, 1975, *11*, 61–70.

Yarrow, L., Rubenstein, J., Pederson, F. & Jankowski, F. Dimensions of early stimulation and their differential effects on infant development, *Merrill–Palmer Quarterly*, 1973, *19*, 205–218.

Yarrow, L., Rubenstein, J., and Pederson, F. *Infant and environment.* Washington, D.C.: Hemisphere Publishing Corp., 1975.

Zigler, E. and Child, I. *Socialization and personality development.* Reading, Mass: Addison–Wesley, 1973.

CHAPTER 8

Understanding Learning Disabilities

HAROLD A. SOLAN, O.D., M.A.

Introduction

The child who is experiencing a learning disability has been identified in the past in various terms such as developmental aphasia, dysphasia, developmental alexia, dyslexia, minimal neurological cerebral dysfunction, and maturational lag—just to name a few. Minimal brain dysfunction (MBD), a diagnostic classification used frequently by neurologists and psychiatrists, psychologists and learning specialists is essentially equivalent to the educational nomenclature, learning disability (LD).

A child who does not respond to instruction in school in the normal manner in spite of average or better than average intelligence, normal motivation, abundant educational opportunities, normal sensory development (auditory and visual), no primary emotional disorder, normal culturation, and no frank brain damage is said to be experiencing a learning disorder. These exclusions, at first, would seem to circumscribe the group to a limited few. As we develop a broader understanding of normal motivation, abundant educational opportunities, normal sensory development, and other concepts, it will be evident that we are dealing with a substantial population of children who are being "classified" daily in schools throughout the United States. Their identification often is based on either "risk factors" such as developmental milestones, or overt failure to learn at a level commensurate with the student's potential, and deficits in attention span, or some combination of the three.

The prevalence of LD children in this country has been variously reported from 4 percent to 15 percent. Most teachers agree that about four children in a heterogenously grouped class of 25 experience learning problems. Based on a school population of forty-six million, we are considering an estimated LD population between 1,840,000 and 6,900,000 children. The size of the group alone tells us that there is no simple solution to this problem. The disability crosses racial lines and all social classes. In the United States, an epidemic of Learning Disability exists.

In this chapter, some of the theoretical, diagnostic, and therapeutic factors customarily associated with the learning disabled child are explored. Etiology and general properties are presented first, manifestations in the middle, and finally a general treatment. A summary in the form of a questionnaire is presented to orient the reader clinically. The subsequent topics enable the reader to develop a holistic appreciation of children who are experiencing learning disabilities by becoming aware of the heterogeneity of the factors that are interfering with their education and development.

Etiological Factors

The Brief Case History Form, Figure 1, (Solan, 1976) enables the clinician to identify developmental abnormalities (or subnormalities) in a number of areas customarily associated with the learning

BRIEF CASE HISTORY FORM

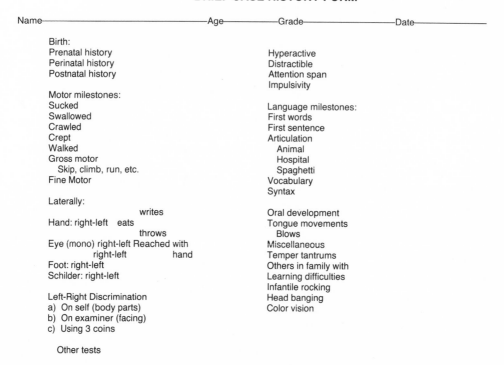

Name—————————————————Age————Grade———————————Date—————

Birth:
Prenatal history
Perinatal history
Postnatal history

Motor milestones:
Sucked
Swallowed
Crawled
Crept
Walked
Gross motor
  Skip, climb, run, etc.
Fine Motor

Laterally:
                writes
Hand: right-left   eats
                throws
Eye (mono) right-left Reached with
        right-left   hand
Foot: right-left
Schilder: right-left

Left-Right Discrimination
a) On self (body parts)
b) On examiner (facing)
c) Using 3 coins

Other tests

Hyperactive
Distractible
Attention span
Impulsivity

Language milestones:
First words
First sentence
Articulation
  Animal
  Hospital
  Spaghetti
Vocabulary
Syntax

Oral development
Tongue movements
  Blows
Miscellaneous
Temper tantrums
Others in family with
Learning difficulties
Infantile rocking
Head banging
Color vision

Figure 1. Brief Case History Form.

disabled child.

Whereas hyperactivity is a major manifestation of children with learning disabilities, not all children who are distractible and have a short attention span are hyperactive. Impulsivity, making decisions too rapidly, is not unusual. Allowing too little time between a thought and its execution often results in the LD child finding himself in one troublesome situation after another. The effect of rapid decisions and responses also reduces the amount of information he is able to acquire in the classroom. Extraneous head, eye, and hand movements (a form of hyperkinesis) round out a cognitive style, characterized by premature closure (Keogh, 1971). Since the learning disabled child often makes rapid decisions and many errors, he must be taught to become more reflective and take longer time to make decisions, resulting in making fewer errors. Reflectivity is clearly more compatible with school learning requirements than is impulsivity (Kagan,

1966). Through the modification of behavior, resulting from motor regulation and perceptual therapy, it is possible to change the conceptual style of the child to the extent that an improved academic performance is evident. Therefore, these factors and the related signs and symptoms are included in the Brief Case History Form.

Abundant research has been presented that has associated prenatal, perinatal, and postnatal disorders with subsequent learning disabilities. For example, Kawi and Pasamanick (1958) completed a study involving 205 children who were poor readers and who had hospital birth records, matched with 205 other children who were good readers for which there were also hospital birth records. It was established that 16.5 percent of the children who were poor readers had mothers who reported histories of two or more episodes during pregnancy or delivery usually involving a reduction of oxygen supply to the fetus or the neonate. The site of the intellectual constellation of the brain, the parietal and occipital lobes, nourished by fine terminal arteries, is particularly vulnerable. Some examples are staining and hemorrhaging by the mother, especially during the first trimester of pregnancy, and extended delivery time. Only 1.5 percent of the normal readers had such histories. Low birth weight, particularly under five pounds, has also been associated with learning problems. Forcipian deliveries have been mentioned also.

Postnatal disorders include: convulsions, concussions, dehydration, extended high temperatures, need for oxygen, and chronic ear infections. Difficulties in sucking and swallowing during infancy are important because of nutritional considerations and, additionally, such difficulties sometimes suggest the possibility of a later articulation problem. While crawling and creeping are not directly associated with learning, it might be said that if almost all children, perhaps 98 percent, learn to crawl and creep in a particular sequential style on their hands and knees, the 2 percent who drag their legs or push themselves across the room in a sitting position are indeed developing differently. Cross-gait creeping requires bilateral integration and proximal muscle development. In addition, the child is aware of stereoscopic vision while engaged in locomotion. The exact age when a child stands unaided and walks is not too predictive. In fact, some of the hyperactive children begin to walk (and run) at nine or ten months, making life very difficult for the mother. On the other hand, a delay in walking beyond 18 months, when walking should have replaced creeping as a means of locomotion, is considered abnormal. Most children are walking at 13 months (Gesell, 1940). Gross motor development at the time the child enters first grade is at best suggestive. Many children who are having learning problems in second grade have histories of clumsy gross motor performance during kindergarten and first grade. Learning to skip is often especially difficult. A lag in fine motor maturation is of greater concern. For example, a child who cannot button his coat, tie his shoe laces, or cut with scissors during the first half of first grade is suspect. All of these tasks are sensorimotor activities requiring either tactual or visual feedback to guide the motor activity.

Delayed speech or dyslalia is another correlate of learning difficulties (Hoffman, 1971). The ability to use two words sequentially for communication is considered speech. An example is *baby ball* when the child means "This is my ball" or "May I have the ball?" Equally important is the spontaneous development of articulation. The child should be understood without undue effort. A combination of delayed speech and poor articulation adumbrates later language disorders. Sometimes, however, a child's first speech may be delayed from age 18 months to 30 months, at which time he speaks in paragraphs. This child usually has no subsequent problems. By contrast, there is the child who may begin to speak at 26 months, but it is difficult to understand him until the age of three and a half or four and a half years. A simple test of echolalia using the words animal, hospital, and spaghetti (Slingerland, 1964) is frequently helpful when evaluating a child in kindergarten or the primary grades. Asking the child to repeat the words several times each sometimes reveals speech blockage: animal becomes *axinal*, hospital becomes *hopsibul*, and spaghetti after two or three repetitious becomes *bisghetti*. The child's speaking vocabulary and syntactical development during the primary grades are frequently indicative of his acquired and innate language developments respectively. While not all children who have good vocabularies and speak grammatically become excellent readers, the absence of these skills is a handicap. DeHirsch (1954), Ingram (1969), and Klasen (1972) have observed that healthy children of average intelligence who showed delayed speech development would later have more difficulty in learning to read and spell than a comparable group of children without delayed speech development. Just as the optometrist observes eye movements for saccadics and pursuits, so does the speech specialist observe tongue movements. The ability of a young child to blow out a light also reflects fine motor facility in this area.

Numerous tests exist to determine whether a child is predominantly right-handed or left-handed. The Brief Case History Form investigates just a few. Some of the simplest examples include writing, throwing, and holding a fork or spoon. Others involve sports such as batting a ball and playing golf and tennis. Using a small tube, a child can be asked to look at a spot on the chalkboard or the wall to identify his sighting eye. When a child reaches for the tube with his right hand and holds it to his left eye, he is said to have mixed dominance. The research has revealed that there is very little relationship between mixed dominance and learning to read (Ayres, 1965; Cohen and Glass, 1968). Ill-defined laterality—using the right hand for some activities and the left for others, revealing a lack of unilateral cerebral dominance—is of greater significance in learning. The Schilder Extension Test (Silver and Hagin, 1967) may assist the clinician in determining whether a child tends to be more right-handed or left-handed. The test is administered by asking the child to raise both arms in front of him at right angles to the body while standing. As the child moves his head from right to left and counts, the examiner observes which arm tends to remain higher. When the right arm remains elevated higher than the left, the child is said to be right-sided and vice versa. Left-right discrimination and a good sense of directionality are also important attributes in learning. When a child can point to his left ear with his right hand or his right ankle with his left hand, the examiner not only knows that he is aware of his body parts, but also that he has internalized left and right. Another technique that Belmont and Birch (1965) included in their modified Piaget Protocol involves asking a child to point to the examiner's left knee with his right hand as the examiner sits facing the child. Also, by placing three coins or three objects in a row, the examiner may secure additional information concerning the child's lateral awareness and sense of directionality. If a nickel, penny, and dime are used in that order, it is not unusual for the child to be able to indicate that the nickel is to the left of the penny and the dime is to the right of the penny, but not understand that the penny is either to the left or right of the

other coins. Often a child answers, "The penny is in the middle," and he will not be swayed.

Children with learning disorders frequently have experienced a great deal of frustration; therefore, temper tantrums (sometimes called catastrophic reactions) are not unusual. Some research seems to indicate that there is a genetic predisposition in certain families for learning disorders. Wender (1971) postulated that this genetic propensity manifests itself when some exogenous factor, such as problems during pregnancy, aggravates an already present tendency. Of course, it just may be that the intellectual values or the educational climate within a household are the all-important factor. For many years, clinicians have reported that children who have learning disorders have histories of rocking in their cribs and high chairs. Head-banging has also frequently been mentioned. Since children are so dependent upon color coding in the many workbooks available to help the child with a reading or arithmetic problem, the absence of color blindness should be confirmed.

The Brief Case History Form makes it possible to develop a profile of an LD child in about ten or fifteen minutes. This clinical impression is helpful to the clinician in establishing a better understanding of the child's attitude and performance in school and at home. One must be particularly cautious about identifying any single deficit as the source of the learning disability. In most children who are experiencing learning problems, a cluster of developmental and behavioral signs is present.

GENETICS

Genetic predilection to learning disability has been explored in a number of "twin studies." One longitudinal study (Matheny, Dolan and Wilson, 1976) confirmed that identical (or monozygotic) twins were more likely than fraternal (or dizygotic) twins to experience academic difficulties. In addition, the identical twins were more concordant than same-sex fraternal twins for all preschool behaviors, including activity level, distractibility, temper, and feeding and sleeping problems. When compared with a matched control group of normal-learning identical twins, the identical experimental twins revealed a higher incidence of breech presentation and a lower rate of weight gain. These findings, and others, support Wender's contention that other random biologic factors are operating in conjunction with the genetic disposition of the children. Compared to singletons, twins are more liable to biologic insult in prenatal and perinatal periods.

While he did not relate hyperactivity to learning disorders, Willerman (1973) concluded that intraclass (within-pair) correlations for activity level in monozygotic (MZ) twins were substantially higher than for dizygotic (DZ) twins. Specifically, when one member was hyperactive, MZ twins showed a high correlation for activity level with DZ twins showed no correlation.

Hallgren (1950) reported on 112 cases of dyslexia who were experiencing learning problems in school. While 10 percent of the controls had parents or siblings with reading and learning difficulties, 90 percent of the 112 cases had parents or siblings with similar problems. One hundred and sixty further cases were ascertained in their families.

Studying the etiopathogenesis of dyslexia, Zahálková and Klobouková (1972) reported the existence of pedigrees with affected individuals in two, three, and ocasionally four generations, suggesting the features of a dominant trait. Based on their study, the authors concluded that the hereditary form of dyslexia is a dominant condition with partial sex limitation, because the gene is manifested less frequently in women. That is, the hereditary form of dyslexia is inherited as an autosomal dominant influenced by sex. Interestingly, more women were found to be gene-carriers, but without clinical manifestations.

Matheny and Dolan (1974) found a bimodal rather than a normal distribution, suggesting a recessive gene influence on lower reading scores. They administered the California Reading Achievement Test to 70 pairs of same-sex twins, ages nine to twelve years. Intraclass correlations were significantly higher for monozygotic than dizygotic pairs. MZ pairs also had significantly less within-pair variability.

The purpose of presenting this information is to alert the reader to specific genetic influences. The hereditary component of intelligence, the high correlation between intelligence and reading, and the possibility that perceptual and attentional disorders may have their own genetic model, all tend to contribute to the outcome of genetic studies. Clinically one cannot distinguish between hereditary and nonhereditary LD or dyslexia without a case history or investigating the occurrence of other affected individuals in the family. Since the condition does not "breed true," the abnormality could manifest itself as dyslexia, hyperactivity, or a sensorimotor disorder. We are possibly dealing with a mode of genetic transmission that is polygenetic. Alternate hypotheses include either a dominant or recessive major gene, the manifestation of which may be influenced by minor genes.

PERCEPTION

Analyzing perceptual maturation can become an exercise in semantics, for it has been difficult for the "experts" to agree upon the scope of "perception." This author's rationale has been influenced by a number of individuals, each of whom has established his own developmental hierarchy. For example, Johnson and Myklebust (1967) stressed that learning disabilities may occur at any or several of the following five levels: sensation, perception, imagery, symbolization, and conceptualization. Since our initial definition precludes sensory deficits, sensation, the antecedent of perception, will not be included in this discussion. We must presume that the appropriate professional attention has been rendered by the eye-care specialist (optometrist or ophthalmologist) or the otolaryngologist to correct any seeing or hearing deficits that may exist. In its pure form, perception involves the processing, integration, and organization of sensory stimuli. The concept of sensory integration includes differentiation, discrimination, memory, and intersensory liaison. Imagery—tactual, auditory, and visual—is also a function of memory. Imagery draws upon our retrieval capacities, enabling us to mentally represent a previous tactual, auditory, or visual experience or sensation such as softness, a noise, or a color. Learning disabled children often experience deficits in imagery. In contrast, symbolization implies the ability to communicate, and it is not dependent upon concrete experience. Symbolization may be either verbal or nonverbal, receptive or expressive, concrete or abstract. Conceptualization is the culmination of this hierarchical shift in language development. Conceptualization is dependent upon the orderly maturation of perceptual skills, imagery, and symbolization. That is, concept formation may be impeded not only if there is a dysfunction at the level of conceptualization, but also if a dysfunction occurs at a lower level of maturation. In practice, the four levels of development beyond sensation are included in developmental and perceptual therapy.

Alfred Strauss, one of the earliest investigators, about forty years ago, provided us with a reservoir of diagnostic information and procedures. For example, Strauss and Lehtinen (1947) "isolated" the *exogenously retarded* child, labeled in more recent times as the brain injured child (BIC) and the learning disabled child (LD). They compared the brain injured child with the *endogenously retarded* child where there existed a family history of retardation. They noted, using the procedures and practices of the time, that the IQs of exogenously retarded children were somewhat lower after training while the IQs of the endogenously retarded children tended to improve slightly. From these observations, the Strauss Syndrome (1947) evolved. In order for a child to be classified as exogenously retarded (i.e. brain injured), the following evidence should be found:

(1) Medical history should reveal evidence of injury to brain before, during or after birth.

(2) There should exist the presence of "slight" (soft) neurological signs which suggest a possible brain lesion.

(3) If mental retardation is present, the immediate family history must be normal indicating he is the only one so affected.

(4) When no mental retardation is present in the child, psychological disturbances can be identified using qualitative and quantitative tests for perceptual and conceptual disturbances (p. 112).

Most important, the fourth condition alone is sufficient for diagnosis. Strauss carefully distinguished between the brain injured child and those demonstrating neurotic and psychotic behavior. He had a good understanding of normal development so that he could recognize easily the signs and impairments related to a disruption in neurological development. By observing a child's performance and analyzing his failures, Strauss decided upon procedures to improve his performance. Most prominent among the perceptual deficits were figure-ground, visual-motor, and auditory-motor disorders. These deficits often existed in combination with such behavioral characteristics as perseveration, distractibility, motor disinhibition, and catastrophic reaction.

Strauss defined perception as an activity of the mind, intermediate between sensation and thought. That is, in the brain, sensation is organized, producing meaning. This processing capacity is dependent upon the organization and integrity of the nervous system.

Strauss first postulated that perceptual organization proceeds from primitive and simple to more complex structures and that, as the nervous system differentiates, more details are integrated into the perceptual processes, enabling the perception of more articulate relationships and more complex unified wholes.

Heinz Werner (1948) pursued this concept of development and distinguished between development and change. Change may merely represent simple growth, as in a coral reef, a stalagmite or stalactite. Development proceeds from a state of relative globality and lack of differentiation to a state of increasing differentiation, articulation, and hierarchical integration. He said that at first there is a fusion of qualities that later become discrete. This concept of syncresis may be applied to motor, sensory, and emotional development. For example, *global excitement* may be differentiated into *joy* and *distress*. Distress may be further differentiated into fear and anger. Development must always involve an increase in complexity as distinguished from simple growth. Articulation represents the sequence of action and relates to the separateness, yet coordination, between parts of an organization as in speech, hearing, seeing, and even thinking. Hierarchical organization describes the dominance of one function or sense over another and will be discussed in more detail.

Herbert Birch postulated an orderly ontogenesis of sensory dominance from the proximoceptive input (gustatory and somatic and tactual) of an infant and toddler to the teleoreceptor control systems (auditory and visual) of a seven-year-old. Birch (1962) stated that, "Reading disability may stem from the inadequate development of appropriate hierarchical organization of sensory systems and so, at least in part, be the product of the failure of visual system hierarchical dominance. . . . Failure for such dominance to occur will result in a pattern of functioning which is inappropriate for the development of reading skills" (p. 164). Birch concurred with Sir Charles Sherrington (1951), who observed that the essential strategy in the evolution of the central nervous system has not been the elaboration of new avenues of sense, but rather the development of increased liaison among the existent major sensory input systems. Children who are experiencing reading and learning disorders more frequently exhibit disturbances in the capacity to develop intermodal or intersensory equivalences, particularly auditory-visual.

No discussion of learning disabilities and perceptual development is complete without referring to the contributions of Newell Kephart. He likened the error control system of the extra pyramidal-cerebellar tracts in the human nervous system to the servomechanisms found in navigational and military electronic guidance programs (1960).

That the amount of feedback (See Figure 2) is variable is particularly significant. For control purposes it is possible that all or almost all of the output be fed back and no motor response takes place permitting the perceptual process to continue until a suitable perceptual-motor match has been made. The delay necessary for successful problem solving is evolved in this manner. This delay distinguishes the reflective child from the impulsive child.

Learning problems most frequently first manifest themselves in kindergarten and grade one. To distinguish development from learning, Piaget (1961) introduced the concept of *Embryogenesis*, which concerns the development of the body, nervous system, and mental functions. He conceptualized development as a total spontaneous process, and each element of learning occurs as a function of total development. Development is *not* the sum of discrete learning experiences. Learning, according to Piaget, is a limited process—limited to

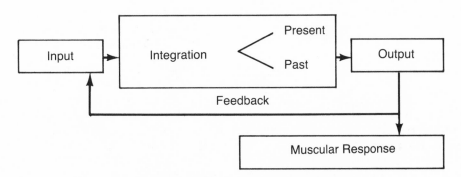

Figure 2. Diagram of feedback mechanisms in perception. From *The slow learner in the classroom* by Newell C. Kephart, Columbus, Ohio: Charles E. Merrill Books, Inc., 1960.

a single structure, situation, or didactic point. Without the development of operational structures, learning achieved by external reinforcement is more likely to be temporary. Lacking a dynamic development structure, isolated learning is less likely to lead to generalizations. Piaget asks, "What more complex structures has this learning succeeded in achieving?" Learning in the absence of suitable developmental structures precludes assimilation or internalization. The resulting associative learning does not result in generalizations.

Like Piaget, Arthur Jensen (1973) emphasized the need to be able to generalize when he defined readiness as the ability to integrate subskills into a cognitive whole, generalize, and transfer previous learning to new learning. Reinforcement of learning depends not upon external reward, but upon the child's own perception of his increasing mastery of the skills he is trying to acquire. Piaget referred to this as intrinsic motivation. Readiness to learn is characterized by the child's ability to perceive discrepancies and approximations in his own behavior in relation to a good model or plan, as when he writes or reproduces a geometric design. The child must be able to conceptualize the learning task and grasp the aim of his efforts long before achieving mastery of the task. All of these abilities and percepts are reinforced by perceptual therapy.

By integrating the concepts of Myklebust, Strauss, Werner, Birch, Kephart, Piaget, and Jensen, the developmental therapist is able to construct a diagnostic and therapeutic regimen. In children who are experiencing learning disorders, the sensory, motor, sensorimotor, processing, and integrating skills necessary to succeed in classroom learning are developed. The child's ability to remember and retrieve information is improved. Attention span is extended, enabling the child to persevere for longer periods of time reinforced by planned successes. Improved intrinsic motivation results and the cycle is self-reinforcing, where originally it had been self-extinguishing. The normal ontogenesis of sensory, motor, and language development is recapitulated. Problem solving and reasoning are stressed. Self-direction and

independence are emphasized. Developmental and perceptual therapy provides a child experiencing a learning disability with those characteristics normally associated with good students who are efficient learners.

According to Kephart, who was a special educator, school is designed for the so-called normal child, and it is expected that each child enters with a certain level of ability which can be used as a base. The skills and abilities represented in this base are the culmination, usually, of a very extensive and rapid period of learning and perceptual development throughout the preschool years. Since later learning is based to a large degree upon these earlier learnings, a child lacking these skills and abilities finds himself in ever-increasing difficulties as the school experience continues. When administering perceptual therapy, we address ourselves to the development of these basic skills and abilities. We attempt to coordinate their growth with efficient cognitive strategies, all of which have a salutary effect not only on the child's classroom learning experiences, but also on his social and emotional development.

REFLECTIVITY AND IMPULSIVITY

Some researchers who have been investigating the causes and treatment of children who are experiencing learning disabilities have cited poor "impulse control" as a frequent characteristic. The child's inability to inhibit the performance of an act long enough to become concerned about the immediate consequences of his behavior results in "social impulsivity" (Wender, 1971). Kagan (1966) noted that these same children "select and report solution hypotheses quickly with minimal consideration for their probable accuracy. Other children of equal intelligence take more time to decide about the validity of solutions. The former group has been called impulsive, the latter reflective." (p. 17) Reflectivity customarily improves with educational and intellectual maturation. Children are constantly presented with situations involving response uncertainty and asked to make a response. The child must choose between answering quickly (quick success) and the anxiety generated by the possibility of committing an error (not making a mistake). These two factors influence decision time. It is important that *anxiety over possible failure* be distinguished from *expectation of failure*. Children who have experienced chronic failure have been habituated to failure and do not experience anxiety from failure or fear of failure. On the contrary, they may answer rapidly *without* any expectation of success, and this constitutes a special entity.

Investigating first- and second-grade children, Kagan (1965) found that subjects with rapid response times and high error scores on visual matching problems made more errors in reading English words than those with longer response times and low error scores.[1] Messer (1970) tested the stability of the cognitive disposition of primary-grade children to be impulsive or reflective over a two and a half year period. The results revealed moderate but significant correlations (absolute range: .25 to .43). Cathcart and Liedtke (1969) noted that teachers of mathematics who require immediate and automatic responses from children who are learning number facts may be doing an injustice to those children who have developed a reflective response style.

Cognitive style is modifiable (Kagan, Pearson, and Welch, 1966), and there are numerous motives that have been effective in mediating behavioral changes. Some, such as external reinforcement (praise, money, toys), the desire to avoid an unpleasant experience, and the personal desire to be competent at a task are familiar. The child's desire to maximize similarity to a desirable adult is an incentive which has been little exploited. Kagan and his associates found that modeling alone may increase the average response time of an impulsive child, but there was no decrease in the error score upon retest. Unfortunately, the modeling was quite brief, about

60 minutes total over three training sessions. One must wonder what the effect of a classroom teacher could be over a ten-month period.

When impulsive children were trained by Egeland (1974) to use more efficient scanning techniques (rather than only delay their responses), the number of errors on the immediate posttest and the delayed posttest were reduced significantly.

One of the most effective ways to modify the behavior of impulsive children has been training impulsive children to talk to themselves. Meichenbaum and Goodman (1971) established the goals of their investigation, "to develop for the impulsive child a cognitive style or learning set in which the child could 'size up' the demands of a task, cognitively rehearse, and then guide his performance by means of self-instructions, and when appropriate reinforce himself." (p. 117) When "modeling" was added to the self-instructional program, not only was the response time significantly increased, but the error score was significantly decreased. By having the subjects self-verbalize, initially aloud and subsequently covertly, the study suggested that the contingencies of reinforcement will result in greater change and more generalization. Clinical experience indicates that a few months of self-instructional training, especially when it is rendered by the appropriate individual who can serve as a suitable model and can bring an impulsive child's overt behavior under his own verbal discriminative control.

Since our original definition restricted the population to children with average or better-than-average intelligence, a positive change in cognitive style often results in an increased attention to detail and high levels of proficiency. The child is also provided with a success-oriented experience. These changes in turn encourage the child to persevere longer with greater effort—necessary for success in school learning. It is not unusual for less social "acting out" to take place as success is experienced and motivation for learning increases. The "academic reflectivity" is generalized to the extent that it also contributes to a reduction in asocial behavior in the learning disabled child.

[1]Matching Familiar Figures Test, Jerome Kagan, Ph.D., Harvard University, Cambridge, Massachusetts.

VISION

All individuals who are experiencing learning disorders should periodically see a vision specialist, optometrist, or ophthalmologist. A complete visual analysis should include: visual acuity tests; examination for ocular pathology; refraction to determine the need for glasses at far and/or at the reading distance; static and dynamic tests to determine the level of binocular coordination and accommodative facility; and measurements to establish the degree of ocular fusion and depth perception. Ocular motility and hand-eye coordination should also be observed. This list certainly does not exhaust the possible areas of investigation for the vision specialist, but rather is intended to indicate those tests most frequently administered. For example, a battery of developmental and perceptual tests is included in some optometric examinations.

It has been this author's experience that there is *not* a high correlation between visual acuity at 20 feet and learning to read. Other investigators have reported similar findings (Pierce, 1977; Wilson and Wold, 1972-1973). Most primary LD children evaluated do not have significantly reduced visual acuity to the extent that they cannot see the relatively large print in a basal reader. On the other hand, there are some primary-grade children who are moderately or severely far-sighted and/or astigmatic. These children often do not perform up to their academic potential, and glasses are recommended. In the primary grades, the frequency of near-sightedness (myopia) is not too great a problem, but when the visual acuity drops to below 20/30, glasses are quite helpful for distance vision. Astigmatism may result in blurred sight at all distances, whereas far-sightedness (hyeropia) causes intermittent blurring, particularly at the reading distance. Far-sightedness is especially insidious, since far-sighted children often have no problem passing the Snellen Test for visual acuity, which is administered at 20 feet in many school vision screening tests. Some children develop significantly different refractive errors in each eye, and this can result in a problem of either uncomfortable vision or poor ocular fusion. Unequal accommodative effort (focusing) causes an individual to tire more easily when reading, and the difference in image size and/or clarity makes it difficult to blend the images of the two eyes in the brain. Sometimes the difference between the two eyes is large enough to cause the poorer eye to suppress or "blank out" its image. Continued suppression at a young age may interfere with the development of the sight in the affected eye, resulting in *amblyopia*, a reduction of sight from lack of use. Even when the appropriate correction is provided for an amblyopic eye, the sight does not return quickly to normal. It is often necessary to patch the good eye and/or provide orthoptic and pleoptic training to improve the sight. Often a contact lens in one or both eyes is helpful in developing binocular fusion.

Binocular coordination difficulties most often refer to *phorias*, the tendency for the eyes to deviate; overt cosmetic deviations are known as *strabismus*. When the eyes tend to underconverge (or diverge), the condition is called *exophoria. Esophoria* is defined as the tendency for the eyes to overconverge. Most often, high phorias cause problems in visual discomfort at the reading distance, although discomfort at far distances (driving and television viewing) is certainly not rare. Sometimes when a person is tired or ill he may experience *diplopia* (double vision), because the ocular fusional reserves are not adequate to compensate for the tendency of the eyes to deviate. The poor ocular fusion that usually accompanies esophoria and exophoria makes it difficult for an individual to concentrate and sustain effort comfortably in reading and study-type activities for extended periods of time. Esophoria may be associated with far-sightedness, and when glasses are prescribed, the tendency for the eyes to turn in is reduced or even eliminated. Accommodative (focusing) disorders are also often present. For example, when Sherman (1973) evaluated 50 children, aged 6 to 13 years, diagnosed and referred as learning disabled, 88 percent had difficulties involving accommodative facility. A reading lens is often effective in ameliorating the symptoms an individual experiences with esophoria and an accommodative insufficiency.

Strabismus conditions are often more complex to treat. *Unilateral convergent strabismus* (one eye turns in) and *unilateral divergent strabismus* (one eye turns out) may also result in amblyopia of the deviating eye, requiring special attention. A strabismus may be *alternating,* in which case either eye is used alternately and the corrected visual acuity usually remains near normal.

In addition to prescription glasses, binocular disorders, both strabismic and nonstrabismic, may be treated with visual training or orthoptic treatments. The training consists of improving the quality and range of ocular fusion (divergence and convergence), developing the facility and range of accommodation, and increasing the precision of ocular fixations. For patients with reduced ranges, increasing vergence ranges with visual training has significant effects upon reading proficiency (Taylor, 1966). Where amblyopia is present, improving the sight in the amblyopic eye is stressed. Sometimes, in cases of strabismus, the deviation of one eye is too great to correct with glasses and/or visual training alone. It is necessary, after developing simultaneous binocular vision and a range of fusion at the angle of deviation, to employ surgery to reposition one or more muscles, after which the range of fusion is extended by visual training so that the eyes remain "straight." The incidence of strabismus is somewhat higher than average among children diagnosed as having minimal brain dysfunction (MBD) (Birch and Gussow, 1970; Kennard, 1960; Millman, 1956) and low birth weight (Goldstein, Henderson, Goldberg, Benitez and Hawkins, 1967).

Visual training has other therapeutic byproducts. Those individuals who are not "visually oriented," a characteristic present in many learning disabled students, are taught to respond more effectively to visual stimuli. In Birch's terms the visual promotes a hierarchical shift in sensory dominance from tactile and auditory to visual. The very nature of visual training and the accuracy of responses it requires tend to improve a child's impulse control. This reduction in impulsivity may be generalized to the extent that the learning-disabled child is less likely to make the rapid decisions in learning that often produce many errors. Attention to task, perseverance, and self-direction, other characteristics of good learners, are also enhanced.

In addition to rendering the customary professional services, the vision specialist can improve the learning-disabled child's ability to sustain effort comfortably in reading and study-type activities. Through visual training and perceptual therapy, he is capable of modifying the student's learning style so that he responds more effectively and efficiently in the classroom.

READINESS FOR READING AND LEARNING

Jensen (1973) noted, "There can be no doubt about the *fact* of readiness. . . . The theoretical explanation of readiness is important, of course, because much of what we do about readiness in educational practice will depend upon our conception of its nature." (p. 4) One may ask why readiness is considered in a discourse dealing with learning disabilities. Thirty years of clinical experience have reinforced the notion that most individuals who experience difficulties in learning began to experience these difficulties in kindergarten or grade one although they may not have been recognized until sometime later. Failure, or near failure, in kindergarten and grade one affects the way in which a child perceives himself as a student. The lack of either external or internal reinforcement at this critical stage of development is crucial and may result in the beginning of a "turning off" process that is difficult to reverse. The variety of psychological problems that may develop from the frustrations associated with persistent learning difficulties will be discussed subsequently.

Although failure to learn to read in first grade is not primarily associated with mental age, research in this area suggests that teaching reading too early can result in a number of problems. For example, Dean's (1939) study of 116 first-grade entrants concluded that a mental age of six and a half years is needed for average success in first grade. Only 29 percent of those with mental ages between six and six and a half years made average progress. Retention is another consideration. Keister (1941) reported that five-year-old children with average intelligence often could attain a first-grade reading level by the end of grade one, but a higher level of regression was evident between June and September than with older children. In addition, by the end of grade two, the incidence of children who were below the norm was greater than older children. Bond and Wagner (1966) cited evidence that showed the progressive influence of mental age on reading ability. Correlation between mental age (as measured by the Stanford-Binet Tests) and reading ability was .35 at the end of grade one, increased to .60 by the end of grade five, and progressed to .80 by high school. The results of an investigation conducted by Cohen and Glass (1968) confirmed these relationships. Although no one questions the advantages of having a high IQ, average or better-than-average intelligence does not ensure learning to read in first grade. Nila (1973) listed four factors in reading readiness in the following order of importance: auditory discrimination, visual discrimination, range of information, and mental age.

Learning to read in grade one is, to a large extent, concrete and mechanical compared to the reasoning skills required later on, when reading becomes the fundamental tool for learning. Jensen (1973) addressed this problem in his monograph, *Understanding Readiness*. Essentially, he described readiness as the ability to integrate acquired subskills into a cognitive whole, generalize, and transfer previous learning to new learning. For example, the grade-one child who is taught the words *peg* and *bit* should be able to derive the words: pe-t, p-it, bi-g, b-eg. Teaching a child to read too early, when he is responding primarily to association learning, creates a cognitive problem with which the child of the mental age of five and a half is not prepared to deal. Customarily, he cannot integrate subskills, generalize, or transfer previous learning to new learning. Usually, there are accompanying perceptual immaturities that interfere with stimulus differentiation

and auditory and visual recall.

In addition to intellectual readiness and sensory and perceptual readiness, there are numerous other general readiness factors. For example, experiential readiness, social development, and emotional maturity all contribute to a child's ability to respond to classroom instruction. The solution to this problem is *not* the mass retention of children who are not ready to learn when they have completed kindergarten or first grade. In the absence of a planned program of intervention during the following year, retention of a child with average intelligence often results in limited improvement since he may be unable to integrate subskills or blend sounds. On the other hand, delaying instruction, while providing the child with an appropriate program to develop a level of readiness for learning that is closer to optimal, reduces the risk of failure. The process of *turning off* begins in kindergarten and first grade, and it is frequently the result of ignoring readiness. The redundant failure and frustration provides negative reinforcement, conditioned inhibition, and (ultimately) experimental extinction. Learning is less efficient. While some skills are learned, the capability of generalizing and transferring these skills to later learning is limited. Also inhibited are those behaviors that promote learning: attention, perseverance, effort, and self-direction. The energy required to reverse the process after three or more years of failure orientation is enormous.

READING

One might possibly say that if there were no children with reading difficulties, the learning-disabled child would no longer be extant. Certainly the work load of the school psychologist and guidance teacher would be significantly reduced. It would be fair to estimate that 90 percent of learning disabled children experience reading difficulties. Most reading problems begin in grades one and two and are often found among children who have average or better than average intelligence. As a group, they have difficulty in conceptualizing the structural relationships of language. Learning to read is learning to blend; at first blending sounds into words, and later blending words into phrases, sentences, paragraphs, and ideas. The thrust of these remarks will exclude special problems, such as those encountered when teaching blacks, Spanish-speaking, and some American Indian children whose speech may involve nonstandard dialects. On the other hand, any child's performance in grammar, syntax, vocabulary, and lexical control needs to be compared to the normal and expected development.

Pedagogically, a reading problem begins when a child fails to develop the necessary word attack strategies. Probably the earliest learning takes place at the associative stage. Preschool children often learn to associate words with pictures. Later on, the initial consonant may be the association cue. Word shapes are also helpful to beginning readers. But the "bottom line" in learning to read is the ability to develop a phonetic approach with strong assistance from context clues and "sight words" that either do not follow the phonic rules (love) or must be introduced early (girl).

Early reading skills represent a fusion of perceptual and cognitive skills. Auditory and visual sequential memory, short- and long-term auditory and visual memory, auditory and visual discrimination, and auditory-visual equivalence are all necessary ingredients of the learning process. Sensorimotor, particularly visual motor, maturation enables the child to accurately write and copy, but understanding what he writes is a cognitive function. Reading comprehension is an outgrowth of the child's ability to decode words and of maturation of this total perceptual-cognitive integration. The child who has learned to read because he is able to integrate subskills into a cognitive whole, generalize, and transfer previous learning to new learning, is also customarily able to integrate the percepts, images, memories, and information to form a concept (Russell, 1956).

The oral reading test provides the reading specialist, psychologist, learning disability specialist, and classroom teacher with an excellent opportunity to evaluate word attack skills rapidly, particularly in the primary grades. Blending, the "final e" rule, vowel pairs, and syllabication may all be included in an informal reading inventory. Excessive substitutions and omissions suggest possible perceptual deficits. Phrasing difficulties often produce comprehension errors. The pitch of the voice and the child's level of "induced" physical activity while reading might lead one to suspect excess anxiety associated with reading. Limited sight vocabulary also becomes evident.

When testing children in the middle grades, using standardized reading tests, the ability to reason and to draw inferences and the recognition of main ideas become paramount, compared to the primary grades when locating answers and identifying facts are most important. Reading in the various content areas, literature, social studies, art, and so forth, becomes progressively more important, as does reading for entertainment. The expansion of reading skills into study skills begins to take place in the middle grades. At this juncture the reading and language insufficiencies of the learning-disabled child become critical, for now he cannot maintain the required rate of progress in his courses. Remediation at this level (and subsequent levels) becomes quite difficult, since it is necessary (continually) to inventory the child's skills. That is, gaps in the continuum of skills usually exist at each of the previous grade levels; and unless a firm foundation is established, remediation will not be successful. The commitment, training, and experience of the instructor are very important, and it is not likely that a significant degree of improvement will be measured unless a skilled specialist is providing the tutoring, preferably on an individual basis.

At any level, the reading program should be success-oriented. Most LD children have experienced much frustration, and their motivation is almost extinguished. They have been measured by parents and teachers, either tacitly or overtly. While they appreciate being complimented for their success, they recognize when they are being patronized.

Occasionally we see a child who truly experiences his initial learning difficulties at the junior high school level. Sometimes, the individual has been an A/B student throughout elementary school. These students are frequently quite bright, and they have been able to compensate for their "average" reading skills because of their superior intelligence. Once in a while a life experience creates an extended emotional impact that interferes with the student's desire and/or ability to learn. Social and peer relationships sometimes result in attitudinal problems that are often very difficult to treat. Among these individuals, the reading and learning disability is in fact merely a symptom of the difficulty.

Finally there is a population of students whose vocabulary and interpretive reading skills are average or above average but whose reading efficiency is poor. Rate of comprehension is slow, and the individual makes too many eye stops and regressive movements while reading. The resulting laborious reading style causes the student to withdraw from reading and study-type activities or procrastinate inordinately before starting an assignment or book. This type of problem can be best identified by an eye movement photograph (see Figure 3). The Controlled Reader[2] and Guided Reader[3] are particularly effective in improving reading efficiency, especially when combined with tachistoscopic training (Solan, 1967).

Teaching reading effectively is indeed a challenge. It requires an approach that is sequential, well-organized, and eclectic; it must be related to general language development and oral and written expression. In order to meet the ever-increasing needs of all students, particularly those who are experiencing learning disabilities, the preparation for the teaching of reading—both preservice and inservice—must provide teachers with a broader theoretical base and more extensive clinical experience.

PSYCHOLOGICAL PROBLEMS

Abundant advice relating to the psycho-

---

[2]Controlled Reader: EDL–McGraw Hill, New York.
[3]Guided Reader: ITC–Taylor Associates, Huntington, New York.

logical management of the child with a learning disability is available to parents and professionals. Much of the advice clearly reflects the diagnostic bias of the writer. In their quest to seek a solution to the academic, social, and emotional problems of a learning disabled child, parents and teachers are exposed to an almost infinite variety of approaches and "solutions." Some clinicians consider learning problems to be solely psychological in origin. On the other hand, Wender (1971) wrote in support of psychostimulants, "It would not be hard to argue that in many instances psychotherapy of children with this syndrome (MBD) virtually constitutes malpractice—a harmful withholding of useful treatment from a child (p. 130)." No one suggests the absence of psychological problems. The treatment of the child depends upon how the treater conceptualizes the problem.

Individuals who have worked extensively with LD children agree that anxiety is an ever-present symptom. At times it is difficult to decide whether the hyperanxious child is experiencing a learning disability and the accompanying hyperactivity because of the anxiety or whether the anxiety is indeed secondary to the child's learning problems. Poor concentration, short attention span, and distractibility may be viewed similarly. Aggressive behavior and depression are observed in 10 to 20 percent of the children (Klasen, 1972).

Children who are experiencing learning disabilities develop adaptive reactions. For example, from becoming passive and withdrawn, the child may develop the *withdrawal reaction*. By reverting to inner fantasy, the LD child can avoid facing the imminent failure that is threatening. Others exhibit a *regressive reaction* that results in a child regressing to an earlier stage of social and emotional development when less sophisticated behavior was expected. Some children generalize their problem and use it as a defense. The child may express his feeling by responding, "I can't learn that, I'm brain injured!" One of the most serious is the *clowning reaction*. Here the child can rationalize that he is not learning because he chooses not to learn. Peer reinforcement is often present. Teacher reinforcement

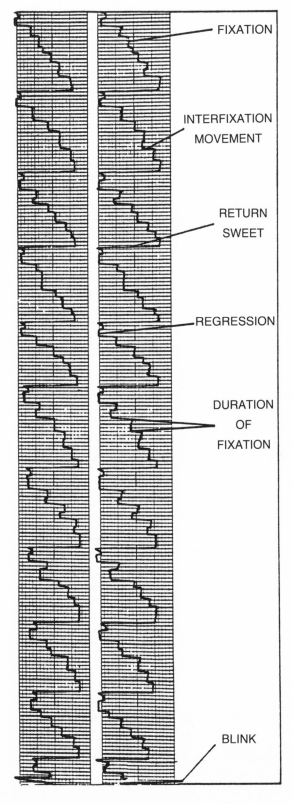

FIXATION

INTERFIXATION
MOVEMENT

RETURN
SWEET

REGRESSION

DURATION
OF
FIXATION

BLINK

Figure 3. Diagram showing how eye-movement characteristics are represented in a Reading Eye II recording. From *Eye-Movement Analysis with the Reading Eye II*, by Helen Frackenpohl Morris. New York: McGraw–Hill, Inc., 1973. Reproduced with the permission of Educational Developmental Laboratories, A Division of McGraw–Hill Book Company.

may also be present if the child is sent out of the room so that he does not have to learn. The various reactions, both acute and chronic, experienced by LD children and their parents are discussed in detail by Gardner (1973) and Silver (1974).

Therapeutic approaches are considered elsewhere in this volume. Operant conditioning has been used successfully alone and in combination with other techniques. Modeling, an effective method of modifying a child's cognitive style, has also proven to be helpful in modifying behavior, particularly with hyperactive children (Bandure, 1969; Ross and Ross, 1976).

Early in life LD children (and probably all children) learn how to test the limits. Because of an inherent lack of organization, it is probably more important for LD children to be subjected to a structured environment. Furthermore, disorganized children are often the product of disorganized parents. This author has found it to be very helpful to provide parents with four simple rules (Wender, 1971):

(1) Establish a hierarchy of importance, distinguishing between misdemeanors and felonies. Parents must decide what is trivial; what is important; what is essential.

(2) Decide in advance upon a plan for rewards and punishment. The rewards and punishments must be commensurate with the behavior. Also it should be remembered that either provides attention, thus punishment is more rewarding than ignoring.

(3) The one time principle: by proscribing or prescribing behavior only once before rewarding or punishing, the child is provided with a predictable environment.

(4) Both parents must abide by a prescribed course of action.

It is sometimes informative to constrast the child's school behavior with his behavior at home. This approach is particularly revealing when it becomes evident that a child is responding to a structured approach in school although unmanageable at home. The structure and the organization in the home can often be improved by applying the four rules. We must remember that the LD child is usually the biological product of the parents who, indeed, may have provided the genetic predispo-

sition for the social and emotional behavior and the accompanying learning problems. Another possibility is that the parents have become disorganized by trying to pursue conflicting plans provided by professionals who are "helping" them deal with the problem. The inability of the parents to reconcile *release therapy*, which further undermines a child's already weak control of his behavior, with a firm approach designed to improve the child's control of his own behavior, is confusing and contributes to the disorganization in the home. On the other hand, therapy that provides the child with additional ego strength, counteracting some of the failure and frustration that has been experienced, is often beneficial.

PSYCHOSTIMULANTS

What are psychostimulants? When are they prescribed for children with learning disabilities? Although other medications are used occasionally to treat children who are experiencing learning disorders and who are also hyperactive, psychostimulants are the current drugs of choice. Central nervous system stimulants have been prescribed with increasing frequency during the past 40 years, long enough to make certain observations. For a thorough discussion of psychostimulant treatment for hyperactive children the reader is referred to Chapter 15.

The medication is effective in reducing hyperactivity, distractibility, and impulsivity in many children under age 13 provided that the dosage is properly regulated. It is not always possible to predict in advance which children will be helped and to what extent they will improve. Some investigators suggest that the psychostimulants provide a useful diagnostic regimen. Those children who do respond to the medication have indeed been experiencing physiological hyperkinesis. Wender (1971) is one of the most outspoken of the group recommending a greater use of central nervous system stimulants in treating children with impulse disorders. There is no question of his diagnostic bias:

I am obviously opting for a trial of stimulant

(amphetamine or methylphenidate) therapy in all children in whom the diagnosis of MBD is suspected. . . . barring the future disclosure of chronic toxic consequences of stimulant drug therapy for such children, one must argue that it is the treatment of choice, and withholding it represents an injury to the patient and his family. (p. 130)

In addition to the experience of many practitioners, there are numerous controlled studies that support Wender's proposal. Knights and Hinton (1969) performed a double-blind experiment with placebo control. They used random assignment of treatment groups and objective measures of several specifically described treatment groups. The statistical analysis was sophisticated, and the conclusions were within the limit of the experimental design. While patient groups appeared to be homogeneous, the sample should have been larger. *Not all studies meet these criteria.* The authors reported a statistically significant improvement in motor control in the methylphenidate group which they hypothesized occurred through increased attention to relevant stimuli (and decreased attention to irrelevant or extraneous cues), leading to an increase in goal-directed behavior. They observed that Ritalin is more effective with some children than others, and it is difficult to predict the efficacy of the medication in advance. A strong placebo effect was noted.[4] To measure motor control the eight-hole Steadiness Test and Porteus Maze Test were used.

There is general agreement that psychostimulants have a "paradoxical" calming effect on prepubertal children. The term "paradoxical" may be a poor choice. Ross and Ross (1976) point out:

The stimulants give the *impression* that a calming effect has occurred in the hyperactive child, but empirical investigations indicate that the actual change in the child's behavior is in more appropriate and better integrated responses in settings characterized by high demands for compliance. (p. 115)

The drugs do not provide a pharmacological sedative action.

[4]Any pharmacologically inert substance that may result in improvement in 20 to 40 percent of subjects.

In addition to improving a child's activity and impulse control, CNS stimulants improve attentiveness and persistence. Social behavior is modified; the child becomes more sensitive to rewards and punishment. Parents become aware of the child's increased need for affection and increased sensitivity to parental approval and disapproval. Perceptual and cognitive learning improve.

Occasionally there are side effects, which include anorexia and insomnia, but these are less noticeable when using methylphenidates rather than dextro-amphetamines. Mild stomachaches and headaches also have been reported. "Bad" responses are reported in 10 percent of Wender's cases. Hyperactivity increases, and if a child is predisposed to schizoid characteristics, the behavior may become intensified. But it should be emphasized that the reaction is temporary, and the symptoms disappear within 12 hours after the last dose of medication.

Since from one-third to one-half of the LD children evince an immediate positive response (Fish, 1971; Wender, 1971), psychostimulants continue to gain acceptance among physicians and parents. Although considerable concern exists, there is a lack of information about the long-term psychological and physiological consequences of stimulant drug intervention. For example, Safer and Allen (1976) reported a "minor" degree of suppression of the growth rate which can occur. They found that children on Dexedrine grow, on average, at 60 to 75 percent of their expected annual rate during the period they are on medication. When abruptly taken off the drug, these children show a distinct growth rebound.

The decision to use psychostimulants for a particular learning disabled child must be based on the individual needs of each child and the ability of the child and the parents to cope with the child's behavior at home and in school, after all possible alternatives have been considered.

NUTRITION

The subject of nutrition, always interesting when related to pregnancy, has in recent years stressed the product of the pregnancy to a greater degree. The influence of malnutrition on the development of the brain, the central nervous system, and intelligence has been investigated fully. Presently under study are the effects of food additives, coloring, natural salicylates, and sugar on the behavior of school-age children. The interrelationships of health, nutrition, and school failure are discussed and abundantly documented in *Disadvantaged Children.* Birch and Gussow (1970) observed:

For poorer children are not merely born *into* poverty; they are born *of* poverty, and are thus at risk of defective development even before their births. . . . A child born of such circumstances is likely to be smaller at birth than his more fortunate contemporaries and is more likely to die at birth or before his second year of life. . . . Throughout the preschool and school years the survivors are likely to be more poorly fed and cared for in their homes, overexposed to disease in their communities and the recipients of little or no medical supervision. The failure of such children in school is not only not a mystery but is virtually forordained. Hence a serious attack on school failure must be an attack on the life conditions which characterize poverty whereever it is found. (p. XII)

Animal studies are valuable to provide guidance, but the results should be extrapolated with caution. The animal evidence is convincing that malnutrition, prenatally and postnatally, results in physical, chemical, and functional changes in the brain, but there are quantitative differences when compared with humans. Winick and Rosso (1975) observed:

In humans, cell division is curtailed by early malnutrition. Later malnutrition will reduce the size of individual cells, but not the number of cells. Again, those areas in which cells are most rapidly proliferating are the areas most affected by undernutrition. In the human, however, cerebrum is such an area, and cell division is profoundly curtailed by early malnutrition in human cerebrum when compared with rat cerebrum. The brain stem is also more markedly affected in the human than in the rat. (p. 50)

The number of cells increases linearly until birth and then more slowly until about 12

to 15 months of age, after which there is little if any increase in the total number of brain cells (Winick, 1968).

It is difficult to discuss malnutrition without considering the economic, sociological, and psychological implications. The environment that produces the malnourished child creates a social barrier and emotional overtones that preclude efficient school learning. How is one to measure the lethargy that results from a history of nutritional deficiency and its accompanying lowered resistance to disease? These children are frequently the product of mothers who themselves were malnourished as children and often during pregnancy; that is, they are the children who probably were at earlier risk of perinatal damage. Psychologically, the hungry, malnourished child is understimulated with a poor self-image and low personal expectations. In school the child finds it difficult to pay attention—often distracted and withdrawn.

Iron deficiency anemia is a widespread deficiency throughout the world. It is the most prevalent nutritional deficiency in the United States, particularly in pregnant women and young children. The incidence of anemia is particularly high in low socioeconomic groups. Since it is associated with a decrease in attention and a reduction in purposeful activity, the effect of anemia on learning is apparent. The teacher may recognize some of the clinical signs by observing the pale, brittle, flat fingernails and the fissures at the corners of the mouth. Iron performs important physiologic functions in oxygen transfer and cellular respiration. Anemia rates from 40 to 80 percent have been reported in preschool children in Washington, D.C., Alabama, and Mississippi (Birch and Gussaw, 1970). Fortunately, the condition is highly reversible. The presence of anemia at the time of testing is the significant variable. It should be remembered, however, that lack of attention, resulting from anemia, is serious since missing one step in the learning process interferes with a child's ability to cope with the next, perhaps more complex, problem.

Several years ago Benjamin Feingold published a preliminary report relating "food additives" to hyperkinesis in childhood. His popular book was published a short time later. Feingold (1974) postulated, "Hyperactive children can be helped—without drugs". He estimated that five million children in the United States suffer from *hyperkinesis-learning disability* (H-LD). Feingold designed a diet to exclude *all foods* and *all drugs* that are artificially flavored and colored. In addition, the diet was salicylate free. Immediately there appeared a spate of cynicism, rejection, and ridicule from nutritionists, physicians, the Nutrition Foundation, et al. Feingold reported numerous case histories but no controlled experiments. He also failed to provide objective measures of change. As in all case histories, the observer of change is not "blind" to the treatment being evaluated and, in fact, has a vested interest in confirming the hypothesis. Overall, Feingold's presentations were criticized as being too anecdotal.

In 1976, a group of investigators, headed by C. K. Connors (1976) at the Department of Psychiatry, University of Pittsburgh, confirmed, with certain reservations, Feingold's hypothesis using a double-blind study. The diets were carefully prescribed and monitored. The results of this study strongly suggest:

A diet free of most natural salicylates, artificial flavors, and artificial colors reduces the perceived hyperactivity of some children suffering from hyperkinetic impulse disorder. Teachers who observed the children over a 12-week period without knowledge of when the child started his diet and without knowledge of the fact that there were two diets which were employed, noted the children as less hyperactive while the children were on the diet recommended by Feingold. The difference obtained between the ratings when the children were on the K-P (Feingold) diet and when they were on the control diet would have occurred by chance only 5 in 1,000 times. Similarly, the teachers rated the children as significantly improved over the baseline period on the K-P diet but not while on the control diet. (p. 161)

The observations and findings of the teachers in school were more clear-cut than those of the parents at home, perhaps because the demands on the child's attention and goal-oriented behavior were greater in the classroom, and therefore any improvements in these areas were more evident.

Another study was conducted by J. I. Williams and his associates (1978) at the Health Care Research Unit, University of Toronto. The relative effects of drugs and diet on hyperactive behavior were explored. They reported, from the results of this brief double-blind cross-over experiment, that stimulant medication was more effective than diet. They confirmed the results of the previous study that school observations by teachers were more positive than at-home observations by parents. The investigators concluded:

A diet free of artificial flavors and colors results in a reduction of symptoms in some hyperactive children. The task is now to find ways of identifying the characteristics of hyperkinetic children most likely to respond to diet, and to have them participate in further clinical evaluation of the diet. (p. 817)

A limited endorsement of the Feingold diet resulted from a double-blind cross-over experiment, conducted by J. P. Harley and his colleagues (1978) at the Department of Food Microbiology and Toxicology, Neurology, Pediatrics, and Psychology, University of Wisconsin, Madison and the Division of Pediatric Neurology, Northwestern University, Children's Memorial Hospital, Chicago. Even though the attitude of the paper appeared to be hostile to the hypothesis being tested, the authors observed:

Nevertheless, objectivity and completeness in reporting our data require us to repeat our finding that ten of ten mothers and four of seven fathers of the preschool sample rated their children's behavior as improved on the experimental (K-P or Feingold) diet. . . . While we feel confident that the cause-effect relationship asserted by Feingold is overstated with respect to school-age children, we are not in a position to refute his claims regarding the possible causative effect played by artificial food colors in preschool children. (p. 827)

Malnutrition is a complex entity: both food quantity and food quality must be considered. Much of the world, including the United States, is exposed to various degrees of protein caloric malnutrition although, in many cases, the total caloric intake may be adequate. Digestive disorders and intestinal diseases (and the medicines used to combat the illnesses) complicate and enhance the problems of malnutrition. Traditional food habits make education difficult at all levels of society, and socio-economic factors compound the problem of malnutrition for the disadvantaged children. Because malnutrition is not a unitary trait and its complexity is shared etiologically with numerous other contributing factors, we have the opportunity and the professional and social responsibility to interrupt this self-reinforcing chain in many places so that all children will be able to achieve their full intellectual and social potential.

CONCLUSION

In this chapter I have provided the reader with a series of "child-oriented" approaches that deal with the diagnosis and treatment of children who experience learning disorders. Thirty years of treating children have taught me that the child is the "identified patient" and that the maximum energy should be directed toward ameliorating the child's problem. In this case, the "problem" is learning disability. My experience has been that children who have learning disabilities:

(1) Often display early neuro-maturational lags that are revealed in the case history by delayed motor and language milestones and a poorly developed sense of directionality and lateral awareness;

(2) Frequently are not able to integrate subskills into a cognitive whole to the extent that they progress normally in reading and arithmetic;

(3) Show evidence of a lag in the development of perceptual and perceptual motor skills, particularly those which are related to learning to read and the evolution of a good body image concept;

(4) Manifest visual functional disorders to a greater extent, making it more difficult for the individual to sustain effort comfortably for extended periods of time in reading and study-type activities;

(5) Show impulse control problems when engaging in a learning situation, which cause them to respond too rapidly (impulsively), resulting in numerous unnecessary errors;

(6) Display aberrant behavior when placed under stress, particularly in learning situations, which in the past has resulted in frustration and failure. Their hyperactivity and distractibility interfere with the development of those learning characteristics which are customarily found in good students. They frequently lack the ability to sustain attention, persevere, and engage in activities requiring self-direction;

(7) Often have not received the quality of individualized supplementary instruction that would enable them to succeed in the classroom.

The treatment and management of children with learning disabilities remains a challenge for psychology, psychiatry, pediatrics, optometry, neurology, and other health practitioners, but most of all, for the educators, who are the primary-care practitioners for the children with learning disabilities, have only recently begun to "put it all together." While other professionals can and should be helpful in enabling the child to respond to instruction more effectively, the bottom line is good teaching which, after all, is the primary responsibility of the educator.

References

Ayres, A. J. Patterns of perceptual–motor dysfunction in children: A factor analytic study. *Perceptual and Motor Skills*, 1965, *20*, 335–368.

Bandura, A. *Principles of behavior modification*. New York: Holt, Rinehart and Winston, Inc., 1969.

Belmont, L., & Birch, H. G. Lateral dominance, lateral awareness, and reading disability. *Child Development*, 1965, *36*, 57–71.

Birch, H. G. Dyslexia and the maturation of visual function. In J. Money (Ed.), *Reading disability*. Baltimore: Johns Hopkins University Press, 1962.

Birch, H. G., & Gussow, J. D. *Disadvantaged children, health, nutrition and school failure*. New York: Harcourt, Brace and World, Grune & Stratton, 1970.

Bond, G. L., & Wagner, E. B. *Teaching the child to read* (4th ed.). New York: Macmillan, 1966.

Cathcart, W. G., & Liedtke, W. Reflectiveness/impulsiveness and mathematics achievement. *Arithmetic Teacher*, 1969, *16*, 563–567.

Cohen, A., & Glass, G. G. Lateral dominance and reading ability. *The Reading Teacher*, 1968, *21* (4), 343–348.

Connors, C. K. Goyette, C. H., Southwick, D. A., Lees, J. M., & Andrulonis, P. A. Food additives and hyperkinesis: a controlled double blind experiment. *Pediatrics*, 1976, *58* (2), 154–166.

Dean, C. D. Predicting first grade reading achievement. *Elementary School Journal*, 1939, *39*, 609–616.

deHirsch, K. Gestalt psychology as applied to language disturbances. *Journal of Nervous and Mental Diseases*, 1954, *120*, 257.

Egeland, B. Training impulsive children in the use of more efficient scanning techniques. *Child Development*, 1974, *45*, 165–171.

Feingold, B. F. *Why your child is hyperactive.* New York: Random House, 1974.

Fish, B. The "one child, one drug" myth of stimulants in hyperkinesis. *Archives of General Psychiatry*, 1971, *25*, 193–203.

Gardner, R. A. *M.B.D.* New York: Jason Aronson, Inc., 1973.

Gesell, A. *The first five years of life.* New York: Harper and Brothers, 1940.

Goldstein, H., Henderson, M., Goldberg, I. O., Benitez, E., & Hawkins C. Perinatal factors associated with strabismus in Negro children. *American Journal of Public Health*, 1967, *57*, 217–227.

Hallgren, B. Specific dyslexia (congenital word blindness). *Acta Psychiat. Scand. Suppl.*, 1950, *65*.

Harley, J. P., Ray, R. S., Tomasi, L., Eichman, P. L., Matthews, C. G., Chun, R., Cleeland, C. S., & Traisman, E. Hyperkinesis and food additives: Testing the Feingold hypothesis. *Pediatrics*, 1978, *61* (6), 818–827.

Hoffman, M. S. Early indications of learning problems. *Academic Therapy*, 1971, *7* (1), 23–25.

Ingram, T. T. S. The nature of dyslexia. *Bulletin of the Orton Society*, Pomfret, Conn., 1969, *19*, 18.

Jensen, A. R. Understanding readiness. In H. A. Solan (Ed.), *The psychology of learning and reading difficulties.* New York: Simon & Schuster, 1973.

Johnson, D. J. & Myklebust, H. R. *Learning disabilities, educational principles and practices.* New York: Grune & Stratton, 1967.

Kagan, J. Reflection–impulsivity: The generality and dynamics of conceptual tempo. *Journal of Abnormal Psychology*, 1966, *71*, 17–24.

Kagan, J. Reflection–impulsivity and reading ability in primary grade children. *Child De-velopment*, 1965, *36*, 609–628.

Kagan, J., Pearson, L., & Welch, L. Modifiability of an impulsive tempo. *Journal of Educational Psycholoay*, 1966, *57* (6), 359–365.

Kawi, A. A., & Pasamanick, B. Association of factors of pregnancy with reading disorders in childhood. *Journal of the American Medical Association*, 1958, *166*, 1420.

Keister, B. V. Reading skills acquired by five year old children. *Elementary School Journal*, 1941, *41*, 587–596.

Kennard, M. A. Value of equivocal signs in neurologic diagnosis. *Neurology*, 1960, *10* (9), 753–764.

Keogh, B. A. Hyperactivity and learning disorders: Review and speculation. *Exceptional Children*, 1971, *38*, 101–109.

Kephart, N. C. *The slow learner in the classroom.* Columbus, Ohio: Charles E. Merrill Books, Inc., 1960.

Klasen, E. *The syndrome of specific dyslexia.* Baltimore: University Park Press, 1972.

Knights, R. M. & Hinton, G. The effects of methylphenidate (Ritalin) on the motor skills and behavior of children with learning problems. *Journal of Nervous and Mental Diseases*, 1969, *148*, 643–653.

Matheny, A. P., Jr. & Dolan, A. B. A twin study of genetic influences in reading achievement. *Journal of Learning Disabilities*, 1974, *7* (2), 99–102.

Matheny, A. P. Jr., Dolan, A. B., & Wilson, R. S. Twins with academic learning problems: antecedent characteristics. *American Journal of Orthopsychiatry*, 1976, *46* (3), 464–469.

Meichenbaum, D. H., & Goodman, J. Training to talk to themselves: A means of developing self–control. *Journal of Abnormal Psychology*, 1971, *77* (2), 115–126.

Messer, S. Reflection–impulsivity: Stability and school failure. *Journal of Educational Psychology*, 1970, *61*, 487–490.

Millman, D. Organic behavior disorder. *American Journal of Diseases of Children*, 1956, *91*, 521–528.

Nila, Sr. Mary. Foundations of a successful reading program. In H. A. Solan (Ed.), *The psychology of learning and reading difficulties.* New York: Simon and Schuster, 1973.

Piaget, J. Development and learning. In R. Ripple and V. Rockcastle (Eds.), *Piaget rediscovered.* Ithaca, New York: Cornell University Press, 1961.

Pierce, J. R. Symposium: Is there a relationship between vision therapy and academic achievement? *Review of Optometry*, 1977, *114* (6), 48–63.

Ross, D. M., & Ross, S. A. *Hyperactivity: Research, theory, action.* New York: John Wiley

& Sons, 1976.

Russell, D. H. *Children's thinking.* Boston: Ginn & Co., 1956.

Safer, D. J., & Allen, R. P. *Hyperactive children, diagnosis and management.* Baltimore: University Park Press, 1976.

Sherman, A. Relating vision disorders to learning disability. *Journal of the American Optometric Association,* 1973, 44 (2), 139–141.

Sherrington, C. *Man and his nature.* Cambridge: Cambridge University Press, 1951.

Silver, A. A., & Hagin, R. A. Specific reading disability: An approach to diagnosis and treatment. *Journal of Special Education,* 1967, 1 (2), 109–118.

Silver, L. B. Emotional and social problems of children with developmental disabilities. In R. E. Weber (Ed.), *Handbook on learning disabilities,* Englewood Cliffs, N.J.: Prentice Hall, Inc., 1974.

Slingerland, B. *Screening tests for identifying children with specific language disability.* Cambridge, Mass.: Educators Publishing Service, 1964.

Solan, H. A. The improvement of reading efficiency: A study of sixty–three *achieving* high school students. *The Journal of the Reading Specialist,* 1967, 7 (1), 1–6.

Solan, H. A. Identifying and treating children with learning disabilities: The role of the optometrist. *New Jersey Journal of Optometry,* 1976, 30 (2).

Strauss, A. A., & Lehtinen, L. E. *Psychopathology and education of the brain–injured child.* New York: Grune & Stratton, 1947.

Taylor, E. A. *The fundamental reading skill* (2nd ed.). Springfield, Ill.: Charles C. Thomas, 1966.

Wender, P. H. *Minimal brain dysfunction in children.* New York: Wiley–Interscience, 1971.

Werner, H. *Comparative psychology of mental development.* New York: Science Editions, Inc., 1948.

Willerman, L. Activity level and hyperactivity in twins. *Child Development,* 1973, 44, 288–293.

Williams, J. I., Cram, D. M., Tausig, F. T., & Webster, E. Relative effects of drugs and diet on hyperactive behaviors: An experimental study. *Pediatrics,* 1978, 61 (6), 811–817.

Wilson, W. K., & Wold, R. M. A report on vision screening in the schools. *Academic Therapy,* Winter 1972–1973, 8 (2), 155–166.

Winick, M. Changes in nucleic acid and protein content of the human brain during growth. *Pediatric Research,* 1968, 2, 352.

Winick, M., & Rosso, P. Malnutrition, growth, and development. In J. W. Prescott, M. S. Read, and D. B. Coursin (Eds.), *Brain function and malnutrition.* New York: John Wiley and Sons, 1975.

Zahalkova, V. V., & Kloboukova, E. Genetical investigations in dyslexia. *Journal of Medical Genetics,* 1972, 9, 48–52.

CHAPTER 9

Childhood Behavior Problems: A Social Learning Perspective

DENNIS R. MOORE, Ph.D.

OVERVIEW OF BEHAVIOR PROBLEMS

This chapter discusses the development and significance of behavior conduct problems of children. This broad-based category of disorders generally includes most forms of problem behavior in children except those originating from neuroses, psychoses, severe retardation, or organic etiologies. As these exclusionary categories suggest, the conduct-problem child is viewed as a "normal" individual who is experiencing social adjustment difficulties. These difficulties may be identified at any age from approximately three years old to late adolescence, and cover a range of severity from disobedience in the home to criminal activity in the community. The discussion of these behavior problems will focus on three major areas that reflect a general correspondence to increasing age

and problem severity.

(1) *Control problems* in young children are characterized by general immaturity and behaviors such as disobedience, high activity rates, complaining, and temper tantrums;

(2) *Aggressive behavior* identified by excessive fighting, verbal attacks, and defiance; and

(3) *Delinquent behavior* that includes behaviors such as truancy, stealing, vandalism, and assault.

It should be noted that these categories do not represent rigid behavioral syndromes. Instead, they are designed to aid in conceptualizing a large, and at times confusing, area of problem behavior. The reader should not assume either a steady progression or a clear separation of identifying problem behaviors across these categories.

A social learning perspective serves as the main theoretical focus of the chapter. This perspective views behavior as the product of learning experiences that occur through interactions within the natural environment. In the present case, liberty has been taken in expanding this perspective to include the interaction of individuals within the family, the interaction of the family system within the community, and the influences of community networks on the family. The family is presented as the primary agent responsible for the socialization of the child with additional influences from peer groups, teachers, and

[1]This chapter was written while the author was supported by NIMH Grants MH29757 and MH31017 from the Center for the Study of Crime & Delinquency and by the Wright Institute, Berkeley, CA. Gratitude is extended to Robert Wahler and Gerald Patterson for filling the roles of mentor and collaborator. Their influence on the ideas presented in this chapter extends far beyond the many references to their work. Also gratefully acknowledged are Judy Arthur and Matthew Fleischman, whose support and interaction aided the process; Hal Herzog and Paula Shilton for their critiques of a previous version of the chapter; and Will Mayer for his superb graphics and manuscript preparation. Family Research Associates is an affiliate of the Wright Institute, Berkeley, CA.

community agencies contributing to patterns of development. Thus, child behavior will be discussed as the product of the interaction of complex social milieus.

In documenting this perspective of child behavior, two primary areas of investigation will be discussed. These are studies based on naturalistic observations of families interacting in the home setting, and sociological studies of longitudinal or retrospective designs that have investigated contributing factors and outcomes of problem behavior in children.

Historical Significance

Clinical recognition of conduct disorders in children is not a recent phenomenon. Studies of child guidance center caseloads from the late 1920s demonstrated that behavior problems constituted the largest single source of referral complaints (Ackerson, 1931; Paynter and Blanchard, 1929). Paynter and Blanchard reported that over 80 percent of their samples were behavior problem referrals. The most frequent complaint for these children was stealing (37 percent), followed by lying, truancy, disobedience, and tantrums (20 percent or more of the combined samples). Ackerson also reported stealing as the most frequent single referral complaint, occurring in 39 percent of 2113 male cases. Thirty percent or more of these cases also had reported problems with disobedience, fighting, temper outbursts, and lying.

This inordinate proportion of behavior-problem children in child service agencies has continued to be reported in studies from great Britain and the United States (Anderson and Dean, 1956; Maclay, 1967; Roach, 1958; Rutter, Tizard, and Whitmore, 1970). It is clear that behavior problem children have been frequent and persistent consumers of mental health resources for the past 50 years. However, the clinical significance of this problem has not been viewed with similar consistency over the years.

Psychiatric focus on child disorders has generally indicated that more severe long-term effects resulted from neurotic or psychotic symptoms in children as opposed to conduct problems. Behavior difficulties

tended to be viewed as problem "stages" that would pass as the child matured. This attitude was reflected in psychiatric nosology. Anderson and Dean (1956) reported that 64 percent of their study sample demonstrated behavior problems that classified them as "*simple* childhood maladjustment" (emphasis added). Such cases required social services (e.g., case work, counseling), but did not warrant professional psychiatric or psychological attention. This view was not entirely unreasonable. The usual presenting problems of behavior disordered children (e.g., tantrums, lying, disobedience) were common to all children. Since most children experienced similar symptoms with no apparent adverse effects, the symptom's relationship to later deviancy could be suspect. In addition, questions of parental accuracy in perceiving the child's deviance could be raised. These issues were addressed in a study by Shepherd, Oppenheim, and Mitchell (1966). They reported a high percentage of remission of child symptoms over time, irrespective of treatment. They also stated that mothers who referred their children for treatment tended to be more nervous, anxious, and unable to cope with ordinary household conflicts, indicating that child referrals depended as much on the mother's abnormal perceptions as on actual problem behavior from the child. Findings such as these promoted the view that "child behavior problems" were as much the product of overly concerned, neurotic parents as they were an identifiable entity.

Questions concerning spontaneous remission of symptoms and the accuracy of parental complaints about child behavior continue to be discussed (see, Johnson et al., 1973; Levitt, 1971). It seems clear that a percentage of parent-referred children do not exhibit observable problem behaviors (Lobitz and Johnson, 1975). Such children and their families require identification and differential treatment. However, given independent documentation of child problem behavior, several concerns are relevant to treating the child. These are the degree to which the problem behaviors create an immediate disrupting influence; the degree to which behaviors result in the identification and exclusion of the child from socializing influences, such as appropriate peer groups; and, most important, the degree to which childhood problems determine adolescent and adult maladjustment. An unruly child who continuously disrupted a classroom would warrant treatment, even though the problem behavior was expected to diminish over a six-month period. If this disrupting pattern of behavior was stable and predictive of continued problem behavior, then it would demand even greater treatment priority. The permanence of behavior problems and the risk of future deviance resulting from these problems have been areas of doubt within psychiatric concerns. Again, disturbances in the personality (e.g., neurosis, schizophrenia) were deemed the areas of deviance with long range implications.

However, differential effects of personality disorders and conduct disorders were reported as early as the 1931 study by Ackerson. This study intercorrelated over 100 specific traits recorded in the case files of clinic-referred children. These problems were grouped as indicators of personality disorder (e.g., incipient psychosis, inferiority, depression) or conduct disorder (e.g., stealing, truancy, disobedience). Ackerson found that the personality traits correlated very little with police arrest records. The conduct disorders, however, correlated .53 with police arrest. It is not surprising that individual items concerned with stealing were among those highly correlated with arrest. Of greater predictive interest was the finding that more innocuous behaviors, such as truancy, loitering, and staying out late, were also highly related to police arrest. Ackerson's study did not attempt to infer causal relationships between events (e.g., loitering leads to staying out late, which leads to stealing and arrest). Perhaps for this reason, or because juvenile misconduct was still not judged to be reflective of serious deviance, Ackerson's findings appear to have had little impact on contemporary psychiatric thinking.

Morris, Escoll, and Wexler (1956) studied a sample of children with conduct problems who had been referred for treatment prior to age 15. These authors reported that 79 percent of the sample interviewed as adults suffered from inadequate social adjustment. Twenty percent of their sample was classified psychotic, indicating that these children were also at risk for more severe psychiatric problems. This study was among the first to relate conduct problems to adult maladjustment. Since that time, other studies have shown that social adjustment problems of very young children were stable throughout childhood. Westman, Rice, and Berman (1967) rated the social adjustment of nursery school children. They found not only that poorly adjusted nursery school children tended still to have social adjustment problems in high school, but that these later problems were highly correlated (.88) with adult use of mental health facilities. Zax, Cowen, Rappaport, Beach, and Laird (1968) also showed that children experiencing adjustment difficulties in the first grade had a high potential for underachievement and poor social adjustment at grade seven.

One of the most thorough studies of the adult adjustment of conduct problem children was a follow-up study by Robins (1966). In this investigation, about 500 adults were interviewed. These adults had recorded histories of antisocial behavior, neurotic symptoms, or normal adjustment as children. A 30-year follow-up showed that the antisocial group was characterized in adult life as having pervasive social and psychiatric adjustment problems. Seventy-one percent had at least one police arrest; 50 percent had multiple arrests; and 50 percent were incarcerated at some point. In addition, this group experienced greater marital difficulty, more frequent unemployment, excessive use of alcohol, and poor social relationships. These sociopathic adults also had a higher incidence of other psychiatric illness and were more likely to be judged disabled by these difficulties at the time of follow-up. It appeared that the best predictors of the adult deviancy pattern reported by Robins were childhood referrals for aggression and theft in which the child had engaged in numerous, diverse antisocial activities. These same children also had a history of disobedience, staying out late, and truancy. Neurotic symptoms (e.g., withdrawal, fear) in children from the Robins study were not helpful in predicting adult psychiatric illness.

It is clear that severe conduct disorders in children, such as those described by Robins (1966), reflect a level of maladjustment that is detrimental to the child, crippling to the adult, and costly to society. The evidence also indicates that less severe behavior problems tend to be stable throughout childhood and may be predictive of escalating deviancy. Obviously, not all behavior problem children are destined to live tumultuous lives. Aspects other than the simple occurrence of a specific problem behavior interact to produce a child at risk for continued deviancy.

Characteristics and Onset of Behavior Problems

Typical referral complaints for problem children usually describe behaviors that are observable and readily defined (e.g., disobedience, disruption, talking back). Other problems having lower rates of occurrence, such as stealing and fighting, may seldom be observed, but still refer to unambiguous behavior. These behaviors, however, are not engaged in only by problem children. Nearly all children at some point disobey their parents, fight, skip school, or engage in petty theft. Therefore, dimensions other than the simple occurrence or nonoccurrence of a behavior must be included in the defining characteristics of problem behavior. These additional dimensions include the number and rate of disturbing behaviors, the setting in which they occur, the age appropriateness of the behaviors, and adult perceptions and tolerances of the behaviors. As an example, a four-year-old child who occasionally displayed a temper tantrum in the home would not be viewed in the same manner as a four-year-old child who averaged five tantrums a day and was generally disobedient (depending, of course, on the parent's tolerance for such behavior). Similarly, an eight-year-old child who had daily tantrums in the classroom would disrupt the setting enough to be considered a problem. Thus, a child's behavior is deemed a problem when it violates assumed, or at times,

explicit normative criteria for age, rate and setting appropriateness. Once such violations are perceived, referral for professional assistance takes place after supervisory adults have failed to alter the problem behavior. These dimensions will have further implications for the identification and treatment of problem children. Increasing the complexity of defining problem behavior also interacts with determining the onset and prognosis of behavior problems. Keeping this in mind, a more detailed description of the problem areas outlined in the introduction can be undertaken.

The appearance of problem behavior can occur at any point as a child develops. However, because of varying stability of behavior patterns, the occurrence of troublesome behavior at specific ages has different prognostic value. The onset and stability of behavior problems has been investigated in a longitudinal study by Gersten, Langner, Eisenburg, Simcha-Fagan, and McCarthy (1976). These investigators sampled groups of children between the ages of six and 18 and examined occurrences of psychological pathology. They re-examined the children five years later. Three types of conduct problems were identified that were predictive of continued deviance. These were intrafamilial aggression, peer-directed aggression (fighting), and delinquency. Gersten et al. reported that patterns of intrafamilial aggression developed before age six and were predictive of family conflict until the child left the home. Peer-directed aggression also developed early in childhood and was predictive of aggressive behavior through adolescence into adulthood. Delinquent behavior was unstable until age ten. At this point, it was increasingly predictive of adult antisocial behavior until age 14, where its prognostic value peaked. As Gersten et al. pointed out, these findings are important for both the understanding and the treatment of problem behavior. Treatment of intrafamilial or peer-directed aggression would be warranted at any point these behaviors appeared because of their early onset and stability. However, treatment of delinquent patterns would not be effective until the child was beyond ten years of age. Since the behavior pattern is unstable prior to this age, treatment effects would be undistinguishable from spontaneous remission of symptoms. In addition, early treatment would not necessarily be expected to affect patterns of behavior that developed later in life. *Control problems* in young children, *aggressive behavior*, and *delinquent behavior* as described in this chapter have approximate correspondence to the Gersten et al. (1976) categories.

Control problems. These problems in young children refer to a group of behaviors that indicate that parents are ineffective in controlling the child: in fact, it is usually the case that the child effectively controls the parents. Typical referral complaints from parents include excessive crying, complaining, temper tantrums, overactivity, disobedience, and enuresis. These behaviors usually appear as problems after the age of three. Up to that point, less appropriate social interaction is expected of the child and many of these behaviors are perceived as permissable. The use of these behaviors at later ages reflects a general immaturity in social interaction. The immediate effect on the family of an out-of-control child is the disrupting and aggravating influence the child has on normal family activities. Usually the parents' ineffectual attempts at control leave them frustrated, angry, and emotionally drained. If the problem is severe enough, the child begins to restrict family activities outside the home because of the inability to control the child in public situations. Recognition of the troublesome nature and inappropriateness of the behavior leads parents to seek professional advice. Under these circumstances, the concern and motivation of the parents create a receptive atmosphere for introducing techniques for altering problem behavior.

Parents do not always perceive such child behavior patterns as indicating abnormal adjustment. Even though the family is experiencing the adverse effects of a control problem child, parents may still take the view that the child will "grow out of it" and tolerate the behavior in the interim. Additional negative effects may accrue in these cases. As these children grow

and interact within the wider community, they are more likely to be identified as out of control by other supervisory adults (such as school personnel and neighbors. The parents of the problem child must then begin to deal with complaints concerning their child's behavior from these sources. These complaints may be received as constructive feedback or as unjust criticism. Eventual treatment of the child can be affected by whether the parents think help is necessary or if help is being forced upon them by community influences.

Aggressive behavior problems. These problems refer to active and excessive physical or verbal assault by the child. Typical referral complaints include fighting, threats, defiance of authority, and frequent arguing. These behaviors are usually noticed about age four to six in peer and adult interactions.

The immediate adverse effects of an aggressive child are again the disruption of the setting and the potential of harm from physical encounters. The child's excessive use of aggressive means of interaction many times results in failure to be socialized into an appropriate peer group. These children, quickly labeled troublemakers by peers and community adults, accrue fewer opportunities for experiencing the positive socializing influences of such groups.

As with control problem children, aggressive children are referred for treatment by their parents or community agencies. However, referral is more likely to be initiated from community sources. This is because these children typically engage in problem behavior outside the home. As will be discussed later, the parents of these children also tend to engage in high rates of aggressive behavior (e.g., Patterson, 1975) and are less prone to view the child's behavior as abnormal. The long-term prognosis for these children is not favorable. The development of an aggressive pattern of interaction is likely to continue into adulthood (Gersten et al., 1976), and may result in poorly socialized, problem-beleaguered individuals (Robins, 1966).

Delinquent behavior. This category refers to problem behaviors such as school truancy, running away, drug and alcohol abuse, sexual misconduct, theft, vandalism, assault, and additional criminal actions. These behaviors are most likely to occur when the child is between 10 and 18 years of age. Many times they are preceded by child histories of poor school performance, inadequate parental control, and inordinate unsupervised time away from home (West and Farrington, 1975). Peer group influence for these children involves other children of similar circumstance, immersing them further within a deviant peer subculture (Cohen, 1955). Both the type of activity engaged in and the increasing age of the child indicate that the problem behavior occurs outside the home to a greater extent than in the previous categories. This results in the delinquent child's identification as such by an increasing network of community adults (e.g., neighbors, teachers, storekeepers, police). This network, in turn, constitutes an additional influence on the child and family. The family must contend with the child's problem actions as well as with complaints and accusations from community sources. Since families of delinquent children are characteristically disrupted and involved in multiple-problem situations, such as marital conflict and unemployment (see Glueck and Glueck, 1968; Robins, 1966), the additional aversive input from community complaints places the parents in a position of coping with an additional problem when they are already overburdened with crises. These families, under duress from school or juvenile authorities, commonly seek professional help.

The prognosis for normative adjustment of delinquent children is poor. Several studies have demonstrated higher incidence of criminal acts, institutionalization, and impoverished social relationships in the adult lives of former delinquents (McCord, 1978; Robins, 1966; West and Farrington, 1977). This is especially true in cases where the child began engaging in delinquent activity at an early age (i.e., nine to twelve) and acquired a history of a variety of offenses throughout adolescence (Polk, 1967; Robins, 1966; West and Farrington, 1975).

Summary

Behavior problems in children constitute a prevalent class of disorders that have been shown to precipitate severe social maladjustment in late adolescence and adulthood. The severity of the later maladjustment can be related to the severity and type of early problem behavior. Here I will describe three categories of problem behavior that correspond to increasing age of the child and decreasing likelihood for favorable adult outcomes. These categories are: control problems in the home, aggressive behavior problems, and delinquent activity. These are not exclusionary or comprehensive categories (e.g., delinquent children are many times also aggressive; children who are control problems may also steal). Instead, they constitute three primary areas of frequent referral in which the problem behaviors have demonstrated stability and the potential for future adverse consequences.

It has been shown that *control problems* in young children are indicative of continued family conflict (Gersten et al., 1976). However, this restricted category of problem behavior does not necessarily indicate continued maladjustment. The problem may be confined to aversive modes of family interaction that are alleviated once the child leaves the home. Patterns of *aggressive behavior* are stable (Gersten et al., 1976) and linked to adult maladjustment (Morris et al., 1956; Robins, 1966). This range of problem behaviors is evidenced in the home and in peer and adult interactions outside the home. An aggressive style of interaction, developed across major environmental settings, increases the likelihood that the child will develop into a hostile, socially unskilled adult. The strongest evidence for severe adult maladjustment comes from the study of *delinquency*. Adult problems of this group include criminal activity, psychiatric disorders, unstable marital and friendship relations, and frequent unemployment (e.g., Robins, 1966; West and Farrington, 1977). This bleak adult outcome is especially prevalent among those having histories of varied, multiple offenses that began at an early age (e.g., Polk, 1967; Robins, 1966). The delinquent pattern of behavior is ubiquitous to all settings and promotes the youth's association with deviant socializing influences.

SOCIAL LEARNING PERSPECTIVE

A social learning perspective of behavior acquisition postulates that individual behavior patterns are acquired through learning processes that take place in the natural environment. This perspective was derived from an impetus in the early 1960s to apply the burgeoning wealth of learning principles to the development of human behavior, particularly abnormal child behavior. In this aspect, it represented an outstanding example of the application of basic laboratory research findings to applied issues in human psychology. The last two decades have witnessed a rapid expansion of these applications, and "social learning" has taken on wide usage and varied meaning. For this reason, it will be beneficial to review briefly the origins and theoretical underpinnings of social learning perspectives and to delineate their meaning.

The earliest consistent use of the term "social learning" (perhaps its origin) comes from the work of Bandura and his associates (Bandura, 1962, 1965; Bandura and McDonald, 1963; Bandura, Ross, and Ross, 1961, 1962; Bandura and Walters, 1963). Much of the research of these investigators focused upon the effects of modeling and imitation on behavior development in young children. They demonstrated increases in aggressive behavior among children who had viewed aggressive models (see, Bandura, Ross, and Ross, 1961, 1962), and modeling effects on moral judgments (Bandura and McDonald, 1963), cognitive processes (Bandura, Adams, and Beyer, 1971), and self-reinforcement (Bandura and Whalen, 1966). Although he described the effects of other principles of learning, Bandura became a major spokesman for the importance of modeling and imitation on the development of behavior repertoires and developed a comprehensive theory of behavior acquisition based on these principles (Bandura, 1962, 1971, 1973, 1977; Bandura and Walters, 1963). Bandura's social learning theory postulates that modeling and imitation are the primary mechanisms through which behavior is acquired. Reinforcement and punishment are of secondary value in developing new

behavior, but may determine the stability and generalizability of behaviors that are acquired through imitation (Bandura, 1977). Social learning theory does not postulate a static process by which the environment shapes behavior. Instead, it describes a dynamic interactional process in which individual behavior and environmental influences are altered in a reciprocal fashion (Bandura, 1962, 1971, 1977). In accounting for human behavior, both overt, observable actions and covert, internal events (such as selfreinforcement) play important roles. Thus, "social learning theory approaches the explanation of human behavior in terms of a continuous reciprocal interaction between cognitive, behavioral, and environmental determinants." (Bandura, 1977, p. vii)

A second area of major influence on social learning perspectives of behavior comes from the more operantly oriented direction that currently fits the rubric of applied behavior analysis. Bijou and Baer (1961, 1965) and their associates and students (Allen et al., 1964; Birnbauer et al., 1965; Wahler et al., 1965; Wolf, Risley, and Mees, 1964) were among the first to apply operant conditioning principles empirically to the study and treatment of child behavior. This group was instrumental in translating operant principles such as reinforcement, punishment, and extinction into applied behavior change techniques such as token economies, time-out from social reinforcement, and differential attention. The early case studies provided convincing, and at times dramatic evidence (see, Wolf, Risley, and Mees, 1964) of the efficacy of these techniques in altering problem behavior. Although most of this work was oriented toward innovation and demonstration of behavioral intervention strategies (Allen et al., 1964; Birnbauer et al., 1965; Wahler et al., 1965), the applied behavioral approach was also integrated into an operant learning theory of behavior development (Bijou and Baer, 1961, 1965).

The major difference in the applied behavior analysis approach and the social learning approach of Bandura is one of emphasis—as opposed to theoretical underpinnings. Both emphasize the importance of behavioral principles in the development and acquisition of behavior. Of primary concern to the applied behavioral approach are traditional operant arrangements of reinforcement and punishment, indicating the emphasis on external contingencies in shaping behavior. Social learning theory (Bandura, 1977) places primary reliance on vicarious learning from modeling and imitation, resulting in an emphasis on internal mediator such as cognitive processes and self-reinforcement. Both of these approaches have had major impact on the course of behavioral psychology and have provided an impetus for new directions and innovative techniques in changing and understanding behavior. They also share common shortcomings that lead to the perspective of social learning presented here.

Studies demonstrating that behavioral techniques can alter, eliminate, or build in behaviors illustrate the power of these procedures to produce behavior change. They do not demonstrate that behavior patterns are caused by such arrangements. The fact that young children act significantly more aggressive after viewing an aggressive model does not necessarily mean that problem levels of aggression stem from a history of inappropriate models. Similarly, the fact that direct manipulation of reinforcement contingencies can change the rate or configuration of problem behaviors does not mean that the behavior originated from mismanagement of contingencies. As related by Willems (1973):

The potential error lies in building a model of behavior on the basis of what works in treatment, or inferring causes from effectiveness of treatment. . . . It is entirely possible that there are fundamental differences between the conditions under which an organism comes to behave in a certain way and the conditions under which he can be *made* to behave in that way or another way. (p. 100.)

Willems (1973, 1977) argues that comprehensive understanding of human behavior will only come from comprehensive investigation of behavior within natural contexts. This requires systematic observation of individuals interacting across multiple settings and conditions. In addition, it would entail comparative analysis of normative and problem populations to demonstrate the differentiating characteristics of various styles of interaction. The accumulation of data on this level would delineate potential cause and effect relationships that could be tested via longitudinal and field-experimental research designs. Through these methods, the role of modeling and contingency arrangements could be tested within the complexity of the natural environment.

The complexity of potential environmental influences comprises a second problem area for simplistically oriented learning theories. The primary emphasis of previous social learning approaches was on dyadic interaction, either in the form of contingency arrangements or modeling experiences, for establishing patterns of behavior. Most environmental settings provide a bombardment of experiential opportunities that fluctuate from day to day along multiple dimensions (e.g., number of interactants, changes in rate and consistency of behavior, different modeling agents). Even within the presumably stable environment of a normal family, fluctuations in setting demand characteristics can require dramatic changes in the response patterns of children. The fluctuations can be as simple as changes in family composition due to the presence or absence of the father, or more severe changes due to the occurrence of high stress levels resulting from acute family crisis (e.g., marital dispute, sudden illness). In addition, the events precipitating emotional and behavioral changes in family members can stem from external influences impinging on the family (unemployment, school problems, harassment from neighbors, and so forth). The sources of influence that can produce daily change in family members are diverse and numerous. In this chapter, the family is viewed as an interactive social system in which the behavior of each individual reflects interdependencies that shape the behavior of the group. In turn, each family member is also influenced by community, school, or work-related systems in which they interact. A developing child is confronted by a continuous array of demand characteristics to which appropriate responses must be learned. This perspective of environmental complexity does not negate the importance of modeling and reinforcement principles of behavior acquisition. However, it does strain simplistic conceptualizations that have tended to accompany such explanations.

The social learning perspective presented here retains the primary importance of learning experiences in behavior acquisition. It is less tied to specific theoretical frameworks and more dependent upon naturalistic investigation of learning processes than previous approaches. In addition, the concept of environmental influences on behavior is expanded. The family remains the primary socializing influence on child development—other socializing influences, such as peer groups and community agencies, providing secondary direct influence on the child. Environmental influences that affect the family system provide indirect influence on child behavior and are also considered. The discussion of these influences on child behavior relies on data from naturalistic observations of families in the home setting and on sociological factors that relate to problem behavior.

FAMILY INFLUENCES ON PROBLEM BEHAVIOR DEVELOPMENT

A social learning perspective of behavior development primarily emphasises the socializing influences of the family. It is assumed that identifiable styles of social attention and interaction (and general childrearing practices) can be shown to relate to patterns of child behavior. Given this assumption, it is reasonable to study families with and without problems to determine the behavior differences that occur within the home environment. These differences can then be studied in more detail to determine the variables that function to produce or maintain problem behavior. Recent interest in examining the dysfunctional aspects of family interaction has led several groups of investigators to develop complex behavior coding systems in order to obtain objective observation data from families (see, Bernal and North, 1977; Patterson, Ray, Shaw, and Cobb, 1969; Reid,

1978; Wahler, House, and Stambaugh, 1976). Data collected using these systems will serve as the basis for describing causal attributes of problem behaviors.

Control Problem Children

Several studies have investigated behavior differences in families having young control problem children and families with matched nonproblem children (Delfini, Bernal, and Rosen, 1976; Forehand et al., 1975; Lobitz and Johnson, 1975; Moore, 1975; Patterson, 1976). These studies demonstrated that the identified problem children engaged in more disruptive, annoying, and noncompliant behavior and, in most cases, in less appropriate social behavior than nonproblem comparison children. They also reported that parents of problem children were more negative and issued more commands than parents of nonproblem children. The studies by Delfini et al. (1976), Forehand et al. (1975), and Lobitz and Johnson (1975) reported that parents of the problem children perceived them as being more abnormal than other children. In these studies, the parents had sought help at a child clinic and thus their perceptions of abnormality would be expected. However, as pointed out by Lobitz and Johnson (1975), the problem and nonproblem children exhibited tremendous overlap in the distribution of problem behavior. Thus, some problem children engaged in less problem behavior than their nonproblem peers and vice versa. Because of this, Lobitz and Johnson (1975) described two types of child referral problems: (1) those in which the children exhibited problem levels of inappropriate behavior, and (2) those in which the parents perceived the child as being a problem, but the child's behavior could not be differentiated from normal children. The second group presents an interesting clinical problem that is not within the scope of this discussion. Of additional interest, however, is the differentiation of a third group of parents; those who perceive their child as normal, when the child has been identified through other sources as engaging in problem levels of inappropriate behavior.

The study by Moore (1975) compared

problem and nonproblem children who were referred by their school teachers. With one exception, the parents of the referred children did not consider them problems in the home. Observations were obtained in both home and school settings, and teachers and parents rated the child daily on overall behavior and recorded the occurrence of low-rate problem behaviors (e.g., fighting, lying, and stealing). School observations showed that the referred children were more oppositional to rules and instructions, engaging in less schoolwork and other appropriate behaviors than the nonreferred children. The teachers rated the referred children more negatively and also reported more problem incidents for this group. In contrast, the home observations did not differentiate groups along obedience dimensions. However, the referred children had significantly lower rates of sustained activity (toy play, work, and so forth) and higher rates of seeking adult attention. Parents of referred children interacted with their children more frequently and were more likely to use aversive styles when interacting. These parents reported much higher rates of problem incidents, but did not rate their children more negatively than parents of nonreferred children. This finding showed that parents were aware of problem episodes, but did not view them as signs of maladjustment. Presumably, such parents would have to witness a wider variety and/or higher rate of deviant actions before seeking assistance.

These studies demonstrated basic differences in the behavior of both control problem children and their parents when compared to nonproblem families. This implies that the mechanisms responsible for problem behavior are interactive in that they reflect dysfunctional processes involving both the child and other family members. Although these comparative studies describe differences, they do not elucidate how such differences develop. More detailed investigation of family interaction is required to determine the functional nature of these patterns of behavior.

During the past 10 years, the work of Patterson and his associates (Patterson, 1973, 1974, 1976, 1979, 1980; Patterson and Cobb, 1971, 1973; Patterson, Littman, and Bricker, 1967; Patterson and Reid, 1970) has been oriented toward investigating the acquisition of problem behavior in children. The main focus of this research has been the relationship of family interaction to problem behavior. Through this line of investigation, Patterson (1976, 1979, 1980; Patterson and Reid, 1970) has developed a theory of coercive interaction in problem families. Coercion theory, based on principles of social learning, postulates that deviant child behavior is the result of inappropriate and inconsistent contingencies applied to child behavior by parents. Within a framework of inconsistency the child learns that the most advantageous method for producing predictable patterns in the environment is to use aversive behaviors to alter the behavior of others. The process of acquiring stable patterns of this type is interactive, since it requires identifiable patterns of behavior on the part of the coercive child and other family members. Patterson has described coercive processes in detail (1976, 1979, 1980). The following description is based on these writings.

OVERVIEW OF COERCION THEORY

"Coercion" indicates that a desired behavioral outcome is achieved through subtle, or at times, forceful aversive manipulation of another individual. Young, nonverbal children commonly use aversive techniques such as crying, demanding, and tantrums to achieve desired outcomes. These behaviors function adequately for such children in bringing their distress to the attention of adults. Although these behaviors are not viewed with alarm in very young children, they represent problem symptoms if they continue in excess much beyond three or four years of age. At about this age social expectations of child behavior require more appropriate verbal methods of communicating. It is assumed that at this age skilled parents start to use consistently methods of punishment and reinforcement to alter their child's behavior to conform to more socially acceptable methods. These skilled parents would also be considered appropriate models for their developing child.

Parents having less skill or those with inappropriate skills or expectations of child behavior proceed in a different manner. Coercion theory postulates that unskilled parents permit coercive child behavior to continue beyond the acceptable age range, or that they intervene only erratically and inconsistently in attempting to change the child. The child's continued use of aversive behaviors within the erratic system would still provide a high percentage of desired outcomes for the child, even though it occasionally resulted in punitive consequences. Thus, the original utility of the aversive patterns of behavior changes from an appropriate functional arrangement to a perseverating response pattern that prevails in the presence of inconsistent or, more appropriately, noncontingent application of consequences. Studies have demonstrated that children experiencing noncontingent consequences for behavior tend not to alter their behavior in situations where consequences are contingently applied (Cairns and Paris, 1971; Warren and Cairns, 1972). Thus, children who have established aversive patterns at this stage are engaging in problem behavior that would be resistant to change by a simple rearrangement of parental consequences.

Although these initial behavior patterns are resistant to change because of their noncontingent reinforcement history, coercion theory postulates additional maintenance effects that derive from contingent arrangements. These are illustrated in the scenario in Figure 1. Here a mother instructs the child to stop an activity. The child ignores the command. The mother repeats the command more sternly, and the child ignores the command again. The mother then confronts the child and yells. At this point, the child yells and cries in response. The mother finally tells the child to stop crying and leaves, after which, the child continues in the activities. In this example, the mother has set up an aversive encounter with the child. By time frame-two, she is displaying irritation, and by time-frame three, anger. The child's response at this point increases the aversiveness of the encounter and sidetracks the intent of the original command. The mother issues a weak command and leaves the situation, thereby escaping the aversive qualities of the encounter. Both the mother and the child were reinforced via a negative reinforcement paradigm. By leaving and giving in to the child the mother removed the noxious qualities of the scene she created. By responding in an aversive manner, the child succeeded in removing the aversive demands of the mother. A second potential ending compounds the reinforcement arrangement for the participants. The mother could have told the child to stop crying and then attended to or comforted the child. The mother and child would have been reinforced for removing the

Figure 1
Coercive Interaction/Reinforcement Trap

aversiveness of this situation and for receiving social affiliative interaction. Thus both negative and positive elements of reinforcement would have been present.

Two main effects stem from this encounter—an immediate effect and a long-term effect. The immediate effect was the end to the aversive situation and its concomitant reinforcing qualities. The long-term effect, however, was an increase in the likelihood of similar response patterns in the future, assuring the continuation of coercive methods. Patterson (1976, 1979) referred to this common family interaction paradigm as a "reinforcement trap," easy to fall into, but difficult to escape from. The reinforcement trap paradigm is the foundation for a spiraling escalation of coercive interaction.

Other tenets of coercion theory become evident as the family system grows more dysfunctional. The reciprocal use of aversive behaviors among family members has been shown to be much higher for problem than nonproblem families (Patterson, 1976). This results in, or is the result of, the increased use of aversive behaviors to end aversive interactions and to coerce attention. The reciprocal use of aversive modes of interaction presents the problem of ending an interaction once it is initiated. Given that one member of an interaction does not readily acquiesce, the conflict should continue until one member stops behaving aversively. Coercion theory postulates that successful termination of an extended aversive interaction would result from the use of behaviors having more intense or severe aversive qualities. The individual who is successful in bringing the interaction to an end is reinforced for having escalated the aversive attack. Thus, the system is characterized by the development of "more and better" coercive behaviors. As this process develops, the family system becomes locked into a continuous cycle of aversive interaction. The emphasis on aversive behavior and negative contingencies results in diminishing or eliminating the effectiveness of positive control techniques. In essence, positive reinforcement is unnecessary due to the success of coercive techniques. Thus, coercion theory predicts that a disrupted family system would

be unaffected by positive behavior change strategies. They should also be resistant to alternative intervention methods (e.g., punishment and reinforcement) because of the early history of noncontingent, or at least erratic, reinforcement schedules.

The demonstration of coercive processes in families requires the identification of several key components in problem family interaction. First, families with behavior problem children should provide erratic, unpredictable contingencies for their child's behavior. Within this context, the identification of reinforcement paradigms (negative or positive) should focus on aversive interactions. Extended aversive exchanges should be characterized by increases in the intensity or aversive qualities of the behaviors. Finally, given a fully disrupted system, all family members should use aversive modes of interaction.

Coercion Research

Research at the Oregon Social Learning Center has been directed toward investigating the coercive dimensions of family interaction. Consistent with previously reported research (see, Lobitz and Johnson, 1975; Moore, 1975), Patterson (1976) reported that problem families engaged in higher rates of aversive behaviors than nonproblem families. This finding was true of all family members except the fathers. Patterson also reported differences in the sequential arrangement of these behaviors. The parents of problem children were more likely than parents of nonproblem children to respond negatively to positive child behavior or positively to negative child behavior. This finding supports the contention that parents of problem children provide unpredictable or inconsistent consequences for child behavior. Patterson (1976) also showed that both problem and nonproblem children were more likely to engage in aversive behavior when responding to aversive intrusions from other family members than at other times. However, the probability for problem children was three times as great as for non-problem children. Continued examination of this sequence (i.e., parent aversive behavior followed by child aversive behavior) showed that in problem families the child's aversive response was more likely to end the aversive behavior of the parent than was true of similar encounters in nonproblem families. This demonstrated a possible advantage for the use of aversive behavior, and indicated that some children may learn aversive modes of responding to terminate the aversiveness of others.

Further investigation of aversive interaction by Patterson and Cobb (1971) showed that specific aversive parent behaviors were effective in suppressing ongoing prosocial behavior of the child. This indicated that the parental behaviors were effective punishers. When these same parental behaviors were engaged in as responses to child aversive behaviors, a different effect was found. In nonproblem families the parent behavior was, again, successful in suppressing the child behavior. However, in problem families the presentation of an aversive behavior from the parents produced an increased likelihood that the child would continue responding in an aversive manner. This phenomenon (the continuation of aversive behavior given aversive input from others) has been labeled "punishment/acceleration" by Patterson (1976), and has been replicated by Kopfstein (1972). The punishment/acceleration paradigm is closely tied to negative reinforcement and increasing levels of aversiveness. Once punishment/acceleration becomes an established pattern, aversive exchanges extend for longer periods. Unlike the simple negative reinforcement paradigm presented earlier (i.e., parent aversive   child aversive   parent withdrawal), the extended exchanges are conceptualized as a unit or chain in which the reinforcing event is the final outcome. Thus, an actual sequence may contain several exchanges of aversive behavior (e.g., parent aversive   child aversive   parent aversive   child aversive   parent aversive   child aversive   parent withdrawal) and may last for longer time periods (30 seconds to several minutes). Both participants are reinforced by terminating the encounter. However, one individual is reinforced by withdrawing participation while the other individual is reinforced for continuing

aversiveness. In disrupted families it is assumed that the child is reinforced for continuing and develops patterns of interaction that manipulate the outcome of aversive interaction.

Chains of aversive interaction have been studied sequentially to determine if these patterns or "strategies" of behavior could be identified. Moore and Patterson (1977) found that a young behavior problem child engaged in statistically reliable sequences of aversive behavior during coercive interactions with her mother. While the mother responded with high rates of aversive behaviors, her response sequences were diffuse and not statistically reliable. It appeared that the child coerced attention, then if the attention was aversive in nature, she employed a strategy that effectively removed the mother's participation. More detailed analysis of the aversive sequences supported this supposition (Patterson and Moore, 1979). For this analysis the interactions were divided into short (one or two child aversive behaviors) and long (three or more child aversive behaviors) aversive sequences. The short sequences significantly increased the probability that the mother would interact with the child in a nonaversive manner. The long sequences resulted when the mother responded aversively. In these cases the child continued to respond aversively, significantly increasing the probability of a positive outcome (mother either withdrawing from interaction or becoming prosocial). This same strategy held for sequences that were initiated by aversive behavior from the mother. A higher proportion of these aversive interactions tended to be long sequences, but the child still increased the probability of a positive outcome by continuing to respond aversively.

Data presented in the above section lend support to the basic tenets of coercive processes in families. Problem families can be identified by their high rates of aversive interaction, by the erratic, noncontingent use of prosocial and aversive attention, and by the tendency to escalate aversiveness in punishing situations. Coercion studies are also beginning to trace interactive family processes that are responsible for the development of inappropriate behavior patterns in children. In problem families the child is immersed in an inconsistent aversive system that would be difficult to arrange coherently. On an immediate level, however, the child learns that a potential advantage comes from the use of aversive behavior. As aversive patterns become established, they predominate in interactions and diminish the use of more prosocial methods. Thus, the family becomes tied to a vicious cycle of inappropriate, aversive styles of communication. At this stage the aversive behaviors acquire different functions in problem and nonproblem families. Problem families use aversive behavior to coerce from others the normal products of social interaction: attention, rewards, and removal of noxious behavior. Nonproblem families achieve the same ends through more socially accepted methods of interaction. Aversive interaction certainly occurs in nonproblem families (as does prosocial interaction in problem families), but more often it fails to achieve desired outcomes.

This depiction of coercive processes has direct relevance for the development of control problem children. Much of the data collected to examine and demonstrate coercion in families was from this problem group. The early age of onset of control problems (three to six years) is indicative of an early failure to use consistent, structured methods for socializing the child. As the child develops in this environment, the phenomena of escalating aversiveness characterize the family. Through this mode of interaction the child learns successfully to manipulate the environment via aversive techniques. Modeling influences are also evident in conduct problem families. As stated above, mothers of conduct problem children engaged in high rates of aversive behaviors (Patterson, 1976). They typically issued excessive commands and disapproving statements to their children but would fail to enforce their demands. Thus, these mothers engaged in high rates of aversiveness, but were ineffective in controlling child behavior (Patterson, 1980). Control problem children emulate the aversive characteristics of these behaviors, but appear to be more effective than the mothers in obtaining positive outcomes

(see Patterson and Moore, 1979).

Aggressive Behavior Problems

Aggressive behavior problems as described in this chapter are viewed as a more severe level of disturbance than control problems. This is because of the higher potential for immediate adverse consequences (e.g., from fighting), and the higher probability of adverse adult adjustment (Gersten et al., 1976; Robins, 1966). The influence of family interactive processes on the development of aggressive behavior problems can still be viewed within the framework of coercion and modeling principles. However, studies have generally not differentiated control problem children from aggressive children. An implicit reason for this is that control problem behaviors have been assumed to develop into aggressive behavior problems. If this were the case, then any differentiation would artificially delineate two stages of a continuous process. Although few appropriate data are available to document continuous or separate developmental tracks, several points of information tend to support the idea of different tracks. The longitudinal study by Gersten et al. (1976) differentiated intrafamilial conflict from peer-directed aggression. These behavior problems had similar ages of onset, countering a position that aggressive behavior progresses from family-oriented conflict. In addition, aggressive behavior problems were diagnostic of adult aggressiveness, whereas intrafamilial conflict was diagnostic of problem behavior only as long as the child remained within the family.

Cross-sectional studies of peer-directed aggression have failed to demonstrate consistent age changes in aggressive behavior (e.g., Feshbach, 1970). While some studies reported increases in aggressive behavior with age (Walters, Pearce, and Dahms, 1957), others have reported decreases (Hartup, 1974; Jersild and Mankey, 1935) or no difference (Ammons and Ammons, 1953; McKee and Leader, 1953). Feshbach (1970) concluded that the most consistent finding was that verbal aggression tended to increase with age. Hartup's (1974) study confirmed this conclusion and indicated that the increased propensity to use verbal aggression was accompanied by a decreased likelihood to use physical aggression. These data imply that aggressive behavior, at best, does not demonstrate a systematic progression with increasing age. However, these studies investigated aggressive behavior in normal children. The development of aggression in deviant children might well progress in a systematic fashion.

A recent study investigated cross-sectional changes in rate and type of aversive behaviors exhibited by problem children (Mukai, 1979). The children in this study ranged in age from 3 to 13 and were largely referred for control problem behavior in home and school settings. The observed child behaviors were combined to reflect physical aggression (e.g., hitting, destroying), verbal aggression (e.g., commands, yelling, humiliating), and passive aggression (e.g., crying, whining). Both physical aggression and passive aggression obtained significant negative correlations with age, indicating decreasing use of these behaviors with increasing age. Verbal aggression obtained zero order correlations, indicating relatively stable use of these behaviors across ages. These findings were congruent with previous research (see Hartup, 1974) and failed to support progressive increases in deviancy for a problem population.

None of these studies provided the appropriate long-term longitudinal design to test developmental processes adequately. However, lack of data supporting a simple progression of deviancy suggests additional complexity in the development of aggressive behavior. Such complexity does not necessarily require new theoretical perspectives for each new problem. Instead, it is more reasonable to apply current knowledge in alternative ways. Aggressive behavior unquestionably constitutes a direct form of coercing desired outcomes from the environment. Therefore, the coercive processes (Patterson, 1976) described for control problem children (e.g., inconsistent parent behavior, negative reinforcement) can be applied to problems of aggression in children. Given that these problem types are different, then differ-

ences in family interaction can be postulated to account for child behavior differences. A potential differentiating factor is the parental role model. An early factor related to problem child behavior has been shown to be inconsistent, erratic parental consequences for child behavior. Parents can exhibit these poor child management skills without necessarily modeling aggressive modes of interaction. A child responding to this environment could easily resort to immature, nagging interactions (e.g., complaining, whining) to coerce more consistent responses from family members. In other instances, parents might couple poor child management skills with active modeling and endorsement of aggressive behavior (e.g., during marital conflicts or parent-child interactions). A child from this environment would gravitate toward coercive techniques of manipulating interactions but, in addition, would have learned an aggressive repertoire of behaviors. This situation provides parental models and learning experiences that portray aggression as an "appropriate" interactive style. Coercive processes again provide the short-term rewards that attach functional qualities to the use of learned aggressive behavior.

Both types of problem children have in common the early absence of environmental structure that results from poor child management. The adverse effects on child behavior of this environment would be expected to occur similarly across families. This explains the similar age of onset for control problems and aggressive problems reported by Gersten et al. (1975). Differences in the response topography for behaviors stem from specific aspects of behaviors modeled and promoted in the home. Thus, the direct modeling and implicit acceptance of aggressive styles of interaction within the family would differentiate aggressive problem children from control problem children. Acceptance of aggressive behavior as normative would also carry implications for parental perceptions of child deviance. If a child was exhibiting behaviors common to all members of the family, then the parents would be less likely to perceive the behavior as a problem than if the child were exhibiting unusual behavior patterns. This, in turn, means that the parents would not attempt to alter the child's behavior. This perspective generates an additional difference between control problem and aggressive children that increases the risk of continued maladjustment for the aggressive child. A control problem child is likely to be identified by the parents as being a problem child. By seeking help for the child's problem behaviors, such parents are demonstrating a knowledge of appropriate child behavior and the motivation to alter current patterns. The combination of early intervention and concerned, knowledgeable parents would predicate a more positive outcome. Conversely, parents who actively modeled problem levels of aggressive behavior would be unlikely to express concern about similar behaviors in their children. A child would engage in learned "appropriate" (aggressive) behavior outside the home where he or she would eventually be identified as a problem by school or community adults. In this case, the parents might seek assistance for their "problem" child partially as the result of community pressure. The aggressive child would have engaged in maladaptive behavior for a longer period of time—across multiple settings. The parents would be motivated to change the child's behavior only to the extent that it alleviated aversive input from the community. This combination of events produces a poorer prognosis for changing the aggressive child than for the control problem child. To some extent, the interaction of such variables may account for the continuance of aggressive behavior patterns into adulthood.

Delinquent Behavior Problems

Delinquent behavior constitutes the most prevalent type of deviant activity for children aged 10 to 18. The occurrence of delinquent behavior per se is common among most children. This is because the "delinquent" label is used for events indicating behavioral status, such as truant, runaway, incorrigible, as well as criminal activity that ranges from petty shoplifting to vandalism to armed theft or assault. As with the previous categories of problem behavior, "de-

linquent" will refer to children who persistently engage in these behaviors and are identified as problems by adults in the community (parents, teachers, police).

The incidence of identified delinquency is usually reported to be approximately 20 percent of the adolescent population (see West and Farrington, 1975; Polk, 1975). Of those children, 45 to 55 percent will commit only one delinquent offense (Collard, 1967; Polk, 1975; Wolfgang, Figlio, and Sellin, 1972). This group of one-time offenders is usually not considered to be a problem population. Instead, the problem population of delinquent children consists of the chronic offenders. Wolfgang, Figlio, and Sellin (1972) defined their chronic group as children with five or more police-identified offenses. This group comprised 6.3 percent of their total sample, but accounted for over 50 percent of all offenses. Multiple-offending adolescents not only account for the majority of delinquent activities, but are also the children most at risk for adult criminality and maladjustment (see Polk, 1975; Robins, 1966). Chronic delinquency is viewed as the most severe and intractable form of childhood behavior maladjustment.

As with control and aggressive problems, few efforts have been made to differentiate delinquent behavior from aggressive behavior. Most studies subsume aggression under delinquency and use these terms interchangeably (see Robins, 1966). Although an intuitive perspective of delinquent children portrays them as aggressive, a developmental perspective may indicate that these behavior problems result from different environmental influences, even though the identifiable characteristics overlap in many children. The Gersten et al. (1976) study indicated separate ages of onset and prognosis for aggression and delinquency. A recent study by Moore, Chamberlain, and Mukai (1979) provided further support for separating these problem types. This study compared the follow-up rates of court-recorded offenses of children who had originally been seen for treatment two to nine years earlier. The children comprised three groups. Those seen for aggression or control problems, those seen for problems with stealing, and a normative comparison sample. At follow-up, all children were over 14 years of age and had been out of treatment for a minimum of two years. Seventy-seven percent of the children originally seen for stealing problems had recorded serious offenses and 67 percent were chronic offenders. Only 13 percent of the sample of aggressive children had court records; a figure slightly lower than the normative comparison groups' rate of 21 percent. Interestingly, a combination of both referral problems did not alter the offense rate. Some of the children who stole showed rates of aversive behavior that also classified them as social aggressors. Conversely, some of the children referred for aggressive behavior later stole. Both of these subgroups encountered high official offense rates, but the addition of aggressive behavior to stealing events did not account for greater variance in court contact than stealing alone. These data were interpreted as indicating that young aggressive children were not at risk for officially identified adolescent delinquency. Rather, it was the child that engaged in more covert asocial actions, such as theft, who encountered a high probability of becoming an official delinquent.

Family variables related to the emergence of delinquent behavior patterns show both similarity to and divergence from family variables discussed previously. Although few studies have directly observed delinquent family interaction, sociological research has investigated family influences for half a century. As early as 1925, the consistency and method of parental discipline was shown to relate to delinquent behavior. Burt (1925) reported that parents of delinquents were characterized by inconsistent, lax, or overly strict disciplinary patterns. The widely-cited study by Glueck and Glueck (1950) provided more detailed analysis of parental discipline. They reported that an increased probability of delinquency was associated with erratic or overly strict paternal discipline, and erratic or lax maternal discipline. In all cases, physical disciplinary practices were associated with increased delinquency.

The most detailed investigation of parent variables comes from the McCord and McCord (1959) reanalysis of data from the Cambridge-Somerville Youth Study (Powers and Witmer, 1951). The Cambridge-Somerville Study was a large scale delinquency treatment and prevention program that collected extensive information on several hundred high-risk boys and their families between 1939 and 1945. McCord and McCord (1959) extracted a series of measures on disciplinary techniques, home atmosphere, and parent characteristics from case notes and records kept on these families. They categorized disciplinary techniques as being punitive, love-oriented, lax, or erratic. Erratic discipline was comprised of inconsistent use of combinations of other techniques (i.e., love-lax, love-lax-punitive, punitive-lax). The McCords found that consistent use of either punitive or love-oriented disciplinary techniques was related to the lowest rates of criminal activity and institutionalization. The lack of discipline or erratic use of methods was associated with high delinquency rates with families using lax discipline and inconsistent punitive-lax discipline having the highest delinquency potential (50 percent and 56 percent, respectively). The McCords concluded that "the *consistency* of parental behavior is more important than the methods parents use for enforcing their demands." (p. 78)

Home atmosphere was characterized as cohesive, quarrelsome but affectionate, broken (i.e., separation or divorce), or quarrelsome and neglecting. The McCords showed that broken and quarrelsome-neglecting homes had the highest rates of delinquency (51 percent and 70 percent, respectively), with significantly more boys being convicted and institutionalized from quarrelsome-neglecting homes. Home atmosphere also interacted with discipline techniques. Love-oriented discipline appeared to mitigate the negative effects of broken or quarrelsome homes while punitive or lax discipline amplified the effects. This was especially true of the combination of quarrelsome-neglecting atmosphere with punitive discipline (75 percent delinquency rate) or lax discipline (100 percent delinquency rate).

The type of parental interaction with the children was also studied by McCord and McCord (1959). They distinguished between loving and nonloving influences from fathers and mothers. Loving fathers were those who were either warm or passive in their interactions. Nonloving fathers were those who were absent or dead, and those who interacted in a cruel or neglecting manner. Overall, children who experienced nonloving paternal influences fared worse than those having loving fathers. The fathers who were present in the family, but provided a rejecting influence (i.e., cruel, neglecting) were associated with the highest rates of delinquency. This was especially true when nonloving fathers and lax or erratic discipline styles were combined. Maternal influences also produced differential effects along the loving/nonloving dimensions, with neglecting mothers being associated with the highest rate of delinquency (70 percent). Unlike fathers, however, passive mothers were also associated with increased delinquency. Lack of maternal affection combined with lax or erratically punitive discipline characterized approximately 40 percent of all delinquent families.

Although the McCord and McCord study was post hoc in nature, it provided a vivid portrayal of potential family influences on delinquency development. A child raised by rejecting parents, inconsistent and punitive in their disciplinary actions and characterized as quarrelsome and neglectful, had little chance of normal development. Various combinations of these maladaptive influences provided differential risk, with inconsistent parental discipline acting as the most pervasive negative influence. These basic findings on family influences have been replicated in a longitudinal study conducted in Great Britain by West and Farrington (1973). Their study reported significant increases in delinquency from families that had (1) cruel, passive, or neglectful parents, (2) very strict or erratic discipline practices, and (3) marked marital conflict. The importance of these parental factors has been consistently implicated in delinquency production.

Direct measures of interaction patterns of delinquent children and their families have been obtained by Reid and Hendricks (1973). This study compared observational data from normal families, families with

aggressive children, and families with children who stole. The families with delinquent children had less interaction overall. This was especially evident for "positive-friendly" interaction in which the mothers and problem children from these families had lower rates of these behaviors than either of the other groups. The "negative-coercive" behaviors for delinquent families demonstrated intermediate rates between the normal and aggressive families. These findings showed that families producing delinquent children had reduced communications between members; little positive exchange when they did interact; and an elevated likelihood of negative exchange. Additional non-systematic information on family organization and operation has come from the comments of the professional observors who enter these homes. From the author's personal communication with observers, families with delinquent children were characterized by the apparent lack of communication between family members. Instead of a family unit, children and parents seemed to comprise a loose, autonomous compilation of individuals. Signs of family organization, such as regular mealtimes, parental knowledge of their children's whereabouts, and scheduled curfews, were typically absent. In essence, these observations corroborated interview data (see McCord and McCord, 1959; West and Farrington, 1973) that portrayed families of delinquent children as lacking warmth, supervision, and cohesiveness.

Although these families provide poor environments for learning socially accepted behavior, evidence exists that modeling influences are important in the acquisition of socially maladaptive behavior. Several studies have investigated the effects of parental deviance, especially fathers' criminality, on delinquency rates (e.g., Glueck and Glueck, 1955; McCord and McCord, 1959; West and Farrington, 1973). This research is also represented by the McCord and McCord findings (1959). They reported a general tendency for criminal fathers to have criminal sons. However, this relationship varied greatly according to other paternal disciplinary characteristics. The effect of the father's criminality was attenuated if the father was considered loving or consistent in disciplinary actions. Forty-seven percent of the criminal but loving fathers had delinquent children compared to 85 percent of criminal and cruel or neglecting fathers. Similarly, 15 percent of criminal fathers who were consistent disciplinarians had delinquent sons compared to 75 percent of criminal fathers who were erratic or lax in their discipline. The mother's role model in the family also affected delinquency rates. Deviant mothers (i.e., criminal, alcoholic, or promiscuous) who were nonloving had an 81 percent probability of having a deviant son, and 94 percent of deviant mothers who were erratically punitive had delinquent sons. Deviant parental role models increased rates of delinquency especially when coupled with additional adverse parental characteristics. It is likely that deviant parents who were nonloving and erratic provided stronger, more consistent deviant role models than those having the incongruous characteristics of deviant histories coupled with consistent discipline and loving atmosphere.

Additional support for the idea that deviant parents raise deviant children comes from an analysis of personality characteristics of mothers of delinquent children. Patterson (1980) studied the Minnesota Multiphasic Personality Inventory (MMPI) scales from mothers of children who were referred for treatment because of problems with high-rate stealing. He showed that the MMPI profile matched the classic profile of young delinquent girls Hathaway and Monachesi (1953) reported. It is unlikely that these mothers actively engaged in delinquent behaviors. However, it is reasonable to speculate that they were implicitly or explicitly supportive of delinquent behavior on the part of their young adolescent children. They would also tend to provide more asocial models of behavior in daily interactions.

The influences of the immediate family on the development of delinquent behavior appear to be pervasive. Although most of the influences discussed were correlative as opposed to causal, they have received wide substantiation. Inconsistent parental discipline, whether punitive or love-oriented, was a common factor in high-risk delinquent groups. The effects of poor discipline were increased or attenuated according to parental styles of interaction. Loving parents tended to attenuate the negative effects of inconsistent discipline, while nonloving parents amplified these effects. Finally, quarrelsome, disrupted families, and deviant parental role models were shown to increase the risk of delinquency. As stated earlier, recidivistic delinquent behavior is viewed as the most severe childhood behavior problem. Both the immediate and the long-term effects are damaging to society and the individual. It appears that familial processes related to delinquency development uniformly represent the antithesis of an appropriate childhood environment. Few opportunities exist for acquiring socially acceptable behavior from family experiences. The children from these home environments, lacking socially adaptive skills, are handicapped in secondary environments. This sets the stage for expulsion from potential normalizing influences outside the family. At a benign level, the children experiencing this high-risk family environment may learn to function adequately with marginal skill levels. At more realistic levels, these children will experience problem beleaguered lives with difficulties running the gamut of social and psychological maladjustment.

Summary of Direct Family Influences

The family environment plays a primary role in the development of a child's behavioral repertoire. Within the family a child learns styles of interaction that must suffice to provide the child with basic and social-affiliative needs, both within the home setting and in environments outside the home. Although each family-child combination provides experiences unique enough to allow for individuality, pervasive common processes shape basic behavior patterns. Evidence of these commonalities is witnessed in the existence of social norms and the ability of individuals to function adequately across diverse, novel situations. In essence, the common learning experiences provide a normative style of interaction from which deviance can be identified. The fact that behavior problem children interact in manners that deviate from the norm also indicates that all or part of their early socializing processes deviated from the norm.

The section on family influences has presented interactive processes that were related to behavior problems in children and that differentiated problem from nonproblem groups. Because of the lack of research continuity across the problem types discussed, the data presented were diverse—ranging from direct observation data from control problem children to sociological survey and interview data from delinquents. However, several dimensions reflecting the quality of the home environment were related to the production of problem behavior across all groups, studies, and data sources. The most noticeable of these dimensions was the degree of consistency or inconsistency of child management. Inconsistent and erratic parental attention and punishment were related to all forms of child maladjustment. This was demonstrated in sequential analysis of parental consequences for child behavior (Patterson, 1976), and the more global ratings of parental disciplinary practices (McCord and McCord, 1959). Although the adverse effect of inconsistent parenting was ubiquitous, the type of maladjustment appeared to be determined by additional modifying factors. These were the type of parental role model and the general home atmosphere.

Parental behavior patterns were related to similar patterns of behavior in problem children. Mothers of control problem children engaged in high rates of aversive "nattering" behaviors, i.e., excessive commands, disapproving statements, and so forth. Likewise, control problem children engaged in high rates of aversive behavior (Patterson, 1976). The connection between aggressive parents and aggressive problem children was not as strongly data-based. However, active teaching and role modeling of aggression was posited as a primary factor differentiating control problem from aggressive problem children. Parental criminality and deviance were shown to be related to delinquent activity in children (McCord and McCord, 1959; West and Farrington, 1973). Social learning theory (Bandura, 1977) places major import on modeling

effects in the home as determinants of child behavior. A diversity of data continues to implicate the importance of these effects.

General home atmosphere was a modifying factor in delinquency production. Cold, rejecting, and oppressive environments increased the likelihood of delinquency, while warm, loving environments attenuated the adverse effects of parental inconsistency and deviant modeling (McCord and McCord, 1959). Unfortunately, comparable data were not available for the other behavior problem types. It is reasonable to postulate similar modifying effects of home atmosphere on aggression and control problems.

The interesting aspect of these variables is the apparent interactive effect of their occurrence on child deviance. Various combinations of variables affected the type and severity of behavioral disturbance. However, *occurrence* alone, especially for inconsistent discipline, seemed to assure some form of problem behavior. The interactive effects of these variables are hypothetically illustrated in Figure 2. Inconsistent child management represents the behavior maladjustment cells (A, B, C, D) with consistent parenting reflecting the four cells of behavior adjustment (E. F. G. H). To simplify the illustration, the parental role model combines the effects of aggressive and deviant models (e.g., criminal, promiscuous). Only the cells characterized by criminal activity demonstrate the effect of deviant models. This is because of data from McCord and McCord (1959) showing that loving parents mitigated the effects of deviant role models. Home atmosphere adds the final variable, and is represented on a rejecting-oppressive to warm-open dimension. The combination of all three adverse effects (cell A) represents the highest probability of severe maladjustment. Cells B, C, and D illustrate the proposed combinations of variables for the remainder of the behavior problems discussed. Consistent child management represents the keystone to behaviorally adjusted children. However, the addition of a rejecting, punitive home atmosphere is illustrated as being indicative of individuals' exhibiting neurotic symptoms.

Undoubtedly, additional variables could

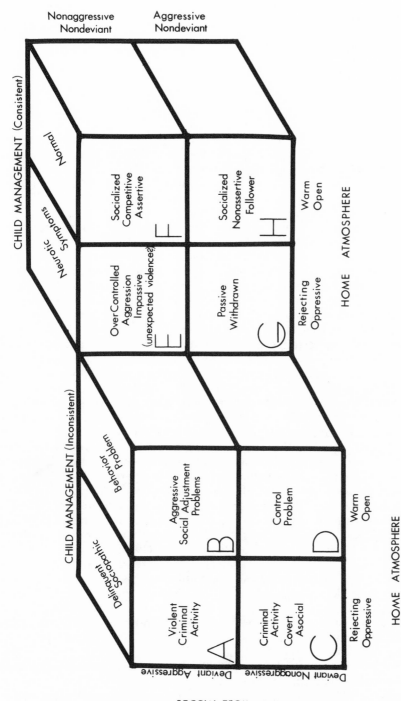

Figure 2
Interactive Influences of Family Variables on Child Behavior

be added to the illustration, thereby increasing the complexity of family influences, and providing finer differentiation among problem types. The three variables presented have a strong data basis and produce both documented and speculative categories of normal and problem behavior. Further clarification of these family influences must await multimeasure longitudinal investigations that are designed to study the development of behavior within the family.

SOCIO/ENVIRONMENTAL INFLUENCES ON CHILD BEHAVIOR

Within a system such as the family, each member experiences reciprocal behavioral influences. Parent behavior modifies child behavior, and child behavior modifies parent behavior. An example of interactive influences was illustrated in the description of escalating coercive processes in families. As one member of the family engages in higher rates and intensity of aversive behavior, the entire family is affected, potentially resulting in a fully disrupted family system. Interactive influences do not apply only to the parent/child relationship. Any influence that alters the behavior of one family member, whether the influence stemmed from within or outside the family, would be expected to affect other family members. Thus, events that occur in the daily experiences of each family member can determine aspects of the quality of family interaction. Given that family members engage in activities within the community, at jobs and through friendship networks, the potential sphere of behavior influence expands exponentially.

Wahler (1976; Wahler, Berland, Coe, and Leske, 1977) has provided a conceptual framework that portrays these influences as expanding and overlapping interactive systems. Figure 3 illustrates three levels of focus within this model. Level I represents the direct influences of the parent/child relationship that have been discussed earlier. It portrays interaction between a parent and child in a dyadic interactive model. Level II expands this view to include interactive effects from all family members.

By expanding the analysis to this level, potential influences become more complex and include indirect effects of familial interaction on child behavior (e.g., marital conflict affects the mother's behavior thus affecting her interaction with the child). Level III places the family within a host of variables that include neighbors, employers, schools, and community agencies. At this level the behavior influences become very complex. A child's behavior can be modified directly through interactions with peers and community adults outside the home. In addition, innumerable indirect effects can accrue to the child from direct community influences on other family members (e.g., job difficulties affect the father's behavior at home which, in turn, affects the father/child relationship). In normal development this expanding sphere of reference provides a diversity of socializing experiences to equip a child with an appropriate diversity of social skills. As influences become further removed from the direct effects of the family, they become less effective in directly altering behavior, but they undoubtedly provide a proving ground for concepts and behaviors learned in the primary environment. Behavior problem children are generally ill-equipped to encounter positive socializing experiences in new environments. Instead, these arenas can provide adverse effects by identifying the child as a problem (disruptive, troublemaker, or aggressive), resulting in overt or covert exclusion of the child from normalizing social interaction.

Few data are available that directly assess the import of influences within the expanding sphere of reference described by Wahler (1976). However, sociological delinquency research and the recent work of Wahler and his associates (Wahler, 1976, 1980; Wahler, Berland, and Coe, 1978; Wahler and Fox, 1980) illustrate the complex interaction of environmental variables.

Indirect Family and Community Influences

Numerous retrospective and longitudinal studies of delinquency have established the importance of specific family demographic characteristics in increasing

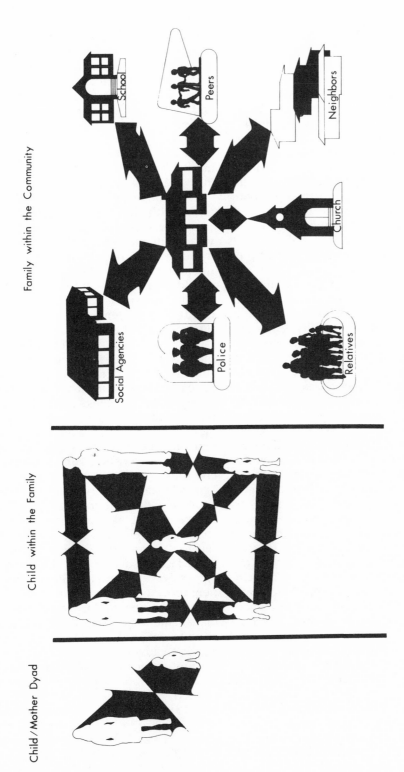

Figure 3
Expanding Realm of Environmental Influences

the risk of delinquency. Characteristics that have consistently related to increased risk include lower socioeconomic status, poor housing conditions, large families, unemployment, and marital conflict or divorce (Robins, 1966; Tonge, James and Hillam, 1975; West and Farrington, 1973). Each of these factors appears to contribute to delinquency, but not necessarily in a direct fashion. Lower socioeconomic levels have disproportionately added to delinquency, but this has been variously interpreted as a reflection of parental criminality (Robins, 1966), poor, overcrowded living conditions, (West and Farrington, 1973), and mental or physical incapacitation of the working adults (Tonge, et al., 1975). It appears evident that membership in poverty-level social classes is associated with delinquency, but that this association interacts with the fact that many adults in this situation are unskilled, and prone to deviant life styles or disability. Although poverty-level existence is neither necessary nor sufficient for delinquency production, it interacts with other family characteristics. In addition, the social class/delinquency relationship has been shown to be strongest for chronic delinquent populations (Robins, 1966; West and Farrington, 1973). Poor, overcrowded housing conditions obviously interact with social class. However, this factor has also demonstrated an independent relationship with recidivistic delinquency (Robins, 1966; West and Farrington, 1973). Within a relatively homogenous lower social class population, Tonge et al. (1975) reported that the most severe problem children were likely to come from families living in the worst housing conditions. Long-standing unemployment was also characteristic of these families.

Family size and risk of child deviance have shown a consistent relationship. Large families were positively correlated with increased rates of aggression and stealing (Rutter, Tizard and Whitmore, 1970) and general delinquency (Douglas, 1966). West and Farrington (1973) controlled for other covarying factors such as family income and still demonstrated a significant increased risk for large families. Children from broken homes in which, typically, the father is absent, have an increased risk for deviant behavior (Quay, 1965; West and Farrington, 1973). West and Farrington (1973) noted that the negative effects were more pronounced in families experiencing divorce as opposed to death of the spouse. Severe marital conflict has adverse effects equal to or greater than divorce. McCord and McCord (1959) reported a stronger relationship to delinquency for children from quarrelsome homes as opposed to broken homes. Tonge et al. (1975) also found that marital disharmony was a pervasive factor in their problem families.

These adverse factors all modify and interact with the more direct influences of family process. It is clear that a home environment characterized by poverty, inadequate, disorganized housing, unemployment, and continuous conflict would provide little in the way of positive socializing experiences. However, not all children experiencing these conditions demonstrate behavior maladjustment. Given basic disruptions in parent management of child behavior, it would be reasonable to expect these additional factors to characterize the most severe and intractable problem families. Tonge et al. (1975) reported that the most severe problem families from their study were multiple-problem families demonstrating most of the above characteristics. Families from these environments appear to be in a continuous "crisis" state, and have been shown to be extremely difficult to treat (Wahler and Moore, 1975). Within such a family, a child's problem behavior would seldom reach the immediate crisis intensity of other factors such as loss of employment, aggressive encounters with a spouse or neighbor, or harassment from welfare agencies. Concern for appropriate child management on a daily basis would not be an expected attribute of parents experiencing these adversities.

Another factor of importance has been the tendency for problem families to be isolated from appropriate, helpful community influences (Garbarino, 1977; Tonge et al., 1975). Social isolation was characteristic of child-abusing families (Garbarino, 1977; Young, 1964), families with conduct problem children (Wahler and Moore, 1975), and families with diverse psychopathology (Tonge et al., 1975). Tonge showed that their problem families had fewer contacts with relatives and neighbors, and participated less in normal social activities than control families in similar circumstances. These authors related social isolation to marital conflict and sociopathic or psychiatric disturbance in the parents, and delinquency in the children. Wahler and Moore (1975) noted that high-risk families who failed to maintain positive treatment effects appeared to be isolated from normal community social constraints. Wahler and his associates pursued the concept of family isolation through a design that directly monitored community contacts of low-income and middle-income families (Leske et al., 1978; Wahler, Leske, and Rogers, 1978; Wahler, 1980). Wahler et al. (1978) collected daily reports on the number, type, and valence (i.e., positive, negative) of contacts with the community experienced by lower and middle-income mothers. They reported that middle-income mothers had nearly four times the number of daily outside contacts, and that the majority of these were rewarding interactions with friends. The majority of the low-income mothers' outside contacts were with relatives or helping agencies. Further analysis indicated that most of the community networks existing for the low-income mothers, who Wahler et al. labeled "insular," were punitive instead of supportive. Within a group of "insular" mothers, Wahler (1980) showed that rates of parent/child aversive behavior covaried inversely with the mothers' daily friendship contacts. Days with high friendship contacts were associated with low rates of aversive interaction between mother and child and vice versa. This established a data-based indirect effect of community influence on child problem behavior. Wahler (1980) interpreted the failure of these insular families to maintain treatment gains to be the result of lack of community support mechanisms for appropriate child management. A similar view of community influence was reported by McCord and McCord (1959). They found that lack of family cohesiveness was highly predictive of delinquency only when the families lived in socially and physically deteriorated

neighborhoods. Supposedly, the supportive influences of good neighborhoods mitigated the negative effect of poor family cohesiveness. It is interesting to note that the children from good neighborhoods who became delinquent were more likely to "reform" as adults than were delinquents from poor neighborhoods. Thus, the positive effects of living in a supportive community may have greater impact on later adult behavior than on adolescent behavior.

The indirect influences on child behavior from these additional family and community sources are viewed as effective due to their direct influence on other family members, especially the parents. This, in turn, is reflected in the parent/child relationship and the general home atmosphere. Although multiple psychological and behavioral alterations undoubtedly result from experiencing these adverse influences, the area of greatest concern for child behavior is the incapacitation of the parent in the role of child manager. The sequencing of the deterioration in family process and community support probably assumes many forms. Parents may demonstrate poor child management and interpersonal skills from the outset. Under these conditions, they might quickly experience failure in maintaining a cohesive marriage, in controlling their children, and in establishing supportive community linkages. Alternatively, parents might demonstrate adequate child management skills, but experience a chronic series of crises (e.g., loss of employment, marital conflict, unwanted pregnancy) that effectively neutralize their parental role. The potential sequences and combinations of events that adversely affect child behavior are limitless. However, the main focus of these events is the impact they hold for increasing the negative dimensions of family interactive variables (see Figure 3).

Direct Community Influences

The final area of influence on child behavior to be discussed concerns the child's interactions in settings outside the home. These settings provide secondary learning environments in which behavior is acquired via the same principles that operated in the home. The wealth of alternative settings provides a diversity of behavior models, consequences, and opportunities to "test" behaviors under novel circumstances. Children who have established normal behavior repertoires in the home carry with them appropriate social skills that are adaptable to a wide variety of situations. Since most children fit within a normal range, interaction among children provides appropriate peer models and social reinforcers. In addition, adults promote appropriate behavior through modeling and explicit and implicit sanctions on behavior. Through these means, children experience social "success" in a variety of settings. ("Success" can be as specific as acquiring a desired toy from a peer or more general concepts, such as social affiliation.) In turn, successful modes of interaction acquire socially functional qualities and greater generality. The more settings and situations in which behavior patterns succeed, the more stable and enduring they should become.

This depiction of increasing generality and stability of behavior patterns is not postulated to culminate in a behaviorally restrictive, rigid individual. On the contrary, in normal development it is reasonable to assume at least two levels of learning—one specific and the other general. Specific learning refers to the acquisition of a particular behavior in a particular situation (e.g., a child may learn to smile and say "hi" when approached by an unknown child, or he/she may learn to ignore the other child until spoken to). General learning refers to more global, conceptual aspects of learning encounters and outcomes. On this level the child learns to "read" the environment, monitor processes and outcomes, and engage in alternative strategies when faced with failure. Given consistent failure to produce desired outcomes, the child would learn to avoid the particular situation. These two levels of social learning would be predicted to result in greater diversification of behavioral repertoires in order to respond appropriately to a diversity of environmental contexts and settings. A classic study by Patterson, Littman and Bricker (1967) illus-

trates these points. In this study Patterson et al. investigated the acquisition of assertive-aggressive behaviors in nursery school children. Their observational data showed that the children could be initially classified as either passive or aggressive. The passive children displayed low rates of assertive behavior overall, and tended to lose in encounters with aggressive children (e.g., an aggressive child could steal a toy from a passive child). Within the first few months, the passive group of children could be further differentiated according to successful use of assertive behavior in aggressive encounters. The passive children who spontaneously counterattacked in an aggressive encounter, resulting in successful termination of the attack, became more assertive in future aggressive situations. However, passive children who were seldom attacked or those who unsuccessfully counterattacked, did not increase their use of assertive behavior. The learning processes for the two groups of passive children receiving high rates of assertive attacks were similar, but resulted in different outcomes. Both groups tried counterattack as an alternative to passivity. One group specifically learned that counterattack succeeded; the other, that it did not. From this specific situation, the successful counterattackers began to "test" and generalize assertive behavior in other contexts. Although not tested in the Patterson et al. study, it would be expected that the children experiencing success by counterattack would generalize this skill to other settings and situations in which attacks occurred. Likewise, it is postulated that the unsuccessful children either employed alternative strategies that were not directly measured, or that the encounters were not perceived as aversive and thus they did not require alteration. Regardless of speculations, it was clear that the successful counterattackers acquired greater diversification of their behavior responses. Although this acquisition might not be socially desirable, it holds realistic value under the specific circumstances.

The adaptation of behavior problem children to secondary settings involves processes similar to normal children but results in different outcomes. The behavior problem child enters alternative environments with socially maladaptive interaction skills. The preponderance of coercive patterns of interaction (Patterson, 1976) and lower levels of prosocial behavior (Moore, 1975, Reid and Hendricks, 1973) that typify problem children in the home carry over into new settings. From the outset, these children are disadvantaged by a restrictive, aversively oriented behavior repertoire. Under ideal circumstances new settings could provide the positive learning experiences and social reinforcers that would help diversify the problem child's interactions toward more socially accepted methods. Unfortunately, this is not always the case, especially for those children from severely disrupted family environments. The description of coercion processes showed that problem children operated under rules of behavior that were not only different from normal children but, at times, counterintuitive (punishment-acceleration paradigm). Additional verification of these differences comes from a study by Wahler (1967) that demonstrated that problem children did not respond to contingent manipulation of social attention. In essence, they could not be changed by the positive means to which normal children responded. Such resistance to change would follow from a history of noncontingent reinforcement. However, it is theorized that other factors, perhaps also counterintuitive, are responsible for maintaining deviant patterns of behavior, restricting the problem child's development in new settings.

Normal children's responsiveness to the manipulation of social attention indicates that they are oriented toward receiving prosocial reinforcement for behavior. This "goal" of behavior is logical and fits within an operant framework. Given that a child is oriented toward the receipt of positive attention (conversely, the removal of negative attention), then new settings promote the generalization of socially accepted behavior and expands the means of acquiring reinforcers. This follows from peer competition for attention that usually occurs in settings outside the home. The peer group would model a broad range of appropriate methods for successfully acquiring reinforcers that could be practiced and tested among peer group members. The prosocial orientation of normal children creates stronger involvement with socially approved and promoted settings, such as schools and community organizations.

I have hypothesized that problem children are not oriented toward prosocial reinforcers and goals. As a result of disrupted family processes, these children develop behavior patterns that allow them to coerce "reinforcers" from the environment that do not have a readily apparent relationship to normal conceptualizations of reinforcement and punishment. When problem children enter new situations, they are able to obtain their goals without competing with peers and the necessity of expanding their behavior repertoire. This produces several detrimental results. Problem children experience their version of success in alternative settings by using only their restrictive, socially maladaptive behavior, and reduce the need to attend to the general aspects of the learning environment. The problem child fails to learn either specific alternative modes of interaction, or general rules for learning to learn (e.g., tracking behavior outcome), because the needed products of interaction are acquired through aversive means. Without specific ties to the prosocial aspects of new settings, problem children would have little stake or involvement in the sanctioned activities of these settings. The typical finding of early school failure for conduct problem children (Polk, 1967; Robins, 1966) would be expected. It would also follow that these problem children would leave settings in which they had minimal commitment earlier than other children. Truancy and early school dropout have consistently shown a relationship to delinquency (Robins, 1966). Once the problem child is out of settings that are socially approved and sanctioned, it becomes increasingly probable that the only available peer group will be children of similar circumstance. Thus, the problem child comes full circle to a reference group that is incapable of modeling or teaching more appropriate means of interaction. This association increases the probability of continued delinquent behavior (McCord and McCord, 1959).

This perspective of community influences is predicated on the assumption that the apparently maladaptive behavior patterns learned by problem children in the home are actually functional in producing desired outcomes. Because the desired outcomes do not fit within a normal conceptualization of social behavior, the problem children succeed in attaining the outcomes in multiple situations without the need to learn more appropriate methods of interaction. The more situations in which these children experience "success," the more stable and enduring the behavior patterns become. At the same time, the problem child drifts further from situations that could potentially orient the child toward more prosocial goals. From the viewpoint of society, the child has failed. However, the child has acquired his or her perceived needs. The outcome of this process is an adult poorly equipped in all dimensions of social and psychological competence. The ability to institute successful change at this point is extremely bleak. In essence, these individuals epitomize the multiproblem, sociopathic adult depicted by Robins (1966) and McCord (1978).

This section has described community influences for the most severe case. It should be clear that this process does not apply to all problem children. Community influences provide beneficial effects any time the problem child is forced to alter behavior in more appropriate directions. This would lead to diversification of the child's behavior repertoire, greater reliance on tracking general setting conditions, and, in favorable outcomes, a reorientation toward prosocial goals. As with the negative effects, the more situations in which the child must develop these skills, the more stable they would become.

CONCLUSION

Childhood behavior problems constitute the largest source of early child deviance. These problems have traditionally been viewed as transient or of minimal psychiatric importance. However, they have emerged as a group of disturbances that are prognostic of some of the most debilitating and pervasive adult disorders. These include psychiatric disturbance, criminality, and general incompetence in normal social functioning. Three areas of problem behavior were delineated in my discussion here. *Control problem* children were young children characterized by immaturity, disobedience, and coercive interaction styles. *Aggressive problem* children were identified from their high rates of physical and verbal assault and general defiance of authority. *Delinquent* children engage in high rates of delinquent behavior that includes truancy, alcohol and drug abuse, sexual misconduct, vandalism, and theft. These three classifications were not designed to portray exclusionary problem syndromes. Instead, they represented common referral areas that correspond to increasing problem severity and poor prognosis. This prognosis results from: (1) increased severity of the immediate consequences of the behavior (e.g., car theft is more severe than fighting with peers, which is more severe than disobeying a command); (2) increased likelihood of establishing the deviant behavior in multiple contexts and situations; and (3) increased likelihood of adult maladjustment.

The social learning perspective presented focused on the family as the primary system responsible for establishing the early behavior patterns of children. Within this environment, children normally learn appropriate modes of social interaction that are linked to common networks of social reinforcers and punishers. For problem children, however, this early experience is disrupted along several dimensions resulting in maladaptive behavior patterns that appear to be linked to alternative networks of reinforcement. Three dimensions of the home environment were depicted as having a causal relationship to the production of child behavior problems. These dimensions were: (1) the consistency of parental management of child behavior; (2) the type of parental role model (normative, aggressive, criminal, and so forth); and (3) the general tenor of the home atmosphere (rejecting/oppressive, warm/open). Inconsistent child management was related to all behavior problem categories. The addition of aggressive modeling to inconsistent child management was related to aggressive behavior problems in children, and the combination of inconsistent child management, deviant role models, and rejecting atmosphere was related to delinquent behavior problems. These dimensions provided a simplistic, global representation of more specific styles of family interaction for which data were presented.

The family represented one sphere of reference that affected child behavior. Since these influences were depicted as interactive or reciprocal (parent behavior affects child behavior, child behavior affects parent behavior), then additional outside influences that affect family members also affect the parent/child relationship. The additional influences were categorized as having indirect or direct effects on child behavior. The indirect effects were depicted as variables that incapacitated the parent as child manager. These included marital conflict, poverty, inadequate, overcrowded housing, and unemployment. Parents experiencing conditions such as these are living in a continuous crisis state in which consistent child management appears as the least of their worries. These multiple problem families also tend to be disconnected from normal community support networks (e.g., friendship networks) that aid in alleviating the crisis state. Wahler and his associates (Wahler et al., 1978) have shown that not only did problem families have fewer community contacts but that these were likely to have aversive qualities that compounded family disruption. Direct influences on child behavior stemmed from the child's experiences in settings outside the home. It was hypothesized that deviant behavior patterns of problem children function to produce desired outcomes from interactions even though these outcomes do not fit normal conceptualizations of social or material reinforcement. Thus, problem children "succeed" in alternative settings without learning more appropriate means of interaction. The more settings in which they establish deviant behavior patterns, the more stable and intractable they become.

These three levels of influence on child behavior (direct from family members, direct from community settings, and indirect from community influence on family members) produce an interactive sphere of reference with infinite combinations of variables. Even though the family represents the primary source of behavior development and maintenance, the additional influences can support or counteract these effects. The complexity of this social milieu holds significance for the treatment of behavior problem children. Social learning–oriented therapy for conduct problem children has generally been based on retraining parents consistently and appropriately to reinforce and punish their children (Bernal, 1971; Patterson, Reid, Jones and Conger, 1975; Wahler, 1969). These treatment programs have taken a strong empirical approach to documenting behavior change and have demonstrated the efficacy of treatment across multiple settings and problem types (Martin, 1977; Patterson, 1974b; Reid and Hendricks, 1973; Wahler, 1969). However, recently some investigators have questioned the ability of parent training programs to demonstrate maintenance of treatment effects (Forehand and Atkinson, 1977; Tavormina, 1974; Wahler and Moore, 1975). Wahler and Moore (1975) showed a sharp distinction in maintenance of treatment effects between "high-risk" and "low-risk" families. The high-risk families were characterized as multiple problem "insular" families while the low-risk families shared only the characteristic of inconsistent child management. The low-risk families showed continued improvement in child behavior at the end of one year follow-up. The high-risk families failed to maintain the behavior improvements.

This differential outcome fits within Wahler's (1976) perspective of expanding systems of influence on child behavior (see Figure 3). Both the high-risk and the low-risk families were dysfunctional at the parent-child level. However, the high-risk families were also dysfunctional on the interpersonal and community levels. Given that problems on these levels incapacitate the parent as child manager, then it would be unreasonable to expect maintenance of improvements that resulted from treatment directed only at the parent-child relationship. As long as a support system (i.e., the therapist) was available to help monitor child behavior, high-risk families improved the behavior of their children. With the removal of constant monitoring, the adverse community influences returned the family to their "normal" state of disruption (Wahler, 1980). Problem children from high-risk families have the bleakest prognosis for normal adult adjustment. Currently, it must be stated that they also have the poorest prognosis for successful therapeutic intervention.

REFERENCES

Ackerson, L. *Children's behavior problems* (Vol. 1). Chicago: University of Chicago Press, 1931.

Allen K. E., Hart, B., Buell, J., Harris, F., & Wolf, M. M. Effects of social reinforcement on isolate behavior of a nursery school child. *Child Development*, 1964, *35*, 511-518.

Ammons, C., & Ammons, R. Aggression in doll play: Interviews of two- to six-year old white males. *Journal of Genetic Psychology*, 1953, *82*, 205-213.

Anderson, F. N., & Dean, H. C. Some aspects of child guidance clinic intake policy and practices. *Public Health Monograph, 42,* 1956.

Bandura, A. Social learning through imitation. In M. R. Jones (Ed.), *Nebraska Symposium on Motivation: 1962.* Lincoln: University of Nebraska Press, 1962.

Bandura, A. Influence of models' reinforcement contingencies on the acquisition of imitative responses. *Journal of Personality and Social Psychology*, 1965, *1*, 589-595.

Bandura, A. Vicarious and self-reinforcement processes. In R. Glaser (Ed.), *The nature of reinforcement.* New York: Academic Press, 1971.

Bandura, A. *Aggression: A social learning analysis.* Englewood Cliffs, N.J.: Prentice-Hall, 1973.

Bandura, A. Self-efficiency: Toward a unifying theory of behavioral change. *Psychological Review*, 1977, *84*, 191-215.

Bandura, A., Adams, N. E., & Beyer, J. Cognitive processes mediating behavioral change. *Journal of Personality and Social Psychology*, 1977, *35*, 125-139.

Bandura, A., & McDonald, F. J. The influence of social reinforcement and the behavior of models in shaping children's moral judgements. *Journal of Abnormal and Social Psychology*, 1963, *67*, 274-281.

Bandura, A., Ross, D., & Ross, S. Transmission of aggression through imitation of aggressive models. *Journal of Abnormal and Social Psychology*, 1961, *63*(3), 575-582.

Bandura, A., Ross, D., & Ross, S. A. Imitation of film mediated aggressive models. *Journal of Personality and Social Psychology*, 1963, *3*, 54-62.

Bandura, A., & Walters, R. H. *Social learning and personality development.* New York: Holt, Rinehart, and Winston, 1963.

Bandura, A., & Whalen, C. K. The influences of antecedent reinforcement and divergent modeling cues on patterns of self-reward. *Journal of Personality and Social Psychology*, 1966, *3*, 373-382.

Bernal, M. E. Training parents in child management. In R. Bradfield (Ed.), *Behavior modification of learning disabilities.* San Rafael, California: Academic Therapy Publications, 1971.

Bernal, M. E., & North, A. J. *Scoring system for home and school* (Rev. 10). Unpublished manuscript, University of Denver, 1972.

Bijou, S. W., & Baer, D. M. *Child development* (Vol. I). New York: Appleton-Century-Crofts, 1961.

Bijou, S. W., & Baer, D. M. *Child development* (Vol. II). New York: Appleton-Century-Crofts, 1965.

Birnbauer, J. S., Wolf, M. M., Kidda, J. D., & Tague, C. E. Classroom behavior of retarded pupils with token reinforcement. *Journal of Experimental Child Psychology*, 1965, *2*, 219-235.

Burt, C. *The young delinquent.* New York: Appleton-Century-Crofts, 1925.

Cairns, R. B., & Paris, S. G. Informational determinants of social reinforcement effectiveness among retarded children. *American Journal of Mental Retardation*, 1971, *76*, 361-369.

Cohen, A. Delinquent boys. Glencoe, Illinois: Free Press, 1955.

Collard, M. P. Significant differences between recidivists and nonrecidivists. *British Journal of Criminology*, 1967, *7*, 93-102.

Delfini, L. F., Bernal, M. C., & Rosen, P. M. Comparison of normal and deviant boys in their homes. In L. A. Hamerlynck, L. C. Handy, & L. J. Mash (Eds.), *Behavior modification and families. 1 Theory and research.* New York: Brunner/Mazell, 1976.

Douglas, J. The school progress of nervous and troublesome children. *British Journal of Psychiatry*, 1966, *112*, 1115-1116.

Feshbach, S. Aggression. In P. H. Mussen (Ed.), *Carmichael's manual of child psychology* (Vol. II). New York: John Wiley & Sons, Inc., 1970.

Forehand, R., & Atkeson, B. Generality of treatment effects with parents as therapists: A review of assessment and implementation procedures. *Behavior Therapy*, 1977, *8*, 575-593.

Forehand, R., King, H. E., Peed, S., & Yoder, D. Mother-child interactions: Comparisons of a noncompliant clinic group and a non-clinic group. *Behavior Research and Therapy*, 1975, *13*, 79-84.

Garbarino, J. The human ecology of child maltreatment: A conceptual model for research. *Journal of Marriage and the Family*, 1977, November, 721-735.

Gersten, J. C., Langner, T. S., Eisenberg, J. G., Simcha-Fagan, O., & McCarthy, E. D. Stability and change in types of behavioral disturbance of children and adolescents. *Journal of Abnormal Child Psychology*, 1976, *4*, 111-127.

Glueck, S., & Glueck, E. *Unraveling juvenile delinquency*. Cambridge: Harvard University Press, 1950.

Glueck, S., & Glueck, E. *Delinquents and non-delinquents in perspective*. Cambridge: Harvard University Press, 1968.

Hartup, W. W. Aggression in childhood: Developmental perspectives. *American Psychologist*, 1974, *29*, 336-341.

Hathaway, S. R., & Monachesi, E. D. (Eds.), *Analyzing and predicting juvenile delinquency with the MMPI*. Minneapolis: University of Minnesota Press, 1953.

Jersild, A. T., & Markey, F. V. Conflicts between preschool children. *Child Development Monographs*, 1935, No. 21.

Johnson, S. M., Wahl, G., Martin, S., & Johanssen, S. How deviant is the normal child: A behavioral analysis of the preschool child and his family. In R. D. Rubin, J. P. Brady, & J. R. Henderson (Eds.), *Advances in behavior therapy*. New York: Academic Press, 1974.

Kopfstein, D. The effects of accelerating and decelerating consequences on the social behavior of trainable retarded children. *Child Development*, 1972, *43*, 800-809.

Leske, G., Afton, A., Rogers, E., & Wahler, R. G. *The interpersonal functioning of insular and non-insular families: Factors related to treatment success and failure*. Unpublished manuscript. Child Behavior Institute, University of Tennessee, 1978.

Levitt, E. E. Research on psychotherapy with children. In A. E. Bergin & S. L. Garfield (Eds.), *Handbook of psychotherapy and behavior change*. New York: Wiley, 1971.

Lobitz, G. K., & Johnson, S. M. Normal versus deviant children: A multimethod comparison. *Journal of Abnormal Child Psychology*, 1975, *3*, 353-374.

Martin, B. Brief family intervention: The effectiveness and the importance of including the father. *Journal of Consulting and Clinical Psychology*, 1977, *45*, 1002-1010.

McCord, J. A thirty-year follow-up of treatment effects. *American Psychologist*, 1978, *33*, 284-289.

McCord, W., & McCord, J. *Origins of crime*. New York: Columbia University Press, 1959.

McKee, J., & Leader, F. The relationship of socio-economic status and aggression to the competitive behavior of preschool children. *Child Development*, 1955, *26*, 135-142.

Moore, D. R. *Determinants of deviancy: A behavioral comparison of normal and deviant children in multiple settings*. Unpublished doctoral dissertation. University of Tennessee, Knoxville, 1975.

Moore, D. R., Chamberlain, P., & Mukai, L. H. Children at risk for delinquency: A follow-up comparison of aggressive children and children who steal. *Journal of Abnormal Child Psychology*, 1979, *7*, 345-355.

Moore, D. R., & Patterson, G. R. *Behavior structure in deviant family systems*. Paper presented at the meeting of the American Psychological Association, San Francisco, August, 1977.

Morris, H. H., Escoll, P. S., & Wexler, R. Aggressive behavior disorders of childhood: A follow-up study. *American Journal of Psychiatry*, 1956, *112*, 991-997.

Mukai, L. M. *Aggression in the home as a function of age and sex in normal and aggressive children*. Unpublished manuscript. Oregon Social Learning Center, 1979.

Patterson, G. R. Changes in status of family members as controlling stimuli: A basis for describing treatment process. In L. A. Hamerlynck, L. C. Handy, & E. Mash (Eds.), *Behavior change: Methodology concepts and practice*. Champaign, Illinois: Research Press, 1973.

Patterson, G. R. A basis for identifying stimuli which control behaviors in natural settings. *Child Development*, 1974, *45*, 900-911. (a)

Patterson, G. R. Intervention for boys with conduct problems: Multiple settings, treatments, and criteria. *Journal of Consulting and Clinical Psychology*, 1974, *42*, 471-481. (b)

Patterson, G. R. The aggressive child: Victim and architect of a coercive system. In L. A. Hamerlynck, L. C. Handy, & E. J. Mash (Eds.), *Behavior modification and families. I. Theory and research*. New York: Brunner/Mazel, 1976.

Patterson, G. R. A performance theory for coercive family interaction. In L. G. Cairns (Ed.), *Social interaction: Methods, analysis, and illustration.* Chicago: University of Chicago Press, 1979.

Patterson, G. R. Mothers: The unacknowledged victims. *Monographs of the Society for Research in Child Development*, 1980, In press.

Patterson, G. R., & Cobb, J. A. A dyadic analysis of "aggressive" behavior. In J. P. Hill (Ed.), *Minnesota Symposia on Child Psychology* (Vol. 5). Minneapolis: University of Minnesota Press, 1971.

Patterson, G. R., & Cobb, J. A. Stimulus control for classes of noxious behavior. In J. Knutson (Ed.), *The control of aggression: Implications from basic research.* Chicago: Aldine, 1973.

Patterson, G. R., Littman, R. A., & Bricker, W. Assertive behavior in children: A step toward a theory of aggression. *Monographs of the Society for Research in Child Development*, 1967, *32*, 1-43.

Patterson, G. R., & Moore, D. R. Interactive patterns as units of behavior. In M. E. Lamb, S. J. Suomi, & G. R. Stephenson, (Eds.), *Social interaction analysis: Methodological issues.* Madison: University of Wisconsin Press, 1979.

Patterson, G. R., Ray, R. S., Shaw, D. A., & Cobb, J. A. *Manual for coding of family interactions* (Rev. 1969). See NAPS Document #01234 for 33 pages of material. Order from ASIS/NAPS, % Microfiche Publication, 440 Park Avenue South, New York, New York, 10016.

Patterson, G. R., & Reid, J. B. Reciprocity and coercion: Two facets of social systems. In C. Neuringer & J. L. Michael (Eds.), *Behavior modification in clinical psychology.* New York: Appleton-Century-Crofts, 1970.

Paynter, & Blanchard. *A study of educational achievement of problem children.* New York: The Commonwealth Fund Division of Publications, 1929.

Polk, K. *Lane County Youth Project: Final report.* Office of Juvenile Delinquency, and Youth Development. U.S. Dept. of Health, Education, and Welfare, 1967.

Polk, K. *Teenage delinquency in small town America. Research Report 5*, Center for Studies in Crime and Delinquency, NIMH, Washington, D.C., 1975.

Powers, E., & Witmer, H. *An experiment in the prevention of delinquency: The Cambridge-Somerville Youth Study.* New York: Columbia University Press, 1951.

Quay, H. Personality and delinquency. In H. Quay (Ed.), *Juvenile delinquency research and theory.* Princeton: Van Nostrand, Col., 1965.

Reid, J. B. (Ed.), *A social learning approach to family intervention: Observation in home settings.*

Eugene, Oregon: Castalia Publishing Co., 1978.

Reid, J. B., & Hendricks, A. F. C. J. A preliminary analysis of the effectiveness of direct home intervention for treatment of predelinquent boys. In L. A. Hamerlynck, L. C. Handy, & E. J. Mash (Eds.), *Behavior therapy: Methodology concepts and practice.* Champaign, Illinois: Research Press, 1973.

Roach, J. L. Some social-psychological characteristics of child guidance clinic caseloads. *Journal of Consulting Psychology*, 1958, *22*, 183-186.

Robins, L. N. *Deviant children grown up.* Baltimore, Maryland: Williams & Wilkins Company, 1966.

Rutter, M., Tizard, J., & Whitmore, K. *Education, health and behavior.* New York: John Wiley and Sons, 1970.

Shepherd, M., Oppenheim, A. N., & Mitchell, S. Childhood behavior disorders and the child guidance clinic: An epidemiological study. *Journal of Child Psychology and Psychiatry*, 1966, *7*, 39-52.

Tavormina, J. B. Basic models of parent counseling. *Psychological Bulletin*, 1974, *81*, 827-835.

Tonge, W. L., James, D. S., & Hillam, S. M. *Families without hope: A controlled study of 33 problem families.* Ashford, Kent: Headly Brothers Ltd, 1975.

Wahler, R. G. *Behavior therapy for oppositional children: Love is not enough.* Paper presented at the Eastern Psychological Association Convention, Washington, D.C., 1968.

Wahler, R. G. Oppositional children: A quest for parental reinforcement control. *Journal of Applied Behavior Analysis*, 1969, *2*, 159-170.

Wahler, R. G. *Generalization processes in child behavior change.* Grant application to National Institute of Mental Health, 1976.

Wahler, R. G. The insular mother: Her problems in parent-child treatment. *Journal of Applied Behavior Analysis*, 1980, *13*, 207-220.

Wahler, R. G., Berland, R. M., & Coe, T. D. Generalization processes in child behavior change. In B. Lahey & A. Kazdin (Eds.), *Advances in child clinical psychology.* New York: Plenum Publishing Corp., 1978.

Wahler, G. R., Berland, R. M., Coe, T. D., & Leske, G. Social systems analysis: Implementing an alternative behavioral Model. In A. Rogers-Warren & S. Warren (Eds.), *Ecological perspectives in behavior analysis.* Baltimore, Maryland: University Park Press, 1977.

Wahler, R. G., & Fox, J. J. Solitary toy play: A desirable family treatment component for aggressive-oppositional children. *Journal of*

Applied Behavior Analysis, 1980, In press.

Wahler, R. G., House, A. E., & Stambaugh, E. E. *Ecological assessment of child problem behavior: A clinical package for home, school and institutional settings*. New York: Pergamon Press, 1976.

Wahler, R. G., Leske, G., & Rogers, E. S. *The insular family: A deviance support mechanism for oppositional children*. Paper presented at the Banff International Conference on Behavior Modification, Banff, Canada, 1978.

Wahler, R. G., & Moore, D. R. *School-home behavior change procedures in a "high risk" community*. Paper presented at the annual meeting of the Association for Advancement of Behavior Therapy. San Francisco, 1975.

Wahler, R. G., Winkel, G. H., Peterson, R. F., & Morrison, D. C. Mothers as behavior therapists of their own children. *Behavior Research and Therapy*, 1965, *3*, 113-124.

Walters, J., Pearce, D., & Dahms, L. Affectional and aggressive behavior of preschool children. *Child Development*, 1957, *28*, 15-26.

Warren, V., & Cairns, R. Social reinforcement satiation: An outcome of frequency of ambiguity. *Journal of Exceptional Child Psychology*, 1972, *13*, 249-260.

West, D. J., & Farrington, D. P. *Who becomes delinquent?* London: Heinemann Educational Books, Ltd., 1973.

Westman, J. C., Rice, D. L., & Bermann, E. Nursery school behavior and later adjustment. *American Journal of Orthopsychiatry*, 1968, 725-731.

Willems, E. P. Go ye into all the world and modify behavior: An ecologist's view. *Representative Research in Social Psychology*, 1973, *4*, 93-105.

Willems, E. P. Steps toward an ecobehavioral technology. In A. Rogers-Warren & S. P. Warren (Eds.), *Ecological perspectives in behavior analysis*. Baltimore, Maryland: University Park Press, 1977.

Wolf, M. M., Risley, T., & Mees, H. L. Application of operant conditioning procedures to the behavior problems of an autistic child. *Behavior Research and Therapy*, 1964, *1*, 305-312.

Wolfgang, M. E., Figlio, R. M., & Sellin, T. *Delinquency in a birth cohort*. Chicago: University of Chicago Press, 1972.

Young, L. *Wednesday's children: A study of child neglect and abuse*. New York: McGraw-Hill, 1964.

Zax, M., Cowen, E. L., Rappaport, J., Beach, D. R., & Laird, J. D. Follow-up study of children identified early as emotionally disturbed. *Journal of Consulting and Clinical Psychology*, 1968, *32*, 369-374.

CHAPTER 10

Child Abuse

ARTHUR H. GREEN, M.D.

The main objective of this chapter is to provide a dynamic understanding of the many facets of the child-abuse syndrome, which, in turn, will provide the framework for the development of an appropriate strategy for its prevention and treatment. Child abuse will be defined, and demographic data will be presented to illustrate the scope of the problem. The major etiological factors in child abuse will be described: the characteristics of the parents that impede their capacity for child-rearing, the child's own contributions to his scapegoating and abuse, and the environmental factors that exacerbate and perpetuate the maltreatment. Data concerning the parents and the children are derived from both behavioral observations and psychodynamic explorations carried out during psychotherapy. The impact of physical abuse on the behavior development and psychological functioning of the children will be outlined in detail. The material is based upon the recent literature on child abuse and the author's extensive clinical and research experience with abused children and their families at the State University of New York, Downstate Medical Center, Brooklyn, N.Y.

SCOPE OF THE PROBLEM

Although the maltreatment and exploitation of children have been recorded throughout history, the phenomenon of child abuse has only recently attracted the attention of child care professionals. It was not until Kempe's classic description of "The Battered Child Syndrome" in 1962 (Kempe, Silverman, Steele, Droegemueller, and Silver, 1962) that child abuse received widespread interest from physicians, social scientists, and the law. Between 1963 and 1965, the passage of laws by all 50 states that required medical reporting of child abuse ultimately subjected the abusing parents to legal process and catalyzed the formation of child protective services throughout the nation. Psychiatric exploration of child battering and the first psychological studies of abusing parents were carried out during this period.

Because of improved reporting procedures, the striking prevalence of child maltreatment in the United States has become apparent. The child abuse law in New York State became effective July 1, 1964. During the first 12-month period, 313 cases of child abuse were reported in New York City with 16 deaths. The latest New York City statistics (1977) included 5,930 reported cases with 77 deaths. An additional 18,309 children were reported to be neglected. The 20-fold increase in reported abuse over a 13-year period obviously reflects an improvement in reporting procedure as well as a substantial increase in the incidence of child abuse. This impression is supported by similar increases in reported child abuse throughout the country. Light (1973) has utilized Gil's 1965 survey and 1970 U.S. Census statistics to project an estimated 200,000 to 500,000 cases of physical abuse annually.

A New York State Department of Social Services estimate of the percentage of cases of severe neglect or sexual abuse enabled Light to project 465,000 to 1,175,000 such incidents in the nation annually. Combining all types of maltreatment leads to an upper projection of over 1,500,000 cases per year. This figure approximates an estimate by Douglas Besharov, Director of the National Center on Child Abuse and Neglect, who calculated 1.6 million annual cases of abuse and neglect with 2,000 to 4,000 deaths (1975), based upon a statistical survey carried out by the Center.

Child maltreatment is currently regarded as a major public health problem and a leading cause of injury and death in children. The proliferation of child abuse and neglect might be related to the general increase of violence in our society demonstrated by the rising incidence of violent crimes, delinquency, suicide, and lethal accidents.

Definition of Child Abuse

The concept and definition of child abuse has been broadened in recent years. In Kempe's pioneering paper, "The Battered Child Syndrome," he and his colleagues (1962) described child abuse as the infliction of serious injury upon young children by parents and caretakers. The injuries, including fractures, subdural hematoma, and multiple soft tissue injuries, often resulted in permanent disability and death. Fontana viewed child abuse as one end of a spectrum of maltreatment that also included emotional deprivation, neglect, and malnutrition. These were all designated as components of the "Maltreatment Syndrome" (1971). Helfer (1975) stressed the prevalence of minor injuries resulting from abuse and estimated that 10 percent of all childhood accidents treated in emergency rooms were consequences of physical abuse. Gil (1974) further extended the concept of child abuse to include any action that interferes with a child's achievement of his physical and psychological potential.

In this chapter, child abuse will refer to the nonaccidental physical injury inflicted on a child by a parent or guardian and will encompass the total range of physical injury. Child abuse will be differentiated from child neglect, and the term "maltreat-

ment" will be used as a general reference to both abuse and neglect. The terms "child abuse" and "neglect" will be based on the following legal definitions stated in the New York State Child Protective Services Act of 1973:

Definition of Child Abuse: An "abused child" is a child less than 16 years of age whose parent or other person legally responsible for his care:
1) inflicts or allows to be inflicted upon the child serious physical injury, or
2) commits or allows to be committed against the child an act of serious injury, or
3) commits or allows to be committed against the child an act of sexual abuse as defined in the penal law.

Definition of Child Maltreatment* A "maltreated child" is a child under 18 years of age who has had serious physical injury inflicted upon him by other than accidental means.

A "maltreated child" is a child under 18 years of age impaired as a result of the failure of his parent or other person legally responsible for his care to exercise a minimum degree of care:
1) in supplying the child with adequate food, clothing, shelter, education, medical or surgical care, though financially able to do so; or
2) in providing the child with proper supervision or guardianship; or
3) by unreasonably inflicting or allowing to be inflicted harm or a substantial risk thereof, including the infliction of excessive corporal punishment; or
4) by using a drug or drugs; or
5) by using alcohol beverages to the extent that he loses self-aid of the family court.

A "maltreated child" is also a child under 18 years of age who has been abandoned by his parents or other person legally responsible for his care.

Detection. The possibility of child abuse must be considered in every child who presents with an injury. A careful history and physical evaluation of the child are warranted when one suspects physical abuse. The physical examination should include a routine X-ray survey of all children under five and laboratory tests to rule out the possibility of an abnormal bleeding tendency. The child, of course, should be hospitalized during this diagnostic evaluation.

While there is no single physical finding or diagnostic procedure that can confirm the diagnosis of child abuse with absolute certainty, the presence of some of the following signs and symptoms derived from the history-taking and physical examination are suggestive of an inflicted injury:

History.

(1) Unexplained delay in bringing the child for treatment following the injury.
(2) History is implausible or contradictory.
(3) History is incompatible with the physical findings.
(4) There is a history of repeated suspicious injuries.
(5) The parent blames the injury on a sibling or a third party.
(6) The parent maintains that the injury was self-inflicted.
(7) The child had been taken to numerous hospitals for the treatment of injuries (hospital-"shopping").
(8) The child accuses the parent or caretaker of injuring him.
(9) The parent has a previous history of abuse as a child.
(10) The parent has unrealistic and premature expectations of the child.

Physical findings.

(1) Pathognomonic "typical" injuries commonly associated with physical punishment, such as bruises on the buttocks and lower back; bruises in the genital area or inner thigh may be inflicted after a child wets or soils, or is resistant to toilet training. Bruises and soft tissue injuries at different stages of healing are signs of repeated physical abuse. Bruises of a special configuration such as hand marks, grab marks, pinch marks, and strap marks usually indicate abuse.
(2) Certain types of burns are typically inflicted, i.e. multiple cigarette burns, scalding of hands or feet, burns of perineum and buttocks.
(3) Abdominal trauma leading to a ruptured liver or spleen.
(4) Subdural hematoma with or without skull fracture.
(5) Radiologic signs, such as subperiosteal hemorrhages, epiphyseal separations, metaphyseal fragmentation, periosteal shearing, and periosteal calcifications.

Etiological Factors. *Parental Characteristics* Numerous theories have been advanced to explain the physical abuse of children by their parents. Early investigations of the "battered child syndrome" (Cohen, Raphling and Green, 1966; Merrill, 1962; Steele and Pollock, 1968) attempted to identify "typical" behavioral characteristics and personality traits in abusing parents that could account for their child battering. They have been described as impulsive (Elmer, 1965); immature (Cohen et al., 1966); rigid, domineering, and chronically aggressive (Merrill, 1962); dependent and narcissistic (Pollock and Steele, 1972); isolated from family and friends (Steele and Pollock, 1968); and experiencing marital difficulties (Kempe et al., 1962). The diversity and lack of specificity of these observations failed to support the notion of a typical child-abusing personality. The fact that these observations were not controlled and were often derived from clinical interviews divorced from the parent-child interaction raised further questions about their reliability and specificity.

More penetrating impressions of the personality defects and underlying psychopathology of abusing parents have been gathered from observations during their psychiatric treatment and while interacting with their children. Steele (1970) stressed the importance of the parent's closely linked identifications with a harsh, rejecting mother and with a "bad" childhood self-image—perpetuated in their relationship with the abused child. Abusing parents inflicted traumatic experiences on their children, similar to those they had endured during childhood. The observation that most abusing parents have frequently experienced physical abuse, rejection, deprivation, and inadequate parenting during their own childhood is one of the few that generates widespread agreement in this field.

Steele (1970) described the abusing parent's tendency to rely on such defense mechanisms as denial, projection, identification with the aggressor, and role reversal. The last, a maneuver by which the abusing parent turns toward the child for the gratification of dependency needs has been reported by other investigators (Morris and Gould, 1963) as well. Galdston (1971) emphasized the importance of unresolved sexual guilt in mothers associated with the conception of the child who is subsequently abused, derived from unconscious oedipal conflicts. Feinstein, Paul, and Pettison (1964) studied the behavior of women with infanticidal impulses in group therapy. These women deeply resented their parents for failing to gratify their dependency needs and demonstrated a hatred of men that could be linked to intense rivalry with their brothers. They also exhibited phobic and depressive symptomatology.

Green (1974, 1976) conducted in-depth interviews with 60 mothers or female caretakers of abused children who were compared with control groups of 30 neglectful and 30 normal mothers. Twenty percent of the abusing mothers participated in follow-up interviews or psychotherapy. The mothers of the abused children could be differentiated from the controls by a more frequent perception of their child as difficult and demanding; the greater emotional unavailability of their parents and spouses; a greater overall lack of childrearing assistance, and the more frequent rejection, criticism, and punishment by their own parents. This mistreatment at the hands of their parents reinforced their feelings of having been burdensome children, and facilitated their identification with a hostile, rejecting parental figure. Typical personality characteristics of the abusing mothers, shared by male abusers, were:

(1) *Unresolved depending conflicts,* resulting from childhood deprivations and the current lack of emotional support from spouse and family.
(2) *Poor impulse control,* based on childhood experience with harsh punishment and identification with violent adult models.
(3) *Low self-esteem,* derived from rejection and criticism by their parents during their childhood.
(4) *Heightened narcissism.* They respond to assaults on their fragile self esteem with a compensatory narcissism. Because of their need to maintain a positive facade, they must defend themselves against the awareness of underlying feelings of worthlessness.
(5) *Use of primitive defense mechanisms.* Primitive defenses such as denial, projection, and splitting are utilized to effect a displacement of unacceptable traits and impulses onto others. The projection of negative parental attributes onto the child results in "scapegoating."
(6) *Disturbances in identity.* Identifications are

shifting and unstable, and dominated by hostile introjects derived from the internalization of "bad" self and object representations of early childhood.

Green's study (1979) of abusing fathers documented the importance of additional factors, such as unresolved dependency on the spouse, excessive drinking, and work-related stress. Paternal child abuse is usually accompanied by spouse abuse and involves its own psychodynamic pattern, which will be described later.

Contributions of the Child

The child's role in the abuse process has become a subject of increasing interest. Usually only a single child in a family is selected for scapegoating and abuse. It is the child, perceived as the most difficult or burdensome, who is the most likely to be abused. The period of infancy and early childhood, during which the child is most helpless and dependent on caretakers, is a particularly stressful time for most parents, especially for those who are "abuse-prone." In fact, the majority of reported cases of child abuse occur in the first two years of life. Infants with sustained crying and irritability may have a devastating effect upon the parent-child relationship. Robson and Moss (1970) noted decreases in mother-infant attachment as a result of sustained crying. Bell and Ainsworth (1972) observed maternal withdrawal in mothers who were unable to control their infants' crying. On the other hand, infants who are relatively unresponsive, passive, lethargic, and slow in development might be equally frustrating to their mothers, tending to provoke abuse. Both the irritable and sluggish infant are readily scapegoated because their mothers perceive their unresponsiveness as a rejection reminiscent of similar experiences with their own parents. This will, in turn, reinforce their sense of inadequacy.

Physically or psychologically deviant children are also vulnerable to abuse. Children with prominent physical defects, congenital anomalies, mental retardation, or chronic physical illness are not only burdensome, they are readily viewed by narcissistic parents as symbols of their own defective self-image.

Low birth weight and premature infants seem to be over-represented in the child abuse statistics (Elmer and Gregg, 1976; Klein and Stern, 1971; Simons et al., 1966). This might be explained in several ways: these infants might be perceived as "unattractive," and are more irritable than their normal counterparts. They are also prone to medical problems and developmental retardation. They manifest feeding disturbances and often require special feeding techniques. Their delayed social responsiveness might be especially frustrating for "abuse-prone" parents with high expectations of their infants. The prolonged separation between the mother and her premature infant during the early postpartum period also interferes with normal attachment behavior or maternal "bonding." Recent studies have indicated that mothers who were permitted greater physical contact with their premature babies in the intensive care nursery demonstrated more effective infant care and attachment behavior following discharge than mothers who were deprived of this contact.

The child also contributes to abuse through aggressive and impulsive behavior which is itself a common sequel of maltreatment. Thus, as the child emulates the violent behavior of his parents, he exhibits the same type of aggressivity and provocativeness that the abuse was designed to prevent. This, in turn, creates a vicious cycle of misbehavior and abuse. The fact that many abused children incite abuse and scapegoating in foster homes attests to their provocativeness.

Environmental Stress

Parental "abuse-proneness" and the special vulnerability of a child for scapegoating and abuse might be insufficient in themselves to result in actual abuse without the presence of a stressful situation of crisis, as a catalyst. A typical childrearing crisis occurs when the equilibrium between the parental capacity and childrearing demands is disrupted. Decreased parental capacity may be caused by a loss or diminution of support from a spouse or key family member involved with child care. Physical or emotional illness in the parent might reduce parenting ability, or the sudden unavailability of child care facilities (daycare center, babysitter) might constitute an inordinate burden for working parents. The pressures of childrearing might be increased by the birth of another child, illness or deviancy of the children, or assuming the care of children of friends of relatives.

Environmental stress has often been associated with lower socioeconomic status. Gil (1970) attributed abuse almost entirely to socioeconomic determinants. A recent study (Justice and Duncan, 1976) has shown a relationship between life change and child abuse, while economic pressures have been associated with child abuse in other investigations (Johnson and Morse, 1968; Kempe et al., 1962). The occurrence of maltreatment has been noticed in middle- and upper-class families as well (Allen, Ten Bensel, and Raile, 1968; Boardman, 1962; Helfer and Kempe, 1968; Young, 1964) The actual impact of poverty on the genesis of child abuse might be somewhat overstated due to the overrepresentation of poor families in child-abuse registers throughout the country. Poor abusers served by municipal agencies are more likely to be reported than their middle- and upper-class counterparts who bring their children to private physicians. In their 1972 review, Spinetta and Riegler (1972) concluded that environmental stress had not been proven to be either necessary or sufficient to cause child abuse. It may however, interact with parental personality traits and child variables to potentiate maltreatment by widening the discrepancy between limited parental capacities and the demands for child care.

Psychodynamics

The psychodynamics in a given case of child abuse are largely determined by the "abuse-prone" personality traits of the parent who interacts with a "difficult" child in an unsupportive nongratifying environment. The relationship between the abusing parent and child is distorted by the cumulative impact of the parent's own traumatic experiences who, as a child was reared in a punitive, unloving environment. Individuals who abuse their children cannot envision any parent-child relationship as a mutually gratifying experience. The task of parenting mobilizes identifications with the parent-aggressors, child-victim dyad of the past. The key psychodynamic elements in child abuse are role reversal; excessive use of denial and projection as defenses; rapidly shifting identifications with pathological identifications with the child; and displacement of aggression from frustrating objects onto the child.

Role reversal occurs when the unfulfilled, abusing parent seeks dependency gratification, which is unavailable from his spouse and family, from his "parentified" child. It is based on an identification with the "child-victim." The child's inability to gratify the parent causes him to be unconsciously perceived as the rejecting mother. This intensifies the parent's feelings of rejection and worthlessness which threaten his narcissistic equilibrium. These painful feelings are denied and projected onto the child, who then becomes the recipient of the parent's self-directed aggression.

This is accomplished by a shift toward identification with the aggressive parent, terminating the role reversal. By beating the child, the abuser assuages his punitive superego and attempts to actively master the traumatic experiences passively endured as a child. The scapegoating process continues as the child becomes the additional target for aggression—displaced from various despised and frustrating objects in the parent's current and past life, such as a rejecting mate or lover, a hated sibling rival, or a depriving parent substitute. These objects are unconsciously linked to the original "parent-aggressor."

The choice of a particular child for scapegoating might depend upon accidental factors such as time of birth, physical appearance, temperament, and/or sex, in addition to actual physical or psychological deviancy. It is ultimately based upon the child's capacity to evoke the negatively perceived characteristics of the parents or of significant others.

Case Illustration Sonia, a six-year-old Puerto Rican girl, was severely beaten by her mother when she was four, resulting in a fractured femur. Sonia was the daughter of Ms. G.'s first husband, who, after frequent quarreling, drinking and "running around," left her when Sonia was one year old. Ms. G. subsequently entered into a common-law relationship with a man who fathered her two young boys.

Ms. G. initially married to escape from her brutal godparents, who had raised her since the age of 18 months after her mother had abandoned her. They had been extremely punitive and restrictive. Ms. G. remembered one occasion in which her godfather had broken a flowerpot over her head. Ms. G.'s marriage was arranged by the godparents. She went to work in a factory and was virtually ignored by her husband. She soon became pregnant but did not want a child since her husband spent no time with her. He deserted her when she was six weeks pregnant, and Ms. G. lived with her sister-in-law to have the baby. She hoped for a boy, stating, "I don't like girls. Boys are more interesting."

In addition to transferring her rage toward her exhusband and godparents onto Sonia, Ms. G. obviously identified with her little girl and brutalized her in the same manner as she had experienced with her godparents. She described her feelings toward Sonia: "Since she was born, I let out all the anger and frustration that I had in myself on her. Whenever she came to me, I sent her away with a beating." It is worth noting that Ms. G.'s relationship with her male children is better.

Nonabusive mothers whose children have been battered by husbands or boyfriends exhibit a slight variation in the psychodynamic pattern. The interaction between mother and child begins in a similar fashion, as the mother endows the child with the attributes of her own rejecting parents. However, the resulting "bad" childhood self-image derived from her parents is partly maintained and partly transferred to the child, while the internalized "parent-aggressor" is projected on to the abusive mate. The mother retains her identification with the "child-victim" rather than with the "parent-aggressor."

These women submit to the physical cruelty of their mates as a masochistic repetition of their childhood victimization by rejecting, aggressive parents. The pain-dependent attachment to the spouse serves as a defense against their hostility toward the child. This is confirmed by the tenacity with which these women cling to brutal and humiliating relationships, and by their tendency to assume the abusive role if the spouse leaves.

KEY PSYCHODYNAMIC ISSUES IN CHILD-ABUSING FATHERS

Special Characteristics of Abusing Fathers

It is striking that although fathers share equal responsibility with mothers for child abuse, psychological investigation of male child abusers has been conspicuously absent from the battered child literature. Most studies of abusing parents fail to clearly differentiate the personality structure and psychodynamics of abusing mothers and fathers.

The study of male child abusers has been neglected for several reasons. First of all, they are physically less available for investigation. Many fathers or father surrogates are only sporadically in the home, while others are forced to leave by court order. Daytime employment prevents them from keeping appointments. Second, their motivation to seek help is less urgent due to their more peripheral involvement with childrearing. This is reinforced by societal attitudes that still minimize the participation of fathers in bringing up their children. Finally, few professionals possess the patience and determination required to overcome these obstacles, since these violent, abusive men are often unpleasant and frightening to deal with. It is easier to refer them to the police or the courts for final disposition.

The following important psychodynamic issues and environmental factors operating in child-abusing fathers and father surrogates are based on their participation in the Comprehensive Treatment Program for Abused Children and their Families at the Downstate Medical Center (Green, 1979).

Unresolved Sibling Rivalry Based Upon Maternal Deprivation

Abusing fathers experienced major frus-
trations during their childhood, such as physical abuse, neglect, and parental abandonment, that prevented the satisfaction of basic needs for nurturance and human contact. This left them with a residue of rage and mistrust.

The father regards the child as a rival for the attention of his spouse due to the lack of previous satisfaction of his own dependency longings. The competitive rivalry with the child for the mother's love is a repetition of the father's unresolved sibling rivalry during his childhood. The father's jealousy of the child usually manifests itself during the first years of life when the child requires the greatest amount of nurturing and attention.

Spouse Abuse

Abusing fathers frequently also abused their wives in addition to the child. Beating the wife often occurs when she threatens to leave or when she tries to protect herself and the children from her husband's aggression. The beatings are designed to further intimidate the spouse and reinforce her passive-submissive behavior. In expressing his rage toward the mother-child dyad, he re-enacts his frustration and anger at exclusion from maternal contact by rivals during his own childhood.

Case History Mr. T., a chronic alcoholic, experienced strong feelings of anger and resentment if his ten-month-old infant cried when he returned home from work. He could not tolerate his wife's feeding and bathing the baby in his presence especially when he was "hungry and tired," and he frequently struck the baby and his wife if the baby cried. Mrs. T. realized that getting the baby fed and put to sleep before her husband returned was the best way of preventing its physical abuse. Mrs. T.'s preoccupation with the crying infant evoked Mr. T.'s childhood memories of having been deprived of food and love by uncaring foster parents whose preoccupation with their five natural children prevented his own cries for nurturance from being satisfied.

A closely related pattern of child abuse based on the theme of sibling rivalry is observed in stepfathers who abuse their stepchildren.

ENVIRONMENTAL ISSUES IN CHILD ABUSE BY FATHERS

Excessive Childrearing Burdens

Some children with gross physical or psychological abnormalities impose a severe burden on their parents by virtue of their inordinate demands for care and attention. They are especially vulnerable to abuse if their deviant behavior is erroneously believed to be willfully motivated.

Child abuse by the father is often provoked by situations in which he is confronted with the sudden and unexpected physical or material burden of child care due to the accidental or intentional unavailability of his spouse. The abuse often takes place while the father is reluctantly caring for the children. At times, the mother's passive manipulation in this type of abuse is obvious.

Case History Mr. M., a hospital maintenance worker, often abused the two oldest of his four daughters when they were left in his care by his chronically alcoholic, psychotic wife. The wife periodically withdrew from her husband, children, and housekeeping responsibilities. Her husband was obliged to assume these responsibilities in her absence. Mrs. M. admitted: "I knew Bill would stop beating them if I took care of the children, cleaned the house, and gave him sex, but this is my way of punishing him."

Abuse of Alcohol

The child and spouse abuse committed by the fathers is often accompanied by excessive drinking. In a study carried out at the Downstate Medical Center (Green 1979), 50 percent of the reports of abuse by fathers indicated that they were drinking heavily or were intoxicated during their assaultive behavior. The vulnerability of these men to alcoholism is consistent with their psychodynamics. Alcohol is perceived as the ultimate source of dependency gratification that cannot be obtained by spouse and family, and it temporarily obliterates feelings of inadequacy, depression, and low self-esteem. Alcohol also enhances the potential for abuse by undermining the inhibitions and brittle defenses against pent-up rage and aggression. Narcotics addiction and use of hard drugs were infrequent in this sample of abusing fathers.

Work-Related Stress

The actual or threatened loss of a job may seriously compromise the father's self-esteem. The possibility of inactivity, financial insecurity, and increased child-rearing responsibilities undermines his feelings of masculinity. The loss of a job also places a great strain on the marital relationship. The father becomes more dependent on his spouse and family for emotional support. He is also prone to depression and excessive drinking, if there is a history of alcoholism.

CHARACTERISTICS OF ABUSED CHILDREN

Previous Observations of Abused Children

Recent efforts to document the psychological damage sustained by abused children have uncovered a variety of cognitive and emotional difficulties, but these have yet to be integrated into a comprehensive psychodynamic understanding of the abused child in the context of his traumatic family environment. Elmer (1965) studied the effects of abuse by comparing abused and nonabused children who had been hospitalized for multiple bone injuries. The abused children showed a higher incidence of mental retardation and speech difficulties. Martin (1972) reported a study in which one-third of a sample of abused children was mentally retarded, 43 percent were neurologically damaged, and 38 percent exhibited delayed language development. Morse, Sahler, and Friedman (1970) discovered mental deficiency in 70 percent of a group of children whose injuries resulted from abuse or neglect.

Behavioral observations of abused children have found them to be stubborn, unresponsive, negativistic, and depressed (Johnson and Morse, 1968), fearful, apathetic, and unappealing, with a blunting of their appetite for food and human contact (Galdston, 1965), and likely to provoke physical attack from others. Green (1968) documented a link between physical abuse and subsequent self-mutilation in schizophrenic children.

The severity and wide range of psychological impairment attributed to abused children clearly warranted further clinical investigation and research in this area. This stimulated the author's interest in exploring the psychological sequelae of abuse in 60 school-aged battered children at the Downstate Medical Center. Comparison groups of nonabused neglected and "normal" children were used in this research study (Green et al., 1974). Psychiatric evaluation and psychological testing of these children documented the cognitive impairment described by others. The abused children exhibited significantly lower mean IQ scores than the comparison group normal children. Twenty-five percent of the abused children were found to be mentally retarded. These children also demonstrated severe deficits in a wide variety of ego functions, such as impulse control, defensive functioning, reality testing, object relations, thought processes, body image, and overall ego competency. The abused children also exhibited a rather typical pattern of depressive affect with low self-esteem, which was often accompanied by self-destructive behavior. In some cases, however, the defects of the child preceded and precipitated the maltreatment (Sandgrund, Gaines and Green, 1974).

Approximately 20 abused children were involved in out-patient individual psychotherapy. The treatment of the children was complemented by various modes of therapeutic involvement with the parents, such as counseling, crisis intervention, and home contact by visiting nurses. The children ranged in age from five to fourteen, and most of them were seen twice weekly for at least one year.

The vast majority of the children had been subjected to recurrent abuse during the first two years of life. There was evidence to indicate that the psychopathology in most of the children had been present prior to latency, but was usually not recognized until schools and daycare centers confronted the parents with the abnormal behavior of the children.

Psychotherapeutic intervention with these abused children provided a better understanding of their psychological functioning and an exploration of the abusive interaction between each child and his family. Child abuse was regarded as a complex experience consisting of several components rather than as a single variable. The following elements were identified:

(1) An acute physical and psychological assault conveying parental rage and hostility which confronted the child with the threat of annihilation and/or abandonment.

(2) This assault was inflicted on a background of poverty, family disorganization, and the interruption of maternal care, resulting in early experiences of object loss and emotional deprivation.

(3) Deviant psychological and constitutional endowment of the child often complemented the pathological environment as a crucial variable associated with abuse.

(4) The abused child was usually a scapegoat and was perceived as the major source of the family's frustrations. The scapegoating process, which consists of the projection of negative parental attributes onto the child, was also influenced by the child's congenital or acquired behavioral deviancy.

These immediate and long-term adverse experiences left a characteristic impact on the cognitive apparatus, ego functions, object relationships, identifications, and libidinal organization of the abused children. Specific disturbances in ego functions, behavior, and character structure with their pathological sequelae may be outlined in the following manner.

PSYCHOPATHOLOGY OF ABUSED CHILDREN

Overall Impairment in Ego Functioning

When viewed globally, the abused children receiving psychotherapy exhibited an overall impairment in ego functioning associated with intellectual and cognitive deficits and a high incidence of delayed development and CNS dysfunction (Green et al., 1974). Many were mentally retarded.

They were often found to be hyperactive and impulsive with minimal frustration tolerance. Motor activity, rather than verbalization, was the preferred mode of expression. Many abused children manifested aberrant speech and language development. Although these children were of latency age, they failed to demonstrate the progressive ego growth and reorganization characteristic of this state. There was an absence of typical latency defenses that enable the normal child to bind anxiety from internal and external sources and cope with phase specific stresses and conflicts. The abused children's preoccupation with external danger and over-stimulated drive activity deprived them of the energy necessary for learning and mastery.

"Traumatic" Reaction with Acute Anxiety State

The frightening physical and psychological assault experienced by these children during an abusive episode exposed them to the threat of annihilation and/or abandonment. Many of the children were overwhelmed by both the quality and quantity of the noxious stimulation, which paralyzed ego functioning and resulted in severe panic. This situation resembled Freud's concept of traumatic neurosis and the breaching of the stimulus barrier (1920). The abused children experienced feelings of helplessness, annihilation, and humiliation, which were often accompanied by a loss of ego boundaries. The anxiety states occurred prior to, or during a beating, or in the anticipation of an attack. These children frequently displayed psychotic behavior at this time, due to the severe ego regressions with the temporary suspension of reality testing.

These children exhibited a striking tendency to re-enact continually the traumatic situation. Repetition of the trauma was observed in overt behavior and in symbolic activities such as fantasy, play, and artistic productions. It was also encountered in the therapeutic relationship in which the children acted out the role of the "bad child" and sought punishment from the therapist. This "fixation to the trauma" may be considered as a defensive reaction that permits the abused child to actively re-create, master, and control the painful affects and anxiety that otherwise might be instigated by the environment.

Case History Sarah, age six, had been a victim of recurrent physical abuse by her mother since infancy. She sustained a broken femur following a severe beating when she was four. On this occasion, her mother attacked her for letting the bathroom sink overflow. During her initial testing, Sarah responded to the examiner's presentation of a hitting scene in a doll family, "The mother hits the baby for playing with water." During a psychiatric interview a short time later, Sarah appeared quite anxious upon returning from the bathroom. She told the psychiatrist that she was afraid he would punish her for spilling water from the sink.

Pathological Object Relationships

Early and pervasive exposure to parental rejection, assault, and deprivation had an adverse effect on the development of subsequent object relationships. Potential new objects were regarded with fear and apprehension. The abused children were not able to achieve Erikson's stage of basic trust (1950). They expected similar frustration and maltreatment from other adults on the basis of previous experience. Violence and rejection were regarded as the major ingredients of human encounters. These children were involved in a perpetual search for "good" objects to protect them from the "bad" ones.

Psychotherapeutic involvement with abused children has provided opportunity to study the vissicitudes of their object relationships in *status nascendi*. The typical abused child initially appeared detached and guarded and was ingratiating to please his therapist and avoid punishment. Once he felt safe, he displayed an enormous object hunger. The therapist was over-idealized, and the child attempted to capture and incorporate this "good parent" as a source of dependency gratification and as a means of protection against his "bad" parental objects. However, the inevitable frustrations and limitations in the therapeutic relationship incited the child's rage and disillusionment.

The child's increasing anger and provocative behavior led to his anticipation of punishment by the therapist, who was rapidly transformed into the "bad parent." The child's projection of his own rage onto the therapist helped to consolidate this negative image and increase his fear of retaliation. At this point he adopted the negative self-image of the "bad child," which represented an "identification with the aggressor" (his own bad parent) in the face of increasing anxiety and helplessness in the treatment situation. The child then proceeded to re-enact with the therapist his relationship with the abusing parent. He sought to achieve mastery and control over anticipated punishment through provocative and testing behavior.

Primitive Defense Mechanism

The abused children relied on an excessive use of primitive defenses such as denial, projection, introjection, and splitting in order to cope with threatening external and internalized parental images. They were unable to integrate the loving and hostile aspects of their parents and others. This accounted for the baffling tendency of some of these children to support completely their parent's transparent denials and rationalizations that concerned inflicted injuries.

While this need to suppress knowledge of parental wrongdoing was occasionally motivated by fear of additional punishment, it also represented the child's need to protect himself from the awareness of the actual and internalized destructive parent and to safeguard the parent from his own murderous rage. Splitting mechanisms were more frequently observed in those children who were abused by the parent who provided most of their nurturing. Their acknowledgment of the destructiveness and malevolence of the primary caretaker, usually the mother, would have placed their tenuous dependent relationship in jeopardy.

Impaired Impulse Control

The abused children were often cited for aggressive and destructive behavior at home and in school. Bullying, fighting, and assaultive behavior were observed in their contact with peers and siblings. The younger children were frequently restless and hyperactive, while the older children and adolescents were commonly involved in antisocial and delinquent behavior. The origin of this problem was overdetermined. The abused children formed a basic identification with their violent parents that faciliated the use of "identification with the aggressor" as a major defense against feelings of anxiety and helplessness. Hyperaggressive behavior typically followed incidents of physical abuse. Loss of impulse control was further enhanced by the presence of CNS dysfunction. These children also lacked the usual superego restraints found in normal children during latency due to inadequate superego models and faulty internalization.

Case History Juan, an eleven-year-old boy, was referred for psychiatric treatment after he persuaded his three-year-old half brother to drink some lye. The half brother required emergency hospitalization and is still in intensive care. Juan returned to his mother and her boyfriend a year ago after living with his abusive father and stepmother in Puerto Rico since the age of two. Juan had been subjected to chronic physical abuse during this period, which consisted of beatings on the head and burns on his body inflicted with a hot iron. Since living with his mother, Juan displayed hyperactive, aggressive behavior in school, frequently hitting and kicking his classmates. Juan conveyed his violent feelings quite dramatically: "Sometimes I hate people because they bother me or hit me. Once I hit a teacher in Puerto Rico because she punished me for hitting a boy. I hit a kid in school who stole my pencil; I knocked him down the stairs. I hit my little brother. When I get nervous I punch the wall and hit my head against the radiator."

Impaired Self-Concept

The abused children were frequently sad, dejected, and self-deprecatory. Their poor self-concept was an end result of chronic physical and emotional scarring, humiliation, and scapegoating, compounded and reinforced by each new episode of physical abuse. One may hypothesize that the preverbal infant who is repeatedly assaulted acquires an unpleasurable awareness of "self," consisting of painful sensation and painful affects linked to primary objects. This painful self-awareness becomes transformed into a devalued self-concept with the development of cognition and language. These children ultimately regard themselves with the same displeasure and contempt that their parents directed toward them. The young children who were repeatedly punished, beaten, and threatened with abandonment assume that it was a consequence of their own behavior, regardless of their actual innocence.

Case History Karen, a seven-year-old girl, was referred to the out-patient child psychiatry clinic because her mother could not tolerate her poor school performance. Her mother continually referred to Karen's stupidity and was certain that the child was retarded. Karen appeared untidy and dishevelled. Her clothes were often torn and stank of urine. Her therapist began to notice evidence of physical injury in the form of a black eye, scratches, and bruises. Her mother admitted that her husband had started to assault Karen and the other children. Karen ascribed her injuries to fights at school and to falls, and persistently defended her parents. She confessed to being stupid and dumb, and expressed guilt over the break up of her family. She lamented, "If I only had done the laundry, my mother wouldn't have been beaten up by my father, and we wouldn't have broken up." Incidentally, Karen's test results indicated an IQ of 108.

Masochistic and Self-Destructive Behavior

Abused children commonly exhibited overt types of self-destructive behavior, such as suicide attempts, gestures, threats, and various forms of self-mutilation. These were often accompanied by more subtle forms of pain-dependent activity in the form of provocative, belligerent, and limit-testing behavior that easily elicited beatings and punishment from parents, adults,

and peers. Accident proneness was considered to be another form of self-destructive activity. Forty percent of our research population of abused children manifested direct forms of self-destructive behavior, a significantly ($p = < .01$) higher incidence than in the neglected and normal controls (Green, 1978). In the majority of cases, the self-destructive behavior was precipitated by parental beatings or occurred in response to actual or threatened separation from parental figures. This finding is of special importance, since self-destructive behavior is seldom observed among latency and pre-adolescent children in the general population. Thus, certain events occurring in normal latency seem to have self-preservative functions which are interfered with in the abused child.

Self-destructive behavior ultimately represented the child's compliance with parental wishes for his destruction and/or disappearance. The child's acting out of parental hostility directed toward him has been described as an important factor in the etiology of adolescent suicidal behavior (Sabbeth, 1969).

Case History Betty, an eight-year-old girl, had been physically abused by her impulsive, schizophrenic mother. Many of the beatings had been triggered by the mother's heavy drinking. When Betty was seven, she jumped off a swing in response to the commands of a "woman's voice." Betty also engaged in self-deprecatory and self-destructive rumination during her psychotherapy sessions. Some of her typical comments were: "I'm terrible; I can't sit still; I always hurt myself; I fall off my bike and lean against a hot radiator." When she was angry with her therapist, Betty would often bang her arm or head against a hard object, stick herself with a pin, or threaten to jump out of the window.

Difficulties with Separation

The abused children often reacted to actual or threatened separation and object loss with intense anxiety. This was frequently traced to numerous experiences of separation and abandonment with parental figures during infancy and early childhood. Hypothetically, chronic physical abuse might have increased the vulnerability of these children to separation, because each beating implies the parent's withdrawal of love and wish to be rid of the child. The abused child's frequent lack of object constancy resulting from cognitive impairment and/or cerebral dysfunction was another contributing factor to the separation problems. Acute separation anxiety was often observed in the treatment situation in response to the therapist's vacations and departure from the hospital. The children were commonly unable to leave the playroom unless they were given a tangible object that they could utilize to represent the absent therapist.

Case History Earl, age six, was hospitalized with severe burns and multiple injuries as a result of abuse by his mother and maternal grandmother. Foster placement was arranged, following his discharge from the hospital. Earl was referred for psychiatric treatment because of unmanageable behavior in kindergarten. Following his therapist's return from vacation at the onset of treatment, he noted with distress that the toys were not in their usual order and that someone had eaten the candies. He complained that someone else would be playing with the therapist the next day when he wasn't there. Near the end of the session, he began to cut erasers off the pencils and attempted to cut off some of the therapist's hair which he wanted to take home.

Difficulties in School Adjustment

Most of the abused children exhibited major problems in school adjustment. Their limited attention span, frequent hyperactivity, and cognitive impairment led to deficient academic performance. At times these children demonstrated specific learning disabilities, such as dyslexia, expressive and receptive language disorders, and perceptual-motor dysfunction on the basis of minimal brain dysfunction or maturational lag. Their aggressivity and poor impulse control contributed to behavior problems with peers and teachers. Their parents were frequently called to school because of their disruptive behavior and learning difficulties, which often led to further abuse. A vicious cycle often ensued, consisting of academic and behavioral problems, parental beatings, and increased disruptiveness in the classroom due to the displacement of anger at the parents onto the teachers.

CENTRAL NERVOUS SYSTEM IMPAIRMENT

Although a high incidence of central nervous system dysfunction among abused children has been reported in the literature (Elmer and Gregg, 1967; Johnson and Morse, 1968; Martin, Beezley and Conway, 1974; Morse, Sahler, and Riedman, 1970), the precise etiology of this impairment has been the subject of considerable controversy. With the exception of obvious cases of massive head trauma resulting in skull fractures with subdural hematomas (as originally described by Kempe et al., 1962, in their seminal paper on the "battered child syndrome"), brain damage alone would not appear sufficient to explain CNS impairment. The uncertain impact of child abuse on neurological development has been noted by Martin et al. (1974), who showed that appreciable numbers of abused children with skull fractures and subdural hematomas were neurologically normal, while numerous abused children without head injury exhibited neurological deficits. Because most abused children manifest a variety of soft tissue injuries as opposed to major skull trauma, it is important to classify this issue.

Several hypotheses have been offered to account for neurological impairment observed in children not known to have sustained massive head injuries. Caffey (1972) described how vigorous shaking of a child's head could result in petechial hemorrhages in the brain. Neglect (Coleman and Provence, 1957), malnutrition (Birch, 1972; Scrimshaw and Gordon, 1968), and maternal deprivation (Bakwin, 1949; Bowlby, 1951; Spitz, 1945) often accompanying child abuse have all been implicated in adverse neurological development. Some observers (Milowe and Lourie, 1964; Sandgrund et al., 1974) have postulated that this impairment may precede and even provoke abuse by rendering these children hyperkinetic and difficult to manage. Most retrospective studies of abuse victims have revealed neurological impairment (Baron, Bejar and Sheaff, 1970; Martin et al., 1974; Smith and Hanson, 1974), mental retardation (Birrell and Birrell, 1968; Elmer and Gregg, 1967; Martin et al., 1974; Morse et al., 1970; Smith and Hanson, 1974), and language deficits (Martin et al., 1974; Smith and Hanson, 1974) that could severely strain the child-rearing capacities of abuse-prone parents (Green et al., 1974). Whether neurological impairment precipitates abuse, is one of the effects of maltreatment, or merely concomitant remains problematic.

There is considerable evidence that the proportion of premature births among abused children is substantially higher than regional averages (Elmer and Gregg, 1967; Klein and Stern, 1971; Martin et al., 1974). Others have noted the prevalence of unrecognized physical handicaps (Ounsted, Oppenheimer and Lindsay, 1974) and congenital anomalies (Birrell and Birrell, 1968) in this population. Several interpretations have been suggested for these findings concerning the role of the child in the abuse process (Friedrich and Boriskin, 1971). The most direct causal inference is that abused children may be less responsive and manageable due to a pre-existing deviancy that renders them vulnerable to scapegoating. These deficits are tolerated poorly by narcissistic parents who respond abusively when their own threshold is breached. Alternatively, prematurity or difficult infant temperaments may impede the establishment of maternal infant bonds. Faranoff, Kennell and Klaus (1972) found that mothers who later abuse or neglect their children visited low-birth-weight infants less frequently than normal control mothers. Ounsted et al. (1974) observed "high-risk" mother-infant dyads characterized by puerperal depression among the mothers and colicky, irritable children who cried excessively and were prone to sleeping difficulties.

Unfortunately, the major weakness thus far in studies to document neurological problems associated with child abuse has been the failure to compare them with control children from otherwise comparable backgrounds.

A study was carried out at the Downstate Medical Center to explore the relationship between the abusive environment and CNS development (Green et al., 1978). The neurological competency of physically abused children who were not known to have sustained severe head trauma was assessed. The neglect, family disorganization, and emotional deprivation were controlled by including nonabused neglected and normal comparison groups. The neurological evaluation of the 120 children (60 abused, 30 neglected, and 30 normal) followed the psychological and psychiatric studies described previously. The children received physical, neurological examinations, including an EEG, and a battery of perceptual-motor tests. On the basis of all available information, the pediatric neurologist assigned each child a global rating of impairment. The results indicated that the abused sample obtained the highest rating of neurological impairment, followed by the neglected and normal controls. Fifty-two percent of the abused children received designations of moderate or severe impairment, as compared to 38 percent of the neglected children, and only 14 percent of the controls.

The higher incidence of neurological impairment among the abused and neglected children was anticipated, but the finding that the abused children were not significantly more damaged than their neglected counterparts was contrary to expectation. The CNS impairment documented in this study indicated relatively subtle neurological dysfunction rather than structural damage. In many instances, these developmental lags and deficits in perception, coordination, and integration of sensory stimuli would not have been detected by the usual neurological examination. These were clearly evident in the careful neurological evaluation and series of perceptual-motor tasks designed explicitly to reveal subtle neurological impairment. Similarities in the nature and prevalence of impairment in the two maltreatment groups in contrast to the relative intactness of the controls suggest that the adverse physical and psychological environment associated with maltreatment may be of greater neurological consequences than the physical assault itself. The combination of behavioral and neurological disability in the maltreated child could result from abnormal child-rearing, poor prenatal and infant care, nutritional deficiency, inadequate medical care, and abnormal (insufficient or excessive) sensory stimulation. Although the control children were also chosen from families on public assistance, more of the control households were intact and had somewhat greater availability of social support systems. The maltreating families appeared to represent the extreme of deprivation and chronic disorganization within their own subculture.

The neurological and developmental sequelae produced by the maltreating environment frequently contribute to the child's vulnerability to abuse by rendering him more difficult to manage. A vicious cycle often unfolds, consisting of inadequate or abnormal parenting, neurological and behavioral impairment, physical abuse, and further impairment, and so on. One may even regard the CNS abnormalities as initial adaptations to the maltreating environment. Martin (1976) suggested that developmental lags in speech and motor development might represent the abused child's inhibitory response to parental admonitions against spontaneous speech and motor expression.

The results of this study implicate poverty, family disorganization, and related environmental factors prevalent in low socioeconomic status maltreating families in the adverse neurological development of abused and neglected children. Because these children are particularly susceptible to subtle neurological impairment, neurological examination of these children should be specifically devised to detect these manifestations.

TREATMENT OF CHILD ABUSE

General Considerations

Unfortunately, efforts toward the rehabilitation of abusing families have not kept pace with the recent nationwide increase in the reporting and public awareness of child abuse. Social scientists have deplored the inability of states and cities to supply services and treatment for the great influx of maltreating families (DeFrancis, 1972; Nagi, 1975; Oviatt, 1972). The impact of punitive societal attitudes toward abusing parents is still reflected in the investigation and management of newly reported cases. In many states, cases of abuse are reported to law enforcement officials rather than to protective service agencies. The initial contact with abusing families emphasizes investigation and confirmation of the alleged incident, which is usually incompatible with the development of a therapeutic strategy. Placement of the children in foster homes and institutions has become the major mode of intervention, owing to the relative scarcity of social and psychiatric services for abusing families and the difficulties experienced in involving abusing parents in traditional counseling and psychotherapy. Abusing parents are too frequently presumed to be unmotivated for help and therefore beyond rehabilitation.

Some progress has recently been made toward the development of child abuse treatment programs through the pioneering efforts of a group of pediatricians, psychiatrists, and social workers at the University of Colorado Medical Center in Denver, Colorado. The Denver group was the first to systematically describe the clinical dimensions and psychology of child abuse and base innovative treatment techniques on this body of knowledge. This group collaborated in the publication of three basic texts on child abuse that were edited by Helfer and Kempe (1968, 1972), and stimulated the development of child-abuse treatment facilities for maltreated children and their families in other parts of the country.

FAILURE OF TRADITIONAL PSYCHIATRIC INTERVENTION

The growing evidence that child maltreatment is associated with severe parental dysfunction and psychiatric disorder has resulted in a steady increase in referrals to psychiatrists for consultation and treatment of abusing parents. The psychiatrists accepted the referrals as they came along and provided whatever treatment was available at their particular clinic or institution, without taking into consideration the special needs of this population. The traditional psychiatric out-patient setting failed to solve the problems of the abusing parent, justifying psychiatry's skepticism and discouraging further referrals from the child protective networks. Traditional psychiatric intervention failed for various reasons. First of all, failure to stabilize the chaotic living conditions of these families by providing social services and home-centered crisis intervention precluded psychiatrists' capacity to explore inner thoughts and feelings. The energies of these parents were absorbed by issues of day-to-day survival, with little energy remaining to invest in a seemingly irrelevant intellectual exercise. Aside from their minimal motivation, abusing parents were often unpleasant to work with because of their hostility, impulsivity, and distrustfulness. They were also quite provocative and frequently missed appointments. These characteristics, coupled with their initial nonresponsiveness and defensiveness, posed a distinct threat to the therapist's narcissism, and usually led to strong countertransference manifestations. Most psychiatric clinics are not equipped to provide the type of outreach and crisis intervention required by these patients. Strengthening of parental functioning and family life through regular home visits by nurses, homemakers, and the therapist are beyond the scope of the average mental health facility. The frequency of missed appointments by these families is an anathema to psychiatric clinics. Aside from their interference with the treatment process and immobilizing the staff, failed appointments are not covered by third party payments. In addition, psychiatrists usually attempt to "analyze" or interpret missed appointments, instead of the aggressive follow-up by telephone or home visit that is required by this patient population.

Treatment of Abusing Parents

The major thrust of treating abusing par-

ents is to protect the children from further injury and to strengthen the family and its child-rearing capacity. To this end, intervention with abusing parents must be designed to modify the major components of the child abuse syndrome: the personality traits of the parents that contribute to the "abuse proneness"; the characteristics of the child that make him more difficult to manage and enhance his scapegoating; and the environmental stresses that either increase the burden of child care or deplete the child-rearing resources of a family. The child abuse syndrome requires a crisis-oriented multidisciplinary approach with a capacity for providing the parents and children with a wide variety of home-based comprehensive services. Innovative techniques such as homemaking assistance; regular home visiting by nurses, social workers, and lay therapists; and a 24-hour hotline for emergencies will assist abusing families to cope with environmental pressures and provide them with child-rearing support. The availability of crisis nurseries and daycare facilities for infants and preschool children will relieve the child care burden and facilitate the identification of pathological or deviant traits that would increase the child's vulnerability to abuse or scapegoating. Child-rearing education, based on an understanding of the child's physical and psychological development, will modify inappropriate parental expectations for precocious and premature performance. Individual and group psychotherapy and counseling attempt to resolve or attenuate parental conflicts and personality traits which contribute to abuse proneness. Family therapy and therapeutic monitoring of parent-child interaction are geared toward the exploration and modification of distorted and inappropriate interactions and communications between parents and children.

Intervention with abusing parents poses special difficulties beyond those usually encountered in poor, unmotivated, and psychologically unsophisticated multiproblem families. The effects of ongoing investigative and punitive procedures inhibit the establishment of a confidential and trusting therapeutic alliance. The suspiciousness and basic mistrust of authority exhibited by these parents, resulting from their longstanding experience of humiliation and criticism by their own parents and authority figures, are intensified by their contact with case investigators and court personnel. This poses a barrier to the development of a therapeutic relationship unless it is dealt with specifically. This problem may be overcome by clearly divorcing the functions of the child protective agency and the courts from those of the therapeutic team. Staff members must be viewed as advocates of the parents. Evaluations and progress reports required by the court or child protective agency should be fully explained and shared with the parents before they are submitted.

The fragile self-esteem of these parents makes it difficult for them to accept advice and help from the therapeutic team. Suggestions concerning child-rearing and household management are frequently construed as criticism and rejection. The parents require continual reassurance and support during the initial stages of treatment. Their own dependency needs must be gratified before "demands" can be placed on them.

Another group of obstacles to treatment is determined by strong feelings of anger and revulsion child abusers elicit in the therapist. Most individuals instinctively condemn and dislike anyone who would intentionally injure an innocent infant or child. Many therapists are additionally burdened by rescue fantasies in which they attempt to save the child from a threatening situation by overidentifying with a "good" parent. Some staff members might feel pressure to "reform" the abuser by transforming him or her into a model parent.

An additional reservoir of negative feelings, or countertransference, toward the abusing parents stems from their provocativeness and masochism. They often exhibit a strong unconscious need to sabotage all therapeutic efforts by regarding them as repetitions of previous humiliating interactions with their parents and spouses. Typical examples of such provocative behavior are arriving late or missing appointments, expressions of overt hostility toward the therapists, and an overall lack of re-

spect or commitment to the treatment process. Needless to say, a successful therapeutic outcome will not be possible unless the treatment personnel are able to recognize and control such feelings of anger and self-righteous indignation toward the parents.

Despite the formidable difficulties encountered during intervention with abusing parents, most of them can be rehabilitated. Pollock and Steele (1972) estimated that 80 percent of these parents can be treated with satisfactory results under optimal conditions. Our own treatment program at the Downstate Medical Center has helped the majority of families involved. Its basic goals and techniques include helping the parent establish a trusting and gratifying relationship with the therapist and other adults, which is facilitated by an initially noncritical need-satisfying therapeutic posture. The parent is "indulged" and permitted to experience the type of dependency gratification he or she was previously unable to obtain. "Giving" to the parent may take the form of child-rearing advice, home visiting, securing medical and social services for the family as an advocate of the parent, and being available in emergencies. The parent is helped to improve his devalued self-image by mobilization of his assets with eventual educational and vocational assistance. The therapist or visiting nurse provides the parent with a model for childrearing. Group therapy has been helpful in facilitating social involvement with peers and the community. As the parents experience gratification and support from the treatment staff and strengthen peer relationships, they will no longer require their children to fulfill a disproportionate share of their dependency needs. The ultimate goal of intervention is to enable the parents to derive pleasure from their children and to increase their capacity for successful nurturing.

Treatment of Abused Children

Numerous studies have recently documented a wide range of cognitive, developmental, neurological, and emotional deficits among abused children that tend to persist after the cessation of maltreatment (Elmer, 1965; Green, 1978a; Martin, 1972; Morse et al., 1970). Green (1978b) described the importance of psychiatric treatment for these children in order to effect changes in the child's pathological inner world by modifying pathological identifications and internalized representations of their violent parents. The abused children also required assistance in improving their impulse control, using verbalization as an alternative to motor discharge; improving their poor self-image; overcoming acute anxiety states and depressive reactions; and learning to trust others. Modifications of psychoanalytically oriented play therapy and psychotherapy have been used effectively to overcome these deficits, while psychoeducational intervention has been used to reverse cognitive defects and learning disabilities. Treatment has been successful in interrupting the vicious cycle in which the abused child re-creates the original sadomasochistic relationship with his parents and others that, if unchecked, leads to further rejection and traumatization. Timely intervention with abused children should be carried out in the context of a multidisciplinary treatment program for the family. The provision of mental health services for abused and neglected children by public mental health agencies has been recently recommended as a federal standard for child abuse and neglect treatment program (Holmes, 1978).

TYPES OF CHILD ABUSE AND NEGLECT TREATMENT PROGRAMS

Child abuse and neglect treatment programs may originate from protective services units of public social service agencies, hospitals, private service agencies, community-based teams, and volunteer organizations. The objectives and focus of each program may vary according to the type of each sponsor organization. The success of any program depends upon the amount of cooperation received from the community and the degree of coordination of its services and resources such as the courts, schools, and social services and welfare agencies.

Protective Services Programs

Protective services units of public social service agencies have become providers of treatment services for abusive and neglectful families in many communities. These units are legally mandated to investigate reports of abuse and neglect and to provide case management and supervision if maltreatment is confirmed. However, due to the large numbers of reported cases, protective services caseworkers have been traditionally burdened with unmanageable caseloads so that the functions of intake and investigation have taken priority over treatment services. The overextended caseworkers were also prone to poor morale and high job "turnover." Certain protective services units have managed to overcome these obstacles by hiring sufficient personnel to ensure smaller caseloads, and expanding their staffs to include trained social workers, nurses, and psychiatrists.

Other units have been able to generate treatment potential by collaborating with hospitals, daycare centers, and mental health facilities in the community offering specialized treatment services. The protective services model has certain advantages. Since the agency is legally mandated to investigate and treat cases of abuse and neglect, it wields authority and a permanent source of funding is ensured. The disadvantages stem from the frequent inefficiency and restrictiveness inherent in a civil service "bureaucracy" and the reluctance of clients to divulge confidential material to an investigative and punitive body that has the power to terminate their parental rights. Some protective services treatment programs attempt to divorce its intake and investigation procedures from the treatment process, but this requires the client to deal with two caseworkers without really eliminating the "punitive" image of the agency.

Hospital-Based Programs

Many hospitals located in inner cities with a high incidence of abuse and neglect have initiated treatment services for the maltreated children and their families. These programs are multidisciplinary, often using existing staff and facilities from the departments of pediatrics, social service, and nursing. Psychiatric consultation is usually available. A child abuse team, usually consisting of a pediatrician, radiologist, social worker, and a child abuse coordinator, reviews suspected cases of abuse and neglect on a regular basis. These cases are usually reported to the local protective services units by the social workers from the department of pediatrics. One of the disadvantages of a hospital-based program is its frequent emphasis on diagnosis and medical management rather than the provision of long-term supportive and psychological services to the families. Most hospitals require additional funding and community support to provide their own treatment services, such as parent groups, child care programs, parent education, home visiting, counseling, and psychotherapy. An effective hospital-based program must maintain a close liaison with the local protective services agency and the family court.

The advantages of the hospital model include access to medical diagnosis and treatment for the maltreated children and their families, its credibility as a service provider, and its separation from investigative and law enforcement functions. Larger academic hospitals may increase their long-term service delivery by mobilizing evaluation and treatment resources from the departments of psychology, psychiatry, and child psychiatry.

Private Nonprofit Agency-Based Programs

These private service programs that often obtain their funding through public social service agencies offer individualized treatment services to abusing and neglectful families. These programs are usually smaller in scope than those sponsored by public agencies and are more selective in their acceptance of referrals. They often maintain a "home"-like atmosphere and offer flexibility in meeting client's needs. They usually provide group and individual therapy, telephone hotlines, and daycare components, and are geared to maintaining client anonymity.

Community-Based Team Programs

These programs are usually located in small rural communities in which no single agency has the resources to provide effective services and rehabilitation to abusive and neglectful families. The public social service agencies in these communities usually limit their involvement to investigations and crisis intervention. The community teams are usually composed of representatives from the department of public welfare, the local hospital and health department, mental health center, elementary and preschool programs, and the county attorney's office. The teams meet regularly to review the reported cases of abuse and neglect. They provide consultation services to the department of public welfare regarding case management and advise the county attorney about recommendations to the court. They frequently coordinate the activities of local agencies interested in maltreatment and are involved in community education and training. Treatment services may be arranged through collaboration with local mental health centers and children's programs.

Volunteer Programs

These programs operate largely through volunteers, who may include former abusing and neglectful parents. These volunteer organizations have small budgets and are quite cost effective. They usually operate independently from other community agencies. Parent Professionals Anonymous is a typical volunteer organization that operates therapy groups for abusing or neglectful parents which is staffed by rehabilitated abusers. The clients can benefit from the nonjudgmental approach, and can readily identify with the nonprofessional staff. Counseling by parent-aides and a 24-hour hotline for emergencies are also typical services provided by volunteer groups. Disadvantages of these programs are a high turnover rate among the volunteers, and their lack of training, which often prevents them from dealing effectively with severe and difficult cases. Some volunteer programs utilize professional consultants to overcome this problem.

Coordination Programs

Some private and public agencies have adopted a coordination model, in which they assume the case management responsibility for clients, but the treatment services are provided by other agencies in the community. Some of these services are obtained on a purchases-of-service basis.

PREVENTION OF CHILD ABUSE

Our objective in studying and treating child abuse on a nationwide scale is, as with any major public health problem, the development of a strategy for prevention. Thus far, early case findings and protective intervention in abusing families have been the primary areas of interest for workers in this field. As more basic knowledge is accumulated about the child-abuse syndrome through clinical experience and research, one can envision a logical shift in focus from treatment and rehabilitation (secondary prevention) to primary intervention. There are several types of preventive measures that may be utilized on a large scale to reduce the abusive potential of a given population.

General Educational Programs

Our society's inadequate preparation for infant and child care has been revealed by the enormous popularity of "how to" books about children and child-rearing. With the demise of the extended family in this country, Spock and other child-rearing specialists have replaced grandparents among the general public as the traditional source of wisdom about raising children. Educational programs concerned with child development and parenting, therefore, might satisfy a basic need of our society. Socioeconomically and educationally deprived segments of the population might particularly benefit from such programs. The subject matter could be introduced into the high-school curriculum and might be presented to the parent population through adult education programs, community organizations, religious groups, daycare centers, and obstetric and pediatric clinics. These programs would include information about community resources for child care and provide education about child abuse and neglect.

More specific programs would be valuable to special groups. Prenatal classes for expectant mothers and fathers could be made available in hospitals as an integral part of prenatal care. The parents would be taught about pregnancy and prenatal and newborn care. Educational programs for the parents should be continued after the birth of the child with a change in focus to infant and early child care. These classes could be held at the same hospital or at a pediatric or well-baby clinic.

Identification of Parents at Risk for Child Abuse

The recent advances in our clinical and theoretical understanding of the child-abuse syndrome, stimulated by an increased national preoccupation with this problem, have facilitated the identification of families at risk for maltreatment. Experienced professionals are now capable of identifying abuse-prone parents who are likely to maltreat their children under certain stressful conditions. Parents with low self-esteem who are isolated and lack gratifying relationships with spouse and family will often make excessive and inappropriate demands on their children in order to fulfill their own unsatisfied needs. These faulty child-rearing practices are more likely to culminate in maltreatment under conditions of stress if the parents are impulsive and had been exposed to violent or exploitative parenting when they were children. It is also possible to predict the child(ren) most likely to be abused or scapegoated in a given "high-risk" family. It is usually the most difficult, demanding, or deviant child who is unable to satisfy the premature expectations of the parents.

Predictive judgments can be made through a variety of techniques. Interviewing the parents, observation of the parent-child interaction, and assessment of the home environment may provide sufficient information to justify an attempt at preventive intervention. There have been recent attempts to develop predictive questionnaires to identify abuse-prone parents (Schneider, Hoffmeister, and Helfer, 1976; Gaines et al., 1978). However, this type of instrument has several drawbacks. Thus far, many nonabusing parents have similar responses to the questionnaire as those parents who have abused their children. The high number of "false positive" responses might indicate that a questionnaire can only detect parents with deviant or unusual child-rearing attitudes and practices, but cannot reliably predict child abuse. Research with predictive instruments carried out at the Downstate Medical Center (Gaines et al., 1978) utilized the Helfer Questionnaire and a similar instrument adapted for use with a low socioeconomic minority group inner-city population. Neither questionnaire was able to differentiate abusing and nonmaltreating control mothers. It is evident that current predictive instruments have yet to achieve the validity and reliability necessary for use as a serious screening device. In addition, (1978) Gaines et al. described several difficulties with the questionnaire format in a low socioeconomic population, where low intelligence, poor reading ability, and a lack of test sophistication could interfere with the validity of the results.

Perhaps the most reliable means of assessing risk for maltreatment is through a sensitive clinical interview of the parent accompanied by careful history taking, which should include the parent's home situation; the nature of relationships with important figures; availability of support systems; attitudes toward and expectation from the children; and the perception of the parent's current self-image and the manner in which the parent viewed his or her own childhood and child-rearing. The interview and history taking should be followed by an observation of the family's communication patterns, which might include interaction between the parents, parents and children, and high-risk parent with target child.

The potentially maltreating parent may be identified at various stages of the child's development, but early detection is preferable. The earliest opportunity for high-risk screening is during pregnancy, where the mother can be assessed during routine prenatal visits. Observations can continue during labor, delivery, and during the postpartum hospitalization.

After the mother returns home with her baby, the next period of contact with a physician is during the infant's visit to the pediatrician for illness of well-baby care. Abuse proneness might also be detected during mother-child interaction in a nursery school, or daycare setting. The staff of preschool programs should receive training in the recognition of children who are at risk for maltreatment. Later in childhood, the elementary school teachers and pediatricians are the professionals in the best position to detect potential maltreatment. Since parents and young children are in frequent contact with preschool and elementary school programs and health care facilities, it is important that teachers, school personnel, and pediatricians receive training in the area of child maltreatment.

Preventive Intervention

Once the high-risk family has been identified an appropriate intervention strategy can be developed according to the relative contributions of each potentiating factor. For example, if a mother exhibits a typical abuse-prone background and personality and is experiencing considerable environmental stress during visits to a prenatal clinic, a visiting nurse might be assigned to the family after the mother gives birth. The situation would entail an even greater potential for abuse if this mother gave birth to a vulnerable "high-risk" child that required a greater amount of care or was viewed as different or unsatisfying due to a physical or congenital abnormality.

This conceptual model could be especially effective in that it identifies those factors that figure most prominently in the abusive process and thus allows preventive interventions to be employed where they will have the greatest impact. For example, if parental personality variables were found to be more significant than either child deviancy or stress, psychotherapy or casework might be considered the treatment of choice. If, on the other hand, family stresses were found to have made the greatest contribution, the deployment of parent aides, homemakers, or visiting nurses could present a more efficient intervention. Kempe and Helfer (1972) described the routine placement of health visitors (visiting nurses) in Aberdeen, Scotland, in all homes following the birth of a child. These nurses were trained to identify families at risk for abuse.

REFERENCES

Bakwin, H. Emotional deprivation in infants, *Journal of Pediatrics*, 1949, 35:512–521.

Baron, M. A., Bejar, R. L., Sheaff, P. J. Neurologic manifestations of the battered child syndrome. *Pediatrics* 1970 45:1003–1007.

Bell, S. M. and Ainsworth, M. D. S. Infant crying and maternal responsiveness. *Child Development* 1972 43:1171–1190.

Besharov, D. Child abuse rate called "epidemic." *The New York Times*, November 30, 1975.

Birrell, R. G. & Birrell, J. H. W. The maltreatment syndrome in children: a hospital survey. *Medical Journal of Australia* 1968 1023–1029.

Birch, H. G. *Malnutrition, learning, intelligence, and behavior.* Cambridge, Mass.: M.I.T. Press, 1968.

Bowlby, J. Maternal care and mental health. *Bulletin of World Health Organization* 1951 355–533.

Caffey, J. On the theory and practice of shaking infants: its potential residual effects of permanent brain damage and mental retardation. *American Journal of Diseases of Children* 1972 124:161–169.

Cohen, M., Raphling, D., & Green, P. Psychological aspects of the maltreatment syndrome of childhood. *Journal of Pediatrics* 1966 69:279–284.

Coleman, R., Provence, S. A. Developmental retardation (hospitalism) in infants living in families. *Pediatrics* 1957 19:285–292.

DeFrancis, V. The status of child protective services. In C. H. Kempe and R. E. Helfer, eds. *Helping the battered child and his family.* Philadelphia: J. B. Lippincott, 1972.

Elmer E. The fifty families study: Summary of phase 1, neglected and abused children and their families. Children's Hospital of Pittsburgh, Pa. 1965.

Elmer, E. and Gregg, C. S. Developmental characteristics of abused children. *Pediatrics*

1967 40:596–602.

Erikson, E. H. *Childhood and society.* New York: Norton, 1950.

Faranoff, A., Kennell, J., & Klaus, M. Follow-up of low birth weight infants—the predictive value of maternal visiting patterns. *Pediatrics* 1972 49:287–290.

Feinstein, H., Paul, N., & Pettison, E. Group therapy for mothers with infanticide impulses. *American Journal of Psychiatry* 1964 120:882–886.

Freud, S. *Beyond the pleasure principle* (std. ed., Vol. 18). London: Hogarth Press, 1955 (originally published, 1920).

Friedrich, W. & Boriskin, J. The role of the child in abuse: a review of the literature. *American Journal of Orthopsychiatry* 1976 46:580–590.

Gaines, R., Sandgrund, A., Green, A. H., & Power, E. Etiological factors in child maltreatment: A multivariate study of abusing neglecting and normal mothers. *Journal of Abnormal Psychology* 1978 87:531–540.

Galdston, R. Observations on children who have been physically abused and their parents. *American Journal of Psychiatry* 1965 122:440–443.

Galdston, R. Violence begins at home. *Journal of the American Academy of Child Psychiatry* 1971 10:336–350.

Gil, D. *Violence against children.* Cambridge, Mass.: Harvard University Press, 1970.

Gil, D. A holistic perspective on child abuse and its prevention, paper presented at the Conference on Research on Child Abuse, National Institute of Child Health and Human Development, 1974.

Green, A. H. Self-destructive behavior in physically abused schizophrenic children. *Archives of General Psychiatry* 1968 19:171–179.

Green, A. H. A psychodynamic approach to the study and treatment of child abusing parents. *Journal of the American Academy of Child Psychiatry* 1976 15:414–429 (a).

Green, A. H. Psychopathology of abused children. *Journal of the American Academy of Child Psychiatry* 1978 17:356–371 (a).

Green, A. H. Psychiatric treatment of abused children. *Journal of the American Academy of Child Psychiatry* 1978 17:92-103 (b).

Green, A. H. Self-destructive behavior in battered children. *American Journal of Psychiatry* 1978 135:579–582.

Green, A. H., Sandgrund, A., Gaines, R., & Haberfeld, H. Psychological sequelae of child abuse and neglect. Paper presented at the 127th annual meeting of the American Psychiatric Association, Detroit, May 1974.

Green, A. H., Voeller, K., Gaines, R., & Kubie,

J. Neurological Impairment in Maltreated Children, paper presented at the Annual Meeting of the American Academy of Child Psychiatry San Diego, California, October, 1978.

Green, A. H. Child abusing fathers. *Journal of the American Academy of Child Psychiatry,* 1979 20,356-371.

Helfer, R. E. The diagnostic process and treatment programs. DHEW publication No. (OHD) 75–69). Washington, D.C.: U.S. Department of Health, Education and Welfare, National Center for Child Abuse and Neglect, 1975.

Helfer, R. E., & Kempe, C. H., eds. *The battered child.* Chicago: University of Chicago Press, 1968.

Helfer, R. E. & Kempe, C. H., eds. *Child Abuse and Neglect: The Family and the Community.* Cambridge, Mass.: Ballinger Publishing Co., 1976.

Holmes, M. Child Abuse and Neglect Programs: Practice and Theory, U.S. Dept. of Health Education & Welfare DHEW Publication No. (ADM) 77–344, 1977.

Johnson, B. & Morse, H. Injured children and their parents. *Children* 1968 15:147–152.

Justice, B. & Duncan, D. F. Life crisis as a precursor to child abuse. *Public Health Reports* 1976 91:110–115.

Kempe, C. H., Silverman, F., Steele, B., Droegemueller, W., & Silver, H. The battered child syndrome. *Journal of the American Medical Association* 1962 181, 17–24.

Kempe, C. H., & Helfer, R. E., eds. *Helping the battered child and his family.* Philadelphia: J. B. Lippincott, 1972.

Klein, M., & Stern, L. Low birth weight and the battered child syndrome. *Am. J. Dis. Child.* (1972) 122:15–18.

Leifer, A. D., Leiderman, P. H., Barrett, C. R., & Williams, J. A. Effects of Mother-Infant Separation on Maternal Attachment Behavior, *Child Development* 1972 43:1203–1218.

Light, R. J. Abused and neglected children in America: A study of alternative policies. *Harvard Educational Review* 1973 43:556–598.

Martin, H. The child and his development. In: C. H. Kempe and R. E. Helfer, eds. *Helping the battered child and his family,* Philadelphia: J. B. Lippincott, 1972.

Martin, H. P., Beezley, P., Conway, E. F., & Kempe, C. H. The development of abused children. *Advances in Pediatrics* (1974) 21:44–73.

Martin, H. *The abused child.* Cambridge, Mass.: Ballinger Publishing Co., 1976.

Merrill, E. Physical abuse of children: An agency study. In V. DeFrancis, ed. *Protecting the battered child,* Denver: American Humane Association, 1962.

Milowe, E. D. & Lourie, R. S. The child's role in the battered child syndrome. *Journal of Pediatrics* (1964) 65:1079–1080.

Morris, M. & Gould, R. Role reversal: A necessary concept in dealing with the battered child syndrome. *American Journal of Orthopsychiatry* 1963 33:298–299.

Morse, W., Sahler, O. J., & Friedman, S. B. A three-year follow-up study of abused and neglected children. *American Journal of Diseases of Children* 1970 120:439–446.

Moss, H. A. & Robson, K. S. The relation between the amount of time infants spend at various states and the development of visual behavior. *Child Development* 1970 41 (2):509–517.

Nagi, S. Child abuse and neglect programs: A National Overview (DHEW publication 75–14). *Children Today,* May–June 1975:13–17.

New York City Central Registry for Child Abuse, 1977.

Ounsted, C., Oppenheimer, R., & Lindsay, J. Aspects of bonding failure: the psychopathology and psychotherapeutic treatment of families of battered children. *Developmental Medicine and Child Neurology* 1974 16:447–456.

Oviatt, B. After child abuse reporting legislation—what? In C. H. Kempe and R. E. Helfer, eds. *Helping the battered child and his family.* Philadelphia: J. B. Lippincott, 1972.

Pollock, C. & Steele, B. A therapeutic approach to parents. In C. H. Kempe and R. E. Helfer, eds. *Helping the battered child and his family.* Philadelphia: J. B. Lippincott, 1972.

Sabbeth, J. The suicidal adolescent! *Journal of the American Academy of Child Psychiatry* 1969 8:272–286.

Sandgrund, A., Gaines, R., & Green, A. H., Child abuse and mental retardation: A problem of cause and effect. *American Journal of Mental Deficiency* 1974 79:327–330.

Schneider, C., Helfer, R., & Pollock, C. The predictive questionnaire: preliminary report. In C. H. Kempe, and R. E. Helfer, eds. *Helping the battered child and his family.* Philadelphia: J. B. Lippincott, 1972.

Scrimshaw, N. S. & Gordon, J. E. *Malnutrition, learning and behavior.* Cambridge, Mass.: M.I.T. Press, 1968.

Simons, B., Downs, E., Hurster, M., & Archer, M. Child abuse. *New York State Journal of Medicine* 1966 66:2783–2788.

Smiht, C. A. & Hanson, R. 134 battered children: a medical and psychological study. *British Medical Journal* 1974 14:666–670.

Spinetta, J. & Rigler, D. The child abusing parent: A psychological review. *Psychological Bulletin* 1972 77:296–304.

Spitz, R. A. Hospitalism. An inquiry into the genesis of psychiatric conditions in early childhood. In the *Psychoanalytic Study of the Child*, vol. 1. New York, International Universities Press, 1945, pp. 53–74.

Steele, B. Parental abuse of infants and small children. In E. Anthony and T. Benedek, eds. *Parenthood: Its psychology and psychopathology*. Boston: Little, Brown & Co., 1970.

Steele, B., and Pollock, C. A psychiatric study of parents who abuse infants and small children. In R. E. Helfer and C. H. Kempe, eds. The battered child. Chicago: University of Chicago Press, 1968.

*In this legal definition, "maltreatment" refers to neglect.

PART III

THERAPEUTIC

APPROACHES WITH

CHILDREN

THERAPEUTIC INTERVENTIONS WITH CHILDREN: OVERVIEW

The third section of the book covers five intervention approaches applied to children: behavioral therapy, problem-solving, psychoanalytic therapy, problem focused family therapy, and psychostimulant treatment for hyperactivity.

Ayllon and Simon discuss basic learning theory assumptions and behavioral techniques to increase behavior and to decrease behavior. These are then applied to specific childhood problems such as self-destructive behavior, feeding and toileting disturbances and speech and language defects.

Kendall and Urbain present a social-cognitive approach to interpersonal problem-solving. The roots of this in behavior therapy are acknowledged as are links to cognitive developmental approches to moral development. The cognitive-behavioral theoretical model is outlined and its use is evaluated in different settings: school, clinic, institutions and family. Problem-solving is looked at as a means of teaching self-control and therefore increasing generalization of behavior change. Research on perspective talking is also reviewed. This chapter is a good source of materials that could be used in further research on the subject of problem-solving or in clinical settings.

Egan and Vandersall write on psychoanalytic approaches to therapy with children: insight-oriented and supportive therapy. Issues of parent work, confidentiality, home visits and school visits are dealt with. The roles of interpretation and play are discussed.

Cole contrasts a problem-focused approach to families based on structural and strategic approaches to a more systems-oriented view. He discusses family assessment and tactics including paradoxical intention. Stages in the life of a family and stages in the therapy process are formulated. Clinical examples are provided and methods are outlined for dealing with the schizophrenic adolescent, school-phobic child, child and adolescent behavior disorders, single parent and adolescent substance abuse.

The final chapter of the book is on hyperactivity and psychostimulants. Whalen presents methodological issues in effectiveness studies, medication procedures and measurement of change. A strong argument is made for the interplay of research and clinical practice. The effects of psychostimulants are categorized as behavioral, including changes in activity level and response modulation, cognitive and learning and social and adaptive behavior. Studies are evaluated and critiqued. Critical questions are raised about side effects of psychostimulants, effect of maturation on hyperactivity and long term improvement due to psychostimulants.

CHAPTER 11

Behavior Therapy with Children

TEODORO AYLLON, Ph.D.
and
STEVEN J. SIMON, Ph.D.

Children who display abnormal behavior have been more amenable to therapeutic change with the use of behavioral procedures than with other forms of treatment (Bellack and Hersen, 1977; O'Leary, Turkewitz, & Taffel, 1973; Patterson, 1974). The fact that children have not had the time to overlearn maladaptive behavior patterns as much as adults, combined with the well-documented efficacy of behavioral procedures themselves, has led Bellack and Hersen (1977) to write that "the behavioral revolution has come closest to fruition in the application of operant conditioning techniques which children (p. 1972)."

It is the intent of this chapter to review some characteristics of an operant approach as well as to describe the procedures themselves as they apply to children. Contemporary clinical research that demonstrates these characteristics, as well as the application of these procedures to a wide variety of abnormal behavior patterns demonstrated by children, will then be reviewed. Entire volumes have been written on this subject (Graziano, 1971; Ross, 1974); hence a chapter of this size and nature must consist of judiciously chosen material. As such, the articles reviewed will, for the most part, consist of those published in the last few years as an attempt to update in a cohesive manner our body of knowledge in this area.

Traditional approaches to children who display behaviors that lead others to interpret them as abnormal typically make use of classification schema involving labels and categories. The *Diagnostic and Statistical Manual-II (DSM-II)* of the American Psychiatric Association (1968) and the classification system proposed by the committee on child psychiatry of the Group for the Advancement of Psychiatry (GAP) (1966) represent two widely used taxonomic systems for classifying types of abnormal behaviors displayed by children. Although the descriptive aspects of these systems are desirable, numerous problems exist with their use. Difficulties in terms of reliability of the categories; iatrogenic effects of labeling; uneven utility in terms of treatment planning or prediction; and the characteristic emphases upon the child as having an illness or some internal type of psychogenic disorder have often been cited as problems that follow from the use of these systems (Ullman and Krasner, 1975; Nathan and Harris, 1975). These and other problems make it difficult to organize a coherent review of behavioral procedures with children according to existing taxonomic systems.

From an applied behavioral perspective, the analysis concerns overt or measurable *behaviors* themselves and their relationship to surrounding external *environments*, rather than with hypothesized internal causative factors. In so doing, the etiological focus is shifted from unmeasurable and hypothesized events assumed to be occurring inside the child to quantifiable factors external to the child that have been substantially demonstrated to influence behavior. Furthermore, this now allows us to simplify the way in which we conceptualize abnormal child behavior. Instead of the need for the numerous and often vague toxonomic categories for describing abnormal behaviors displayed by children (which might range from "other special symptom" to "adjustment reaction of childhood" to "other social maladjustments, nonspecific conditions," as in the *DSM–II*), we can alternatively conceptualize problematic children's behavior in terms of maladaptive behavior that occurs too frequently or desirable behaviors that occur too infrequently or not at all. Our therapeutic objectives then become straightforward. The therapeutic task becomes one of increasing or strengthening skill in areas where *behavioral deficits* occur or decreasing or eliminating problematic *behavioral excesses* (Kanfer and Saslow, 1968; Ross, 1974). This, then, describes the first half of the behavioral perspective mentioned above—the conceptualization of the abnormality as the frequency of the problematic *behaviors* themselves.

It was stated that the behavioral perspective also focuses on the *environments* in which these behaviors occur (as in behavioral excesses) or do not occur (as in behavioral deficits). Children typically spend the preponderance of their time in one of two types of environments: the home environment or the educational environment. The behaviorally-oriented therapist will thus attempt to analyze any problematic child behavior in terms of its frequency of occurrence and when and where the problem behaviors occur. Accordingly, this review of operant approaches to abnormal child behavior will be organized not according to traditional taxonomic systems, but according to whether the problems are one of behavioral excesses or deficits, with an emphasis upon whether they are displayed in the home or educational environment.

CHARACTERISTICS OF A BEHAVIORAL APPROACH

There are several major characteristics of

a behavioral approach to abnormal behaviors displayed by children that set it apart from more traditional approaches to such problems. These include: (1) a focus upon overt behaviors; (2) treatment conducted in the natural environment; (3) the use of key personnel in the child's environment in therapeutic implementation; (4) the systematic assessment of target behaviors before, during, and after treatment; (5) the use of experimentally validated psychological principles as the basis for treatment procedures; and (6) an emphasis upon positive, humane, and growth-expanding procedures aimed at treatment objectives of social importance to the child.

Focus upon behavior

The subject matter of a behavioral approach, not surprisingly, is behavior itself. That is, publicly observable overt behaviors comprise the primary datum of a behavioral approach. The level of analysis of the behavior therapist, therefore, is strictly upon what the child does that is observable to others. This is in marked contrast to more traditional, psychodynamic approaches that focus upon hypothesized underlying causes of the overt or "symptomatic" behavior. According to this internal model of pathology, the level of analysis is upon unobservable processes thought to occur within the child. It is logical and meaningful within this framework that treatment should focus primarily upon curing the hypothesized, underlying causes that are inferred from the observed behaviors. Treatment aimed exclusively at the symptoms directly and not at "root" causes would be thought to result in a new or different set of symptoms. This is known as the "symptom substitution" hypothesis. The review that follows is comprised of applied research reports—all of which demonstrate that remediation of "symptomatic" behavior through *direct* treatment approaches does not lead to "symptom substitution." We will return to this issue later.

Treatment in the natural environment

The behavioral practitioner does not attempt to deal with presumed internal events believed to be occurring *within* the child. Rather, he focuses upon the overt behavior of the child as it occurs in his natural surrounding environment. The premise here is that behavior is functionally related to events that occur *outside* of the individual in his environment. The traditional tactic of focusing upon hypothesized intrapsychic agents tends to shift practitioners away from focusing upon the dynamic interplay that exists between behavior and environment. That such relationships exist has been unequivocally supported by extremely large areas of basic and applied psychological research (*Journal of the Experimental Analysis of Behavior; Journal of Applied Behavior Analysis*). Such research has demonstrated how behavior is functionally related to past and present antecedent and consequent events that surround behavior and that occur in the environment. It is the unique and idiosyncratic combination of such experiences that influences, for the most part, how an individual behaves.

With this emphasis upon analyzing behavior relative to environment comes the characteristic behavioral approach of treating problematic behaviors in the natural environments in which they occur. This is in large contrast to traditional approaches that generally involve bringing the child within the "artificial" confines of a therapeutic office and working with him within the restrictive context of the "office visit." An important advantage to treatment in the natural environment is that it is more realistic and meaningful to the child and will, therefore, promote generalization and maintenance of therapeutic gains beyond the course of treatment. Another advantage of attempting to provide treatment in the environment where the behavior is problematic, in addition to the fact that it is more realistic to the child, is that this allows the therapist to make use of the many potential resources existing in the environment that can be imaginatively applied in the pursuit of therapeutic objectives.

Significant others as change agents

Some of the most potentially powerful therapeutic resources that typically exist within the environment of children are the significant people, such as parents, teachers, guardians, and others, who play such a prominent role in their day-to-day existence. It is characteristic of a behavioral approach to enlist the active support and participation of key personnel in the child's world with regard to treatment planning and implementation. This is because effective and meaningful reinforcers are typically centered on such individuals. Thus, along with the shift from the office to the natural environment, a behavioral approach transfers emphasis from a "one-to-one" therapeutic relationship between therapist and child to a multilevel system (Tharp and Wetzel, 1969), wherein the therapist designs a suitable program that is then acted upon by the significant people in the child's natural environment. In this regard, parents can be trained to carry out home-based treatment programs with their children; teachers can be trained to carry out behavioral treatment programs in their classrooms; ward attendants or paraprofessionals can be taught to implement programs in institutional facilities and so forth. The advantages to such an approach are greater economy in terms of allowing larger numbers of children to receive help as well as greater promotion of generalization and maintenance of therapeutic gains since treatment occurs in the child's real environment through the intervention of key personnel.

Systematic assessment

A fourth major characteristic of a behavioral approach is its unremitting insistence upon systematic assessment. One of the advantages of focusing upon overt behavior is that it allows for quantification and measurement. Unobservable intrapsychic processes cannot be systematically measured in any direct sense—they can only be inferred. This does not mean that feelings, emotional states, or cognitions are ignored. On the contrary, these states are considered as they relate to overt behavior. That is, it is assumed that they will be reflected in behavior. For example, a child who is feeling insecure will in all probability display few behaviors associated with independence. More likely, he will stay around the house, having few friends or outside activities. By focusing upon these *behaviors* it is assumed that successful treatment will also effectively increase feelings of security, worth, and self-esteem.

With an emphasis upon quantifying overt behaviors, the behavioral practitioner can now evaluate the effects of a treatment program upon one or more target behaviors that have been precisely defined. Unambiguous assessment procedures that are continuously applied prior to, during, and following a program of treatment are essential in order to answer two important questions: Was there a change in the target behavior and was the change directly due to the treatment procedure that was used?

The first question is answered by comparing levels of behavior obtained from behavioral measures during and after treatment with levels obtained prior to treatment (baseline). It is only through this process of using sensitive measurement procedures to assess levels of carefully defined target behaviors that a therapist may reliably state whether or not any behavioral changes have taken place. Furthermore, this process provides a self-corrective function. By continuously monitoring the effects of treatment, changes, and improvements in the therapeutic program itself may be made based upon data. This allows for more responsive *and* responsible treatment and enhanced therapist accountability.

Although it is imperative that behavioral assessment be carried out for the sake of observing progress from the individual client's point of view, it is also important that the second question be answered to ascertain the efficacy of treatment procedures themselves. Behavioral practitioners typically evaluate the effectiveness of a treatment program by assessing it within the context of a within-subject experimental design. A reversal design, in which periods of treatment and nontreatment are alternated, or a multiple baseline design, which involves the implementation of a particular treatment at two or more different, but consecutive points in time across individuals, behaviors, or situations (see

Hersen and Barlow, 1976 for a fuller discussion of within-subject methodology), have often been used. It is only through the judicious use of these and other experimental designs that we can answer the question raised above regarding treatment effectiveness. It is from the point of view of the profession itself that the answer to this question becomes important. Well-controlled demonstrations of a treatment procedure's effectiveness add much to the confidence of other practitioners in their use of the procedure with other clients.

Thus, from a behavioral point of view, careful assessment is viewed as an integral part of the treatment process with importance from both the individual patient's and the profession's points of view.

Treatment based upon validated psychological principles

A behavioral approach makes the assumption that lawful processes are operating in the acquisition and maintenance of behavior. As such, behaviors judged by others to be "abnormal" are not considered to be *qualitatively* different from behaviors considered to be "normal." All behaviors are said to be a function of the same psychological principles that behavioral practitioners refer to as the "laws of learning." Abnormal behaviors are learned in much the same manner that normal behaviors are learned. The difference between behaviors considered by others to be abnormal from those which are considered normal, instead, is a *quantitative* one. Abnormal behaviors are considered inappropriate because they occur too frequently or too infrequently with regard to contexts of time, place, and social milieu.

Based upon this assumption—that *all* behavior is a function of the same lawful psychological processes—a behavioral approach seeks to utilize these same processes in the therapeutic pursuits of teaching adaptive skill repertoires to replace maladaptive, abnormal ones. Consequently, behavioral treatment programs are based on and make use of experimentally validated principles of learning. The procedures themselves are not "amorphous" or whimsically determined. Instead, a behavioral approach to treatment "is part of a highly technical system, based upon laboratory investigation of the phenomena of conditioning for describing behavior and specifying the conditions under which it is acquired, maintained, and eliminated (Michael and Meyerson, 1962, p. 382)." This will become more evident as the basic behavioral treatment procedures are described later.

BEHAVIOR THERAPY PROCEDURES

Behavior modification is currently defined as "the application of learning and conditioning principles and techniques to the understanding and remediation of human problems (Ayllon and Milan, in press)." For the most part, behavioral procedures and the learning principles upon which they are based, result in one of two outcomes: an *increase* in the probability of behavior or a *decrease* in the probability of behavior. In keeping with the behavioral approach's conceptualization of abnormal child behavior as involving a problem of either a behavioral excess or a behavioral deficit, not surprisingly, procedures that increase behavior are used for the problem of deficits, while procedures that decrease behavior are used with the type of problem defined as excessive.

TECHNIQUES FOR INCREASING BEHAVIOR

Reinforcement

The major strategy for increasing behavior involves a variety of techniques whose basis is the principle of *reinforcement*. There are two types of reinforcement procedures: one that increases a response that leads to the *presentation* or continuation of a pleasant or desirable event or condition (positive reinforcement), and one that increases a response that leads to the *removal* or discontinuation of an unpleasant or undesirable event or condition (negative reinforcement). The defining characteristic of reinforcement is that behavior increases in some manner as a function of the pro-

cedure.

An example of positive reinforcement is provided by Whaley and Mallott (1971) who described a case involving a boy who never listened to his mother when she called him in from play. Television-viewing was made contingent on heeding the mother's calls, and the behavior of responding to the calls dramatically increased in probability. Positive reinforcement is, perhaps, the most widely used and the most potent behavioral procedure for increasing behavior.

Examples of the second class of reinforcement procedures, those of negative reinforcement, are more difficult to encounter, since, by definition, they involve exposing the child to something unpleasant. For this reason, behavior therapists are reluctant to employ these procedures with children and instead prefer to use positive reinforcement tactics. However, the procedures do have some utility with children for whom traditional, positive reinforcers are not effective (Williams, 1973). For example, Sajwaj, Libet, and Agras (1974) taught a six-month-old infant to stop regurgitating her food by squirting small amounts of lemon juice in the infant's mouth contingent on rumination or its precursors. The behavior of swallowing food without regurgitating was reinforced, since it resulted in the avoidance of the harsh-tasting lemon juice. Because examples of such procedures are rare and because behavior therapists primarily use tactics that are pleasant and desired by the child, such as positive reinforcement, the remainder of this discussion will focus upon some guidelines for and characteristics and types of positive-reinforcement strategies.

There are a number of important guidelines that should be followed in the design and implementation of a reinforcement program with children (Bellack and Hersen, 1977). First, the stimulus or event that is to be used as a positive reinforcer must increase the behavior upon which it is contingent. Reinforcers can be very idiosyncratic, since what is reinforcing to one child (increases his behavior) may not be reinforcing to another (does not increase his behavior). In the above example, if television-viewing for heeding the mother's calls was used with a child who did not like TV but preferred to read books, it is unlikely that any behavior change would have been effected. Thus, it becomes important to check out the "reinforcing potential" of the stimulus or event. This can be done by directly asking the child or parent about things he likes to do or observing him over a period of time in order to determine those activities the child likes to engage in. Second, after a reinforcer is selected, it should be ensured that this same reinforcer is not available from other sources. If the child has access to the reinforcer in some other manner, this will likely decrease his motivation to try to earn it in the manner specified by the therapist. A third guideline, similar to the second, involves the need to avoid satiation effects in a reinforcement program. Although M & Ms candy might be extremely reinforcing to a child, after he has earned and eaten five bags or hoarded away 15 bags within a short period of time, it is likely that his motivation to earn more M & Ms by way of the reinforcement program will decrease. Thus, if reinforcement is given on a continuous basis (i.e., one unit of reinforcement after each response), it should be given in small amounts. In addition, it is well to have a variety of reinforcers available since this will further effectively guard against the possibility of satiation. Fourth, when initiating a program of reinforcement, reinforcement should initially be delivered on a continuous or nearly continuous basis, with the schedule of reinforcement being thinned out shortly thereafter. One of the primary objectives of most behavioral programs is the eventual fading out of the program itself by "weaning" the child from programmed reinforcement while allowing natural contingencies of reinforcement to take over. By gradually thinning out levels of reinforcement as the program proceeds, three things are occurring: the "weaning" process has begun; satiation effects are being avoided; and stronger patterns of behavior are being established, since research has demonstrated that intermittent reinforcement leads to more enduring behavior change. A fifth and related guideline is that as reinforcement is delivered, it should always be accompanied by some

form of affection, praise, or approval from the person delivering it. It is in this manner that social approval itself becomes a powerful reinforcer and thus can be used as a more natural reinforcer available in the child's environment which can be used to maintain positive behavior changes.

Contingency contracting. A special type of reinforcement procedure involves the use of a negotiated and clearly specified agreement between the child and the parent, teacher, or therapist that outlines the behaviors the child is expected to engage in and the consequences that will be received as a result. All the details of the agreement are typically put in writing and are signed by the parties concerned. The agreement is referred to as a "contingency contract" since it specifies in advance the contingencies that will occur for appropriate behavior or misbehavior.

Contingency contracts have been found to be most useful with children and adolescents who have some sort of interpersonal problem with authority figures. Such problems usually can be reduced to perceived misbehavior on the part of the child. Behavior changes are thus aimed at by way of the contingency contract, which is based upon a *quid pro quo* system of reciprocal reinforcement. When the child changes from undesirable behavior to the agreed upon desired behavior, which is reinforcing to the parent or therapist, the parent or therapist responds in kind by providing the stipulated reinforcement for the child's newly displayed desired behavior. An example of this procedure is provided by Frederiksen, Jenkins, and Carr (1976) who treated a teenage boy with a three-year history of regular polydrug abuse. The contract was aimed at increasing appropriate behaviors that were incompatible with drug abuse, such as enrolling, preparing for, and attending a vocational training school. For these behaviors, as stipulated by a contractual arrangement made by the boy with his parents, he received such reinforcers as allowances, use of the car, and less stringent curfew restrictions. Weekly sessions were held to monitor execution of the contract. The outcome of this procedure was a marked, lasting decrease in drug usage as well as increased ratings of family happiness. In addition, contingency contracting has been found to be useful with children in classroom settings (Homme, Csanyi, Gonzalez, and Rechs, 1969), with adolescent behavioral problems (Tharp and Wetzel, 1969), with juvenile delinquents (Stuart, 1971), and with school dropouts (MacDonald, Gallimore and MacDonald, 1970).

Token economies. Another special type of reinforcement procedure involves the use of conditioned generalized reinforcers. There are several different types of reinforcers. Primary reinforcers are unlearned reinforcers and are exemplified by such biological necessities as food, water, and warmth. Objects or events that become reinforcing by virtue of our experience are conditioned or secondary reinforcers. Such reinforcers typically acquire their reinforcing properties by being paired with events that are already reinforcing such as primary reinforcers. Conditioned reinforcers that are reinforcing because they are readily paired with *many* other reinforcers are referred to as "generalized conditioned reinforcers." Examples of these are social praise, money, and grocery-store trading stamps.

The token economy is based upon the therapeutic use of generalized conditioned reinforcers, which are known as "tokens" (Ayllon and Azrin, 1968). Tokens may take the form of points, stars, poker chips, or anything that lends itself to immediate, convenient delivery after reinforcible behavior has been observed. Tokens, themselves, are of relatively little or no reinforcing value but attain their reinforcing properties by serving as a medium of exchange for objects or events, known to be reinforcing. The imaginative and appropriate use of token procedures can serve as a motivational vehicle for effecting behavior change. Three steps are involved: (1) specification of target behaviors that are to receive token reinforcement; (2) specification of a medium of exchange (i.e., type of tokens to be used); and (3) the availability of one or more backup reinforcers for which the tokens may be exchanged (Ullman and Krasner, 1975).

The advantages of token-economy treatment are numerous (Ayllon and Azrin,

1968; Kazdin, 1977). First, tokens are much more conveniently administered than other reinforcing events. Their delivery does not interrupt ongoing behavior and this allows them to be delivered immediately after desirable behavior. Second, the delivery of tokens serves as a bridge for any time delay that might have occurred between the reinforcible behavior and the reinforcing event. A yearly trip to the circus or a new bicycle might be highly reinforcing events, yet are inconveniently administered and might be so delayed that appropriate behaviors would go virtually unreinforced. As a result of these advantages, a third advantage is that numerous or component behaviors may now become subject to reinforcement. Reinforcement is not always an "all-or-none" process as when new behavior is being shaped through reinforcement of successive approximations. (This will be discussed more fully in the next section). Similarly, token reinforcement allows for a "parceling" of otherwise large reinforcing events that might have been earned in an "all or none" fashion. For example, a trip to the circus might cost 100 tokens that could be earned by displaying numerous appropriate behaviors or displaying a single appropriate behavior many times over an extended period of time. Without the aid of a token system, a large reinforcer, such as a trip to the circus, might have to be used in this all-or-none manner by delivering it after a single or short-term display of desired behavior. The guideline that a well-designed token economy should involve a variety of backup reinforcers allows for several other advantages, such as the reduced possibility of satiation effects occurring and the adaptability of the system to a variety of individuals—each with their own unique reinforcer preferences. Finally, tokens used in a well-designed system can become potent reinforcers which can maintain behavior at higher levels than other conditioned reinforcers, such as praise and approval (Kazdin, 1975; 1977).

A review of token economy treatment with children is beyond the scope here. The procedure has been used on a widespread basis with a variety of types of children and adolescents who display a variety of abnormalities in a variety of settings. Its widest application has been in the class-room with children who display academic deficiencies and learning disabilities. It has been successfully used in decreasing class-room disruption with such populations as hyperactive children (Ayllon, Layman, and Kandel, 1975), mentally retarded children (Simon, Robertson, Pachman and Drab-man, in press), and deaf children (Simon, unpublished), as well as for increasing academic behaviors that have been found to be inversely related to classroom disruption (Ayllon and Roberts, 1974; Kirby and Shields, 1972; Winnett and Roach, 1973). In addition to school settings, token economies have been used in halfway houses for predelinquents (Phillips, 1968), in juvenile detention facilities (Burchard, 1967), and in facilities for the mentally retarded (Thompson and Grabowski, 1972). Token economy treatment has also been adapted to such natural environments as the home and playground within the context of outpatient therapy (Ayllon and Skuban, 1974; Ayllon et al., 1975; Patterson, 1974). The interested reader is referred to Kazdin's (1977) scholarly review of this area for a more in-depth discussion.

The above discussion has made the assumption that the child has the target response(s) in his behavior repertoire (i.e., he knows how to do it) and all that is needed is the appropriate use of reinforcement to increase the probability of the behavior. Unfortunately, this is not always the case. In many situations, the child simply does not know how to engage in the behavior, and a different tactic is therefore necessary—one that teaches the child what to do. For example, young children who have toileting problems either do not have the component skills or have the skills but display them inconsistently. As an example of the latter case, Ayllon, Simon, and Wildman (1975) described the successful treatment of an "encopretic" boy who at one time had been toilet-trained. Since the boy, therefore, had the skills, all that was needed was an appropriately designed reinforcement program to increase appropriate toilet behaviors. In the former case, the child needs to be actively taught how to effectively use the bathroom. Azrin and Foxx (1974) have described an efficient

package for accomplishing this. This package includes several additional procedures for increasing behavior, such as instructions, shaping, and modeling.

Instructions, shaping and modeling. Whereas the above reinforcement procedures may be used to increase behaviors that already exist within the child's repertoire of skills, several additional procedures exist for teaching entirely new skills. A widely used procedure for teaching new behavior simply involves the presentation of instructions or prompts, in verbal or written form, which detail the behavior the child is expected to learn. As the child begins to display proficiency in the new skill, typically, the necessity for continuing the instructional or prompting process diminishes, and these procedures are then gradually faded out.

When such instructional or prompting procedures also involve the use of reinforcement for behaviors that successively approximate the ultimate target behavior, this procedure is known as "shaping." An example of the shaping procedure in the teaching of a new skill is provided by O'Neil (1972). In this report, a five-year-old girl afflicted by cerebral palsy, whose only form of locomotion was scooting, was taught to walk in an upright posture with the aid of a crutch. First, the girl was reinforced for achieving a kneeling position. Second, she was reinforced for moving from a kneeling position to a standing position with the aid of a nearby piece of furniture. Next, she was reinforced for transferring herself from the nearby furniture to a crutch. This, in itself, was accomplished in several steps involving the use of hand support, a specially designed harness and a weighted crutch. Gradually these aids were faded out until the girl achieved the terminal behavior of upright ambulation with the use of a crutch. A similar procedure was used by Horner (1971) to teach a mentally retarded *spina bifida* child to walk.

In addition to the above types of procedures, a parent, teacher, or therapist can actually demonstrate for the child the behavior that is expected. This may be done either physically or by way of videotape—known as *modeling*. An example of the use of modeling for teaching new response patterns or skills is provided by Kelly, Furman, and Phillips (in press), who used a modeling procedure to teach retarded adolescents various social skills. In this study, two moderately retarded adolescents were taught such conversational skills as fully answering questions when asked , asking their own questions, and extending social invitations by way of a procedure based largely upon the observation of a skillful videotaped model engaging in these behaviors. Again, this exemplifies the use of modeling to teach new behavior. However, the use of modeling in therapy is not necessarily restricted to the simple teaching of new behavior. Modeling may also be used to increase existent behaviors as a result of observing a model experience positive consequences after engaging in the desired behavior (i.e., vicarious reinforcement). For example, Bandura, Grusec, and Menlove (1967) demonstrated this "disinhibitory effect" of modeling in an experiment with children who were highly fearful of dogs. This study showed that approach responses of such children to dogs could be increased by having them observe fearless models playfully interact with dogs.

We have now reviewed techniques to increase behavior in situations where either skill deficits were present or the child had the skill but displayed it too infrequently. These situations represent only half of what may be considered "abnormal child behavior." The other half involves situations in which children display maladaptive behavior to an excessive degree. Procedures for decreasing inappropriate excessive behavior will now be reviewed.

TECHNIQUES TO REDUCE BEHAVIOR

Extinction

Behavior that is supported or maintained by positive reinforcement may be reduced or eliminated simply by withholding delivery of the reinforcing events that maintain the behavior. This procedure is known as extinction. Up until now, the reinforcement procedures described above or the punishment procedures described in a subsequent section involve the programming of *new* outcomes that either reinforce desirable behaviors or inhibit undesirable ones. Extinction consists of the identification and discontinuation of *existing* consequences that reinforce the target behaviors to be reduced. An example of this process that was used to reduce the bedtime "tantruming" behavior of a 21-month-old boy is provided by Williams (1959). In this case study, the young boy refused to go to sleep unless one of his parents stayed by his bedside until he fell asleep. Failure of the parent to do this would result in tantruming behavior that stopped only after one of the parents "gave in" and stayed at his bedside. The extinction procedure simply allowed the child to continue without a parent yielding to it by going in the room. Going to sleep alone shortly increased, as tantruming behavior quickly dropped out. The use of simply "ignoring" inappropriate child behavior is a form of extinction widely used by parents and teachers (Drabman and Jarvie, 1977). Indeed, Madsen, Becker and Thomas (1968); Becker, Madsen, Thomas, and Arnold (1967); Allen et al., (1964) have found "ignoring" to be an effective method of reducing classroom disruption.

Although extinction has been shown to be effective in reducing undesirable behavior, from an applied point of view, there are problems with its use. First, it is sometimes difficult to ascertain and ultimately control consequences that might maintain inappropriate behavior. Second, extinction may produce emotional side effects such as frustration, anger, and a temporary increase of undesirable behavior, known as "response bursts" or "extinction bursts". Finally, since extinction of undesirable behaviors usually occurs gradually, the extinction process may be too slow, especially when quick behavior changes are needed. For example, extinction has been found to result in gradual reductions in self-injurious behavior of autistic children (Lovaas and Simmons, 1969); however, it is much less rapid in achieving these outcomes than direct punishment of such behavior. With behaviors that are dangerous to the child or others or that are highly disruptive to others, the exclusive use of an extinction tactic would not be recommended because of its potentially slow nature.

Extinction of Undesirable Behavior Combined with Reinforcement for Alternative Desirable Behavior

Because extinction alone may be slow, combining it with a reinforcement program for desirable behaviors that compete with undesirable ones will hasten the desired behavior change. Simultaneously, the child will accrue academic or social benefits from a positive-oriented program designed to teach or strengthen desirable behaviors. The best evidence comes from research showing that disruptive, and, in some cases, hyperactive behavior may be reduced in the classroom simply by providing reinforcement for "on-task" behavior (Ayllon, Layman, and Burke, 1972; Ayllon and Roberts, 1974; Ayllon et al., 1975; Kirby and Shields, 1972; Marholin, Steinman, McInnis, and Heads, 1975; and Winnet and Roach, 1973). When a child is busy engaging in appropriate academic behaviors such as solving math problems or reading a textbook, he cannot be simultaneously acting out in class.

Punishment

Whereas reinforcement procedures increase behavior by presenting a pleasant or desirable event contingent on desired behavior, a group of procedures that is collectively referred to as "punishment procedures" decreases or suppresses behavior by making an unpleasant or undesirable state of affairs contingent on undesired behavior. Punishment occurs in one of four forms: (1) presentation of unconditioned physical noxious stimulus contingent upon the occurrence of the undesired response; (2) intensive practicing of correct responses contingent on the occurrence of the undesired response (response cost); (3) removal from a reinforcing situation for a certain period of time contingent on the occurrence of the undesired response (timeout); and (4) removal of a positive reinforcer in the form of a penalty that is contingent on the undesired response (response

cost). The first two strategies involve the *presentation* of some aversive event while the last two involve the *withdrawal* of some positive event.

Before detailing these procedures, it is useful to explain the use of punishment in general. From the general public's point of view, punishment is perhaps the most controversial and most misunderstood of the behavioral procedures. For example, the therapeutic use of punishment by a trained professional should be differentiated from punishment used by a parent. Whatever its merits, parental punishment has been a time-honored means to engender discipline in children. Unfortunately, parental punishment tends to be unsystematic and is typically used more as a means for gaining retribution and expressing anger than as a means for altering the child's behavior (Bellack and Hersen, 1977). However, the current criticisms directed at the use of punishment are not toward parents, but rather to its use by individuals whose contact with children is of a professional or caretaking capacity. For example, punishment is regarded as dehumanizing to the child in that it is a coercive means of influencing him; its effects are transitory and short-lived; it teaches children what *not* to do but neglects teaching them positive behaviors; and it engenders negative feelings and avoidance with regard to authority figures. Furthermore, regardless of who uses physical forms of punishment, an unfortunate by-product of its use is that the punished child may learn a variety of aggressive responses as a means of resolving interpersonal problems. This occurs because of modeling processes. This may be one way of understanding the "battered child syndrome" since there is some evidence to indicate that parents of battered children were physically abused (Oliver and Taylor, 1971).

Bearing these negative aspects of punishment in mind, it is equally important to state that research has shown that the judicious use of appropriately applied punishment can result in positive and lasting behavior changes that can be made minimally aversive (or "dehumanizing") to the child. When punishment is considered to be necessary, as when the undesired behaviors are physically dangerous to the child or others, it should *always* be used in accordance with the following empirically based guidelines. First, punishment should always be delivered as early as possible within the undesirable response sequence (Aronfreed and Rever, 1965) or immediately following the undesirable response. Delayed punishment might not only have a weak effect upon prior undesirable behavior, but might also suppress desirable behavior that might have occurred in the interim. Second, punishment should always be used consistently—that is, each occurrence of the undesired response should result in the immediate presentation of the punishing event. Third, it is important that the behavior that is being punished does not also result in reinforcement. Potentially reinforcing events for deviant behavior should be withdrawn (extinction). For example, when a parent or teacher admonishes a child for misbehavior by way of an extended "talk," the child is also receiving a good deal of potentially reinforcing social attention from the so-called punishing event. Finally, and perhaps most importantly, whenever punishment is to be used to suppress undesirable behavior, reinforcement for *alternative desirable behavior* should also be made available. Punishment should never be used alone: it should always be used in concert with some program of reinforcement. In this manner, the child is also taught *what to do* (as well as *what not to do*) and, as a result, has an appropriate and adaptive means of displaying behavior with positive outcomes. As such, the child can now avoid punishing outcomes altogether. This last guideline ensures that the therapist uses a punishment strategy, where deemed necessary, within the overall context of a humane, positive, and more effective approach to therapy. (The interested reader is referred to Johnston (1972) for a more detailed analysis of the various parameters and guidelines for applying punishment to human problems.)

In spite of the large body of contemporary research on human punishment, it should be kept in mind that the overwhelming majority of behavior therapists prefer to use positive therapeutic strategies, such as reinforcement over punishment. Again, punishment is used on a limited basis for serious behavior problems resistant to nonaversive strategies.

Punishment involving unconditioned physical noxious stimuli. This type of punishment includes events such as unpleasant-tasting stimuli, shock, a slap on the wrists, and so forth, which are made contingent on the occurrence of undesirable behavior. One example of this form of punishment has already been mentioned in the case involving the use of lemon juice contingent on regurgitation. Some other apparently "lifesaving" applications of these procedures are presented by Lang and Melamed (1969), who successfully terminated the persistent vomiting of a nine-month-old baby who weighed only 12 pounds, and by Bucher and Lovaas (1968), who suppressed the self-mutilating behavior of a seven-year-old autistic boy by using several brief, low-intensity electric shocks (Johnston, 1972).

From a practical point of view, *learned*, conditioned, rather than unconditioned, aversive stimuli are more widely used. Verbal reprimands, yelling, and the like, are examples of acquired punishing stimuli. For example, O'Leary, Kaufman, Kass, and Drabman (1970) found that soft, privately delivered reprimands were an effective means of reducing classroom disruption. Interestingly, this procedure was found to be more effective than loud reprimands delivered publicly. The louder type of reprimands may have had some reinforcing characteristics in terms of attention from the teacher and peer approval of being yelled at by the teacher. Indeed, Madsen, Becker, Thomas, Koser, and Plager (1970) have found such perceived forms of "punishment" to be more reinforcing than punishing in that they increased disruptive behaviors rather than decreased them.

Overcorrection. Azrin and his associates (Azrin and Wesolowski, 1974; Foxx and Azrin, 1972, 1973) have described a punishment procedure, known as overcorrection, which requires the child to expend effort toward correcting instances of misbehavior contingent on its occurrence. *Positive practice overcorrection* requires the child to extensively practice the correct response after the occurrence of the undesirable response. An example of this is provided by Foxx and Azrin (1973), who eliminated such self-stimulatory behaviors as head-weaving and hand-clapping in autistic children by having them intensely practice (about five minutes) keeping these body parts stationary or moving them only for functional reasons contingent on instances of self-stimulatory behavior. Another form of overcorrection, *restitutional overcorrection*, requires the child not only to correct any environmental damage produced by his misbehavior, but he must correct it to a better than normal state. For example, Duker and Seys (1977) drastically reduced the high-frequency vomiting behavior of an institutionalized retarded teenage girl by requiring her to go through a 20-minute procedure that involved washing her face and cleaning the area of the floor affected by the vomiting (as well as unaffected surrounding areas), and changing her clothes.

Time-out from reinforcement. When access to positive reinforcement is withdrawn for a certain period of time contingent on the display of inappropriate behavior, this is known as time-out from reinforcement or, more briefly, "time-out." The procedure most closely associated with the time-out strategy is the contingent use of brief periods of social isolation, although other forms of time-out have also been used. Time-out in the form of putting a child in social isolation basically entails sending the child to a nonstimulating, boring, and otherwise uneventful environment—that is void of reinforcers—for a predetermined, brief period of time. The time-out interval generally ranges from about two to fifteen minutes in length. Longer time-out intervals such as 30 minutes have been found to be no more effective than briefer intervals and, in some respects may be detrimental to the child (i.e., keeping him out of potentially desirable learning situations) (White, Nielsen, and Johnson, 1972).

The appropriate use of time-out in the form of social isolation is to be distinguished from the "time-honored" parental procedure of telling a child to "go to your room!" Appropriately applied time-out is more systematic, disallows the presence of any reinforcers such as toys, TV sets, and other objects, in the time-out situation, and is generally briefer in duration. Furthermore, an important rule to be followed in the use of this type of punishment procedure is that the child should be allowed out only after he has displayed desirable behavior. Failure to heed this rule might allow for the reinforcement of undesirable behavior. For example, if a 10-minute time-out interval is decided upon and a child released precisely at the end of this interval even though he tantrumed throughout the entire period, tantruming behavior would probably be negatively reinforced since it was, in this example, paired with his release from an undesirable situation. A more appropriate use of the procedure would involve the dual requirements of a 10-minute time-out with release coming only after two or three minutes without tantruming. For example, Wolf, Risley, and Mees (1964) reduced temper tantrums, food stealing, and eyeglass throwing of an institutionalized three-year-old autistic boy by placing him in his hospital room with the door closed for a 10-minute interval contingent on throwing his eyeglasses or stealing food or until tantruming behavior had ceased in the case of temper tantrums.

As mentioned earlier, social isolation is not the only form of time-out. Any strategy that involves the contingent removal of the opportunity to gain reinforcement for some period of time is a time-out procedure. In this regard, contingent discontinuation of a cartoon for thumbsucking (Baer, 1962), removal from a dining room for food stealing (Ayllon, 1963), physical restraint for aggressive behavior (Vukelich and Make, 1971), and brief cessation of attention from a therapist after self-injurious behavior (Tate and Baroff, 1966), also exemplify the application of time-out to the reduction of inappropriate child behavior.

Response cost. A procedure related to time-out, in that it involves the withdrawal of positive reinforcers to suppress undesirable behavior, is known as response cost. The use of this procedure basically entails a fine, penalty, or loss of something valued contingent on the occurrence of inappropriate behavior. Although several authors have included time-out and response cost together in their discussion of punishment, Kazdin (1972) made the distinction that in time-out the essential feature "is a period of time after responding in which reinforcement is no longer available (while) with response cost there is no necessary temporal restriction on available reinforcement (p. 534)." In addition, with time-out procedures there is a temporal period during which *all* reinforcers are made inaccessible, while with response cost procedures a specified amount of a *single*, discrete type of reinforcer is withdrawn after each instance of the undesirable behavior.

Response cost has predominantly involved the contingent withdrawal of conditioned reinforcers such as points, tokens, or money. It has been most frequently applied within the context of a token economy, wherein token fines can be levied for inappropriate behavior. Phillips (1968), for example, reduced aggressive statements, tardiness, and use of the word "ain't" by enforcing point fines for these behaviors within a token program for predelinquent boys, while Wolf, Hanley, King, and Lachowicz (1970) reduced classroom out-of-seat behavior of an overly active boy by using a similar tactic.

Briefly, the preceding discussion on four different types of punishment procedures indicates that these procedures have as common elements the contingent delivery of an unpleasant state of affairs and their use to suppress inappropriate behavior. Again, these procedures should be used in the most discriminating sense; they should be applied only when inappropriate behaviors are highly maladaptive (e.g., dangerous) and resistant to the exclusive use of less aversive strategies. When they are implemented, they should be used along with such safeguards as careful specification of the behaviors to be punished, the punishing consequences, and their contingent relationships. At the outset, the child should be informed of the various consequences, positive as well as negative, that will follow his desirable and undesirable behaviors. Finally, punishment procedures should *always* be used in conjunction with positive reinforcement programs for increasing adaptive and desirable behavior.

BEHAVIORAL PROCEDURES FOR ANXIETY MANAGEMENT

A number of procedures exist that have been found to be helpful in reducing excessive levels of anxiety in children, typically displayed in the form of avoidance, fearful, or phobic behavior. The procedures discussed until now have generally been based upon operant learning. The operant model of learning focuses upon behavior as it is influenced by contingencies between antecedent events and behavioral consequences. Another type of learning is based upon the respondent model that focuses upon behavior as it is influenced by associations between stimuli. Although the distinction between operant and respondent forms of learning is less clear than was once thought (Miller, 1975), behavioral procedures used for reducing anxiety are based, in large part, upon the respondent conditioning model.

Behavioral theory maintains that anxiety responses are conditioned or learned on the basis of pairings between a formerly neutral stimulus and an aversive stimulus. Through repeated pairings of these two stimuli, the formerly neutral stimulus attains some aversive or anxiety-provoking properties. The classic report of Watson and Rayner (1920) illustrated how a fear may be conditioned in this manner. These researchers conditioned a fear of white rabbits in a five-year-old boy by pairing a startling, loud noise with a previously unfeared white rabbit. After several such pairings, the boy came to fear the white rabbit. Once fear is conditioned, it is maintained by negative reinforcement of escape and avoidance responses. That is, such behaviors prevent the onset of or lead to the termination of the feared stimulus and are therefore strengthened. To this behavioral conception of fear and avoidance behavior, Bandura (1969) has emphasized the importance of vicarious or modeling influences upon the learning of fears.

Since behavioral theory maintains that fears are developed as a result of direct or observed pairings of the feared stimulus with something aversive, the basic behavioral strategy involves exposing the child to the fear arousing situation under nonaversive contexts or without the possibility of experiencing any aversive consequences from the exposure to the feared situation. One of the most widely used procedures involves the gradual exposure of the child to the feared stimulus while it is paired with very pleasant stimuli, such as deep states of relaxation. This procedure is known as *systematic desensitization*. Another procedure that attempts to expose fearful children to high levels of feared situations in the absence of aversive consequences is known as *implosive therapy* or *flooding*. A third type of strategy that has been used to reduce childhood fear responses is based on *modeling* procedures. The disinhibiting effect of having a fearful child observe a nonfearful model engage in positive interactions with the feared stimulus has already been discussed.

Systematic desensitization

In the late fifties, Wolpe (1958) pioneered a procedure for reducing severe anxiety and phobic behavior which he called systematic desensitization. The technique basically involves three procedural steps: (1) training in deep muscle relaxation; (2) construction of a hierarchy of scenes revolving around the feared situation with each scene becoming progressively more anxiety-arousing than the previous; and (3) pairing of the imaginally visualized scenes with the state of relaxation. The objective is to have the patient successfully visualize each scene in the hierarchy without experiencing any anxiety. A large body of analogue and applied research has found this strategy to be highly successful in reducing phobic behavior (Bandura, 1969; Kazdin and Wilcoxon, 1976; Paul, 1969a, b; Wilson and Davison, 1971). Furthermore, several variations of the basic procedure have also been applied to the reduction of maladaptive anxiety responses. For example, *in vivo desensitization* involves the client in relaxing while actually confronting the anxiety-arousing situation, while *contact desensitization* adds to this a nonfearful model who helps the client approach the feared situation. These extensions of the original systematic desensitization procedure are often useful with young children since children may not yet display the cognitive and lin-

guistic skills necessary for the basic systematic desensitization process. For example, Jones (1924) successfully eliminated a young boy's fear of rabbits by pairing the feared stimulus with candy. This was done by having the boy eat candy while the rabbit was gradually moved closer to the child. These and similar procedures, including positive reinforcement for approach responses to feared situations, have been successfully applied to a wide variety of childhood phobias such as fear of water (Bentler, 1962), fear of toilets (Neale, 1963), fear of riding in cars (Lazarus, 1960), and school phobia (Ayllon, Smith, and Rogers, 1970; Lazarus, Davison, and Polefka, 1965; Patterson, 1965).

Implosive therapy or flooding.

An alternative tactic for reducing maladaptive avoidance behavior is to present the feared situation to the patient all at once and in sufficiently high levels so as to cause anxiety to be experienced. Escape or avoidance responses are prevented so that the patient must confront the feared situation and experience the anxiety until it dissipates as a function of extinction. In so doing, the patient learns that nothing aversive will happen as a result of confronting the feared situation and that it can indeed be coped with. Heretofore, this could not be learned since the patient always engaged in escape or avoidance behavior. This procedure is generally referred to as implosive therapy when the feared situation is presented symbolically in imagination, while it is referred to as flooding (or response prevention) when done *in vivo*. Although this strategy is infrequently employed with children, Kandel, Ayllon, and Rosenbaum (1977) reported a unique adaptation of this procedure to a four-year-old boy who was described as a social isolate. The procedure involved reinforcing *other* children to play with the isolate boy. In this manner, the boy "was flooded with children eager to interact with him (p. 77)." This procedure produced marked increases in social interaction in two separate settings.

The preceding discussion was centered around descriptions of various behavior therapy procedures used with children. For purposes of clarity, each procedure was described separately. However, it would be misleading to infer that in the behavioral treatment of children, therapy would be this "compartmentalized." In actual practice, behavioral problems displayed by children are rarely circumscribed or unidimensional so as to be adequately handled by a discrete type of procedure. Instead, applications of behavior therapy to children are more correctly characterized as consisting of a variety of sometimes overlapping or complementary procedures arranged within a comprehensive approach to the often complex problems displayed by a child. The basic objectives, however, always remain the same: to decrease inappropriate behaviors that are excessively displayed *and* to increase appropriate forms of behavior that are deficiently displayed.

Since many reviews on behavior therapy with children already exist (Graziano, 1972; Sherman and Baer, 1969), the remainder of this chapter will illustrate the previously described procedures in a selective review of the more recent behavior therapy literature with children.

APPLICATIONS

Reduction of Behavioral Excesses

When children display problematic behaviors on an all too frequent basis, the goal of therapy, naturally, is to reduce these behaviors. Behavioral procedures for achieving this goal were previously reviewed. However, what kind of excessive behaviors are these behavior reduction procedures typically applied to? In general, a behavioral excess may be considered as any behavior pattern that is socially and/or physically detrimental to the child himself or to the social environment in which he lives. Self-injurious behavior, feeding disturbances, nocturnal disturbances, toileting disturbances, antisocial behaviors, and phobias are just some examples of classes of behavior that indicate the need for procedures to reduce or eliminate them. Furthermore, these areas represent the research

and clinical interests currently being pursued and published in major behavioral journals.

Children who display self-destructive behavior, such as mentally retarded or autistic children who engage in *self-injurious behavior* (SIB), provide a dramatic example of instances in which quick and effective behavior reduction procedures are required. According to Altman, Haavik, and Cook (1978), two literature reviews have concluded that "the most successful procedure to eliminate self-injurious behavior was contingent electric shock (p. 85)." However, because of the potential legal and ethical ramifications of the use of this procedure, alternative effective methods have been sought. For example, Altman et al. (1978) treated a three-year-old retarded boy, who chronically bit the index fingers of his hands, by contingently delivering aromatic ammonia following each occurrence of hand-biting. The entire treatment consisted of 28 such deliveries of broken ammonia capsules, which resulted in a complete and lasting suppression of self-injurious behavior.

Overcorrection procedures represent another tactic that has been used to eliminate self-injurious behavior. Harris and Romanczyk (1976) treated the chronic head-banging of an eight-year-old retarded boy by using a positive practice overcorrection procedure. This consisted of physically guiding the child's head in an up-down then left-right sequence every five seconds for five minutes following an instance of head-banging. A head-banging response during overcorrection reset the five-minute overcorrection interval. During the nine-month period following implementation of this procedure, head-banging was reduced to zero or near zero levels. Kelly and Drabman (1977) reduced the eye-poking behavior of a partially blind three-year-old retarded boy using a similar type of procedure.

An alternative tactic for reducing SIB has been reported by Favell, McGimsey, and Jones (1978). These authors conducted several studies on the tactic of providing positive reinforcement for increasing periods of time during which no self-injurious behavior occurred. Interestingly, with the profoundly retarded children who participated in these studies, physical restraint was used as the positive reinforcer. According to McGimsey et al. (1978), there is previous literature to indicate that certain self-injurers enjoy being physically restrained. Indeed, it was found that self-injury was reduced by providing this form of reinforcement contingent on periods of time without self-injurious behavior. Furthermore, in one of the studies, lemon juice was initially used to reduce SIB and was moderately effective in reducing such behavior. However, the addition of the positive reinforcement strategy was much more effective than the aversive, lemon juice strategy alone. This study illustrates the importance of combining positive reinforcement for appropriate behavior with any form of punishment procedure for inappropriate behavior. A study by Evans (1976) also illustrates the use of this important strategy in the reduction of a special type of SIB, chronic hair-pulling (trichotillamania). In this study, an eight-year-old nonretarded, psychotic girl's hair-pulling was eliminated by using a token economy in the home, with tokens being earned for increasing periods of time without hair-pulling *plus* five-minute time-out periods (in the bedroom) contingent on hair-pulling. This specialized form of SIB has also been treated successfully by the procedures developed by Altman et al. (1978) and Favell (1978) described earlier.

Feeding disturbances represent another general category of maladaptive excessive behaviors. Ruminative vomiting, overeating, and eating nonedible objects (pica) are all forms of disordered feeding behavior requiring reduction or elimination. Several recent case studies illustrate the behavioral treatment of potentially life-threatening ruminative behavior. The effectiveness of aversive faradic shock for infants who display this problem has previously been mentioned. Successful replications of this procedure have been reported by Toister, Condrin, Worly, and Arthur (1975) and Cunningham and Linscheid (1976). Although lemon juice as an aversive stimulus has been reported to be effective in the treatment of ruminative feeding disturbances (Sajwaj et al., 1974), Murrey, Keele,

and McCarver (1977) described the successful application of tabasco sauce as an alternative physically noxious punishing stimulus. In addition, these authors emphasized the importance of "massive" use of social reinforcement contingent on nonemetic behaviors as well as its withdrawal when emetic behaviors were displayed. Ruminative vomiting is a behavior that always results in some form of immediate attention contingent on its occurrence. Hence, lack of attention for several minutes following rumination constitutes an extinction procedure, while social attention for nonvomiting constitutes the very important procedure of reinforcing behaviors that are incompatible with the behavior to be reduced. In fact, Wright, Brown, and Andrews (1978) used the reinforcing procedure exclusively in the successful treatment of a nine-month-old ruminative child. They suggested that this nonaversive procedure should be used with children whose ruminative behaviors have not yet placed their lives in jeopardy, while the punishment procedures described above would be more appropriate for the more severe cases.

Another form of feeding disturbance involves either the overeating of food (resulting in childhood obesity) or the eating of nonedible objects (pica). Food preferences and eating patterns are shaped early in life and largely determine the likelihood of becoming obese. Although much behavioral work has been undertaken in the adult weight reduction area, relatively little has been done with children. Wheeler and Hess (1976) described a treatment strategy for children that emphasized re-education of the obese child *as well as their mothers* aimed at reducing inappropriate and excessive eating behaviors. Treatment emphasized the modification of situations that lead to excessive eating, as well as modification of the consequences that follow it, in a strategy described as a "long-term, successive approximation approach to control eating patterns within the family and social context of the patient (p. 235)." It was found that this approach resulted in significant improvements with not only the children, but the mothers as well who remained with the program as compared to those who dropped out or were untreated controls.

The other type of maladaptive feeding response which is often a severe and potentially dangerous problem among the profoundly mentally retarded is pica, the eating of small objects off the floor and walls. Bucher, Reykdal, and Albin (1976) successfully reduced pica behavior in two profoundly retarded children by consequating such behavior with 30 seconds of physical restraint contingent on the earliest detectable part of a pica response.

In addition to feeding disturbances, *disordered sleep behaviors* represent another form of abnormal behavior displayed by children in the home setting. Therapeutic objectives in this area typically take the form of reducing behaviors that may be incompatible with sleeping such as hyperactivity, ritualistic behavior, thumbsucking, and so forth. Ayllon, Garber, and Allison (1977), for example, described the treatment of a five-year-old child who would frequently get up during the night, walk into his parents' room and lie down between them. This behavior was effectively eliminated by instructing the parents to provide token reinforcement for remaining in bed the entire night. When he crawled into his parents' bed as they were asleep, the parents were instructed to respond by making it naturally uncomfortable for the boy by rolling over, extending their arms over his body, and so forth, while simulating typical sleep movements. Bergman (1976) treated a seven-year-old "hyperactive" boy who stayed up during most nights and frequently lay in bed with his parents. Complete elimination of such insomniac behavior was effected simply by disallowing the boy from entering the parents' bedroom and returning him to his own bedroom with little or no attention or admonishing from the parents.

Chronic thumbsucking is another nocturnal behavior which is maladaptive to the extent that it can result in malocclusion as well as delaying the onset of orthodontal work. Ross (1975) eliminated such behavior in a severely maloccluded child with five minute time-outs from television watching contingent on thumbsucking during the daytime, combined with painting the thumb with a commercially prepared aversive tasting substance before bedtime. Lassen and Fleet (1978) treated a child with a similar problem by having her wear a glove to sleep. This resulted in lasting elimination of thumbsucking even after the glove was no longer used.

Finally, Martin and Conway (1976) described the treatment of a different type of sleep disturbance—nocturnal rocking. The rocking behavior of a 25-month-old girl who displayed over 1,000 instances of nocturnal rocking was completely eliminated by connecting a bright light to a noise-operated relay which turned on the light (the punishing stimulus) contingent on the child's rocking.

Toileting disturbances displayed by children, such as bedwetting (enuresis) or fecal soiling (encopresis), represent another class of behavioral excess that requires the use of behavior reduction procedures. The behavioral treatment of enuresis has had a long and often successful tradition. Two types of treatments have been used primarily. The Mowrer and Mowrer (1938) method attempts to classically condition waking by pairing it with a full bladder through the use of an alarm that sounds when moisture comes into contact with the bed. Retention control training (Kimmel and Kimmel, 1970) attempts to strengthen or "train the bladder" to be able to retain urine by operantly reinforcing the child for increasing periods of time (up to 30 to 45 minutes) without urination. Both procedures have been found to be reasonably successful in the elimination of this problem (Yates, 1975), although the retention control method has met with more mixed results (Harris and Purohit, 1977). Some researchers have found that the increased bladder capacity that often results from retention control training does not yield generalization in terms of decreased nocturnal enuresis (Doleys et al., 1977; Jehu et al., 1977). A different and more recent means of reducing enuretic behavior, known as "dry-bed training," has also been found to be effective in eliminating this problem (Azrin, Sneed, and Foxx, 1974; Azrin and Thienes, 1978). This form of treatment involves a package of procedures, such as positive practice in going from bed to toilet, hourly awakenings, the use of an alarm, as well as making the child responsible for cleaning himself and the affected area. A comparison of this treatment strategy with retention control training by Doleys et al. (1977) found the dry-bed training procedure to be clearly superior. Yet another tactic in the treatment of enuresis has been described by Singh, Phillips, and Fischer (1976). In this report, the chronic enuresis of a 13-year-old girl was eliminated by awakening her to use the bathroom two hours after falling asleep and then progressively earlier (e.g. one hour and 45 minutes, one and one-half hours, and so forth).

A different type of toileting disturbance referred to as encopresis described the habitual soiling of a child beyond the normative toilet training years. As mentioned previously, when the encopretic child has never been taught how to use the toilet, he simply needs to be toilet trained. However, if the child already is competent in these skills, yet still soils his clothing, this behavior needs to be eliminated. The behavioral treatment of this problem typically involves reducing encopretic behavior by increasing appropriate toileting behaviors that are incompatible with encopresis. This generally takes the form of providing reinforcement for correct use of the toilet as well as for increasing periods of time without soiling (Ayllon et al., 1975; Wright and Walker, 1978). For example, Plachetta (1976) completely eliminated the soiling behavior of a six-year-old encopretic boy by arranging a "contingency contract" with the parents whereby the boy would be reinforced for four ten-minute "attempts" to use the toilet which the child was to make throughout the day. Such procedures could just as well have been reviewed in the subsequent section on illustrations of procedures used to increase behavior since in these cases appropriate use of the toilet is being strengthened and increased. However, the approach of *reducing* inappropriate behavior by *increasing* appropriate behavior illustrates that well-planned, comprehensive behavioral treatments rarely make use of one treatment strategy without the other.

For lack of a better term, a wide variety of problematic child behaviors that are troublesome or disturbing to others are often grouped together and referred to as *antisocial behavior*. These behaviors, by definition, are excessive and, therefore, are suitable targets for behavior elimination or reduction. For example, Stumphauzer (1976) described the successful treatment of a 12-year-old girl who displayed almost daily "uncontrollable stealing" behavior for a five-year period. Treatment consisted of teaching the girl how to symbolically reinforce herself for instances of not stealing ("I am a good girl"), as well as a family contingency contract that specified daily and weekly rewards for the passage of time periods without stealing. As a result, stealing behavior was decreased to zero or near zero levels. Stawar (1976) treated a seven-year-old boy who displayed persistent fire-setting behavior by, again, teaching and increasing a response that was incompatible with such behavior—bringing matches to mother. The boy was imaginatively taught this response vicariously within the context of fables in which the hero of the fable was rewarded for bringing matches to his mother. In actual practice, the boy was subsequently reinforced for performing this response. The mother was instructed to leave a pack of matches lying around the house twice a day so that the boy could receive much practice and reward for engaging in this newly acquired, desirable response. In two weeks, the boy returned matches to the mother on 19 out of 23 trials and had not set a fire from the time treatment was carried out to a seven month follow-up. Another form of antisocial behavior, chronic swearing, was eliminated in a young boy by punishing each instance of swearing with an aversive, naturally available chore—window washing. Swearing was effectively eliminated as a result of this punishment contingency (Fisher and Nehs, 1978).

Public masturbation is yet another form of antisocial behavior frequently exhibited by self-stimulating retarded children. Cook et al. (1978) successfully used lemon juice as a punishing stimulus in the elimination of this type of behavior from both home and school settings. Similarly, Matson and Ollendrick (1976) used the contingent spraying of *Listerine* in the mouths of nine, otherwise normal children, who displayed frequent biting of others when they did not get their way, as a means of reducing this type of aggressive behavior. Finally, children who engage in other forms of antisocial behaviors, such as verbally abusive temper tantrums of disruptive behavior in the classroom, represent other targets for behavior reduction procedures. Withdrawal of social attention, e.g. "ignoring" (Ayllon and Skuban, 1973); social isolation time-out (Drabman and Spitalnik, 1973); time-out in the form of becoming ineligible to receive predetermined rewards (Spitalnik and Drabman, 1976); time-out modified for public places, e.g. use of a restroom, car backseat, and so forth (Murray, 1976), as well as various combinations of these procedures along with the teaching of social skill and reinforcement for nontantruming (Ayllon and Skuban, 1973) have all been successfully applied in the elimination of these forms of maladaptive social behavior.

The reduction of excessive fear and avoidance responses in children, commonly referred to as phobias, represents the last type of behavioral excess to be reviewed. Croghan and Musante (1975) eliminated a seven-year-old boy's phobia of tall buildings by way of a variant of *in vivo* desensitization. Treatment consisted of having the boy gradually approach the feared objects (several tall buildings) within the context of game-playing. In a similar manner, Freeman, Roy, and Hemmick (1976) used *in vivo* desensitization in the successful treatment of a phobia of medical examinations displayed by a seven-year-old retarded boy. A hierarchy of procedures that comprise a physical examination was created with the first several steps being administered by a friendly and trusted nurse. After several such sessions, the nurse administered the entire examination. Next, the nurse administered the examination with a physician present. Finally, the physician followed the hierarchical procedure with the nurse present until the boy's fear was ultimately deconditioned to the point where a different physician was able to administer a complete physical examination without incident. Luiselli (1978) reported another treatment consisting of

in vivo desensitization with a seven-year-old autistic boy who feared school buses. Initially, the boy was reinforced for approaching and boarding a stationary bus along with his mother. This was gradually changed to reinforcement being provided for sitting on a moving school bus without the mother—the ultimate goal of treatment.

These case studies represent relatively unidimensional approaches to children's fears that rely heavily upon the *in vivo* desensitization process. MacDonald (1975), on the other hand, described a multiple treatment approach in the elimination of a child's phobia of dogs so intense that the child was reluctant to leave the house. Imaginal systematic desensitization, modeling, *in vivo* desensitization, dog-interaction skills training, programmed outdoor activity, and restructuring the child's social environment—primarily the parents, which previously served to cue and reinforce dog phobic behaviors—were all components of this successfully administered comprehensive treatment package.

INCREASING SKILLS WHERE BEHAVIORAL DEFICITS EXIST

One of the most prominent examples of a type of behavioral deficit that requires procedures aimed at teaching new or strengthening existing but infrequently displayed behaviors is in the area of *speech and language deficits*. Children without verbal or linguistic skills, such as the deaf, autistic or profoundly retarded, often display a wide variety of deficits that, to a large extent, are related to deficits in communicative abilities. For example, nonverbal, retarded children who often do not display verbal imitation skills have been taught these skills that are prerequisite for the learning of language itself. Hung (1976) taught three such nonimitative, nonverbal retarded children to imitate ten single-syllable verbal responses through a shaping procedure. That is, reinforcement was provided for successive approximations to the terminal behavior of correct imitation until all three subjects were correctly imitating the verbal prompts presented to them by the trainer. Similarly, Stevens-Long, Schwarz, and Bliss (1976) taught a six-year-old autistic boy whose language consisted primarily of two-word phrases to use both simple and compound sentence structure. Seventeen different pictures were used as prompts with training being given on ten of the pictures, while the other seven were used to assess generalization. Imitative prompts, food reinforcement for correct responses, and ten-second time-outs (therapist turned away) contingent on incorrect responses were successfully used to teach this boy the generative use of simple and compound sentence structure.

Children who talk in some situations (e.g. at home) but not in others (e.g. at school) present another type of speech and language disorder known as elective mutism. The treatment of this problem provides another good example of the need to increase behavior, in this case verbal behavior, in areas where it is deficiently displayed or nonexistant. Richards and Hansen (1978), for example, described the treatment of an eight-year-old girl who never spoke to a teacher or staff member in the school setting but talked regularly at home. This seemingly strange behavior pattern led some school personnel to believe that she was retarded. A stimulus fading procedure was used along several stimulus and response dimensions. Initially, treatment began in the home with just the girl and the teacher. Gradually, treatment shifted from the home to the school route and into the classroom; from requiring the girl to talk initially in whispers and in one-word responses to full, audible verbal responses; from the situation involving just the girl and the teacher to situations including one, two, three friends, and ultimately the entire class; and requiring the girl to respond only once during a session to requiring several dozen responses per session. This graduated approach of fading new response requirements into the therapeutic sessions resulted in complete and lasting "verbosity" in the classroom, along with a part in a school play, as well as the finding that the girl had an IQ of 117.

Academic deficits represent another type of behavioral deficit which serve as targets for behavior strengthening procedures. For example, Aaron and Bostow (1978) increased both the academic productivity and on-task behavior of three students with defective academic repertoires by making "free time" a reinforcer contingent on a specified percentage of responding in six different academic areas. The use of reinforcement to increase academic behaviors in the classroom has an extensive and distinguished tradition (O'Leary and O'Leary, 1972). Although reinforcement has been the primary strategy for increasing academic skill where deficits exist, there is no reason that this "prosthetic" procedure itself could not be imaginatively applied in the teaching process per se. For example, Kincaid and Weisberg (1978) demonstrated how a token economy, with tokens labeled with letters of the alphabet, could teach economically disadvantaged children alphabet recognition while the program itself was used to strengthen other desirable classroom behaviors.

Although reinforcement, in one form or another, is the primary procedure for increasing academic skill, it is not the only procedure. The manipulation of antecedent events can also result in improved academic performance. Ayllon, Garber, and Pisor (1975), for example, demonstrated that *decreased* time limits could result in increased academic performance. Likewise, Rainwater and Ayllon (1976) increased the academic performance of first graders simply by introducing a timer to the academic work situation.

A number of classes of behavior disorders reviewed in the preceding section on reducing behavioral excesses may also have various types of behavioral problems that require procedures for increasing skill in deficit areas. It was mentioned that when a child displays *toileting disturbances*, such as enuresis, if he does not have the necessary component skills in his behavioral repertoire, these behaviors need to be shaped and strengthened. Butler (1976), for example, successfully shaped toileting skills in a four-year-old spina bifida child who had some degree of bladder impairment. Foxx and Azrin's (1973) shaping procedure, which included positive practice in using the toilet, reinforcement for correct elimination as well as for maintaining dry pants, and cleanliness training (i.e. cleaning up after an accident), comprised the treatment package.

A *feeding disturbance*, sometimes known as anorexia, characterized by a refusal to eat, has as its treatment object increased self-feeding behavior. Ives, Harris, and Wolchik (1978) treated such a child by way of a multicomponent forced-feeding procedure. The child in this case refused to consume any type of food other than an instant breakfast or an occasional animal cracker. Treatment consisted of requiring the child to eat 20 small meals throughout the day by placing morsels of food in his mouth and physically prompting chewing movements. Spitting out was not allowed, and if it occurred simply resulted in another morsel of food being placed into his mouth. Swallowing was reinforced with social attention and sips of the favored instant breakfast drink. This procedure was first conducted in the school and later in the home, with the outcome being self-feeding in both situations as food gradually took on its naturally reinforcing characteristic.

Finally, the *antisocial behaviors* spoken of previously may also be treated with procedures aimed at increasing adaptive, prosocial behaviors. Behaviors such as swearing, stealing, physical aggression, and so forth, which were discussed in the section on reducing inappropriate behaviors, are too often associated with individuals referred to as juvenile delinquents. Recently, it has become increasingly clear that it is also important to teach such individuals skills that will help them adapt in a socially acceptable manner. In this regard, Mills and Walter (1976) conducted a study assessing the effects of developing employment skills with 76 adjudicated juvenile delinquents to see what effect it had upon their antisocial modes of behavior. The "Behavioral-Employment Intervention Program" used in this study involved teaching basic job skills as well as "positive job attitudes," reflected in such behaviors as good attendance, grooming, and performance; contingency contracting procedures; and training participating employers to reinforce desirable behaviors displayed by the delinquent. The results of this study

indicated that increasing positive employment skills was indeed an effective means of reducing delinquent behavior, as 85 percent of the participants had no further arrests and stayed on the job for at least three months over the one year follow-up.

CONCLUSION

Traditionally, a review of some approaches to children's therapy would have to include some mention of such aspects as projective testing; one-to-one therapist-child interaction; therapist interpretation of the child's deviant behavior, play therapy, and so forth. It should have been apparent that these elements of traditional therapy with children were not discussed. Their omission is not accidental. The above procedures belong to a view in which the child's problem is of an intrapsychic nature, requiring therapist interpretation, and, perhaps, reliving of important past experiences of a traumatic nature. The procedures reviewed here are all derived from a different conceptual view of what is wrong with the child. The behavioral view is based on the premise that the child's behavior (or its absence) is what causes him to get into trouble in his environment. Consequently, reducing problematic behaviors or equipping him with new and adaptive ones will enable him to cope effectively with his environment.

Although the child's behavior is the primary focus of treatment, it must be kept in mind that the behavior of a child does not exist within a social vacuum. There exists a dynamic social interaction between the child and the immediate environment. Most notable is the ongoing interrelationship of the child's behavior with that of the parents or teachers. Effective treatment requires a blending of the social environment and does not easily take place in the absence of an integrated program involving the reactions of those individuals who are most significant to the child. For example, a child who displays abnormal behavior because of physical abuse by parents will certainly require that the parents be retrained to cope with the child's behavior without the use of physical abuse (Sandler,

Van Dercar, and Milhoan, 1978). Hence, effective treatment of the child almost always requires some types of changes in the behavior of the significant others in his life. There are two important reasons for this. The daily experience of the child is one of learning new behavior through countless interactions with important socializing agents—as parents and teachers. Second, the integral involvement of these individuals will promote the generalization of positive behavior changes across settings, situations, and time.

Finally, it should be mentioned that the area of child behavior therapy is a burgeoning one. Increasingly complex research is being conducted in the area, and it is not unreasonable to expect in the near future new behavioral procedures being advanced toward more economical and enduring treatment involving greater degrees of self-control and autonomy for the child.

REFERENCES

Aaron, B. A. & Bostow, D. E. Indirect facilitation of on-task behavior produced by contingent free-time for academic productivity. *Journal of Applied Behavior Analysis*, 1978, *11*, 197.

Allen, K. E., Hart, B. M., Buell, J. S., Harris, F. R., & Wolf, M. M. Effects of social reinforcement on isolate behavior of a nursery school child. *Child Development*, 1964, *35*, 511–518.

Altman, K., Haavik, S., & Cook, J. W. Punishment of self-injurious behavior in natural settings using contingent aromatic ammonia. *Behaviour Research and Therapy*, 1978, *16*, 85–96.

American Psychiatric Association. *Diagnostic and statistical manual of mental disorders* (*2nd ed.*). Washington, D.C.: American Psychiatric Association, 1968.

Aronfreed, J., & Reber, A. Internalized behavioral suppression and the timing of social punishment. *Journal of Personality and Social Psychology*, 1965, *1*, 3–16.

Ayllon, T. Intensive treatment of psychotic behavior by stimulus satiation and food reinforcement. *Behaviour Research and Therapy*, 1963, *1*, 53–61.

Ayllon, T. & Azrin, N. H. *The token economy: A motivational system for therapy and rehabilitation.* New York: Appleton-Century-Crofts, 1968.

Ayllon, T., Garber, S. W., & Allison, G. Behavioral treatment of childhood neurosis. *Psychiatry*, 1977, *40*, 315–322.

Ayllon, T., Garber, S., & Pisor, K. Reducing time limits: A means to increase behavior of retardates. *Journal of Applied Behavior Analysis*, 1976, *9*, 247–252.

Ayllon, T., Layman, D., & Burke, S. Disruptive behavior and reinforcement of academic performance. *Psychological Record*, 1972, *22*, 315–323.

Ayllon, T., Layman, D., & Kandel, H. A behavioral-educational alternative to drug control of hyperactive children. *Journal of Applied Behavior Analysis*, 1975, *8*, 137–146.

Ayllon, T. & Milan, M. *Correctional rehabilitation and management: The psychological approach.* New York: Wiley & Sons, in press.

Ayllon, T. & Roberts, M. Eliminating discipline problem by strengthening academic performance. *Journal of Applied Behavior Analysis*, 1974, *7*, 71–76.

Ayllon, T., Simon, S. J., & Wildman, R. W. Instructions and reinforcement in the elimination of encopresis: A case study. *Journal of Behavior Therapy and Experimental Psychiatry*, 1975, *6*, 235–238.

Ayllon, T. & Skuban, W. Accountability in psychotherapy: A test case. *Journal of Behavior Therapy and Experimental Psychiatry*, 1973, *4*, 19–30.

Ayllon, T., Smith, D., & Rogers, M. Behavioral management of school phobia. *Journal of Behavior Therapy and Experimental Psychiatry*, 1970, *1*, 125–138.

Azrin, N. & Foxx, R. M. *Toilet training in less than a day.* New York: Simon and Schuster, 1974.

Azrin, N. H., Sneed, T. J., & Foxx, R. M. Dry bed: Rapid elimination of childhood enuresis. *Behaviour Research and Therapy*, 1974, *12*, 147–156.

Azrin, N. H. & Thienes, P. M. Rapid elimination of enuresis by intensive learning without a conditioning apparatus. *Behavior Therapy*, 1978, *9*, 342–354.

Baer, D. Laboratory control of thumbsucking by withdrawal and representation of reinforcement. *Journal of the Experimental Analysis of Behavior*, 1962, *5*, 525–528.

Bandura, A., Grusec, J., & Menlove, F. Some social determinants of self-monitoring reinforcement systems. *Journal of Personality and Social Psychology*, 1964, *69*, 1–9.

Becker, W. C., Madsen, C. H., Arnold, C. R., & Thomas, D. R. The contingent use of teacher attention and praising in reducing classroom behavior problems. *Journal of Special Education*, 1967, *1*, 287–307.

Bellack, A. S. & Hersen, M. *Behavior modification: An introductory textbook.* Baltimore, Md.: Williams & Wilkins Co., 1977.

Bentler, P. M. An infant's phobia treated with reciprocal inhibition therapy. *Journal of Child Psychology and Psychiatry,* 1962, *3,* 185–189.

Bergman, R. L. Treatment of childhood insomnia diagnosed as "Hyperactivity." *Journal of Behavior Therapy and Experimental Psychiatry,* 1976, *7,* 199.

Bucher, B. & Lovaas, O. I. Use of aversive stimulation in behavior modification. In *Miami symposium on the prediction of behavior: Aversive stimulation,* M. R. Jones, ed. Coral Gables, Fla.: University of Miami Press, 1968.

Bucher, B., Reykdal, B., & Albin, J. Brief physical restraint to control pica in retarded children. *Journal of Behavior Therapy and Experimental Psychiatry,* 1976, *7,* 137–140.

Burchard, J. D. Systematic socialization: A programmed environment for the habilitation of antisocial retardates. *Psychological Record,* 1967, *17,* 461–476.

Butler, J. F. Toilet training a child with spina bifida. *Journal of Behavior Therapy and Experimental Psychiatry,* 1976, *7,* 63–66.

Cook, J. W., Altman, K., Shaw, J., & Blaylock, M. Use of contingent lemon juice to eliminate public masturbation by a severely retarded boy. *Behavior Research and Therapy,* 1978, *16,* 131–133.

Croghan, L. & Musante, G. J. The elimination of a boy's high building phobia by *in vivo* desensitization and game playing. *Journal of Behavior Therapy and Experimental Psychiatry,* 1975, *6,* 87–88.

Cunningham, C. E. & Linscheid, T. R. Elimination of chronic infant ruminating by electric shock. *Behavior Therapy,* 1976, *7,* 231–234.

Doleys, D. M., Ciminero, A. R., Tollison, J. W., Williams, C. L., & Wells, K. C. Dry-bed training and retention control training: A comparison. *Behavior Therapy,* 1977, *8,* 541–548.

Drabman, R. & Jarvie, G. Counseling parents of children with behavior problems: The use of extinction and time-out techniques. *Pediatrics,* 1977, *59,* 78–84.

Drabman, R. & Spitalnik, R. Social isolation as a punishment procedure: A controlled study. *Journal of Experimental Child Psychology,* 1973, *16,* 236–249.

Duker, P. C. & Seys, D. M. Elimination of vomiting in a retarded female using restitutional overcorrection. *Behavior Therapy,* 1977, *8,* 255–257.

Evans, B. A case of trichotillomania in a child treated in a home token economy program. *Journal of Behavior Therapy and Experimental Psychiatry,* 1976, *7,* 197–198.

Favell, J. E., McGimsey, J. F., & Jones, M. L. The use of physical restraint in the treatment of self-injury and as positive reinforcement. *Journal of Applied Behavior Analysis,* 1978, *11,* 225–241.

Fischer, J. & Nehs, R. Use of a commonly available chore to reduce a boy's rate of swearing. *Journal of Behavior Therapy and Experimental Psychiatry,* 1978, *9,* 81–83.

Foa, E. Flooding. In *Psychotherapy Handbook,* R. Hernik, ed. New York: Jason Aronson, 1980.

Foxx, R. M. & Azrin, N. H. Restitution: A method of eliminating aggressive-disruptive behavior of retarded and brain damaged patients. *Behaviour Research and Therapy,* 1972, *10,* 15–27.

Foxx, R. M. & Azrin, N. H. The elimination of autistic self-stimulatory behavior by overcorrection. *Journal of Applied Behavior Analysis,* 1973, *6,* 1–14.

Frederiksen, L., Jenkins, J. O., & Carr, C. R. Indirect modification of adolescent drug abuse using contingency contracting. *Journal of Behavior Therapy and Experimental Psychiatry,* 1976, *7,* 377–378.

Freeman, B. J., Roy, R. R., & Hemmick, S. Extinction of a phobia of physical examination in a seven-year-old mentally retarded boy—a case study. *Behaviour Research and Therapy,* 1976, *14,* 63–64.

Graziano, A. M. *Behavior therapy with children.* Chicago: Aldine-Atherton, 1971.

Group for the Advancement of Psychiatry. *Psychopathological disorders in childhood: Theoretical considerations and a proposed classification.* (Vol. VI), GAP Report No. 62, 1966.

Harris, L. S. & Purohit, A. P. Bladder training and enuresis: A controlled trial. *Behaviour Research and Therapy,* 1977, *15,* 485–490.

Harris, S. L. & Romanczyk, R. G. Treating self-injurious behavior of a retarded child by overcorrection. *Behavior Therapy,* 1976, *7,* 235–239.

Hersen, M. & Barlow, D. H. *Single-case experimental designs: Strategies for studying behavior change.* New York: Pergamon Press, 1976.

Homme, L., Csanyi, A., Gonzales, M., & Rechs, J. *How to use contingency contracting in the classroom.* Champaign, Ill.: Research Press, 1969.

Horner, R. D. Establishing use of crutches by a mentally retarded spina bifada child. *Journal of Applied Behavior Analysis,* 1971, *4,* 183–190.

Hung, D. W. Teaching mute retarded children vocal imitation. *Journal of Behavior Therapy and Experimental Psychiatry,* 1976, *7,* 85–88.

Ives, C. C., Harras, S. L., & Wolchik, S. A. Food refusal in an autistic type of child treated by a multi-component forced feelings procedure. *Journal of Behavior Therapy and Experimental Psychiatry*, 1978, 9, 61–64.

Jehu, D., Morgan, R. T. T., Turner, R. K., & Jones, A. A controlled trial of the treatment of nocturnal enuresis in residential homes for children. *Behaviour Research and Therapy*, 1977, 15, 1–16.

Johnston, J. M. Punishment of human behavior. *American Psychologist*, 1972, 27, 1033–1054.

Jones, M. C. The elimination of children's fears. *Journal of Experimental Psychology*, 1924, 7, 382–390.

Journal of Applied Behavior Analysis. Lawrence, Kan.: Society for the Experimental Analysis of Behavior. 1968–.

Journal of the Experimental Analysis of Behavior. Ann Arbor, Mich.: Society for the Experimental Analysis of Behavior, 1958–.

Kandel, H. J., Ayllon, T., & Rosenbaum, M. S. Flooding or systematic exposure in the treatment of extreme social withdrawal in children. *Journal of Behavior Therapy and Experimental Psychiatry*, 1977, 8, 75–81.

Kanfer, F. & Saslow, G. Behavioral diagnosis. In C. M. Franks (Ed.), *Behavior therapy: Appraisal and status*. New York: McGraw-Hill, 1969, pp. 417–444.

Kazdin, A. E. Response cost: The removal of conditioned reinforcers for therapeutic change. *Behavior Therapy*, 1972, 3, 533–546.

Kazdin, A. E. *Behavior modification in applied settings*. Homewood, Ill.: The Dorsey Press, 1975.

Kazdin, A. E. *The token economy*. New York: Plenum Press, 1977.

Kazdin, A. E. & Wilcoxen, L. A. Systematic desensitization and nonspecific treatment effects: A methodological review. *Psychological Bulletin*, 1976, 83, 729–758.

Kelly, J. A. & Drabman, R. S. Generalizing response suppression of self-injurious behavior through an overcorrection punishment procedure: A case study. *Behavior Therapy*, 1977, 8, 468–472.

Kelly, J., Furman, W., & Phillips, J. Teaching conversational skills to retarded adolescents. *Behavior Therapy*, in press.

Kincaid, M. S. & Weisberg, P. Alphabet letters as tokens: Training preschool children in letter recognition and labelling during a token exchange period. *Journal of Applied Behavior Analysis*, 1978, 11, 199.

Kimmel, H. D. & Kimmel, E. An instrumental conditioning method for the treatment of enuresis. *Journal of Behavior Therapy and Experimental Psychiatry*, 1970, 1, 121–123.

Kirby, F. D. & Shields, F. Modification of arithmetic response rate and attending behavior in a seventh-grade student. *Journal of Applied Behavior Analysis*, 1972, 5, 79–84.

Lang, P. J. & Melamed, B. G. Avoidance conditioning therapy of an infant with chronic ruminative vomiting. *Journal of Abnormal Psychology*, 1969, 74, 1–8.

Lassen, M. K. & Fluet, N. R. Elimination of nocturnal thumbsucking by glove wearing. *Journal of Behavior Therapy and Experimental Psychiatry*, 1978, 9, 85.

Lazarus, A. A. The elimination of children's phobias by deconditioning. In H. J. Eysenck (Ed.), *Behaviour therapy and the neuroses*. London: Pergamon Press, 1960.

Lazarus, A. A., Davison, G. C., & Polefka, D. A. Classical and operant factors in the treatment of school phobias. In A. M. Graziano (Ed.), *Behavior therapy with children*. Chicago: Aldine-Atherton, Inc., 1971.

Lovaas, O. I. & Simmons, J. Manipulation of self-destruction in three retarded children. *Journal of Applied Behavior Analysis*, 1969, 2, 143–157.

Luiselli, J. K. Treatment of an autistic child's fear of riding a school bus through exposure and reinforcement. *Journal of Behavior Therapy and Experimental Psychiatry*, 1978, 9, 169–172.

MacDonald, M. L. Multiple impact behavior therapy in a child's dog phobia. *Journal of Behavior Therapy and Experimental Psychiatry*, 1975, 6, 317–322.

MacDonald, W. S.; Gallimore, R.; MacDonald, G. Contingency counseling by school personnel: Economical mode of intervention. *Journal of Applied Behavior Analysis*, 1970, 3, (3), 175–182.

Madsen, C. H., Becker, W. C., & Thomas, D. R. Rules, praise and ignoring: Elements of elementary classroom control. *Journal of Applied Behavior Analysis*, 1968, 1, 139–150.

Madsen, C. H., Becker, W. C., Thomas, D. R., Koser, L., & Plager, E. An analysis of the reinforcing function of "sit down" commands. In R. K. Parker (Ed.), *Readings in Educational Psychology*, Boston: Allyn & Bacon, 1970.

Marholin, D., II, Steinman, W. M., McInnis, E. T., & Heads, T. B. The effects of a teacher's presence on the classroom behavior of conduct-problem children. *Journal of Abnormal Child Psychology*, 1975, 3, 11–25.

Matson, J. L. & Ollendick, T. H. Elimination of low frequency biting. *Behavior Therapy*, 1976, 7, 410–411.

Michael, J. & Meyerson, L. A behavioral approach to counseling and guidance. *Har-*

vard Educational Review, 1962, *32,* 382–401.

Miller, N. E. Clinical applications of biofeedback: Voluntary control of heart rate, rhythm, and blood pressure. In H. I. Russek (Ed.), *New Horizons in Cardiovascular Practice,* Baltimore, Md.: University Park Press, 1975.

Mills, C. M. & Walter, T. L. A behavioral employment intervention program for reducing juvenile delinquency. *Behavior Therapy,* 1977, *8,* 270–271.

Mowrer, O. H. & Mowrer, W. M. Enuresis: A method for its study and treatment. *American Journal of Orthopsychiatry,* 1938, *8,* 436–469.

Murray, M. E. Modified time-out procedures for controlling tantrum behavior in public places. *Behavior Therapy,* 1976, *7,* 412–413.

Murray, M. E., Keele, D. K., & McCarves, J. W. Treatment of ruminations with behavioral techniques: A case report. *Behavior Therapy,* 1977, *8,* 999–1003.

Nathan, P. & Harris, S. *Psychopathology and society.* New York: McGraw-Hill Book Co., 1975.

Neale, D. H. Behaviour therapy and encopresis in children. *Behaviour Research and Therapy,* 1963, *1,* 139–149.

O'Leary, K. D., Kaufman, K. F., Kass, R. E., & Drabman, R. S. The effects of loud and soft reprimands on the behavior of disruptive students. *Exceptional Children,* 1970, *37,* 145–155.

O'Leary, K. D. & O'Leary, S. G. *Classroom management: The successful use of behavior modification.* New York: Pergamon, 1972.

O'Leary, K. D., Turkewitz, H., & Taffel, S. Parent and therapist evaluation of behavior therapy in a child psychological clinic. *Journal of Consulting and Clinical Psychology,* 1973, *41,* 279–283.

Oliver, J. E. & Taylor, A. Five generations of ill-treated children in one family pedigree. *British Journal of Psychiatry,* 1971, *119,* 473–480.

O'Neal, S. The application and methodological implications of behavior modification in nursing research. In M. Batey (Ed.), *Communicating nursing research: The many sources of nursing knowledge.* Boulder, Col.: WICHE, 1972.

Plachetta, K. E. Encopresis: A case study utilizing contracting, scheduling and self-charting. *Journal of Behavior Therapy and Experimental Psychiatry,* 1976, *7,* 195–196.

Patterson, G. R. A learning theory approach to the treatment of the school phobic child. In L. P. Ullman and L. Krasner (Eds.), *Case studies in behavior modification.* New York: Holt, Rinehart and Winston, 1965.

Patterson, G. R. Interventions for boys with conduct problems: Multiple settings, treatments, and criteria. *Journal of Consulting and Clinical Psychology,* 1974, *42,* 471–481.

Paul, G. Outcome of systematic desensitization I: Background procedures and uncontrolled reports of individual treatment. In C. M. Franks (Ed.), *Behavior therapy: Appraisal and status.* New York: McGraw-Hill, Inc., 1969 (a).

Paul, G. Outcome of systematic desensitization II: Controlled investigation of individual treatment, technique variations and current status. In C. M. Franks (Ed.), *Behavior therapy: Appraisal and status.* New York: McGraw-Hill, Inc., 1969 (b).

Phillips, E. L. Achievement place: Token reinforcement procedures in a home-style rehabilitation setting for "pre-delinquent" boys. *Journal of Applied Behavior Analysis,* 1968, *1,* 213–223.

Rainwater, N. & Ayllon, T. Increasing academic performance by using a timer as antecedent stimulus: A study of four cases. *Behavior Therapy,* 1976, *7,* 672–677.

Richards, C. S. & Hansen, M. K. A further demonstration of the efficacy of stimulus fading treatment of elective mutism. *Journal of Behavior Therapy and Experimental Psychiatry,* 1978, *9,* 57–60.

Ross, A. O. *Psychological disorders of children: A behavioral approach to theory research and therapy.* New York: McGraw-Hill Book Co., 1974.

Ross, J. A. Parents modify thumbsucking: A case study. *Journal of Behavior Therapy and Experimental Psychiatry,* 1975, *6,* 248–249.

Sajwaj, T., Libet, J., & Agras, S. Lemon juice therapy: The control of life-threatening rumination in a six-month-old infant. *Journal of Applied Behavior Analysis,* 1974, *7,* 557–563.

Sandler, S., Van Dercar, C., & Milhoan, M. Training child abusers in the use of positive reinforcement practices. *Behavior Research and Therapy,* 1978, *16,* 169–175.

Sherman, J. A. & Baer, D. M. Appraisal of operant therapy techniques with children and adults. In C. M. Franks (Ed.), *Behavior therapy: Appraisal and status.* New York: McGraw-Hill Book Co., 1969.

Simon, S. J. *Behavioral compensation: The effects of contrast manipulations on the classroom behavior of deaf children.* Unpublished doctoral dissertation. Georgia State University, Atlanta, Georgia, 1978.

Simon, S. J., Robertson, S., Pachman, J., & Drabman, R. Self-control token procedures with a class of mentally retarded disruptive children. *Behavior Therapy*, in press.

Singh, R., Phillips, D., & Fischer, S. C. The treatment of enuresis by progressively earlier waking. *Journal of Behavior Therapy and Experimental Psychiatry*, 1976, 7, 277–278.

Spitalnik, R. & Drabman, R. A classroom time-out procedure for retarded children. *Journal of Behavior Therapy and Experimental Psychiatry*, 1976, 7, 17–22.

Stawar, T. L. Fable mod: Operantly structured fantasies as an adjunct in the modification of fire-setting behavior. *Journal of Behavior Therapy and Experimental Psychiatry*, 1976, 7, 285–288.

Stevens-Long, J. S., Schwarz, J. L., & Bliss, D. The acquisition and generalization of compound sentence structure in an autistic child. *Behavior Therapy*, 1976, 7, 397–404.

Strober, M. & Bellack, A. S. Multiple component behavioral treatment for a child with behavior problems. *Journal of Behavior Therapy and Experimental Psychiatry*, 1975, 6, 250–252.

Stuart, R. B. Behavioral contracting with the families of delinquents. *Journal of Behavior Therapy and Experimental Psychiatry*, 1971, 2, 1–11.

Stumphauzer, J. Elimination of stealing by self-reinforcement of alternative behavior and family contracting. *Journal of Behavior Therapy and Experimental Psychiatry*, 1976, 7, 265–268.

Tate, B. G. & Baroft, G. S. Aversive control of self-injurious behavior in a psychotic boy. *Behavior Research and Therapy*, 1966, 4, 281–287.

Tharp, R. G. & Wetzel, R. J. *Behavior modification in the natural environment*. New York: Academic Press, 1969.

Thompson, T. & Grabouski, J. *Behavior modification of the mentally retarded*. New York: Oxford University Press, 1972.

Toister, R. P., Condrin, C. J., Worley, L., & Arthur, D. Faradic therapy of chronic vomiting in infancy: A case study. *Journal of Behavior Therapy and Experimental Psychiatry*, 1975, 6, 55–59.

Ullman, L. P. & Krasner, L. *A psychological approach to abnormal behavior* (2nd ed.). Englewood Cliffs, N.J.: Prentice-Hall, 1975.

Vukelick, R. and Make, D. F. Reduction of dangerously aggressive behavior in a severely retarded resident through a combination of positive reinforcement procedures. *Journal*

of Applied Behavior Analysis, 1971, 4, 215–225.

Watson, J. B. and Rayner, R. Conditioned emotional reactions. *Journal of Experimental Psychology*, 1920, 3, 1–14.

Whaley, D. & Mallott, R. *Elementary principals of behavior*. Englewood Cliffs, N.J.: Prentice-Hall Inc., 1968.

Wheeler, M. E. & Hess, K. W. Treatment of juvenile obesity by successive approximation control of eating. *Journal of Behavior Therapy and Experimental Psychiatry*, 1976, 7, 235–242.

White, G. D., Nielsen, G., & Johnson, S. M. Timeout duration and the suppression of deviant behavior in children. *Journal of Applied Behavior Analysis*, 1972, 5, 111–120.

Williams, C. D. The elimination of tantrum behavior by extinction procedures. *Journal of Abnormal and Social Psychology*, 1959, 59, 269.

Williams, J. L. *Operant learning: Procedures for changing behavior*. Monterey, Cal.: Brooks/Cole Publishing Co., 1973.

Wilson, G. T. & Davison, G. C. Processes of fear-reduction in systematic desensitization: Animal studies. *Psychological Bulletin*, 1971, 76, 1–14.

Winnett, R. A. & Roach, E. M. The effects of reinforcing academic performance on social behavior. *Psychological Record*, 1973, 23, 391–396.

Wolf, M. M., Hanley, E. L., King, L. A., Lachowicz, J. & Giles, D. K. The timer-game: A variable interval contingency for the management of out of seat behavior. *Exceptional Children*, 1970, 37, 113–117.

Wolf, M. M., Risley, T., & Mees, H. L. Application of operant conditioning procedures to the behavior problems of an autistic child. *Behaviour Research and Therapy*, 1964, 1, 305–312.

Wolpe, J. *Psychotherapy by reciprocal inhibition*. Stanford, Cal.: Stanford University Press, 1958.

Wright, D. F., Brown, R. A., & Andrews, M. E. Remission of chronic ruminative vomiting through a reversal of social contingencies. *Behaviour Research and Therapy*, 1978, 16, 134–136.

Wright, L. & Walker, C. E. A simple behavioral treatment program for psychogenic encopresis. *Behaviour Research and Therapy*, 1978, 16, 209–212.

Yates, A. J. *Theory and practice in behavior therapy*. New York: Wiley, 1975.

CHAPTER 12

Social-Cognitive Approaches to Therapy with Children

PHILIP C. KENDALL, Ph.D. and EUGENE URBAIN, Ph.D.

SOCIAL PROBLEM-SOLVING

How can we account for the large differences in the ways children go about solving the interpersonal problems they encounter in their day-to-day lives? To what extent are such differences a matter of general intellectual capacity of the sort measured by IQ tests? Are children's ways of thinking about social situations related to their level of actual behavioral adjustment? And, perhaps, most important, can social-cognitive, problem-solving skills be taught and will such training result in more adjusted behavior?

It seems reasonable to assert that a person's positive mental health is related to the way in which the social/interpersonal problems that come up in day-to-day living are handled. Prior to the 1970s, there had been surprisingly little systematic research into the processes concerning *how people think* when confronted with personal and interpersonal problems in their lives. Until recently, research into human problem-solving processes focused almost exclusively on problems of nonsocial content, such as puzzle-type tasks, anagram prob-

NOTE: The authors wish to thank David Pellegrini for his valuable comments made on an earlier version of this manuscript. This chapter was prepared while the first author's research was supported by University of Minnesota Graduate School Grant #440-0160-4909-02 and Grant #441 0749 5236 02. Portions of this paper were adapted from an article by Urbain and Kendall (1980).

lems, and intellectual creativity tasks of various kinds (see Simon and Newell, 1971, for a review). Jahoda (1953, 1958) was among the first to place explicit theoretical emphasis on the relation of effective interpersonal problem-solving to social and emotional adjustment and proposed that psychological health is related to a problem-solving sequence. The sequence includes the tendency to recognize and admit a problem, reflect on possible solutions, make a decision, and take action.

The social-cognitive, problem-solving approach in general is unique in its emphasis on adaptive *thinking processes*, as opposed to an emphasis on internal psychodynamics or specific overt behaviors per se as major factors in psychological adjustment. To understand what is meant here by the concept of a "problem," D'Zurilla and Coldfried (1971) have provided us with the following working definition:

The term *problem* will refer here to a specific *situation* or set of situations to which a person must respond in order to function effectively in his environment. To point up this situational emphasis (as opposed to the traditional "intrapsychic" connotation to the word "problem" in clinical psychology), the term *problem situation* will be used in most instances in place of "problem". A situation is considered problematic if *no effective response alternative is immediately available to the individual confronted with the situation.* (p. 107–108)

The internal cognitive processes that lead to successful problem-solving are highlighted—processes akin to "the operation of cognitive strategies or 'learning sets' which enable an individual to 'create' or discover solutions to a variety of unfamiliar problems (p. 108)." The authors are careful to point out, however, that the emphasis on the situation should not lead to the mistaken assumption that all relevant stimulation is seen to originate in the external environment. A given problem situation should be viewed as reflecting an interaction of both external situational events as well as personal reactions resulting from "feedback" from the person's own prior responses. The authors proceed to a definition of interpersonal problem-solving:

Problem-solving may be defined as a behavioral process . . . which (a) makes available a variety of potentially effective response alternatives for dealing with problematic situations and (b) increases the probability of selecting the most effective response from among these various alternatives. (p. 108)

It is readily apparent that the interpersonal problem-solving approach overlaps to some extent with the early attempts by Thorndike (1920) and Guilford (1967) to define a domain of "social intelligence" that was presumably related to competence in interpersonal situations. However, efforts to discover a unitary domain of behavior reflecting this "social intelligence" factor have met with little success (Keating, 1978). Present research in the area of social-cognitive problem-solving has subsequently placed greater emphasis on attempts to delineate a variety of discrete yet interrelated interpersonal cognitive problem-solving (ICPS) skills that are hypothesized to be important components of social problem-solving processes.

Mention should be made at this point of the relationship of the social-cognitive problem-solving approach to the field of behavioral psychology in general. In the first place, this approach is congruent with the increasing emphasis on the role of internal cognitive events evident in behavior modification research. Problem-solving is a "cognitive-behavioral" process; it deals with cognitive processes and their relationship to behavioral adjustment (Kendall and Hollon, 1979). Problem-solving interventions, however, place greater emphasis on training at the level of covert thinking processes themselves—for example, generating alternatives, evaluating consequences, and so forth—in contrast to intervention methods aimed specifically at the training of discrete behavioral responses to a situation—such as relaxation responses, assertive responses, affiliative responses, and so forth. Second, the social-cognitive approach attempts to speak directly to a recurrent problem in numerous "traditional" studies of discrete response training, namely, the lack of generalization of treatment effects to situations other than the training situation (Kazdin, 1975). The essential hypothesis, based on the social-cognitive problem-solving model, is that training at the level of the cognitive processes that presumably mediate competence across a broad range of situations will in fact "build in" generalization as an inherent part of treatment. On the other hand, problem-solving treatments share with other behavioral interventions an emphasis on social-learning processes involved in response acquisition (Bandura, 1977; Rotter, 1954). Consequently, social-cognitive therapy is aimed at the remediation of response deficits and at the direct teaching of component problem-solving skills, as opposed to being directed primarily toward affect release and the uncovering of dynamic complexes and unconscious motivation.

Assuming the large number of studies being published under the general rubric of "social skills training," some effort at initial classification seems in order. As an initial step, we propose that the variety of existing approaches to the direct teaching of social behavior may be usefully classified along a continuum of response generality, with studies emphasizing training of discrete observable social behaviors at one end and studies emphasizing training in general covert cognitive problem-solving *processes* at the other. Although clearly no general social-cognitive thinking skills can be taught without reference to some specific social content, we will be concerned here mainly with studies that place more explicit emphasis on training general strategies for dealing with a wide variety of interpersonal situations.

We have excluded from the present review studies involving more specific response training, examples of which might include modeling studies to increase the social participation of withdrawn children (Evers and Schwartz, 1973; Keller and Carlson, 1974; O'Connor, 1969, 1972); studies involving direct coaching in skills for friendship making (Oden and Asher, 1977); assertiveness training studies with children (Bornstein, Bellack, and Hersen, 1977); and studies of the effects of various types of environmental reinforcement on children's peer interactions (Nelson, Worrell, and Polsgrove, 1973; Scott, Burton, and Yarrow, 1967; Slaby and Crowley, 1977; Solomon and Wahler, 1973). (The interested reader is referred to Combs and Slaby (1978) for a review of studies of this genre.)

In this survey of the research on social-cognitive interventions we have divided the studies into those that (1) involve training in interpersonal problem-solving in the school and institutional setting; (2) involve training in family problem-solving; (3) focus on verbally mediated self-control; and (4) emphasize social perspective–taking training. Our final observations and comments will concern the issues pertinent to the broader literature on social-cognitive therapy.

SOCIAL-COGNITIVE PROBLEM-SOLVING IN SCHOOLS

One of the most extensive research programs to date on the assessment and training of interpersonal cognitive problem-solving skills in children has been conducted by Spivack and Shure and their coworkers at the Hahnemann Community Mental Health Center in Philadelphia (Spivack and Shure, 1974; Spivack, Platt, and Shure, 1976; Shure and Spivack, 1978). The investigators have previously published a fairly extensive review of the various interpersonal cognitive problem-solving (ICPS) abilities that have been investigated (Spivack et al., 1976). Among a number of proposed ICPS abilities, the following have

been found to bear the most consistent relationships to measures of overt social adjustment in children (when they report controlling for the effect of IQ):

(1) *Alternative thinking*: the ability to generate multiple potential alternative solutions to a given interpersonal problem situation.
(2) *Consequential thinking*: the ability to foresee the immediate and more long-range consequences of a particular alternative and to use this information in the decision-making process.
(3) *Means-ends thinking*: the ability to elaborate or plan a series of specific actions in order to reach a given goal, and to recognize potential obstacles within a realistic time framework.

These component ICPS skills have been measured in various ways in different age samples of children and young adults. Two of the assessment devices have been standardized and manuals are available from the investigators. The Preschool Interpersonal Problem-Solving (PIPS) test is used as a measure of alternative thinking in early childhood. The PIPS test is a technique that requires the child to generate alternative solutions to two age-relevant interpersonal problems (a child wants a toy another child is playing with; a child breaks the mother's favorite flowerpot, and she might be angry). A child's score consists of the combined total of different, relevant alternatives. The second instrument, the Means Ends Problem Solving (MEPS) procedure, was used to study means-ends thinking in middle childhood, adolescent, and adult groups. The procedure consists of a series of problem situations in story format, in which only the problem situation and the final outcome of the problem are presented. The subject is then asked to fill in the middle of the story, indicating means by which the problem outcome might be reached. The protocols are scored for the total number of relevant means; the number of potential obstacles the subject perceives toward carrying out a particular means; and for use of a relevant time sequence in coordinating the specific actions involved in a given means.

The investigators report that alternative thinking appears quite consistently related to adjustment in the age span from the preschool years into adolescence. Means-ends thinking appears to play an important role in adjustment beginning in middle childhood around age nine and increasing into the adolescent and adult years. On the other hand, consequential thinking showed a less consistent relationship with adjustment, although it did appear to play some role in the preschool years—particularly in adulthood. The investigators have also looked at a number of other potential ICPS abilities, including sensitivity to interpersonal problems and accuracy of causal reasoning in an interpersonal situation. These variables did not relate with any consistency to adjustment in childhood, although the negative findings might in part be due to the nature of the specific measurement tasks used.

The problem-solving training programs developed by Spivack, Shure, and associates are presented in the form of specific training scripts, consisting of structured daily activities and discussion to teach component ICPS skills. The training script for preschoolers (Spivack and Shure, 1974) involves a sequence of 46 short (20–30 minute) daily lessons, activities, and games conducted by the preschool teacher. The program involves initial teaching of a number of skills felt to be prerequisite for instruction in problem-solving, namely, linguistic concepts such as "same-different" and "if-then," and the ability to identify basic emotions (happy, angry, sad). The main portion of the program is then devoted to a series of hypothetical interpersonal problem situations, and is divided sequentially into three parts: enumerating solutions only; enumerating consequences only; and pairing specific solutions with specific consequences. Extensive use is made of teacher demonstration and puppet play to illustrate the training concepts, and whenever possible the problem-solving methods are applied to actual problems that arise among the children in school.

Outcomes from the problem-solving training indicated that the treated children, relative to a no-treatment control group, improved on measures of alternative and consequential thinking, as well as on ratings of behavioral adjustment. Moreover, an improvement effect was maintained at follow-up one year later when children were rated by new teachers who were unaware of the experimental conditions. A very similar program has since been developed for use in the kindergarten classroom, with similarly strong positive results reported at the conclusion of the training period (Shure and Spivack, 1978).

Chittenden (1942) reported a classic study of the modification of dominance patterns in preschool children. Children were selected on the basis of high-dominance and low-cooperation scores derived from behavioral observations of the children in the preschool laboratory. Training consisted of a series of 11 sessions where the adult experimenter met individually with each child. In each session, the child and the experimenter worked out solutions to interpersonal problem situations presented in the context of doll play. For example, two dolls, playing the roles of preschool children, would be faced with the problem of finding a way to play successfully with only one toy. Emphasis was placed on learning alternative responses to aggressive and dominant behaviors. Aggressive and cooperative interaction were acted out in the doll play, and the child judged the consequences of the "play" as satisfactory or unsatisfactory based on the criterion of whether the dolls had a "good time" or a "bad time" playing together. The data were analyzed using two methods. First, an analysis was conducted of the covariance of scores of the trained and control children made on the initial test with those made on a post-test after the training period. The results showed that the trained children received significantly lower domination scores than the controls. A trend toward increases in cooperation scores for the trained children was apparent but did not reach statistical significance. The second method involved an analysis of variance of the domination and cooperation scores from observations of the trained children in the preschool play group. This analysis showed that the trained children were significantly less dominative and significantly more cooperative immediately after training. The decrease in domination scores was evident a month later, while the increase in cooperation was no longer significant. Since the control group (nontreatment) was not observed at the posttesting and follow-up periods, it was not possible to establish definitively that the changes in the experimental group were due to the training specifically.

Zahavi (1973) and Zahavi and Asher (1978) applied a somewhat similar technique with aggressive nursery school children. Zahavi and Asher reported that the preschool teacher employed rational methods, explaining to the children that hitting others causes hurt; other children do not like children who hit; and it is wise to think of alternatives to hitting. Modeling and doll-play components were specifically avoided, however, as the focus of the study was on the effect of the teacher's verbal instructions on the children's behavior. Post-treatment observations indicated reduced aggressiveness in these children as opposed to aggressive children who did not receive the instructions. Subsequent training of the control children led to reduced aggression in these children as well.

The problem-solving approach developed by Spivack and Shure and associates is similar in many respects to the model of interpersonal problem-solving proposed for behavior modification by D'Zurilla and Goldfried (1971). Drawing from the previous literature on nonsocial problem-solving, these investigators proposed the following sequence of interpersonal problem solving stages:

(1) *General orientation or "set"*: that is, recognition that a problem exists and inhibition of the initial tendency to respond impulsively or to do nothing at all.
(2) *Problem definition and formulation*: this stage involves classifying elements of the situation appropriately so as to separate relevant from irrelevant information, identifying one's primary goals, and specifying the major subproblems, issues, or conflicts.
(3) *Generation of alternative solutions*: the emphasis here is on the quantity (versus quality) of ideas that can be generated, and a noncritical or nonevaluative attitude is seen as important at this stage.
(4) *Decision making*: this stage involves the evaluation of possible short-term and long-term consequences of a given alternative. The value (positive, negative, neutral) of the consequences is assessed along with a subjective evaluation of the likelihood of success of a particular alternative (highly likely, likely, unlikely).
(5) *Verification*: the final stage involves monitoring the plan, that is, obtaining information about the actual consequences as a strategy is implemented in order to make self-correction possible.

Allen et al., (1976) have reported on the results of a training program using the D'Zurilla and Goldfried model in an intervention with third- and fourth-grade elementary school children. Sessions were conducted by the classroom teacher in the elementary school. A total of 24-30-minute sessions were conducted over a period of 18 weeks. The assessment of problem-solving included a Problem-Solving Measure (PSM), a Structured Real-Life Problem Situation (SRLPS), and a series of modular In-Class Measures (ICMs). The PSM was a modified version of the Means-Ends Problem-Solving procedure. On the PSM, children were presented with hypothetical problem situations, and their responses were scored for number of alternative solutions, the number of specific steps elaborated to implement the solutions, and potential obstacles generated that limit the effectiveness of a given solution. The SRLPS consisted of the following simulated real-life problem: on approaching the testing room, the child was told that it was occupied and that it could not be used, although the experimenter really wanted to play the story-telling games with the pupil. A child received a score for the number of solutions generated to the simulated problem. The ICMs, in turn, were designed to assess the specific problem-solving skill being taught in the training sequence. They were administered in the classroom in the form of short games or quizzes. The intervention made use of modeling, role-play, and behavior rehearsal techniques. Exercises were included for teaching in divergent thinking (brainstorming alternative uses for an object), problem identification (the teacher helped clarify the problem in a series of unfinished problem stories), alternative thinking, consequential thinking, and elaboration of solutions. Alternative solutions and consequences were discussed about common interpersonal problems that arise in school, and children were encouraged to give feedback to one another about the adequacy of various solutions.

Results of the program indicated that children improved on the combined measure of alternative thinking and means-ends thinking—the problem-solving measure (PSM). They also improved on a locus of control scale in the direction of increased feelings of internal control. However, no effect of training was evident on ratings of overt behavioral adjustment on the Walker Problem Behavior Checklist or on a sociometric measure of peer status. Whether the lack of enhancement of adjustment following training was due to the insensitivity of the measures, to the intractability of behavior problems among nine-year-olds, or to the weakness of the intervention is not known.

McClure (1975; McClure, Chinsky and Larcen, 1978) tested an elaborated version of the training program. Four experimental conditions were employed: videotape modeling only, videotape plus discussion, videotape plus role-played exercises, and a nontreatment control group. McClure found that the training conditions generally enhanced internal locus of control and problem-solving on the Problem Solving Measure (PSM) and in a structured group peer interaction measure (FCI). The FCI measure (Friendship Club Interaction) was an experimental analogue of problematic peer group situations. Subjects were asked to participate in a "Friendship Club" contest, in which an award was promised to the team that gave the best answers to a series of contest questions. The rules were: (1) all six team members must agree on the team's best answer; (2) all six members must help answer the question; and (3) all six members must be club officers. In addition to contest questions centering on interpersonal problem situations, the subjects were confronted with a number of actual problems embedded in the FCI-setting. These additional problems included: (1) five chairs for six subjects (chair problem); (2) five officer cards for six subjects (missing role problem); and (3) the process of distributing officer titles (role distribution

problem). The entire procedure was videotaped and scored for problem-solving responses.

Using the term "problem sensing," McClure was also interested in how obvious a problematic situation must be before a child would recognize its existence as a problem and begin to problem-solve. Problem sensing was assessed through a simulated Dyadic Interaction (DI) task, for example, a "mother" (an experimental confederate) explains that "her child" has never had a chance to make friends at school. The "mother" then makes various "prods" to induce problem-solving in the subject, if the child fails to problem-solve after the initial introduction to the problem. "Prods" included a restatement of the problem ("Mike is really concerned about making friends here at school"), followed by more directive statements, as required ("I wish I could help him make friends"; "How do you think Mike could make some friends?"). Problem sensitivity was indicated by the number and intensity of prods required. McClure found that the number of alternative solutions offered was the best predictor of problem sensitivity relative to other predictors such as IQ, verbosity, locus of control, or step-by-step elaboration. The number of alternative solutions was also the best predictor of a child's problem-solving persistence in the face of obstacles presented by the experimenter to the child's solutions. The ability to conceptualize alternatives was also related to judges' ratings of solution effectiveness, indicated by maximum positive consequences and minimum negative consequences.

Measures of general behavioral adjustment were not included in the McClure et al. study. He found, however, that video modeling, combined with role-play exercises, led to higher scores for the peer interaction measure (FCI) than did the conditions involving videotape only, videotape plus discussion, or the no-treatment control group. Overall treatment effects were evident for the PSM, the FCI, and locus of control, but not for the Dyadic Interaction (DI) task. McClure et al. (1978) interpreted the overall findings as indicating that problem-solving training, combining both observational learning and behavior rehearsal, is more likely to transfer to everyday social interactions.

A seven-week program for training social and nonsocial problem-solving skills with third, fourth, and fifth graders was reported by Stone, Hinds, and Schmidt (1975). The program involved some interesting procedures, such as videotaped presentation of problem situations, after which the children discussed problem-solving with a character named "Bonnie the Bunny." Picture games were used to teach the children to distinguish between facts, choices, and solutions. Treatment produced significant gains for the total experimental versus no-treatment control group on generation of facts (gathering of information relevant to the problem before attempting to generate solutions), choices, and number of alternative solutions. Behavioral adjustment was not assessed. Closer inspection of the data revealed that the differences were not significant for the third graders in the areas of choices and solutions, nor for the fifth graders in the area of facts. The program was possibly too sophisticated for the third graders to make fine discriminations among facts, choices, and solutions. The lack of significant results for the fifth graders in generating facts is more difficult to explain. The authors suggested that "one hypothesis may be that at this age children are more action or outcome-oriented and do not want to get bogged down with isolated facts (p. 38)."

Pitkanen (1974) reported decreases in aggressive behavior in a sample of eight-year old boys using a cognitive problem-solving approach. The experimental and control (no-treatment) groups were each comprised of 12 subjects. The experimental group met for eight sessions over a period of four weeks. Subjects initially discussed filmstrips of interpersonal conflicts, followed by role-playing of conflict situations. Emphasis was directed toward the generation of alternatives to aggressive behavior and toward the consideration of consequences of various alternatives, including consideration of the feelings of the various persons in the interaction. Aggression was measured by composite scores on a series of laboratory-type games and activities. Although both experimental and control groups improved on their aggression scores, the experimental group improved significantly more than the control group. There was also some indication of improvement on tasks measuring strategies of problem solution.

Feldhusen, Houtz, and Ringenbach (1972) and Feldhusen and Houtz (1975) have been active in the assessment and training of problem-solving skills. Feldhusen et al. (1972) have reported on the construction of the Purdue Elementary Problem-Solving Inventory (PEPSI), an instrument designed to assess the general problem-solving ability of disadvantaged elementary-school children from various ethnic backgrounds and grade levels (one through six). The test consists of 49 problems that are presented as slides (cartoon form) portraying children in a variety of real-life situations. The inventory was designed to measure the following abilities: sensing that a problem exists; defining the problem; asking questions; guessing causes; clarifying the goal of the problem situation; judging if more information is needed; analyzing details; redefining familiarl objects for unusual uses; seeing implications; solving single and multiple-solution problems; and verifying solutions. Further information on the components measured by the PEPSI is available in Speedie, Houtz, Ringenbach, and Feldhusen (1973) and Feldhusen and Houtz (1975).

Houtz and Feldhusen (1976) reported on a problem-solving training study in which children from 12 classrooms participated in either a training-plus-reward, training-only, or a no-treatment control condition. Those students receiving training were exposed to 15-30 minute daily sessions of problem-solving worksheets for nine weeks. These in-class worksheets covered a wide variety of component problem-solving skills, including sensing whether a problem exists; defining the problem; asking questions; and identifying causes; suggesting possible solutions; noticing critical details; and verifying solutions. Those children in the training-plus-reward condition were also provided with 30-45 minutes of free time twice per week as a reward for working on the problem-solving materials. The authors reported that PEPSI posttraining scores, with Verbal IQ and PEPSI pretraining scores used as covariates, differed significantly. The training-only group outperformed both other groups. Further analysis of the effects of training employed scores on a transfer test of problem-solving ability that consisted of two, open-ended verbal questions. Analysis of transfer-test scores, with Verbal IQ as a covariate, indicated that the three experimental groups differed significantly from one another. Again, the training-only group outperformed the other groups.

The results of the Houtz and Feldhusen (1976) training program indicate that the training exercises were effective in increasing children's abilities to generate a number of different alternatives to a variety of types of problem situations. The lack of an additional effect due to training-plus-reward was attributed to the weakness of the contingency between effort on the problem-solving worksheets and the free time reward. The use of additional measures, such as behavioral observations, teacher ratings of adjustment, or peer sociograms seems indicated in future studies of this type.

Schneider and Robin (Note 1; Schneider, 1975) have developed a procedure to foster self-control in impulsive children in a special education classroom. Using a story format (the story of a turtle that learns to go into his shell and relax when he is angry), they have children use imagery, relaxation, problem-solving, and peer support to control disruptive behavior. The teaching of the technique took 15 minutes every day for about three weeks, after which training sessions were gradually thinned out to twice a week. The procedure was effective in reducing aggression in seven out of eight children during one school year.

SOCIAL-COGNITIVE PROBLEM-SOLVING IN INSTITUTIONS AND CLINICS

The work of Sarason and his associates (Sarason, 1968; Sarason and Ganzer, 1969, 1973) has involved the direct training of social skills with institutionalized delinquents. While the emphasis has not been on the training of cognitive problem-solv-

ing skills per se, a substantial problem-solving component was probably involved. The focus of the research has been to examine the potential differential effects of modeling and group discussion as treatment methods with this population. The training content centered around common social, educational, and vocational situations—for example, learning what to do in a job interview. That an emphasis was placed on alternative and consequential thinking is suggested by the fact that boys "were given examples of desirable and undesirable ways of coping with social, vocational, and educational situations (1973, p. 443)." Results showed that, compared to an untreated control group, both modeling and discussion approaches had greater positive effects on self-descriptions, locus of control, and on counselors' behavioral ratings of prosocial and negative behavior. Decreased recidivism was reported for the two treatment conditions over controls a full two to three years following intervention. Treatment effects did not differ to a significant extent between the two experimental groups.

Ollendick (Note 2) employed a somewhat similar approach with 18 incarcerated juvenile delinquents. Subjects were matched on age, IQ, and locus of control scores and assigned randomly to a Social Skills or a Discussion group. Sessions were held once a week for 10 weeks and lasted approximately 75 minutes. Subjects in the Social Skills training were instructed to bring to the group problems they were having with each other and with the staff. They subsequently received instructions concerning alternate ways of responding; rehearsed the situation with other group members; observed the therapist and other groups members modeling appropriate behavior; and received feedback from both the group and the therapist on their performance. Social reinforcement was given contingent on the appropriateness of their behavior, and the subjects were provided with homework tasks of graduated difficulty to practice the newly learned behaviors during the week. Members of the Discussion group were instructed to bring to the group problems they were having with each other and the staff and ways to circumvent these problems were discussed, both the behavioral procedures used in the Social Skills group were not used. Results at post-testing showed significant increases for the Social Skills group over the Discussion-only group on a number of measures: increased eye contact, increased requests for new behavior, increased spontaneous positive responses, and decreased aggressive comments in a series of role-played social situations that were videotaped. Improvement was also noted on self-report scales of state anxiety and locus of control. While the Social Skills group also increased their earning of points for appropriate behavior in the institutional token economy system, they showed only a nonsignificant trend toward a decrease relative to the Discussion group in the number of acting-out behaviors (Insubordination and fighting) observed in the two weeks that followed treatment.

Giebink, Stover, and Fahl (1968) reported on a program for modifying responses to frustration for six boys in a residential treatment setting. Specifically, the investigators sought to increase the number of alternative solutions given to four frustrating situations commonly found in such settings. Training consisted of the repeated playing of a special board game in which winning was contingent on using all the possible solutions when landing on "frustration squares." Repeated exposure to the alternative solutions resulted in increased use of the solutions in the residential settings. Frequency data on the occurrence of trained responses after treatment were encouraging, although the sample size was small and no control group was available.

Some encouraging results regarding treatment effectiveness appear in the studies reviewed thus far. However, the reader must appreciate the substantial differences across studies with respect to the evaluation procedures employed. While some significant progress has been made in the development of new measures of interpersonal problem-solving, the relations of these various instruments to observed types of adaptive and maladaptive behavior need to be more firmly established (Butler and Meichenbaum, 1981; Kendall and Fischler,

Note 3). Long-term outcome data are scarce, further limiting our current knowledge of the intensity and durability of impact such interventions may have on developmental processes in children. There also are a limited number of investigators employing attention control groups or control conditions other than no-treatment groups. Future research will need to be concerned more specifically with demonstrating effects of intervention above and beyond the effects of subjects' motivation, exposure to the assessments, and therapist attention without the specific training. The reader is referred to O'Leary and Borkovec (1978) for a discussion of issues in the selection of control groups.

FAMILY APPLICATIONS

Several reports currently exist in which training in problem-solving processes has been extended to intervention in the areas of childrearing and family problems. Since human beings learn a great deal about interpersonal behavior from growing up in their particular family context, family systems provide a logical focus for therapeutic interventions. The increasing interest in approaches to family therapy reflects a growing awareness of early interpersonal influences on individual adaptation. As the family unit is the context in which numerous significant and possibly prototypic interpersonal problems arise, it is reasonable to propose that facilitating family problem-solving strategies would have an impact on individual adjustment.

Alexander and Parsons (1973) and Parsons and Alexander (1973) have reported on the effectiveness of a short-term intervention applying a social problem-solving model to family therapy for adolescent status offenders. Although the teaching of problem-solving per se was not the stated goal of the program, the treatment procedures bore considerable resemblance to problem-solving training procedures in other studies. For example, the authors reported that therapists "actively modeled, prompted, and reinforced in all family members: clear communication of substance as well as feelings, and clear presentation of demands and alternative solutions—all leading to negotiation, with each family member receiving some privilege for each responsibility assumed to the point of compromise (Alexander and Parsons, 1973, p. 221)." Families were seen in two therapy sessions a week for a period of four weeks.

The program produced significant improvement over control groups in a number of family interaction measures derived from videotape observations of the families during a problem-solving task. Specifically, the four interaction measures were aimed at measuring activity level (silence, frequency, and duration of simultaneous speech), as well as verbal reciprocity (equality of verbalization). In the first study (Alexander and Parsons, 1973), the treatment program demonstrated superiority of effects over a short-term, client-centered therapy approach, a psychodynamic family program, and a no-treatment control group. In the second study (Parsons and Alexander, 1973), the treatment was superior to a no-treatment control group and to a placebo control group that consisted of group discussions, focused mainly on the expression of feelings and that was led by a professional psychologist. In a later follow-up report of the two treatment studies (Klein, Alexander, and Parsons, 1977), the problem-solving focus of treatment was more directly stated: "The ultimate goal of the therapeutic process then becomes one of training the family in effective problem-solving techniques in order for the family unit to more adaptively meet the developmental changes occurring as children reach adolescence (p. 471) . . ." The follow-up, two and a half to three and a half years after treatment, indicated that the problem-solving intervention resulted in sibling involvement with the courts of one-third to one-half below that of the comparison groups, as well as resulting in a continued significantly lower rate of recidivism for the original problem adolescents.

Quite impressively, both the Alexander and Parsons (1973) and Parsons and Alexander (1973) projects have evidenced improvements among a group of children that are considered to be unyielding to most treatments. However, not all of the cognitive-behaviorally oriented efforts with delinquents have been as successful (see Little and Kendall, 1979). One aspect of these two successful projects, the emphasis placed upon treatment within the family context, may be an important component that facilitates both the learning of the social/interpersonal cognitive problem-solving skills and their application in the real world.

Robin et al., (1977) have researched the assessment and training of problem-solving skills in mother-child dyads. They reduced the D'Zurilla and Goldfried (1971) model of problem-solving to four steps for treatment application:

(1) *Defining the problem* included pinpointing specific parent and adolescent behaviors which made a particular subject a source of disagreement.
(2) *Listing the solutions* included generating as many alternatives for resolving the disagreement as possible.
(3) *Evaluation of options* included a detailed review of the positive and negative consequences of the previously listed ideas, culminating in a negotiated agreement.
(4) *Planning the implementation of a solution* consisted of deciding upon the logistic details for executing the selected option.

The therapist taught the dyad to self-monitor negative communication patterns (teasing, put downs, interrupting, sarcasm, lack of eye contact) and to replace these patterns with effective communication skills, such as reflective listening, visual and nonverbal attention, appropriate voice tone, and verification of meaning. Treatment took place during five one-hour sessions. Modeling, guided practice, role-playing, feedback, and social reinforcement were used to teach the problem-solving and communication skills. The treatment produced highly significant increases in problem-solving behavior during audiotaped discussions of hypothetical and real problems over a no-treatment control group. A methodological strength of the study was the investigators' effort to measure individually the component problem-solving and communication skills. Reliable measures were obtained of problem definition, option listing, evaluation (of consequences), agreement (interchanges in which the dyad explicitly adopted a particular solution), and negative behavior (curses, commands, threats). Improvement was noted in all measures at posttesting, with the exception of negative behavior, which was unexpectedly low at the preassessment.

A further outcome measure involved a checklist completed by parents and adolescents involving five-point ratings of the quality and frequency of problem-solving behaviors, communication skills, and specific conflicts at home. The generally nonsignificant results on the checklist suggest either a lack of clear-cut generalization of treatment effects to the home environment or the insensitivity of the measures used to assess generalization. In either case, the authors provided several useful suggestions for enhancing generalization in further applications of similar treatment programs: (1) assignment of homework practice trials in problem-solving, to be audiotaped for review in the next treatment sessions; (2) assisting the family in planning regular family conferences to integrate problem-solving into their daily routines; and (3) inclusion of fathers and other relevant family members in treatment.

The issue of generalization was examined in greater detail by Foster (1979) in a recent study in which 28 families complaining of excessive arguing and family conflicts were randomly assigned to one of three groups: skills training, skills training plus generalization, and a waiting-list control group. The treatment was conducted with either one or both parents and a 10-14 year-old son or daughter. Families were seen individually for a total of seven sessions. The skills training program was modeled after Robin et al. (1977) and focused on family problem-solving and communication skills. The second training group received skills training with additional efforts to facilitate generalization: (1) assignment and discussion of homework tasks of graduated difficulty each week, and (2) discussion of the use of the specific ways the problem-solving and communication skills could be used at home. Content analysis of the therapy sessions revealed that

discussions of home behavior and communication occurred more often in the generalization treatment than in the skills-training-only group. However, results based on interactional data, derived from 10-minute audiotapes of the family discussing a distressing problem, yielded generally negative results: no treatment effect was observed on a problem-solving code designed to measure the components of the problem-solving model. This finding may have been due to the fact that a number of families displayed some surprisingly good problem-solving skills on this measure even prior to intervention. All groups, including the control group, improved on several questionnaire measures: Conflict Behavior Questionnaire, a Decision-making Questionnaire, and an Issues Checklist.

Several specific effects due to treatment emerged, however. Adolescents and parents concurred that improvement toward specific goals was greater in the two treatment groups. Maternal reports of conflict behavior and intensity of discussions of a variety of issues decreased significantly for the two treatment groups. These changes were maintained at a six to eight-week follow-up period, with only self-reports of communication goals showing consistent "backsliding" effects from posttreatment to follow-up. Little evidence for increased effectiveness of generalization training methods over the skills-training method alone was provided. There were no differences between the two treatment groups in problem improvement; in self-reported improvement in communication skills in the session or at home; in the audiotaped generalization problem; or in instructor evaluations.

The Family Contract Game has been developed by Blechman and associates (Blechman, Olson, Schornagel, Halsdorf, and Turner, 1976a; Blechman, Olson, and Hellman, 1976b), using a board game format to instruct family members in component problem-solving skills. These skills include pinpointing of family problems in specific behavioral terms; collecting information relevant to a problem; generating action alternatives; selecting a course of action; and evaluating the consequences of the action. The procedure has been evaluated using six individual conflicted parent-child dyads (Blechman et al., 1976b) with eight- to fifteen-year-old children. There were five 40-minute treatment sessions. Within the Family Contract Game sessions, each game play produced a behavioral contingency contract that resolved a previously designated problem. The results of behavioral observations indicated that on-task problem-solving behaviors increased and off-task antagonistic behavior decreased during game play. However, there was no posttreatment generalization of the increased problem-solving skills to a nonstructured discussion of family problems without using the game format.

Shure and Spivack (1978) have reported on a series of investigations of problem-solving skills in mother-child dyads. Training studies were conducted to instruct mothers in the use of problem-solving methods with their preschool children. The training consisted of 43 suggested daily lessons in which mothers were guided in teaching ICPS skills to their children at home. The training led to substantial increases in alternative and consequential thinking by the experimental children over a no-treatment control group. Increases in ICPS skills in the children were also associated with significant improvement on behavior ratings completed by preschool teachers, who were blind to the treatment conditions. No difference between trained and untrained groups was apparent on the measure of sensitivity to interpersonal problems, perhaps because the task was developmentally too sophisticated to be enhanced by training at the preschool level. Trained mothers improved in their means-ends thinking about hypothetical mother-child and child-child problems, but not in their means-ends thinking about adult problems. The trained mothers also exhibited significant changes in their self-reported childrearing approach toward a more problem-solving style. The effects of training on the children's behavior was substantial and is comparable to the magnitude of effects obtained for teacher-trained children in a previous study (Spivack and Shure, 1974).

The results of research on the effectiveness of social-cognitive problem-solving training within the context of the family unit have, in general, been fairly encouraging. There are, however, numerous additional questions that require further investigative efforts. Do trained family units subsequently produce increased adjustment in siblings? What are the factors that contribute most strongly to the durability and generalization of training effects? The studies reviewed do suggest the utility of problem-solving interventions within the family, and point to the importance of incorporating significant other persons into the process of teaching those cognitive-behavioral skills that lead to improved adjustment.

VERBALLY MEDIATED SELF-CONTROL AND INTERPERSONAL PROBLEM-SOLVING TRAINING

In this section we will discuss self-instructional methods and examine training studies that investigate the role of linguistic processes in the development of children's self-control over their own behavior. In emphasizing the role of language and self-verbalizations in regulating behavior, such a review necessarily excludes discussion of the potential influence of other nonlinguistic cognitive processes. However, we note in passing an observation made by Meichenbaum (1976):

Some argue that language is essentially a weak instrument in the modification of behavior while others treat language and thought as equivalent. It is necessary to remind ourselves of Furth's (1976) observation, following Piaget, that thinking can occur without language but that language can greatly enhance thinking and in turn affect behavior. That is the promise of the self-instructional CBM (Cognitive Behavior Modification) treatment approach. (p. 17)

The investigation of the normal development of self-control processes in children owes considerably to the studies of verbal mediation by Soviet investigators (Luria; Vygotsky). Luria (1961) has extensively studied the processes by which language acquires a function of self-regulation over motor behavior in young children. He postulated the following sequence of events in the acquisition of verbally mediated control of behavior:

(1) A young child's behavior is initially directed by the spoken speech of other persons in the environment, particularly parents.
(2) The child gradually begins to regulate his/her own behavior through the use of his/her own *overt* speech and spoken self-verbalizations.
(3) Gradually a child's self talk "goes underground" and self-regulation is maintained through internalized speech or *covert* self-instruction.

Vygotsky (1962) has expanded upon the important role that internalized language seems to play in the development of abstract and symbolic thinking processes. He emphasized the continuing importance of internalized linguistic processes in the self-regulation of behavior through childhood and into the adult years. Kohlberg, Yaeger, and Hjertholm (1968) summarized a considerable body of supporting evidence concerning the importance of private speech in the self-regulation and directing of ongoing overt motor behavior. The period of middle childhood in the approximate age range from seven to ten years appears to be a time of particularly rapid development of verbal mediational capacity across a wide range of content areas (Jensen, 1971). In the Piagetian viewpoint (Flavell, 1963), this is a time of development and consolidation of concrete cognitive operations in preparation for later formal operative thinking.

Meichenbaum and Goodman (1971) developed an intervention strategy to teach verbally mediated self-control to young impulsive children. Based on the research of a number of previous investigators, they deduced that a breakdown of normal self-regulation could occur in several different ways. First, a child could show a *comprehension* deficiency, that is, he (or she) may not comprehend the nature of the problem or task and thus be unable to discover what mediating responses to produce. Second, the child may have the correct mediators in his (or her) repertoire but fail to spontaneously and appropriately use them—i.e., the child may show a *production* deficiency.

Third, the mediators that the child produces may not be successful in actually guiding his (or her) ongoing behavior—what Reese (1962) has called a *mediational* deficiency. The remedial approach involved training children in the explicit use of appropriate strategies for self-verbalization, using the following sequence:

(1) An adult model performed a task while talking to himself out loud (cognitive modeling).
(2) The child performed the same task under the direction of the model's instructions (overt, external guidance).
(3) The child performed the task while instructing himself aloud (overt self-guidance).
(4) The child whispered the instructions to himself as he went through the task (faded, overt self-guidance).
(5) The child performed the task while guiding his performance via private speech (covert self-instruction) (from Meichenbaum, 1977, p. 33).

The subjects were 15 hyperactive and disruptive boys (ages seven to nine) in a remedial classroom in a public elementary school. Results demonstrated the effectiveness of the method in producing a more cognitively reflective approach in the trained subjects over control children, leading to improved scores on a series of nonsocial problems tasks (Porteus Mazes, WISC-Performance IQ, Matching Familiar Figures Test). Both attention and assessment control groups were used. A follow-up assessment one month later indicated that the improvement in the trained versus untrained groups had been maintained. However, no generalization of training effects was apparent on classroom observations of inappropriate (off-task) behavior or on teacher ratings of self-control, activity level, and cooperativeness.

Subsequent studies using similar verbal selfinstructional (VSI) procedures to train children in problem-solving on nonsocial academic-type problem tasks have generally demonstrated positive results on outcome measures similar to the training tasks (Douglas, Parry, Marton, and Garson, 1976; Kendall and Finch, 1978). The evidence for generalization to other classroom behaviors and situations outside the training situation is inconsistent, however, and the reader is referred to Kendall (Note 4) and Meichenbaum and Asarnow (1979) for a discussion and analysis of the enigma of generalization.

The application of self-instructional training methods to the modification of social behavior has also begun to be explored. Goodwin and Mahoney (1975) used modeling of covert self-instructions to foster impulse control for three aggressive boys in the face of verbal taunts by other children. Children observed a videotaped model engaging in ongoing coping self-statements during a verbal taunting game, a procedure in which one person was asked to go to the center of a circle and was exposed to verbal taunts by other members of the group. Following the modeling procedures, children were exposed to the game situation and coached in the use of appropriate self-instructions. A substantial decrease in observed disruptive classroom behaviors was apparent one week following training. There was no control group.

In a single-subject investigation, Kendall and Finch (1976) treated an overactive / impulsive nine-year-old boy with verbal self-instructions provided via modeling and a response-cost contingency during training. Three target behaviors were identified: inappropriate "switches" in topics of conversation, switches in games played, and switches in rules for play. Each of these socially disruptive switches was reduced when the cognitive-behavioral intervention was applied. Use of a multiple baseline design permitted reasonable assurance that the treatment was responsible for the observed improvements. The successful modification of overactivity, also demonstrated by a multiple baseline design, was reported by Bornstein and Quevillon (1976).

Self-instructional methods were used by Gottman, Gonso, and Schuler (1976) as part of a training program to teach social skills to two isolated third-grade girls. The children initially viewed a 10-minute videotape depicting a coping self-statement squence by a same age model. The sequence consisted of the soliloquy of an inner debate which proceeded as follows: (1) statement of wanting to initiate interaction; (2) worrying about negative consequences;

(3) self-debate; (4) the decision to go ahead; (5) the approach; (6) the greeting; and (7) asking to join in (or requesting help). The film was followed by role-played rehearsal of friendship-making skills with an adult coach. Relative to two control subjects who received an equal amount of adult attention but no training, the experimental girls showed improved peer sociometric status nine weeks after training. Observational measures revealed a change in the distribution of attention to popular versus unpopular peers for the experimental girls, although no differences between experimental and control subjects was observed in the absolute frequency of peer interactions.

Camp, Blom, Herbert, and Van-Doorninck (1977) have developed a program entitled "Think Aloud" for young aggressive boys of elementary school age (Bash and Camp, Note 5). The Think Aloud program was presented in daily, 30-minute sessions over a period of six weeks. The subjects were 12 second-grade boys selected on the basis of their aggression scores on the Miller School Behavior Checklist. Treatment involved self-instructional practice on a variety of both social and nonsocial problem tasks. The social problem-solving component employed a number of the games and activities used by Spivack and Shure (1974) to teach alternative and consequential thinking. Emphasis was placed throughout the intervention period on modeling of cognitive strategies and developing answers to four basic questions: "What is my problem?"; "What is my plan?"; "Am I using my plan?"; and "How did I do?" To initially engage the children in the process of rehearsing the self-instructions, a "copycat" game was used in which the children repeated self-statements modeled by the experimenter. The copycat procedure was gradually faded, and the child was encouraged to verbalize strategy and eventually to fade the problem analysis and strategy planning to a covert level. Training also employed a series of games providing practice in identifying emotions, considering what might happen next in various situations, and generating multiple alternatives in a given situation. The general problem-solving approach was also incorporated into conversations in problem situations, as such situations arose naturally in the course of training. Although role-plays were not used, the trainer suggested that "thinking out loud" could help in the classroom and asked the child to think of ways he could use thinking out loud in doing his schoolwork and in getting along with others.

Two control groups were employed in this study: an aggressive control group and a normal control group, both of which received no treatment. Results showed that both trained and untrained aggressive groups improved in aggressive behavior as rated on the Miller School Behavior Checklist. While no differences in aggression ratings appeared between the experimental subjects and aggressive controls, teachers rated the experimental group as showing improvement on a significantly larger number of prosocial behaviors. On the cognitive test battery, experimental subjects showed improvement over aggressive controls on certain measures (WISC-R mazes, MFF reaction time) but not on others (WRAT-reading). At the posttest, the pattern of test scores for the experimental group had moved in the direction of greater similarity to the pattern of scores of the normal control group. One factor that may have limited the potential effectiveness of the program was the high level of verbal output and silliness shown by the aggressive boys. Chatter, silliness, and inappropriate verbal activity were handled mainly by ignoring them, rather than attacking them directly through some form of negative consequences. In this context, we are reminded of Kendall's (1977) argument for the inclusion of systematically applied behavioral contingencies to enhance the effectiveness of cognitive training programs with impulsive children. A second potential concern of the Camp et al. (1977) study involved the absence of a placebo or attentional control group. The reliance on no-treatment control groups does not permit us to rule out the possibility that any observed changes in the trained group may be attributable to increased individual adult attention rather than to the specific training procedures per se. Nevertheless, the Camp

et al. (1976) study is a relatively encouraging illustration of the clinical application of a cognitive problem-solving treatment with children.

Drummond (1974) assessed the relative effectiveness of self-instructional training versus a discussion control group and an assessment control group using a sample of school behavior problem children. The children received two training sessions a week for three weeks, followed by an immediate posttest assessment and a follow-up 13 weeks later. The self-instructional training took place in groups of five children, and centered around simulated classroom situations, such as talking out, hitting other students, leaving the desk, and inattentive behaviors. The children would offer examples of such situations and then rehearse self-controlling responses. The words "Wait! What? How? Reward!" were printed on the chalkboard as mnemonic devices, and were also printed on notecards the children took to class and used to record when they had successfully applied their own kind of "self-talk." The discussion control group spent its time discussing general topics, such as getting along, problems in school, and so forth. The results indicated that on teacher ratings of classroom behavior, the self-instructional group performed significantly better, especially immediately after training. No differences were found on classroom observation measures, although these measures did not focus specifically on behaviors that were taught in the training sessions. No group differences were evident on the MFF or on Coopersmith's self-esteem inventory. The training in this study was not aimed specifically at training children in cognitive problem-solving processes per se. However, in so far as the training was directed at teaching children to be more reflective in a given situation and to consider alternative courses of action, a problem-solving component was probably involved.

The combined cognitive-behavioral procedures of verbal self-instructions, therapist modeling, and contingency management (Kendall and Finch, 1979) have also been applied to social / interpersonal problem-solving. Kendall and Wilcox

(1980) compared two self-instructional training strategies with an attention control group. One of the self-instructions groups received *concrete* training, i.e., self-instructions were worded so as to be specific and to apply only to the task at hand. The other self-instructions group received *conceptual* training. Conceptual self-instructions, by contrast, were worded globally and abstractly such that they represented general thinking strategies and could potentially apply to a wider range of situations. The control group received an equal amount of therapist time and exposure to the training materials, but without the therapist-modeled self-instructions and without the behavioral contingencies. As part of this treatment procedure, children were first trained in the use of self-instructions on psycho-educational tasks; later sessions were devoted to the use of self-instructional problem solving in social / interpersonal contexts. Thirty-three teacher-referred children who scored at the nonself-controlled end of a Self-Control Rating Scale (Kendall and Wilcox, SCRS, 1979) were involved. Each of the six treatment sessions lasted 40 minutes. Results indicated that although the child's self-report did not show change, and several performance measures evidenced improvements for subjects in all three groups, blind teacher ratings of both self-control (SCRS) and hyperactivity (Connors, 1969) showed therapeutic generalization at posttreatment and at one-month follow-up. These treatment effects were stronger for the conceptual labeling group than for the concrete labeling group. No specific assessment of social skills was made in this study, however, and this limits the conclusions we may draw, regarding the potential effectiveness of self-instructional methods in modifying social behavior per se.

While early investigations of self-control training tended to focus on nonsocial problem tasks, recent research efforts have been adapted to the social/interpersonal domain. Conclusions regarding the utility of self-instructional methods in the treatment of social and interpersonal problems would be premature at this time, given the limited nature of the evidence. Although clinical interest in this area is growing, there is still a paucity of research that has systematically evaluated treatment effectiveness with multiple dependent measures. Long-term follow-up data are also scarce at the present. Several studies currently in progress should add significantly to our understanding of the efficacy of these therapeutic procedures in promoting effective social behavior in children.

PERSPECTIVE-TAKING THEORY AND TRAINING

Studies that emerged from research into the development of a child's cognitive ability to take the perspective or role of another person in a social interaction (see Shantz, 1975) are our concern here. Our coverage will include a brief review of perspective-taking theory and a more detailed analysis of perspective-taking training studies. The relationship of perspective-taking to other social-cognitive problem-solving skills will also be considered briefly.

Research into the development of children's understanding of their social environment and their concepts of interpersonal relationships has grown extensively in the last 10 to 15 years. Piagetian theory provided the basis for a series of pioneering studies (Feffer and Gourevich, 1960; Flapan, 1968; Flavell, Botkin, Fry, Wright, and Jarvis, 1968) investigating the role of "egocentrism" in a child's verbal communication with others and in his/her comprehension of social interactions. The basic idea is that children, as they develop, emerge from a relative state of "egocentrism" in which they were unable to differentiate their own internal emotional states, thoughts, and perceptions from those of other persons. Although the unitary nature of the "social egocentrism" construct has been challenged (Hudson, 1978; Kurdek, 1977; Kurdek and Rodgon, 1975; Shantz, 1975), there exists a fair amount of concurrence among investigators regarding the sequence of emergence of certain cognitive reasoning structures related to perspective-taking in children. These basic levels of perspective-taking logic are summarized as follows (Selman and Byrne, 1974; Selman, 1976; Shantz, 1975):

Level 0. The child does not consider another's point of view. For example, if the child likes candy, then he/she thinks that everyone must like candy.

Level 1 (ages 4 to 9) The child can consider another person's thoughts and realizes that the other may think differently about a given situation. The child at this level has only a rudimentary awareness of the possible existence of different perspectives and has difficulty in accurately taking the role of the other.

Level 2 (ages 6 to 12) The child can *sequentially* consider his own perspective and the perspective of another, and therefore can consider himself in part as an object of the other's perception. Because the child knows his thoughts are being considered by others, his own behavior and view of himself are partially based on that awareness. However, the child has great difficulty in considering different perspectives *simultaneously* in time and in coordinating them as a more objective observer of the interaction.

Level 3 (ages 9 to 15) This level is characterized by the ability to simultaneously coordinate various social perspectives in a social interaction. As this ability develops, the child begins to form a concept of the "generalized other" from which a broader societal perspective and a consistent view of the self presumably emerge (Mead, 1934). Selman (1976) has termed this the development of the "third person perspective" in a social interaction.

Selman (Selman and Byrne, 1974; Selman, 1976) has conceived of these perspective-taking levels as underlying cognitive *structures* that undergo an invariant sequence of development through the various stages just described. The concept of perspective-taking abilities as underlying *structures*, however, needs to be differentiated from the concept of perspective-taking *activity*, which refers to the actual application of the underlying cognitive structure to a particular social content area or to a particular social situation. Selman describes perspective-taking activity as "role-taking *in action.*"

The literature contains a number of studies that attempt to foster children's cognitive role-taking (knowledge of anothers' thoughts or intentions) and affective role-taking (knowledge of anothers' feelings) through training programs of various kinds. An often-cited series of training studies is that of Chandler and his associates (Chandler, 1973; Chandler, Greenspan, and Bar-

enboim, 1974). In the Chandler (1973) study, training of role-taking skills was conducted with a group of 15 chronically delinquent boys ages 11 to 13. The children met on a daily basis for three hours during a 10-week summer period, and received payment for their participation. Training involved the boys in writing and videotaping role-plays of skits of events involving persons of their own age. Each skit was replayed until each participant had occupied each different role of the characters in the skit, and videotapes were reviewed at the end of each set in an effort to determine ways of improving them. Relative to no-treatment controls and to a placebo control group who watched animated and documentary films, results revealed that the experimental children improved significantly on a measure of social cognitive role-taking skill (Chandler bystander cartoons). The experimental group also showed significantly lower recidivism rates at an 18-month follow-up period. In a second study (Chandler et al., 1974) with institutionalized emotionally disturbed children, cognitive-role-taking skill increased following both social role-taking training and referential communication training. Referential communication refers to a child's accuracy of verbal communication by taking into account the needs of the listener. Mean comparisons on a measure of behavioral improvement 12 months after training showed only a trend toward greater improvement in the two treatment groups as compared to no-treatment controls. There were, however, significant correlations between the degree of behavioral improvement and the degree of improvement on the social-cognitive tasks.

Little (1979) randomly assigned 18 institutionalized females aged 13 through 16 (matched on the basis of role-taking deficits using Chandler's [1973] measure) to treatment and attention control groups that met twice a week for three weeks. The treatment groups improvised skits about the types of people they might encounter in everyday living, both adults and peers. Each skit had a part for every girl in a group of five or six girls. After the skits were performed and videotaped, the group watched the tape, and each girl reported what it was like to play the role she had enacted. The procedure was repeated until every girl had played every part, and new skits were developed as needed. The attention control group spent an equal amount of time in creating a videotaped documentary about their institution, but control subjects were not allowed to appear on camera in an active role. The results indicated a significant reduction in role-taking errors for both groups. Although the treatment group showed the greater change, differences were not significant. Other dependent variables did not show meaningful change. Perhaps, since both treatment and control groups improved significantly in role-taking ability, factors in the cooperative effort of making a film may have facilitated the acquisition of some role-taking skills.

A year-long social development curriculum with fourth- and fifth-grade elementary school subjects has been prepared by Elardo and Caldwell (Note 6). The program, termed Project AWARE (Elardo and Cooper, 1977), included training components aimed at facilitating both perspective-taking and interpersonal problem-solving abilities. The perspective-taking component included activities designed to enhance children's ability to identify emotions and their awareness of the thoughts and feelings of themselves and others. Emphasis was placed on developing awareness and acceptance of individual differences among people. The problem-solving component involved formulating alternatives to social problem-situations through role play. The options available, the consequences of each option, and the thoughts and feelings of all people involved were discussed. Two 25-minute sessions were held on a weekly basis, led by trained classroom teachers, for approximately ten months. For the first month the senior investigator conducted the discussions, with the teacher as participant, and then conducted a session once a week for two additional months. Thereafter, the sessions were conducted entirely by the homeroom teacher. The outcome data to date indicate that the program was successful in producing significantly higher scores for the experimental children, versus no-treatment controls, on measures of cognitive role-taking, alternative thinking, and classroom adjustment, as measured by the Devereux Elementary School Behavior Rating Scale. The AWARE children were rated by their teachers as evidencing more respect and concern for the teacher and for others; as having better strategies in dealing with problems; as less likely to blame the teacher or classroom materials for problems; and as more creative in verbal expressions and more willing to share experiences with the group. No direct assessment of the relation between the amount of change on behavior ratings and the amount of change in role-taking or alternative thinking skill was made. However, the children with the lowest initial scores in classroom adjustment showed the greatest improvement from treatment. Posttesting was conducted after five and a half months of the experimental program. Evaluation of the program with other groups of children of different ages is currently in progress.

Iannotti (1978) found a role-taking training procedure to be effective in increasing children's scores on standardized tasks of helping and cooperation, but no effect was evident on a measure of aggression requiring children to describe how they would act in hypothetical social situations (such as being pushed out of line). The subjects were 30 normal six-year-old boys and 30 normal nine-year-old boys. The groups met for 25 minutes daily for 10 days. The experimental conditions included: (1) *role-taking*—a social situation was role played, after which the experimenter asked questions about the motives, thoughts, and feelings of the characters; (2) *role-switching*—a social skit was replayed until each child had assumed the role of each character in the role play, and discussion emphasized the experience of changing perspectives (that is, "What would you do (or feel) if you were X ? Why do you think X did that to you?"); (3) *control group*—the control groups met with the experimenter on the same schedule as the other groups and discussed stories without an emphasis on role-taking. Both experimental groups showed increases in cooperation and altruism measures relative to the attention controls. No effect was evident for a measure of empathy in which photographs were presented in which the character's emotions were either appropriate or inappropriate to the depicted context and affective matching by the child to the character's emotional state was measured. Improvement on a cognitive role-taking task was evident for the training groups in one school, but not in another.

VanLieshout, Leckie, and VanSonsbeck (1976) have reported on the effectiveness of a training program to enhance social role-taking skills in preschool children. Children in the training group discussed the feelings of others in stories and puppet play, enacted roles, and were socially reinforced for being helpful and altruistic toward other children. The experimental program was conducted in 30-minute daily sessions by the nursery school teacher for a total of 18 weeks. With mental age controlled, trained three- and four-year-old children showed considerably higher scores on a battery of cognitive and affective role-taking tests relative to controls. The control group was a nursery school program without the special emphasis on perspective-taking training. No significant effect of treatment was apparent for the group of five-year-olds. Unfortunately, as Shantz (1975) noted, some aspects of training may be fairly specific to the battery of role-taking tests, and thus some of the changes may simply represent specific practice effects. In addition, the study leaves open the question as to what aspect of training—role-taking, prosocial behavior training, or both—produced the effects observed.

Working within a structural model of development, Selman (Jaquette, Parkhurst, and Selman, Note 7; Selman, 1976; Selman and Byrne, 1974) set out to examine the role of perspective-taking ability across a variety of different social content areas. He examined the sequential development of role-taking ability in such areas as children's concepts of persons, friendships, and groups, and has described a sequence of interpersonal awareness levels. While a detailed review of Selman's efforts is beyond the scope of this chapter, one finding is of particular relevance. Selman (1976) reported that institutionalized emotionally disturbed children did not differ from a normal reference group with regard to the absolute *capacity* for using the higher levels of perspective-taking logic. Rather, the clinical group failed to *apply* the higher levels of reasoning consistently across different social content areas, and their typical level of functioning was usually at the lower stages of interpersonal reasoning. However, a minority of the disturbed children actually showed levels of interpersonal awareness comparable to or even exceeding the level of the adjusted group. This finding led Selman and his associates to conclude that while some level of perspective-taking skills may be necessary for adaptive social functioning, it is not, by itself, sufficient for social adjustment.

Jaquette et al. (Note 7) have recently reported on a pilot study of an intervention program aimed at fostering more mature levels of interpersonal awareness in 12 to 13-year-olds at a school for emotionally disturbed youngsters with peer relationship difficulties. The approach, termed "Developmental Peer Therapy," was implemented via weekly class meetings with eight children throughout the school year. Emphasis was placed on adequacy of interpersonal communication, supportive peer feedback, and democratic group decision-making. Children participated in setting the weekly agenda for the meetings, which usually involved discussion of real-life interpersonal problems that had arisen during the week. The children also engaged in planning group activities, selecting group leaders on a rotating basis, and making up petitions for changes they believed were necessary in the way the staff ran the school. An effort was made to structure the group discussion at the level of the children's capacity for interpersonal awareness—based on pretest assessments. Results indicated that children demonstrated an increased capacity for developmentally more mature forms of interpersonal reasoning on the Selman (Note 8) measure of interpersonal awareness.

Enright and McMullin (1977) reported on the outcome of a cross-age training program based on Selman's levels of interpersonal awareness. The experimental group consisted of 12 randomly selected sixth-grade children who met in pairs, with each pair leading discussion groups of four or five first graders. Meetings were held on a twice a week basis for 22 weeks. The training group of sixth graders met once a week with the first graders and once with the experimenters to discuss their experience as discussion leaders. Three basic training methods were used in the experimental group. The first method involved the use of hypothetical interpersonal dilemmas, stories in which conflicting alternatives are read or shown for the children to discuss. The sixth-grade leader tried to induce "cognitive conflict" by introducing responses one level above a child's current level of interpersonal awareness. The sixth graders presumably experienced such interpersonal cognitive conflict through selecting filmstrips or story books to use with their first grade students. The dilemma was also used as a means of discussing with the sixth graders how younger children may solve a given dilemma, the hypothesis being that this would add to the sixth-graders' understanding of persons in general. The second training method focused on the process of behavioral interaction between the sixth- and first-graders in promoting growth. Instead of concentrating on story content, the sixth-graders would discuss the quality of first-grade interactions that they saw as discussion leaders. This aspect of the training was aimed at fostering a greater understanding of *interactions* among people on the part of the sixth-graders. The final method involved an attempt to bridge discrepancies observed between what the sixth-graders could conceptualize cognitively and their actual behavior with the first-graders. For instance, if a child was capable of inferring that it hurts the first-graders when she yells at them, but then he/she continued to yell, the experimenters would concentrate on pointing out the discrepancies between thought and action. The discussions were audiotaped and videotaped, and planning for the next week was based on weekly examination of the tapes by the experimenters. The results showed improvement by the experimental sixth-grade subjects over a nontreatment control group on the Selman measures of interpersonal awareness. No generalization was evident to measures of communicative role-taking,

means-ends thinking, or to another cognitive role-taking task. Some evidence of improvement on a moral development measure was apparent. The pattern of results suggests that the intervention procedure produced results specific to only certain types of social-cognitive stage thinking rather than to other types of social-cognitive processes.

Another approach to fostering higher levels of perspective-taking ability in children has recently been reported by Silvern, Waterman, Sobesky, and Ryan (1979). Fourth- and fifth-grade children, with scores below age norms on a measure of perspective-taking logic, engaged in discussions of videotaped vignettes in which something in the interaction "went wrong" due to a perspective-taking error by one of the actors. Each problem required solution at a more mature level of perspective-taking than that required by the preceeding problem. Children actively discussed alternative solutions to provide a more desirable outcome based on appropriate perspective-taking, and they acted, videotaped, and viewed their own versions. The training increased scores of the experimental subjects versus a nontreatment and a placebo control group on measures of cognitive-role-taking, affective role-taking, and self-esteem, and led to lower scores on a measure of defensiveness. No behavioral outcome measure of adjustment or actual peer interaction was used.

Several other studies are broadly relevant to the area of role-taking training, and should be given brief mention. Staub (1971) found that the role-playing of "helper-victim" roles substantially increased girls' tendency to respond to audiotaped distress signals of another child from outside the experimental room. The procedure produced increases for boys on a measure of sharing. There were two treatment sessions, and the subjects were 75 kindergarten children. Each child in the role-play group was given an opportunity to role-play both "helper" and "victim" roles in a role-switching procedure. The role-play group was superior to an induction group (discussion of helpful acts without role play) and to a control group in which children enacted scenes unrelated to helping.

Clore and Jeffrey (1972) found that direct and vicarious emotional role-playing in college students led to increased positive responses to a disabled person and to a series of issues concerning disabled students in general. Furness (1976) has provided a practical guide to role-playing of social situations with elementary school children, although she reported no statistical outcome data. Dupont (Note 9) has developed programs for enhancing emotional development in children ages seven to fifteen (toward Affective Development, TAD I and II). The programs include components to enhance awareness of individual differences, emotional and body awareness, social perspective-taking, and awareness of career opportunities. Some preliminary outcome data indicate that children who participate in the training program score higher relative to untrained children on measures of self-esteem and on a test requiring a child to generate alternatives in psychosocial situations (Dupont, Note 9). Dinkmeyer (1973) has also developed an extensive program series for enhancing social development in young children (Developing Understanding of Self and Others; DUSO D1 and D2) that include numerous perspective-taking activities. However, no data regarding evaluation of the program's effectiveness has been published to our knowledge.

Other investigations (Ojemann, Levitt, Lyle, and Whiteside, 1955; Muuss, 1960a) have examined the effects of programs designed to enhance children's causal reasoning about the social behavior of others. The "causal" training program used by Ojemann et al. (1955) was conducted by instructing teachers in the application of the causal approach to understanding human behavior in their handling of everyday classroom problems among their students. Typical classroom situations were presented to the teachers to give them some experience in understanding what would be "surface" as opposed to "causal" ways of handling these situations. Teachers were also presented with an instructional unit to develop their own awareness of developmental problems of the normal child. The subjects were 19 children in each of four classrooms, grades four to six. The

teachers' training consisted of one month of intensive work during the summer, followed by group conferences every three weeks during the school year. Relative to untrained control children, the children in the experimental classrooms improved significantly in their understanding of the dynamics of social behavior as measured by a Problem Solving Test and a Causal Test of social-causal reasoning. Ojemann et al. (1955) and Muuss (1960a) did not include any measure of overt behavioral adjustment in their studies. Muuss (1960a) found a decrease in antidemocratic attitudes after a two-year exposure to a similar causal program, but not after only one year of exposure to the program. No changes in the children's Manifest Anxiety Scale (Castanda, McCandless, and Palermo, 1956) were evident in this study, although this measure was sensitive to training effects in a previous study (see Muuss, 1960b and Ojemann, 1967 for a review of such studies).

A program is currently being developed by Feshbach and Feshbach (Feshbach, Note 10) in the Los Angeles public schools in an attempt to train empathic abilities in aggressive inner-city boys. The guiding rationale is that an empathic response is presumably incompatible with aggression—that is, that affective responsiveness to another's distress will serve as an inhibitor of aggressive acts. The initial pilot training study involved 30 hours of exercises and activities of twenty to fifty minutes in length, and assessed the results of a pilot comparison of several different varying conditions.

It was found that half of the subjects in the experimental groups showed considerable change on both aggression and prosocial measures, while only one subject in the control groups showed a marked improvement on both of these dependent measures. There was also some evidence of a relationship between improved behavior ratings and improved scores on perspective-taking measures. The investigators are now involved in an even more extensive application of these training methods with third- and fourth-grade subjects.

The interventions that have focused on perspective-taking skills have often been successful in improving performance on measures that attempt to assess perspective-taking abilities. In addition, studies have at times found improvements on ratings of behavioral adjustment, and in one case an impact on recidivism rates was found (Chandler, 1973). Although there are less impressive outcomes in some studies, training in perspective-taking does appear in some cases to offer a valuable contribution to the remediation of social cognitive defects. Nevertheless, issues in need of attention in future research include more extensive examination of these procedures with clinical samples; inclusion of behavioral observations or ratings from outside the treatment setting to assess generalization; and further explanation of the precise nature of the perspective-taking deficits.

The Relation of Perspective-Taking to Other Social Cognitive Problem-Solving Abilities

To date, research in human perspective-taking and research into other social cognitive problem-solving abilities have proceeded along fairly independent lines. On the one hand, we find a growing body of perspective-taking training research based on cognitive developmental theories that have arisen out of a structural approach to understanding cognitive development. The primary emphasis of these studies is on acquiring knowledge about changes in children's internal cognitive structures as they grow older, and on attempting to specify the processes or mechanisms of change. The emphasis is a developmental one. We have, however, an increasing body of research looking into other interpersonal cognitive problem solving (ICPS) abilities, including alternative and consequential thinking, problem identification, and means-ends thinking.

Inasmuch as perspective-taking and the other ICPS skills mentioned are processes that operate on social content, they can all logically be classified as processes in social cognition. Moreover, while we may rightly make a conceptual distinction between perspective-taking and other ICPS skills for purposes of research and analysis, it seems quite likely that these processes are inter-

dependent in the actual performance of daily social-cognitive acts. Stated another way, it is likely that making cognitive inferences about the thoughts, feelings, and perceptions of other persons is closely related to other aspects of the problem-solving processes, such as appropriate "self-talk" during alternative and consequential thinking, when one is faced with a situation of interpersonal conflict. However, it is conceptually possible for a perspective-taking inference to be made in a situation without subsequent generation of alternatives and evaluation of consequences. We recall the Enright and McMullin (1977) finding that training that led to increased interpersonal awareness did not generalize to means-ends thinking or to another role-taking task. It might in fact be useful to view inferences about the perspective of others as part of the processes involved in the recognition and identification of a problem, prior to subsequent decision making. Spivack et al. (1976) suggested that role-taking ability may be a necessary yet not sufficient component for the successful solution of an interpersonal problem. Shure and Spivack (1978) also suggested that good role-taking abilities should increase the quality and range of alternative solutions available for problem-solving.

To our knowledge, there is only one reported study (Platt and Spivack, 1973, reported in Spivack et al. (1976) in which a measure of social perspective-taking was included in an investigation along with other ICPS measures and the intercorrelations between them examined. Platt and Spivack found that perspective-taking on Feffer's cognitive role-taking task (Feffer, 1959) loaded on the same factor as means-ends problem-solving scores for a sample of normal adults as well as for a sample of adult psychiatric inpatients. Intercorrelations between the role-taking task and the means-ends thinking task were .38 (nonpsychiatric sample, N = 47) and .52 (Psychiatric patients, N = 105). Perspective-taking correlated with alternative thinking with coefficients of .34 and .30 respectively for the two samples. Correlations between measures of problem recognition and alternative thinking were .39 and .45. Unfortunately, intercorrelational data are only available for the adult samples. The data do suggest a relationship between various social cognitive skills, however. Moreover, the moderate nature of the correlations argue against the notion that the proposed ICPS abilities reflect a unitary social cognitive ability akin to "social intelligence."

CONCLUSION

The literature on the training of social-cognitive skills that we have reviewed offers some encouraging evidence of therapeutic effectiveness, although some equivocal findings are apparent in the literature as well. The use of nonclinical samples, the limited use of optimal control groups, and the absence of measures of overt behavioral adjustment limits the value of a number of studies in terms of their practical utility for therapy at present.

A more systematic inclusion of multiple-response measures (self-report, task performance, teacher ratings, sociometrics, and behavioral observations) for assessing therapeutic outcomes is needed in future research. There is also the need for future research that will assist in highlighting the "active ingredients" of complex multifaceted training programs that are responsible for reported treatment effects. Studies aimed at training single-component processes in isolation (e.g., generating alternatives, evaluating consequences, affect recognition) and at training limited rational combinations of these processes should help us further to separate out the more effective from the less effective components of particular training programs.

Another factor that would benefit future training studies, as Brown, Campione, and Barclay (Note 11), Kendall (Note 4), and Meichenbaum and Asarnow (1979) have suggested, might be to build more intensive procedures for generalization of treatment effects into the main body of the training programs themselves. One example of this would be to supplement cognitive self-control training with operant reinforcement procedures in the classroom. Another point to be emphasized is the need for more longitudinal assessment

of long-term outcomes in training studies.

The reader must appreciate at this point the diversity of theoretical backgrounds that have contributed to the interventions that aim to teach social-cognitive abilities to children. Let us emphasize, however, some points of similarity that do exist among the different training programs when put into actual practice. While differing in specific training content, the studies usually involve several of the following instructional methods:

(1) Direct verbal instructions to the child
(2) Modeling
(3) Environmental reinforcement (material rewards, social praise, response-cost)
(4) Role-play and behavior rehearsal
(5) Self-instruction
(6) Self-reinforcement
(7) Feedback and group discussion

Most of the studies reviewed utilize a combination of these methods, particularly modeling and role-playing, despite differing theoretical perspectives. There also appears to be a considerable amount of overlap of training content at times across the different training approaches. For example, studies of perspective-taking training often describe generation of alternative solutions as a component of the training. Conversely, several authors included practice in role-taking components (identifying feelings and emotional causality) as part of their problem-solving training programs. Given the likelihood that social cognitive problem-solving skills function together to a considerable extent in real-life social problem situations, it is not surprising to find such overlap of components in studies that aim at broad-based remedial social development.

To advance our efforts to remediate disturbed interpersonal behavior, we will need to know more about the exact nature of the skill deficits of our clients. Consider the following questions:

(1) Does the child in fact lack the basic skills required for solution to a given problem situation X? If so, which skills does he/she lack?
(2) Does the child have the adequate social-cognitive abilities in his/her re-

sponse repertoire but simply fail to employ them? If so, what situational or motivational factors account for this?

(3) Are there children who in fact are considered socially competent by their parents and teachers in most interpersonal situations who nonetheless *lack* well-developed social-cognitive skills appropriate for their age?

It seems apparent that the ability to perform cognitive problem-solving or role-taking operations does not necessarily ensure competent performance in a given interpersonal situation. A child may be able to think of alternatives but lack the component skills or information required to carry out a specific plan of action. Or perhaps a child may be quite capable of alternative thinking in most situations but be incapable of accurately identifying a given problem situation due to distortion caused by strong emotions or exaggerated states of emotional need (Jahoda, 1953). Presumably, however, the competent problem-solver is able to recognize what is missing in the situation or in him/herself and then actively formulate some specific means to remediate the deficit. Alternative thinking might possibly be viewed as a necessary yet insufficient component for effective means-ends planning, just as perspective-taking may be a necessary but not sufficient component to guarantee good overall social adjustment in children. Stated differently, problem-solving processes appear hierarchically organized, and probably involve multiple subunits and feedback loops between components in the system.

Another important series of unanswered questions revolves about the broad issue of developmental change. Developmental psychology has for some time been concerned with the changing organization and development of cognitive structures, as reflected in the perspective-taking literature. Behavioral psychology, on the other hand, has in the past focused largely on observed behavioral responses and on the manner in which they can be learned and changed. Some of the current interest of behavioral psychologists in internal cognitive events unfortunately retains the restricted focus on thoughts as response products or out-

comes, with little emphasis on the cognitive developmental *processes* or mechanisms that produce the substantial differences in cognition between children and adults. Combs and Slaby (1978) have commented on this lack of a truly developmental focus in the behavioral literature. It is here that the social-cognitive problem-solving approach offers some promise. The approach represents an attempt to bridge part of the gap between internal cognitive events and observed social behaviors by specifying a series of general interpersonal cognitive processes. The cognitive problem-solving components have internal structural properties that should lend themselves to developmental theorizing as in the case of perspective-taking. However, they can also be viewed as cognitive *processes* from the standpoint of information-processing theories. The structural properties of social-cognitive skills are probably best subsumed under the rubric of the "existence" component in the Flavell et al. (1968) information-processing model. The basic questions here would be: To what extent do the basic cognitive problem-solving structures or abilities exist in the child's repertoire? Are the child's cognitive capacities up to the requirements for solving a specific problem X? The second element of Flavell's model, the "need" element, refers to the motivational component, that is, recognition by the child that a particular situation requires that the social-cognitive machinery be set in motion. The third component, Flavell's "inference" component, would then involve the actual execution of social-cognitive processes (i.e., the actual process of infering a particular perspective, generating alternatives and consequences, and so forth, in a given situation). Finally, the "performance" component involves analysis of the factors that lead to successful implementation or failure of implementation of these social-cognitive operations in actual overt social acts.

A final comment regarding the role of children's affect in therapy seems in order. The problem-solving approach, although fundamentally cognitive in nature, provides a vehicle for more systematic inclusion of the role of children's emotions in behavior modification research. The approach highlights the importance of research into the processes by which children develop the cognitive abilities to identify emotions in themselves and others and to understand the causes behind these feelings. Sensitivity to recognizing emotional cues may well be an important basic step toward recognizing the existence of a problem which needs to be solved.

REFERENCE NOTES

Schnieder, M. & Robin, A. Turtle manual. Unpublished manuscript, State University of New York at Stony Brook, 1975.

Ollenidick, T. H. *Social skills training for juvenile delinquents.* Unpublished manuscript, Indiana State University, 1978.

Kendall, P. C. & Fischler, G. *Interpersonal cognition and behavior.* National Institute of Mental Health Grant, University of Minnesota, 1980.

Kendall, P. C. *Self-instructions with children: An analysis of the inconsistent evidence for treatment generalization.* Address presented to the Second National Conference on Cognitive Behavior Therapy Research, New York, October, 1978.

Bash, M. & Camp, B. *Think aloud program: Group manual.* Unpublished manuscript, University of Colorado School of Medicine, 1975.

Elardo, P. T. & Caldwell, B. M. *The effects of an experimental social development program on children in the middle childhood period.* Unpublished manuscript, University of Arkansas at Little Rock, 1976.

Jaquette, D., Parkhurst, V., & Selman, R. *Class meetings and developmental peer therapy: An interpersonal problem-solving approach for remedial social development.* Unpublished manuscript, Harvard University, 1978.

Selman, R. L. *The development of conceptions of interpersonal relations: A structural analysis and procedures for the assessment of levels of interpersonal reasoning based on levels of social perspective-taking.* Unpublished manuscript, Harvard, Judge Baker, Social Reasoning Project, 1974.

Dupont, H. *Toward affective development: Theory, program development, and learner verification.* Unpublished manuscript, University of Wisconsin, Eau Claire, 1976.

Feshbach, N. D. *Empathy training: A field study in affective education.* Address presented at the American Educational Research Association Meetings, Toronto, Canada, March 1978.

Brown, A., Campione, J., & Barclay, C. *Training self-checking routines for estimating test readiness: Generalization from list learning to prose recall.* Unpublished manuscript, University of Illinois, 1978.

REFERENCES

Alexander, J. F. & Parsons, B. V. Short-term behavioral intervention with delinquent families. *Journal of Abnormal Psychology,* 1973, *81,* 219–225.

Allen, G., Chinsky, J., Larcen, S., Lochman, J. E., & Selinger, H. *Community psychology and the schools: A behaviorally oriented multilevel preventive approach.* Hillsdale, New Jersey: Lawrence Erlbaum Associates, Publishers, 1976.

Bandura, A. *Social learning theory.* Englewood Cliffs, N.J.: Prentice-Hall, 1977.

Blechman, E., Olson, D., Schornagel, C., Halsdorf, M., & Turner, A. The family contract game: Technique & case study. *Journal of Consulting & Clinical Psychology,* 1976, *44,* 449–455 (a).

Blechman, E., Olson, D., & Hellman, I. Stimulus control over family problem-solving behavior: The family contract game. *Behavior Therapy,* 1976, *7,* 686–692 (b).

Bornstein, M., Bellack, A., & Hersen, M. Social-skills training for unassertive children: A multiple-baseline analysis. *Journal of Applied Behavior Analysis,* 1977, *10,* 183–195.

Bornstein, P. & Quevillon, R. The effects of a self-instructional package on overactive preschool boys. *Journal of Applied Behavior Analysis,* 1976, *9,* 179–188.

Butler, L. & Meichenbaum, D. Assessing interpersonal problem-solving. In P. C. Kendall & S. D. Hollon (Eds.), *Assessment strategies for cognitive-behavioral intervention.* New York: Academic Press, 1981.

Camp, B., Blom, G., Herbert, F., & Van Doorninck. "Think Aloud": A program for developing self-control in young aggressive boys. *Journal of Abnormal Child Psychology,* 1977, *5,* 157–168.

Castaneda, A. McCandless, B., & Palermo, D. The children's form of the manifest anxiety scale. *Child Development,* 1956, *27,* 317–326.

Chandler, M. Egocentrism and antisocial behavior: The assessment and training of social perspective-taking skills. *Developmental Psychology,* 1973, *9,* 326–332.

Chandler, M., Greenspan, S., & Barenboim, C. Assessment and training of role-taking and referential communication skills in institutionalized emotionally disturbed children. *Developmental Psychology*, 1974, *10*, 546–553.

Chittenden, G. E. An experimental study in measuring and modifying assertive behavior in young children. *Monographs of the Society for Research in Child Development*, 1942, 7 (Whole No. 31).

Clore, G. L. & Jeffery, K. M. Emotional role playing, attitude change, and attraction toward a disabled person. *Journal of Personality and Social Psychology*, 1972, *23*, 105–111.

Combs, M. L. & Slaby, D. A. Social skills training with children. In B. Lahey and A. Kazdin, (Eds.), *Advances in Child Clinical Psychology*, Vol. 1. New York: Plenum Press, 1978.

Conners, C. K. A teacher rating scale for use in drug studies with children. *American Journal of Psychiatry*, 1969, *126*, 884–888.

Dinkmeyer, D. *Developing understanding of self and others manual*. Circle Pines, Minn.: American Guidance Service, 1973.

Douglas, V., Parry, P., Marton, P., & Garson, C. Assessment of a cognitive training program for hyperactive children. *Journal of Abnormal Child Psychology*, 1976, *4*, 389–410.

Drummond, D. *Self-instruction training: An approach to disruptive classroom behavior*. Unpublished doctoral dissertation, University of Oregon, 1974.

D'Zurilla, T. & Goldfried, M. Problem-solving and behavior modification. *Journal of Abnormal Psychology*, 1971, *78*, 107–126.

Elardo, P. T. & Cooper, M. *Project aware: A handbook for teachers*. Menlo Park, Calif.: Addison-Wesley, 1977.

Enright, R. & McMullin, I. A social-cognitive developmental intervention with sixth and first graders. *Consulting Psychologist*, 1977, *6*, 10–12.

Evers, W. & Schwartz, J. Modifying social withdrawal in preschoolers: The effects of filmed modeling and teacher praise. *Journal of Abnormal Child Psychology*, 1973, *1*, 248–256.

Feffer, M. H. The cognitive implications of role-taking behavior. *Journal of Personality*, 1959, *27*, 152–168.

Feffer, M. H. & Gourevich, V. Cognitive aspects of role-taking in children. *Journal of Personality*, 1960, *28*, 383–396.

Feldhusen, J., Houtz, J., & Ringenbach, S. The Purdue elementary problem-solving inventory. *Psychological Reports*, 1972, *31*, 891–901.

Feldhusen, J. & Houtz, J. Problem-solving and the concrete-abstract dimension. *Gifted Child Quarterly*, 1975, *19*, 122–129.

Flapan, D. *Children's understanding of social interaction*. New York: Teachers College Press, 1968.

Flavell, J. H. *The developmental psychology of Jean Piaget*. New York: D. Van Nostrand Co., 1963.

Flavell, J., Botkin, P., Fry, C., Wright, J., & Jarvis, P. *The development of role-taking and communication skills in children*. New York: Wiley, 1968.

Foster, S. L. Family conflict management: Skill training and generalization procedures. (Doctoral dissertation, State University of New York at Stony Brook, 1978). *Dissertation Abstracts International*, 1979, *39*, 5063B-5064B. (University Microfilms No. 79-08,689)

Furness, P. *Role play in the elementary school, a handbook for teachers*. New York: Hart Publishing Co., 1976.

Furth, H. *Thinking without language*. New York: The Free Press, 1976.

Giebink, J. W., Stover, D., & Fahl, M. Teaching adaptive responses to frustration to emotionally disturbed boys. *Journal of Consulting and Clinical Psychology*, 1968, *32*, 366–368.

Goodwin, S. & Mahoney, M. Modification of aggression through modeling: An experimental probe. *Journal of Behavior Therapy and Experimental Psychiatry*, 1975, *6*, 200–202.

Gottman, J., Gonso, J., & Schuler, P. Teaching social skills to isolated children. *Journal of Abnormal Child Psychology*, 1976, *4*, 179–197.

Guilford, J. P. *The nature of human intelligence*. New York: McGraw-Hill, 1967.

Houtz, J. & Feldhusen, J. The modification of fourth graders' problem-solving abilities. *Journal of Psychology*, 1976, *93*, 229–237.

Hudson, L. M. On the coherence of role-taking abilities: An alternative to correlational analysis. *Child Development*, 1978, *49*, 223–227.

Iannotti, R. J. Effect of role-taking experiences on role-taking, altruism, empathy, and aggression. *Developmental Psychology*, 1978, *14*, 119–124.

Jahoda, M. The meaning of psychological health. *Social Casework*, 1953, *34*, 349–354.

Jahoda, M. *Current concepts of positive mental health*. New York: Basic Books, 1958.

Jensen, A. R. The role of verbal mediation in mental development. *Journal of Genetic Psychology*, 1971, *118*, 39–70.

Kazdin, A. E. *Behavior modification in applied settings*. Homewood, Ill.: Dorsey Press, 1975.

Keating, D. K. A search for social intelligence. *Journal of Educational Psychology*, 1978, *70*, 218–223.

Keller, M. & Carlson, P. The use of symbolic modeling to promote social skills in preschool children with low levels of social responsiveness. *Child Development*, 1974, *45*, 912–919.

Kendall, P. C. On the efficacious use of verbal self-instructional procedures with children. *Cognitive Therapy and Research*, 1977, *1*, 331–341.

Kendall, P. C. & Finch, A. J., Jr. A cognitive-behavioral treatment for impulse control: A case study. *Journal of Consulting and Clinical Psychology*, 1976, *44*, 852–857.

Kendall, P. C. & Finch, A. J., Jr. A cognitive-behavioral treatment for impulsivity: A group comparison study. *Journal of Consulting and Clinical Psychology*, 1978, *46*, 110–118.

Kendall, P. C. & Finch, A. J. Developing non-impulsive behavior in children: Cognitive-behavioral strategies for self-control. In P. C. Kendall and S. D. Hollon (Eds.) *Cognitive-behavioral interventions: Theory, research, and procedures*. New York: Academic Press, 1979.

Kendall, P. C. & Hollon, S. D. Cognitive-behavioral interventions: Overview and current status. In P. C. Kendall and S. D. Hollon (Eds.) *Cognitive-behavioral interventions: Theory, research, and procedures*. New York: Academic Press, 1979.

Kendall, P. C. & Wilcox, L. E. Cognitive-behavioral treatment for impulsivity: Concrete versus conceptual training in non-self-controlled problem children. *Journal of Consulting and Clinical Psychology*, 1980, *48*, 80–91.

Kendall, P. C. & Wilcox, L. E. Self-control in children: Development of a rating scale. *Journal of Consulting and Clinical Psychology*, 1979, *47*, 1020–1029.

Kendall, P. C., Pellegrini, D., & Urbain, E. S. Approaches to assessment for cognitive-behavioral interventions with children. In P. C. Kendall and S. D. Hollon (Eds.), *Assessment strategies for cognitive-behavioral interventions*. New York: Academic Press, 1981.

Kendall, P. C. & Hollon, S. D. (Eds.) *Cognitive behavioral interventions: Theory, research, and procedures*. New York: Academic Press, 1979. (b)

Klein, N. C., Alexander, J. F., & Parsons, B. V. Impact of family systems intervention on recidivism and sibling delinquency: A model of primary prevention and program evaluation. *Journal of Consulting and Clinical Psychology*, 1977, *45*, 469–474.

Kohlberg, L., Yaeger, J., & Hjertholm E. Private speech: Four studies and a review of theories. *Child Development*, 1968, *39*, 671–690.

Kurdek, L. A. Structural components and intellectual correlates of cognitive perspective taking in first through fourth grade children. *Child Development*, 1977, *48*, 1503–1511.

Kurdek, L. A. & Rodgon, M. M. Perceptual, cognitive, and affective perspective-taking in kindergarten through sixth-grade children. *Developmental Psychology*, 1975, *11*, 643–650.

Little, V. L. The relationship of role-taking ability to self-control in institutionalized juvenile offenders (Doctoral dissertation, Virginia Commonwealth University, 1978). *Dissertation Abstracts International*, 1979, *39*, 2992B. (University Microfilms No. 78-22,701)

Little, V. L. & Kendall, P. C. Cognitive-behavioral interventions with delinquents: Problem-solving, role-taking and self-control. In P. C. Kendall and S. D. Hollon (Eds.) *Cognitive-behavioral interventions: Theory, research, and procedures*. New York: Academic Press, 1979.

Luria, A. *The role of speech in the regulation of normal and abnormal behaviors*. New York: Liveright, 1961.

McClure, L. F. *Social problem-solving training and assessment: An experimental intervention in an elementary school setting*. Unpublished doctoral dissertation, University of Connecticut, 1975.

McClure, L. F., Chimsky, J. M., & Larcen, S. W. Enhancing social problem-solving performance in an elementary school setting. *Journal of Educational Psychology*, 1978, *70*, 504–513.

Mead, G. *Mind, self, and society*. Chicago: University of Chicago Press, 1934.

Meichenbaum, D. (Ed.) *Cognitive behavior modification newsletter*, Number 2, April, 1976.

Meichenbaum, D. *Cognitive-behavior modification: An integrative approach*. New York: Plenum Press, 1977.

Meichenbaum, D. & Asarnow, J. Cognitive behavior modification and metacognitive development: Implications for the classroom. In P. C. Kendall and S. D. Hollon (Eds.) *Cognitive-behavioral interventions: Theory, research, and procedures*. New York: Academic Press, 1979.

Meichenbaum, D. & Goodman, J. Training impulsive children to talk to themselves: A means of developing self-control. *Journal of Abnormal Psychology*, 1971, *77*, 115–126.

Muuss, R. The effects of a one- and two-year causal-learning program. *Journal of Personality*, 1960, *28*, 479–491. (a).

Muuss, R. Mental health implications of a preventive psychiatry program in the light of research findings. *Marriage and Family Living*, 1960, *22*, 150–156 (b).

Nelson, C. M., Worell, J., & Polsgrove, L. Behaviorally disordered peers as contingency managers. *Behavior Therapy*, 1973, *4*, 270–276.

O'Connor, R. Modification of social withdrawal through symbolic modeling. *Journal of Applied Behavior Analysis*, 1969, *2*, 15–22.

O'Connor, R. Relative efficacy of modeling, shaping, and the combined procedures for modification of social withdrawal. *Journal of Abnormal Psychology*, 1972, *79*, 327–334.

Oden, S. & Asher, S. R. Coaching children in social skills for friendship making. *Child Development*, 1977, *48*, 495–506.

Ojemann, R. H. Incorporating psychological concepts in the school curriculum. *Journal of School Psychology*, 1967, *5*, 195–204.

Ojemann, R. H., Levitt, E., Lyle, W., & Whiteside, M. F. The effects of "causal" teacher training program and certain curricular changes on grade school children. *Journal of Experimental Education*, 1955, *24*, 95–114.

O'Leary, K. D. & Borkovec, T. D. Conceptual, methodological, and ethical problems of placebo groups in psychotherapy research. *American Psychologist*, 1978, *33*, 821–830.

Parsons, B. V. & Alexander, J. F. Short-term family intervention: A therapy outcome study. *Journal of Consulting and Clinical Psychology*, 1973, *41*, 195–201.

Pitkanen, L. The effect of simulation exercises on the control of aggressive behavior in children. *Scandinavian Journal of Psychology*, 1974, *15*, 169–177.

Reese, H. Verbal mediation as a function of age. *Psychological Bulletin*, 1962, *59*, 502–509.

Robin, A. L., Kent, R., O'Leary, D., Foster, S., & Prinz, R. An approach to teaching parents and adolescents problem-solving communication skills: A preliminary report. *Behavior Therapy*, 1977, *8*, 639–643.

Rotter, J. B. *Social learning and clinical Psychology*. Englewood Cliffs, N.J.: Prentice-Hall, Inc., 1954.

Sarason, I. G. Verbal learning, modeling, and juvenile delinquency. *American Psychologist*, 1968, *23*, 254–266.

Sarason, I. G. & Ganzer, U. J. Developing appropriate social behaviors of juvenile delinquents. In J. Krumholtz and C. Thoresen (Eds.), *Behavior Counseling Cases and Techniques*, New York: Holt, Rhinehart & Wilson, 1969.

Sarason, I. G. and Ganzer, V. J. Modeling and group discussion in the rehabilitation of juvenile delinquents. *Journal of Counseling Psychology*, 1973, *20*, 442–449.

Schneider, M. Turtle technique in the classroom. *Teaching Exceptional Children*, 1974, *8*, 22–24.

Scott, P. M., Burton, R. V., & Yarrow, M. R. Social reinforcement under natural conditions. *Child Development*, 1967, *38*, 53–63.

Selman, R. L. Toward a structural analysis of developing interpersonal relations concepts: Research with normal and disturbed preadolescent boys. In A. D. Pick (Ed.) *Minnesota Symposia on Child Psychology* (Vol. 10) Minneapolis: University of Minnesota Press, 1976.

Selman, R. & Byrne, D. A structural-developmental analysis of levels of role-taking in middle childhood. *Child Development*, 1974, *45*, 803–806.

Shantz, C. V. The development of social cognition. In E. M. Hetherington (Ed.) *Review of Child Development Research* (Vol. 5). Chicago: University of Chicago Press, 1975.

Shure, M. B. & Spivack, G. *Problem-solving techniques in childrearing*. San Francisco: Jossey Bass, 1978.

Silvern, L. E., Waterman, J. M., Sobesky, W., & Ryan, V. L. Effects of a developmental model of perspective taking training. *Child Development*, 1979, *50*, 243–246.

Simon, H. A. & Newell, A. Human problem-solving: The state of the theory in 1970. *American Psychologist*, 1971, *26*, 145–159.

Slaby, R. G. & Crowley, C. G. Modification of cooperation and aggression through teacher attention to children's speech. *Journal of Experimental Child Psychology*, 1977, *23*, 442–458.

Solomon, R. W. & Wahler, R. G. Peer reinforcement control of classroom problem behavior. *Journal of Applied Behavior Analysis*, 1973, *6*, 49–56.

Speedie, S. M., Houtz, J., Ringenbach, S., & Feldhusen, J. Abilities measured by the Purdue elementary problem-solving inventory. *Psychological Reports*, 1973, *33*, 959–963.

Spivack G. & Shure, M. B. *Social adjustment of young children*. San Francisco: Jossey-Bass, 1974.

Spivack, G., Platt, J., & Shure, M. B. *The problem-solving approach to adjustment*. San Francisco: Jossey-Bass, 1976.

Staub, E. The use of role-playing and induction in children's learning of helping and sharing behavior. *Child Development*, 1971, *42*, 805–816.

Stone, G., Hinds, W., & Schmidt, G. Teaching mental health behaviors to elementary school children. *Professional Psychology*, 1975, *6*, 34–40.

Thorndike, R. L. Intelligence and its uses. *Harper's Magazine*, 1920, *140*, 227–235.

Urbain, E. S. & Kendall, P. C. Review of social-cognitive problem-solving interventions with children. *Psychological Bulletin*, 1980, *88*, 109–143.

VanLieshout, C., Leckie, G., & Van-Sonsbeck, B. Social perspective-taking training: empathy and role-taking ability of preschool children. In K. F. Riegel and J. A. Meacham (Eds.) *The Developing Individual in a Changing World.* Chicago: Aldine, 1976.

Vygotsky, L. *Thought and Language.* New York: Wiley, 1962.

Zahavi, S. *Aggression control.* Unpublished master's thesis. University of Illinois, 1973.

Zahavi, S. & Asher, S. R. The effect of verbal instructions on preschool children's aggressive behavior. *Journal of School Psychology*, 1978, *16*, 146–153.

CHAPTER 13

Psychoanalytic Psychotherapies with Children

JAMES H. EGAN, M.D.
THORNTON A. VANDERSALL, M.D.

Psychotherapy is a term used to describe the psychological treatment of emotional disorders. Psychotherapy is often divided into supportive, educative and reconstructive types.

We will begin with a discussion of reconstructive psychoanalytic psychotherapy of children. This type of treatment is also called dynamic psychotherapy, exploratory psychotherapy or insight oriented psychotherapy and relies heavily on the theoretical principles of psychoanalysis.

Supportive psychotherapies also draw upon this theoretic framework. For this reason we will discuss supportive psychotherapies in the second section of this chapter.

REVIEW OF THEORETICAL CONCEPTS

Psychoanalysis is a theory of the mind, a tool for scientific exploration, and a form of treatment. It is largely derived from the work of Sigmund Freud, and embodies a rich and complicated conceptual framework.

Basic to the differing theoretical points of view are two postulates: the concepts of psychic determinism and that of the dynamic unconscious (Brenner, 1955). Psychic determinism suggests that no mental activity is random, and that all psychic events have multiple determinants; that is, all behaviors are overdetermined. The second postulate or basic assumption of psychoanalytic theory is the concept of the dynamic unconscious.

The concept of the unconscious was familiar in biblical times, but Freud's great contribution was to understand that there are unconscious, dynamic forces and conflicts which account for many or most of the determinants of even "conscious" thought and behavior; that is, thought and behavior are generally determined by unconscious, and dynamic influences.

As a means of appreciating the complexity of behavior, it is necessary to view these behaviors from a number of major, and different theoretical points of view. (Greenson, 1967). These are:

1. The topographic
2. The dynamic
3. The economic
4. The genetic
5. The structural and
6. The adaptive

The Topographic Point of View. The topographic point of view stresses the location of mental activity with regard to consciousness, and unconsciousness. It implies that some behaviors reflect conflicts regarding access to consciousness.

The Dynamic Point of View. The dynamic

point of view assumes that mental phenomena are the result of a number of interacting, and opposing forces. It also assumes that observed behaviors represent the final common pathway of these competing and opposing forces.

The Economic Point of View. Drives and energetic concepts are embodied in the economic point of view. Drives are thought to have energy and direction and are described in terms of their source, aim, and object.

The source is presumed to be in the various erogenous zones of the body, the aim is the discharge of the energies, and the object is that to which the energy is directed. In the case of the thumb sucking, for example, the oral mucosa would be the source of oral libido (the mental representation of the sexual drive). The aim would be stimulation of the mucosa with drive discharge (gratification) and the thumb (or nipple) would be the object. Thus many behaviors, both normal and deviant, can be understood in terms of shifts of objects and the transformation of the sources of energies, as well as by the interaction among the different drives.

The Genetic Point of View. The genetic point of view refers to the origins and development of mental activities and structures. Implicit is the assumption that current behavior is influenced by the past.

The Structural Point of View. The structural point of view is concerned with the three major (macro) structures of the mind; the ego, id, and super ego. A psychic structure is defined as a mental function(s) that is stable; relatively impervious to change. The structural point of view emphasizes the interrelationships among the ego, id, and super ego.

The id is the mental representative of the instinctual drives, and is thus viewed as the source of energies that will fuel the other structures. Drives are unconscious, press for discharge, and are organized according to the laws of the primary process; that is according to the principles of condensation and displacement.

The ego is both conscious and unconscious, and is characterized by its many and diverse functions. Prominent ego functions would include memory, language, perception, speech, thought, object relations, control of instinctual drives, defensive functions, and reality testing.

The super ego like the ego is both conscious and unconscious and is composed of the conscience and the ego ideal. The conscience shapes behavior by the use of guilt when its standards are threatened. The ego ideal is the view of the self to which an individual aspires. Failure to meet one's ego ideal is greeted by shame. Violation of the conscience elicits guilt.

The Adaptive Point of View. The adaptive point of view is supra-ordinate to the others. This view states that there is an inborn preparedness on the part of an individual for the average expectable environment, and that at any given moment the individual makes the best "choice", the most adaptive "decision", given the total of inner and outer experience. Thus all behavior must be viewed as adaptive or maladaptive in light of outer as well as inner realities.

INDICATIONS FOR PSYCHOANALYTIC PSYCHOTHERAPY

Psychotherapy is indicated when development is adversely interfered with by an emotional disorder. Thus transient developmental or reactive disorders would not usually be considered indications for treatment.

Generally children tend not to perceive themselves in emotional distress. Their capacities to externalize are legendary and thus they tend to perceive themselves as victims of outside forces rather than suffering from internalized conflicts. Hence it is often parents, pediatricians or teachers who desire treatment for them. Common conditions suggesting psychotherapeutic interventions would include those disorders whose pathogenesis significantly reflects intrapsychic conflict: poor social relationships, inhibitions, some learning disturbances, serious regressions, maladaptive behaviors, and disturbances in mood, and self esteem to name a few.

To put it simply, psycho-analytic psychotherapy is a treatment for the resolution of intrapsychic conflict. It is indicated in situations where there is no major regression in ego or super ego functions (Scharfman, 1978). It is generally not the primary treatment of choice for disturbance in capacities (deficient repertoires).

Insight-oriented psychotherapy is indicated for academic failure due to fears of success or failure, or when the failure is a reflection of oppositional behavior, while it is not indicated for the treatment of poor academic performance due to limited capacities (low intelligence) or a specific learning disturbance. Similarly exploratory psychotherapy is indicated for elective mutism or hysterical aphonia, but not for aphasia. And as a final example, insight-oriented psychotherapy is indicated for antisocial behavior when it is due to an inordinate need to be punished, but it is generally of little value when the antisocial behavior reflects serious ego, and super ego deficiencies (poor impulse control, little capacity to tolerate frustrations, and reduced capacities for guilt, remorse or empathy).

From the foregoing, three facts of importance emerge: first, a careful assessment is necessary to highlight areas of conflict, and relative areas of diminished capacities. Second, it will be necessary to include the child as a participant observor of the proceedings as a means of educating him into the process of becoming a patient, as well as a means of enlisting his cooperation and motivating him for treatment. Third, it will be necessary to provide some method of enlisting the parents as allies of the treatment process.

INSIGHT-ORIENTED PSYCHOTHERAPY

Psychotherapy with the child is often done one, two, or three times per week. The more frequent the sessions, theoretically, the more intensive the work possible, and the more the expectation is for shifts in psychic structures. The fewer the sessions the less the work will be considered reconstructive and the more it will be considered supportive, abreactive, educative and directive in nature. Many therapists find a twice weekly schedule for the child to be highly useful in many cases.

In the early sessions of the child's treatment it is necessary to introduce him to the role of patient, and to help him develop a therapeutic alliance with the therapist. This process is facilitated when the therapist is seen as a warm, empathic, helpful, concerned, honest, non-judgmental person who is persistent in his efforts to help the child understand himself. The stance of the therapist as a helper who will not censure or humiliate the patient and who will continue to respect the dignity and work of the child in spite of what he says is of critical importance.

The child begins treatment with an expectation of help and optimism which is both reality based and a manifestation of an early positive transference. After the first week or two of relatively open and spontaneous communication the child often appears to have little to communicate. Beginning therapists often become discouraged at this point, and begin to doubt their capacities and technique, or to wonder if their original assessment that this child would benefit from psychotherapy was correct. This state of affairs usually reflects the emergence of resistance.

Resistance is a defense employed during the course of treatment that serves to interrupt the unfolding or progress of the treatment. A resistance (defense) it must be remembered is an unconscious mental mechanism designed to ward off intrapsychic danger or pain. Thus a patient is not aware that he is resisting.

A common countertransference problem is to feel that a patient is resisting the therapist rather than to perceive resistance as an unconscious intrapsychic reaction on the part of the patient.

Frequently therapists feel that if only a patient would reveal what he is defending against, or stop resisting, the treatment would progress. It is far more correct to say that the process of analyzing the patient's (defenses) resistances is the essence of the treatment. If a patient says "I had a dream, but I can't tell you what it was about," the content of the dream is not as important as analyzing the resistance to telling the dream: the defenses against telling it.

CONFIDENTIALITY

Beginning psychotherapists are frequently concerned about issues of confidentiality and their parent contacts. They are generally surprised to learn that children ten and under usually do not share their concern. To a considerable degree the therapist's anxiety reflects an "adulto-pomorphism." Issues of confidentiality are more prominent with adolescents or adults than with children. It is most unusual for a child to be significantly upset by the therapist seeing the parents. I suspect that this reflects the fact that children tend to presume a certain parental omniscience anyway. In addition, latency aged children are so highly defended that their conflicts are out of their awareness and hence they are not so concerned about exposure as the adolescent or adult with many conscious "secrets". (Sarnoff, 1976).

INTERPRETATION

The analysis of resistances or defenses is accomplished by interpretation. Interpretation is the major tool available to the psychotherapist. It is a complicated and difficult process that is effected over a considerable period of time. Greenson (1967) suggests that the process of "analyzing" can be thought of as comprising four components: confrontation, clarification, interpretation proper and working through.

Confrontation is a process by which a patient is made aware of a particular behavior; "I see you're late today", or "I notice on Friday's you generally have little to say." It goes without saying that in order for a patient to analyze a particular resistance he must first be aware of its presence.

Clarification is an elaboration of confrontation. "I see you're often late in coming to your session, is it generally difficult for you to get places on time?" or "We've noticed on Friday's that you have little to say, how do you respond to imminent separations from others?" Thus clarification is a process of documenting how a particular behavior is manifested in other aspects of a patient's life.

The issue of timing interventions is always a concern to a therapist. As a general rule one may almost always make comments at the level of confrontation or clarification, as relatively little preparatory work need be done. Indeed one often does these two procedures in the very first interview;—"I can see how upset you are at coming to see me."

A little later in the interview when the nature of the particular distress has been clarified (anxiety on meeting a new person, for example) one might ask "Is it generally hard for you to meet new people?"

Interpretation proper is a process of making unconscious issues conscious, of conveying dynamic meanings to behaviors, and of making genetic reconstructions. This is a phase of psychotherapeutic work that requires considerable skill.

In general there is but one rule for making an interpretation although it is often stated in multiple different forms. The general rule is to deal with surface issues before depth issues. It is sometimes restated as deal with ego before id, or as defense before impulse.

In general when analyzing defenses one first analyzes the defenses against affects. When that has been accomplished, it is then possible to analyze the conflicts and impulses, with which they are associated.

One six year old boy with multiple neurotic symptoms, and intense castration anxiety (he slept in his mother's bed nightly) told one of the authors of having been to the dentist. He became increasingly anxious as he related that he had a "needle", and then a tooth drilled. When he was asked about the experience, he replied that the drill "tickled."

It was clear that he was unable to deal with the intense fear associated with the procedure; instead he denied the fear and reversed the affect. One could have told him that needles and drills don't tickle, etc; an educative but nonanalytic intervention. Or one could have done an end run around the defense and told him that he was really terrified, but that he couldn't acknowledge it, and so he reversed or substituted the affects. This type of intervention only increases the sense of danger to the ego, and hence will result in a strengthening of the defenses.

Instead one would do better to respect the defense, (Bornstein, 1951) and work from the side of the defense, or ego. One might accomplish this by saying something like "Wouldn't it be nice if needles and drills tickled?" One might even add, "Why if they tickled, one wouldn't mind them so." Similar attempts to create an "alliance" are well described by Bornstein (1949).

The six year old boy in this example said, "But they do Doctor. The therapist replied, "Yes wouldn't it be nice" whereupon he said, "Yes it tickles, tickles, tickles . . ." (with increasing tension and aggression) until the tickle melted away into a loud buzz sound for the drill with him being the dentist shoving the drill into a patient's mouth.

At this point the therapist was able to exclaim, "No wonder you said tickle, why it's so scary the way you do it." With that he proceeded to tell other tales of the dentist and what they do, culminating in how dentists extracted teeth. Thus by hinting at the defense against the fear this little patient was able to recognize his repressed affect (fear). The next step would be to help him understand his conflicts regarding his mother. That is his wish to have his mother, and dispossess his father. His conflict stems from his fear of retaliation in the form of castration by the father for such impulses.

During the following session the six year old patient talked of doubles and triples and multiples of things. He stated a "cat has nine lives" so if he loses one he still has eight left. He then added that when he has a cold he wishes he had nine noses so that if he were to blow his nose and one fell off he would have eight left. The therapist commented how safe he would feel if there were multiples of everything, and how upsetting it is to have only one of something because if he lost that . . . "Yes like my wee wee", he shouted.

A few sessions later he played a game of "I'm the king of the castle" and another one of a young man trying to rob valuables from the king. We then spoke of how the king might get mad, and how the robber would be punished. After playing the king for awhile and telling me how he would

stab the robber in the eye, or punch him or chop off his wee wee, the therapist made a thorough interpretation concerning his wishes regarding his mother and father, and his castration fears. Thus his successive defense against affects, conflicts and finally wishes were analyzed.

Working through is a process of analyzing the material over and over, from a number of different points of view, and with varying emphasis in an effort to fully analyze the multiple determinants of behaviors, and the many associated defenses.

Play

The child therapist often uses play as a means of understanding his child patient. Play to child analysis is somewhat similar to the dreams of adults. The major difference is that adults have a conviction that their dreams are about them, whereas children in play have rather successfully projected their inner lives in the play. Thus they do not tend to see the play as a part of them, or as depicting themselves. This is both a help and a hinderance to our work. It is a help in that the child is not so self conscious in what he portrays. It is an obstacle in that we must now carefully work to assist him in becoming aware of those aspects of himself as revealed to us in the play. The logical step would seem to be to tell our young patient exactly that. If one were to do so, which would be to symbolically analyze the play directly, the play would very likely cease. In fact one of the best ways to stop a specific piece of play is to interpret it directly.

The task of the therapist then is to attempt to understand the play, and to have the child elaborate upon it. We do not, however, make our intervention directly from it. As close as one would come to doing so would be to observe the play and perhaps say, "The poor boy he's so lonely—tell me Joey—have you ever felt that way?"

Except for this use of play, we tend to make our interventions upon interactional material (between therapist and patient) or upon the other material that the child provides. Play then is a precious source of information for the therapist; so precious that one dares not run the risk of having it cease in response to intense symbolic interpretation (Freud, A., 1945).

Child therapists who have also had considerable adult training frequently find themselves in the position of making only the most innocuous, open-ended, non-directive statements to a child. The hope is that the child will be encouraged to follow through with his own ideas; ideas that have not been contaminated by the therapists directive questioning. Alas the child often fails to follow the lead and offers instead an exasperating "I don't know—or "No."

Berta Bornstein (1945) in describing adult analysts experience in treating children said,

"About twenty years ago the suggestion that the training of every analyst should include child analysis was seriously discussed. Since every analytic case leads into the conflicts of childhood, and since every neurosis in an adult is based on a childhood neurosis, this idea seemed not without justification. The analyst who had had first-hand experience with children would be on less strange ground in analyzing adults. His understanding of the adult's unconscious would be increased and it would be easier for him to comprehend the strange character of the transference reactions. Since the unconscious is less concealed and seems to be less repressed in children we expected to penetrate to material of the very first years, which in adult analysis could only be concluded and reconstructed. However, this expectation was disappointed. The suggestion to analyze children was taken up only by a few analysts, but even these dropped the experiment after one or two cases. It was difficult for them to find any access to the child. The child neither talked of his current experiences nor seemed in the least interested in his past. He even brought far fewer recollections than the adult patient. And worst of all, the adult analyst felt helpless against the child's refusal to bring free associations."

Margaret Mahler coined the term "running commentary" to refer to the action of the therapist who comments without actually expecting a confirmatory statement from the patient. Rather the therapist will review some likely possibilities or meanings and muse out loud. It goes something like this—"I wonder how come you're so silent today—could it be that you feel you have nothing to say. . . , or is it rather that you don't want to talk to me, or is it perhaps that today is Friday?"

How hard it is to talk on Friday's—almost like it's hardly worth talking to me since I won't see you until next Tuesday."

A running commentary of this type is not only helpful, but often essential, yet it often causes therapists some anguish that they are being too directive. A corrective for that is to realize how limited one's powers are to direct people's lives and thoughts, and therefore not to see the therapy as a major intrusion.

Parent Work

One of the most painful decisions any parent has to make is to take his child for a psychological consultation. Most parents enter this process with trepidation and feelings of guilt, shame, and failure. It is not surprising, therefore, that they are often highly ambivalent about accepting a recommendation for treatment since to do so will often confirm for them their fears that "they have caused" the disorder.

Most therapists find it useful to have regular visits with the parents during the course of the child's treatment. This is often at weekly intervals initially but is frequently reduced to bi-weekly or monthly contacts as the treatment progresses.

In addition, it serves to enlist the parents as helpers of the treatment. A therapist may tell the parents that they are his or her eyes and ears at home, and that they are needed in order to do work. This is true, and it serves to increase parental support for the treatment. These meetings also permit the parents an opportunity to voice their concerns about issues of parenting, and hence to help them clarify their decisions.

Parent work is sometimes done by a person other than the therapist, but this is far less frequent an occurrence than it once was. In some instances when there is significant parental pathology, the parent should be referred for treatment. This is generally intended to help the parent and not the child patient, since even if the parent pathology was initially responsible for the child's difficulties it is rare for a shift in the parent's difficulties after one or more years of treatment to be sufficient to rectify the already internalized problems of the child.

When doing parent work, it is important not to treat them or respond to them as patients. The stance is rather that of treating them as a "colleague" who is interested along with them in the child. One should no more treat a parent as a patient than the pediatrician would who also treats their child. The pediatrician would surely not propose giving the parent an injection of an antibiotic without permission, when the parent has brought the child to the doctor.

Likewise parents would feel insulted if when they consulted their child's teacher, the teacher also proceeded to teach or evaluate them without an explicit invitation to do so. The therapist's stance towards the parents is that of a teacher or pediatrician whom they have consulted regarding their child. In short, inexperienced clinicians frequently cause parent enmity by assuming a therapeutic stance towards the parents. This often compounds the parent's already high degree of guilt. If this becomes too great for the parent to bear, they often sabotage or terminate the treatment.

Termination

The decision to terminate is a difficult one that is usually arrived at by a consensus. Generally the therapist, patient and parents are involved. The patient and parents usually base their decisions upon the degree to which the original presenting problems have been resolved.

The therapist's decision will be based on an assessment of the degree to which the obstacles to development have been removed. Thus, the therapist will not expect the patient to approach some idealized version of normality, but rather to be able to cope adequately with the age appropriate developmental tasks. A common technical error is for the therapist to attempt to maintain the patient in treatment in order to resolve all problems, before termination.

When a decision to terminate is made a date should be agreed upon. Several months should be allotted to permit an adequate analysis of the problems of separating from the therapist. It frequently happens that there will be a recrudescence of symptoms. The therapist should not be alarmed but rather continue to do analytic work to the end. Considerable skill is required to differentiate a transient recurrence of symptoms in response to termination from a severe and more permanent regression. If one's impression is the former, one terminates on schedule. If it is the latter, the therapist, patient, and parents will obviously have to reconsider their decision.

SUPPORTIVE PSYCHOTHERAPY

The child therapist who is trained in explorative therapy or child analysis, and who finds the verbal, bright, and intact-for-developmental-level child in his office is indeed fortunate. The therapist may then proceed along the reconstructive lines outlined in the first section of this chapter with a reasonable expectation of terminating after the child has improved and is better equipped to meet future hurdles. What of the child (much more common among referrals) who, by nature of defect, experience, of lack of current needed support, is enmeshed in maladaptive behavior and is unable to participate in uncovering therapeutic adventures? What does the child psychotherapist have to offer this child and his family or school, that will be helpful and facilitate development? When psychoanalytic technique cannot be used, is psychoanalytic theory helpful?

ASSESSMENT

In an earlier section we noted the importance of careful assessment in selecting the child who can be seen with insight as a goal. Through examples we suggested that those handicaps and inhibitions that are produced by psychic conflict are those that can be approached by a truly corrective model. If the assessment reveals that the child's silence, for example, is due to an aphasia based on brain damage rather than an elective, conflict-based, oppositional or controlling attitude, our efforts must take a different tack. One cannot assume there are no psychological difficulties, but the assessment must continue so as to understand the inner reactions of the child to this handicap.

In most situations where supportive work will be done, assessment begins with a phone call or office visit with the available parents. During the initial assessment with the parents one must obtain an idea of the problem, the nature of the symptoms, their onset and duration, how they have changed over time, what factors have exacerbated, and what have alleviated the symptoms.

Next to the history taking, an interview with the child, with or without the parents according to the child's age and ability to separate, with the use of toys and drawings or without such supports with an older verbal child, establishes the other half of the data base needed for a clear conceptual understanding of the difficulties the child is experiencing. The Goodman and Sours (1967) book on *The Child Mental Status Examination* and the Assessment chapters in the Chess and Hassibi (1978) and Barker (1971) books are several of many good and varied accounts that detail the process of psychological evaluation of a child prior to treatment planning.

The assessment of the child must be more than a random collection of facts as outlined in a textbook. It must be organized around some principle that will enhance our understanding and indicate a rational approach toward correction or amelioration of the symptom and problems. In the authors' experience the normal development pattern and thrust of the average child provides the best framework for the understanding of the symptom and the planning of intervention. Anna Freud's (1965) invaluable book on assessing development is mandatory reading for clear comprehension of the crucial relationship of symptom to development. The therapist must obtain information relating to the child's overall progress along developmental lines such as those progressing from dependency to self-reliance and adult object relations along with others listed by Freud: suckling to rational eating, soiling to bowel control, irresponsibility to re-

sponsibility in body management, egocentricity to companionship, body to toy, and play to work.

The child's psychiatric assessment would be characterized as an attempt to understand the inter-relationships between development delays in specific areas and (a) symptoms caused by intra-psychic conflict, (b) traumatic failures in the care taking environment, and (c) constitutional handicaps.

SYMPTOMS WITH INNER CONFLICT

The patient with dental fears discussed earlier in this chapter can be characterized as a child with no developmental delays of significance, but with some threat posed in the developmental line working toward responsibility in body management. Were the patient to persist in irrational fears that prohibited reasonable dental attention, a definite arrest in this area might result. The same patient's symptom is well understood as based upon conflict due to age appropriate intrapsychic developmental tasks. No indications of significant constitutional handicaps or deficits were found and the evaluation of the family, school, and the environmental supports revealed all were doing their job in ways that might be reasonably expected. This then represents that case where explorative analytic therapy is most clearly indicated.

DIFFICULTY IN THE SUPPORTING ENVIRONMENT

Let us look at a case where problems in the supporting environment are the main determinates of the problem. This eight year old girl was referred for evaluation for therapy because of presumed difficulty in making friends, an "antisocial" attitude, violent extremes of sibling rivalry, underachievement in school and manipulative and oppositional behavior directed toward her parents at home. The parents' history, the school anecdotal reports, psychological testing, and data derived from several extensive interviews and play sessions with the child revealed no evidence of constitutional problems. While friendships and alliances had frequently changed, more careful evaluation revealed there was no real impairment in the capacity for companionship. To the extent that this young patient was able to relax her over-attention to the relationship with her parents, she was able to do well with friends and school work as well. Her difficulty in progressing smoothly along the developmental line from dependency to self-reliance and overall satisfying, age-adequate peer relationships seemed based on her great preoccupation over the attention she received from her parents. The mother spoke at length of her own childhood deprivations and of the difficulty in providing appropriate care to three small children, the child in question being the oldest. There had been some physical abuse of this child in response to her behavior upon the arrival of siblings and, after counseling, this later changed to a total "hands off" attitude in the manner of rearing the child.

The developmental delays in this situation seemed moderate and related clearly to inconsistencies and indecision in the caretaking environment. The patient was intensely alloplastic in her approach to problems and explorative work with her seemed light-years away. The parents were advised to continue in a modified family therapy that was directive and was aiding them toward a management of their child that showed promise of opening the developmental bottleneck.

CONSTITUTIONAL HANDICAP

An adolescent girl with Cerebral Palsy was seen for depression, learning problems, and social isolation. Neuropsychological evaluation confirmed that a number of specific learning disabilities were concomitants of the brain damage that also produced the hemiplegia at birth. Developmental delays were present to a moderate degree in the lines of dependency to mature object relations, egocentricity to companionship, and in play and work. The family and school were uniquely perceptive and supportive of the girl during her

childhood, early adolescence, and later adolescence. The constitutional deficits were real but improved some with medical, surgical, and special educational aid throughout elementary school, junior high school, and senior high school years. What remained were some inner hurts that could only be shared in a supportive way during the patient's childhood. During early adolescence, as the patient used small slights as an excuse to withdraw or over reached toward difficult goals that resulted in failure, one could be more directive and educational in approach. Finally, when in college and away from home, the patient was finally able, with a new therapist, to begin working on the inner conflicts leading to her depression. Finally a therapeutic model that utilized insight and could be called reconstructive was indicated and useful.

The foregoing examples are intended to show the uses of a developmental diagnostic evaluation as an aid and organizational guide for understanding and rational treatment planning. The developmental level of the child, the ability of the child to work in one or another type of therapy, the quality and nature of the supports that are or are not available to the child, and the resources and skills of the therapist and the community all must be understood and utilized in the best way possible in fielding a supportive or educative therapeutic plan. The Group for the Advancement of Psychiatry (1973) has published a report that discusses in excellent detail the factors involved in rational treatment planning and in the kind of decision making involved in beginning the supportive therapy discussed above.

Only in the first case, where symptoms were based on inner conflict and the patient was available for such work because of intact ego functions, could a psychoanalytic therapy apply. Although the latter two cases were not treated by an insight oriented approach with the child, psychoanalytic, developmental theories provided a model for understanding the behavior and symptoms of the child, as well as indicating where intervention was possible or would be effective.

HOME VISITS

Families vary in their ability to convey information about themselves. As a way of acquiring more insight, home visits have been espoused by many child therapists, and more recently strongly advocated by one school of family therapy. Schomer (1978) has commented upon the value of a home visit as a useful tool in understanding the family and establishing a working relationship. Erikson (1963) spoke about the value of having a meal with the family prior to initiating therapy with the child. The experienced observer will learn much indeed, often quickly, from the home visit. There may be questions raised as to how much is learned that would not surface during regular sessions, as well as the uses to which materials obtained can be put during the course of therapy. The family that is open to a home visit and able to reveal itself there is likely to give the information readily during office interviews. The closed family may reveal little during home visits (other than their insularity, if they even permit the visit) that can be used in any helpful way toward later therapeutic change. Kanner (1972) looked with undisguised disdain at the practice of taking a meal with the family prior to therapy or during a therapeutic situation, terming it "noodle soup psychiatry." Yet the polite and welcomed entry into the home—particularly the chaotic or violent home—may provide a great impetus to change in the family and a keen awareness by the therapist of the dimensions of the problem.

SCHOOL VISITS

Information from schools and communication with schools command a key role in the psychiatric assessment of most children in supportive psychotherapy. In spite of this, little detail about such exchanges is available in the child psychiatric literature. Berlin (1975) points out that psychoanalytic psychiatry can aid the schools in extending their cognitive approaches into areas involving the child's feelings, in recognizing how their surrogate parent role in development is increasing in a fluid, changing society, and in an enriched awareness of their facilitating work in the development of competence by the child. The role of the psychotherapist as consultant to the school will be touched upon later in this chapter. Here, however, we would like to draw attention to the uses of the school as a source of information for assessment of the child. Since the child spends many hours in the school, following a separation from the security of the home and parents, with new and varied peers, and is asked to perform difficult tasks that are novel and challenging, the school does represent a kind of stress test for the child. The child's behavior and function in school provide valuable information about adaptation and supportive or confirmatory (at times contradictory) information about progress in developmental lines or signs of delay that may not be found by a look at the home and family situation alone.

How best to obtain this information from the school? Concerns in the family about confidentiality and the child's pride or fears of embarrassment must be kept in mind as "releases" are obtained and the more meaningful permissions should be obtained prior to contact with the school. Oftimes the school report precedes the child's evaluation, usually delivered by a distressed parent fresh from a "teacher conference" or bearing a suspension notice. This may represent only the "tip of the iceberg" of the school's concern and it may be distorted by parental anxiety. In almost all cases it is important to tap the source of information the school possesses about the child.

Written reports from schools may be helpful. Cohen (1979), in a discussion of the evaluation of the school age child, includes a comprehensive form that may be used to obtain information from the schools. One should be aware of who produces the report and their professional training and relationship to the child in the school. Based on experience, school reports regarding behavior have often been found to be biased or distorted to some degree. This is not to discredit them, but to point out that these reports often pass quickly from observation to inference and bear more the mark of concern and alarm than of dispassionate professional psychological observation.

Telephone conversations with a person in school who has significant contact with the child is a more valid method of gaining information. Questions can be asked and areas explored that are often missing from reports. Furthermore, much can be learned about the dynamic interaction of the child with the adult environment of the school, including some sense of whatever evocative dimensions there may be to the child's operations in school.

A visit to the school is perhaps the most valuable method by which this part of the task of assessing the child may be approached. Younger children usually view a school visit as supportive interest rather than spying upon them. They can be observed in the classroom usually without obtrusiveness and an excellent sense thereby gained of function with peers and at tasks. The school/classroom visit, however, is most helpful in establishing a positive relationship between the therapist and the school. This may not only be useful, but necessary, in the supportive treatment that is to follow. By such a visit, we demonstrate both our interest and our intention to truly understand. The school is able to sense us as an ally rather than an adversary (as they often view the parents). Future supportive work with the child and family is thus bolstered by a cooperative and trusting attitude by the school.

SUPPORTIVE PSYCHOTHERAPY WITH THE CHILD

The descriptions of insight-oriented work with a child will apply in many respects to the child who is seen supportively. Indeed, many of the "rules" given regarding therapy with one type of child will pertain with another. Kestenbaum (1978), discussing the psychotherapy of the psychotic child, often sounds very much like Barker (1971) or Chess and Hassibi (1978) as they described therapy of a supportive or "eclectic" type.

Perhaps the first dictum has to do with creating an accepting, respectful, and noncritical atmosphere. This is not always easy. Children rarely come of their own accord. They have often acquired, in spite of young years, perjorative views of the function of the therapist as a "shrink." The very prospect of a therapeutic visit implies something is wrong, thus a criticism is inherent.

The therapist should not press directly toward the symptom or problem, but efforts are much better directed toward getting to know the child by way of learning about the child. Their activities, talk, and play should be savored as much as possible. Some children permit this and are open to enjoying, others are more careful or suspicious and require more patience from us.

In supportive work the therapist will most often be a real object rather than a transference object. Limits may have to be set regarding conduct during the session. The therapist will often need to be directing and involved with the child, even physically. This can be done without insinuation of ourselves into the child's space, provided we maintain a respectful stance and—in so far as possible—a cherishing attitude toward the child. The therapist is thus asked to walk a fine line between intervention and holding back, between watching from a distance and being close and between accepting the child and pointing out difficulties. To the extent that a trusting alliance can be formed with the child, there is greater hope that our interventions will be incorporated by the child in a useful and corrective way. The therapist may be acting as a caring teacher whose level of concern for the development and welfare of the child approaches that of a parent.

Play In Supportive Psychotherapy

As pointed out in the first section on analytic work with children, play may provide rich indications of the child's conflicts. If one must be chary in the interpretation of play in child analysis, the rule holds as much for supportive therapy. To some extent "play is the work of the child" and may have a problem solving and competence-developing function in the child. Experienced child psychiatrists (Allen, 1942) have written instructively about the uses of play in child therapy. Some therapists have very elaborately equipped playrooms to depict every imaginable symbolic or fantasy situation. Games have occupied many hours of therapeutic time, to a purpose that might well be questioned as serving defense more than change. A well selected, small, and varied supply of play materials will be useful, if not mandatory, for the passage of some sessions with nonverbal or constricted children. Perhaps a few crayons and ample paper represent the helpful minimum of play materials the supportive therapist should possess.

Work With Parents

Our section on insight-oriented therapy dealt with the parents as helpers in that kind of treatment. Parents play an even larger role in supportive therapy. There are situations where work with the child is well nigh impossible or nonproductive. In these situations advice to the parents may represent the major contribution the supportive therapist can make. In past years, and continuing in many child guidance centers, work with the parents was relegated to a second member of the team. The therapist and the case worker would then conference regularly regarding the progress of the child. The supposed advantage of this method of treatment, even though expensive and time consuming, was that each child had their own person with whom to work and a respectful and confidential alliance could be more readily formed. The disadvantage of this method of treatment, beyond that alluded to earlier, is that all members of the therapeutic team tend to see themselves as therapists for their particular individual, are reluctant to play a supportive role to other therapists, and often become competitive with other members of the therapeutic team. This can produce many breakdowns in the communication that is essential for this type of conjoint treatment. Supportive therapists, over the years, through a number of reality pressures, have become more comfortable and adept at integrating work

with the parents into their therapy with the child.

Barker (1971) has commented that it is important to accept the parents as concerned individuals who have often reluctantly and with much ambivalence brought a child to the therapist for consideration of a problem. They need an explanation of the child's problem that corresponds to the best understanding the therapist can muster about the child. And, as noted before, they often will be the major people with whom the therapist works in those many situations where the child is unavailable. They surely are entwined with the child and their personality configurations or psychopathology are intimately related to the child's behavior and difficulties. In most instances, however, we should still be able to approach them in a fact-giving, information-seeking, and objective directing manner. If their anxieties or complex personalities present major deterrants to the child's progress, that should be approached as diplomatically and directly as possible. If a straight forward, information-giving approach does not work, it may at times be necessary to move the parents into therapy for themselves. Child therapists can recount many instances wherein a child referral has led to a parent treatment.

Work With Schools

In closing, we would like to return to consider the opportunity of working with the school as a supportive and preventive model for intervention in the life of the child. Berlin (1975, 1979) has commented repeatedly about the salutory role the child therapist may play in the life of the school, and, in turn, in the life of the child. To the extent that schools can become better aware of the developmental hurdles of the child at different ages and can more appropriately tune their sensitivity to feelings and struggles of the child, rather than maintaining an exclusive focus on cognitive development or rote acquisition of knowledge, they will become a primary preventive instrument. In the majority of cases where this idealized goal will never be realized, the supportive therapist can play a useful role with the child and the school if the school can become aware of the struggles of the child and utilize its understanding, patience, teacher-pairing, peer-matching, and activities-selecting functions in ways that will work toward support and benefit of the child rather than creating hurdles and conflict for the child. In many instances, the therapist can do little more than recommend specific kinds of class placement or other concrete items. It is fortunate when the therapist has such a relationship with the school or classroom teacher that the therapist may direct attention to the negative reactions of the teacher or school personnel to certain behaviors of the child, reactions that may create major road blocks in the development and function of the child in the school. It is important to recognize that such information giving or "interpretation" can only be offered to school personnel in a useful way within the context of an ongoing, positive relationship between the school and the therapist-consultant.

Work with the school does provide the kind of true model of supportive work. The effects of this can be helpful to the child's development and should be approached in a positive and enthusiastic manner by the child therapist. To the extent that such distant interventions can be viewed as challenging and helpful we can approach them with a greater likelihood of success rather than having them resemble a futile gesture by a therapist who is unable to help the child in the usual one to one situation.

CONCLUSION

This chapter has reviewed psychoanalytic concepts briefly. It focused primarily on two types of analytically oriented psychotherapy with children: insight oriented therapy and supportive theory, using case illustrations and addressing practical issues involved in intervention.

REFERENCES

Allen, F. H. *Psychotherapy with children.* New York: Norton, 1942.

Barker, P. *Basic child psychiatry,* London: Crosby Lockwood Staples, 1971.

Berlin, I. N. Psychiatry and the school. In A. Freedman, H. Kaplan & B. Sadock (Eds.) *Comprehensive textbook of psychiatry*—II (Vol. 2) (2nd Ed.). Baltimore: Williams & Wilkins, 1975.

Berlin, I. N. Primary prevention. In J. Noshpitz (Ed.), *Basic handbook of child psychiatry* (Vol. IV). New York: Basic Books, Inc., 1979.

Bornstein, B. Clinical notes on child analysis. *Psychoanalytic study of the child* (Vol. I). New York: International Universities Press, 1945.

Bornstein, B. The analysis of a phobic child, some problems of theory and technique in child analysis. *Psychoanalytic study of the child* (Vol. III/IV). New York: International Universities Press, 1949.

Bornstein, B. On latency, *Psychoanalytic study of the child* (Vol. VI). New York: International Universities Press, 1951.

Brenner, C. *An elementary textbook of psychoanalysis.* New York: International Universities Press, 1955.

Chess, S. & Hassibi, M. *Principles and practice of child psychiatry.* New York: Plenum Press, 1978.

Cohen, R. L. Examination of the preschool and school-age child. In J. Noshpitz (Ed.) *Basic handbook of child psychiatry* (Vol. I). New York: Basic Books, Inc., 1979.

Erikson, E. H. *Childhood and society.* New York: Norton, 1963.

Freud, A. Indications for child analysis. *Psychoanalytic study of the child* (Vol. I). New York: International Universities Press, 1945.

Freud, A. *Normality and pathology in childhood, assessments of development.* New York: International Universities Press, 1965.

Goodman, J. D. & Sours, J. A. *The child mental status examination.* New York: Basic Books, Inc., 1967.

Greenson, R. E. *The technique and practice of psychoanalysis* (Vol. I). New York: International Universities Press, 1967.

Group for the Advancement of Psychiatry. *From diagnosis to treatment: an approach to treatment planning for the emotionally disturbed child.* New York: Report No. 87, Sept. 1973.

Kanner, L. *Child psychiatry* (4th Ed.). Springfield, Ill.: Thomas, 1972.

Kestenbaum, C. Childhood psychosis: psychotherapy. In B. Wolman, J. Egan, & A. Ross (Eds.) *Handbook of treatment of mental disorders of childhood and adolescence.* Englewood Cliffs, N.J.: Prentice-Hall, Inc., 1978.

Sarnoff, C. *Latency.* New York: Jason Aronson, Inc., 1976.

Scharfman, M. Psychoanalytic treatment. In B. Wolman, J. Egan, & A. Ross (Eds.) *Hand-*

book of treatment of mental disorders in child-hood and adolescence. Englewood Cliffs, N.J.: Prentice-Hall, Inc., 1978.

Schomer, J. Family therapy. In B. Wolman, J. Egan, & A. Ross (Eds.) *Handbook of treatment of mental disorders in childhood and adolescence.* Englewood Cliffs, N.J.: Prentice-Hall, Inc., 1978.

CHAPTER 14

Problem-Focused Family Therapy Principles and Practical Applications

STEPHEN A. COLE, M.D.

INTRODUCTION

This chapter will present a discussion of the principles of structural and problem-oriented family therapy. Special consideration will be given to clinical situations involving the problems of children. This approach to family therapy is action-oriented, pragmatic, and goal-directed and is particularly suitable for public clinic settings concerned with providing cost-effective services. The exclusion of long-term family therapy, insight-oriented approaches, and of behavior therapy reflects the author's therapeutic orientation.

We will define family therapy as any psychosocial therapeutic intervention in which the family is conceived of as the unit of change. In other words, therapy with an individual alone and conjointly with several members of the family are both considered family therapy if the therapist's goal is conceived of in family terms. In this model of family therapy, change is considered not in intrapsychic terms, but rather in terms of the behavior of family members toward one another and of the transactions between family members.

As a social movement within the mental health field, family therapy is growing rapidly. Given the wealth of material published on families and family therapy within the past few years, it would seem that this is a well-established and secure field within

clinical and academic settings. Yet barely 20 years have passed since the first articles appeared on the families of patients with schizophrenia. This work drew its conceptual strength from the models of cybernetics, general systems theory, and communications theory and from sociological constructs concerning the sick role and the dynamics of deviance in small groups (Wiener, 1961; Ashby, 1956; Ruesch and Bateson, 1951; Parsons, 1951; von Bertalanffy, 1951; Lemert, 1961; Goffman, 1959; Merton, 1968a).

The Palo Alto Group (Gregory Bateson, Don Jackson, and co-workers) studied the place of paradox in human relations, and elaborated therapeutic techniques to clarify the confused communication and to loosen the rigidity characteristic of schizophrenic families (Jackson, 1969a; 1969b). Several years later, Minuchin, Montalvo, and others at the Wiltwyck School applied these principles as they struggled to help families of juvenile delinquents (Minuchin, Montalvo, Guernery, Rosman and Schumet, 1967a). Employing a structural model of family role dysfunction, the Wiltwyck group developed directive techniques to alter the role performance of family members to establish a more smoothly functioning family system (Minuchin, 1974). Minuchin hoped to restore the leadership, cohesion, and sense of belonging these families appeared to lack.

Central to the thinking of these writers was the notion that family dynamics must contribute to the maintenance of symptomatic behavior. The identified patient's "illness" appeared to serve unintentionally as a tension-relieving mechanism, preserving the stability of the family system. Furthermore, family members frequently were unaware how their behavior and that of the identified patient maintained the family "homeostasis" as indicated (Jackson, 1957). Observing the here-and-now, redundant patterns of interaction between family members, and between them and the members of their informal support system outside the family, family therapists began formulating hypotheses linking family behavior patterns to symptom maintenance and began to develop therapeutic strategies and techniques to influence family members to change their behavior. In contrast to insight-oriented therapists, these family therapists chose not to provide patients with a "scientific" rationale, and instead framed explanations in terms of the family's own language and point of view (Haley, 1969).

The techniques to be described in this chapter follow the hypothesis that individuals undergo a persistent change in attitude, behavior, and understanding following an experience in which they, together with members of groups with which they identify and to which they belong, have altered their behavior patterns in a particular manner (GAP, 1970). The therapist joins the family group as its leader during the therapeutic encounter; directs the flow of interaction between family members; "reframes" their original problem; and guides them out of their old reality toward new rules, new myths, and a new family structure. Since the therapy is problem-focused and bound by the initial contract to a brief series of meetings (usually ten), there is little likelihood that families will become unduly dependent upon the therapist, as has been reported for other modalities of psychotherapy (Tennov, 1975). What follows in this chapter is a brief description of the theory and clinical applications of this approach to family therapy.

HOW FAMILIES COPE WITH STRESS

Stressful Life Events

Recent evidence indicates that the emergence of symptoms follows unsuccessful attempts by individuals and families to cope with stressful life events (Cassel, 1975; Holmes and Rahe, 1967; Rabkin and Struening, 1976). Hill has classified life stresses according to the extent to which they result in depletion or accretion of status or resources, or lead to demoralization (Hill, 1965). Hospitalization, going off to war, the accidental breaking of a limb, being laid off at work, and change of residence to a place far from a supportive social network are examples of temporary depletion. A young adult leaving home, impairment due to chronic illness, war injury, retirement, and death result in permanent depletion. Birth, adoption, college acceptance, job promotion, and the addition of in-laws through marriage are examples of accretion. Rituals exist in every culture to assist individuals and families through the stressful rites of passage resulting in depletion or accretion.

Demoralizing events occurring within the family are associated with socially devalued, deviant behavior of family members and include violence, infidelity, desertion, nonsupport, marital separation, divorce, imprisonment, substance and alcohol abuse, delinquency, illegitimacy, runaway, mental hospitalization, and suicide. There are no recognized rites of passage for these events. Families cope with them alone, along with the occasional support of family, friends, and neighbors. Demoralizing events occurring outside the family include burglary, assault, rape, fire, flood, and holocaust. The few social mechanisms protecting families from their effects—among them the court system, insurance policies, and emergency relief—can never fully repair the damage done or heal the wounds to the inflicted.

Family Development

A consideration of the normal, natural troubles to be faced by client families at their particular stage in the family life cycle is an important aspect of family assessment (Carter and McGoldrick, 1980; Duvall, 1971; Haley, 1973a).

State one: courtship. Mastery of the courtship stage requires that a young man or woman exercise initiative and be adept in the social skills necessary to meet and develop a relationship with a member of the opposite sex. He or she should succeed in school or employment, and have friends of the same sex. Those without the requisite skills to master this developmental milestone may never leave home. Historically, this is the first generation of women to go through this phase of the life cycle (Gluck, Danneter, and Milea, 1980).

Stage two: marriage. The decision to marry requires a formal declaration of loyalty and embeds the relationship of the young couple within the life of the community through the ritual of the marriage ceremony and feast. Since the marriage ceremony is often a union of families with quite different rules and customs, the early months or years of marriage may be marked by conflicts stemming from the "invisible loyalties" (Boszormenyi-Nagy and Spark, 1973) of the spouses to their respective family traditions.

Stage three: childbirth and dealing with the young. This stage is fraught with peril to the marriage. Recent studies show that two-thirds of divorces occur within the first ten years of marriage and two-thirds of these occur within the first five years (Reilly, 1976). With the birth of the first child, each spouse now becomes a parent. The addition of parental role responsibilities signals the final end of adolescence and the irreversible onset of adulthood. What may have been a comfortable dyadic relationship between two persons now becomes a triad. One parent may now enter into a coalition with an attentive and loving infant against a busy and inattentive spouse.

With the birth of the first child, the grandparents become involved in the young family, as they assert their rights of access to their grandchildren. During the preschool years, parents may disagree with one another and with the grandparents over the proper way to bring up the children. When some children develop recur-

rent symptoms of colic or asthma, one parent, usually the one at home, may become more involved in the care of the child during the child's periods of acute distress. During this stage, some children develop temper tantrums that their parents seem unable to control. The early years of child-rearing are quite costly to parents, who must cope with energy depletion and little privacy.

When the eldest child is sent to school for the first time, this product of the parents' efforts to teach their child about the world will be exposed to the critical eye of the wider community. If a marital conflict resulting in the formation of a stable coalition between the child and one of the parents has preceded the child's departure for school, one might expect the emergence of symptomatic behavior in either the child or the parent. For instance, the child may experience a flare-up of a preexisting asthmatic condition or develop a school phobia in response to the mother's sense of loss. Some young couples' relationships are marked by overt or covert conflict over rules of discipline and their enforcement. When parents fail to form a strong and united executive, their children may develop conduct disturbances, as they test their parents' limits of tolerance both at home and at school.

Stage four: the middle marriage years. By this time, all the children are in school. The marital couple now may reassess whether the rewards of married and family life are worth the cost of their respective efforts to maintain the life of the family. A wife may become dissatisfied with a husband unavailable to her through his overinvolvement in work, overindulgence in alcohol, or overattention to television programs. She may seek moral support from her extended family and friends, increase her involvement in community activities, may return to school, find a job, or join the local church. She may also become depressed, enter psychotherapy or resort to pills and/or alcohol. Families at this stage usually come for treatment when one of the *children* becomes symptomatic through psychosomatic illness, delinquent behavior, trouble at school, or drug abuse. The situation reaches crisis proportions when adolescents defy their parents' rules and thereby threaten the family's social order.

Stage five: weaning parents from children. This stage, when the American family becomes a "launching center" (Arensberg, 1962), demands that parents release their children into the worlds of work, college education, military service, and/or marriage, with appropriate financial assistance and observance of the rituals associated with these rites of passage. While preparing for their own lives in the "empty nest," parents must also provide a supportive home base for their children. Difficulties arise when parents cannot let go, and in subtle or overt ways undermine their children's efforts to leave home. This problem is exacerbated when children do not possess the skills needed to succeed at college, in an occupation, or in acquiring a mate.

If the parents' marriage was unsatisfactory to begin with, the empty nest becomes a cold place indeed. To a woman whose identity has predominantly been her role as mother, the arrival of a grandchild may save her from the predicament of having to find other absorbing interests and activities that enhance her self-esteem. Some women welcome the arrival of the empty nest as an opportunity to enrich their life experiences through the establishment of a career outside the home.

When the family is not successful in launching a child, and the child subsequently develops an acute, remitting form os schizophrenia, one of the goals of the family therapist should be to help the parents establish the kind of home environment from which the young person can be launched, while conveying the expectation that the child could live a relatively normal life. However, if the child's schizophrenia is of a severe and chronic nature, the therapist should explain the medical aspects of the disorder to the parents, giving a diagnosis, prognosis, and probable course of treatment. When the child and parents fully understand the extent of their child's disability, they may set realistic expectations, and avoid the vicious cycle of intensifying demoralization when their child fails repeatedly to complete an education, find a job and mate, and leave home.

Stage six: retirement and old age. If the par-

ents have married early and have entered the empty nest stage while still in their forties, there may be a period of several years during which they have the opportunity to rebuild a marriage relationship set aside during the years of child-rearing. Although the incidence of divorce during this stage in the family life cycle is relatively low, long-lasting resentments and unfulfilled expectations regarding the marriage will now become exaggerated, especially if the parents are no longer involved with their children. Divorce at this stage may present less of a problem to the man than the woman, since it appears to be the social custom for men to marry down in age and social class. People in their late forties and early fifties may choose to remain in an unsatisfactory marriage rather than face the prospect of living the rest of their lives alone. Conversely, once divorced, individuals (particularly women) may actually choose to remain unmarried.

The late fifties and early sixties often mark the emergence of the first symptoms of chronic physical illness, as the aging process begins to impose real limitations on the physical and emotional resources of the couple. Retirement adds to the progressive process of role depletion and withdrawal from the world of parenting and work. Accompaniments of this process are a reduction in earning power and social isolation through curtailment of social activities and separation from friends and family through relocation and death. Depression in one or both partners may result from this process of role depletion and social isolation.

Specific Coping Mechanisms and Social Support

A family's adjustment to life stress depends upon its pooled resources of energy, skill, and information, and upon whether family members expect to succeed or to fail at meeting challenges. A crisis may result when family members fail to control the threatening environment by adjusting their coping strategies to the new set of demands (Janis, 1974; Langsley and Kaplan, 1968; Mechanic, 1974; Parad and Caplan, 1965; White, 1974).

In one study of normal adults by Green and co-workers, a cluster analysis suggested that individuals resort to seven different coping styles: (1) talking with friends and relatives; (2) becoming more involved in work-related activities; (3) doing something pleasurable; (4) partaking in religious activities; (5) getting away from it all; (6) resorting to smoking, drugs, and/or alcohol; and (7) seeing a health professional (Green, Mellinger, Figa-Talemanca, Kalmer, and Bertera, 1978).

The literature on coping and adaptation suggests that one of the most important factors contributing to the successful mastery of a difficult situation is the "social support" perceived by and available to individuals and families (Cobb, 1976). Whether people will cope successfully (and asymptomatically) or resort to strategies accompanied by the emergence of symptoms depends on a number of factors, including their biological predisposition and whether they perceive the event as stressful (Weiner, 1977) and themselves as part of a network of mutual obligation, care, and concern, and can call on family and friends for information, advice, and moral support.

Families unable to cope with difficulties may seek advice from extended kin and from friends, neighbors, and various nonprofessionals whose expertise rests with having experienced or known someone with a similar problem (Sussman and Burchinal, 1971). Families involved in voluntary community activities beyond employment and attending school will often have more information for problem-solving purposes than families who are not "joiners" and are distrustful of outside advice.

If family members can provide one another with adequate social support, they may prevent the outbreak or exacerbation of illness. Otherwise, as some investigators have speculated, a shared sense of hopelessness and helplessness may trigger, in constitutionally predisposed individuals, either disordered and deviant behavior or violent alterations in the sympathetic and parasympathetic nervous systems, resulting in the physiological dysfunction of vulnerable organ systems (Engel, 1960). Once a family member behaves in a deviant manner or develops a symptom that is noticed by others and so labeled, demoralized relatives may seize the opportunity to experience satisfaction and a boost to a failing sense of self-esteem by providing care for the sick member (Sampson, Messinger and Towne, 1962; Anthony, 1970; Livsey, 1972). For instance, the gratitude an asthmatic child bestows upon devoted parents may encourage their becoming more intensely involved in the caring process, and the attention given the child may induce him or her to remain short of breath, out of school, and away from playmates.

Through this process, symptom development serves the interests of both the sick and the care-providers. Freud wrote of the "secondary gain" neurotics achieved through extrinsic rewards and increased attention paid to them by significant others (Freud, 1916–1917). Many years later, Haley discussed how patients use symptoms knowingly or unknowingly to gain advantage over others, resort to the sick role, and disclaim responsibility for the behavior (Haley, 1963a). Kai Erikson has written that deviant members help ensure the cohesion of social systems by clarifying the limits of tolerable behavior and thereby reassuring nondeviant members that they belong to the group (Erikson, 1971). For instance, some children receive more attention from their parents and "get their way" more often through temper tantrums than by being nice and polite.

When the benefits of deviant behavior exceed the costs of punishment, a vicious cycle ensues, as a greater proportion of the family's resources is spent providing care, and less is available for carrying out essential family activities. This leads to an impairment of family functioning, increasing social isolation and a decline in coping performance (Strauss, 1975). Eventually, the family may fail even in its role as caretaker and resort in desperation to hospitalization for the management of acute episodes of the illness or behavior disorder.

Family disorganization under stress may be seen as an "initiating factor," leading to symptom expression in a member. Ineffective individual and family coping strategies may then sustain exacerbations of the physiological or behavioral abnormalities associated with the symptom pattern.

THE "SYSTEMS" MODEL AND FAMILY GROUP DYNAMICS

Let us now consider in some detail the "systems model" of how families cope with the environment. One cannot fully appreciate problem-focused family therapy without some acquaintance with these concepts (Gray, Duhl, and Rizzo, 1969; Haskell, 1972; Iberall, 1972; Odom, 1971; von Bertalanffy, 1968).

Consider the family as a system of mutually interacting units (in this case family members), where a change in any one will result in a change in every other member of the family system (Miller, 1965). Unlike physical systems that may be experimentally "closed" to the environment, the family is an "open system" with a *boundary* to the environment which is "semipermeable," permitting the entry and exit of information, energy, and matter in various states of organization. The laws of thermodynamics predict the conservation of matter and energy. They also predict the tendency of every physical system to move irreversibly toward a state of greater disorder (increasing "entropy"). Living systems, however, constantly struggle against the entropy principle, and do so by "ingesting" matter and energy in a state of higher order than that which is eliminated. Schroedinger once said that living systems "eat information" in order to survive (Schroedinger, 1944). It is through the intake, processing, and rearrangement of matter, energy, and information that family members perform the work that creates and preserves the stability of the family unit.

To survive, living systems must also achieve a "steady state" in relationship to the environment. This steady state is a state of relative equilibrium, steady at an instant of time, but responsive to changes in the external environment. Pursuing this notion further, we can speak of the "equilibrium" of the family interior, as family members interact with one another in predictable, patterned sequences of behavior that have developed over time, perhaps years and generations, and which have served to ensure the survival of the family unit (Arensberg, 1972; Chapple, 1970; Collins and Collins, 1973). These sequences of behavior can be studied and mapped out, and the family's rules of interaction can be determined inductively.

The major purpose of living systems is their own survival. Survival is possible only within certain limits. Just as a thermostat functions to maintain the temperature of physical systems within allowable limits, so do "governors" exist to preserve the "homeostasis" of family systems by maintaining the adherence of family members to implicit and explicit rules of behavior (Jackson, 1957). For instance, families vary in their tolerance of loud and vigorous activity. To keep behavior within bounds, someone (say a rival sibling) must: (1) notice that the "rules" have been violated; (2) transmit the information to the family executives (parents); (3) decide upon the proper corrective measures; and (4) execute these measures.

The degree to which family homeostasis is maintained will depend upon: (1) the permeability of the boundary to the environment—it will be more difficult to maintain adherence to rigid rules when the boundary is highly permeable and less difficult when the permeability is low; (2) the range of deviation from prescribed rules—the lower the family's tolerance of deviant behavior, the greater the amount of work that family will exert to maintain equilibrium; and (3) the "tightness" of communication linkages between family members—the tighter the linkages, the more rapidly are deviations noticed, reported, and corrected (Hoffman, 1975).

Let us look more closely at these corrective processes. Just as a beehive would collapse into chaos without a queen bee, most human societies appear to require the presence of a "chieftain" who makes the laws and gives the orders that delegate to others the authority to enforce the laws of the society (Chapple and Coon, 1942). Some human groups differ according to whether their laws or rules reflect a consensus or will of the majority, as in democratic societies, and in others the rules are created arbitrarily, as in authoritarian societies.

In small groups or families, authoritarian patterns occur when members communicate more frequently with a "central," initiating member than with one another. Here, the communication pattern resembles a "wheel," and the system is organized around the person at the center, who is seen as the expert and is responsible for directing the behavior of persons on the periphery (Bavelas, 1951; Shaw, 1964). Here, the central person is "fed" information and suggestions from the peripheral persons, makes decisions, and then gives orders to the peripheral members. This contrasts with a group in which no clearly central figure emerges, which, by definition, is more democratic and which

depends on group consensus for cohesive decision making (Bavelas, 1948).

One method of determining leadership patterns in small groups is to look for patterns of behavior sequence initiation and response among group members. In a two-person or dyadic system, one person provides or requests support, information, or an opinion. The other may respond by first acknlowedging the initiator and then following the initiator's lead, by accepting what was offered or suggested, or by providing what was requested (Bales, 1951). Here, we can say that the first person is in charge when the second responds as requested most of the time.

Three hypotheses emerge from this model of immediate relevance to family therapy (Figure 1):

Figure 1
Range of Family Process and Structure

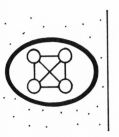 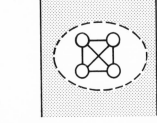 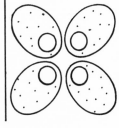

	Consensus-Sensitive	Environment-sensitive	Interpersonal distance sensitive
Reiss:	Consensus-Sensitive	Environment-sensitive	Interpersonal distance sensitive
Bowen:	Fusion, undifferentiated ego mass	Differentiation	Emotional Cut-Off
Minuchin:	Enmeshment		Disengagement
Kantor and Lehr:	Closed	Open	Random
Epstein:	Rigid	Flexible	Chaotic
Wynne and Singer:	Pseudomutuality, Rubberm Fence.		
Lidz:	Schism & Skew		
Olson et al.	Rigidly Enmeshed		Chaotically Disengaged
Leff:	Overinvolvement, Critical Comments		
KIND OF FAMILY	Families of schizophrenics Families with psychosomatic illness	No serious pathology	Families of delinquents
CLINICAL MANIFESTATIONS	Fear, suspicion, confusion Environment unpredictable. Brittle family equilibrium. Crisis from trivial events. Low level of autonomy.	Experienced mastery over environment: predictable. Self-sufficiency	Competition, impulsiveness, loneliness. Absence of rules and responsibility. Crises unnoticed
THERAPEUTIC APPROACH	Separate fused members. Break pathological coalitions. Strengthen Subsystems. Mobilize network support and teach family to cope competently. Encourage age-appropriate involvement outside the family.		Recruit strong executive from within family to impose rules. Encourage teamwork and supportive involvement. Encourage age-appropriate role functioning.

(1) We would assume that families with little tolerance for deviance; tight communication linkages; a high frequency of interaction with family members; relatively "closed" boundaries; and a high degree of centralized communication and decision making would be very sensitive to small deviations in family members; would exaggerate the importance of mild symptoms; would discourage autonomy for individuals, and be relatively unresponsive to therapeutic intervention (Epstein, Bishop and Levin, 1978; Kantor and Lehr, 1975; Lidz, et al., 1957; Minuchin, Baker, Rosman, Liebman, Milman and Todd, 1975; Olson, Sprenkle and Russell, 1979; Reiss, 1971; Vaughn and Leff, 1976; Wynne, et al., 1958). This has been called the "Enmeshed Family" and has been found frequently when the identified patient has a schizophrenic or psychosomatic disorder that is out of control.

(2) Families where everyone is going his or her "own thing"; with loose interpersonal linkages; little awareness of what others are feeling or doing; few discernible rules or patterns of enforcing them, and with completely permeable boundaries, would be insensitive to symptomatic change in family members until a crisis occurred. This has been called the "Disengaged Family," and occurs more often when the identified patient is a delinquent (Minuchin, et al., 1967b).

(3) "Normal" families then would not be overly sensitive to deviation, having close but not tight communication linkages, with boundaries relatively open to external input and with a definite but nonauthoritarian leadership pattern, encouraging both autonomy and participation in family decision making and enforcement. This family would cope effectively with symptomatic members, and would welcome appropriate assistance from sources outside the family (Westley and Epstein, 1969a).

The model suggests the following therapeutic strategy: (1) For enmeshed families, one would attempt to increase distance and decrease communication frequency between family members, open up closed boundaries to the outside world, and decentralize overly authoritarian family power structures. (2) For disengaged families, one would try to encourage a higher frequency of communication between family members, impose stricter rules for proper behavior and create a stronger sense of shared identity and a tighter and more efficient organization.

In order to apply this model to clinical situations, we need a more complete understanding of how the family does its work. We need to know more about the kinds of tasks family members are expected to perform and about how family members interact when carrying them out.

A role may be defined as a set of normative expectations associated with a particular position or status in the social structure (of the family) (Merton, 1968b). For instance, the roles of parents in an intact family may consist of wage-earning, housekeeping, teaching the young, nurturing, sexual relations, problem-solving or "therapy" (for one another and the children), recreation, and maintaining ties with extended kin (Nye, 1976). Proper assessment of family functioning would then involve determining whether these roles are being carried out adequately by family members, and if there is some defect, whether this is due to inadequate assignment, coordination, or individual performance of family roles.

Clinical evidence and some research findings suggest that children are healthier when their parents are in agreement rather than conflict over the carrying out of role responsibilities, and when this agreement is arrived at through consensus rather than arbitrary decision (Pratt, 1976; Westley and Epstein, 1969b). Difficulties might arise when role expectations are not met by one or both parents, and the parents are in open or covert conflict.

If parents disagree and do not resolve the conflict, one parent may form a *coalition* with one or more of the children against the other parent. Coalitions are an inevitable product of three-person group interactions: two persons of lesser status or strength frequently join together against the more powerful third member (Caplow, 1968). In formal organizations with a three-tiered hierarchy of manager-foreman-worker, three kinds of coalitions are possible:

(1) Manager-foreman versus worker. This is *conservative* because it preserves the social structure.

(2) Foreman-worker versus manager. This is *revolutionary* because between them, the foreman and worker can overpower and thwart the purposes of the manager and bring production to a standstill.

(3) Manager-worker versus foreman. This is an *improper* coalition, because it strips the foreman of power and thus makes his position untenable.

In normal families one's position in the hierarchy is usually determined by generation. In the nuclear family, parents are the recognized leaders. Parents have a greater opportunity for exerting successful leadership when their relationship as husband and wife (the "spouse subsystem") is harmonious. However, when one, e.g., the wife, decides that her rewards in the form of praise, attention, encouragement, and assistance from her husband do not recompense her for the work she is performing for the family, she may either confront her husband directly and try to bargain for a fairer *exchange*; resort to sabotage by forming coalitions with the children, who are usually more openly expressive of their appreciation; or withdraw and become demoralized and depressed (Osmond, 1978).

In some situations cross-generational alliances can become "frozen," resulting in the overly close tie of one parent to one or more children and the relative uninvolvement of the other parent (Haley, 1967). Frozen alliances place the child in a highly vulnerable position with severely restricted autonomy, having to side with one parent against the other on virtually every point of disagreement between them. This situation then resembles the three-tiered hierarchy of formal organizations, with an absent manager-father having to contend with the revolutionary coalition of foreman-mother-plus-children.

To summarize, effective family functioning takes place when the following "systems" properties are satisfied:

(1) System boundaries are strong enough to protect the family from a hostile environment and ensure its survival, but open enough to allow family members to learn how to cope with the outside world.

(2) Family roles are coordinated to ensure that family members perform the necessary tasks for maintaining the system.

(3) Leadership is effective and flexible, based on consensus, and is neither authoritarian nor chaotic.

(4) Linkages between family members are loose enough to permit individual growth and autonomy, but tight enough to prevent a sense of loneliness and alienation.

(5) Rules of proper behavior are neither overly strict (encouraging the emergence of family scapegoats and "identified patients") nor overly lax (where problems must grow to crisis proportions before they are recognized).

(6) Coalitions between family members are primarily fluid and within generations, rather than fixed and cross-generational.

(7) Family members have the capacity to form novel perceptions, understandings, and problem-solving strategies when their former coping patterns are inadequate to the task at hand. While the first six properties are concerned with the maintenance of family stability or *morphostasis*, the seventh concerns the family's capacity for change or *morphogenesis* (Hoffman, 1971; Maruyama, 1968; Wertheim, 1973).

FAMILY THERAPY: ITS CONTEXT

As has been explained, family therapists with a systems orientation are interested in how people in primary groups (persons meeting together face-to-face on an informal basis over an extended period of time) interact to maintain problematic situations. We may contrast this approach with the "biomedical" orientation, in which symptoms are seen as products of subcellular, cellular, and organ-level physiological deviations from a homeostatic norm, and with the "intrapsychic-developmental" orientation, in which symptoms are viewed primarily as stress-induced maladaptive behavior responses whose form is dictated by a developmentally arrested intrapsychic organization.

A therapist's theoretical orientation or "paradigm" (Kuhn, 1970) inevitably influences his or her goals and therapeutic techniques. Systems-oriented family therapists work to alter family interaction patterns; biomedical therapists seek to effect changes in body physiology; and intrapsychic-developmental therapists endeavor to help patients achieve new insights concerning their experience in the world. The family therapist conceives of goals in terms of new patterns of interactions enabling the family to solve problems more effectively; the biomedical therapist wishes to correct physiological imbalance; and the intrapsychic-developmental therapist seeks to secure lasting alterations in a person's cognitive functioning. The three approaches do not exclude one another. All are directed toward helping people improve their coping responses to stressful life events. Each operates at a different level of organization, whether somatic, psychic, or social. All are relevant to the provision of services meeting the total needs of patients or clients, and all must be considered in developing comprehensive case assessment and treatment plans.

A therapist, approaching a case with a comprehensive view of patient dysfunction and treatment needs, would consider four levels of functioning:

(1) *Biomedical.* If the child is acutely ill, provide immediate medical or psychiatric attention. If the child is chronically ill, see that a regime of medication, diet, and exercise has been prescribed.

(2) *Sociocultural.* See that the child and family are clothed, fed, and housed. Secure basic life supports. See that children are attending school and are receiving medical care. Secure community support systems to provide financial supports and day care. Encourage participation in self-help groups and voluntary activities.

(3) *Family and interpersonal.* Help the family members enhance their relationships and organizational structure. Offer family and network therapy, multiple-family therapy.

(4) *Personal.* Help family members achieve personal growth and differentiation. Offer individual and group therapy.

Several writers have attempted to reduce the "hodge-podge" of theory and technique in family therapy to a set of simple, understandable types (Zuk, 1976). For instance, Beels and Ferber divided family therapists into "conductors" and "reactors" (Beels and Ferber, 1969). Conductors are therapists who direct families according to a set routine or pattern of their own invention, while reactors use a more indirect approach, allowing themselves to experience the family "doing its own thing," before attempting to clarify and alter underlying family dysfunction.

In 1970, the Group for the Advancement of Psychiatry categorized family therapists on a spectrum from *A* to *Z* (GAP, 1970) (see Figure 2). *A* therapists tend to follow the medical model, emphasizing etiology and diagnosis and believing that insight into problems precedes change. *Z* therapists are more interested in the behavior through which a particular problem is maintained, and believe that insight fol-

Figure 2

A versus Z Orientations in Family Therapy

	Intrapsychic	*Social Field*
1. Unit of analysis	Individual	Family or primary group
2. Theoretical perspective	Psychoanalysis	Social and behavioral sciences
3. Process of change	Insight (subjective experience) The past (history)	Change of behavior patterns
4. Time frame of evidence	Etiology: What *created* the problem? (cause-effect)	The present
5. Focus of investigation	Dynamics and diagnosis.	Identify repeating patterns of behavior that help *maintain* the problem.
6. Goal of investigation	Long-term, person-oriented	Strategy.
7. Style of therapy	Clarify problem, work through resistances.	Short-term, problem-oriented.
8. Role of therapist	The problem is in the patient. Important. May be crucial.	Therapist becomes part of the problem. Not crucial.
9. Place of feelings	A victim.	Part of the problem.
10. The child is ——	Similar approach to all problems.	Continual reevaluation.
11. Technique	Central	Peripheral.
12. Position of therapist	Growth, personality change.	Problem-solving.
13. End result		

lows a change in behavior. Whereas the *A* therapist focuses on history, the working through of feelings and fixed ideas and transference, the *Z* therapist emphasizes observable, recurrent patterns of behavior that seem to perpetuate or intensify maladaptive coping responses on the part of the family and the identified patient. While the *A* therapist reconstructs a linear, historical sequence through which the maladaptive behavior came about, in order to effect change in the individual personality, the *Z* therapist adopts therapeutic strategies merely to bring about either a resolution of the patient's presenting problem or a change in the current pattern of family relationships. The rationale and goals of the *Z* therapist described here would appear to be more applicable to clinical situations in which brief interventions are mounted toward the rapid resolution of presenting symptoms.

FAMILY THERAPY: ASSESSMENT

The family therapist's goals will be generated by assessment of family dysfunction. This assessment is based upon the gathering of information concerning family development, family structure ("systems properties"), the influence of culture and social class,* and the solutions family members have resorted to in coping with the presenting problem and with stressful life events.

The stages of family therapy include:

(1) gathering information from (a) reports of family members and (b) observations of family members' interactions in the session;

(2) joining;

(3) problem-setting;

(4) promoting interactions;

(5) setting a contract;

(6) planning strategy; and

(7) tactical implementation of the strategy.

There are certain principles that guide most experienced therapists. The therapist

*Due to the complexity of social class and cultural factors, this discussion is left to other writers.

should appear confident and expert in his craft (Frank, 1963), conveying a spirit of warmth, genuine interest in and empathy for the clients' problems (Matarazzo, 1971; Rogers, 1970). He should be in charge of the interview, and should proceed according to his own accustomed routine for helping the family determine what problems can be worked on in the therapy. Before the family leaves the first session (or at least by the third session for beginning therapists), the therapist and family should arrive at a contract in which the process of therapy is clarified, the problems are agreed upon, and a specified number of sessions is set aside for the work of solving them (Epstein and Bishop, 1979).

Gathering Information Prior to the First Session

Information gathering is an important part of any therapeutic process. It should begin with the first telephone call and continue until the terms of the contract have been completed. A great deal of data can be collected by telephone (Napier, 1976). While this may involve forming temporary coalitions with family "informants," it saves time, and enables the therapist to anticipate communication and behavior patterns and to formulate preliminary hypotheses which he or she can then test out in the first session.

(1) **Demographic data.** Find the names, birthdates, birthplaces, occupations, and education of every family member of the household and of important extended family members as far back as three generations. Determine the country of origin, ethnicity, religion, and whether family members originally lived in rural or urban areas.

(2) **Chief complaint.** Have the informant describe the reason for the consultation. It is very important to get a detailed description of the presenting problem and to determine exactly what the patient and family members have been doing to cope with it.

(3) **Characteristic coping patterns.** Find out what family members usually do to cope with everyday stressful life events. Typical questions might be:

"What do you usually do when you are under a lot of pressure? . . . How is that similar to or different from what your husband, wife, son or daughter does? . . . Has your family faced any particular difficulties in the past year or so? . . . Have there been any births, deaths, marriages, illnesses, divorces, relocations, changes in jobs?"

Ask how family roles are allocated, and whether family members are satisfied with the distribution. Find out what stressful life events have occurred within the past year or so in the family.

(4) **Use of social networks.** (Beels, 1978; Tolsdorf, 1976.) Ask the informant whether family members consult with anyone outside the household about their troubles. Find out who these people are; how frequently they are consulted; what kind of advice they give; and whether the family uses the advice (incidentally, this will also give a good indication of how the family will respond to family therapy).

(5) **Historical information.** Look for patterns of physical and mental illness as far back as three generations. Look for developmental difficulties in the identified patient and siblings. What was the family's response to delays in reaching milestones in physical and cognitive development? Was a minor delay the cause for expression of major concern and overinvolvement, or were major defects overlooked until pointed out by a teacher? Find out whether other members of the nuclear or extended family exhibited patterns of illness or disordered behavior similar to those of the identified patient. Try to assess the approximate contributions of biological, psychological, and social factors to the presenting problem.

Clinical Example A 34-year-old mother, Rose, was referred to the clinic by her son's pediatrician because she was depressed. Rose quit her job as a paramedic four months earlier because her seven-year-old son, Billy, was so often in *status asthmaticus* that she had to leave work to take care of him at home. Rose had held this job for two years—since Billy had entered kindergarten. Rose's mother, Beatrice, had died unexpectedly in her sleep eight months earlier. Grandma Beatrice had been living with the family for years and did much of the housework and caring for the children. In a telephone interview prior to the first session, Rose described her mother as controlling and critical of her, but indulgent with the children, especially Billy. Billy developed asthma two months after his grandmother's death. Rose's husband, George, was an accountant who worked long hours on the job, often bringing work home or spending his evenings watching television. George's mother, Mae, lived nearby, and called George several times a week. Rose described her husband as "overworked and tired" and his mother as "interfering." Rose's daughter, Debby, was apparently a typical 13-year-old, and recently had become more involved with friends and activities at school, and was often away from home.

Rose was recently spending her days doing housework, waiting for the school nurse to call requesting that she bring Billy home or to the community hospital emergency room. If Billy needed to be hospitalized, Dr. Brown, the pediatrician, would be called in. By now, Dr. Brown and Rose were old friends. Because of Billy's problem with breathing, Rose spent many sleepless nights sitting by his bedside. Becoming increasingly demoralized, Rose sought advice from her friend, Doris, who recommended counseling. Rose then consulted Dr. Brown, who suggested she try family therapy.

(6) **Family network genogram and social network diagram.** A family network genogram is a map based on information from family members and significant others in which the patient is located schematically among the important persons in his or her life (Guerin and Pendagast, 1976). The map usually includes the names, ages, relationships, relocations, occupations, and even the personality or interactional characteristics of all network members. A rather complete genogram can usually be constructed following a half-hour interview or telephone conversation. This information is often quite useful for planning strategy to help the family cope with the presenting problem. The following genogram can be constructed from the foregoing information.

Figure 3 NETWORK GENOGRAM

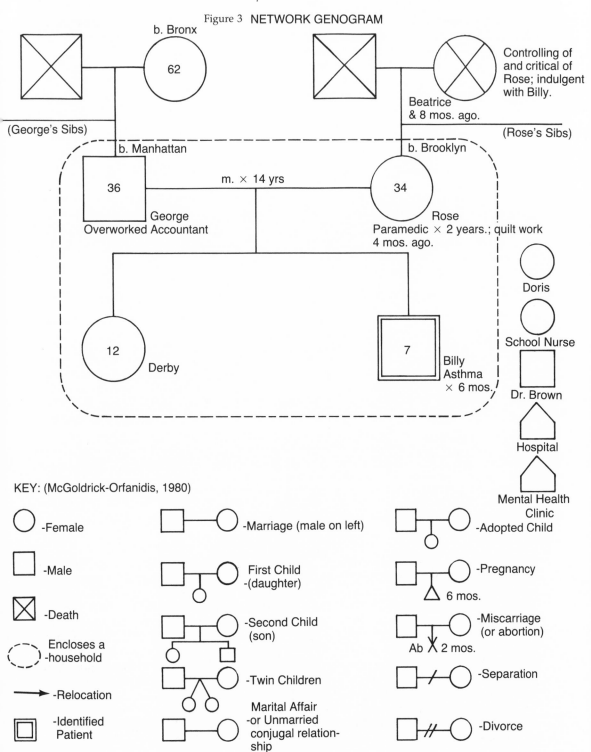

KEY: (McGoldrick-Orfanidis, 1980)

Network Diagram The degree of participation of the principal actors in the presenting problem can be further clarified by the use of a social network diagram re- cording the frequencies of interaction of persons appearing in the genogram (Capildeo, Court, and Rose, 1976).

Figure 4

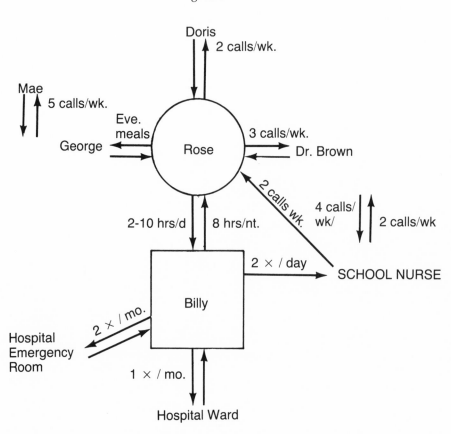

From the foregoing information, and with the aid of the network genogram and social network diagram, we can construct the following hypothesis. The untimely death of Grandma Beatrice deprived the home of someone to do the housework, give orders, and care for Billy. The emergence of the symptom presumably brought on by this stressful life event, now conveniently organized the household around Billy's asthma, and provided Billy with someone else to care for him. It forced Rose to remain at home, doing the housework. As Billy was not held responsible for his shortness of breath, a pediatrician was found to organize the management of Billy's treatment. The family had found a

way to replace Beatrice, but at a high cost: Billy's asthma was placing in jeopardy his performance at school, the development of peer relations, and Rose's new career in the health field. Clearly, the principal goal for the therapy would be to help the family find ways to do the things that Beatrice did for them without the pain, disability, and sacrifice that accompanied the psychosomatic illness.

Gathering Information in the First Family Session

The most important data in problem-focused family therapy concerns the interaction of family members during the therapeutic encounter.

(1) Observing patterns of communication. The therapist looks for persistent patterns of communication throughout the interview. He or she notices who signals whom, verbally and nonverbally, with what frequency and intensity, for how long and over what issues. The therapy can be viewed as a dance between family members in which the therapist first tries to learn their steps, dances them, and then endeavors to teach the family new steps (Beels and Ferber, 1969; Napier and Whittaker, 1978).

The therapist realizes that one cannot *not* communicate and that every message, whether verbal or nonverbal, conveys information. Each message, by giving or requesting a command or support, attempts to define the nature of the relationship between the speaker (sender) and those who are spoken to (receivers) (Watzlawick, Beavin and Jackson, 1967a). The person(s) receiving the message may accept the speaker's information as true, act upon the command and accept the support, and in so doing confirm the speaker. This kind of relationship is called *complementary*, where the one-up person initiates, the one-down responds, and both acknowledge the expertise of the person initiating the behavioral sequence.

However, the responder may choose to disagree with the speaker over the validity or relevance of the information, refuse to follow the command, or turn down the support. Here, the responder has answered with a disconfirmation. The responder may even supply new information and a different opinion about what should be done and urge the original initiator to accept a new approach. This kind of competitive relationship is called *symmetrical*, and may escalate into intense conflict unless one side either agrees to let the other prevail, withdraws from the field (leaving the matter unresolved), or the two work out a compromise.

While situations of complementarity are inherently more stable, clinical evidence indicates that when stability is preserved in families at the expense of leaving conflicts unresolved as in "pseudomutual" families (Wynne et al., 1958), the dissatis-fied responder may form a coalition with a third person, often a child. As we have seen, children often provide dissatisfied parent(s) with both a secure source of attention and a target for the indirect expression of resentment against the other parent. A child may side first with one and then with the other parent, depending upon the issue in question, or may be caught in a stable, freedom-restricting alliance with one parent against the other. When a "triangulated" child develops a symptom, parents often seem to avoid resolving their differences by becoming overinvolved in the caring process (Bowen, 1976; Minuchin et al., 1975).

Communication is "masked" when messages are qualified verbally or nonverbally by the sender in ways that render their meaning ambiguous (Epstein et al., 1978). For instance, a wife, instead of clearly asking her husband to help with the housework, may relate how the husband of a friend has recently begun doing the vacuuming, or tell him that she has read an article describing how modern couples share housecleaning chores. She might add to the ambiguity by disqualifying the statement, "You know, George, I really don't mind washing the dishes," with a hint of sarcasm or irony through an inflection of the voice, with a sigh, a grin, or a despairing look at the floor.

Masking leads to outright confusion when people speak in paradoxes. The conditions setting up a "pragmatic paradox" (Watzlawick, Beavin and Jackson, 1967b) are:

(1) a clearly complementary relationship;

(2) an order given to the subordinate that must be disobeyed to be obeyed;

(3) the subordinate is not permitted to leave the "frame," that is, is not allowed to tell his superior that the order is absurd (in other words, by making a *metacomment*). Everyday examples of paradoxical statements are,

"Don't do what I tell you to do. I'm only making suggestions."

"Be spontaneous."

"Just let your mind wander freely and tell me your free associations."

"Don't believe what I tell you."

In the classical double-bind situation, the "victim" is exposed to repeated paradoxical injunctions; is verbally threatened with punishment for disobedience while being nonverbally encouraged to disregard the original message; and is further prohibited from escaping from or commenting on the situation. This may lead to rage, panic, or inappropriate, vague or even wildly metaphorical responses (Bateson et al., 1956; Wilden, 1977).

(2) Observing patterns of interaction: the family program. The therapist looks for patterns of communication, for family rules that preserve family homeostasis and that may contribute to an exacerbation of the patient's symptomatic behavior (Satir, 1971). The therapist is interested in determining who communicates with whom, over what issues, for how long, with what intensity, and with what frequency. The therapist may ask direct questions of family members, but the most important information often comes from watching the family do its "dance." Paying close attention to what family members are doing, the therapist must stop listening to the content of what they are saying. Therapists trained to listen closely to content frequently encounter considerable difficulty making this adjustment. The task requires a gestalt reversal, an inversion of foreground and background, of figure and ground.

This approach highlights therapeutic work with what Scheflen calls the "behavioral program" of the family (Scheflen, 1968). The basic assumption is that all family interactions are "programmed," and that it is the task of the therapist to identify and then change the order of these programs. According to Scheflen, programs have the following qualities:

(1) Programs are composed of units of behavior that are hierarchically integrated and performed in steps.

(2) Programs are specific to subcultural units (e.g. ethnic, class, regional, and institutional).

(3) Programs are context-specific (e.g. to a given situation, task and social organization).

(4) Programs have variants and alternative units to meet specific contingencies.

(5) Programs have common meanings to their experienced performers.

(6) Programs prescribe the social organization and the division of labor, with an elaboration of roles within the primary group.

(7) Programs must be responsive to the values and purposes of the larger social context and cultural traditions within which the primary group is embedded.

(8) Programs provide for the integration of behavior and communication on three levels:

(a) *simple coordination*, not requiring consciousness for synchrony;

(b) *irregular corrective signals* dealing with ambiguity and contingencies, which pace the interaction, identify the categorical membership (ethnic, class, age, sex, status, occupation, skill, and so forth), and readiness for participation of the performer, coordinate the performers by monitoring deviance, inattention, and improper relationships, and modify the program to fit the demands of the external context;

(c) *metacommunications* (conscious comments about what is or has been said or done), which may have no apparent relationship to the program at hand, and may accompany the program and enhance its performance, or may accompany the program and distort, rationalize, or disguise it (metacommunications of this kind often change the program by confusing the participants, as in the double bind or by disconnecting their intentions from the apparent goals of the group).

(9) Programs are performed through multiple verbal and nonverbal channels.

Family therapists can readily apply this model to the assessment of family dysfunction. The therapist looks for:

(1) programs that are inappropriate to the demands of the situation;

(2) family members who assume inappropriate roles; and

(3) units and sequences of behavior that are clumsily performed.

The goal of the therapist will then be to help the family to change the relevance, coordination, and performance of its programs. In carrying out these tasks, the therapist should recognize the uniqueness of each family member and mobilize the motivation of each individual toward the therapeutic goal. The therapy may not succeed unless the proposed changes offer some promise of meeting the needs of each family member.

FAMILY THERAPY: TREATMENT

The Healer and the Sick Role

Healers exist in every society, and provide both a psychological benefit to the individual, that of restoration of morale, and a social function for the society, that of reintegration of the sick individual into the formal social structure (Cole, 1976; Totman, 1979). Persons who perceive themselves as sick are entitled to be relieved of their role responsibilities in job and family if they agree to cooperate with the physician in order to get well (Parsons, 1951). The physician's role is to name the illness, give the patient a prognosis, and prescribe the steps the patient must take to overcome the acute manifestations of the disease process. The physician restores morale to the individual; he rescues the individual from the fear, uncertainty, and hopelessness generated by a symptom pattern out of his control by giving a diagnosis, a prognosis, and a ritual through which the patient is expected to recover. The "cure," however, resides within the patient. It is the function of the therapist to elicit the behavioral responses from within the patient, to demonstrate to the patient that he has the resources to initiate the desired change (Zeig, 1978).

However, this contract may only succeed when the patients implicitly accept a one-down, inferior position, from which they will accept suggestions from the therapist (Haley, 1963b). When the patient agrees to let the physician define the nature of their relationship, the above description of the sick role and the role of the physician is fairly accurate. However, when patients or families do not follow this prescribed ritual, the effectiveness of the treatment is impaired, the process of recovery is prolonged, and both physician and patient may become dissatisfied with the treatment.

Patients and families may fail to follow prescribed regimens because:

(1) The professional language in which the ritual is framed is not understood or misunderstood by the patient or family.

(2) Families and patients are distrustful of advice coming from persons or agencies outside their family system (such persons or families may unintentionally oppose all professional advice) (Kantor and Lehr, 1975).

(3) The cost to the patient or family of changing their ways seems greater than the benefit gained from relief.

(4) A "self-fulfilling prophecy" mutually held by family members predicts the unsuccessful outcome of any form of intervention (individuals raised in an environment where frustration is more often encountered than satisfaction may be unwilling to try new approaches to problems).

Family therapists interested in developing brief therapy techniques for rapid interventions with families with problems of crisis proportions need to become experts in quickly overcoming these kinds of resistance, rather than interpreting and "working through" them. One important means many experienced family therapists use to begin the process of neutralizing family opposition to change is to "join" or enter, as a participant-observer, into the emotional and behavioral process of the family. This basic *joining* maneuver enhances the effectiveness of any form of brief psychotherapy. If the therapist can convince the family that he is "one of us" and demonstrate this through participation in their nonverbal "dance" and by using their characteristic patterns of speech, family members may be less inclined to regard him as an outsider whose suggestions are not to be trusted.

At the very least, a good therapist should offer his clients the possibility of an enhanced sense of self-esteem through the therapeutic encounter by demonstrating personal qualities of warmth, genuineness, and the capacity to achieve an empathic understanding of persons in distress. If the therapist can convey to family members the message that their encounter with him will be an "experience of significance" that enhances self-esteem, quite unlike the frustrating and discouraging attempts they have made to solve the presenting problem, he or she may convince the family that there is a "way out."

Attendance at the First Session

It is important to invite to the first session everyone concerned with the presenting problem. Usually, this should include at least everybody living in the household of the identified patient. Network therapists also invite important friends, extended kin, and involved professionals (Ruveni, 1975; Speck and Attneave, 1971).

The absence of an important member may indicate that:

(1) The family is not fully participating in the therapy and that at least one member is actively opposing the activity.

(2) The absent individual has "special" needs and a low expectation that they will be met in the therapy.

(3) There is dissension in the family. When a member does not show up, the therapist may:

(1) Define this as a problem and either encourage fuller participation of the absent member or (paradoxically) recommend continued absence of the member so that the therapy will not be hindered by his presence;

(2) Announce that the therapy will be restricted to the "family" that attends the sessions (implicitly realizing that the absent member inevitably will be affected by the family therapy, anyway);

(3) Maintain contact with the absent member by letter; or

(4) Agree to see whatever family members appear, and continue to make inquiries about those who are absent.

Conducting the First Session

The first meeting with the family is the most important. Here, you must arrive at a therapeutic contract and establish ground rules for the therapeutic process. If you succeed, the family will return for the next meeting. One routine that is easily taught to beginners consists of three stages:

(1) joining or socializing;

(2) defining the problem;

(3) establishing a contract (Epstein and Bishop, 1979; Haley, 1976a).

(1) Joining. The therapist wishes to achieve maximal recruitment of member motivation and energy toward the work, and to win the acceptance of every family member as their leader in the therapy (Minuchin, 1974). As a participant, the family therapist enters the ongoing dance and flow of the family's activities, and as an observer, the therapist looks for functional and dysfunctional patterns in the performance, coordination, and relevance of the family's attempts to solve the presenting problem.

Starting with the person appearing least involved in the session, and moving rapidly from one person to another, generation by generation, ask each one's name, age, occupation, interests, and hobbies. If you or people you know have similar occupations or interests, share this knowledge openly but discreetly. When joining with children, adapt your approach to fit each child's developmental Stage. You might pick up and cuddle and talk baby talk to an infant, bounce a toddler on your knee, play a game with a latency child, and talk to a teenager about the latest pop record or ballgame. Keep a few toys on hand, for example, a blackboard and chalk or paper and crayons, dolls, puppets, model cars, and building blocks. In some "closed" families, school-age children may be the primary connection with outsiders, and in such situations, the therapist may have to join the family through the children. Children are often more responsive to playful actions than to words, and usually like to be touched. Relate to them as not-too-distant relatives, with respect, humor, and fondness.

Find something you like about each member of the family and communicate this. Look for and subtly mimic their mannerisms of speech and gesture, their metaphors, grammar, idioms, and dialect. Participating in the family experience in this way may enable the therapist to "neutralize" built-in family resistance to outsiders. If the therapist can experience the world from the family's point of view, interventions can be framed in language that family members understand and then phased into ongoing behavioral sequences in a way that feels natural to the family. This approach resembles Lewin's explanation of how group leaders successfully alter attitudes of group members: by applying pressure on group members to change while simultaneously working to lessen member resistance (Lewin, 1948; 1965).

This discussion brings up an important caveat. Many therapists frequently have difficulty maintaining their objectivity once they become involved in the family process. This problem is most often encountered with families of schizophrenics, which seem to exert a kind of "suction" upon the therapist. When this happens, therapists may find themselves overcome with intense emotion, confused, and unable to retain control of the session. Here, the family has won the struggle for control and has virtually incorporated the therapist into a position or role in the family program. Therapists alert to this foreseen danger can either seek consultation from a colleague or supervisor or employ a cotherapist. Use of a cotherapist allows one member of the therapy team to be the participant and the other the observer. The cotherapist may remain in the room or watch the therapy from behind a one-way mirror. Cotherapy may create difficulties unless the nature of the relationship is quite clearly spelled out and the cotherapists meet regularly to plan their joint strategy and tactics (Roman and Meltzer, 1977).

(2) Defining the problem. The therapist once more speaks with each family member in turn, to come to a mutual understanding of the presenting problem (Haley, 1976). To get things going, start with the family member who has appeared most supportive of your efforts. You may tell this person:

Now, let's find out the main reason why you are all here today, what the problems are in the family that I can help you with so that we can together find a way to make things better for the family. I am interested in what each one of you thinks is the matter, and I'd like to start with you. Could you say what you think the main problems are in the family right now?

If one person refuses an opinion, go right on to the next, while suggesting that that person may later think of something to say. Be sure to convey your interest in each member's separate and unique view of the situation and summarize your understanding of each person's version of the family problem aloud as you go around. Move fairly rapidly from person to person, and immediately stop all diversions and arguments. There will be ample time later on for family *enactment* of their behavioral sequences. A diversity of opinions may suggest either the presence of a high level of overt conflict or that alternative solutions can be readily generated from within the family in the therapy process. Conversely, a consensus concerning the nature of the problem may indicate either a low level of overt conflict or family intolerance for alternative solutions (which bodes poorly for the therapy). The therapist should sum up the range of opinions expressed and add his own understanding, "reframed" to provide a family systems perspective.

(3) Establishing a contract. It is important that the therapist and family come to a mutual agreement, and then arrive at a contract concerning the nature of the problem, the goals to be worked toward, the times of the sessions, who should attend and the length of treatment. Problems should be framed concretely, with goals or expectations set in terms of objectively reportable alterations in behavioral sequences (Stanton and Todd, 1976; Woodward, Santa-Barbara, Levin and Epstein, 1976).

Promoting interactions. This phase of the therapy begins after you have negotiated a contract with the family—toward the end of the first session or in the second session. Your goal for this stage of the therapy is to direct the family to *enact* the family drama. You are looking for visual evidence to further clarify your assessment of the family problem. Until now, you have relied primarily on the reports of family members. To attain this new objective, you will have to withdraw from your central position in the therapy process.

To emphasize that the family is now center stage, you pull your chair back a little, toward the edge of the circle and avoid gazing directly at any family member. Using simple, concrete words, short phrases, long pauses, and an action-directing orientation (Guntern, 1976), you gently but firmly tell two or more family members to discuss how they attempted to cope with the presenting problem in the last acute episode. Tell family members who are not "acting" to carefully observe what takes place, since you will shortly ask them for their opinions.

As the family performs, becoming less self-conscious and gradually letting go of their public presentations of self, what takes place will begin to resemble what happens at home. The experienced family therapist now looks for recognizable pattern configurations that together form the dynamic family structure. One checklist of categories of behavior to observe includes (Epstein et al., 1978; Kantor and Lehr, 1975; Weakland, Fisch and Watzlawick, 1974):

(1) *Communication patterns.*

(a) Are they clear or masked? Do people say what they mean, or do they resort to inuendo, vague metaphors or paradox? Is there confirmation or disconfirmation between verbal and nonverbal modes of communication?

(b) Are they direct or indirect? Do family members speak directly to the person the message is intended for, or do they resort to gossip, complaining about one person to another?

(2) *Dyadic interaction patterns.*

(a) Frequency. Do certain family members speak more often with one particular person?

(b) Intensity. Does the relationship appear to involve a heavy investment of affect, marked by the expression of anger, sadness, laughter, joy, or fear?

(c) Duration. How long does the exchange last before others are included or a new transaction is begun with someone else?

(d) Dominance. Is one member clearly the initiator and the other the responder, or are the two in competition?

(e) Conflict. If the exchange involves a disagreement, is the conflict resolved without overt expression of emotion, does it escalate into an uproar with no resolution or the withdrawal of one from the field, or is it left unresolved?

(f) Pursuing-Distancing (Bowen, 1976). Does one member, dissatisfied and seeking attention, understanding or affection, approach or initiate a relationship with the other, who responds with disinterest, withholding, and withdrawal?

(3) *Coalitions and alliances.* Do you notice the formation of coalitions, where two or more family members are more closely involved with one another than with one or more "peripheral" persons? Are the coalitions overt or covert? Are they within generations or do they cross generational lines?

(4) *Tightness of linkages: behavior control.* What are the mechanisms by which family members recognize and correct deviant behavior? Are small deviations picked up and corrected at once, or do problems grow into crises before they are attended to? Is the family political structure authoritarian, democratic but with an acknowledged leader, laissez-faire, or chaotic? Does the family run a "tight ship" with little individual privacy or are members encouraged to express their own opinions and suggestions?

(5) *Role performance: skill and satisfaction.* Do family members competently perform the duties called for by their family roles, both instrumental and affective (Epstein et al., 1978; Parsons and Bales, 1955)? Are the roles appropriate to their respective positions (by age and status) in the family, as parents, grandparents, and children? To what extent do family members feel satisfied that the rewards they receive are just compensation for the efforts they are making in the family's behalf?

(6) *Problem-Solving* (Miller, Pribram, and Galanter, 1960). How successfully do family members complete several interrelated steps necessary for all problem-solving operations, namely:

(a) recognition of dissonance;

(b) communication of this to other members of the family;

(c) mobilization of information and resources;

(d) construction of alternative action solutions;

(e) choosing one course of action or plan;

(f) observing the extent to which the

plan is effective in solving the problem; and

(g) adjusting the plan, sticking with it, or trying out a new one.

(7) *Openness to environmental input: morphogenetic potential*. Do family members seek alternative plans or solutions only from within the family or a discreet and confined social network, or are they open to suggestions from outside their system? Is the family able to generate creative solutions spontaneously, or are their alternatives merely repetitions of previous attempts in different dress, that is, only "more of the same?" (Watzlawick, Weakland, and Fisch, 1974a).

Planning an Strategy

An experienced therapist observes family members who are discussing and enacting their presenting problem, and then concentrates on those particular behavioral configurations that appear to be more closely related to the expression of the symptom. We assume that the pattern of symptom expression is merely one manifestation of a rather complex cybernetic chain, regulated by numerous microevents generating positive and negative feedback. The therapist wishing to interrupt the chain searches for maneuvers to interrupt the cycle that replace the patterns of symptomatic behavior with more effective coping responses to the sources of stress presumed responsible for precipitating the symptom (Weakland et al., 1974).

Since a dysfunction in one category is often accompanied by dysfunctions in other categories of the family's behavioral program, the therapist may choose to work in several categories at once, or in one area that is both related to the expression of the symptom and is likely to have a favorable outcome early in the therapy. Many families referred for therapy have experienced considerable frustration and failure, expecting little of their new venture. The therapist tries to coach the family from one small, successful step in the right direction to the next, each step becoming gradually more difficult. In this manner, the therapist hopes to increase the family's level of satisfaction and mutual esteem and to raise their expectations.

The therapist designs strategies to overcome deficits in the various categories of family functioning. Here are several suggestions.

(1) **Role performance and satisfaction.** Help family members readjust the allocation of family roles so that tasks are age and status-appropriate and fairly distributed (Tharp and Otis, 1966). Help family members to determine whether their respective shares of family *benefits* (e.g., material goods, privacy, use of the car, and TV, free time, affection, attention, understanding, companionship, advice, help with projects, allowance, educational opportunities, sexual satisfaction, worldly success) are just recompense for the *cost* or work devoted to the family enterprise (e.g. housework and chores, earning a living, planning family activities, managing social relations with family and friends, teaching and disciplining the children, helping family members with problems). Members who are more powerful arrange for others to work excessively in exchange for a meager distribution of benefits, while contributing relatively little front-line effort themselves.

(2) **Coalitions and linkages.** Family members dissatisfied with their share of the cost-benefit exchange often enter cross-generational coalitions against the member with the greatest overt power. Overinvolvement between a parent and a symptomatic child can be teased apart in three stages: (1) bring the peripheral parent in closer to the child to lighten the burden of the overinvolved parent; (2) encourage a closer relationship between the parents and support increased autonomy for the child; and (3) encourage the child to become more involved with siblings and peer group.

During this three-stage process, you gradually encourage the parents to become less dependent on the health-care provider, and help the child to assume a greater share of responsibility for independent management of the illness. As we have seen, when the family is enmeshed, you try to encourage a greater tolerance of differences, greater autonomy, more privacy, and more involvement of the wife and children in activities outside the home. When the family is disengaged, you prescribe a higher frequency of interaction between family members, teaching them to give each other attention, understanding, and companionship—and then recruit one or more of them as leaders who must be taught how to set and enforce family rules.

(3) **Communications and dyadic interactions.** Encourage the use of clear and direct communication, and help the family to openly express and resolve conflicts (many of which originate in unfair role allocation). Teach family members how to stop recurrent, symmetrical escalations. Exaggerate differences and promote disagreement to bring about the open expression of previously "buried" conflict in "pseudomutual" and psychosomatic couples; sustain the conflict by preventing members from withdrawing from the conflict prematurely. Encourage "pursuers" to become involved in satisfying, independent activities, and to leave "distancers" alone. Promote more interruptions by silent members to democratize sessions characterized by speeches or monologues.

(4) **Problem-solving and morphogenesis.** Teach family members to work as a team and to adopt an empirical approach to problem-solving. Using the Socratic method, help family members arrive at novel understandings of their presenting problem, framing it as one event in a cybernetic cycle, rather than as an outcome of a linear chain of cause-and-effect. Encourage family members to propose alternative solutions that bring about a change in family rules and roles and not merely a substitution of actors. When members of the nuclear family fail to find creative solutions, suggest that they seek the advice of extended kin, friends, colleagues, or other members of their natural support system. When the family and its natural support system fail to generate an alternative to the symptomatic behavior pattern, then the therapist should be ready with a prescription for change. However, the family may not follow your suggestions: they may refuse to even try the task; they may try and repeatedly fail; or they may just forget to do it. When you are quite sure that the family is resisting change, you may either confront them and refuse to continue the therapy until they are ready to try out al-

ternative solutions, or you may resort to paradox. The use of paradoxical injunctions has become fashionable, and even beginning therapists are attempting to put families into therapeutic double-binds, so that continued disobedience will result in positive change. While intellectually appealing, paradox is heavy ammunition, and should be used cautiously and by experts. (Keep this caveat in mind when reading the sections on paradox.)

Positive and Paradoxical Reframing

The therapist endeavors to provide patients with opportunities to make their own changes (Erickson, 1978). Participants in a frustrating cycle of symptom expression from which there appears to be no escape are often unable to see beyond their frame of reference or to view their behavior at a more abstract, *meta*, level of conceptualization (Watzlawick, Weakland and Fisch, 1974b). The first step toward helping families to escape consists of redefining the nature of the problem.

A problem-focused family therapist is not interested in tracing the historical origins of the problem, but rather in what family members are doing and will do to sustain or exacerbate the problem. The therapist does not allow family members to persist in viewing themselves as passive, helpless victims, but rather focuses on how they actively arrange for other family members to treat them that way. The therapist shows how each family member is involved in perpetuating the current situation.

When family members reject positive redefinitions of the situation, the therapist may choose to present the new definition with a paradoxical twist (Palazzoli et al., 1977; Papp, 1977). For instance, you may praise a symptomatic child for sacrificing him or herself to preserve family stability and then caution the family against changing due to the difficulties (spelled out in detail) particular family members will experience should the change occur. Here, the therapist redefines symptom expression as a positive family coping response and encourages the family not to change. To the extent that family members value spontaneous action and oppose outside influence, reframing the problem in this manner may provide family members with the opportunity to make their own changes in the situation by disproving the therapist's definition and disobeying his orders.

Family Therapy as a Rite of Passage

The emergence of symptoms in family members often follows the occurrence of stressful life events that are a natural accompaniment of the family life cycle. The process of family therapy may then function as a process in which family members are guided through difficult life transitions. It is important for the therapist to be aware of and to orient the therapeutic strategy toward successful accomplishment of the developmental tasks faced by each family member.

Useful Tactics in Family Therapy

(1) Clarifying Communications. Therapists often invoke ground rules for how family members may speak during the family session (Sluzki, 1978). These rules are usually enforced only when they are broken. A basic set of rules might consist of: (1) each person should speak directly to the person for whom the message is intended—gossip should be discouraged; (2) each person should speak only for him or herself; (3) each person should make "I" statements concerning the expression of intentions and feelings—"you" statements should be discouraged (we call this "mind reading"); and (4) when family members appear not to have heard one another correctly, have them repeat back to the original speaker what was said, and then obtain the original speaker's agreement.

(2) Forming temporary coalitions with family members. Whenever the therapist interacts with a family member, he or she is either strengthening or weakening a bond with that member. While it is essential to avoid entangling alliances, intentional temporary side-taking with family members frequently facilitates the process of change (Minuchin, 1974; Sluzki, 1975; Zuk, 1967). Here, the therapist reinforces or disagrees with, confirms or disconfirms, accepts or

disqualifies a member's statements of information, interpretation, or opinion. In so doing, the therapist seeks to strengthen those sources of potential change that appear likely to foster the realization of strategic goals. For instance, a therapist may side with the weaker parent (without explaining to the family that this is what is happening), hoping to liberate the family from adherence to an overly rigid set of rules.

To illustrate this, we return to the situation of the overinvolved parent-child coalition with the peripheral parent. When we consider coalitions formed by the therapist, a three-stage strategy may be expanded into six stages: (1) Therapist sides with mother over her burden of assuming the role of caretaker; (2) Therapist sides with father over the importance of his potential contribution to managing the child's symptoms; (3) Therapist encourages the husband to seek advice from the wife, to assume specific duties in the caring process, and then report back to her for further corrective instructions; (4) While continuing to encourage close cooperation between husband and wife, the therapist sides with the child and helps the child to assume a greater responsibility for care of the illness; (5) Therapist encourages the child to spend more time with siblings and peers, and encourages the parents to spend an evening, then a weekend, alone without the child; and (6) Therapist tells the family they can now continue on their own, but leaves the door open should further problems arise.

(3) Utilizing the power of the small group. Small groups are an effective means for influencing their members to adopt new attitudes and behavior. Many family therapists seek to bring about family change utilizing techniques originally developed in experimental work with small groups. These changes are thought to occur in the following ways: (1) members persuade themselves to change by urging others to make the same changes (the "helper therapy principle") (Riessman, 1965); (2) group discussion followed by public commitment to a course of action is effective in achieving individual behavior change (Coch and French, 1948); and (3) the probability that group members will adopt problem-solving orientations and work together under stress depends upon the degree of their cognitive and emotional involvement in the issue; the extent of their perceived participation in the decision-making process (Cartwright and Zander, 1968; Kelley and Thibault, 1969); and the achievement of successful results (Sherif and Sherif, 1956).

Characteristically, the therapist will choose a task for the family to perform in the session. Usually, the purpose of the task is to solve a particular problem, often an unresolved conflict between two or more persons. The therapist, hoping to mobilize maximal member attention and involvement in the issue, tells the two persons most closely identified with the opposing points of view (often the parents) to discuss the matter, and arranges the seats in the room so that the parents are facing each other, and instructs everyone else to watch and form their own opinions about what will take place. After a few minutes, the therapist asks the others to give their opinions and observations. The therapist helps family members come to a consensus over the nature of the parents' problem and what should be done about it. The therapist then helps the family to design a homework task in which family members are instructed to make a small change in the pattern of conflict. It is especially important that everyone agree to the task. Sometimes consensus can be formalized by taking a voice vote.

(4) Escalating stress. Family members in conflict may act to reduce emotional tension or conflict through premature capitulation or withdrawal or by being diverted from the conflict by the behavior of a third person, often a symptomatic child. The therapist may intervene to prevent the operation of these homeostatic mechanisms (Minuchin and Barcai, 1969). For instance, a parent who usually withdraws will be encouraged to keep up the fight and hold out for greater gains. An overworked and underappreciated wife may be told that her husband has neglected her needs because she has been too meek. The therapist will encourage the wife "to drive a harder bargain," and suggest that she up the ante by threatening to do less work around the house unless he shows more appreciation in readily palpable ways. The therapist may tell the husband that his reward might be a livelier and less depressed wife who spends more of her time with him.

In family lunch sessions with anorectic children and adolescents, therapists instruct parents to try to make their child eat, pushing them beyond the point at which they would normally have given up. This "unbalances the system," and produces a highly dramatic event in which either the parents win or the child wins (Rosman, Minuchin and Liebman, 1975). The therapist intends to create a crisis by escalating the conflict situation to such emotional intensity that the family can no longer depend upon its normal rules to preserve order. At this point, new ways of handling the situation may occur to the family or may be proposed to the family by the therapist and given to the family as homework tasks.

(5) Giving directives. Setting tasks for the family, both within the therapy session and as homework, the therapist attempts to bring about change through the performance of new behavioral sequences. The therapist wishes to direct the active involvement of family members with one another by altering the frequency, quality, intensity, duration, and direction of their verbal and nonverbal patterns of communication. The therapist may choose to pose directives in one or more of three ways: direct, indirect and paradoxical.

(a) *Direct* (metonymy). The therapist prescribes specific behavior sequences that are to be followed by each family member. For instance, a distant father will be asked to help his 15-year-old son with his homework for at least two hours weekly. Overinvolved parents will be asked to take a "night off," hire a baby-sitter, and spend the evening together.

(b) *Indirect* (metaphor). The therapist discusses the case of a family with a similar problem and the changes they made that worked out, or tells a seemingly unrelated story that illustrates the same point. Milton Erickson tells illustrative stories while deliberately utilizing a trance-induction technique in which he tries to confuse his patients' sequential processing mechanisms. In one story, he tells how a girl with eneuresis cured herself, where the therapy merely provided her with the opportunity to learn "what she needed to know, what she already knew, but didn't yet know she knew, but learned on that day she had really known for a long time (Erickson, 1978)."

Paul Watzlawick tells this story:

Some hunters are trying to catch monkeys in the tropics. They place the monkey's favorite fruit inside a hollow gourd, and tie the gourd to the ground. The monkey comes, somehow discovers the fruit inside, and reaches in. Now, the opening of the gourd is wide enough for him to put his hand and arm in, but the moment he grabs the fruit he can no longer extricate the hand with the fruit through the narrow opening. In order to become free he would have to get go of the fruit which, in his greed, he cannot do. So he becomes his own prisoner. The hunters come and throw a net over him and then he has to let go, but it's too late (Wilder, 1978).

This form of "indirect suggestion" is a well-known hypnotic technique (Bandler and Grinder, 1975); the effectiveness has been attributed to its utilization of the learning capacity of the nondominant hemisphere of the brain (Watzlawick, 1978).

(c) *Paradoxical* (see caveat, page 00). The therapist prescribes the symptom or the system, and then depends upon the family to disobey (Frankl, 1960; Haley, 1976b; Hoffman, 1976; Palazzoli, et al., 1978; Raskin and Klein, 1976). The therapist can spice his interventions with paradox, from mild to heavy flavoring, depending upon the magnitude of the family's opposition to change and the therapist's comfort in using this technique.

(1) *Mild paradox.* Caution the family. Anticipate difficulty in carrying out tasks; if possible, anticipate all the possible ways the family might defeat successful completion of the homework. When giving the task prescription, question whether the family is ready to undertake it.

(2) *Moderate paradox.* Prescribe the symptom. Tell the family that the first step toward eliminating a symptom is being able to bring it on voluntarily or to make it worse (Haley, 1973; Hare-Mustin, 1975). Tell the family that you are interested in

getting all the information you can about the symptom, and that the patient should keep a careful diary recording everything he can remember when he is symptomatic. Or you can pair the symptom with an unpleasant task or chore. For example, you might tell a man with insomnia to take half an hour before his usual bedtime and write down all the thoughts he can remember that kept him awake the night before, and then take an extra half hour past his bedtime to write down all the thoughts that he anticipates will keep him awake again. After the symptom or problem seems to have been resolved, you may prescribe a relapse, suggesting that the family should practice the original symptom pattern occasionally for a short period of time, and then discuss how they were able to stop doing it.

(3) *Heavy paradox.* Prescribe the symptom. Congratulate the symptom-bearer for this sacrifice to preserve the family stability (whose quid pro quo you describe in some detail) and then suggest that the family not change because of certain potential dangers to particular family members, which you rather hesitantly describe. The reason you give for coming to this conclusion is that you doubt whether the particular family members are ready to cope with the dangers. The identical message may be mailed in letter form to each family member a few days later. This approach has been successfully utilized to keep absent members informed of events occurring in therapy sessions which they are congratulated for not attending (sometimes this may result in their attending the meetings).

Directives as Therapeutic Probes: Sources of Failure

Just as a scientist attempts to discover natural laws predicting changes in physical or biological systems by carefully altering certain conditions while keeping others constant, so a family therapist uses directives or tasks as experimental probes to uncover the laws of family systems (Minuchin, 1977). When the directive is successful and results in the predicted change, the therapist goes on to the next step. But when the directive fails, the therapist tries to discover the reason for the failure to plan a more successful next move (Pittman, 1977).

Four typical sources of failure include: (1) the therapist has not joined properly and is still regarded by the family as a stranger; (2) the therapist has made an incorrect assessment of the family problem, and is therefore working with the wrong strategy; (3) the therapist has not deployed his tactical maneuvers skillfully enough; and (4) the family's opposition to change is too great for the therapist to overcome.

If you are having trouble, the problem may be that you have been "sucked into" the family interior from whence you can no longer take an objective, problem-solving approach. When this happens, make a videotape of a session and study what you are doing wrong. Or go behind a one-way mirror and watch the family for awhile. Ask another family therapist for advice, a consultation, or supervision.

Simple Prescriptions for Typical Situations

(1) The symmetrical power struggle. Two parties disagree over the rules of their relationship; neither accepts the one-down position. Result: repeating symmetrical escalations or a stand-off. Prescription: assign days and situations in which one is clearly in charge, taking responsibility for initiating the disputed activity while the other is told to obey. A paradoxical twist may be added, by having the couple stage a typical argument for a few minutes and then hold a discussion about it. This may be followed by a task in which the two are instructed to say only complimentary things to one another.

(2) The psychosomatic child. In this typically enmeshed family, the child is triangulated between parents who have unresolved conflicts and become overinvolved in caring for the illness, overprotective of the child, and overdependent on the pediatrician (Liebman et al., 1977). Result: focus on the child's symptoms is accompanied by repeated exacerbations of the acute phase of the illness. Prescription: Increase the "social distance" between parents and children (Leff, 1976) by strengthening the parental "executive" coalition,

thereby encouraging the child to assume more responsibility for managing the illness and to make closer ties with siblings and peers. Encourage the parents to be less dependent on the pediatrician and to spend more intimate time with one another. Encourage the parents to join a self-help group composed of parents of children with the same illness, where they can trade advice, experiential knowledge, and emotional support.

(3) The schizophrenic adolescent. The approach is similar to that of the psychosomatic child with these exceptions: recognize the real limitations to the child's assuming greater responsibility for managing the illness. In a selected number of first-break schizophrenics, the therapist may encourage the parents to work closely in setting and enforcing household rules. If the parents remain united, the adolescent may not resort to psychosis to prevent their separation, and may respond to an orderly homelife by an age-appropriate move away from the nest (Haley and Lande, 1974). Long-term, multiple-family groups are helpful for assisting families of chronic schizophrenics with the social isolation and frustration accompanying the illness (Beels, 1975).

(4) School phobia. The disorder is reframed as the child's way to make the parent, usually the mother, feel less lonely so that the parent at work, usually the father, will not feel guilty. The child is told that persistence in this behavior will have dire consequences later on. Prescription: the therapist tells the mother that she must insist that her child go to school, and that both parents be willing to bodily carry their child to school and arrange with the teachers to prevent an escape home (Pittman, Langsley and De Young, 1968).

(5) Childhood and adolescent behavior disorders. Delinquency often occurs in "blended," remarried, or single-parent families, where members are disengaged from one another, rules are non-existent or arbitrarily enforced and family members often feel lonely and isolated. Prescription: encourage parents and step relations to openly discuss family rules. Give family members tasks to do together and encourage them to show one another attention, understanding, and companionship. Appoint a "strong man" or parental executive to set and enforce rules.

(6) Single parent family. The parent (usually the mother) is overwhelmed with duties that leave her little time for rest or recreation outside the home. Frequently one child, the eldest, assumes the role of "parental child," helping mother as her foreman, to keep the other children in line, performing various household chores, and becomes mother's little man or woman by listening to mother's troubles and offering advice. Prescription: mother is encouraged to arrange her life so that she can make and stay in touch with friends and relatives outside of her immediate family. She may be encouraged to attend a self-help group of other single parents, such as Parents Without Partners, to join a baby-sitting cooperative, and to place her preschool children in a daycare center. The liberated parental child may miss the frequent contact with mother, and will have to be encouraged to make age-appropriate peer and sibling relationships (Montalvo, 1969).

(7) Teenage substance abuse. The therapist defines drug abuse as a family problem, arranges for the family to manage the patient's detoxification at home, and works toward the expectation that the patient will become normal (Haley, 1978; Stanton and Todd, 1978). The therapist sides with the parents against the "problem young person" and helps the parents to strengthen their executive roles in the family. The remainder of the strategy is nearly identical to that of the psychosomatic child.

Stages in the Therapy Process

Since we are working within a brief therapy model, the changes we have been discussing should occur within 10 or 20 sessions (the first 10-session contract may be followed by another, if the family has shown a good response to the first contract). The sessions are usually held weekly in the early and middle phases of treatment and are held less often toward termination. Therapists concentrating on paradoxical symptom prescription may meet with the family on a once-a-month basis throughout the therapeutic encounter.

(1) Initial Stage. Set common goals for treatment. Focus on the presenting problem and do not get side-tracked. Keep the parents working together on the problem with the child, and do not allow the parents to discuss their marital difficulties. It may be necessary to meet separately with the parents to formulate a therapeutic strategy, and separately with the child (and sometimes with each family member alone) to secure cooperation with the therapeutic work. Forming too close an alliance with the child may undermine the parents' influence, while joining too closely with the parents may result in the refusal of the child to go along with the plan.

(2) Middle stage. As the child begins to get better, the parents may begin to struggle, or another person in the family may develop a symptom. During this crisis, the therapist should be readily available to the family and should continue to prevent the parents from escalating their conflict so that the problem can be confined to the child. The therapist should not be distracted by the symptoms of other family members unless they are directly related to the original problem.

(3) End stage. Sessions are spaced more widely apart. Issues related to the child's problem are dealt with, such as school performance, vocational placement, and peer relations. Once the presenting problem has been effectively resolved, through a dramatic decrease in the level of symptomatic behavior, the therapist announces that the family has completed its contract. The family is then told that they may return after awhile to work on other problems that may arise, or at this point a new contract may be agreed upon to work on matters such as the parents' marital relationship, or the newly emerging symptoms of a sibling.

Training in Family Therapy: Live Supervision

The kind of family therapy described here is best learned by practice. Trainees often interview their assigned families in front of a one-way mirror (Malcolm, 1978). The supervisor(s) and other trainees sit behind the mirror. The group behind the mirror listens, observes, and critically discusses the encounter while the beginning therapist attempts to carry out the strategy decided upon with the training group before the session. The questions they ask as they witness the proceedings include: Has the therapist joined properly? Have the major problems been discussed and a contract agreed upon? Does the therapist appear to be in charge of the meeting or has the family already made the therapist "one of them?"

Live supervision provides a dynamic learning arena where trainees are actively taught the technique of family therapy by the supervisor while the actual therapy unfolds. The supervisor wishes to demonstrate the proper use of the technique—and then to correct the trainee's first efforts. During live supervision, the trainee realizes that at any time during the session with the family the supervisor may telephone a suggestion, enter the room with a comment to anyone present, join the trainee as cotherapist for a brief period of time, or call the trainee out of the session for a consultation with the group behind the mirror.

At first, the trainee may be self-conscious and attentive to the last small detail of technique which can be viewed on videotape. As trainees become more comfortable, their moves become less self-conscious. Like many human endeavors, for instance athletics, once the technique is mastered the individual moves or plays may be executed more or less automatically (Herrigel, 1953). At this point, again as in sports, strategy becomes the primary object of interest.

While the therapist-in-training endeavors to help client families find their own unique solutions to their problems, the supervisor simultaneously tries to help the therapist develop and master his or her own therapeutic style (Montalvo, 1973).

Comparison of Problem-Focused Family Therapy with the Bowen Method.

Problem-focused family therapy differs from the other major systems-oriented family therapy approach, that of Murray Bowen, in several ways (Bowen, 1976; Carter and Orfanidis, 1976). (1) "Bowen-

ites" see the three generational family system as the unit of change, rather than that portion of the family group which "lives with" the presenting problem. (2) Pursuing the goal of family wide improvement in cognitive functioning, Bowen-oriented therapists help individual family members to "differentiate," rather than assisting the family group to solve problems more effectively. "Differentiation of self" may be achieved through an often lengthy process of "detriangulation" from highly charged, fused relationships in one's family of origin. Here the therapist serves as a coach, teaching patients how to discover and then cease their participation in problematic multigenerational relationship patterns which are hypothesized to recur in subsequent relationships with spouse and children. (3) Unlike problem-focused therapy, which includes the children and encourages family members to enact their drama in the therapy session, Bowen therapy frequently does not involve the children directly, and features a process where the therapist is always central. Family members, usually the marital couple, engage in dialogues with the therapist. While one spouse is speaking to the therapist, the other is told to listen and then tell the therapist his or her reaction to what the partner said.

In this way, the therapy is designed to help family members become less impulsively controlled by their emotional reactions to one another, and more cognitively aware of the nature and extent to which they have been controlled by their emotions. Patients are coached to plan strategies and tactics that will help liberate them from fusion, triangulation, pursuing distancers, and overfunctioning. Tasks consist of homework in which patients go back to important members of their families of origin, trying to unravel themselves from emotional entanglements.

Some of these concepts have been successfully applied for the crisis intervention and long-term treatment of families of chronic psychotics (Flinn and Brown, 1977). The primary goal is not resolution of specific problems but the long-term management of persons whose disordered behavior is presumably the result of a primarily biological malfunction. Here the two approaches might be profitably combined, using problem-focused techniques to help the family manage the psychotic member and Bowen techniques to help more competent siblings escape the "undifferentiated family ego mass."

Since the technique of change in the Bowen approach concerns individual growth and cannot be easily achieved in brief family treatment, this method of family therapy may be more suitable for long-term therapy in a private practice setting. We need evaluation studies with definitive results comparing the different methods of family therapy before we can be confident of this assertion.

Outcome Studies

A recent exhaustive review of outcome research in family therapy reported surprisingly high improvement rates (90 percent) for patients with psychosomatic illness and substance abuse from the Philadelphia Child Guidance Clinic where structural and strategic family therapy (the basis of the problem-focused approach) are practiced exclusively (Gurman and Kniskern, 1978). This same review also reported that the McMaster Group has found that action-oriented family therapy, in which the therapist stimulates interaction, gathers information and gives support, has been found more effective for achieving a good outcome early in treatment than insight-oriented family therapy, where the therapist clarifies motivation and labels unconscious motives. Mosher and Keith recently concluded that family therapy can be recommended for newly diagnosed schizophrenics (Mosher and Keith, 1979).

Gurman and Kniskern, in the review previously cited, further concluded that: (1) Brief family therapy is not inferior to long-term, open-ended family treatment; (2) "Family therapy appears to be at least as effective and possibly more effective than individual therapy for a wide variety of problems, both apparent 'individual' difficulties as well as more obvious family conflicts."; and (3) compared to pure control groups, family therapy was found superior in 18/31 comparisons, equal in 11/31, and inferior in only 2/31 studies.

CONCLUSION

While the outcome data do not yet fully justify the current surge of enthusiasm for brief and problem-focused structural and strategic family therapy, these techniques do appear to be particularly appropriate for brief interventions in clinic settings where the child is presented as the problem (Haley, 1973b). The therapy is directed towards changing the interactional processes which maintain the exacerbation of illness and behavior disturbances. The approach attempts to change the social forces affecting the patient in the here-and-now through a rapid mobilization of appropriate social supports from the family and the patient's natural support system (Beels, 1978). These family therapy techniques have been successfully taught to general practitioners (Epstein and Levin, 1973) and have been recently utilized for the formation of self-help groups of patients with chronic illness (Cole, 1979). The next several years may see a greater collaboration among family therapists of different outlooks and between family therapists and clinicians of biomedical and psychodynamic orientations, as all work together to securely establish a biopsychosocial orientation to health care.

BIBLIOGRAPHY

Anthony, E. J. The mutative impact of serious mental and physical illness in a parent on family life. In *The child in his family*, E. J. Anthony and C. Koupernick (Eds.) New York: Wiley, 1970.

Arensberg, C. M. The American family in the perspective of other cultures. In Winch, R. F. & Goodman, L. W. (Eds.) *Selected studies in marriage and the family*, New York: Henry Holt, 1962, (revised ed.).

Arensberg, C. M. Culture as behavior: structure and emergence. *Ann. Rev. Anthropol* (1972) 1:1–26.

Ashby, W. R. *An introduction to cybernetics.* London: Chapman and Hall, 1956.

Bales, R. F. *Interaction process analysis.* Cambridge, Mass.: Addison-Wesley, 1951.

Bandler, R. & Grinder, J. Accessing the nondominant hemisphere. In Bandler R. and Grinder J. (Eds.) *Patterns of the hypnotic techniques of Milton H. Erickson, M.D. Vol. 1.* Cupertino, Calif.: Meta Pubs., 1975.

Bateson, G., Jackson, D. D., Haley, J., & Weakland, J. Toward a theory of schizophrenia. *Behavioral Science* (1956) 1(4):251–264.

Bavelas, A. A. A mathematical model for group structures. *Applied Anthropology* 1948 VII(3):16–30.

Bavelas, A. A. Communication patterns in task-oriented groups. In Lerner D., & Lasswell H. D. (Eds.) *The policy sciences,* Stanford, Calif.: Stanford Univ. Press, 1951.

Beels, C. C. & Ferber, A. Family therapy: a view. *Family Process* (1969) 8:280–318.

Beels, C. C. Family and social management of schizophrenia. *Schizophrenia Bull.* (1975) 1(13):97–118.

Beels, C. C. Social networks, the family and the psychiatric patient: an introduction to the issue. *Schizophrenia Bull.* (1978) 4(4):512–521, 522 ff.

Boszormenyi-Nagy, I. & Spark, G. *Invisible loyalties.* New York: Harper & Row, 1973.

Bowen, M. ("Anonymous") Toward the differentiation of a self in one's own family. In Framo J (Ed.) *Family interaction.* New York: Springer, 1972.

Bowen, M. Theory in the practice of psychotherapy. In Guerin P. J. *Family therapy: theory and practice,* New York, Gardner Press, 1976.

Capildeo, R., Court, C., & Rose, F. C. Social network diagram. *British Medical J.* (1976) 1:143–144.

Caplow, T. *Two against one: Coalitions in the triad.* New York: Prentice-Hall, 1968.

Carter, E. & Orfanidis, M. M. Family therapy with one person and the family therapist's own family. In Guerin P. J. (Ed.) *Family therapy: Theory and practice.* New York: Gardner Press, 1976.

Carter, E. A. & McGoldrick, M. (Eds.) *The family life cycle: A framework for family therapy.* New York: Gardner Press, 1980.

Cartwright, D. & Zander, A. Motivational processes in groups: introduction. In Cartwright D. & Zander A. (Eds): *Group dynamics: Research and theory,* 3rd. ed., New York: Harper & Row, 1968.

Cassel J. Social science in epidemiology: psychosocial processes and stress. In Struening, E. L., Guttentag M. (Eds.) *Handbook of evaluation research I,* Beverly Hills: Sage Publishers, 1975.

Chapple, E. & Coon, C. S. Political institutions. In Chapple E, & Coon C. S. *Principles of anthropology,* New York: Henry Holt, 1942,

Chapple, E. D. *Culture and biological man.* New York: Holt, Rinehart & Winston, 1970.

Cobb, S. Social support as a moderator of life stress. *Psychosomatic Medicine* (1976) 38:300–314.

Coch, L. & French, J. R. P., Jr. Overcoming resistance to change. *Human Relations* (1948) 11:512–532.

Cole, S. Liminality and the sick role. *Man and Medicine* (1976) 2(1):41–53, 71–73.

Cole, S. Self-help groups for clinic patients with chronic illness. *Primary Care* (1979) 6(2):325–340.

Collins, O. & Collins, J. L. *Interaction and social structure.* The Hague: Mouton, 1973.

Duvall, E. M. *Family Development.* Philadelphia: Lippincott, 1971.

Engel, G. L. A unified concept of health and disease. *Perspec. Biol. Med.* (1960) pp. 459–485.

Epstein, N. B. & Levin, S. Training for family therapy within a faculty of medicine. *Canad. Psychiat. J.* (1973) 18(3):203–207.

Epstein, N. B., Bishop, D. S., & Levin, S. The McMaster Model of family functioning. *J. Marr. Fam. Counsel.* (1978) 4(4):19–31.

Epstein, N. B. & Bishop, D. S. Problem-centered systems therapy of the family. Unpublished manuscript. Providence, R.I., Brown University, Butler Hospital, 1979.

Erikson, K. T. The social construction of deviants. In E. Rubington & Weinberg, M. S. (Eds.): *The study of social problems: Five perspectives.* New York: Oxford Press, 1971,

Erickson, M. H. Personal communication. Dr. Erickson's private office, Phoenix, Ariz., April, 1978.

Flinn, S. K. & Brown, L. O. Opening moves in crisis intervention with families of chronic psychotics. In T. J. Buckley, J. J. McCarthy, E. Norman, & M. A. Quaranta, (Eds.) *New directions in family therapy.* Oceanside, N.Y.: Dabor Science Pubs, 1977, pp. 90–102.

Frank, J. *Persuasion and healing.* New York: Schocken, 1963, pp. 62, 72.

Frankl, V. Paradoxical intention: a logotherapeutic technique. *Am. J. Psychother.* (1960) 14:520–535.

Freud, S. The common neurotic state. Lecture XXIV of S. Freud *Introductory Lectures on Psycho-Analysis.* Transl., J. Strachey (Ed.). vol. XVI of *The Standard Edition.* London: Hogarth Press, 1916–17,

Bluck, N., Danneter, E., & Milee, K. Women in families. In E. A. Carter and M. McGoldrick (Eds.) *The family life cycle: A framework for family therapy.* New York: Gardner Press, 1980.

Goffman, E. The moral career of the mental

patient. *Psychiatry* (1959) 22:127ff.

Gray, W., Duhl, F. J., & Rizzo, N. D. (Eds.) *General systems theory and psychiatry*. Boston: Little Brown, 1969.

Green, L. W., Mellinger, G. D., Figa-Talamanca, I., Manheimer, D. I., Kalmer, H., & Bertera, R. Coping and self-care patterns of urban adults in response to symptoms of stress. Paper delivered at Annual Meeting of The American Psychiatric Association, May 10, 1978, Atlanta, Georgia.

Group for the Advancement of Psychiatry *The field of family therapy*. New York: Group for the Advancement of Psychiatry, 1970.

Guerin, P. H. & Pendagast, E. G. Evaluation of family system and genogram. In Guerin, P. J. (Ed.) *Family therapy: Theory and practice*, New York: Gardner Press, 1976,

Guntern, G. Personal communication. Externship seminar with Salvador Minuchin, Philadelphia Child Guidance, Fall, 1976.

Gurman, A. S. & Kniskern, D. P. Research on marital and family therapy: progress, perspective and prospect. In S. L. Garfield & A. E. Bergin (Eds.) *Handbook of Psychotherapy and Behavior Change*, 2nd ed. New York: Wiley, 1978,

Haley, J. *Strategies of Psychotherapy*. New York: Grune & Stratton, 1963.

Haley, J. Toward a theory of pathological systems. In C. Zuk (Ed.) *Family therapy and disturbed families*. Palo Alto: Science and Behavior Books, 1967, pp. 11–27.

Haley, J. An editor's farewell. *Family Process* (1969) 8(2):149–158.

Haley, J. The family life cycle. *Uncommon Therapy: The Psychiatric Techniques of Milton H. Erickson, M. D.* New York: Norton, 1973, pp. 41–64 (a).

Haley, J. Strategic therapy when the child is presented as the problem. *J. Amer. Acad. Child Psychiat.* (1973) 12(4):641–659 (b).

Haley, J. & Lande, G. *Coming Home From the Mental Hospital*. Training Videotape. Philadelphia, Pa., Phila. Child Guidance Clinic, 1974.

Haley, J. Conducting the first interview. Chapt. 1 In Haley, J.: *Problem-Solving Therapy*. Washington, D.C., Jossey Bass, 1976, pp. 9–47 (a).

Haley, J. Passage from *Young Eccentrics: The Therapy of Mad Young People*. Quoted in Stanton, M. D. and Todd, T. C., Structural family therapy with heroin addicts. In Kaufman E. & Kaufmann P. (Eds.) *The Family therapy of drug and alcohol abusers*, New York: Gardner Press, 1978.

Hare-Mustin, R. T. Treatment of temper tantrums by a paradoxical intervention. *Family Process* (1975) 14(4):481–485.

Haskell, E. *Full circle: The moral force of unified science*. Current Topics of Contemporary Thought, vol. 8. London: Gordon and Breach, 1972.

Herrigel, E. *Zen in the art of archery*. New York: Pantheon, 1953.

Hill, R. Some generic features of families under stress. In H. J. Parad, Ed. *Crisis intervention*, New York: Family Service Assn. of America, 1965,

Hoffman, L. Deviation-amplifying processes in natural groups. In Haley J. (Ed.) *Changing families: A family therapy reader*, New York: Grune and Stratton, 1971,

Hoffman, L. Enmeshment and the too prickly cross-joined system. *Family Process* (1975) 14:457–468.

Hoffman, L. Breaking the homeostatic cycle. In Guerin P.J. (Ed.) *Family therapy: Theory and practice*. New York: Gardner Press, 1976,

Holmes, T. H. & Rahe, R. The social readjustment rating scale. *J. Psychosomatic Res.* (1967) 11:213–218.

Iberall, A. S. *Toward a general science of viable systems*. New York: McGraw-Hill, 1972.

Jackson, D. D. The question of family homeostasis. Reprinted In Jackson D. D. (Ed.) *Communication, Family and Marriage*. Human Communication, vol. 1, Palo Alto: Science and Behavior Books, 1957,

Jackson, D. D. Ed. *Communication, family and marriage*. Palo Alto: Science and Behavior Books, 1969 (a).

Jackson, D. D., ed. *Therapy, communication and change*. Palo Alto: Science and Behavior Books, 1969 (b).

Janis, I. L. Vigilance and decision-making in personal crisis. In G. V. Coelho, D. A. Hamburg, and J. E. Adams, eds. *Coping and adaptation*. New York: Basic Books, 1974,

Kantor, D. & Lehr, W. Family types: structural arrangements. In Kantor D, Lehr W (Eds.) *Inside the family*, San Francisco: Jossey-Bass, 1975,

Kelley, H. H. & Thibault, J. W. Group problem solving. In B. Lindzey and E. Aronson, *Handbook of social psychology IV*, 2nd ed., Reading, Mass.: Addison-Wesley, 1969,

Kuhn, T. S. *The Structure of scientific revolutions*, 2nd ed., enlarged. International Encyclopedia of Unified Science 2(2). Chicago: University of Chicago Press, 1970.

Langsley, D. G. & Kaplan, D. M. *The treatment of families in crisis*, New York: Grune and Stratton, 1968.

Leff, J. Schizophrenia and sensitivity to the family environment. *Schizophrenia Bull.* (1976) 2(4):566–574.

Lemert, E. M. Paranoia and the dynamics of exclusion. *Sociometry* (1962) 25(1):2–20.

Lewin K. *Resolving Social Conflicts*, New York: Harper, 1948, p. 68.

Lewin, K. Group decision and social change. In *Basic Studies in Social psychology*, H. Proshansky & B. Seidenberg, eds. New York: Holt, Rinehart & Winston, 1965.

Lidz, T., Cornelison, A. R., Fleck, S., & Terry, D. The intrafamilial environment of schizophrenic patients. II. Marital schism and marital skew. *Amer. J. Psychiat.* (1957) 114:241–248.

Liebman, R., Minuchin, S., Baker, L., & Rosman, B. Chronic asthma: a new approach to treatment. In *Child psychiatry: Treatment and research*, M. F. McMillan and S. Henao, eds. New York: Brunner/Mazel, 1977,

Livsey, C. Physical illness and family dynamics. *Advances in Psychosomatic Medicine* (1972) 8:237–251.

Malcolm, J. A reporter at large: the one-way mirror. *The New Yorker*, May 15, 1978: 39–114.

Maruyama, M. The second cybernetics: deviation-amplifying mutual causal processes. In *Modern systems research for the behavioral scientist*, W. Buckley, ed. Chicago: Aldine, 1968,

Matarazzo, R. G. Research on the teaching and learning of psychotherapeutic skills. In A. Bergin and S. Garfield, (Eds.) *Handbook of psychotherapy and behavior change*, New York: Wiley, 1971,

McGoldrick-Orfanidis. Personal communication, 1980.

Mechanic, D. Social structure and personal adaptation. In G. Coelho, D. A. Hamburg, and J. E. Adams, Eds. *Coping and adaptation*, New York: Basic Books, 1974,

Merton, R. K. *Social theory and social structure*, New York: Free Press, 1968,

Miller, G. A., Galanter, E., & Probram, K. H. *Plans and the structure of behavior*. New York: Henry Holt, 1960.

Miller, J. G. Living systems: basic concepts. *Behavioral Science* (1965) 10(3):193–237.

Minuchin, S., Montalvo, B., Guernery, B. G., Rosman, B. L., & Schumer, F. *Families of the slums*. New York: Basic Books, 1976.

Minuchin, S. & Barcai, A. Therapeutically induced family crisis. In J. Masserman, Ed. *Science and psychoanalysis* vol. XIV, New York: Grune and Stratton, 1969,

Minuchin, S. *Families and family therapy*. Cambridge, Mass.: Harvard University Press, 1974 (a).

Minuchin, S., Baker, L., Rosman, B. L., Liebman, R., Milman, L., & Todd, T. C. A conceptual model of psychosomatic illness in children. *Arch. Gen. Psychiat.* (1975) 32:1031–1038.

Minuchin, S. Constructing a therapeutic reality. In T. J. Buckley, J. J. McCarthy, E. Norman, and M. A. Quaranta, eds. *New Directions in family therapy* Oceanside, N.Y.: Dabor Science Pubs., 1977,

Montalvo, B. *Family with a little fire*. Training Videotape. Philadelphia, Pa.: Philadelphia Child Guidance Clinic, 1969.

Montalvo, B. Aspects of live supervision. *Family Process* (1973) 12(4):343–360.

Mosher, L. & Keith, S. Research on the psychosocial treatment of schizophrenia: a summary report. *Am. J. Psychiatry* (1979) 136(5):623–631.

Napier, A. Y. Beginning struggles with families. *J. Marr. and Family Counseling* (1976) 2(1):3–12.

Napier, A. Y. & Whittaker, C. A. The basic conflict. In A. Y. Napier & C. A. Whittaker *The family crucible*, New York: Harper & Row, 1978.

Nye, F. I. *Role structure and analysis of the family* Beverly Hills: Sage Pubs, 1976.

Odom, H. T. *Environment, power and society*. New York: Wiley, 1971.

Olson, D. H., Sprenkle, D. H., Russell, C. S. Circumplex model of marital and family systems: I. Cohesion and adaptability dimensions, family types and clinical adaptation. *Family Process*, 1979, 18, 3–28.

Osmond, M. W. Reciprocity: a dynamic model and a method to study family power. *J. Marr. and the Family* (1978): 49–61.

Palazzoli, M. S., Cecchin, G., Prata, G., & Boscolo, L. *Paradox and counterparadox*. New York: Aronson, 1978.

Parad, H. J. & Caplan, G. A framework for studying families in crisis. In Parad, H. J. (ed.) *Crisis intervention*. New York: Family Service Assn., 1965, pp. 53–72.

Parsons, T. Illness and the role of the physician: a sociologic perspective. *J. Am. Orthopsychiat. Assn.* (1951) 21:454–460.

Parsons, T. & Bales, R. F. *Family, socialization and interaction process*. Glencoe, Ill.: Free Press, 1955.

Pittman, F. S., Langsley, D. G., & De Young, C. D. Work and school phobias: a family approach to treatment. *Amer. J. Psychiat.* (1968) 124:1535–1541.

Pittman, F. S. The family that hides together. In Papp, P. (ed.): *Family therapy: Full length case studies*. New York: Gardner Press, pp. 1–21.

Pratt, L. *Family structure and effective health behavior: The energized family*, P. Papp, ed.

Boston: Houghton-Mifflin, 1976,

Rabkin, J. G. & Struening, E. L. Life events, stress and illness. *Science* (1976) 194:1013–1020.

Raskin, D. E. & Klein, Z. E. Losing a symptom through keeping it. *Arch. Gen. Psychiat.* (1976) 33:548–555.

Reilly, M. E. The family. *Population Profiles 17.* Washington, Conn.: Center for Information on America, 1976.

Reiss, D. Varieties of consensual experience III. Contrasts between families of normals, delinquents and schizophrenics. *J. Nerv. and Mental Dis.* (1971) 152(2):73–95.

Riessman, F. The "helper" therapy principle. *Social Work* (1965) 10:27–32.

Rogers, C. R. *On becoming a person.* Boston: Houghton Mifflin, 1970,

Roman, M. & Meltzer, B. Cotherapy: a review of current literature (with special reference to therapeutic outcome). *J. Sex and Marital Ther.* (1977) 3(1):63–77.

Rosman, B. L., Minuchin, S. & Liebman, R. Family lunch session: an introduction to family therapy in anorexia nervosa. *Amer. J. Orthopsychiat.* (1975) 45(5):846–853.

Ruesch, J. & Bateson, G. *Communication: The social matrix of psychiatry.* New York: Norton, 1951.

Ruveni, U. Network intervention with a family in crisis. *Family Process* (1975) 14(2):193–203.

Sampson, H., Messinger, S. L., Towne, R. D. Family processes and becoming a mental patient. *Amer. J. Sociol.* (1962) 68:88–96.

Satir, V. M. The family as a treatment unit. In. J. Haley, Ed. *Changing Families,* New York: Grune and Stratton, 1971, pp. 127–132.

Scheflen, A. Human communication: behavioral programs and their integration in interaction. *Behavioral Science* 13(1) (1968); reprinted in *Family therapy: An introduction to theory and technique,* G. D. Erickson and T. P. Hogan, eds. New York: Aronson, 1976.

Schrödinger, E. *What is life?* Cambridge: Cambridge University Press, 1944.

Shaw, M. E. Communication networks. In L. Berkowitz, ed. *Advances in social psychology,* New York: Academic Press, 1964,

Sherif, M. & Sherif, C. M. *An Outline of Social Psychology* (rev. ed.). New York: Harper & Row, 1956,

Sluzki, C. The coalitionary process in initiating family therapy. *Family Process* (1975) 14(1):67–77.

Sluzki, C. Marital therapy from a systems theory perspective. In T. J. Paolino and B. S. McCrady, eds. *Marriage and marital therapy,* 1978, New York: Brunner/Mazel.

Speck, R. V. & Attneave, C. L. Social network intervention. In J. Haley, (Ed.) *Changing families,* New York: Grune and Stratton, 1971,

Stanton, M. D. & Todd, T. C. Structural family therapy with heroin addicts: some outcome data. Paper presented at the Society for Psychotherapeutic Res. Meeting, San Diego, June, 1976.

Stanton, M. D. & Todd, T. C. Structural family therapy with heroin addicts. In E. Kaufman and P. Kaufman, eds. *The family therapy of drug and alcohol abusers,* New York: Gardner Press, 1978.

Strauss, A. *Chronic illness and the quality of life.* St. Louis: Mosby, 1975, pp. 1–67.

Sussman, M. B. & Burchinal, L. Kin family network: unheralded structure in current conceptualization of family functioning. In J. R. Eshelman, ed. *Perspectives in marriage and the family,* Boston: Allyn and Bacon, 1971.

Tennov, D. *Psychotherapy: The hazardous cure.* New York: Abelard-Schuman, 1975.

Tharp, R. G. & Otis, G. D. Toward a theory for therapeutic intervention in families. *J. Counseling Psychol.* (1966) 30(5):426–434.

Golsdorf, C. Social networks, support and coping: an exploratory study. *Family Process* (1976) 15(4):407–417.

Totman, R. *Social causes of illness.* London: Souvenir Press, 1979.

Vaughn, C. E. & Leff, J. P. The measurement of expressed emotion in the families of psychiatric patients. *Brit. J. of Social and Clin. Psychol.* (1976) 15(Part 2):157–165.

von Bertalanffy, L. General systems theory: a new approach to the unity of science. *Human Biology* (1951) 23:339.

von Bertalanffy, L. *General systems theory.* New York: Braziller, 1968.

Watzlawick, P. The psychotherapeutic technique of "reframing." In *Successful Psychotherapy,* J. L. Claghorn, ed. New York: Brunner/Mazel, 1976, pp. 119–127.

Watzlawick, P. *The Language of Change: Elements of Therapeutic Communication.* New York: Basic Books, 1978, pp. 48–90.

Watzlawick, P. Beavin, J. H. & Jackson, D. D. *Pragmatics of human communication.* New York: Norton, 1967,

Watzlawick, P., Weakland, J., & Fisch, R. *Change: Principles of Problem Formation and Problem Resolution.* New York: Norton, 1974,

Weakland, J. H., Fisch, R., Watzlawick, P., & Bodin, A. M. Brief therapy: focused problem resolution. *Family Process* (1974) 13(2):141–168.

Weiner, H. *Psychobiology and human disease.* New York: Elsevier, 1977,

Wertheim, E. S. Family unit therapy and the science and typology of family systems. *Family Process* (1973) 12:361–376.

Westley, W. A. & Epstein, N. B. *The silent majority*. San Francisco: Jossey-Bass, 1969,

White, R. W. Strategies of adaptation. In *Coping and adaptation*, G. Coelho, D. A. Hamburg, and J. E. Adams, eds. New York: Basic Books, 1974,

Wiener, N. *Cybernetics or control and communication in the animal and the machine*, 2nd ed. Cambridge, Mass.: M.I.T. Press, 1961.

Wilder, C. From the interactional view—a conversation with Paul Watzlawick. *J. Communication* (1978) 28(4):35–45.

Wilden, A. The double bind: schizophrenia and Gödel. In *System and structure*. London: Tavistock, 1977, p. 120.

Woodward, C. A., Santa-Barbara, J., Levin, S., & Epstein, N. B. The role of Goal Attainment Scaling in evaluating family therapy outcome. *Amer. J. Orthospcyhiat*. (1978) 48(3):464–476.

Wynne, L., Rjckoff, I. M., Day, J., & Hirsch, S. I. Pesudo-mutuality in the family relations of schizophrenics. *Psychiatry* (1958) 21:205–220.

Zeig, J. K. Symptom prescription and Ericksonian principles of hypnosis and psychotherapy. Paper delivered to the 1978 Annual Meeting of the American Psychiatric Assn., May 9, 1978, Atlanta, Ga., unpublished Text, p. 21.

Zuk, G. H. Family therapy. *Arch. Gen Psychiat*. (1967) 16:71–79.

Zuk, G. H. Family therapy: clinical hodepodge or clinical science. *J. Marr. and Fam. Counseling* (1976) 2(4):299–303.

CHAPTER 15

Hyperactivity and Psychostimulant Treatment*

CAROL K. WHALEN, Ph.D.

In almost any elementary school classroom today, an observer will find at least one child who has been diagnosed—either formally or informally—as hyperactive. The chances are good that two or three additional children have received similar labels or are considered "borderline cases." Problematic social transactions and lags in academic learning often characterize these youngsters. Although it is impossible to make definitive prevalence determinations, current estimates suggest that between 5 and 12 percent of school-aged children are considered hyperactive, and that boys are from three to nine times more likely than girls to receive this label (Jones et al., 1975; Miller, Palkes, and Stewart, 1973; Safer and Allen, 1976; Sprague, Cohen, and Eichlseder, Note 1).

Diverse treatment procedures have been used for children considered hyperactive. A token economy might be developed in which specific contracts are made with the child and appropriate behavior earns points that can be exchanged for desired items and activities. Or, a cognitive behavioral approach may focus on teaching children self-instruction strategies for guiding their own behavior. Special education programs may be implemented in the classroom.

Child management training, counseling, or traditional psychotherapy may be recommended for parents. Other approaches include play therapy, family therapy, dietary regulation, megavitamins, biofeedback, relaxation training, and chelation to relieve the body of excessive amounts of lead. A large number of psychoactive drugs has also been prescribed for these children, including a variety of central nervous system stimulants (Ritalin, Dexedrine, Cylert, Deaner, Benzedrine, and Desoxyn), tranquilizers (Atarax, Mellaril, Thorazine), antidepressants (Tofranil, Elavil), and antihistamines (Benadryl). Children and their families often receive several of these treatments, either concurrently or sequentially.

Within this variegated therapeutic armamentarium, psychostimulants are clearly considered the treatment of choice (Bosco and Robin, 1980; Krager and Safer, 1974; Sandoval, Lambert, & Sassone, 1980), and most children diagnosed hyperactive probably receive psychostimulant therapy at some time during their school-age years. It has been estimated that about 1.5 to 2 percent or about 600,000 school-aged youngsters per year take psychostimulants (Sprague and Gadow, 1976), and in most cases the specific drug is either Ritalin (methylphenidate) or Dexedrine (dextroamphetamine). These two drugs, very similar in terms of their behavioral effects, have the best-documented, most positive, and least toxic influence on the largest

*Portions of the research for this chapter were supported by National Institute of Mental Health grant MH 29475 and National Institute of Drug Abuse grant DA–01070.

number of hyperactive children. Alternate stimulant medications or nonstimulant medications are used primarily when children are unable to tolerate Ritalin or Dexedrine, when little or no behavioral improvement is observed, or when there is serious concern about potential drug abuse in the child or his family. Nonpharmacologic intervention strategies are used primarily as adjuncts and often as "second thoughts" rather than as integral components of a treatment plan, although there are some notable exceptions to this pattern (Satterfield, Cantwell, and Satterfield, 1979). This chapter focuses primarily on the treatment of hyperactivity with the psychostimulants Ritalin or Dexedrine. Readers interested in information about other psychoactive drugs are referred to Werry (1978b) and Wiener (1977), and those interested in nonpharmacologic intervention strategies are referred to Chapter 10 through 13 of this volume as well as to Douglas, Parry, Marton, and Garson (1976), Kendall and Finch (1979), Mash and Dalby (1979), Meichenbaum and Asarnow (1979), Pelham (1978), and Ross and Ross (1976).

METHODOLOGICAL ISSUES

What are the effects of methylphenidate and dextroamphetamine? In what ways do these psychostimulants regulate the behaviors of hyperactive children? It is tempting to begin this chapter with a list of drug-facilitated changes. However, such a list could be quite misleading if presented independently of the methods used to generate the list. In the field of pediatric psychopharmacology, there are few (if any) standard methods. Procedural diversity pervades this area, and clinical conclusions about the effects of psychostimulants on children must be interpreted within the context of specific methodologies. For this reason, a few of the major methodological dimensions are highlighted before the behavioral effects of psychostimulant treatment are described.

Diagnostic complexities and sample heterogeneity.

The diagnosis of hyperactivity is not a very objective procedure. There are no definitive quantitative indicators, such as amount of movement per minute, length or breadth of attention span, or cortical response to specific stimuli. The identification of hyperactivity is a social-environmental process; one child may receive this diagnosis in a specific ecosystem at a particular point in time and escape the labeling process in an entirely different setting. Despite the lack of definitive diagnositic procedures, there is some consensus among child health specialists on the core characteristics of hyperactivity (Schrager et al., 1966; Werry, 1972). Children likely to receive this diagnosis are perceived as restless, inattentive, impulsive, irritable, and intractable. They often have academic problems in the classroom and difficulties getting along with peers and adults. Children who more or less fit this pattern may receive one or several diagnostic labels from a large set of clinical terms, including hyperactivity, hyperkinetic impulse disorder, minimal brain dysfunction (MBD), and attention deficit disorder. In this chapter such terms are used interchangeably. Although there is less than perfect overlap among the groups included under each rubric, the behavioral differences between a child diagnosed hyperactive and another diagnosed MBD will probably be no greater than the differences between two children given any one of these labels.[1]

More important than the diagnostic labels are the specific criteria used to select children for drug treatment studies. Some investigators require signs of physiological dysfunction, while others rule out children who show such signs. Family pathology may be assessed or ignored during the selection process. Normal intelligence may be a selection criterion, or mentally retarded children may be grouped with those whose IQs are average or above. In other

---

[1]A complete discussion of the diagnostic dilemmas revolving around the hyperactivity construct is beyond the scope of this chapter. The interested reader is referred to Achenbach and Edelbrock (1978) and Gittelman-Klein, Spitzer, and Cantwell (1978) for detailed discussions of the classification of child psychopathology. The elusive search for the syndrome of hyperactivity is illustrated in Langhorne, Loney, Paternite, and Bechtoldt (1976), Routh and Roberts (1972), and Werry (1968).

words, there are no standard selection procedures, and heterogeneity of the research sample is always a prime suspect when contradictory findings emerge, particularly since we know very little about how individual differences and treatment modalities interact.

One promising research strategy is the division of hyperactive children into more or less homogeneous subgroups according to specific characteristics. When distinctive clusters of behavior characteristics and outcomes are analyzed, heterogeneity within an original sample of children becomes a useful aid to inquiry rather than an impediment to interpretation. Diverse variables are being used to distinguish among subgroups of hyperactive children, including suspected neurological dysfunction (Satterfield, Cantwell, Saul, Lesser, and Podosin, 1973), situation-specificity or generality of behavior problems (Campbell, Endman, and Bernfeld, 1977; Schleifer et al., 1975), presence or absence of aggressive behaviors (Loney, Langhorne, and Paternite, 1978), levels of lead in the body (David et al., 1977), and specific patterns of psychological test scores (Conners, 1973). Intriguing findings are emerging from these subgroup studies, and additional research along these lines should help facilitate the match between child characteristics and intervention strategies.

Medication procedures: Dosage and time of action.

The standard method of determining dosage is to begin with a minimal amount (2.5 to 5 mg of dextroamphetamine or 5 to 10 mg of methylphenidate) and then increase the dosage until either a satisfactory response is noted, undesirable side effects occur, or a maximum limit is reached (Cantwell and Carlson, 1978; Katz et al., 1975). Sprague and Sleator (1973, 1976) have criticized these procedures, not only because of the potential hazards of using side effects as cues, but also because this individual titration method does not allow determination of specific dose-response relationships. These investigators recommend use of standard doses on a milligram of drug per kilogram of body weight (mg/kg)

basis. Their precise dose-response studies using this approach have indicated that optimal dosage levels for many children are lower than those typically recommended and that the optimal amount of medication varies with the specific target behavior that is measured (Sprague and Sleator, 1977). These important findings are detailed in a later section. The relevant point here is that variations in dosage procedures and levels may account for some of the inconsistencies in the research literature.

These complexities are further compounded by the fact that average daily dosages of methylphenidate, for example, may vary 15 or 20 mg across studies and 40 or even 60 mg from one individual to the next. There is no direct way to assess the impact of such large dosage differences when interpreting discrepant findings. Drug response is an individual matter, especially in children. One child will show a dramatic behavioral or toxic effect from a single, small dose while another will appear unaffected by multiple, large doses, and these differences cannot yet be predicted. Numerous developmental and individual difference factors influence drug uptake and distribution in the body (e.g., relative sizes of certain organs and tissue masses, fat development, body water), and there is little definitive information about how these and other variables interact to influence the range of drug responses (Briant, 1978).

The timing of medication is also an important consideration, since the period of peak effectiveness for typical doses of methylphenidate and dextroamphetamine is about four hours (e.g., Swanson, Kinsbourne, Roberts, and Zucker, 1978). Most specialists recommend two to three doses a day at four-hour intervals, while others feel that children can get along on a single morning dose that carries them through most of the school day. Time of day must be considered in evaluations of medication effects. Unless a late afternoon dose is given, medication often "wears off" by the time the child and his family are reunited at the end of the day. From a treatment standpoint, the morning and midday dose procedure is often ideal, since (1) most hyperactive children have greater difficulty at school than at home; (2) most parents and physicians desire to use the smallest amount of medication that is effective; and (3) late afternoon doses may interfere with sleep. From a research standpoint, however, temporal factors complicate integration of data from different sources. For example, when teachers report improvement and parents report no change, it is difficult to know how much of the discrepancy is due to setting differences (e.g., a high-demand school environment versus a low-demand home situation); how much is due to personality differences between teacher and parent; and how much is due to differences in time since medication.

Measurement of change.

The problem of assessing treatment efficacy has plagued researchers for decades, whether the focus is on pharmacological, psychological, or educational interventions. First, decisions must be made about which behavioral domains are relevant. Should a treatment program be considered successful when a child reports that he feels better? When his parents or teachers report global improvement? When scores on objective tests of attention and cognition improve? When he fidgets less and stays seated longer? When he gets better grades? When the frequency of undesirable social behaviors decreases? Once these general decisions are made, the next step is to find or develop reliable and valid assessment instruments. Each assessment modality has its own inherent pitfalls. Checklists and ratings are global, subjective, and easily influenced by characteristics of the respondent, as well as by behavior change in the target child. Direct behavior observations are difficult to obtain and are often too specific, time-limited, or reactive to accurately reflect a child's problematic patterns. Laboratory measures of attention and learning tend to be more objective than ratings and more sensitive than behavior observations. They are also the most comparable from study to study. However, the impressive reliability of laboratory measures is often achieved at the expense of validity, and the relationship between precise changes in

the laboratory and behavioral improvement in the natural environment must be documented. Fully aware of these and many other measurement problems, most investigators use multimodal assessment strategies that include batteries of diverse instruments and procedures. Assessment instruments and issues are discussed further below and in Conners (1977), Knights (1974), Loney (1980), and Werry (1978a).

Research procedures and designs.

A placebo-controlled, double-blind procedure is the sine qua non of drug studies. Placebos are inert chemical substances that look and taste the same as the active medication. Double-blind methodology requires that neither the patient-subject nor the clinician-researcher knows when active drugs versus placebos are taken. In the treatment of children, it is also important that parents and teachers remain blind to drug conditions. The obvious reason is that the expectancies created by knowledge of drug condition could bias the ratings obtained from a child's significant others, independently of the child's actual behaviors. Perhaps a less obvious reason is that adults can—quite subtly and inadvertently — influence a child to behave in line with their own expectancies (Johnson and Lobitz, 1974).

It is important to note that double-blind conditions are relative rather than absolute achievements. Sophisticated observers who are looking for drug effects can often "break" the double-blind code since behavior changes or side effects may signal the presence of active medication (Werry and Sprague, 1974). Failure to maintain perfect double-blind conditions does not necessarily invalidate findings on drug effectiveness, however. Henker, Whalen, and Collins (1979) found that ratings of child behaviors obtained from adults able to partially break the double-blind code were quite similar to those obtained from adults who did not even know that a medication study was in progress.

Another important consideration is whether between-groups or crossover designs are used. In a between-groups comparison, different groups of children are given placebo and active medication, while in a crossover study the same children are tested under both placebo and drug conditions. Crossover designs have several advantages over between-groups designs. Because each subject serves as his own control, individual differences among subjects are less likely to obscure drug-related changes. Thus, crossover designs typically require fewer subjects than group designs and are more sensitive to medication effects. However, crossover designs also have their pitfalls. For example, if sufficient wash-out time is not allowed between drug conditions, the effects of the drug may carry over into the placebo trials. Also, unless behavior changes can be easily reversed, the medication-placebo sequence, and thus the entire crossover design, is inappropriate. Finally, puzzling sequence effects that cannot be attributed to insufficient wash-out time or irreversibility of effects have been found in some crossover studies. For example, Conners, Eisenberg, and Barcai (1967) found much stronger effects of dextroamphetamine when the placebo was given first than when the drug was given first. It is impossible to interpret such discrepancies, although there are several feasible explanations, including individual differences in the groups of children who received the two drug-placebo sequences. More detailed discussions of these design issues appear in Conners (1977), Sprague (1978), and Levine, Schiele, and Bouthilet (1971).

Another design option is to focus intensively on a single individual rather than on groups. Single-subject methodology involves stepwise application of several treatment conditions to an individual, such as placebo and several drugs or several dosage levels of one drug. These designs are particularly appropriate when there are ethical or practical constraints on withholding treatment for lengthy periods of time or on giving specific treatments to large numbers of people. Single-subject designs are also useful when the target problems are rare and idiosyncratic. Unlike group designs, single-case studies can highlight rather than mask the unique characteristics of specific individuals and settings.

Used frequently in behavior modification studies, single-subject procedures were limited until recently because it was difficult to assess the statistical significance of treatment-induced changes. Appropriate statistical techniques are now being developed (Kazdin, 1976), however, and single-subject approaches are becoming viable alternatives in drug evaluation studies. See Hersen and Barlow (1976) for a comprehensive discussion of specific experimental procedures, as well as of the advantages and limitations of single-subject methodologies.

Summary: The interplay between research and clinical practice.

Methodological intricacies and inconsistencies make it difficult to reach general conclusions about psychostimulant effects. When one group of investigators reports positive medication responses and another group fails to find such effects, we must examine details about the specific children in each study, medication procedures and dosages, target behaviors, assessment instruments, experimental designs, and so forth. Each clinical conclusion discussed below is embedded in—and qualified by—the specific methodologies applied in reaching the conclusion.

BEHAVIORAL EFFECTS

To illustrate the direct effects of psychostimulants, this section focuses on four major behavioral domains: activity level, attention, cognition and learning, and social adaptation. It should be noted that psychostimulant effects have been documented in several additional areas, including cognitive styles, perceptual-motor performance, biochemical functions, and psychophysiological processes. For more detailed information about these other areas, the reader is referred to Aman (1978), Barkley (1977a), Conners (1975b), Rosenthal and Allen (1978), Silbergeld (1977), and Sroufe (1975).

Activity level and response modulation.

As the term hyperactivity itself suggests,

excessive motor activity has often been considered the prime characteristic of hyperactive children, and reduced activity level is expected following psychostimulant medication. Several systematic studies have indicated that psychostimulants do in fact reduce motor activity—as perceived by parents and teachers, as measured by mechanical devices, or as observed directly in classrooms and playrooms (Barkley, 1977b; Rapoport, Buchsbaum, Zahn, Weingartner, Ludlow, and Mikkelsen, 1978; Whalen, Collins, Henker, Alkus, Adams, and Stapp, 1978). However, other investigators report no significant medication effects or even drug-related increases in motor activity (Ellis et al., 1974; Millichap and Boldrey, 1967; Routh, 1975).

The issues are quite complex, and the activity area is replete with both conceptual and methodological problems. First, activity level is often treated as a unidimensional phenomenon, even though ample evidence attests to the multidimensional nature of this construct (Bell, 1968; Cromwell, Baumeister, and Hawkins, 1963; Routh, Schroeder, and O'Tuama, 1974). What aspects of motor activity are most relevant for hyperactive children? Should we be concerned with the particular body part that is moving, the proportion of the body that moves, the amount of time motion continues? Should we focus on qualitative aspects of motor activity such as intensity, suddenness, or situational appropriateness?

In a systematic comparison of several measures of activity, Barkley and Ullman (1975) found only low to moderate intercorrelations. It is not unusual for medication to affect one type of activity and have no influence on other types. For example, Sprague, Barnes, and Werry (1970) found that methylphenidate reduced amount of wiggling during a laboratory task but had no significant effect on classroom behaviors such as "out of seat" or turning around in chair. Similarly, Whalen et al. (1978) found a methylphenidate-related decrease in body movements and fidgeting but no effects on leaving one's seat or traveling around the classroom.

A second problem is that, even when investigators focus on a single type of activity and a single measuring instrument, reliability is often difficult to achieve. Johnson (1971) systematically studied the actometer, a modified wristwatch that records amount of motion rather than passage of time. He found that two presumably identical actometers could not be relied upon to yield identical results, and that minor differences in where the child wore the actometer could have a major impact on the readings.

Even when reliability is achieved within a single research setting, comparisons across laboratories are often impossible since investigators use different instruments and procedures. Global ratings of activity may be obtained from parents, teachers, clinicians, or trained observers, and these respondents may or may not know that a medication study is in progress. Classroom observers may be instructed to count each instance of movement or only those instances that appear inappropriate or disruptive. Actometers may be attached to a child's dominant or nondominant wrist or ankle, or these instruments may be worn over the chest or on the back. Some stabilimetric chairs ("wiggle cushions") are sensitive only to "seat" movements, while others record movements of the arms, legs, and trunk as well. It is hoped that recent refinements in rating systems and instrumentation will lead to better standardization of procedures and, consequently, greater commensurability of findings.

A third issue stems from the increasing evidence attesting to the importance of task demands and situational contexts. Psychostimulants may have no effects on motor activity during free play (Ellis et al., 1974; Sleator and von Neumann, 1974) but may systematically reduce motoric behavior under highly structured, task-oriented situations (Sleator and von Neumann, 1974; Sprague et al., 1970; Whalen, Henker, Collins, Finck, and Dotemoto, 1979a). Such findings have led to the hypothesis that the critical feature is not the quantity of gross motor activity but rather the modulation of such behaviors, particularly the child's ability to regulate his activity in accord with externally imposed demands (Conners, 1976a; Kaspar et al., 1971; Keogh, 1971). However, this attractive hypothesis was not supported in a recent demonstration by Barkley (1977b) that methylphenidate reduced motor activity in four different types of environmental contexts: free play, restricted play, structured testing, and movie viewing. Similarly, Rapoport, Abramson, Alexander, and Lott (1971) reported dextroamphetamine-related reductions in motor activity during a playroom session that involved no task demands. These disparate findings on environmental influences underscore the complexities of situational analysis. Environmental contexts *do* appear to moderate medication-induced changes in various types of activity, but additional research is needed to map specific drug-by-situation interactions.

A fourth consideration that must be entered into this activity level puzzle is the fact that not all children referred for "hyperactivity" have problems with activity level—regardless of measuring instrument or context. The diagnostic label may, in fact, be a misnomer (Whalen and Henker, 1976). Most child health specialists now agree that the core difficulties experienced by hyperactive youngsters involve sustained attention and response modulation rather than excesses in gross motor activity per se, and it has been suggested that decreases in activity level—when they occur—may be "side effects" of enhanced attention and goal orientation (Conners, 1976a; Douglas, 1976; Rapoport et al., 1978; Sykes et al., 1971). This decreased focus on activity level is clearly reflected in the current draft of the *American Psychiatric Association's Diagnostic and Statistical Manual (DSM-III)*. The previous diagnostic label "Hyperkinetic Reaction of Childhood" has been replaced by the term "Attention Deficit Disorder" (ADD), and two subtypes have been identified, ADD with hyperactivity and ADD without hyperactivity (Gittelman-Klein, Spitzer, and Cantwell, 1978).

Attention.

One of the conclusions about psychostimulants that enjoys considerable consensus is that these drugs improve attention. As a construct, however, "attention" is even more complex and multidimensional than "activity level" (Keogh and Margolis,

1976a, 1976b), and diverse measures are used to document drug-related improvements in this domain. One procedure is to send objective observers into a classroom and ask them to record how frequently a given child is "on task" in contrast to "off task." The observers are, of course, blind as to medication status and, preferably, naive about the purposes of the study. When this type of procedure is used, hyperactive children taking placebo or no medication are more likely than their peers to be observed staring out of the window, talking to a neighbor, working on a nonassigned activity, or doing just about anything other than the assigned task (Abikoff, Gittelman-Klein, and Klein, 1977; Whalen et al., 1979a). In contrast, hyperactive children who are taking psychostimulants show enhanced task attention (Sprague et al., 1970) and may be indistinguishable from their peers (Whalen et al., 1979a).

Medication effects have also been found on laboratory measures designed specifically to assess attentional patterns. Perhaps the best known examples are the vigilance or continuous performance tasks, first developed to study why detection accuracy of radar operators declined during a prolonged watch (Kupietz and Richardson, 1978; Mackworth, 1948). The objective is to detect relatively rare signals against a background of irrelevant stimuli. For example, a child may be asked to observe a pair of flashing lights and respond only when a red-green combination appears (Anderson, Halcomb, and Doyle, 1973). Or, he may be asked to watch or listen to a string of letters and press a button each time he sees or hears the letter *A* followed by the letter *X* (Sykes et al., 1971). Errors of omission (failure to respond to a signal) and errors of commission (false alarms) are measured, and changes in performance accuracy over time are also monitored. Compared to their peers, hyperactive children tend to make more errors of both omission and commission, and their performance deteriorates more rapidly over time. Psychostimulant-related improvements have been reported for all three types of measures (Conners and Rothschild, 1968; Douglas, 1976; Kupietz and Balka, 1976; Sykes et al., 1971; Werry and

Aman, 1975; Yepes, Balka, Winsberg, and Bialer, 1977).

Vigilance tasks are quite routine and monotonous, and questions have been raised about their relevance to the real-life demands placed on children in everyday environments. In a recent attempt to relate laboratory and naturalistic measures of attention, Kupietz and Richardson (1978) found significant correlations between errors on a visual vigilance measure and "off task" behavior in the classroom. Although the correlations were only of moderate strength, these findings provide some support for the validity of vigilance tasks as analog measures of academically relevant attentiveness.

Studies of cortical evoked responses, cardiac changes, and other psychophysiological functions provide additional evidence of psychostimulant effects on attentional mechanisms (e.g., Conners, 1976a). Porges (1976) is using a two-component model of attention quite reminiscent of a model delineated almost a century ago by William James (1890). The first component involves passive, reflexive, reactive attention, while the second involves active, voluntary, and sustained attention. According to Porges, each component is characterized by distinct heart rate patterns and specific behavioral responses. A reaction time task, presented as a race track game, is used to assess these two attention components. Both the child and the adult have matchbox cars that are presumably competing against each other. A "ready" (warning) signal initiates a preparatory interval, and a "go" signal terminates the interval. The goal is to press a button as quickly as possible following the "go" signal in order to release the car onto a track. To maintain the child's motivation, the adult's car is released automatically in a way that allows the child to "win" most races. According to the two-component model, reactive attention occurs immediately following the warning signal, while sustained attention is required during the second part of the preparatory interval, as the child awaits the "go" signal.

Porges and his colleagues (Porges and Smith, 1980; Porges, Walter, Korb, and Sprague, 1975) are finding that during re-active attention phases, heartrate responses of hyperactive children do not differ from those of their peers and psychostimulants have no effects. During active (sustained) attention phases, however, some hyperactive children show heart rate responses (e.g., increased heart rate variability) that are theoretically incompatible with sustained task attention. Moreover, for a subgroup of children, methylphenidate produces parallel changes in psychophysiological and behavioral responses, decreasing heart rate variability and enhancing task performance.

To summarize, psychostimulant-related improvements have been documented on a wide variety of measures presumed to tap attention. There are, of course, real questions about what these measures have in common and how they differ from measures that fail to show drug effects. The picture that is emerging suggests that psychostimulants facilitate focal attention and over time and under highly structured task conditions that require systematic nonresponse to extraneous stimuli. In other words, the drugs appear to enhance sustained, selective attention and active response inhibition in the service of task performance (Conners, 1976a; Douglas, 1972).

Cognition and learning.

The literature describing psychostimulant effects on cognition and learning is contradictory, with some investigators reporting drug-facilitated increments and others failing to find such effects. It appears that short-term laboratory learning tasks are more likely to yield psychostimulant effects (Dalby et al., 1977; Sprague and Sleator, 1976) than are longer-term measures such as achievement and intelligence tests (Barkley and Cunningham, 1978; Rapoport, Quinn, Bradbard, Riddle, and Brooks, 1974; Rie, Rie, Stewart, and Ambuel, 1976; Weiss, Minde, Douglas, Werry, and Sykes, 1971).

Sprague and his colleagues use a picture recognition test of short-term memory. First the child views a slide containing a matrix of several individual pictures taken from children's books. Next, a single probe picture is presented, and the child's task is to indicate whether or not the single picture appeared in the matrix presented earlier. Difficulty level (or information load) can be adjusted quite easily by varying the number of pictures presented in the matrix. A green reinforcement light flashes following each correct response, and the child earns points that are later exchanged for small toys. Several studies have indicated that methylphenidate improves accuracy on this task (Sprague and Sleator, 1976). The changes also appear to be dose-related when the task becomes difficult (Sprague and Sleator, 1977), a finding that later will be discussed further.

In a systematic study of temporal parameters, Rie and Rie (1977) had children learn a story and then tested their recall two hours and again two days later. Ritalin enhanced story recall two hours after the learning experience, but there were no medication-related differences two days later. Findings of short-lived drug effects are consistent with data emerging from long-term follow-up studies indicating that the academic difficulties of hyperactive youngsters persist into late childhood and adolescence, regardless of type, intensity, and duration of treatment (Mendelson, Johnson, and Stewart, 1971; Riddle and Rapoport, 1976; Weiss, Kruger, Danielson, and Elman, 1975). In summary, medication often induces immediate improvements in learning and cognition, but these improvements may not be maintained over time.

One intriguing finding is that psychostimulants often result in improved teacher ratings and better academic grades in the absence of improved achievement test scores (Gittelman-Klein and Klein, 1975). It is quite likely that some medication-related changes in cognitive performance are secondary effects of enhanced attention and improved social-adaptive behavior rather than direct effects of learning per se (Barkley and Cunningham, 1978; Conners, 1976a; Weiss et al., 1971).

Social-adaptive behavior.

Improved interpersonal functioning is one of the most frequently reported effects of psychostimulant treatment. The primary data sources are rating scales and checklists obtained from teachers and parents, measures which have proven remarkably valid in distinguishing between placebo and medication under carefully controlled, double-blind conditions (Conners, 1976b; Dykman et al., 1976; Rapoport et al., 1974; Sleator and von Neumann, 1974).

The global perceptions of smoother social transactions in hyperactive children given psychostimulants have raised questions about the *specific* behavior changes that attend the medication. Humphries, Kinsbourne, and Swanson (1978) used a cooperative ("Etch-a-Sketch") tracking task to study mother-child interaction. The mother was given control of the knob that makes horizontal lines, and the child controlled the knob that makes vertical lines. The goal was to trace specific mazes that require simultaneous or sequential use of both knobs. Thus, this task generated interdependence and provided an excellent setting for the assessment of communication and cooperation. Humphries et al. (1978) found that children and their mothers exchanged more praise and less criticism when the children were on methylphenidate than when they had taken placebos. Moreover, the mothers were less directive and the children more directive in the medication than in the placebo condition. Barkley and Cunningham (1978) also found significant medication effects on mother-child interaction. When on methylphenidate, hyperactive boys were more attentive and responsive to maternal commands, and mothers tended to be more positive and less directive. These changes in maternal, as well as child behaviors, illustrate the reciprocal nature of medication effects; the impact is observed not only on the child, but also on others in his social environment.

Much less information is available about medication effects on peer interaction than on adult-child patterns. We recently developed a referential communication task to study peer communication in school-aged boys. Working in pairs, one boy serves as "mission control" (message sender) and the other as "astronaut" (message receiver). Mission control is given a photograph of a block design, and the astronaut has a set of blocks ("equipment parts") but no cues as to their correct placement. The task is for mission control to guide the astronaut in the correct placement of each block (See Figure 1). Described as an exercise to teach astronauts how to repair their own spaceship in case of equipment failure during an actual space mission, this game has proven highly engaging to young boys. In our initial study using this task, several interesting differences between hyperactive and comparison boys emerged (Whalen, Henker, Collins, McAuliffe, and Vaux, 1979b). The hyperactive boys were less efficient in their communications; they showed higher rates of task-irrelevant chatter and disagree-

ment; and they were less likely to modulate their verbal messages in accord with shifts in role demands, i.e., from mission control (leader) to astronaut (follower) status. More differences between the two groups emerged in the relatively ambiguous astronaut role than in the more task-guided mission control role. Perhaps the most interesting finding was that medication had little effect on measures of communicative competency. In this particular study, methylphenidate exerted a stronger influence on communicative style than on content, decreasing behavioral intensity without increasing performance adequacy. Given the paucity of data on peer interaction, it is not yet possible to determine the situa-

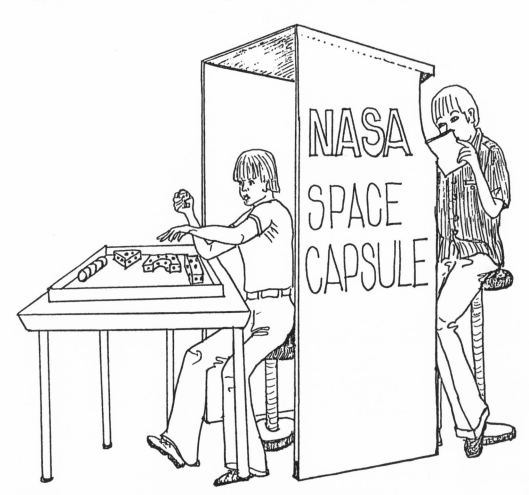

Figure 1. Illustration of "Space Flight," a dyadic referential communication game for assessing peer communication patterns.

tional specificity or generality of these findings.

Medication-related changes in social behaviors have also been documented in naturalistic classroom settings. For example, in a recent set of studies comparing various dimensions of classroom environments we found that, under some conditions, hyperactive children on placebo (compared to those on methylphenidate) showed higher rates of verbalization, social initiation, disruption, physical contact, and so forth. (Whalen et al., 1978, 1979a). These studies are described in greater detail below.

The research just reviewed indicates that specific changes in interpersonal behaviors do, in fact, attend psychostimulant treatment. Additional research is necessary, however, to assess the value and impact of these changes. Several studies have documented medication-related increases in moodiness or dysphoria as well as overall decreases in the amount of social interaction (Barkley and Cunningham, 1979; Schleifer et al., 1975; Whalen et al., 1978, 1979a, 1979b). It is too early to determine whether (or under what conditions) psychostimulants decrease sociability, but such potential effects should be considered when making treatment decisions and monitoring outcomes.

Summary of behavioral effects.

The most consistently reported effects of psychostimulant therapy are improved regulation (rather than decreased levels) of motor activity, enhanced attention and concentration, and smoother interpersonal transactions. These improvements are reported in 60 to 90 percent of hyperactive children treated with psychostimulants. There is no consistent evidence that stimulants enhance long-term cognitive functioning as assessed by standard intelligence or achievement tests.

CRITICAL QUESTIONS

Psychostimulant treatment of hyperactivity is probably the most extensively and intensively studied of all the child thera-

pies. Many talented clinical investigators have addressed trenchant questions over the past two decades, with results that are at times intriguing, at times surprising, and at times disappointing. Several assumptions about the causes and course of hyperactivity have been invalidated through confrontation with empirical reality, and many studies have raised more questions than they have answered. Now, some of these critical areas and their implications are examined.

What are the side effects of psychostimulants? Most drugs that produce therapeutic effects also have unintended and undesirable consequences (Werry, 1978a). The two most common side effects of stimulants are decreased appetite (anorexia) and sleep disturbances (insomnia). Many other side effects have been reported, including headaches, abdominal pains, skin rashes, dysphoria, lethargy, and irritability (Barkley, 1977a; Katz et al., 1975; Millichap, 1975a). Such side effects typically respond quite rapidly to dosage decreases. In some cases continuation of side effects dictates either a shift from one drug to another or the discontinuation of pharmacotherapy. In other instances, a second drug may be prescribed to counteract the side effects of the primary drug (Cantwell, 1977; Katz et al., 1975), and the clinical and social ramifications of this trend toward polypharmacy merit careful examination.

Given their rapid response to dosage adjustments, most psychostimulant side effects have been viewed as inconsequential. However, recent research on growth rates has led to uneasiness about potentially serious long-term effects. After analyzing data on the heights and weights of hyperactive children taking psychostimulants, Safer and his colleagues (Safer and Allen, 1973; Safer, Allen, and Barr, 1972) concluded that these children were not growing as rapidly as expected for their ages; that growth suppression was greater at higher dosage levels; and that the effects were more apparent with dextroamphetamine than with methylphenidate. Accelerated or rebound growth occurs when drugs are discontinued (Safer, Allen, and Barr, 1975; Weiss et al., 1975), but it is unclear whether such growth spurts are sufficient to counteract the effects of years of stimulant therapy.

Numerous growth rate reports have been published since the initial Safer et al. (1972) study, with some investigators documenting growth retardation (Schain and Reynard, 1975) and others failing to find any signs of delayed growth (McNutt, Boileau, and Cohen, 1977). In a recent review of the literature on growth rates, Roche, Lipman, Overall, and Hung (1979) concluded that there is good evidence for *temporary* growth retardation during the first few years of treatment, but no evidence that *adult* stature or weight is affected by stimulant treatment during childhood. Growth retardation is more apparent at high than at low dosage levels and in children who take medication continuously than in those who are given "drug holidays" during the summer months. Roche et al. emphasized the fact that results thus far available apply only to the prepubertal period; the effects of stimulants on growth rates during pubescence are unknown.

Recent evidence on cardiovascular changes is also somewhat disquieting. Studying heterogeneous groups of children in different research settings, numerous investigators have documented stimulant-induced increases in heart rate and blood pressure (Aman and Werry, 1975; Ballard, Boileau, Sleator, Massey, and Sprague, 1976; Barkley, 1977a; Rapoport et al., 1974). The increases are quite small, and most physicians feel that they pose no immediate health hazards. There is always the possibility, however, of atypical toxic responses in a minority of children. Moreover, the long-term effects of prolonged increases in heartrate and blood pressure are unknown. Cardiovascular functions are easy to assess and should be monitored routinely while children are taking psychostimulants. Cardiac and other side effects are also dose-related—another indication that dosage levels should be kept to a minimum.

Do hyperactive children outgrow their problems? Until recently it was believed that the problems encountered by hyperactive youngsters were age-specific and time-limited; the difficulties were assumed to disappear during adolescence, presumably as a consequence of physiological maturity. The evidence emerging from long-term follow-up studies refutes this proposition—at least for a significant proportion of hyperactive children. Many of these youngsters continue to have serious interpersonal and academic difficulties during adolescence and adulthood. The problems do tend to change in form and intensity. In many instances difficulties are less severe during adolescence and especially adulthood than during childhood, perhaps because individuals have more options and greater opportunities to select compatible living and working environments. However, continued restlessness, difficulties sustaining attention, interpersonal problems, and self-denigration are often reported (Ackerman, Dykman, and Peters, 1977; Borland and Heckman, 1976; Butter, 1977; Hoy et al., 1978; Weiss, Hechtman, Perlman, Hopkins, and Wener, 1979).

Do psychostimulants produce enduring improvements? If many hyperactive children do not outgrow their problems spontaneously, questions about long-term effects of psychostimulant treatment become quite important. Follow-up studies of hyperactive children given psychostimulants yield results similar to studies of untreated hyperactive children: many of these youngsters continue to experience interpersonal and academic difficulties whether or not they are still taking medication at the time of follow-up evaluation (Huessy, Metoyer, and Townsend, 1974; Mendelson et al., 1971; Weiss et al., 1975). In an interview study of hyperactive children during adolescence, Stewart, Mendelson, and Johnson (1973) found that a large proportion reported that they say things without thinking, have quick tempers, have difficulty studying, are too talkative, restless, irritable, and so forth. In addition, many appeared disgusted with themselves and pessimistic about their futures.

Weiss, Hechtman, and Perlman (1978) recently reported results of a 10-year follow-up study of hyperactive children. At the time of follow-up evaluation the hyperactive individuals were between 17 and 24 years of age. Ratings were obtained from teachers and employers as well as from the hyperactive subjects themselves, and a similar set of ratings was obtained for a normal comparison group of young adults. It is noteworthy that the hyperactive group was perceived as more competent on the job than at school, and there were no significant differences between the two groups in ratings obtained from employers. However, self-ratings of interpersonal competence, self-control, and achievement were significantly lower in the hyperactive than in the comparison group, and teacher ratings of the hyperactive group were also markedly inferior to those of the control group.

The unwelcome consensus is that psychostimulants facilitate short-term improvements in many hyperactive children but have no enduring benefits. In other words, this treatment may ease the friction between a child and his environment without altering long-term prognoses. Short-term gains should not be discounted—they can be quite momentous in the lives of troubled children, families, and teachers. Additional treatment modalities are clearly needed, however, to enhance the functioning of hyperactive individuals throughout their life spans.

Many fathers (and some mothers) of hyperactive children describe difficulties during their own childhoods that match those currently experienced by their children. Some also report continued problems in their own lives, for example, inability to concentrate and frequent interpersonal conflicts. These adult self-descriptions, in combination with the disappointing long-term (and posttreatment) outlook for many hyperactive youngsters, have led some clinicians to recommend psychostimulant treatment during adulthood, perhaps throughout the entire life span. In other words, the traditional practice of discontinuing psychostimulant treatment at puberty is no longer followed routinely. Moreover, adults never identified as hyperactive during childhood are now being treated with psychostimulants (or antidepressants) for such problems as "adult hyperkinesis" or "adult brain dysfunction" (Huessy, Cohen, Blair, and Rood, 1979; Mackay, Beck, and Taylor, 1973; Maletzky, 1974; Mann and Greenspan, 1976; Safer and Allen, 1975; Wood et al., 1976).

The "appropriate" age range is not only creeping forward through adulthood but also backward to the preschool and toddler levels (Conners, 1975a; Nichamin, 1972; Schleifer et al., 1975). In addition, psychostimulants are being used in the treatment of nonhyperactive children, for example, those considered to have conduct disorders, special learning disabilities, or attention deficit disorders without hyperactivity (Cantwell and Carlson, 1978). In summary, a "slippery slope" is developing, with an increasing number of problems over an increasing time span prompting psychostimulant treatment. The implications and potential dangers of such slippery slopes are discussed elsewhere (Whalen and Henker, 1980). At this time, the data are still sparse and often quite subjective, and thus evaluation of these practices has just begun. It will be important to scrutinize the methodology and findings of psychostimulant treatment research with these new groups as additional controlled studies begin to appear in the literature.

Are psychostimulant effects state dependent? Research with laboratory animals has demonstrated that learning that occurs while an organism is under the influence of a specific drug may not transfer to the drug-free state (Overton, 1973). These findings raise questions about whether the learning achievements of medicated hyperactive children can be applied only as long as medication is continued. The assumption has been that state-dependent learning (or learning dissociation) does not occur with hyperactive children. However, empirical studies are limited in number as well as scope, and both state dependency (Swanson and Kinsbourne, 1976) and failure to find state dependency (Aman and Sprague, 1974) have been reported. The question is still open—no definitive conclusions can be drawn from the paucity of data now available. The issue is indeed an important one, since state dependency would have implications for dosage adjustments (Aman, 1978) and for the long-term consequences of psychostimulant therapies.

What is the optimal medication response? At first blush, the complexity of this question may not be apparent. If a child behaves better while taking medication, he is said to show a positive medication response. But, for some children this means less "bouncing around" and fewer "weird" noises; for others it means fewer fights with peers; and for still others it means better concentration on school work. What is at once puzzling and intriguing is the fact that changes in various behavioral domains tend not to be related. In a comprehensive study of behavioral and psychometric changes, Gittelman-Klein and Klein (1975) found few significant correlations either within or across the two realms. For example, changes on a continuous performance test tended not to correlate with changes on the WISC, the Porteus Mazes, or a series of achievement tests. Parental assessment of global improvement was not related to parental ratings of specific behaviors or traits, and there was no agreement between parent and teacher ratings. There are, of course, numerous possible reasons for nonrelationships, including errors in the measuring instruments, context effects, and heterogeneity of the children studied—as well as actual independence of target behaviors. The important point is that there is no single pattern of medication responses: children often change in a particular behavioral domain without showing concomitant changes in other domains, and different children show different types of behavior change.

The importance of studying specific target behaviors was recently highlighted in the Sprague and Sleator (1977) elegant study of dose-response relationships. These investigators measured four different target behaviors simultaneously: learning performance (short-term memory), social behavior (teacher ratings), wiggling (stabilimetric cushion), and cardiovascular functioning (heartrate). A double-blind crossover design was used in which each measure was obtained for each child under three dosage conditions: placebo, low dosage (.3 mg/kg), and high dosage (1.0 mg/kg). The dose-response curves for the various measures were quite different. Teacher ratings improved as a direct function of dosage; children were rated as least manageable on placebo and most manageable on the high (1.0 mg/kg) dosage. A similar pattern

emerged for wiggling, with the smallest amount of movement occurring under the high dosage condition. If the study had been limited to these two measures, the conclusion would be that the higher dosage is clearly preferable. However, optimal performance on the short-term memory task was found with the low (.3 mg/kg) dosage, and performance actually deteriorated when dosage was increased. Moreover, tachycardia (increased heart rate) emerged only with the high dosage; there were no differences in heart rate between the placebo and low dose conditions.

These findings underscore the need to conduct a cost/benefit analysis when making treatment decisions. What is the relative importance of short-term learning versus teacher perceptions of social behavior? What are the long-term implications of each type of change for each individual child? One might even ask how many extra heart beats will be accepted for how much improvement in classroom ratings. The answers are not simple ones.

Can we predict how children will respond to psychostimulants? Not all hyperactive children show a favorable response to psychostimulant therapy. The 10 to 40 percent who prove unresponsive continue to spur studies of prognostic indicators, signs that will allow specialists to predict treatment outcomes. Two prominent conclusions emerge from an examination of this research literature. First, many carefully conducted studies that include multimodal assessment procedures have failed to yield *any* significant correlations between child or family variables and treatment outcomes (Werry and Sprague, 1974). Second, although intriguing relationships are sprinkled throughout the literature, the results of different studies using similar measures are often contradictory. Not only is agreement across laboratories difficult to achieve, but at times a single investigator is unable to replicate previous findings using a new or expanded sample.

For example, the results of some studies suggest that children with putative signs of central nervous system dysfunction respond most favorably to stimulants (Millichap, 1975b; Satterfield et al., 1973; Steinberg, Troshinsky, and Steinberg, 1971).

Other investigators report either no relationships between physiological signs and behavioral outcomes (Hechtman, Weiss, and Metrakos, 1978; Rapoport et al., 1974) or the opposite result, i.e., more favorable response in children with no signs of "organicity" (Schain and Reynard, 1975). Family "adequacy" (e.g., parenting style, psychological health of parents) has also been implicated as a predictor in some studies, with best medication response found in children whose parents appear to be the most competent (Conrad and Insel, 1967; Loney, Comly, and Simon, 1975). Once again, however, we find that this relationship does not hold up across studies (Loney, Prinz, Mishalow, and Joad, 1978). Similar inconsistencies are found for a wide array of additional variables, including age of child at referral and other demographic factors, types of behavior problems, and psychological test scores. Following a detailed review of the literature, Barkley (1976) concluded that the common theme underlying the few promising predictive indicators is their relationship to attentional processes; children with clear attentional problems seem to be those most likely to benefit from psychostimulants. This hypothesis certainly merits further examination, and more information is needed about the interrelationships among the diverse psychophysiological, psychological, and behavioral measures presumed to assess attentional styles and competencies.

Do psychostimulants have a paradoxical effect on hyperactive children? Since Ritalin and Dexedrine are central nervous system stimulants that appear to exert a calming influence on hyperactive children, these drugs have been said to have a paradoxical effect, i.e., to function as "downers" rather than as "uppers" (Bradley, 1937; Millichap, 1975b; Wender, 1971). This argument takes two alternate forms. The first is simply that immature organisms respond differently than mature organisms to stimulant drugs. The second focuses exclusively on hyperactive children, postulating biochemical or neurological dysfunctions that cause these youngsters to respond differently than either normal children or adults.

There is no supportive evidence for either form of the "paradoxical effect" hypothesis. At appropriate dosage levels, stimulants do not sedate hyperactive children (Barkley, 1977a; Cantwell, and Carlson, 1978; Sroufe and Stewart, 1973). It is only at atypically high dosages — or in unusually stimulant-sensitive youngsters —that signs of cognitive or motoric "slowing" emerge. As discussed above, the clinical description of these children as "calmer" when on medication probably results from enhanced ability to selectively attend to relevant stimuli and inhibit inappropriate behavior. In fact, there are striking parallels in the ways adults and hyperactive children respond to stimulants. Both groups show improved attention and concentration, greater capacity to sustain performance over time, and similar side effects (Rapoport, Buchsbaum, Weingartner, Zahn, Ludlow, Mikkelsen, 1980; Sroufe and Stewart, 1973).

The question about whether hyperactive children respond differently than normal agemates has been more difficult to answer because of ethical concerns about giving stimulants to children free of learning and behavior problems. One careful study was conducted with normal prepubertal boys. Using placebo-controlled, double-blind crossover procedures, Rapoport et al. (1978) studied the effects of a single dose of dextroamphetamine (.5 mg/kg). The results were strikingly similar to those found for hyperactive children, including short-term improvements on attention and learning tasks, reduced rates of task-irrelevant verbalization, and less movement during structured task activity. In addition to casting serious doubt on paradoxical effect hypotheses, these findings underscore the dangers of reasoning backward from treatment to etiology, i.e., assuming that a positive medication response confirms a physiological deficit (Whalen and Henker, 1976, 1977).

Is psychostimulant treatment of school children increasing at an alarming rate? In the early 1970s a loud furor was raised about psychostimulant treatment when sensational reports that 10 to 20 percent of America's school children were being medicated suddenly were published (Sprague and Gadow, 1976). Since that time, child health specialists have been accused of drugging children into submission and using chemical straitjackets to suppress natural ebullience and protests against intolerable social conditions (Brown and Bing, 1976; Conrad, 1975; Schrag and Divoky, 1975; Witter, 1971). The errors of both evidence and logic inherent in these views are detailed elsewhere (Whalen and Henker, 1977, 1980). The relevant point here is that recent prevalence studies indicate that only between 1 and 2 percent of school age children are receiving psychostimulants, and that there are no indications of dramatic increases in stimulant treatment rates (Bosco and Robin, 1980; Krager and Safer, 1974; Krager, Safer, and Earhart, 1979; Sandoval et al., 1980).

This discussion, however, is not meant to imply that psychostimulant treatment practices are problem-free. Drugs may be prescribed unnecessarily, at inappropriate dosages, or for excessive periods of time. There are serious inadequacies in drug monitoring procedures (Solomons, 1973; Sroufe, 1975; Weithorn and Ross, 1975). For example, many physicians do not consult with teachers about a child's problems or treatment responses, even though recent research indicates that teachers are the best detectors of medication effects (Sleator and von Neumann, 1974). It is also difficult to get parents and teachers to follow through with nonchemical means of helping hyperactive children once they "succumb" to the ease and convenience of pills (Sandoval, Lambert, and Yandell, 1976). In summary, the data on prevalence and medical management of stimulant treatment justify neither alarmism nor complacency at this time.

Should psychostimulants be used as a first or as a last resort? The short-term positive effects of psychostimulants are quite seductive. In the large proportion of hyperactive children who respond favorably, behavioral improvements are often rapid and profound. These findings have led some professionals to recommend drug treatment as a "first resort" (Wender, 1971), and the result is often exclusive reliance on this single treatment modality.

There are, of course, serious concerns about psychostimulant treatment. Not all children show short-term improvements, and many have unfavorable long-term outcomes. There are uncertainties about the eventual effects of physiological changes such as increases in heart rate and blood pressure. As will be discussed below, there are also concerns about possible emanative effects of using medication as an explanatory schema for behavioral successes and failures. These apprehensions have led some clinicians to advocate withholding psychostimulants until all other intervention strategies have failed. As a general policy, however, neither the "last resort" nor the "first resort" stance is justified by either the research literature or ethical and clinical concerns for individual children.

Clearly what is needed is systematic research on nonchemical intervention strategies. Early results of some programs are quite promising, particularly those using operant or cognitive behavior modification procedures (Ayllon, Layman, and Kandel, 1975; Douglas et al., 1976; Gittelman-Klein, Klein, Abikoff, Katz, Gloisten, and Tates, 1976; O'Leary, Pelham, Rosenbaum, and Price, 1976; O'Leary, and Pelham, 1978; Wolraich et al., 1978). Data from a comparative study by Gittelman-Klein and her colleagues indicate that Ritalin alone is generally superior to behavior modification with placebo, but the optimal approach combines Ritalin and behavior modification (Gittelman-Klein, Abikoff, Pollack, Klein, Katz, and Mattes, 1980). Additional research is needed on tailoring treatment packages to individual children, optimizing the temporal sequencing of intervention strategies, and increasing the palatability and cost-effectiveness of nonpharmacologic treatments.

THE SOCIAL ECOLOGY OF PSYCHOSTIMULANT TREATMENT

Psychostimulants are not discrete change agents that have unilateral effects on circumscribed behavioral domains. Rather, psychostimulant treatment is embedded in social and physical environments, and the behavior-environment interplay is bidirectional. Treatment outcomes are mediated by environmental factors, and drug therapy programs modify the environments in which they occur. Examples of relevant environmental antecedents, mediators, and outcomes are provided below.

Behaviors in contexts. There are probably no 24-hour hyperactive children — youngsters who are perceived as inattentive, impulsive, and difficult to manage at any time and in any setting. There are probably a few children who would be perceived as inappropriate or disruptive regardless of setting. There are probably also a few settings that would elicit difficult behavior from almost any child. In most cases, however, the critical feature is an interaction between personal and environmental characteristics; most children diagnosed as hyperactive have problems in some settings and do not differ from their peers in other settings. This view is quite similar to the one that has evolved from the temperament studies by Thomas, Chess, and Birch (1968) and Thomas and Chess (1977) and the trait-state studies by personality and social psychologists (Mischel, 1973).

Very little is known about the influence of situational dimensions on the behavior patterns of hyperactive children before and during psychostimulant treatment. The best guess from the research literature is that hyperactive youngsters are most likely to have difficulties—and psychostimulants are most likely to be beneficial—in settings that are paced or regulated by an external source (teacher, parent) and that demand sustained attention to designated tasks (Douglas, 1972, 1976). Thus, positive effects of psychostimulants should be more apparent during a structured reading assignment than a free activity period in the classroom. At home the results should be more apparent when the child is eating dinner with guests than when he is constructing a model airplane by himself. In other words, the hypothesis is not that hyperactive children have specific behavioral deficits, but rather that they have difficulty modulating their behavior in accord with external cues, and psychostimulants are thought to aid these response modulation processes (Conners, 1976a).

Despite the attractiveness of this hypothesis, there have been few attempts to test it directly. In a recent set of studies, we crafted classroom environments to create both (1) "provocation ecologies" designed to foster "hyperactive" behaviors and psychostimulant effects, and (2) "rarefaction ecologies" designed to attenuate differences between medicated and nonmedicated hyperactive boys. In one classroom experiment, for example, ambient stimulation and source of regulation were systematically varied in a 2 × 2 experimental design. Children were exposed to either regular classroom noise or to excessive amounts of noise (rock music) while they were working either on activities paced by themselves or activities paced by an external source (a prerecorded audiotape that dictated instructions). Under double-blind conditions, a randomly assigned half of the hyperactive children were on methylphenidate (average dosage = .41 mg/kg), and the other half were on placebo. Normal comparison children also participated in these studies.

Medication-by-situation interactions emerged for both classroom conditions. For example, hyperactive boys on placebo initiated more social interchanges than either hyperactive boys on methylphenidate or comparison peers, but only under self-paced conditions (see Figure 2). As can be seen in Figure 3, the generally higher rate of noisemaking (e.g., tapping a pencil, kicking a chair leg) in the placebo group was most apparent during the high stimulation classroom periods. Hyperactive children on placebo also tended to show more gross motor movement than either those on medication or the comparison group, but these excesses were *not* seen during the quiet/self-paced period. In addition, youngsters on placebo were more likely to "stand out" from their peers (i.e., behave inappropriately) when confronted with other-paced than with self-paced classroom tasks. Variations in these classroom dimensions also had a predictable impact on the behavior patterns of normal comparison youngsters. Additional details about the methods and results of these studies are presented in Whalen et al (1978, 1979a).

These findings underscore the need to explore alternative routes to specific be-

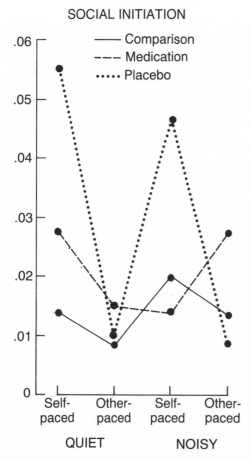

Figure 2. Probability of social initiation in comparison boys, hyperactive boys on methylphenidate (Ritalin), and hyperactive boys on placebo. Reprinted by permission from the *Journal of Applied Behavior Analysis*, 1979, 12, 65–81.

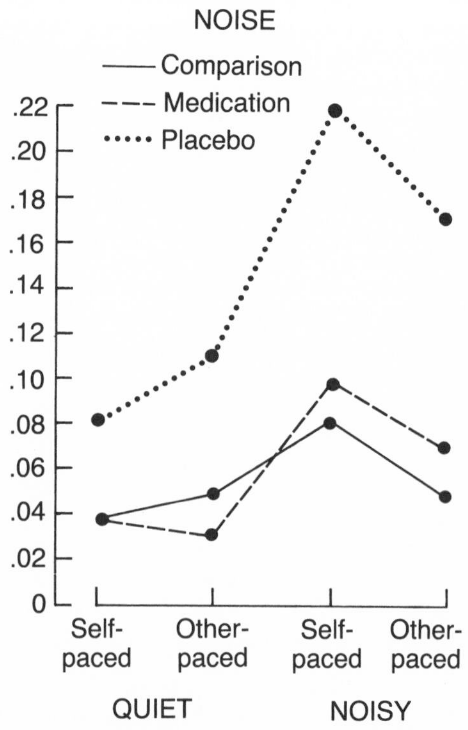

Figure 3. Probability of noise-making in comparison boys, hyperactive boys on methylphenidate (Ritalin), and hyperactive boys on placebo. Reprinted by permission from the *Journal of Applied Behavior Analysis*, 1979, 12, 65–81.

havioral goals; desired changes can be effected through various mixtures of pharmacotherapy and environmental restructuring, and there is no advantage to exclusive reliance on a single treatment modality. When buttressed by additional research, these indications of medication-by-situation interactions will have important implications for the design of both pharmacologic and nonchemical intervention programs.

Emanative effects on the child and his significant others. The unintended consequences of psychostimulant treatment extend far beyond the side effects discussed above. In a previous article we de-

scribed the sociocognitive sequelae or emanative effects that often accompany medication programs (Whalen and Henker, 1976). People (including children) are active construers of their worlds, generating hypotheses to explain and predict day-to-day events (Kelly, 1955). When children are given psychostimulants to help them learn or "behave," they need to explain the treatment to themselves. They also generate causal explanations for the behavioral improvements they notice—as well as for the changes in the ways other people respond to them. What is the message of the medication? A child taking psychostimulants may attribute improvement to factors under his own control, and he may begin to view himself (perhaps for the first time) as acquiring skills and gaining competence. Or, the changes may be attributed solely to the medication—to processes beyond his own control. One 11-year-old girl we interviewed described how her medication enabled her to make 20 friends and to finish her math assignment within the allotted time. A 10-year-old boy reported that his legs and feet "just started moving" when he did not take his medication. Another youngster told us that his medication allowed him to apologize to his dog for getting mad and being mean. On several occasions children have told us that they take pills so that people will like them better.

Such external attributions are often modeled by parents and teachers. A child who earns a "B" in spelling after a string of failures may be told that his medication is really working well, and one who misbehaves in the classroom may be asked whether he forgot to "take his little trip to the office" to receive his midday medication. Such messages may serve as inadvertent encouragement for the child to relinquish responsibility for his actions and to decrease his own efforts toward behavioral improvement.

There is no single message conveyed by medication. Psychostimulants can be described as magic pills or as a crutch that will help the child learn, but only if he works along with the medication. Successes can be attributed to a child's developing skills or to correct dosage adjustments. Unfortunately, cognitive contexts are not usually considered when psychostimulant treatment programs are implemented. What is the optimal way to introduce such a program to a child and his parents? How can guilt over past failures be discouraged at the same time motivation for future efforts be enhanced? How can medication be presented without reducing perceived personal causation and responsibility for behavior change? Additional research is needed to unravel the complex network of causal constructs generated by psychostimulant treatment and to facilitate cognitive structuring that enhances rather than decelerates a child's

personal efforts and self-perceptions of competence. These issues—and their long-term treatment implications—are discussed more fully in Whalen and Henker (1980).

Another potential emanative effect on the child that has been widely debated is an increased probability of substance abuse, including alcohol and licit, as well as illicit, drugs. The concern is that when we give children drugs to enhance everyday functioning we may be teaching them that life's problems can be most easily and effectively ameliorated by chemical coping. It is, of course, quite difficult to collect valid data on substance use patterns, particularly from individuals such as hyperactive youngsters who have already been socially stigmatized. Although no definitive conclusions can be drawn, none of the available evidence substantiates these substance abuse concerns; as far as we know at this time, hyperactive youngsters previously treated with psychostimulants do not seem to be at risk for substance abuse (Beck et al., 1975; Henker, Whalen, Bugental, and Barker, 1981; Laufer, 1971; Weiss, 1975). More comprehensive empirical studies are indicated, particularly since the probabilities of treatment-facilitated substance abuse may increase with the growing trend toward stimulant treatment of adolescents and adults.

Emanative effects on communities, institutions, and the fabric of society. The effects of psychostimulant treatment emanate beyond individual children and their immediate ecosystems. The relative success of this treatment modality has potential professional and social consequences that are just beginning to be scrutinized. Unfortunately, competent research is much more difficult to conduct at macrocosmic than at microcosmic levels of analysis, and thus we know much more about psychostimulant effects on the overt behaviors of children than about their effects on social policies and institutions. In the following paragraphs some concerns about potential emanative effects on society will be illustrated. It should be kept in mind that these macrocosmic effects have not been well documented; they are presented as possibilities in need of consideration rather than as realities in need of redress.

Many of the concerns that have been raised about psychostimulants (and other drug treatments for behavior problems) are based on their very effectiveness. Drug-induced improvements can be so salient and welcome that they mask more serious problems. For example, when children become more manageable in the classroom, their learning deficits will be less apparent. A child who cannot read is less likely to attract attention when he sits quietly at his desk than when he throws spitballs or wanders aimlessly around the classroom. The result of increased manageability may be a failure to diagnose learning difficulties and a reduction in efforts to improve academic programs and teaching techniques (Rie, 1975). This fear has also been expressed at a much broader level. For example, Conrad (1975) has asserted that disruptive or undesirable behaviors may be signs of malfunctioning social systems. According to this argument, medication serves to suppress such signs and thus obscures the need to correct basic social problems. In other words, effective drug therapy may camouflage the fact that we are treating the wrong symptoms—and perhaps even the wrong patients.

A second, related concern is that society may be substituting chemistry for coping and over-relying on easy but short-sighted solutions. Are we turning into a society of prescription shoppers, demanding instant, push-button solutions for every discomfort or inconvenience (Bok, 1974; Silverman and Lee, 1974)? The possibility that effective medication may interfere with a child's acquisition of self-management skills was suggested above. This risk may extend to the societal level, the concern being that psychoactive drugs decrease society's motivation to develop better self-regulation strategies (Lennard, Epstein, Bernstein, and Ransom, 1971). The use of ready remedies may interfere with the development of alternative options for action such as programs for enhancing interpersonal competencies, improving educational technologies, or redesigning various aspects of physical and social environments. Lennard and Bernstein (1974) pointed out that drugs change nonusers as well as users and may

lead society to new and less human modes of transaction. These concerns increase with each technological advance, as additional drugs are developed to alleviate an increasing number of problems in living.

In summary, effective drug treatment is seductive. It is difficult to imagine feasible nonchemical interventions that can be applied at a cost of approximately 20 cents and five minutes per day and generate short-term success rates of 60 to 90 percent. As cost-effectiveness increases, long-term hazards become less salient and evaluations of alternative solutions less probable. Drug treatment programs for behavior disorders are not specific, isolated phenomena. They can have far-ranging effects on social systems, leading to shifts in one segment and reverberative shifts in other segments. In the long run, a functional evaluation must consider the multidimensional and interdependent consequences of drug treatment and generate a social cost accounting or cumulative benefit/risk/cost analysis. For a more comprehensive discussion of these and other macrocosmic emanative effects, see Lennard and Bernstein (1974), Silverman and Lee (1974), and Whalen and Henker (1980).

MYTHOLOGY, MYSTIFICATION, AND THE RIGHTS OF CHILDREN

Children diagnosed hyperactive are most typically those who disturb other people. The diagnostic label has broad semantic elasticity and is applied using subjective-social rather than objective-impersonal criteria. At the present time the most effective intervention is pharmacologic, and the drugs used to treat hyperactive children are the same as (or similar to) those widely abused by adolescents and adults. The immediate medication-induced benefits are often so satisfying to a child's parents and teachers that remaining or emerging problems may be overlooked and nonpharmacologic approaches underutilized. Finally, research methodology in pediatric psychopharmacology is replete with problems, and published findings often appear inconsistent and contradictory.

Although it is an oversimplified description of the state of the art and science of psychostimulant treatment, this brief synopsis highlights the probable reasons that psychostimulant treatment has become a major arena for diverse and fervent battles, including controversies over the rights to be different, to maintain privacy, to receive an education, and to receive or refuse treatment. In both popular and professional publications, the practice of giving psychostimulants to school-aged youngsters has been widely criticized. Some of these critiques are quite sound, pointing out tendencies toward the overlabeling of hyperactivity and the overprescribing of psychostimulants. Others, however, are hyperbolic, uninformed, and highly politicized. Critics who ignore data can attract quite a following by coining colorful phrases and drawing loose links between psychostimulant treatment and such unwelcome social forces as political suppression, industrial greed, and professional territoriality. Uncritical acceptance of such dysfunctional fictions poses dangers to both effective clinical practice and productive scientific inquiry.

From the perspective of troubled children, the major concern is the probability of increasing the distance between problem and solution. Denying a somewhat effective treatment before establishing comparable or superior alternatives is both practically and ethically unsound. And refusing to treat overt problems while engaging in an interminable search for underlying social maladies raises similar practical and ethical concerns. Children have a right to the best available treatment even when it is far from perfect. The fact that society's deficits may have enhanced the need for treatment does not cancel this right. Nor does the fact that some people abuse a treatment justify denying it to all. A child's family, classmates, teachers, and communities also have certain rights, including nonchaotic conditions for living and learning. The rights to refuse treatment and to be protected from incursions into individual liberties are equally valid. The critical questions concern the modes and morals of balancing these rights—and the inevitable tradeoffs involved (Koocher, 1976; Wells, 1973).

The politicization of psychostimulant treatment can also have unsalutary effects on scientific research. In an enlightening discussion of legal and ethical issues, Sprague (1978) points out the absurdity of recent legislation in Massachusetts "banning" research on pediatric psychopharmacology (Brown and Bing, 1976). Sprague's concern is that the constraints are confined to clinical research in the schools and have no implications for practitioners in the field. Thus the acquisition of systematic knowledge about drug effects is impeded, while the clinical use of these drugs continues unabated and largely unmonitored. Given the numerous unanswered questions about psychoactive drugs, the passage of such legislation is quite lamentable. As Lockhart has warned, "In our concern for preventing and stopping pediatric drug research because of ethical dilemmas, we should not lose sight of the ethical issues raised by research that never gets done (1977, p. 10)."

CONCLUSION

Psychostimulant medication is the most common treatment modality for children diagnosed hyperactive, and short-term improvement rates range between 60 and 90 percent. Consensus is developing about the beneficial influences of psychostimulants on attentional patterns, response modulation, and interpersonal functioning. Psychostimulant effects are moderated by a wide range of variables including individual differences among children and families, medication dosage and timing, and types of assessment instruments and procedures. The effects on an individual are strongly influenced by environmental parameters, and information about person-by-drug-by-situation interactions is slowly emerging. Psychostimulants appear to be most effective in situations that require sustained attention and response inhibition while working on tasks structured and paced by someone other than the child himself.

For many hyperactive children, the short-term behavioral gains induced by medication tend not to translate into enduring benefits. These disappointing long-term results are quite puzzling, and many questions remain unanswered despite high research density during the past two decades. Additional studies are needed to delineate predictors of treatment outcomes; refine nonpharmacologic intervention strategies; and map the sociocognitive sequelae or emanative effects of medication on a child and his ecosystem. Neither sensational alarmism nor complacent reliance on pharmacologic solutions is justified. Serious consideration should be given to the rights of children and to the emanative effects of chemical coping on society's policies, practices, and potential.

REFERENCE NOTE

1. Sprague, R. L., Cohen, M. H., and Eichiseder, W. *Are there hyperactive children in Europe and the South Pacific?* Paper presented at the meeting of the American Psychological Association, San Francisco, August 1977.

REFERENCES

Abikoff, H., Gittelman-Klein, R., & Klein, D. F. Validation of a classroom observation code for hyperactive children. *Journal of Consulting and Clinical Psychology*, 1977, *45*, 772–783.

Achenbach, T. M., & Edelbrock, C. S. The classification of child psychopathology: A review and analysis of empirical efforts. *Psychological Bulletin*, 1978, *85*, 1275–1301.

Ackerman, P. T., Dykman, R. A., & Peters, J. E. Teenage status of hyperactive and nonhyperactive learning disabled boys. *American Journal of Orthopsychiatry*, 1977, *47*, 577–596.

Aman, M. G. Drugs, learning and the psychotherapies. In J. S. Werry (Ed.), *Pediatric psychopharmacology—The use of behavior modifying drugs in children*. New York: Brunner/Mazel, 1978.

Aman, M. G., & Sprague, R. L. The state-dependent effects of methylphenidate and dextroamphetamine. *The Journal of Nervous and Mental Disease*, 1974, *158*, 268–279.

Aman, M. G., & Werry, J. S. Methylphenidate in children: Effects upon cardiorespiratory function on exertion. *International Journal of Mental Health*, 1975, *4*, 119–131.

Anderson, R. P., Halcomb, C. G., & Doyle, R. B. The measurement of attentional deficits. *Exceptional Children*, 1973, *39*, 534–539.

Ayllon, T., Layman, D., & Kandel, H. J. A behavioral-educational alternative to drug control of hyperactive children. *Journal of Applied Behavior Analysis*, 1975, *8*, 137–146.

Ballard, J. E., Boileau, R. A., Sleator, E. K., Massey, B. H., & Sprague, R. L. Cardiovascular responses of hyperactive children to methylphenidate. *Journal of the American Medical Association*, 1976, *236*, 2870–2874.

Barkley, R. A. Predicting the response of hyperkinetic children to stimulant drugs: A review. *Journal of Abnormal Child Psychology*, 1976, *4*, 327–348.

Barkley, R. A. The effects of methylphenidate on various measures of activity level and attention in hyperactive children. *Journal of Abnormal Child Psychology*, 1977, *5*, 351–369 (a).

Barkley, R. A. A review of stimulant drug research with hyperactive children. *Journal of Child Psychology and Psychiatry*, 1977, *18*, 137–165 (b).

Barkley, R. A., & Cunningham, C. E. Do stimulant drugs improve the academic performance of hyperkinetic children? A review of outcome research. *Clinical Pediatrics*, 1978, *17*, 85–93.

Barkley, R. A., & Cunningham, C. E. The effects of Ritalin on the mother-child interactions of hyperactive children. *Archives of General Psychiatry*, 1979, *36*, 201–208.

Barkley, R., & Ullman, D. A comparison of objective measures of activity and distractibility in hyperactive and nonhyperactive children. *Journal of Abnormal Child Psychology*, 1975, *3*, 231–244.

Beck, L., Langford, W. S., Mackay, M., & Sum, G. Childhood chemotherapy and later drug abuse and growth curve: A follow-up study. *American Journal of Psychiatry*, 1975, *4*, 436–438.

Bell, R. Q. Adaptation of small wristwatches for mechanical recording of activity in infants and children. *Journal of Experimental Child Psychology*, 1968, *6*, 302–305.

Bok, S. The ethics of giving placebos. *Scientific American*, 1974, *231*, 17–23.

Borland, B. L., & Heckman, H. K. Hyperactive boys and their brothers: A 25-year follow-up study. *Archives of General Psychiatry*, 1976, *33*, 669–675.

Bosco, J., & Robin, S. Hyperkinesis: How common is it and how is it treated? In C. K. Whalen & B. Henker (Eds.), *Hyperactive children: The social ecology of identification and treatment*. New York: Academic Press, 1980.

Bradley, D. The behavior of children receiving benzedrine. *American Journal of Psychiatry*, 1937, *94*, 577–585.

Briant, H. An introduction to clinical pharmacology. In J. S. Werry (Ed.), *Pediatric psychopharmacology—The use of behavior modifying drugs in children*. New York: Brunner/Mazel, 1978.

Brown, J. L., & Bing, S. R. Drugging children: Child abuse by professionals. In G. P. Koocher (Ed.), *Children's rights and the mental health professions*. New York: Wiley, 1976.

Butter, H. J. Attention, sensory reception, and autonomic reactivity of hyperkinetic adolescents: A follow-up study. *The Psychiatric Journal of the University of Ottawa*, 1977, *2*, 105–111.

Campbell, S. B., Endman, M. W., & Bernfeld, G. A three-year follow-up of hyperactive preschoolers into elementary school. *Journal of Child Psychology and Psychiatry*, 1977, *18*, 239–249.

Cantwell, D. P. Psychopharmacologic treatment of the minimal brain dysfunction syndrome. In J. M. Wiener (Ed.), *Psychopharmacology in childhood and adolescence*. New York: Basic Books, 1977.

Cantwell, D. P., & Carlson, G. A. Stimulants. In J. S. Werry (Ed.), *Pediatric Psychopharmacology—The use of behavior modifying drugs in children*. New York: Brunner/Mazel, 1978.

Conners, C. K. Psychological assessment of children with minimal brain dysfunction. *Annals of the New York Academy of Sciences*, 1973, *205*, 282–302.

Conners, C. K. Controlled trial of methylphenidate in preschool children with minimal brain dysfunction. *International Journal of Mental Health*, 1975, *4*, 61–75 (a).

Conners, C. K. Minimal brain dysfunction and psychopathology in children. In A. Davids (Ed.), *Child personality and psychopathology: Current topics* (Vol. 2). New York: Wiley, 1975 (b).

Conners, C. K. Learning disabilities and stimulant drugs in children: Theoretical implications. In R. M. Knights & D. J. Bakker (Eds.), *The neuropsychology of learning disorders. Theoretical approaches*. Baltimore: University Park Press, 1976 (a).

Conners, C. K. Rating scales for use with children. In W. Guy (Ed.), *ECDEU assessment manual for psychopharmacology* (Rev. ed.). (DHEW Publication No. ADM 76–338). Washington, D.C.: U.S. Department of Health, Education and Welfare, 1976 (b).

Conners, C. K. Methodological considerations in drug research with children. In J. M. Wiener (Ed.), *Psychopharmacology in childhood and adolescence*. New York: Basic Books, 1977.

Conners, C. K., Eisenberg, L., & Barcai, A. Effect of dextroamphetamine on children: Studies on subjects with learning disabilities and school behavior problems. *Archives of General Psychiatry*, 1967, *17*, 478–485.

Conners, C. K., & Rothschild, G. H. Drugs and learning in children. In J. Hellmuth (Ed.), *Learning disorders* (Vol. III). Seattle: Special Child Publications, 1968.

Conrad, P. The discovery of hyperkinesis: Notes on the medicalization of deviant behavior. *Social Problems*, 1975, *23*, 12–21.

Conrad, W. G., & Insel, J. Anticipating the response to amphetamine therapy in the treatment of hyperkinetic children. *Pediatrics*, 1967, *40*, 96–98.

Cromwell, R. L., Baumeister, A., & Hawkins, W. F. Research in activity level. In N. R. Ellis (Ed.), *Handbook of mental deficiency: Psychological theory and research*. New York: McGraw-Hill, 1963.

Dalby, J. T., Kinsbourne, M., Swanson, J. M., & Sobol, M. P. Hyperactive children's under-use of learning time: Correction by stimulant treatment. *Child Development*, 1977, *48*, 1448–1453.

David, O. J., Hoffman, S. P., Sverd, J., & Clark, J. Lead and hyperactivity: Lead levels among hyperactive children. *Journal of Abnormal Child Psychology*, 1977, *5*, 405–416.

Douglas, V. I. Stop, look and listen: The problem of sustained attention and impulse control in hyperactive and normal children. *Canadian Journal of Behavioral Science*, 1972, *4*, 259–282.

Douglas, V. I. Effects of medication on learning efficiency. Research findings review and synthesis. In R. P. Anderson & C. G. Halcomb (Eds.), *Learning disability/minimal brain dysfunction syndrome*. Springfield, Ill.: Charles C. Thomas, 1976.

Douglas, V. I., Parry, P., Marton, P., & Garson, C. Assessment of a cognitive training program for hyperactive children. *Journal of Abnormal Child Psychology*, 1976, *4*, 389–410.

Dykman, R. A., McGrew, J., Harris, T. S., Peters, J. E., & Ackerman, P. T. Two blinded studies of the effects of stimulant drugs on children: Pemoline, methylphenidate, and placebo. In R. P. Anderson & C. G. Halcomb, (Eds.), *Learning disability/minimal brain dysfunction syndrome*. Springfield, Ill.: Charles C Thomas, 1976.

Ellis, M. J., Witt, P. A., Reynolds, R., & Sprague, R. L. Methylphenidate and the activity of hyperactives in the informal setting. *Child Development*, 1974, *45*, 217–220.

Gittelman-Klein, R., Abikoff, H., Pollack, E., Klein, D. F., Katz, S., & Mattes, J. A controlled trial of behavior modification and methylphenidate in hyperactive children. In C. K. Whalen & B. Henker (Eds.), *Hyperactive children: The social ecology of identification and treatment*. New York: Academic Press, 1980.

Gittelman-Klein, R. & Klein, D. F. Are behavioral and psychometric changes related in methylphenidate-treated, hyperactive children? *International Journal of Mental Health*, 1975, *4*, 182–198.

Gittelman-Klein, R., Klein, D. F., Abikoff, H., Katz, S., Gloisten, A. C., & Tates, W. Relative efficacy of methylphenidate and behavior modification in hyperkinetic children: An interim report. *Journal of Abnormal Child Psychology*, 1976, *4*, 361–379.

Gittelman-Klein, R., Spitzer, R. L., & Cantwell, D. P. Diagnostic classifications and psychopharmacological indications. In J. S. Werry (Ed.), *Pediatric psychopharmacology — The use of behavior modifying drugs in children*. New York: Brunner/Mazel, 1978.

Hechtman, L., Weiss, G., & Metrakos, K. Hyperactive individuals as young adults: Current and longitudinal electroencephalographic evaluation and its relation to outcome. *Canadian Medical Association Journal*, 1978, *118*, 919–923.

Henker, B., Whalen, C. K., & Collins, B. E. Double-blind and triple-blind assessments of medication and placebo responses in hyperactive children. *Journal of Abnormal Child Psychology*, 1979, *7*, 1–13.

Henker, B., Whalen, C. K., Bugental, D. B., & Barker, C. Licit and illicit drug use patterns in stimulant treated children and their peers. In K. D. Gadow & J. Loney (Eds.), *Psychosocial aspects of drug treatment for hyperactivity*. Boulder, CO: Westview Press, 1981.

Hersen, M., & Barlow, D. H. *Single case experimental designs: Strategies for studying behavior change*. New York: Pergamon, 1976.

Hoy, E., Weiss, G., Minde, K., & Cohen, N. The hyperactive child at adolescence: Cognitive, emotional, and social functioning. *Journal of Abnormal Child Psychology*, 1978, *6*, 311–324.

Huessy, H. R., Cohen, S. M., Blair, C. L., & Rood, P. Clinical explorations in adult minimal brain dysfunction. In L. Bellack (Ed.), *Psychiatric aspects of minimal brain dysfunction in adults*. New York: Grune & Stratton, 1979.

Huessy, H. R., Metoyer, M., & Townsend, M. Eight to ten year follow-up of 84 children treated for behavioral disorder in rural Vermont. *Acta Paedopsychiatrica*, 1974, *40*, 230–235.

Humphries, T., Kinsbourne, M., & Swanson, J. Stimulant effects on cooperation and social interaction between hyperactive children and their mothers. *Journal of Child Psychology and Psychiatry*, 1978, *19*, 13–22.

James W. *Principles of psychology*. New York: Holt, 1890.

Johnson, C. F. Hyperactivity and the machine: The actometer. *Child Development*, 1971, *42*, 2105–2110.

Johnson, S. M., & Lobitz, G. K. Parental manipulation of child behavior in home observations. *Journal of Applied Behavior Analysis*, 1974, *7*, 23–31.

Jones, N. M., Loney, J., Weissenburger, F. E., & Fleischmann, D. J. The hyperkinetic child: What do teachers know? *Psychology in the Schools*, 1975, *12*, 388–392.

Kaspar, J. C., Millichap, J. G., Backus, R., Child, D., & Schulman, J. L. A study of the relationships between neurological evidence of brain damage in children and activity and distractibility. *Journal of Consulting and Clinical Psychology*, 1971, *36*, 329–337.

Katz, S., Saraf, K., Gittleman-Klein, R., & Klein, D. F. Clinical pharmacological management of hyperkinetic children. *International Journal of Mental Health*, 1975, *4*, 157–181.

Kazdin, A. E. Statistical analyses for single-case experimental designs. In M. Hersen & D. H. Barlow (Eds.), *Single case experimental designs: Strategies for studying behavior change*. New York: Pergamon, 1976.

Kelly, G. A. *The psychology of personal constructs* (2 vols.). New York: Norton, 1955.

Kendall, P. C., & Finch, A. J., Jr. Developing nonimpulsive behavior in children: Cognitive-behavioral strategies for self-control. In P. C. Kendall & S. D. Hollon (Eds.), *Cognitive-behavioral interventions. Theory, research, and procedures*. New York: Academic Press, 1979.

Keogh, B. Hyperactivity and learning disorders: Review and speculation. *Exceptional Child*, 1971, *38*, 101–109.

Keogh, B. K., & Margolis, J. S. A component analysis of attentional problems of educationally handicapped boys. *Journal of Abnormal Child Psychology*, 1976, *4*, 349–359 (a).

Keogh, B. K. & Margolis, J. Learn to labor and to wait: Attentional problems of children with learning disorders. *Journal of Learning Disabilities*, 1976, *9*, 276–286 (b).

Knights, R. M. Psychometric assessment of stimulant-induced behavior change. In C.

K. Conners (Ed.), *Clinical use of stimulant drugs in children.* New York: American Elsevier, 1974.

Koocher, G. P. (Ed.). *Children's rights and the mental health professions.* New York: Wiley, 1976.

Krager, J. M., & Safer, D. J. Type and prevalence of medication used in the treatment of hyperactive children. *New England Journal of Medicine,* 1974, *291,* 1118–1120.

Krager, J. M., Safer, D., & Earhart, J. Follow-up survey results of medication used to treat hyperactive school children. *Journal of School Health,* 1979, *49,* 317–321.

Kupietz, S. S., & Balka, E. B. Alterations in the vigilance performance of children receiving amitriptyline and methylphenidate pharmacotherapy. *Psychopharmacology,* 1976, *50,* 29–33.

Kupietz, S. S., & Richardson, E. Children's vigilance performance and inattentiveness in the classroom. *Journal of Child Psychology and Psychiatry,* 1978, *19,* 155–160.

Langhorne, J. E., Jr., Loney, J., Paternite, C. E., & Bechtoldt, H. P. Childhood hyperkinesis: A return to the source. *Journal of Abnormal Psychology,* 1976, *85,* 201–209.

Laufer, M. W. Long-term management and some follow-up findings on the use of drugs with minimal cerebral syndromes. *Journal of Learning Disabilities,* 1971, *4,* 519–522.

Lennard, H. L., & Bernstein, A. Perspectives on the new psychoactive drug technology. In R. Cooperstock and S. L. Lambert (Eds.), *Social aspects of the medical use of psychotropic drugs.* Toronto, Canada: House of Lind, 1974.

Lennard, H. L., Epstein, L. J., Bernstein, A., & Ransom, D. C. *Mystification and drug misuse.* San Francisco: Jossey-Bass, 1971.

Levine, J., Schiele, B. C., & Bouthilet, L. (Eds.). *Principles and problems in establishing the efficacy of psychotropic agents.* PHS Publication No. 2138, 1971.

Lockhart, J. D. Pediatric drug testing: Is it at risk? *Hastings Center Report,* 1977, *7,* 8–10.

Loney, J. Childhood hyperactivity. In R. H. Woody (Ed.), *Encyclopedia of clinical assessment.* San Francisco: Jossey-Bass, 1980.

Loney, J., Comly, H. H., & Simon, B. Parental management, self-concept, and drug response in minimal brain dysfunction. *Journal of Learning Disabilities,* 1975, *8,* 187–190.

Loney, J., Langhorne, J. E. Jr., & Paternite, C. E. An empirical basis for subgrouping the hyperkinetic/MBD syndrome. *Journal of Abnormal Psychology,* 1978, *87,* 431–441.

Loney, J., Prinz, R. J., Mishalow, J., & Joad, J. Hyperkinetic/aggressive boys in treatment: Predictors of clinical response to methylphenidate. *American Journal of Psychiatry,* 1978, *135,* 1487–1491.

Mackay, M. C., Beck, L., & Taylor, R. Methylphenidate for adolescents with minimal brain dysfunction. *New York State Journal of Medicine,* 1973, *73,* 550–554.

Mackworth, N. H. The breakdown of vigilance during prolonged visual search. *Quarterly Journal of Experimental Psychology,* 1948, *1,* 6–21.

Maletzky, B. M. d-Amphetamine and delinquency: Hyperkinesis persisting? *Diseases of the Nervous System,* 1974, *35,* 543–547.

Mann, H. B., & Greenspan, S. I. The identification and treatment of adult brain dysfunction. *American Journal of Psychiatry,* 1976, *133,* 1013–1017.

Mash, E. J., & Dalby, J. T. Behavioral interventions for hyperactivity. In R. L. Trites (Ed.), *Hyperactivity in children: Etiology, measurement, and treatment implications.* Baltimore: University Park Press, 1979.

McNutt, B. A., Boileau, R. A., & Cohen, M. N. The effects of long-term stimulant medication on the growth and body composition of hyperactive children. *Psychopharmacology Bulletin,* 1977, *13,* 36–38.

Meichenbaum, D., & Asarnow, J. Cognitive-behavioral modification and metacognitive development: Implications for the classroom. In P. C. Kendall & S. D. Hollon (Eds.), *Cognitive-behavioral interventions: Theory, research and procedures.* New York: Academic Press, 1979.

Mendelson, W., Johnson, N., & Stewart, M. A. Hyperactive children as teenagers: A follow-up study. *The Journal of Nervous and Mental Disease,* 1971, *153,* 273–279.

Miller, R. G., Palkes, H. S., & Stewart, M. A. Hyperactive children in elementary schools. *Child Psychiatry and Human Development,* 1973, *4,* 121–127.

Millichap, J. G. *The hyperactive child with minimal brain dysfunction: Questions and answers.* Chicago: Yearbook Medical Publishers, 1975 (a).

Millichap, J. G. The paradoxical effects of CNS stimulants on hyperkinetic behavior. *International Journal of Neurology,* 1975, *10,* 241–251 (b).

Millichap, J. G., & Boldrey, E. E. Studies in hyperkinetic behavior II. Laboratory and clinical evaluations of drug treatments. *Neurology,* 1967, *17,* 467–471.

Mischel, W. Toward a cognitive social learning reconceptualization of personality. *Psychological Review,* 1973, *80,* 252–282.

Nichamin, S. J. Recognizing minimal cerebral dysfunction in the infant and toddler. *Clinical Pediatrics*, 1972, *11*, 255–257.

O'Leary, K. D., Pelham, W. E., Rosenbaum, A., & Price, G. H. Behavioral treatment of hyperkinetic children: An experimental evaluation of its usefulness. *Clinical Pediatrics*, 1976, *15*, 510–515.

O'Leary, S. G., & Pelham, W. E. Behavior therapy and withdrawal of stimulant medication in hyperactive children. *Pediatrics*, 1978, *61*, 211–217.

Overton, D. A. State dependent learning produced by addicting drugs. In S. Fisher & A. M. Freedman (Eds.), *Opiate addictions: Origins and treatment*. Washington, D.C.: V. H. Winston & Sons, 1973.

Pelham, W. E. Behavior therapy with hyperactive children. *Psychiatric Clinics of North America*, 1978, *1*, 227–245.

Porges, S. W. Peripheral and neurochemical parallels of psychopathology: A psychophysiological model relating autonomic imbalance to hyperactivity, psychopathy, and autism. In H. W. Reese (Ed.), *Advances in child development and behavior* (Vol. 11). New York: Academic Press, 1976.

Porges, S. W., & Smith, K. M. Defining hyperactivity: Psychophysiological and behavioral strategies. In C. K. Whalen & B. Henker (Eds.), *Hyperactive children: The social ecology of identification and treatment*. New York: Academic Press, 1980.

Porges, S. W., Walter, G. F., Korb, R. J., & Sprague, R. L. The influences of methylphenidate on heart rate and behavioral measures of attention in hyperactive children. *Child Development*, 1975, *46*, 727–733.

Rapoport, J., Abramson, A., Alexander, D., & Lott, I. Playroom observations of hyperactive children on medication. *Journal of the American Academy of Child Psychiatry*, 1971, *10*, 524–534.

Rapoport, J. L., Buchsbaum, M. S., Weingartner, H., Zahn, T. P., Ludlow, C., Mikkelsen, E. J., Dextroamphetamine: Cognitive and behavioral effects in normal and hyperactive boys and normal adult males. *Archives of General Psychiatry*, 1980, *37*, 933–943.

Rapoport, J. L., Buchsbaum, M. S., Zahn, T. P., Weingartner, H., Ludlow, C., & Mikkelsen, E. J. Dextroamphetamine: Cognitive and behavioral effects in normal prepubertal boys. *Science*, 1978, *199*, 560–563.

Rapoport, J. L., Quinn, P. Q., Bradbard, G., Riddle, K. D., & Brooks, E. Imipramine and methylphenidate treatments of hyperactive boys. *Archives of General Psychiatry*, 1974, 30, 789–793.

Riddle, K. D., & Rapoport, J. L. A 2-year follow-up of 72 hyperactive boys. Classroom behavior and peer acceptance. *The Journal of Nervous and Mental Disease*, 1976, *162*, 126–134.

Rie, E. D., & Rie, H. E. Recall, retention, and Ritalin. *Journal of Consulting and Clinical Psychology*, 1977, *45*, 967–972.

Rie, H. E. Hyperactivity in children. *American Journal of Diseases of Children*, 1975, *129*, 783–789.

Rie, H. E., Rie, E. D., Stewart, S., & Ambuel, J. P. Effects of methylphenidate on underachieving children. *Journal of Consulting and Clinical Psychology*, 1976, *44*, 250–260.

Roche, A. F., Lipman, R. S., Overall, J. E., & Hung, W. The effects of stimulant medication on the growth of hyperkinetic children. *Pediatrics*, 1979, *63*, 847–850.

Rosenthal, R. H., & Allen, T. W. An examination of attention, arousal, and learning dysfunctions of hyperkinetic children. *Psychological Bulletin*, 1978, *85*, 689–715.

Ross, D. M., & Ross, S. A. *Hyperactivity: Research, theory, and action*. New York: Wiley, 1976.

Routh, D. K. The clinical significance of open field activity in children. *Pediatric Psychology*, 1975, *3*, 3–8.

Routh, D. K., & Roberts, R. D. Minimal brain dysfunction in children: Failure to find evidence for a behavioral syndrome. *Psychological Reports*, 1972, *31*, 307–314.

Routh, D. K., Schroeder, C. S., & O'Tuama, L. A. Development of activity level in children. *Developmental Psychology*, 1974, *10*, 163–168.

Safer, D. J., & Allen, R. P. Factors influencing the suppressant effects of two stimulant drugs on the growth of hyperactive children. *Pediatrics*, 1973, *51*, 660–667.

Safer, D. J., & Allen, R. P. Stimulant drug treatment of hyperactive adolescents. *Diseases of the Nervous System*, 1975, *36*, 454–457.

Safer, D. J., & Allen, R. P. *Hyperactive children: Diagnosis and management*. Baltimore: University Park Press, 1976.

Safer, D., Allen, R., & Barr, E. Depression of growth in hyperactive children on stimulant drugs. *New England Journal of Medicine*, 1972, *287*, 217–220.

Safer, D. J., Allen, R. P., & Barr, E. Growth rebound after termination of stimulant drugs. *Journal of Pediatrics*, 1975, *86*, 113–116.

Sandoval, J., Lambert, N., & Sassone, D. The identification and labeling of hyperactivity in children: An interactive model. In C. K. Whalen and B. Henker (Eds.), *Hyperactive children: The social ecology of identification and treatment*. New York: Academic Press, 1980.

Sandoval, J., Lambert, N. M., & Yandell, W. Current medical practice and hyperactive children. *American Journal of Orthopsychiatry*, 1976, *46*, 323–334.

Satterfield, J. H., Cantwell, D. P., Saul, R. E., Lesser, L. I., & Podosin, R. L. Response to stimulant drug treatment in hyperactive children: Prediction from EEG and neurological findings. *Journal of Autism and Childhood Schizophrenia*, 1973, *3*, 36–48.

Satterfield, J. H., Cantwell, D. P., & Satterfield, B. T. Multimodality treatment: A one-year follow-up of 84 hyperactive boys. *Archives of General Psychiatry*, 1979, *36*, 965–974.

Schain, R. J., & Reynard, C. L. Observations on effects of a central stimulant drug (methylphenidate) in children with hyperactive behavior. *Pediatrics*, 1975, *55*, 709–716.

Schleifer, M., Weiss, G., Cohen, N., Elman, M., Cvejic, H., & Kruger, E. Hyperactivity in preschoolers and the effect of methylphenidate. *American Journal of Orthopsychiatry*, 1975, *45*, 38–50.

Schrag, P., & Divoky, D. *The myth of the hyperactive child*. New York: Pantheon, 1975.

Schrager, J., Lindy, J., Harrison, S., McDermott, J., & Wilson, P. The hyperkinetic syndrome: Some consensually validated behavioral correlates. *Exceptional Children*, 1966, *32*, 635–637.

Silbergeld, E. K. Neuropharmacology of hyperkinesis. In W. B. Essmann & L. Valzelli (Eds.), *Current developments in psychopharmacology* (Vol 4). New York: Spectrum, 1977.

Silverman, M., & Lee, P. R. *Pills, profits, and politics*. Berkeley: University of California Press, 1974.

Sleator, E. K., & von Neumann, A. W. Methylphenidate in the treatment of hyperkinetic children. *Clinical Pediatrics*, 1974, *13*, 19–24.

Solomons, G. Drug therapy: Initiation and follow-up. *Annals of the New York Academy of Sciences*, 1973, *205*, 335–344.

Sprague, R. L. Principles of clinical drug trials and social, ethical and legal issues of drug use in children. In J. S. Werry (Ed.), *Pediatric psychopharmacology: The use of behavior modifying drugs in children*. New York: Brunner/Mazel, 1978.

Sprague, R. L., Barnes, K. R., & Werry, J. S. Methylphenidate and thioridazine: Learning, reaction time, activity, and classroom behavior in disturbed children. *American Journal of Orthopsychiatry*, 1970, *40*, 615–628.

Sprague, R. L., & Gadow, K. D. The role of the teacher in drug treatment. *School Review*, 1976, *85*, 109–140.

Sprague, R. L., & Sleator, E. K. Effects of psychopharmacologic agents on learning disorders. *Pediatric Clinics of North America*, 1973, *20*, 719–735.

Sprague, R. L. & Sleator, E. K. Drugs and dosages: Implications for learning disabilities. In R. M. Knights & D. J. Bakker (Eds.), *Neuropsychology of learning disorders: Theoretical approaches*. Baltimore: University Park Press, 1976.

Sprague, R. L., & Sleator, E. K. Methylphenidate in hyperkinetic children: Differences in dose effects on learning and social behavior. *Science*, 1977, *198*, 1274–1276.

Sroufe, L. A. Drug treatment of children with behavior problems. In F. D. Horowitz (Ed.), *Review of Child Development Research* (Vol. 4). Chicago: University of Chicago Press, 1975.

Sroufe, L. A., & Stewart, M. A. Treating problem children with stimulant drugs. *New England Journal of Medicine*, 1973, *289*, 407–413.

Steinberg, G. G., Troshinsky, C., & Steinberg, H. R. Dextroamphetamine-responsive behavior disorder in school children. *American Journal of Psychiatry*, 1971, *128*, 66–71.

Stewart, M. A., Mendelson, W. B., & Johnson, N. E. Hyperactive children as adolescents: How they describe themselves. *Child Psychiatry and Human Development*, 1973, *4*, 3–11.

Swanson, J. M., & Kinsbourne, M. Stimulant-related state-dependent learning in hyperactive children. *Science*, 1976, *192*, 1354–1357.

Swanson, J., Kinsbourne, M., Roberts, W., & Zucker, K. A time-response analysis of the effect of stimulant medication on the learning ability of children referred for hyperactivity. *Pediatrics*, 1978, *61*, 21–29.

Sykes, D. H., Douglas, V. I., Weiss, G., & Minde, K. K. Attention in hyperactive children and the effect of methylphenidate (Ritalin). *Journal of Child Psychology and Psychiatry*, 1971, *12*, 129–139.

Thomas, A., & Chess, S. *Temperament and development*. New York: Brunner/Mazel, 1977.

Thomas, A., Chess, S., & Birch, H. G. *Temperament and behavior disorders in children*. New York: New York University Press, 1968.

Weiss, G. The natural history of hyperactivity in childhood and treatment with stimulant medication at different ages. *International Journal of Mental Health*, 1975, *4*, 213–226.

Weiss, G., Hechtman, L., & Perlman, T. Hyperactives as young adults: School, employer, and self-rating scales obtained during ten-year follow-up evaluation. *American Journal of Orthopsychiatry*, 1978, *48*, 438–445.

Weiss, G., Hechtman, L., Perlman, T., Hopkins, J., & Wener, A. Hyperactives as young adults. A controlled prospective ten-year follow-up of 75 children. *Archives of General Psychiatry*, 1979, *36*, 675–681.

Weiss, G., Kruger, E., Danielson, V., & Elman, M. Effects of long-term treatment of hyperactive children with methylphenidate. *Canadian Medical Association Journal*, 1975, *112*, 159–165.

Weiss, G., Minde, K., Douglas, V., Werry, J., & Sykes, D. Comparison of the effect of chlorpromazine, dextroamphetamine and methylphenidate on the behavior and intellectual functioning of hyperactive children. *Canadian Medical Association Journal*, 1971, *104*, 20–25.

Weithorn, C. J., & Ross, R. Who monitors medication? *Journal of Learning Disabilities*, 1975, *8*, 458–461.

Wells, W. W. Drug control of school children: The child's right to choose. *Southern California Law Review*, 1973, *46*, 585–616.

Wender, P. H. *Minimal brain dysfunction in children*. New York: Wiley, 1971.

Werry, J. S. Studies on the hyperactive child. IV. An empirical analysis of the minimal brain dysfunction syndrome. *Archives of General Psychiatry*, 1968, *19*, 9–16.

Werry, J. S. Organic factors in childhood psychopathology. In H. C. Quay & J. S. Werry (Eds.), *Psychopathological disorders of childhood*. New York: Wiley, 1972.

Werry, J. S. Measures in pediatric psychopharmacology. In J. S. Werry (Ed.), *Pediatric psychopharmacology—The use of behavior modifying drugs in children*. New York: Brunner/Mazel, 1978 (a).

Werry, J. S. (Ed.) *Pediatric psychopharmacology: The use of behavior modifying drugs in children*. New York: Brunner/Mazel, 1978 (b).

Werry, J. S., & Aman, M. G. Methylphenidate and haloperidol in children: Effects on attention, memory, and activity. *Archives of General Psychiatry*, 1975, *32*, 790–795.

Werry, J. S., & Sprague, R. L. Methylphenidate in children: Effect of dosage. *Australian and New Zealand Journal of Psychiatry*, 1974, *8*, 9–19.

Whalen, C. K., Collins, B. E., Henker, B., Alkus, S. R., Adams, D., & Stapp, J. Behavior observations of hyperactive children and methylphenidate (Ritalin) effects in systematically structured classroom environments: Now you see them, now you don't. *Journal of Pediatric Psychology*, 1978, *3*, 177–187.

Whalen, C. K., & Henker, B. Psychostimulants and children: A review and analysis. *Psychological Bulletin*, 1976, *83*, 1113–1130.

Whalen, C. K., & Henker, B. The pitfalls of politicization. A response to Conrad's "The discovery of hyperkinesis: Notes on the medicalization of deviant behaviors." *Social Problems*, 1977, *24*, 590–595.

Whalen, C. K., & Henker, B. The social ecology of psychostimulant treatment: A model for conceptual and empirical analysis. In C. K. Whalen & B. Henker (Eds.), *Hyperactive children: The social ecology of identification and treatment*. New York: Academic Press, 1980.

Whalen, C. K., Henker, B., Collins, B. E., Finck, D., & Dotemoto, S. A social ecology of hyperactive boys: Methylphenidate (Ritalin) effects and medication by situation interactions in systematically structured classroom environments. *Journal of Applied Behavior Analysis*, 1979, *12*, 65–81 (a).

Whalen, C. K., Henker, B., Collins, B. E., McAuliffe, S., & Vaux, A. Peer interaction in a structured communication task: Comparisons of normal and hyperactive boys and of methylphenidate (Ritalin) and placebo effects. *Child Development*, 1979, *50*, 388–401.

Wiener, J. M. (Ed.), *Psychopharmacology in childhood and adolescence*. New York: Basic Books, 1977.

Witter, C. Drugging and schooling. *Trans-Action*, 1971, *8*, 30–34.

Wolraich, M., Drummond, T., Salomon, M. K., O'Brien, M. L., & Sivage, C. Effects of methylphenidate alone and in combination with behavior modification procedures on the behavior and academic performance of hyperactive children, *Journal of Abnormal Child Psychology*, 1978, *6*, 149–161.

Wood, D. R., Reimherr, F. W., Wender, P. H., & Johnson, G. E. Diagnosis and treatment of minimal brain dysfunction in adults: A preliminary report. *Archives of General Psychiatry*, 1976, *33*, 1453–1460.

Yepes, L. E., Balka, E. B., Winsberg, B. G., & Bialer, I. Amitriptyline and methylphenidate treatment of behaviorally disordered children. *Journal of Child Psychology and Psychiatry*, 1977, *18*, 39–52.

Authors Index

Subject Index